EXPERIENCING THE WORLD'S RELIGIONS

Tradition, Challenge, and Change

MICHAEL MOLLOY

University of Hawai`i

Kapio`lani Community College

MAYFIELD PUBLISHING COMPANY

Mountain View, California
London • Toronto

My love to Lucy and Paul
who taught us all to dance.

Copyright © 1999 by Michael Vincent Molloy

Library of Congress Cataloging-in-Publication Data

Molloy, Michael
    Experiencing the World's Religions: Tradition, Challenge, and Change / Michael Molloy.
        p.   cm.
    Includes bibliographical references and index.
    ISBN 1-55934-494-6
    1. Religions.   I. Title.
    BL80.2.M65   1998
    291—dc21   98-6183
                                                                                  CIP

Manufactured in the United States of America
10 9 8 7 6 5 4 3 2 1

Mayfield Publishing Company
1280 Villa Street
Mountain View, California 94041

Sponsoring editor, Ken King; *production editor,* Carla White Kirschenbaum; *manuscript editor,* Andrea McCarrick; *text designer,* Anna George; *design and art manager,* Jean Mailander; *illustrators,* Natalie Hill and Joan Carol; *photo research,* Brian Pecko; *manufacturing manager,* Randy Hurst. The text was set in 10/12 Palatino by Carlisle Communications and printed on 50# Somerset Matte by R.R. Donnelley & Sons Company.

Cover image: Copyright © 1998 Umon Fukushima/Panoramic Images, Chicago, All rights reserved.

Contents

Preface   *xv*

1 Understanding Religion   *1*

❦ FIRST ENCOUNTER   *1*
WHY IS THERE RELIGION?   *2*
Speculations on the Sources of Religion   *3*
Key Characteristics of Religion   *6*
The Sacred   *7*
Religious Symbolism   *8*

PATTERNS AMONG RELIGIONS   *10*
First Pattern: Focus of Beliefs and Practices   *11*
Second Pattern: Religious Views of the World and Life   *12*
Third Pattern: Religious Views of Male and Female   *14*
Box: Is Goddess Worship Still Alive?   *15*
Multidisciplinary Approaches to the Study of Religion   *16*
Why Study the Major Religions of the World?   *18*
Box: Exploring Religion Beyond the Classroom   *19*

THE PILGRIMAGE   *20*

RELIGION BEYOND THE CLASSROOM   *22*

FOR FULLER UNDERSTANDING   *22*

RELATED READINGS   *22*

KEY TERMS   *23*

2 Oral Religions   25

❈ FIRST ENCOUNTER   *25*

DISCOVERING ORAL RELIGIONS   *27*
Past Obstacles to the Appreciation of Oral Religions   *28*
The Modern Recovery of Oral Religions   *28*

STUDYING ORAL RELIGIONS: LEARNING FROM PATTERNS   *31*
Human Relationships with the Natural World   *31*
Box: Spirits Within   *32*
Sacred Time and Sacred Space   *33*
Respect for Origins, Gods, and Ancestors   *34*

SACRED PRACTICES IN ORAL RELIGIONS   *37*
Life-Cycle Ceremonies   *37*
Taboo and Sacrifice   *39*
Shamanism, Trance, and Magic   *40*
Artifacts and Artistic Expression in Oral Religions   *43*
Box: Halloween: "Just Good Fun" or Folk Religion?   *46*

❈ PERSONAL EXPERIENCE: GODS IN HAWAI'I   *47*

ORAL RELIGIONS TODAY   *50*

RELIGION BEYOND THE CLASSROOM   *51*

FOR FULLER UNDERSTANDING   *52*

RELATED READINGS   *52*

KEY TERMS   *53*

3 Hinduism   55

❈ FIRST ENCOUNTER   *55*

THE ORIGINS OF HINDUISM   *57*
The Earliest Stage of Indian Religion   *58*
The Aryans and Their Religion   *60*
The Vedas   *61*

THE UPANISHADS AND THE AXIS AGE   *62*
The Origin of the Upanishads   *63*
Important Concepts of the Upanishads   *64*

LIVING SPIRITUALLY IN THE EVERYDAY WORLD   *68*
The Bhagavad Gita   *68*
The Caste System   *70*

The Stages of Life   *72*
The Goals of Life   *73*
The Yogas   *73*
Box: Hindu Meditation: More Than Emptying the Mind   *75*
DEVOTIONAL HINDUISM   *77*
The Trimurti: Brahma, Vishnu, and Shiva   *79*
Worship of the Divine Feminine: Devi   *83*
The Guru as Object of Devotion   *84*
Devotion to Animals   *85*
Box: Hindu Celebrations   *86*
Other Forms of Religious Devotion   *86*

❧ PERSONAL EXPERIENCE: GAZING INTO THE
MOTHER'S EYES   *87*

HINDUISM AND THE ARTS   *88*

HINDUISM: MODERN CHALLENGES   *90*
Mohandas Gandhi   *92*
Hindu Influence Beyond India   *94*

RELIGION BEYOND THE CLASSROOM   *97*

FOR FULLER UNDERSTANDING   *98*

RELATED READINGS   *98*

KEY TERMS   *98*

4 Buddhism   *101*

❧ FIRST ENCOUNTER   *101*

THE BEGINNINGS OF BUDDHISM: THE LIFE OF THE
BUDDHA   *102*

THE BASIC TEACHINGS OF BUDDHISM   *107*
The Three Marks of Reality   *108*
The Four Noble Truths and the Noble Eightfold Path   *110*

THE INFLUENCE OF INDIAN THOUGHT ON EARLY
BUDDHIST TEACHINGS   *113*
Ahimsa: "Do No Harm"   *113*
The Soul and Karma   *114*
Nirvana   *114*
Box: Was the Buddha an Atheist?   *115*

THE EARLY DEVELOPMENT OF BUDDHISM   *115*

THERAVADA BUDDHISM: THE WAY OF THE
ELDERS   *118*

Theravada Teachings and Literature *120*
Theravada Art and Architecture *121*

MAHAYANA BUDDHISM: THE "BIG VEHICLE" *123*
Mahayana Teachings and Practice *123*
Mahayana Thought and Worldview *125*
Mahayana Literature *130*
Mahayana in China *130*
Mahayana in Korea *133*
Mahayana in Japan *133*
Some Major Schools of Mahayana *134*

ZEN BUDDHISM: ENLIGHTENMENT THROUGH
EXPERIENCE *138*
Zen Techniques for Enlightenment *140*
Buddhism and the Arts of Japan *142*

VAJRAYANA BUDDHISM: THE "DIAMOND
VEHICLE" *146*
Origins, Practice, and Literature of Tibetan Buddhism *146*
Box: Buddhist Festivals *147*
Ritual and the Arts *149*

❧ PERSONAL EXPERIENCE: VISITING THE DALAI
LAMA *152*

BUDDHISM, THE WEST, AND MODERN
CHALLENGES *154*

RELIGION BEYOND THE CLASSROOM *158*

FOR FULLER UNDERSTANDING *159*

RELATED READINGS *159*

KEY TERMS *160*

5 Jainism and Sikhism *163*

❧ FIRST ENCOUNTER *163*

SHARED ORIGINS *164*

JAINISM *165*

BACKGROUND *165*

MAHAVIRA AND THE ORIGINS OF JAINISM *165*

WORLDVIEW *167*

JAIN ETHICS *168*
Box: Jains and Gentle Suicide *170*

THE DEVELOPMENT OF JAINISM AND ITS
BRANCHES   *171*

Digambaras   *171*

Shvetambaras   *171*

Sthanakavasis   *172*

JAIN PRACTICES   *172*

JAIN SCRIPTURES   *172*

JAIN ART AND ARCHITECTURE   *174*

SIKHISM   *174*

BACKGROUND   *174*

NANAK AND THE ORIGINS OF SIKHISM   *176*

THE WORLDVIEW AND TEACHINGS OF NANAK   *177*

Box: The "Five K's" of the Sikhs   *178*

THE DEVELOPMENT OF SIKHISM   *178*

SIKH SCRIPTURES   *180*

SIKHISM AND THE MODERN WORLD   *181*

PERSONAL EXPERIENCE: A VISIT TO THE GOLDEN
TEMPLE   *182*

RELIGION BEYOND THE CLASSROOM   *184*

FOR FULLER UNDERSTANDING   *184*

RELATED READINGS   *184*

KEY TERMS   *185*

6 Taoism and Confucianism   187

FIRST ENCOUNTER   *187*

BASIC ELEMENTS OF TRADITIONAL CHINESE
BELIEFS   *189*

TAOISM   *191*

THE ORIGINS OF PHILOSOPHICAL TAOISM   *192*

Laozi (Lao Tzu)   *192*

The Tao Te Ching   *193*

Zhuangzi (Chuang Tzu)   *195*

Box: The Seasons of Life   *196*

THE BASIC TEACHINGS OF PHILOSOPHICAL
TAOISM   *197*

TAOISM AND THE QUEST FOR LONGEVITY   *198*

RELIGIOUS TAOISM   *199*

TAOISM AND THE ARTS   *201*

TAOISM AND THE MODERN WORLD   *204*

Box: The Chinese Garden—Bridge to the Infinite   *205*

CONFUCIANISM   *206*

THE TAO IN CONFUCIANISM   *206*

THE LIFE OF CONFUCIUS   *206*

Box: Confucianism: Philosophy or Religion?   *208*

LIVING ACCORDING TO CONFUCIAN VALUES   *208*

The Five Great Relationships   *209*

The Confucian Virtues   *212*

Box: The Ideal Human Being   *214*

CONFUCIAN LITERATURE   *215*

The Five Classics   *215*

The Four Books   *217*

THE DEVELOPMENT OF CONFUCIANISM   *218*

Schools of Philosophy   *218*

The Development of Confucianism as a Religious
    System   *221*

CONFUCIANISM AND THE ARTS   *223*

Box: Friends from Far Away   *224*

❧ PERSONAL EXPERIENCE: AT A CONFUCIAN
    TEMPLE   *226*

Confucianism and the Modern World   *228*

RELIGION BEYOND THE CLASSROOM   *231*

FOR FULLER UNDERSTANDING   *231*

RELATED READINGS   *232*

KEY TERMS   *232*

7 Shinto   *235*

❧ FIRST ENCOUNTER   *235*

THE ORIGINS OF SHINTO   *236*

THE HISTORICAL DEVELOPMENT OF SHINTO   *239*

Accommodation with Buddhism and Confucianism   *239*

Shinto and Japanese National Identity   *241*

Box: Kamikaze Pilots and Shinto   *243*

ESSENTIALS OF SHINTO BELIEF   *245*

Box: Shinto Ethics: Basic Rules for the Twenty-First
  Century   *247*

SHINTO RELIGIOUS PRACTICE   *247*

Worship at Shrines   *247*

Celebration of the New Year   *250*

Observances of the Seasons and Nature   *250*

Other Practices   *251*

PERSONAL EXPERIENCE: A TEMPLE HIGH ABOVE
KYOTO   *252*

SHINTO AND THE ARTS   *254*

Architecture   *254*

Music and Dance   *255*

SHINTO OFFSHOOTS: THE NEW RELIGIONS   *256*

SHINTO AND THE MODERN WORLD   *259*

RELIGION BEYOND THE CLASSROOM   *260*

FOR FULLER UNDERSTANDING   *261*

RELATED READINGS   *261*

KEY TERMS   *261*

8 Judaism   263

FIRST ENCOUNTER   *263*

AN OVERVIEW OF JEWISH HISTORY   *265*

THE HEBREW BIBLE   *267*

Box: Books of the Hebrew Bible   *268*

BIBLICAL HISTORY   *269*

In the Beginning: Stories of Origins   *269*

The World of the Patriarchs and Matriarchs   *272*

Moses and the Law   *274*

Box: The Ten Commandments   *278*

The Judges and Kings   *279*

Exile and Captivity   *280*

Return to Jerusalem and the Second Temple   *281*

Box: Zoroastrianism   *282*

CULTURAL CONFLICT DURING THE SECOND-TEMPLE
ERA   *283*

The Seleucid Period   *283*

Responses to Outside Influences   *284*

THE DEVELOPMENT OF RABBINICAL JUDAISM   *286*
The Canon of Scripture and the Talmud   *286*
Islam and Medieval Judaism   *288*
The Kabbalah   *289*
Christianity and Medieval Judaism   *290*

QUESTIONING AND REFORM   *291*

JUDAISM AND THE MODERN WORLD   *292*
Hitler and the Holocaust   *293*
Creation of the State of Israel   *294*

❧ PERSONAL EXPERIENCE: A VISIT TO ANNE FRANK'S
HOUSE   *295*

JEWISH BELIEF   *297*

RELIGIOUS PRACTICE   *298*
The Jewish Sabbath   *298*
Holy Days   *299*
Jewish Dietary Practices   *302*
Other Religious Practices   *303*

DIVISIONS WITHIN CONTEMPORARY JUDAISM   *305*
Culturally Based Divisions   *305*
Observance-Based Divisions   *307*

THE CONTRIBUTIONS OF JUDAISM   *310*

JEWISH IDENTITY AND THE FUTURE OF JUDAISM   *314*

RELIGION BEYOND THE CLASSROOM   *314*

FOR FULLER UNDERSTANDING   *315*

RELATED READINGS   *315*

KEY TERMS   *316*

9 Christianity   *319*

❧ FIRST ENCOUNTER   *319*
Box: The Christian System of Chronology: B.C. and A.D.   *321*

THE LIFE AND TEACHINGS OF JESUS   *321*
Jesus in the New Testament Gospels   *324*
The Two Great Commandments   *327*

EARLY CHRISTIAN BELIEFS AND HISTORY   *328*
Paul and Pauline Christianity   *329*
The New Testament: Its Structure and Artistry   *332*

Box: The Books of the New Testament   *333*

THE ESSENTIAL CHRISTIAN WORLDVIEW   *338*

THE EARLY SPREAD OF CHRISTIANITY   *342*

INFLUENCES ON CHRISTIANITY AT THE END OF THE
ROMAN EMPIRE   *345*
Augustine   *345*
Benedict and the Monastic Ideal   *346*

THE EASTERN ORTHODOX CHURCH   *349*
Early Development   *350*
Monasticism in the Eastern Church   *350*
Eastern Orthodox Beliefs   *351*
Box: Inside a Greek Orthodox Church   *353*

❧ PERSONAL EXPERIENCE: INSIDE THE MONASTERIES ON
MOUNT ATHOS   *353*

CHRISTIANITY IN THE MIDDLE AGES   *355*
Christian Mysticism   *356*
The Crusades, the Inquisition, and the Founding of Religious
    Orders   *357*
The Late Middle Ages   *359*

THE PROTESTANT REFORMATION   *360*
Martin Luther   *362*
Box: Essential Beliefs of Protestant Christianity   *363*
Forms of Protestantism   *364*

THE DEVELOPMENT OF CHRISTIANITY FOLLOWING
THE PROTESTANT REFORMATION   *367*
The Catholic Reformation (Counter Reformation)   *367*
The International Spread of Christianity   *368*
Box: Essential Beliefs of Catholic Christianity   *369*
Nontraditional Christianity   *370*

CHRISTIAN PRACTICE   *373*
Sacraments and Other Rituals   *373*
The Christian Year   *377*
Devotion to Mary   *379*

CHRISTIANITY AND THE ARTS   *380*
Architecture   *380*
Art   *384*
Music   *387*

CHRISTIANITY FACES THE TWENTY-FIRST
CENTURY   *389*
The Challenge of Science   *389*
Contemporary Influences and Developments   *391*

RELIGION BEYOND THE CLASSROOM   *396*

FOR FULLER UNDERSTANDING   *397*

RELATED READINGS AND MUSICAL RECORDINGS   *397*

KEY TERMS   *398*

10 Islam   *401*

❧ FIRST ENCOUNTER   *401*

THE LIFE AND TEACHINGS OF MUHAMMAD   *402*

ESSENTIALS OF ISLAM   *408*

The Five Pillars of Islam   *410*

Additional Islamic Religious Practices   *416*

Box: The Islamic Religious Calendar   *417*

Scripture: The Qur'an   *421*

THE HISTORICAL DEVELOPMENT OF ISLAM   *422*

Expansion and Consolidation   *422*

The Shiite and Sunni Division within Islam   *424*

SUFISM: ISLAMIC MYSTICISM   *427*

Sufi Beliefs   *427*

Al-Ghazali and Sufi Brotherhoods   *429*

Sufi Practice and Poetry   *430*

PERSONAL EXPERIENCE: RAMADAN IN MOROCCO   *432*

ISLAMIC LAW AND PHILOSOPHY   *434*

Islamic Law and Legal Institutions   *435*

Islamic Philosophy   *436*

ISLAM AND THE ARTS   *438*

Architecture   *438*

Fine Art   *440*

ISLAM AND THE MODERN WORLD   *445*

Islam and Contemporary Life   *445*

Box: Women in Islam: Contrasting Notions of
    Liberation   *448*

Islam in the West and Beyond   *449*

RELIGION BEYOND THE CLASSROOM   *452*

FOR FULLER UNDERSTANDING   *452*

RELATED READINGS   *453*

KEY TERMS   *453*

11 The Religious Search in the Modern World *455*

❧ FIRST ENCOUNTER   *455*

MODERN INFLUENCES ON THE FUTURE OF RELIGION   *456*
The New World Order   *457*
Multiculturalism and Interfaith Dialogue   *459*
Box: Religion and Rock Music   *460*
Women's Rights Movements   *462*
Reassessment of Human Sexuality   *464*
Science and Technology   *467*
Secularism   *469*
Environmentalism   *472*

THE RECURRING CHALLENGE OF CHANGE   *472*

NATURISM: A NEW RELIGIOUS PHENOMENON?   *472*

ECLECTIC SPIRITUALITY   *480*
Box: Religion and Movies   *481*
Box: Religion and Pop Culture   *483*

❧ PERSONAL EXPERIENCE: *2001* AND BEYOND   *488*

RELIGION BEYOND THE CLASSROOM   *489*

FOR FULLER UNDERSTANDING   *489*

RELATED READINGS   *489*

NOTES   *490*
CREDITS   *499*
INDEX   *501*

Publisher's Foreword

The publisher would like to commemorate Alden Paine, who died in November 1997. Alden had a long and illustrious career in college publishing, and *Experiencing the World's Religions* was one of the last projects he initiated. After beginning his career with other publishers, Alden began to build Mayfield's lists in the Humanities and Social Sciences and helped to lay the foundation of the company with his work. He had a particular talent for anticipating areas of study in which new types of books would be needed, such as women's studies, death and dying, and sexuality, and for initiating texts dealing with such subjects before the courses were firmly fixed in college curricula. Alden had more than good publishing instincts, however; he devoted himself to campus work and developed strong personal as well as professional relationships with generations of teachers. We will miss Alden's creativity—and his occasional contentiousness.

We believe this dedication is an appropriate way to honor and remember a man who had a great impact on both the people and the business he loved.

Mayfield Publishing Company

Preface

I am often made aware of how intrigued students are by the study of religion. They fill the many sections of the world religions course offered at my college, and at the end of the course they invariably write in their evaluations that the course should be taken by every college student because it has made them see so many things in new ways.

The approach that I follow in this text began when I first viewed postcards and photos from Asia, Africa, and Europe collected by my artist grandmother. The cards featured some of the most colorful religious sights of the world—temples, masked dancers, paintings. Those pictures were the door through which I entered the larger world encompassed by religion. Later, in college, I saw other sides of religions—their broad intellectual content, their appreciation for rare states of emotion and understanding, their influence on cultures, and their sometimes healing, sometimes frightening power in the lives of individuals. From that point on, studying religions for me also meant exploring music, literature, philosophy, psychology, and art. I saw that religions offer ways not only to experience the world, but also to appreciate it. Since college, my investigation of religions has led me to fascinating places and to extraordinary people. As I look back on my encounters, I feel grateful for the kindness of the many who took me in even though I was a stranger. This book tries to share some of the joy that these people and experiences have brought.

With students in mind, I have been guided by several ideals in writing this book:

1. *The ideal of the educated person.* What, I ask myself, should we expect "the educated person" to know about religions? What would a person seeking to be an "educated person" actually want to know about religions? What should the study of religions lead to for those who want to continue their education? This book tries to present that essential content, then point to places, texts, and people through which more can be discovered.

2. *The ideal of clarity.* I often think of the ironic axiom, "When you see the spark of ambition, water it." And indeed a student's initial enthusiasm for religions can quickly be smothered by wave upon wave of specialized terms, names of goddesses and gods, significant dates, and

historical figures. Thus I have tried here to fan rather than water readers' natural inquisitiveness by emphasizing the social issues and human concerns that provide contexts for terms, names, and dates with detailed description. To enhance clarity, chapters include maps and timelines as well as key terms with definitions and pronunciation guides.

3. *The ideal of a multidisciplinary approach to religion studies.* A religion is not just a system of beliefs, but is a combination of ways in which beliefs are expressed in ceremony, food, clothing, art, architecture, pilgrimage, scripture, and social organization—to name only a few. This book tries to make the multifaceted nature of religions explicit. The photographs have been chosen to help achieve this ideal.

4. *The ideal of experience.* Religions are better understood through first-hand experience. This book invites readers both to imagine and to seek the experiences of many religions both at home and abroad. Each chapter begins with a First Encounter that encourages the reader to imaginatively apprehend some aspect of a religion. Later in each chapter a description of a personal experience suggests additional possibilities for experience. Each chapter ends with ideas for experiencing the focal religion at home and abroad.

5. *The ideal of scholarship blended with respect.* Adherents to a particular religion frequently assume that their histories and accounts of their tradition are factual, their texts unique and sacred, and their belief system true. While this inside view may be limited, it often provides adherents with deeply meaningful experiences. In contrast, scholars who study religions seek objectivity through the use of methods that emphasize proof, emotional distance, and even doubt. Their approach—although it may downplay the fact that religions belong to the heart as well as the head—provides valuable tools for making significant distinctions and seeing shared patterns. Because this is a secular textbook about multiple religions, I necessarily follow an academic approach and give precedence to the insights that come from modern scholarly inquiry. At the same time, I try to portray each religion in ways that convey some of the awareness of adherents. My hope is that, through this blending of scholarship and respect, I can accomplish the goal set forth by the book's title—to help readers understand the experience of each religion.

Supplemental materials, available to help students and teachers, include a study guide, an electronic study guide, and an instructor's manual. The study guide gives chapter summaries, learning objectives, and review questions in several formats. The unique CD-ROM Study Guide offers for each chapter: guided tours that highlight important concepts, pronunciation guides for key terms, flash cards, as well as true false, multiple choice, and fill-in-the-blank questions, and mini-lectures that provide an in-depth study of selected concepts. The study guide can be used with either Windows- or Macintosh-based computers. The instructor's manual provides learning objectives, chapter outlines, lecture supplements, notes on using exercises in the textbook, lists of relevant videos and websites, sample examination questions, essay topics, and pages for use as transparencies or handouts.

Many teachers have shared their wisdom with me; I am grateful particularly to Lucy Molloy, Walter Daspit, Winfield Nagley, Sobharani Basu, and David Kidd. I thank Thomas Hilgers for the use of many fine photographs. A grant from the East-West Center in Honolulu made possible much of the initial travel and study necessary for this book. Several monasteries were kind in allowing me to stay and participate in their life: Songgwang-sa in South Korea, Engakuzan in Japan, Saint John's Abbey in Minnesota, and Saint Andrew's Abbey in California.

This book began at the request of a legendary editor, Alden Paine, who like a good Taoist united persistence with gentleness. Work on the manuscript became like a square dance, as I was partnered at different stages with skillful editors and assistants working for Mayfield Publishing Company. Ken King guided the entire project insightfully and invited me to meet the staff in Mountain View. Sheryl Fullerton helped me to "cut to the chase" in my writing. Kate Engelberg reviewed the manuscript and selected auxiliary materials. Susan Shook worked hard to make the instructor's manual practical. Joshua Tepfer organized supplemental material for the instructor's manual. And in the earliest stage Jim Bull initiated the contract process. The student's manual was written by Richard Trussell. The CD-ROM was created by Jack Jackson. Jeff Ruff prepared the lecture supplements and Joshua Tepfer compiled and annotated the video lists for the instructor's manual. Brian Pecko did the photo research and Anna George designed the book and cover. I thank them for their collaboration and creativity. Special thanks to Carla White Kirschenbaum for her sense of beauty and her sensitivity as production editor; and to copy-editor Andrea McCarrick, whose face I never saw but whose laughter on the phone I came to know so well.

Thanks also go to these teachers and scholars who offered their ideas: Robert Platzner, CSU Sacramento; Brannon M. Wheeler, University of Washington; Thomas F. MacMillan, Mendocino College; George Alfred James, University of North Texas; Dr. D. Kerry Edwards, Red Rocks Community College; R. F. Lumpp, Regis University; Ramdas Lamb, Assistant Professor, University of Hawaii; R. C. Trussell, Pikes Peak Community College; G. David Panisnick, Honolulu Community College; Prof. Madhav M. Deshpande, University of Michigan; Robert J. Miller, Midway College; Mark MacWilliams, Saint Lawrence University; David D. Waara, Western Michigan University; John G. Spiro, Illinois Wesleyan University; Gerald Michael Schnabel, Bemidji State University; Rita M. Gross, University of Wisconsin—Eau Claire; Wendell Charles Beane, University of Wisconsin—Oshkosh; Dr. Ann Berliner, CSU Fresno; and Dr. Dan Breslauer, University of Kansas. The book is far better as a result of their reviews. Because our (and my) understanding of religions is constantly expanding, I will appreciate new suggestions, and I ask readers who wish to offer any to send them to me via the publisher.

Although it is a truism, this book has been shaped by hundreds of other people who are also owed my thanks. They planted in me seeds that I hope have come to flower in this book.

OCEAN

ASIA

PACIFIC

OCEAN

INDIAN

OCEAN

AUSTRALIA

CHRISTIANITY

ISLAM

HINDUISM

JUDAISM

CHRISTIANITY and NATIVE RELIGIONS

BUDDHISM

CHINESE RELIGIONS

SHINTO and BUDDHISM

NATIVE RELIGIONS

CHAPTER **1**

Understanding Religion

 FIRST ENCOUNTER

For months you have wanted to take a break from work and the monotony of everyday life, and recently some friends invited you to vacation with them at their mountain cabin. At first you hesitate. This is not the kind of trip you had in mind. After reconsidering, you realize that a remote getaway with friends is just the change of pace you need.

Now, three weeks later, you have been driving all day and have just arrived at the cabin. It is late afternoon, and the air is so cold you can see your breath. Your friends welcome you warmly, and there's a nice fire in the living room. Your hosts show you to your room and give you a short tour. Soon you are all fixing supper together—pasta, wild mushrooms, salad—and during the meal you talk of your work, your zany relatives, and your mutual friends. Everyone is laughing and having a good time. It's confirmed: coming here was a great idea.

After supper, your friends won't let you help with the dishes (of course there is no dishwasher). "I think I'll go out for a walk," you say, putting on your heavy jacket with the hood. As the front door closes behind you, you step into a world transformed by twilight.

What strikes you first is the smell in the air. There is nothing quite like the scent of burning wood—almost like incense. It fits perfectly with the chill. You walk farther, beyond the clearing that surrounds the house, and suddenly you are on a path beneath tall pine trees. As a strong breeze rises, the trees make an eerie, whispering sound. It is not exactly a rustle, more like a rush. You recall reading once that the sound of wind in pines is "the sound of eternity."

Moving on, you find yourself walking along the mountain's ridge. To your left you see the evening star against the blue-black sky. To your right, it's still light and you see why you are cold: you are literally above the clouds. You sit down on a flat rock, pull on your hood, and watch the pine tree silhouettes disappear as darkness spreads its thickening veil.

It's difficult to pull yourself away. All around you stars begin to pop out, and soon they are blooming thick as wildflowers. Overhead, the mass of stars resembles a river—it must be the Milky Way. You get up and slowly turn full circle to take it all in.

You had almost forgotten about stars. You don't see them much back home, let alone think of them. Where you live, stars appear in movies. Here, though, stars are mysterious points of light. You remember what you once learned: stars are so distant that their light can take millions of years to reach earth. You realize that some of the stars you see may no longer exist; only their light remains.

At last you begin to walk back to the cabin. A cluster of clouds emerges on the horizon, lit from behind by the rising moon. You see your friends' wooden cabin in the distance. From here it looks so small. The stars seem like the permanent, real world, while the house appears little and temporary—more like a question mark in the great book of the universe. Questions flood your mind. Who are we human beings? Do we make any difference to the universe? Are we part of any cosmic plan? Is there any point to the universe at all? What is it all about?

WHY IS THERE RELIGION?

One of the world's most mysterious paintings, by French artist Paul Gauguin (1848–1903), depicts a group of people who stand or sit in a kind of timeless primeval world, arms lifted up to the sky.[1] Gauguin painted the work toward the end of his life and considered it to be his masterpiece. The title of the painting is an odd one: *Where Do We Come From? What Are We? Where Are We Going?* Like us when we look out at the night sky with wonder, Gauguin's

---

Note: This text uses the time designations B.C.E. ("before the common era") and C.E. ("of the common era") in place of the Christianity-biased abbreviations B.C. ("before Christ") and A.D. (*anno Domini,* "in the year of the Lord").

figures appear as strangers in the cosmos. Gauguin's vision expresses amazement at how great we human beings are, yet also how small we are within the galaxy and how short our lives are.

In his painting *Where Do We Come From? What Are We? Where Are We Going?* Paul Gauguin uses the images of a religious statue and people in postures of prayer to express the deepest human questions.

Why do we sometimes feel disjointed, unconnected, alone? Where do we fit? Religion is among the greatest of human efforts to answer these questions. It helps unite us in communities that bring meaning to our lives; it offers answers to our deepest questions; and it helps give us a sense of place in the universe.

Speculations on the Sources of Religion

Why does religion exist? An evident answer is that it serves many human needs. One of our primary needs is having to deal with our mortality. Because we and our loved ones must die, we have to face the pain of death and the inevitable questions it brings about whether there is any soul, afterlife, or rebirth. People often look to religion for the answers. Religion can help us cope with death, and religious rituals can offer comfort. Human beings also desire good health, a regular supply of food, and the conditions necessary (such as suitable weather) to ensure these things. Before the development of modern science, human beings looked to religion to bring about these practical benefits, and they often still do.

Human beings are also social by nature, and religion offers companionship and the fulfillment that can come from belonging to a group. Moreover, religion often provides a way to care for the needy.

Human beings have a need to seek out and create artistic forms of expression. Religion stimulates art, music, and dance, and has been the inspirational source of some of the most imaginative buildings in the world. Religion not only makes use of multiple arts but also integrates them into a living, often beautiful whole.

Perhaps the most basic function of religion is to respond to our natural wonder about ourselves and the cosmos—our musings on a starry night. Religion helps us relate to the unknown universe around us by answering the basic questions of who we are, where we come from, and where we are going.

Death is inevitable. In different ways, religion helps people understand and deal with that certainty.

Issues relating to the origins of religion have engaged thinkers with new urgency since the dawn of the age of science. Many have suggested that religion is a human attempt to feel more secure in an unfeeling universe. The English anthropologist E. B. Tylor (1832–1917), for example, saw religion as being rooted in spirit worship. He noted how frequently religions see "spirits" as having some control over natural forces and how commonly religions see those who die—the ancestors—as passing into the spirit world. Fear of the power of all these spirits, he thought, made it necessary for people to find ways to please them. Religion offered such ways, thus allowing the living to avoid the spirits' dangerous power and to convert that power into a force that worked for the good of human beings. Similarly, the Scottish anthropologist James Frazer (1854–1941), author of *The Golden Bough,* saw the origins of religion in early attempts by human beings to influence nature and identified religion as an intermediate stage between magic and science.

Sigmund Freud (1856–1939) theorized that belief in a God or gods arose from an adult's projection of powerful and long-lasting childhood experiences with his or her parents. These experiences, of fear as well as of security, were the basis for the adult's attempts to deal with the anxieties of a complicated present and an unknown future. Freud thought that since a major function of religion is to help human beings feel secure in an unsafe universe, religion would become less necessary as human beings gained greater physical and mental security. Freud's major works on religion include *Totem and Taboo* and *Moses and Monotheism.*

Another psychologist, William James (1842–1910), came to his ideas on religion via an unusual course of study. Although he began his higher education as a student of art, he made a radical switch in fields and turned to the study of medicine. Finally, when he recognized the influence of the mind on the body, he was led to the study of psychology and then of religion, which he saw as growing out of psychological need. James viewed religion as a positive way of fulfilling needs and praised its positive influence on the lives of individuals. He wrote that religion brings "a new zest" to living, provides "an assurance of safety," and leads to a "harmonious relation with the universe."[2]

The German theologian Rudolf Otto (1869–1937) argued in his book *The Idea of the Holy* that religions emerge when people experience that aspect of reality which is essentially mysterious. He called it the "mystery that causes trembling and fascination" (*mysterium tremendum et fascinans*). In general, we take our existence for granted and live with little wonder, but occasionally something happens that disturbs our ordinary view of reality. For example, a strong manifestation of nature—such as a violent thunderstorm—may startle us. It is an aspect of reality that is frightening, forcing us to tremble (*tremendum*) but also to feel fascination (*fascinans*). The emotional result is what Otto called "numinous awe."[3] He pointed out how often religious art depicts that which is terrifying, such as the bloodthirsty Hindu goddess Durga.[4]

Carl Gustav Jung (1875–1961), an early disciple of Freud, broke with his mentor because of fundamental differences of interpretation, particularly about religion. In his books *Modern Man in Search of a Soul, Memories, Dreams, Reflections,* and *Psychology and Alchemy,* Jung described religion as something that grew out of the individual's need to arrive at personal fulfillment, which he called *individuation.* According to Jung, many religious insignia can be seen as symbols of personal integration and human wholeness: the circle, the cross (which is made of lines that join at the center), and

The mandala, says Jung, illustrates "the path to the center, to individuation."

the sacred diagram of the mandala (often a circle within or enclosing a square), which he called "the path to the center, to individuation."[5] He pointed out that as people age, they can make a healthy use of religion to understand their place in the universe and to prepare for death. For Jung, religion was a noble human response to the depth of reality and to its complexity.

Scholars have made various attempts to identify "stages" in the development of religions. Austrian ethnographer and philologist Wilhelm Schmidt (1868–1954) argued that all humankind once believed in a single High God and that to this simple **monotheism** (a belief in one God) later beliefs in lesser gods and spirits were added. The reverse has also been suggested, namely, that **polytheism** (a belief in many gods) led to monotheism. Influenced by the notion of evolution, some have speculated that religions "evolve" naturally from **animism** (a worldview that sees all elements of nature as being filled with spirit or spirits) to polytheism and then from polytheism to monotheism. Critics of this view feel it is biased in favor of monotheism, in part because it is a view originally advanced by Christian scholars who presented their belief system as the most advanced.

Scholars today hesitate to speak of any "evolution" of religion from one form to another. To apply the biological notion of evolution to human belief systems seems biased, oversimple, and speculative. Even more important, such a point of view leads to subjective judgments that one religion is more "highly evolved" than another—a shortsightedness that has kept many people from appreciating the unique insights and contributions of every religion. Consequently, the focus of religious studies has moved from the study of religion to the study of religions, a field that assumes that all religions are worthy of study.

Key Characteristics of Religion

When people begin their study of religions, they bring ideas from the religion in which they were raised or from the predominant religion of their society. They may assume, for example, that every religion has a sacred book or that it worships a divine being or that it has a set of commandments. Indeed, many religions do share all these characteristics, but some do not. Shinto, for example, does not have a set of commandments, nor does it preach a moral code; Zen Buddhism does not worship a divine being; and many native religions have no written sacred scripture. Nevertheless, we call them all religions. What, then—if not a common set of elements—must be present for something to be called a religion?

An obvious starting point for many scholars is to examine linguistic clues: What are the linguistic roots of the term *religion*? Intriguingly, the most common interpretation of *religion* is "to join again," "to reconnect." The Latin roots of the word *religion* are thought to be *re-*, meaning "again," and *lig-*, meaning "join," or "connect" (as in "ligament").[6] If this derivation is correct, then the word *religion* suggests the joining of our natural, human world to the sacred world. In classical Latin, the term *religio* meant awe for the gods and concern for proper ritual.[7] We must recognize, though, that the term *religion* arose in Western culture and may not be entirely appropriate when applied across cultures—*spiritual path,* for example, might be a more fitting designation to refer to other religious systems. We will keep these things in mind when we use the long-established term *religion.*

New religions—new attempts to "reconnect" people with their origins and a "deeper" reality—sometimes grow out of the ashes of older religions. Here we see the ruins of a temple from the Roman religion with a church tower from the supplanting Christian religion.

Traditional dictionary definitions of *religion* read something like this: A system of belief that involves worship of a God or gods, prayer, ritual, and a moral code. But there are so many exceptions to that definition that it is neither comprehensive nor accurate. So instead of saying that a religion *must* have certain characteristics, it is now thought more useful to list a series of characteristics that are found in what are commonly accepted as religions. We may accept as a "religion" whatever manifests a reasonable number of the following characteristics:[8]

Belief system Several beliefs fit together into a fairly complete and systematic interpretation of the universe and the human being's place in it; this is also called a worldview.

Community The belief system is shared, and its ideals are practiced by a group.

Ethics Rules about human behavior are established, often having been revealed from a supernatural realm, but they can also be viewed as socially generated guidelines.

Characteristic emotions Among the emotions typically associated with religions are dread, guilt, awe, mystery, devotion, liberation, ecstasy, inner peace, and bliss.

Ritual Beliefs are enacted and made real through ceremonies, ritual objects, and specialized locations or buildings.

Sacredness A distinction is made between the sacred and the ordinary; ceremonies often emphasize the differentiation between the sacred and the ordinary through the deliberate use of different language, clothing, and architecture. Certain objects, actions, people, and places may share in the sacredness or express it.

> Religion [is] a way of life founded upon the apprehension of sacredness in existence.
> —Julian Huxley, biologist[9]

The Sacred

All religions are concerned with the deepest level of reality, and most say that the core or origin of everything is sacred and mysterious. This sense of a mysterious, originating holiness is called by many names: Brahman, Tao, Great Mother, Divine Parent, Great Spirit, Ground of Being, the Ultimate, the Absolute, the Divine, the Holy. People, however, experience and explain sacred reality, referred to by these names, in different ways, as we shall see in the chapters that follow.

One familiar term for the sacred reality, particularly in the Western world, is *God*, and *monotheism* is the term that means a belief in one God. In some systems, the term *God* often carries with it the notion of a cosmic Person—a divine being with will and intelligence who is just and compassionate and infinite in virtues. God is also called omnipotent (having total power over the universe). While God may be said to have personal aspects, all monotheistic religions agree that the reality of God is beyond all categories: God is said to be pure spirit, not fully definable in words. This notion of a powerful God, distinct from the universe, describes a sacredness that is active in the world but also distinct from it. That is, God is **transcendent,** unlimited by the world and all ordinary reality.

In some religions, however, the sacred, ultimate reality is not viewed as having personal attributes but is more like an energy or mysterious power. Frequently, the sacred is then spoken of as something **immanent** within the universe. In some religions, there is a tendency to speak of the universe not just as having been created but also as a manifestation of the sacred nature itself, in which nothing is separate from the sacred. This view, called **pantheism** ("all divine" in Greek), sees the sacred as being discoverable within the physical world and its processes. In other words, nature is holy.

Some religions worship the sacred reality in the form of many coexisting gods, a view called **polytheism.** The multiple gods may be fairly separate entities, each in charge of an aspect of reality (such as nature gods), or they may be multiple manifestations of the same basic sacred reality.

In recent centuries, we find a tendency to deny the existence of any God or gods (**atheism**), to doubt belief in God (**agnosticism**), or simply to take no position (**nontheism**). (Such tendencies are not strictly modern; they can also be found in some ancient systems, such as Jainism; see Chapter 5.) However, if one sees religion broadly, as a "spiritual path," then even systems based on these three views—particularly if they show other typical characteristics of a religion—can also be called religions.

Religious Symbolism

Religions present views of reality, and most speak of the sacred. Nevertheless, because religions show so much variety in their teachings and because the teachings of some religions, when taken at face value, conflict with those of others, it is common to assert that religions express truth *symbolically.* A symbol is something fairly concrete, ordinary, and universal that can represent—and help human beings intensely experience— something of greater complexity. For example, water can represent spiritual cleansing; the sun, health; a mountain, strength; and a circle, eternity. We frequently find symbolism, both deliberate and unconscious, in religious art and ritual.

Symbols—and their interpretation—have long played an important part in analyzing dreams. It was once common to think of dreams as messages from a supernatural realm that provided a key to the future. Although this type of interpretation is less common nowadays, most people still think that dreams are significant. Sigmund Freud introduced his view of the dream as a door into subconscious levels of the mind; he argued that by understanding dreams symbolically we can understand our hidden needs and fears. For example, a dream of being lost in a forest might be interpreted as distress over losing one's sense of direction in life, or a dream of flying could be interpreted as a need to seek freedom.

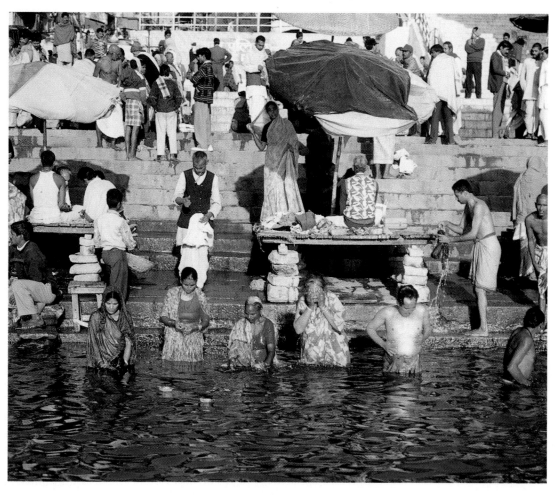

Washing with water is a universal symbol of inner purification.

Carl Gustav Jung extended the symbol-focused method of dream interpretation to the interpretation of religion. Some religious leaders have been cautious about this approach—popularized during the last half of the twentieth century by Joseph Campbell—lest everything be turned into a symbol and all literal meaning be lost. And religion specialists oppose the view that two religions are basically the same because similar symbols appear in both.

Nevertheless, there are many scholars and religious leaders who recognize the importance of symbolic interpretation, because the use of religious symbols may point to some structure that underlies all religions. There is no doubt that many of the same symbolic images and actions appear repeatedly in religions throughout the world. Water, for instance, is used in all sorts of religious rituals: Hindus bathe in the Ganges River;

To ascend one of the pyramids in Teotihuacán was to seek a place where one could encounter the sacred.

Christians use water for baptisms; Jews use water for ritual purification; and Muslims and followers of Shinto wash before prayer. Ashes also have widespread use to suggest death and the spirit world: ashes are used by tribal religions in dance ceremonies, by Hindu holy men to represent asceticism and detachment, and by Christians, whose foreheads are marked by ashes in observance of Ash Wednesday. Likewise, religious buildings are placed on hills or are raised on mounds and reached by stairs—all suggesting the symbol of the holy mountain, where the sacred can be encountered. We also see in various religions the recurrence of a symbolic story of transformation: a state of original purity degenerates into pollution or disorder; a battle to fight disorder culminates in a sacrificial death; and the result is a renewed sense of purity and order. When viewed this way, symbols and symbolic myths at times suggest a universal symbolic "language" that all religions speak, and those interested in religious symbolism hope that understanding the "language" of symbols will help uncover what is universally important in all religions.

PATTERNS AMONG RELIGIONS

When we study religions in a comparative and historical sense, we are not looking to validate them or to disprove them or to enhance our own belief or practice—as we might if we were studying our personal religious tradition. Instead, we want to comprehend the particular religions as thoroughly as possible and (as we emphasize in this book) to understand the experience of people within each religion. Part of that process of understanding leads us to see patterns of similarity and difference among religions.

While we do look for patterns, we must recognize that these are only patterns, not conceptual straightjackets. Religions, especially those with long histories and extensive followings, are usually quite complex. Furthermore, religions are not permanent theoretical constructs but are constantly in a process of change—influenced by governments, thinkers, historical events, changing technology, and, especially, the shifting values of the cultures in which they exist.

First Pattern: Focus of Beliefs and Practices

Realizing the limitation of all generalizations, we nonetheless might look for orientations shown by individual religions as a way of gaining some perspective on them. When we look at the world's dominant religions, we see three basic orientations in their conception and location of the sacred.[11]

> Religion is the substance of culture, and culture the form of religion.
>
> —Paul Tillich, theologian[10]

> *Sacramental orientation* The sacramental orientation emphasizes carrying out rituals and ceremonies regularly and—importantly— correctly as the path to salvation; in some religions, correct ritual is believed to influence the processes of nature. All religions have some degree of ritual, but the ceremonial tendency is predominant, for example, in most tribal religions, in Roman Catholic and Eastern Orthodox Christianity, in Vedic Hinduism, and in Tibetan Buddhism. Making the Catholic sign of the cross, for example, is done in a certain way: only with the right hand, beginning with a touch on the forehead, then on one's chest, and finally on each shoulder, left to right.[12]

> *Prophetic orientation* The prophetic orientation stresses that contact with the sacred is ensured by proper belief and by adherence to moral rules. This orientation also implies that a human being may be an important intermediary between the believer and the sacred; for example, a prophet may speak to believers on behalf of the sacred. Prophetic orientation is a prominent aspect of Judaism, Protestant Christianity, and Islam, which all see the sacred as being transcendent but personal. Billy Graham, the famous evangelist, has often urged personal conversion with these rhyming words: "The Bible commands it; our Savior demands it." The television crusades of ministers like him are a good example of the prophetic orientation in action.

> *Mystical orientation* The mystical orientation seeks union with a reality greater than oneself, such as with God, the process of nature, the universe, or reality as a whole. Often techniques for lessening the sense of one's individual identity (such as seated meditation) help the individual experience a greater unity. The mystical orientation is a prominent aspect of Upanishadic Hinduism, Taoism, and some

schools of Buddhism. (Master Kusan [1901–1983], a Korean teacher of Zen Buddhism, described the disappearance of self in the enlightenment experience of unity with this memorable question, "Could a snowflake survive inside a burning flame?"[13]) Although the mystical orientation is more common in religions that stress the immanence of the sacred or that are nontheistic, it is a less prominent tendency in Judaism, Christianity, and Islam as well.

Any one of these three tendencies may be dominant in a religion, yet the other two tendencies might also be found in the same religion to a lesser extent and possibly subsumed into a different purpose. For example, ceremony can be utilized to help induce mystical experience, as in Catholic and Orthodox Christianity, Japanese Shingon Buddhism, Tibetan Buddhism, Taoism, and even Zen Buddhism, which has a strongly ritualistic aspect of its own.

Second Pattern: Religious Views of the World and Life

Given the great variety in their worldviews, it is not surprising that each religion defines differently the nature of sacred reality, the universe, the natural world, time, and human purpose. Religions also differ in their attitudes toward the role of words in expressing the sacred and in their relations to other religious traditions. By examining different views on these concepts, we will have further bases for comparison that will lead us to a more complete understanding of the world's religions.

The nature of sacred reality Some religions, as we have seen, speak of the sacred in terms that characterize it as being transcendent, existing primarily in a realm beyond the everyday world. In other religions, though, sacred reality is spoken of as being immanent; that is, it is within nature and human beings and can be experienced as energy or holiness. Sometimes the sacred is viewed as having personal attributes, while elsewhere it is seen as an impersonal entity.

The nature of the universe Some religions see the universe as having been begun by an intelligent, personal Creator who continues to guide the universe according to a cosmic plan. Other religions view the universe as being eternal, that is, having no beginning or end. The implications of these two positions are quite important to what is central in a religion and to how the human being acts in regard to this central belief. If the universe is created, especially by a transcendent deity, the center of sacredness is the Creator rather than the universe, but human beings imitate the Creator by changing and perfecting the world. If, however, the universe is eternal, the material universe itself is sacred and perfect and requires no change.

The human attitude toward nature At one end of the spectrum of attitudes on this topic are religions or religious schools that see nature as the realm of evil forces that must be overcome. Nature is gross and contaminating, existing in opposition to the nonmaterial world of the spirit—a view, known as **dualism,** held by some forms of Christianity and Hinduism. At the other end of the spectrum, as in Taoism and Shinto, nature is considered to be sacred and needs no alteration. Other religions, such as Judaism and Islam, take a middle ground, holding that the natural world originated from a divine action but that human beings are called upon to continue to shape it.

Time Religions that emphasize a creation, such as Judaism, Christianity, and Islam, tend to see time as being linear, moving in a straight line from the beginning of the universe to its end. Being limited and unrepeatable, time is important. In some other religions, such as Buddhism, however, time is cyclical. The universe simply moves through endless changes, which repeat themselves over grand periods of time. In such a religion, time is not as crucial or "real," because, ultimately, the universe is not moving to some final point; consequently, appreciating the present may be more important than being oriented to the future.

Human purpose In some religions, human beings are part of a great divine plan, and although each person is unique, individual meaning comes also from the cosmic plan. The cosmic plan may be viewed as a struggle between forces of good and evil, with human beings at the center of the stage and the forces of good and evil at work within them. Because human actions are so important, they must be guided by a prescribed moral code that is meant to be internalized by the individual. This view is significant in Judaism, Christianity, and Islam. In contrast, other religions do not see human life in similarly dramatic terms, and the individual is only part of much larger realities. In Taoism and Shinto, a human being is a small part of the natural universe, and in Confucianism, an individual is part of the family and of society. Such religions place less emphasis on individual rights and more emphasis on how the individual can maintain harmony with the whole. Actions are not guided by an internalized moral system but by society, tradition, and a sense of mutual obligation.

Words and scriptures In some religions, the sacred is to be found in written and spoken words, and for those religions that use writing and create scriptures, reading, copying, and using sacred words in music or art are important. We see the importance of words in native religions (which pass on their traditions orally), in Judaism, in Christianity, in Islam, and in Hinduism. Other religions, such as Taoism and Zen Buddhism, which show a certain mistrust of words, value silence and wordless meditation. Although Zen and Taoism utilize language in their practices and have produced significant literature, each of these religions finds language limited in expressing the richness or totality of reality.

Exclusiveness and inclusiveness Some religions emphasize that the sacred is distinct from the world and that order must be imposed by separating good from bad, true from false. In that view, to share in sacredness means separation—for example, withdrawal from certain foods, places, people, practices, or beliefs. Hinduism, Judaism, Christianity, and Islam are among the religions that have been generally exclusive, making it impossible to belong to more than one religion at the same time. In contrast, other religions have stressed inclusiveness. Frequently, such religions also have emphasized social harmony, the inadequacy of language, or the relativity of truth, and they have accepted belief in many deities. Their inclusiveness has led them to admit many types of beliefs and practices into their religions, to the point that it is possible for an individual to belong to several religions—such as Buddhism, Taoism, and Confucianism—simultaneously. This has led to misunderstanding at times, as when a Christian missionary has "converted" a Japanese follower only to find the new convert still visiting a Shinto shrine.

Third Pattern: Religious Views of Male and Female

Because gender is such an intrinsic and important part of being human, religions have had much to say about the roles of men and women, both on earth and in the divine spheres. Thus, views of what is male and what is female provide another basis for comparing religions.

Bishop Barbara Harris, shown here at her consecration in 1989, became the first female bishop of the Episcopal Church.

Is Goddess Worship Still Alive?

Although male imagery is dominant in contemporary religions, traces—and current practices—of Goddess worship are abundant.

- In India, the divine is worshiped in its female aspects as the Great Mother (also known as Kali and Durga) or as lesser female deities.
- In Catholic and Orthodox Christianity, Mary, the mother of Jesus, although not venerated as a divinity, is held to possess suprahuman powers and is a strong role model for women's behavior.
- In the Mahayana Buddhist pantheon, Guanyin (Kannon) receives special veneration as a female ideal of mercy.
- In Japan, the premier Shinto divinity is the goddess Amaterasu, patroness of the imperial family. In contrast to many other religion systems, the goddess Amaterasu is associated with the sun, while a male god is associated with the moon.
- In Korea and Japan, shamans are frequently female.
- In Africa, India, and elsewhere, some tribal cultures remain matriarchal.
- In Wicca, a contemporary restoration of ancient, nature-based religion, devotees worship a female deity they refer to as the Goddess.
- Symbolic forms of the female divine are still prominent in the rites of several religions. Common symbols include the moon, the snake, spirals and labyrinths, the egg, *yoni* (symbolic vagina), water, and earth. These symbolic representations of the female suggest generation, growth, nurturance, intuition, and wisdom.

In many influential religions of today, male imagery and control seem to dominate: the sacred is considered male and the full-time religious specialists are frequently male. But this may not always have been the case. Tantalizing evidence suggests that female divinities once played an important role in many cultures and religions. The most significant female deity was particularly associated with fertility and motherhood and has been known by many names, such as Astarte, Asherah, Aphrodite, and Freia (after whom Friday is named). Statues of a Mother-Goddess—sometimes with many breasts to suggest the spiritual power of the nurturing female—have been found throughout Europe, as well as in Turkey, Israel, and the Middle East.

Why has patriarchal religion, at least for now, so overcome matriarchal elements? It is possible that matriarchy and Goddess worship were frequent in early societies but that matriarchal cultures were suppressed by male-led nomadic cultures, by the development of the tools and strategies of war, and by the growth of populous city-states that needed defense.

It appears that male domination spread significantly after 2000 B.C.E. In India, the Aryans who entered the subcontinent were led by males on horseback who worshiped gods that were almost exclusively male. In Israel, worship of the Goddess was stamped out by prophets who preached exclusive worship of the male god Yahweh and by kings who wanted loyalty paid to them and their offspring. We read passages like this in the Hebrew Scriptures: "They abandoned the Lord and worshipped Baal and the Astartes. So the anger of the Lord was kindled against Israel" (Judg. 2: 13–14).[14] The Christian New Testament forbids women to preach: "I do not allow them to teach or to have authority over men; they must keep quiet. For Adam was created first, and then Eve. And it was not Adam who was deceived; it was the woman who was deceived and broke God's law" (I

Tim. 2:12–14).[15] In Asia, Confucianism has been distrustful of women in general and has ordinarily refused them leadership roles. In Buddhism, despite recognition in scripture that women can be enlightened, in practice the great majority of leaders have been men.[16] This patriarchal tendency has shaped religious life, for good or bad, for the last three to four thousand years.

Nevertheless, changes—inevitable in religion, as in everything else—are occurring. As women take leadership roles in business and civic life, they are assuming similar leadership roles in religion in some societies. The study of comparative religion has helped this process by opening people's eyes to those religions of the past in which goddesses were worshiped and women played leading roles. Students of art, literature, and the history of religion are finding abundant evidence of female mystics, poets, shamans, and prophets. It is possible that religion in general is turning away from exclusively patriarchal patterns and beginning to include once again matriarchal values and practices.

MULTIDISCIPLINARY APPROACHES TO THE STUDY OF RELIGION

One of the most fascinating things about religion is that it has influenced so many areas of human life. Consequently, religion can be studied from the point of view of several disciplines. History and literary study have provided two traditional ways of approaching religion, and more recently the fields of anthropology, psychology, and sociology have offered a new look at religion from the perspective of human behavior.

There are other approaches, too. We can focus our study on a single religion or look at several religions at the same time. Believers may opt to explore their own religion "from the inside," while nonbelievers may want to concentrate on the answers that several religions have given to a single question, such as life or death. Following is a list of some common approaches to religion.

Psychology Psychology (Greek: "soul study") deals with human mental states, emotions, and behaviors. Despite being a fairly young discipline, psychology has taken a close look at religion because it offers such rich human "material" to explore. A few areas of study include religious influences on child rearing, human behavior, and self-identity; group dynamics in religion; trance states; and comparative mystical experiences.

Mythology The study of religious tales, texts, and art has uncovered some universal patterns. Mythology is full of recurrent images and themes found in all religions, such as the tree of knowledge, the ladder to heaven, the fountain of life, the labyrinth, the secret garden, the holy mountain, the newborn child, the suffering hero, initiation, rebirth, the cosmic battle, the female spirit guide, and the aged teacher of wisdom. The word *myth* in ordinary language usually refers to a story that may be meaningful but is historically untrue. In religion the word *myth* simply means a story that is central to a religion. For example, the story of the Buddha's enlightenment is the central myth of Buddhism.

Philosophy Philosophy (Greek: "love of wisdom") in some ways originated from a struggle with religion; although both arenas pose many of the same questions, philosophy does not automatically accept the answers given by any religion to the great questions. Instead, philosophy seeks answers independently, following reason rather than religious authority, and it tries to fit its answers into a rational, systematic whole. Some questions philosophy asks are, Does human life have any purpose? Is there an afterlife? and How should we live? Philosophy is essentially the work of individuals, while religion is a community experience; philosophy tries to avoid emotion, while religion often nurtures it; and philosophy is carried on without ritual, while religion naturally expresses itself in ceremony.

Theology Theology (Greek: "study of the divine") is the study of topics as they relate to one particular religious tradition. A theologian is an individual who usually studies his or her own belief system. For example, a person who is in training to become a minister might study Christian doctrine.

The arts Comparing patterns in religious art makes an intriguing study. For example, religious architecture often uses symmetry, height, and archaic styles to suggest the sacred; religious music frequently employs a slow pace and repeated rhythms to induce tranquillity; and religious art often incorporates gold, haloes, equilateral designs, and circles to suggest perfection or otherworldliness.

Anthropology Anthropology (Greek: "study of human beings") has been interested in how religions influence the ways a culture deals with issues such as family interaction, individual roles, property rights, marriage, child rearing, social hierarchies, and division of labor.

Archeology Archeology (Greek: "study of origins") explores the remains of earlier civilizations, often uncovering the artifacts and ruins of religious buildings from ancient cultures. When possible, archeologists translate writings left by these people, much of which can be religious in origin. Archeology occasionally sheds light on how one religion influences another. For example, the excavation of a cuneiform library at Nineveh 150 years ago revealed a story (in the epic of *Gilgamesh*) that is similar to—and may have influenced—the biblical story of Noah and the flood. Archeology can also reveal religious material that allows scholars to decipher an entire writing system. For example, the discovery in the early nineteenth century of the Rosetta Stone (which contained the same inscription in three different scripts) led researchers to unlock the meaning of Egyptian hieroglyphics.

Comparative religion Over the last century, the academic study of religion has intensified as a result of the increasing interaction between different cultures, as well as the translation of religious documents from around the world. Scholars attempt to examine objectively all elements of specific religions, and departments of religious studies have been set up by universities to analyze, teach, and publish the growing body of knowledge.

WHY STUDY THE MAJOR RELIGIONS OF THE WORLD?

> Science investigates; religion interprets. Science gives man knowledge which is power; religion gives man wisdom which is control.
>
> —Martin Luther King, Jr.[17]

Because religions are so wide-ranging and influential, their study helps round out a person's education, as well as enrich one's experience of many other related subjects. Let's now consider some additional pleasures and rewards of the study of religions.

Insight into religious traditions Each religion is interesting in its own right, as a complex system of values, relationships, personalities, and human creativity.

Insight into what religions share The study of religions requires sympathy and objectivity. While it is true that being a believer of a particular religion brings a special insight that an outsider cannot have, it is also true that an outsider can appreciate things that are not always obvious to the insider. This is particularly true of shared patterns of imagery, belief, and practice.

Tolerance Because human beings are emotional creatures, their religions can sometimes allow inflamed feelings to override common decency. As history shows, religious communities have sometimes relied on censorship and authoritarianism to impose their will. Examining the major religions of the world helps one develop a certain objectivity and tolerance.

Appreciation of differences In a multicultural world, tolerance of differences is valuable, but enjoyment of differences is even better. Variety is a fact of nature, and the person who can enjoy variety—in religion and everywhere else—is a person who will never be tired of life.

Insight into everyday life Religious influences can be found everywhere in modern culture, not just within religious buildings. Politicians make use of religious images, for example, when they speak of a "new covenant" with voters. Specific religions and religious

Exploring Religion Beyond the Classroom

Travel, which at one time was affordable for only the very rich, is now an option for a broad spectrum of the population—and something wonderful for people interested in religion. Studying religions from books is somewhat limited, as compared to a firsthand experience of the great religious art, architecture, music, and ceremony to be found across the globe. The difference between studying books about religion and actually experiencing the living expressions of religion throughout the world is like the transforming experience in the film *The Wizard of Oz*: when the main character Dorothy (Greek: "gift of God") begins her mythic journey, accompanied only by her dog Toto (Spanish: "all"), her black-and-white world suddenly turns to color. (This book encourages such firsthand experience; sections titled "Religion Beyond the Classroom" that appear at the end of each chapter will offer suggestions for specific places to visit.)

There are innumerable programs designed specifically for young travelers. Many colleges offer study-abroad programs, with summer courses scheduled that include travel; and some have semester and year-long study programs abroad. Scholarships and other financial aid may be available for these programs. Large travel companies also offer summer tours for students, particularly to Europe and Asia; these companies are able to offer affordable tours by scheduling charter flights and inexpensive hotel accommodations. Programs such as these often make an excellent first trip abroad for students. Young travelers touring on their own can join the Youth Hostel Association of their country and make use of a worldwide network of inexpensive youth hostels, which is quite extensive in Europe but also exists in the United States and many other countries around the world.

Senior citizens (55 years and above) can take advantage of Elderhostel programs. Elderhostel offers a wide variety of programs—educational courses, excursions, and service projects—all around the world, usually lasting from one to several weeks. Among the various religious programs offered are studies of Jerusalem, English cathedrals, and religious art.

Travelers who have limited time should look into travel packages that include the costs of the flight, hotel, and car or tour bus. Many countries also sell railroad passes. The Eurailpass and Britrail Pass are the best known and can be purchased through any travel agent. Retirees, often with more time and open schedules, might consider cruises that include sightseeing opportunities on land. Moreover, there are agencies and clubs through which homeowners can exchange the use of their house or apartment with people from another region or country.

Information on travel, youth hostels, and home exchanges can be found in the travel sections of libraries and bookstores. There are also many fine guidebooks for travelers, some for the general traveler and others for quite specialized audiences. Good guidebooks should be read in preparation for travel, and at least one should be carried along on the trip. Intellectual preparation and practical planning before travel makes the journey an even richer experience. Recommended guidebooks for students are the *Lonely Planet* series and the *Let's Go* series from the Harvard Student Agencies. Specialized travel books relating to religion are also available, such as guides to English cathedrals, Japanese temples, and pilgrimage sites around the world. The Internet is another good source of travel information, with several thousand sites to choose from. And, of course, travel agents can help in planning and making reservations.

denominations take public positions on moral issues, such as abortion and war. Our weekly routines are regulated by the originally Jewish practice of a six-day work week followed by a day of rest, and the European-American school calendar is divided in two by the originally Christian Christmas holidays. Even comic strips use religious imagery: animals crowded onto a wooden boat, a man holding two tablets, angels on clouds, a person meditating on a mountaintop. The value of the study of religions is that it helps us recognize and appreciate the religious influences that are everywhere.

Appreciation for the arts Anyone attracted to painting, sculpture, music, or architecture will be drawn to the study of religions, because various religious traditions have possibly been the most significant patron of these arts. The study of religions is a gateway to these forms of art and many others.

Enjoyment of travel One of the great pleasures of our age is travel. Walking through Chartres Cathedral in France is quite different from reading about it. The study of world religions gives travelers the background necessary to fully enjoy the many wonderful places they can now experience directly.

Insight into family traditions Religions have influenced most earlier cultures so strongly that their effects are readily identifiable in the values of our parents and grandparents—even if they are not actively religious individuals. These values include attitudes toward education, individual rights, gender roles, different ethnic groups, different religions, and elders.

Help in one's own religious quest Not everyone is destined to become an artist or a musician or a poet, yet each one of us has some ability to appreciate visual arts, music, and poetry. In the same way, although some people may not be explicitly religious, they may have religious instincts, a sense of the sacred, and a desire to seek ways to feel at home in the universe. Those who belong to a religion will have their beliefs and practices enriched by the study of the world's religions, since they will learn about their religion's history, major figures, scriptures, and influence from different points of view. Others may have little interest in traditional religions yet nonetheless insist that they have a strong interest in spirituality and describe their lives as a spiritual quest. For any person involved in a spiritual search, it is extremely helpful to study a variety of religions. Stories of others' spiritual quests provide insights that we may draw on for our own spiritual journey.

THE PILGRIMAGE

With open minds, eager for the many benefits of studying religions, we now begin an intellectual pilgrimage to many of the world's important living religions. We will first look at a sample of religions often associated with native peoples across the globe. We will then go on to study religions that emerged on the Indian subcontinent and then to the religions that arose in China and Japan. Next we will travel to the area east of the Mediterranean Sea—a generally arid region that nonetheless has been fertile in supporting new religious ideas. Finally, we will consider the modern religious search.

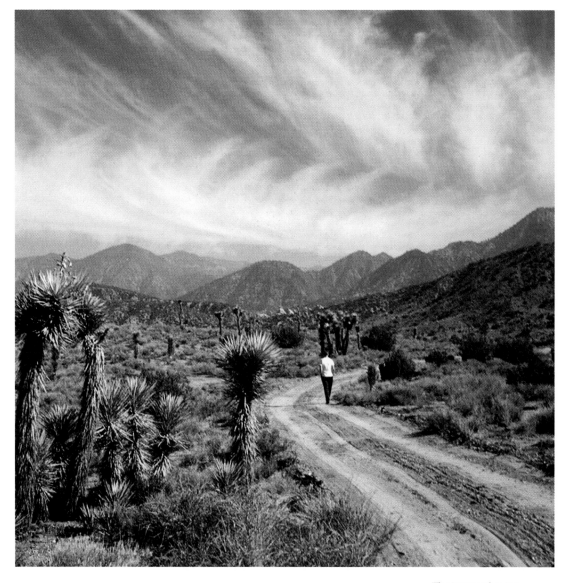

The journey begins.

Our journey, though academic and intellectual, may prompt strong emotions in some readers. For some it will be a prelude to an actual physical pilgrimage. For others it will be an intellectual pilgrimage that will provoke both doubt and insight.

We begin with the knowledge that at the end of every journey we are not quite the same as we were at the beginning. Ours is a journey of discovery, and through discovery, we hope to become more appreciative of the experience of being human in the universe.

RELIGION BEYOND THE CLASSROOM

You can learn a great deal about religious practice and the artistic manifestations of religion without having to travel far from home. For example, you only have to look up "church" in the yellow pages of a telephone book to find listings that will probably extend for pages. In addition, Saturday newspapers often have religious news and announcements of upcoming events.

What were once considered "minority" religions are becoming widespread, and any city will have meeting places for a variety of religions. North America, in particular, has many Chinese and Tibetan Buddhist temples, Catholic monasteries and retreat houses, Zen meditation centers, Muslim mosques, Greek and Russian Orthodox churches, Hindu temples, and Hindu or Buddhist vegetarian restaurants. Cities and counties with a diversity of ethnic minorities are particularly rich in religious places of worship and meditation. All you have to

do is call up and ask about making a visit. People in religious centers are almost invariably welcoming to outsiders, and they will direct you to other people and places within their tradition. Find out when there are services, concerts, and meetings; and if you are seriously interested, you can ask to be put on their mailing list.

Although travel abroad requires more planning, effort, and money, it provides unforgettable experiences. It can be done more easily than most people think and at virtually any age. Most religions encourage travel for religious reasons—this is the meaning of a pilgrimage, an ancient custom that is still very much alive. The goal of a pilgrimage is not only to visit a particular place but to grow spiritually. Even if your reason for travel is not conventionally religious, the experience will surely result in personal growth.

FOR FULLER UNDERSTANDING

1. Explore the insights of Freud or Jung about religion, and use those insights to examine the religious tradition with which you are most familiar. How would Freud or Jung understand that religion?

2. Early in this chapter there was a list of human needs religion sometimes fulfils. Can you add to that list?

3. In this book we will focus on architecture and travel as two ways of studying religions. Make a list of interesting religious buildings and travel destinations in your area.

4. Keep a notebook or journal of references to religion that you see in newspapers and on television. What patterns do you see? What issues recur?

RELATED READINGS

Campbell, Joseph. *The Power of Myth.* New York: Doubleday, 1988. An investigation of myths, fairy tales, and religious symbols in readable style. See also Campbell's more difficult *The Hero with a Thousand Faces* (Princeton, NJ: Princeton University Press/Bollingen, 1968), which focuses on the journey of the mythic hero in several religions and cultures.

Eliade, Mircea. *The Sacred and the Profane: The Nature of Religion.* New York: Harper & Brothers, 1959. A seminal work by a major scholar of comparative religion that cites examples from many cultures of universal religious symbols, of ways of establishing sacred space and sacred time, and of techniques for initiation and rebirth.

Huxley, Aldous. *The Perennial Philosophy.* New York: Harper & Row, 1945. A book that quotes much mystical religious literature to argue that all mystical experience is basically similar, despite different religious language. Although Huxley's argument is much debated, the book is an important contribution to the topic.

Jung, Carl G. *Memories, Dreams, Reflections.* London: Fontana, 1972. The author's account of his own life, focusing on his religious search and his understanding of religious symbolism. It is a dense but fascinating classic that anyone with an interest in religious symbolism will enjoy.

Stone, Merlin. *When God Was a Woman.* San Diego: Harcourt Brace Jovanovich, 1976. An important book that brought attention to ancient worship of the divine in female form.

KEY TERMS

Agnosticism: Literally meaning "not know"; the position that holds that the existence of God cannot be proven.

Animism: From the Latin *anima,* meaning "spirit," "soul," "life force"; a worldview common among oral religions (religions with no written scriptures) that sees all elements of nature as being filled with spirit or spirits.

Atheism: Literally meaning "not God"; the position that holds that there is no God or gods.

Dualism: The belief that reality is made of two different principles (spirit and matter); the belief in two gods (good and evil) in conflict.

Immanent: Existing and operating within nature.

Monotheism: The belief in one God.

Nontheistic: Not asserting or denying the existence of any deity; unconcerned with the supernatural.

Pantheism: The belief that everything in the universe is divine.

Polytheism: The belief in many gods.

Transcendent: Not limited by the physical world.

CHAPTER **2**

Oral Religions

 FIRST ENCOUNTER

As it is for most visitors, your first stop in Hawai`i is Waikiki, on the island of O`ahu. After four days of swimming, sightseeing, and viewing the sunsets, you fly south to the much less populated island of Hawai`i—called the Big Island by local residents. From the airport in Hilo, you begin to drive upcountry, toward the little town of Volcano. The area around Hilo, on the rainy side of the island, resembles the tropical paradise of fantasy: the leaves of the trees are bright lime-colored flames, and houses are fronted by vanda orchids and fragrant white-flowered plumeria trees.

As you drive inland and upward, lawns and homes yield to fields of beige grass and clusters of dark brown rock. Banyan trees give way to small silver-leaved `ohi`a lehua, as delicate as their red flowers. Now you are closer to the volcanoes that are still producing the island. The land here

Note: The glottal stop (`okina) is used throughout this book in the spelling of certain Hawaiian words. It is indicated by an inverted apostrophe.

is raw and relatively new. You check into the old lava-rock hotel near the volcanic crater and look forward to settling in for the night. After supper you listen to ukulele music in front of the big fireplace in the lobby and watch a man and two women perform a slow hula for the guests.

The next morning, after a good sleep, you walk out to the rim of the crater. You are a bit startled by the steam rising through cracks and holes in the rock. Then you hike down a trail that leads to a bed of old lava, passing yellow ginger and tiny wild purple orchids on the way. The lava in the crater at this spot is dry; it crunches underfoot. Here and there you see stones wrapped in the broad leaves of the *ti* plant and wonder why they're there.

On the way back up the trail, you fall in step with a woman who explains that she was raised on the Big Island but now lives on another island. She is here just for a few days, to visit the volcano area and to see old friends. She tells you about Pele, the goddess of fire, whose place of veneration is the volcano.

"When I was young I learned that Pele came from the island of Kaua`i to Maui, where she lived in Haleakala Crater before she moved to this island. Nowadays, people here are mostly Buddhist or Christian, but they still respect Pele. I know a man who says Pele once appeared to him. He told me she had long hair and was surrounded by fire. Other people have seen her on the road. Pele gets a lot of offerings—mostly *ti* leaves and food. But when the lava is flowing toward Hilo, people also bring out pork and gin," the woman says with a little grin, "and my friends tell me that the offerings work."

The lava, she explains, is active now at the other end of a series of craters, closer to the ocean. She suggests that you drive to the lava flow before dark and adds, "Be sure to have good walking shoes, as well as a flashlight in case it gets dark before you go back to your car. Be sure not to take any lava rock away with you. They say it brings bad luck, you know."

In midafternoon, you drive down the curving Chain of Craters Road, past old lava flows, to the highway near the ocean. You stop and park near the cars of other lava watchers, then begin hiking with a few people across the fresh lava, toward the ocean. About half a mile in, you encounter yellow caution strips and overhear an officer warning one man to stop. "Further on it's just too dangerous. It looks solid on top, but you can slip through the crust." You and the others crowd up next to the barriers and see steam rising on the right up ahead. Through the rising steam you glimpse a bright orange band of molten lava underneath the dry crust as it falls into the ocean.

Sunset comes quickly, and even more people arrive, some with blankets around their shoulders. As darkness falls, the flowing lava becomes more visible and the steam takes on a reddish glow. "Look over there," someone says. In the distance a bright stream of orange lava slides down a hill, a slow-motion waterfall of fire. You watch at least an hour as the sky becomes completely dark. Now the only light comes from the flowing lava and a few flashlights. It is, you think, like being present at creation: this land is being born.

The next morning in the lobby you see the Hawaiian woman again. "Well, did you see Pele last night?" she asks, smiling. You smile back. For all the rest of your stay you wonder about Pele, about what else might remain of native Hawaiian religion. Isn't hula, you ask as you think back over what you've read, an expression of Hawaiian beliefs? Why do people make offerings of *ti* leaves? How much of the ancient religion lives on?

DISCOVERING ORAL RELIGIONS

All around the world, native people follow their spiritual traditions. Among the Ainu in far northern Japan, the Inuit (Eskimo) in Canada, the aboriginal peoples of Australia, the Maori of New Zealand, the Yoruba of Africa, and the many indigenous peoples of the Americas, religious teachings are passed on by word of mouth rather than through written texts. In some areas, the ancient religious ways of native peoples may be endangered or lost, but their influence is evident to an observant eye, and certain characteristics are likely to live on in stories and local customs. There is as yet no agreement on how to categorize these religions. Various alternative terms include *traditional, aboriginal, indigenous, tribal, nonliterate, primal,* and *basic,* but because of each term's connotative limitations, no single descriptive word seems quite appropriate. However, for the purposes of this text, the terms *oral religion* and *native religion* will refer to those cultures that have used spoken language (versus written language) to hand down their religious traditions from generation to generation.

This mask from Gabon in Africa may well be appreciated by outsiders as a work of art. However, its creators understood it as part of a ritual stilt dance associated with funeral ceremonies of the BaPunu and Ashira peoples.

Oral religions are found in every climate, from the tropical jungle to the arctic tundra, and some are far older than today's dominant religions. Because most of them developed in isolation from each other, there are major differences in their stories of creation and origin, in their beliefs about the afterlife, in their marriage and funeral customs, and so on. In fact, there is as much variation among oral religions as there is, for example, between Buddhism and Christianity. In North America, for instance, there are several hundred Native American nations and more than fifty Native American language groups. The variety among oral religious traditions is stunning and each religion deserves in-depth study. But because of the limitations of space, this book must focus on shared elements; regrettably, we can barely touch on the many differences.

Past Obstacles to the Appreciation of Oral Religions

Up until the early part of the twentieth century, scholars focused more on religions that had produced written texts than on those that expressed themselves through orally transmitted stories, histories, and rituals. This lack of attention may have been due in part to the fact that religions with written records are easier to study primarily because they don't necessarily require travel or physically arduous research; moreover, when scholars master their particular languages, they can study, translate, and teach the original writings either at home or to students anywhere. Finally, text-based religions are easier to study because they tend to be large-scale and influential, whereas oral traditions are usually very local in scope and are often meaningful only to those familiar with the spoken language in which the teachings are conveyed.

There has also been a bias toward text-based religions because of an assumption that they are complex and that oral religions are simple. Greater research into oral religions, however, has dispelled such notions of simplicity. Consider, for example, the sandpaintings of the Navajo people and the ceremonies of which the paintings are a part. "In these ceremonies, which are very complicated and intricate, sandpaintings are made and prayers recited. Sandpaintings are impermanent paintings made of dried pulverized materials that depicted the Holy People [supernatural beings] and serve as a temporary altar. Over 800 forms of sandpaintings exist, each connected to a specific chant and ceremony."[1]

Sandpaintings are impermanent; gothic cathedrals are not. It is possible that the traditional bias toward written religions may also reflect an unconscious attraction to material permanence. Written religions often produce manuscripts, musical notation, stone sculpture, and fairly permanent buildings. Oral religions, in contrast, tend to express themselves in ways that have less permanence: dance, masks, wood sculpture, paintings that utilize mineral and plant dyes, tattoo, body painting, and memorized story and chant. Perhaps we have to begin to see these transitory expressions of religious art as being equal in stature to more permanent sacred writings and artistic creations. Geoffrey Parrinder, for example, writes that "African art provides a kind of scripture of African religion." He calls African art the "indigenous language of African belief and thought."[2]

The Modern Recovery of Oral Religions

We know about native religious traditions through the efforts of a number of disciplines, particularly anthropology. One pioneer was Franz Boas (1858–1942), a professor at Columbia University and curator at the American Museum of Natural History in New York. Another was Margaret Mead (1901–1978), a curator at the same institution, whose major contributions included such books as *Coming of Age in Samoa* and *Growing Up in New Guinea.*

The ecological movement has also hastened our study of oral religions. Environmentalist David Suzuki argues that we must look to native peoples and religions for insightful lessons in the relationship between human beings and nature. In his introduction to the book *Wisdom of the Elders,* he writes that the earth is rapidly moving toward what he calls "ecocrisis." He quotes the ecologist Paul Ehrlich in saying that solutions will have to be "quasi-religious." Suzuki argues that "our problem is inherent in the way we perceive our relationship with the rest of Nature and our role in the grand scheme of things. Harvard biologist E. O. Wilson proposes that we foster *biophilia,* a love of life. He once told me, 'We must rediscover our *kin,* the other animals and plants with whom we share this planet.' "[3]

The development of recording technology (especially photography and sound recording) has helped the recovery of native religious traditions. Photography captures native styles of life and allows them to be seen with a certain immediacy. Ethnomusicology involves the recording of chants and the sounds of musical instruments that might otherwise be lost. Gladys Reichard, a specialist in Navajo ceremony, has written that chanters in the Navajo religion need to know thousands of songs by memory, and remarks that the number of Navajo songs is "incalculable."[4] The fact that listeners can replay such recordings has no doubt added to the appreciation of this music.

Interest in native music has come from composers as well as anthropologists. Previously unrecorded folk music, much of it rooted in oral religions, became available in Europe in the early twentieth century and made its way into the compositions of such musicians as Ralph Vaughan Williams (1872–1958) and Béla Bartók (1881–1945). The influence of native music continues today, such as in the songs of Paul Simon that are inspired by South African tribal music. In the last one hundred years, recordings have been made all over the globe, to be appreciated and studied virtually anywhere.

Artists around the world have begun in the last century to find inspiration in native wood sculpture, masks, drums, and textile design. Pablo Picasso (1881–1973), for example, often spoke of the strong influence that African religious masks had on his work. By early 1900, West African masks had found their way to Paris and the artists there. A scholar describes the

All our histories, traditions, codes were passed from one generation to another by word of mouth. Our memories must be kept clear and accurate, our observation must be keen, our self control absolute.

—Thomas Wildcat Alford, Shawnee[5]

The Hawaiian chanter typically has learned chants orally from a *kupuna,* an esteemed elder who passes on what he or she knows to worthy disciples.

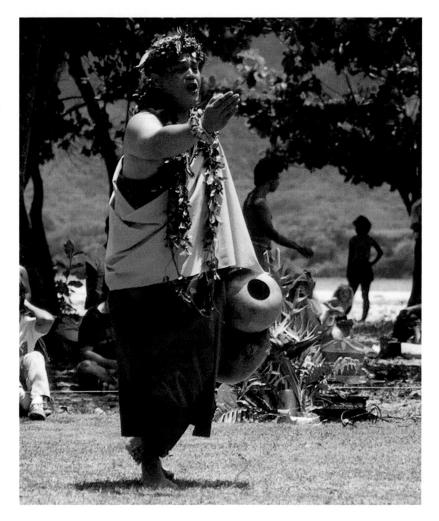

effect of one African work on several artists who were close friends. "One piece . . . is a mask that had been given to Maurice Vlaminck in 1905. He records that [André] Derain was 'speechless' and 'stunned' when he saw it, bought it from Vlaminck and in turn showed it to Picasso and Matisse, who were also greatly affected by it."[6] French artist Paul Gauguin moved to Tahiti and the Marquesas to find and paint what he hoped was a fundamental form of religion there, and some of his paintings allude to native Tahitian religious belief.[7] The work of artists like Picasso and Gauguin helped to open eyes to the beauty produced by oral religions.

The religious art of native peoples of course needs no authentication from outsiders. And outsiders present a problem: they tend to treat native religious objects as purely secular works of art, while people within an oral religious tradition do not make such a distinction. Oral religions exist generally within **holistic** cultures, in which every object and act may have religious meaning. Art, music, religion, and social behavior within such cultures can be so inseparable that it is hard to say what is distinctly religious and what is not.

Fortunately, the bias that once judged native religions to be "primitive" manifestations of the religious spirit—as opposed to the literate, so-called higher religions—is disappearing. It is an inescapable fact that the span of written religions is relatively brief—barely five thousand years—yet scientists now hold that human beings have lived on earth for at least a million (and possibly two or three million) years. Although we do not know how long human beings have been manifesting religious behavior, we believe it goes back far more than a few thousand years.

STUDYING ORAL RELIGIONS: LEARNING FROM PATTERNS

The study of oral religious traditions presents its own specific challenges. Our understanding of oral religions comes primarily from the various methods described in Chapter 1, yet some of these approaches have proven less effective in the study of oral religions than they have in the examination of large-scale literate religions. Hence, we depend on more recent tools to learn about oral religions.

Because oral religions are most often far less visible than their large-population counterparts, scholars often approach them with the methods commonly used to study indigenous cultures. Studies by anthropologists, sociologists, and cultural historians are presently changing the way we make sense of many of the phenomena associated with oral religions and will continue to reshape our understanding of these traditions over the next decades.

It would be ideal if we could study and experience each native religion separately; barring that, however, one workable approach is to consider them collectively as "sacred paths" that share common elements. Thus, in this chapter we will concentrate on finding patterns in native religions—while keeping in mind that beyond the patterns there is enormous variety. The patterns we identify in oral religions will also enrich our encounter with other religions in later chapters. Three key patterns we will consider are the human relationship with nature, the framing of sacred time and space, and the respect for origins, gods, and ancestors.

Human Relationships with the Natural World

Most oral religions have sprung from tribal and small-scale cultures where survival requires a harmonious and respectful relationship with nature. In the worldview of oral religions, human beings are very much a part of nature. People look to nature itself (sometimes interpreted through traditional lore) for guidance and meaning.

In fact, native religions often see everything in the universe as being alive, a concept known as *animism*. The life force (Latin: *anima*) is present in everything and is especially apparent in living things—trees, plants, birds, animals, and human beings—and in the motion of water, the sun, the moon,

Spirits Within

Among many peoples, certain objects—a rock, a tree, a bird—are thought of as being animated by an individual spirit that lives within. And in particular native traditions, we find deities that care about a whole category of reality—such as the earth, water, or air. Here are three examples from Africa:

- Among the Yoruba, storms are the work of the deity Shango, a legendary king with magical powers who climbed to heaven.

- The Ibo pray to Ala, an earth-mother deity, for fertility of the earth. Women also pray to her for children, and men pray to her to increase their herds.
- In Ashanti belief, Ta Yao is the god of metal. The work of blacksmiths and mechanics is under his charge.[8]

clouds, and wind. But life force is also present in static mountains and soil. Frequently there is a sense that everything on earth has some sort of perception and feeling, as if one might talk to rocks and trees and animals and expect them to respond.

In this worldview, everything is part of the same reality. There are no clear boundaries between the natural and supernatural and between the human and nonhuman. Everything has both its visible ordinary reality and a deeper, invisible sacred reality. To say that nature is full of spirits can be a way of affirming the presence of both a universal life force and an essential, underlying sacredness.

In a world that is animated by spirits, human beings must treat all things with care. If a spirit is injured or insulted, it can retaliate. Human beings must therefore show that they respect nature, especially the animals and plants they kill to eat. Human beings must understand the existence and ways of the spirit world so that they can avoid harm and incur blessings. (We will revisit this spirit world later, when we discuss contacting it through trance states and the spiritual specialist the shaman.)

Native American religions are frequently cited for their reverential attitude toward the natural world; human beings and animals are often pictured as coming into existence together, and sun, moon, trees, and animals are all considered kin. Hehaka Sapa, or Black Elk, an Oglala Sioux, who dictated his autobiography in 1930, explains what this means. He points out that his community, which traditionally lived in *tipis* (circular tents made of animal skins and poles), arranges itself in a circle—as does all nature, which is constantly making circles, just like the sun, the moon, and the whirlwind.

For Black Elk there is no strong distinction between the human and animal worlds but rather a sense of kinship. To exploit nature mindlessly is as sacrilegious as harming one's own mother. As Smohalla of the Nez Perce people said, "You ask me to plow the ground. Shall I take a knife and tear my mother's breast? Then when I die she will not take me to her bosom to rest."[10]

In native religions there is also frequently an ethic of restraint and of conservation concerning nature's resources. One is expected to take only

Birds make their nests in circles, for theirs is the same religion as ours.

—Black Elk, Oglala Sioux[9]

what one needs and to use all the parts of an animal or plant. In traditional Hawai`i, for example, fishing in certain areas would be temporarily forbidden (*kapu*, or taboo) in order to allow the fish population to be replenished. Of course, the ideal was not universally maintained, and even native peoples have sometimes been unaware of the destructive effects of their actions. We think, for example, of how the native people of Easter Island virtually deforested their entire island. Despite an example like this, it is clear that native peoples who did not live in harmony with nature could not long survive.

It is difficult, perhaps, for human beings today to experience fully the intimate connection with the rest of nature that has been a common aspect of oral religions. The predominant contemporary view sees human beings as fundamentally different from other animals. Perhaps this tendency is a result of our modern culture, which emphasizes the skills of writing and reading. We also have little connection with the origins of our food, and we live and work indoors. Electric light diminishes our awareness of day and night and obstructs the light of the moon and stars. Except for insects, rodents, and the most common birds, we seldom see wildlife firsthand. Traffic noise drowns out the sounds of wind, rain, and birdsong. In contrast, consider the sense of kinship with animals found, for example, among the Haida people of the Pacific Northwest: "the Haida refer to whales and ravens as their 'brothers' and 'sisters' and to fish and trees as the finned and tree *people*."[11]

Sacred Time and Sacred Space

Our everyday lives go on in ordinary time, which we see as moving forward into the future. Sacred time, however, is "the time of eternity." Among the Koyukon people of the Arctic it is called Distant Time, and it is the holy ancient past in which the gods lived and worked.[12] Sacred time is cyclical, returning to its origins for renewal. By recalling and ritually reliving the deeds of the gods and ancestors (as, familiarly, Christians do through the yearly celebration of Christmas and Easter), we enter into the sacred time in which they live. Oral religions even tend to structure daily lives in ways that make them conform to mythic events in sacred time; this creates a sense of holiness in everyday life.

A good example of sacred time is the traditional Hawaiian observance of the four-month winter period *Makahiki,* dedicated to the agricultural god Lono. During this time, all war and heavy work were forbidden and Hawaiians told stories of Lono, whom they symbolized with a pole, an image, and white barkcloth banners that they carried throughout the islands. The fact that the British explorer Captain James Cook arrived during Makahiki encouraged the native people to accept him as the god Lono, bodily returned to the islands.

Like ordinary time, ordinary space exists in the everyday. Sacred space, however, is the doorway through which the "other world" of gods and

Ayers Rock, known as Uluru to native Australians, rises abruptly from the desert floor. It is a sacred mountain and symbolic center for native religion in Australia.

ancestors can contact us and we can contact them. Sacred space is associated with the center of the entire universe, where power and holiness are strongest and where we can go to renew our own strength.

In native religions, sacred space is established by a great mountain, a volcano, a valley, a lake, a forest, a single large tree, or some other striking natural site. For Black Elk and his people it was Harney Peak in South Dakota. In Australian aboriginal religion, Uluru (Ayers Rock) has served as this sacred center; in Africa, Mount Kilimanjaro and other high mountains have done the same.

Sacred space can also be constructed, often in a symbolic shape such as a circle or square, and defined by a special building or by a boundary made of rope or of rocks, such as Stonehenge in England. It can even be an open area among trees or buildings, such as the great open space between the temples of Teotihuacán, near Mexico City.

Respect for Origins, Gods, and Ancestors

Origins   Most oral religions have cosmic tales of their origins that are regularly recited or enacted through ritual and dance. Some tell how the world originated from a supernatural realm beyond this one. Other emergence stories speak of the earth arising out of previous earths or from earlier, more chaotic material forms. Often the land and creatures emerge from watery depths. One creation story among the Hopi says that the earth, before it took shape, was mist. Stories of the origin of a tribe may be connected with its story of the earth's creation. Among the Acoma Pueblo there is a story of two sisters who lived entirely underground. Eventually they climbed up the roots of a tree and into the sunlight through a hole in the ground, to become the first human beings on earth. One became mother of the Pueblo.[13]

Gods   Native religions frequently speak of a High God who is superior to all other deities and is considered to be wise, ancient, and benevolent. The Inuit speak of a Great Spirit living in the sky who is female and to whom all human spirits eventually return. In a few African religions, too, the High God is either female or androgynous; and in some religions there are two complementary High Gods, characterized as male/female, brother/sister, or bad/good. The Bakuta of central Africa speak of the twins Nzambi-above and Nzambi-below, although in their myths the lower twin disappears and Nzambi-above becomes the High God.[14]

In some African religions, stories of the High God, who is almost always also the creator of the world, offer some explanation for the ills of the world or the distance between human beings and the divine. Many African religions tell how the High God created the world and then left it—sometimes out of dismay at human beings or simply for lack of interest. "Many people of central and southern Africa say that God (Mulungu) lived on earth at first, but men began to kill his servants and set fire to the bush, and so God retired to heaven on one of those giant spiders' webs that seem to hang from the sky in morning mists. In Burundi, however, it is said that having made good children God created a cripple, and its parents were so angry that they tried to kill God and he went away."[15]

Although oral religions often revere a High God, altars and imagery dedicated to a High God are not common. Instead, native religions tend to focus on lesser deities, especially those associated with forces of nature, in their prayer, ritual, and art.

In a few cultures, such as in Mexico and West Africa, large temples have been built, temple rituals are held, and priesthoods have been created to carry out religious ceremonies, but such developments are relatively rare. More commonly, ceremonies in oral religions are performed at small shrines, either in the home or outdoors, at a river bank, a large tree, or a rock formation, for example.

Ancestors   Oral religions make little distinction between a god and an ancestor. Both are important, because living people must work with both for success in life. Spirits of ancestors must be treated well out of love for them and out of respect for their potentially dangerous power. The way they are treated can determine what they bring to human beings. In African religions, ancestor spirits are commonly thought to bring health,

Native peoples of North America have produced a wide variety of images such as this stone figure of the Aztec moon goddess, Coyolxauhqui.

Some indigenous peoples of western Canada erect a totem pole to honor an ancestor. Images on the totem pole are related to the ancestor's life story.

wealth, and children if they are pleased, and disease and childlessness if they are not. The way to appease angry ancestors is through ritual, sometimes including sacrifice. The ancestors often live in an afterlife that is a state of existence much like earthly life. Belief in reincarnation is found sometimes, as in native Tahitian religion. In traditional Hawaiian religion, it was believed that the spirits of the dead went to an underworld, while the spirits of cultural heroes ascended into the sky.

SACRED PRACTICES IN ORAL RELIGIONS

In oral societies, everyday religious activity and practice are significant because their primary purpose is often to place individuals, families, and groups in "right relationships" with gods, ancestors, other human beings, and nature. Rituals are the basic way in which human beings ensure they are living in harmony with each other and with nature. Rituals are frequently devoted to major aspects of human life: key events in the life cycle, rules concerning certain kinds of behavior, sacrifice, and access to the spirit world. In addition, artifacts such as masks and statues are an essential part of specific rituals.

Life-Cycle Ceremonies

In oral societies, the human journey through life is aided and marked by rites of passage. In addition to being important to the individual, these rites also help hold the society together by renewing bonds and admitting new members to the community.

Rites of passage mark an important life event, such as the birth of a child. In some native religions, a woman about to give birth goes off by herself to bear her child at a sacred site or in a house built for such purpose. Birth is considered a powerful time for the mother and child, and the blood associated with it is believed to have dangerous power.

After the birth, the newborn is often celebrated with a public event that may occur immediately or anytime from a week to a year after the actual birth. In some parts of Africa, babies do not become members of the community until they receive their names in a special public ceremony that is accompanied by song, dance, and a meal. A name is chosen carefully because of the influence it is thought to have on the child's future.

Special rituals also mark a person's entry into adulthood. They may include a period of instruction in tribal history and belief, in sex, and in adult responsibilities. They often involve an initiation ritual that may be experienced in seclusion or in the company of other initiates. Rites can include a symbolic death—painful and frightening—meant to turn the boy into a man. Across Africa, circumcision for boys is a common rite for entering adulthood.

Read myths. They teach you that you can turn inward, and you begin to get the message of the symbols. Read other people's myths, not those of your own religion, because you tend to interpret your own religion in terms of facts—but if you read the other ones, you begin to get the message.

—Joseph Campbell[16]

In western Africa, initiation societies oversee coming-of-age rituals. "The Poro [a secret initiation society] is for boys, controlled by a hierarchy of elders, different in each village, which meets in a sacred grove where the clan founder was buried. The purpose of the initiation is the rebirth of the youths, who are said to be swallowed by the Poro spirit at the beginning and returned to their parents as reborn at the end of the initiation."[17] A parallel initiation society exists for girls, who receive sexual instruction and training in the skills necessary for marriage.

A girl's first menstrual period may also be marked publicly. For example, among the Apache, a four-day ceremony marks a girl's menarche (first menstruation). During the ceremony, which is long and elaborate, the girl performs a dance, receives a massage from her female sponsor, kneels to receive the rays of the sun, and circles repeatedly around a ceremonial cane.

In Native American religions, a common ritual of early maturity is the vision quest, or dream quest, which may involve prolonged fasting and some kind of preliminary cleansing, such as washing or undergoing a sweat bath. For years before the vision quest the young person may receive training in fasting, to prepare for the experience. Commonly, a tribal religious specialist will create a sacred space by ritually marking the four directions of the compass and the center. The sacred space, set apart from the community, may be a place of natural beauty, such as a hilltop or a platform of branches in a tree.

The seeker remains in the sacred space until a vision, or dream, comes; in the event the vision doesn't come, the seeker may be instructed to return the following year. The vision is believed to show the appropriate direction that the young person's life must take, and sometimes a spirit guide or animal guardian appears to offer help. Although the vision quest is often a part of the coming-of-age ceremonies for males, among some peoples it is also employed for females. The vision quest may be used at other times, too—particularly when the individual or the group must make an important life decision.

In oral societies, as in almost all other cultures, marriage is a ritual that not only publicly affirms and stabilizes a union but also cements economic arrangements and, through the ceremony, ensures fertility. In both Africa and North America, however, marriage in tribal cultures has been primarily a practical arrangement. Among Native American peoples, marriage has usually been celebrated simply as a social contract that is worked out by the families. Monogamy has been the norm, but divorce is acceptable when a marriage is not successful. In African native religions, although marriage is a rite of passage, marking the transition from one state to another, it may not be marked by religious ceremony. In fact, "its religious side is not distinctive. It is regarded as the normal sequel to rites of adolescence, whose purpose was to prepare for this state."[19]

As the final passing from this life, death is accompanied by rituals that serve to comfort close relatives, assist the spirit of the dead person in moving on, and protect the living from bad influences that could come from an

> There, when I was young, the spirits took me in my vision to the center of the earth and showed me all the good things in the sacred hoop of the world.
>
> —Black Elk, speaking of his vision quest at Harney Peak[18]

unhappy spirit. Because the spirit of the dead person may be sad to leave the family circle, it must be helped to make its trip to the spirit world by placing clothing, food, money, and favorite objects with the body. In the case of a chief or other notable person, the body may be embalmed or mummified for public display until a large funeral can be arranged. In the past, great African chiefs have had wives, children, and servants buried alongside them. Among Native American tribes, the sacrifice of relatives and attendants to accompany a dead leader has also occurred. For example, after the death of the Natchez leader Tattooed Serpent in 1725, two of his wives and six others, after preparation by fasting, were strangled as a part of the funeral ritual.[20] In Native American religions, bodies of the dead are usually buried, but sometimes they are placed on platforms or in trees.

Taboo and Sacrifice

A **taboo** is a rule that forbids specific behavior with regard to certain objects, people, animals, days, or phases of life. Taboos represent a codification of the social and religious order. In our language, "taboo" means, often negatively, something that is prohibited. This is essentially the viewpoint of an outsider. From inside native religions, a taboo is often better seen as a way of protecting the individual and of safeguarding the natural order of things.

Taboos frequently relate to sex and birth. Blood, too, is always an element of mysterious power—both helpful and dangerous. For example, in some but not all groups, menstruating women are expected to remain separate from everyone else because menstrual blood is considered powerful and dangerous. In contrast, a few cultures (such as the Apache) hail a girl's menarche as a time when a girl has power to heal illness.

Probably because of the blood involved, a woman giving birth in some native cultures must remain alone or in the company of women only—not even the woman's husband may be present. In traditional Hawai`i, for example, women of high rank gave birth in isolation, at the site of special large stones used only for this purpose. Oral societies also frequently forbid husbands from resuming sexual relations with a wife for some time after childbirth—this period can even last until the child is weaned.

Like birth, death is also surrounded by taboos concerning the spirit of the dead person, who may seek to reward or take revenge on the living because of the way he or she was treated in life. The afterlife can be a shadowy, uncertain realm that the departing spirit is reluctant to enter, especially if the spirit is leaving a happy family circle. Proper rituals must be performed, accompanied by public mourning, to avoid angering the dead person's spirit.

A number of taboos regulate other social behavior. One common taboo relates to rank: people of high position, such as chiefs, nobility, priests, and shamans, must be treated with extraordinary care because of their special powers; taboos protect them from insult or inappropriate action. In traditional Hawaiian culture, for example, the shadow of a commoner could not fall on a member of the nobility. In a strongly hierarchical native culture, such as in many African tribes, the health of the people and the fertility of the land are believed to depend on the health of the sacred king. To maintain his health, the king is protected by taboos—particularly regarding the people with whom he may associate. Because of these taboos and the fear his role inspires, the sacred king may live a life quite separate from his subjects.

Foods and food sources in many cultures are governed by taboos. Among African tribes, commoners have been forbidden to touch or eat the food of a king. In traditional Hawai`i, women were forbidden to eat coconuts and most types of bananas, nor could they touch fishhooks.

Antisocial actions may also be subject to taboo. In Native American religions, taboos and rules encourage a sense of harmony with other members of one's people. Strong taboos against adultery and stealing within the tribal unit, for example, are enforced by shame, warnings, shunning, and expulsion, often administered by a tribal council. Nevertheless, although harmony is important, warfare against another people has at times been considered justified.

When a taboo has been broken or a spirit must be placated, the person or group must atone for the lapse, often through sacrifice. The usual offering is food and drink. A **libation** (the act of pouring a bit of drink on the ground as an offering) may be made or a portion of a meal set aside for a spirit. An animal may be sacrificed and its blood poured out on the ground or on an altar as an offering of the life force to the deity. Sacrificial animals ordinarily are food animals, such as chickens, pigs, and goats.[22] After the sacrifice, all the participants (including ancestral and nature spirits) may eat the cooked animal—thus pleasing the spirits by feeding them and including them in the meal.

Although it has been rare, human sacrifice (and sometimes cannibalism) has occurred in some native cultures. The sacrifice of human beings was practiced (at least for a time) for specific purposes in Aztec religion, Hawaiian religion, and among tribal peoples of New Guinea; it was much less common among native peoples of North America and Africa.

Before leaving the topic of taboos, it might be good to note that taboos exist plentifully in every society, including our own. Many are associated with sex, marriage, and parenthood. In modern societies, for example, taboos exist against polygamy, incest, and marriage between close relations. Such taboos may seem "natural" to the society that enforces them but "unusual" to outsiders. Taboos are not inherently valid across groups and societies but are culturally determined.

Shamanism, Trance, and Magic

As we have seen, native religions take for granted that a powerful and influential but invisible spirit world exists and that human beings can have access to it. A **shaman** acts as an intermediary between the visible, ordinary world and the spirit world. The shaman can contact this realm, receive vi-

> Do not kill or injure your neighbor, for it is not him that you injure. Do not wrong or hate your neighbor, for it is not him that you wrong, you wrong yourself. Moneto, the Grandmother, the Supreme Being, loves him also as she loves you.
>
> —Shawnee rules[21]

sions of it, and transmit messages from it, often to help or heal others. As one commentator remarks, "The shaman lies at the very heart of some cultures, while living in the shadowy fringes of others. Nevertheless, a common thread seems to connect all shamans across the planet. An awakening to other orders of reality, the experience of ecstasy, and an opening up of visionary realms form the essence of the shamanic mission."[23] Sometimes the spirits speak through the shaman, who knows entry points to their world, which may be reached in dreams or trances by climbing a sacred tree, descending through a cave into the underworld, flying through the air, or following a magical map.

The shaman understands the primordial unity of things and experiences a shared identity with animals and the rest of nature. Thus the shaman can interpret the language of animals, charm them, and draw on their powers. The shaman gains the powers of animals and the rest of nature by wearing items taken from important animals, such as deer antlers, lion skins, and eagle feathers.

Part of becoming a shaman is having one or more encounters with the spirit realm in the form of a psychological death and rebirth. A person may have experienced some great loss—of sight, of a child, or of something equally precious. He or she may have had a mental breakdown, been terribly sick, or suffered a serious accident and come close to dying. Upon recovering from such an extreme experience, this person can have new powers of insight and healing, which can lead to becoming a shaman. Those who have experienced vivid dreams and visions that are thought to be manifestations of the spirit world are also sometimes trained as shamans.

The shaman often blends the roles of priest, oracle, psychologist, and doctor. A common English term for the shaman is *medicine man*, yet it stresses only the therapeutic role and obscures the fact that shamans are

The twentieth-century shaman often mingles elements from native religion with practices of the dominant religion. Here, a Taiwanese shaman uses firecrackers to drive away unwelcome spirits.

I enter the earth. I go in at a place like a place where people drink water. I travel a long way, very far. When I emerge, I am already climbing threads [up into the sky]. I climb one and leave it, then I climb another one. . . . You come in small to God's place. You do what you have to do there. . . . [Then] you enter, enter the earth, and you return to enter the skin of your body.

—Bushman trance dancer[24]

both female and male. In Korean and Japanese native religious paths, in fact, shamans are frequently female.

The shamanic trance state that brings visions, both to the shaman and to others, can be induced in several ways: weakening the visual boundaries (for example, by sitting in the darkness of a cave or hut for prolonged periods); fasting, experiencing sensory deprivation, making regular rhythmic sounds (such as drumming, rattling, bell ringing, and chanting), and dancing in a repetitive way, especially in circles. The ingestion of natural substances is also common; peyote cactus, datura, cannabis (marijuana), coca, opium, and the mushroom *Amanita muscaria* have all been used to induce trance states both by the shaman alone and sometimes by participants in a ceremony.

Some Native American peoples have used a **calumet**—a long sacred pipe—for smoking a special kind of tobacco that is far stronger than commercial cigarette tobacco—so strong that it can have a hallucinatory effect. The bowl of the pipe is usually made of clay but sometimes of bone, ivory, wood, or metal; and the stem is usually made from a reed. The calumet is an object that gives protection to the person who carries it. The pipe is smoked as part of a shared ceremony that establishes strong bonds among all the participants, and oaths sworn at these ceremonies have the greatest solemnity.

Rituals involving the use of peyote have developed primarily within the last two centuries in some native North American tribes.[25] The practice seems to have moved north from Mexico, where peyote grows easily and has long been used for religious purposes. When the fruit of the peyote cactus is eaten, it provides a psychedelic experience that lasts six or more hours and produces a forgetfulness of the self and a sense of oneness with all of nature. Ceremonies commonly begin in the early evening and last until dawn. Among North American tribes, the rituals are often mixed with Christian elements. For example, a member of the Native American Church described his preparation for the ceremony: "First we set up an altar—a Mexican rug and on it a Lakota Bible in our own language. We use only the revelations of St. John in our meetings. It's . . . full of visions, nature, earth, stars. . . . Across the Bible we put an eagle feather—it stands for the Great Spirit. . . . On the left is a rawhide bag with cedar dust to sprinkle on the fire. That's our incense."[26] The blending of elements, he says, is intentional, because it illustrates that at their core all religions are the same. It is interesting to note that the religious use of peyote by the Native American Church has been upheld by the United States Supreme Court.

Magic plays a powerful role in many oral religions. In native African religions and their Caribbean offshoots, powerful, invisible, ever-present spiritual forces that can do either tremendous good or bad are directed and diffused by diviners, healers, and others through incantations, potions, and figurines used for sympathetic magic. Magic in the hands of certain individuals can be used, as African scholar John Mbiti remarks, "for harmful ends, and then people experience it as bad or evil magic. Or they may use it for ends which are helpful to society, and then it is considered as good magic or 'medicine.' These mystical forces of the universe are neither evil nor good in themselves, they are just like other natural things at [our] disposal."[27]

Magic and trance states are believed to make it possible to look into the past and future, a process called **divination** (from the Latin *divus*, "god," and *divinare*, "to foretell"). Looking into the past helps determine the causes of illness and other misfortune, while looking into the future guides an individual to act wisely. It is a common belief in African religions that an individual has a predetermined future that can be discovered through divination.

The magical worldview common to native religions can create a number of specialized religious roles. A diviner looks for causes of sickness, depression, death, and other difficulties. A healer works with a person afflicted with physical or mental illness to find a cure. A rainmaker ends drought. Malevolent witches and sorcerers transmit magic to cause damage; as Mbiti describes it, they take fingernails, hair, clothes, or other possessions of the victim, then burn or harm them or bury an object that is believed to cause harm in the victim's path. He adds that "another belief is that the spirit of the witches leaves them at night and goes to eat away the victim, thus causing him to weaken and eventually die. It is believed, too, that a witch can cause harm by looking at a person, wishing him harm or speaking to him words intended to inflict harm on him."[28] Not all who practice magic do so for evil ends. Others use their power to counteract disease and evil forces through good-luck charms.

Artifacts and Artistic Expression in Oral Religions

The masks, drums, statues, rattles, and other objects that are important in oral religions were once seen as curiosities to be collected and housed in anthropological museums. Today, however, we view them differently; we realize that we must respect their importance to the cultures that produced them as well as their inherent artistic value. The arts of oral religions are not created by "artists" as "art" but as functional objects to be used in particular settings and special ways. Navajo sandpaintings, for example, are often photographed and reproduced in books as though they are permanent works of art. In fact, when used by a healer, they are temporary creations that are made and then destroyed as a part of the ritual. And unlike art in most Western cultures, sacred objects and images in native religions are not separate endeavors but an essential part of the religious expression itself. Modern secular culture does not usually think of dance or tattoo or body painting as religious expression, but in many native religions these art forms all fulfill that role.

In religions that do not rely on the written word, artistic expressions take on unique significance because they are filled with meaning and remind practitioners of the specifics of the oral tradition. Statues and paintings,

Although hula is still a form of entertainment that travelers can enjoy at tourist hotels in Waikiki, it is also a key element of Hawaiian religious and cultural celebrations.

of course, are common in a great many religions, both oral and written. Dance, which takes on particular importance in oral religion, incorporates religious objects such as carved and painted masks, headdresses, costumes, ornaments, and musical instruments. In native Hawaiian religion, *hula kahiko* (ancient hula) is danced in conjunction with chanting to honor the gods. Instruments for marking rhythm and *lei* (wreaths of flowers or other plants worn around the head, wrists, and ankles) when used in hula are considered religious objects.

Chants, too, are essential because they capture many of the stories and words of the tradition so they can be memorized and used properly in sacred ceremonies. Chanters must not only have prodigious memories and be able to recall thousands of chants, they must also be able to create special variations on traditional chants and oral texts for individual occasions.

Masks play a significant role in oral religions, especially when used in dance. When a dancer is wearing a mask and any accompanying costume, the spirit is not merely represented by the masked dancer. The dancer actually becomes the spirit, embodied on earth, with the spirit's powers. Among the BaPunu in Africa, for example, dancers not only wear masks but walk on stilts—the overall psychological effect must be intense. Particularly complex masks have been produced in the Pacific Northwest by such tribes as the Haida, Tsimshian, and Kwakwaka`wakw (Kwakiutl).[29] Some of their masks, especially those depicting animal spirits, have moveable parts that make them even more powerful for those who wear and see them.

Sacred images are reinterpreted on this contemporary blanket from the Pacific Northwest coast. The white borders, which originally would have been made of shells, are today made of buttons.

Besides masks and statues, other forms of wood carving can manifest religious inspiration. Perhaps the most famous of all wood carvings is the carved pole, commonly called totem pole, found in the Pacific Northwest. The totem pole usually depicts a group of **totems** (animal figures that are revered for their symbolic meaning such as bear, beaver, thunderbird, owl, raven, and eagle, among the most common) stacked one on top of another. The animals may memorialize ancestors or represent badges of kinship groups, with specialized meaning for the individual or the family responsible for the totem pole.[30] Some totem poles are a part of the structure of a traditional wooden house or lodge. Others—apparently a later development—are raised to stand alone, frequently to mark an important event.

Other important arts that can have religious meaning are weaving, clothing decoration (such as beading), and basketry. These creations may seem to have less obvious religious significance, but the imagery used is frequently of religious derivation, particularly figures from tribal myths, nature deities, and guardian birds and animals.

Feathers and featherwork are also a major part of many oral religions because of their powerful association with flight and contact with the world above and beyond our own. Richard W. Hill, in an essay on the religious meaning of feathers, remarks that "some cultures associate certain birds with spiritual or protective powers. Birds are believed to have delivered songs, dances, rituals, and sacred messages to humankind. Feathers worn in the hair blow in the wind and evoke birds in flight. For followers of the

Halloween: "Just Good Fun" or Folk Religion?

Although many of us may think of oral religions as having no connection to our modern, everyday life, elements from them persist, particularly in our celebrations of traditional folk holidays.

- "Halloween" means the evening before All Hallows' (All Saints') Day, which falls on November 1. Although Halloween gets its name from Christianity, the celebration is, in fact, a continuation of *Samhain,* the new year festival celebrated in pre-Christian England and Ireland. There is a strong theme of death and rebirth, as winter comes on and the old year disappears. It was believed that spirits of ancestors roamed free at this time and needed to be fed and placated. We see this underlying the practices of children going door to door, receiving food. We also see it in the many Halloween costumes that suggest death (skeletons) and communication with the spirit world (angels, devils, and religious figures).
- Although the festival has a Christian name and purpose, the origins of Christmas, too, are pre-Christian. It began as a festival of the winter solstice, when the days are the coldest and shortest in the northern hemisphere. People compensated by celebrating a holiday of extra light, warmth, and abundance. The Christmas tree with its lights and the evergreen wreaths and decorations have nothing to do with the story of Jesus' birth; rather, they are clear symbols of fertility and life, which the celebrants hope will persist through a cold winter. The giving of presents is related to this idea of abundance, and the Christian Saint Nicholas has been transformed in the last two hundred years into the grandfatherly Santa Claus. Like a

Awe of the spirit world is prominent in folk religions. In the United States, this awe comes alive at Halloween.

wizard, Santa Claus flies through the air, carried by his magical reindeer, dispensing presents from his overflowing bag to children all around the earth.

- Easter's Christian meaning is mixed with elements that derive from the Jewish Passover, but underlying this tradition are symbols of fertility and new life—eggs, flowers, and rabbits. (The name *Easter* is Old English and derives from a spring festival in honor of Eastre, goddess of the dawn.) Easter has maintained a close tie to nature in that it is always celebrated at the time of the full moon.

We can see in these examples of contemporary folk religion the "universal language" of religious symbols. It is the same language, whether found in folk religion, native religions, or the other religions we will take up in the chapters ahead.

Ghost Dance religion of the late nineteenth century, birds became important symbols of rebirth."[31] Feathers are worn in the hair, made into headdresses, and attached to clothing. In Native American cultures, they are also attached to horse harnesses, dolls, pipes, and baskets.

The symbols that appear in myths and in dreams are the basic vocabulary of oral religious art. Common symbols include a great mountain located at the center of the universe, the tree of life (also called the world tree), the sun and moon, fire, rain, lightning, a bird or wings, death's head and skeleton, a cross, and a circle. These images, however, often appear in unusual forms; for example, lightning may be a zigzag, and the sun may look like a swastika or the tree of life like a ladder. Colors are universally used with symbolic meaning, although the exact meaning differs from culture to culture.

PERSONAL EXPERIENCE: GODS IN HAWAI`I

On the southernmost island of the Hawaiian Islands lies *Pu`uhonua `o Honaunau* ("place of refuge"), once a sanctuary for Hawaiians who had done something that was *kapu* ("taboo," "forbidden"). They could escape punishment and be purified if they could reach *Pu`uhonua `o Honaunau,* or one of its sister sanctuaries, by water or land.

Seeking refuge from the frenzy of life in Honolulu, I fly to the Kona airport and drive my rental car down the Big Island's southwest coast to *Pu`uhonua `o Honaunau,* now run by the United States National Park Service. After a short walk toward the shore, I see the tall, long stone wall of the sanctuary. Closer to the ocean are its *heiau* (temples) made of large, nearly black lava rock, around which grow *ti* plants, to demarcate a sacred space and to ward off evil spirits. Most dramatic to my outsider's eyes are the tall carved wooden images (in Hawaiian, called *ki`i,* and in English, commonly called *tikis*) that once no doubt beckoned to the refugee who sought out this place at the ocean's edge. The offering platform and thatch houses near the ki`i have been restored so that I can see what it might have been like when this was a sacred site within traditional Hawaiian religion. Because the official kapu system was dissolved in 1819 by King Kamehameha II, the place is not used for seeking sanctuary any more—at least officially.

Even on this sunny day, the stone wall, the tall images, and the stark landscape speak not of the "peace and comfort" we may typically associate with a refuge but rather of power, law, and awesome majesty. The ground is hard, black lava rock and white coral, and except for the coconut trees here and there amid the few structures, there is little green vegetation. Ocean waves lap at the shore, but an almost eerie quiet reigns.

Late afternoon: I'm the only person here. It is not hard for me to imagine being a native who has fled from home and now awaits a priestly blessing in order to be made safe for the return. I sense that the Hawaiian religion drew its power from the land, from this very place. The rocks that make up the heiau are petrifications of fire, water, air, and earth. This is not the tour director's tropical fantasyland. Nor, I realize, is it a place of living religious practice. But that doesn't matter, at least to me, today: what I sense in the land is alive, even in this religious museum.

As I drive back up the hill toward the main road, I see a small directional sign that says "Painted Church." Ready for an experience of contrast, I follow its arrow and soon arrive at Saint Benedict's Catholic Church—a

The fierce looks of the ki`i at Pu`uhonua `o Honaunau may have been intended to ward off unwanted visitors, from this or the spirit world.

tiny, white wooden structure that has elements of Gothic style. A sign near the door says that its interior was painted a century ago by a Belgian missionary priest. The church sits on a grassy hillside, with a small cemetery spreading out below. I ascend the wooden stairs of the church and walk in.

The interior is "tropical Gothic." Ten small windows have pointed Gothic arches. The wooden pillars are candy canes, painted with red and white swirls; their tops turn into palm trees, with fronds like painted feathers on the pastel sky of the ceiling. Behind the altar is a mural of Gothic arches, stretching back into an imaginary distance, creating the pretense of a European cathedral. On one side wall, Saint Francis experiences a vision of Jesus on the cross. In another painting, Jesus is being tempted by Satan. The other wall shows a man on his deathbed, his face bathed in heavenly light. A cross of execution, the pains of death—these are not pleasant experiences, but they are softened by the way they are depicted here. Near the exit, I'm tempted by the bell rope that hangs through a hole in the choir-loft floor overhead, but I resist. Kapu.

Back outside, from the top of the stairs I see the shining ocean below and can even make out the Hawaiian place of refuge at its edge. This little church, charming as it appears, presents old familiar themes: a High God, a sacrificial victim, an offering of blood, a restoration of justice. The themes

In a painting at Saint Benedict's Church, Jesus wards off temptations offered by Satan.

may not be obvious, but they are there. This, I reflect, is the religion that re-placed the native Hawaiian religion; the cycle of replacement evident here is typical, I think, of what has happened to so many other native religious traditions. Does it make all that much difference how religions die and rise? I am deep in thought as I pass a stone grotto enclosing a statue of Mary and then walk past the resident priest's small house. From inside come the sounds of a roaring crowd and of a radio announcer. "Strike two!" the voice shouts. I get in my car and drive away, still seeking refuge.

ORAL RELIGIONS TODAY

Oral religions, like the rainforests and jungles of the earth, are endangered. As modern urban culture spreads across the earth, it tends to dominate everyone's worldview. It would be hard to convince today's young people to fast and undergo deprivation in preparation for a vision quest when all they need to visit other worlds painlessly are a videotape and a television set. Everywhere we go, we find blue jeans, T-shirts, rock music, pizza, and Coca-Cola taking over the world. (Some even believe that popular culture is becoming a religion of its own, displacing all others.)

One of the greatest threats to oral religions is the destruction of native habitat. Because so much personal and tribal identity comes from trees, birds, animals, and one's direct experience of nature, the destruction of na-tive habitat means the destruction of native peoples and their religions. Logging interests are an almost universal problem, but especially in Malaysia, Indonesia, New Guinea, western Canada, and the northwestern United States, where fights are intense over land ownership and govern-mental protection. Mining and oil interests are a second source of habitat destruction, particularly in Brazil, Alaska, and the western part of the con-tinental United States. Finding sound economic ways to protect native habi-tat is one of the challenges of our time. Ecotourism is one possible solution, but it brings its own problems through the introduction of nonnative peo-ples to these fragile cultures.

Another cause of the weakening of oral religions is the spread of pros-elytizing religions, especially Christianity and Islam. In sub-Saharan Africa, probably less than ten percent of the population still practices the older oral religions; the rest practice Christianity or Islam. Today, for example, there are more black members of the Anglican Church than there are white mem-bers. The same phenomenon appears true in many Pacific cultures, where oral religions have been supplanted by forms of Christianity.

Nevertheless, oral religions still thrive in some places of the world, ex-isting in their purest forms in those pockets where modern influence has penetrated the least. Native religions also coexist, occasionally diluted, alongside other religions or intermixed with them. In Taiwan, Korea, and Japan, for example, shamanism may exist side by side with other religions. (Because the shamans in Korea are often female, their oral religious practices allow them roles that are not open to them in Buddhism and Christianity.) In Central America, people who otherwise are practicing Catholics worship deities of earlier native religions. In the Caribbean, the gods of African religions have sometimes been combined with forms of French and Spanish Catholicism in the oral religions of Voodoo and Santería.

In North America, in the Pacific, and in Africa, people have continued or are attempting to restore the practices of their ancestral ways. In New Zealand, for example, there is a revival of Maori culture in canoe building, tattooing, dance, and wood sculpture. This attempt at revival is complicated by debates over such issues as land ownership and the introduction of Maori language into schools and public life. In Hawai`i, a renaissance of Hawaiian culture, language, and hula necessarily means retelling the stories of the gods and goddesses of Hawaiian mythology. Some schools now teach all their lessons in Hawaiian, and hula schools are flourishing. The island of Kaho`olawe is no longer used by the U.S. military for bombing practice and has been restored as a place for traditional Hawaiian religious services. Citizens of many native nations in North America are instructing their young in traditional dance and other religious practices. Nevertheless, how to deal with a traditional belief in deities in the face of some dominant monotheistic religions presents intriguing questions. One result, as in the Native American Church, is that beliefs and practices now often incorporate both oral and text-based traditions.

Interest in oral religions is a potential restorative for cultures that have moved quickly from their traditional rural homes to concrete high-rise apartments in the city. In oral traditions, we see religion before it was compartmentalized. These holistic traditions help us see the religious dimensions that can be found in our own everyday life and expand our sensitivity to nature. Their remembrance of the sacred past makes holy the present and the future.

RELIGION BEYOND THE CLASSROOM

Places of interest for those who want to explore oral religions include sacred natural sites, places where native religious life persists, the remains of native religious buildings, and museums that display the arts of oral religions. Powwows are held in the summer in many places in Canada and the United States, especially the Southwest. Religion and anthropology departments of local colleges are a good source for finding regional places of interest and ceremonies open to nonnatives. The following list is a small sample of sights in North America available to the general traveler.

United States

California—Los Angeles: Southwest Museum

Colorado—Mesa Verde National Park (contains native dwellings and kivas); Dolores: Anasazi Heritage Center

Hawai`i—Big Island: Pu`uhonua `o Honaunau (a place of refuge and several reconstructed temples); Oahu: Kane`aki Heiau in Makaha Valley (a reconstructed temple)

Minnesota—sites at Red Lake, Leech Lake, and White Earth

New Mexico—Bandelier National Monument (contains remnants of native cliff dwellings); Canyon de Chelly and Monument Valley (feature native cliff dwellings), Taos: Navajo Indian Reservation; Santo Domingo Pueblo

New York—New York City: Museum of Natural History

Canada

'Ksan, British Columbia: Gitskan village (includes seven tribal houses, a longhouse, and many totem poles)

Ottawa: Canadian Museum of Civilization

Vancouver: Museum of Anthropology at the University of British Columbia (houses a large collection of totem poles, masks, and other artifacts)

Victoria: Royal British Columbia Museum (features a fine collection of masks); Thunderbird Park (displays totem poles outdoors)

Mexico

Davisadero (Tarahumara native community)

Mexico City: National Anthropological Museum and recently uncovered sites next to the cathedral

Oaxaca and Monte Albán (sites of Zapotec and Mixtec ruins)

Teotihuacán (near Mexico City): Temple of Quetzalcoatl and the Pyramids of the sun and moon

---

FOR FULLER UNDERSTANDING

1. Where you live is now or once was home to native peoples. Make up a list of their traditional religious sites, beliefs, and practices. Visit the sites with friends or classmates, and make a report to your class.

2. Are there any museums or galleries in your area that house special examples of oral religious objects? Visit one and do a drawing of a single object. Explain in writing its background, use, and maker as well as you can.

3. Investigate the relatively new festival of Kwanzaa. Who created it and why? What are its rituals? How would you compare it to a longstanding folk celebration such as Thanksgiving, Christmas, or New Year?

RELATED READINGS

Abbott, Isabella Aiona. *La`au Hawai`i: Traditional Hawaiian Uses of Plants.* Honolulu: Bishop Museum Press, 1992. A demonstration by a Hawaiian botanist of the holistic nature of traditional religion. Abbott specifically discusses the religious dimensions of Hawaiian agriculture and the use of plants in religious ceremony and hula.

Charlot, John. *Chanting the Universe: Hawaiian Religious Culture.* Hong Kong: Emphasis International, 1983. A well-illustrated presentation of a creation chant, with reflections on the culture from which it was born.

Halifax, Joan. *Shaman: The Wounded Healer.* London: Thames and Hudson, 1994. A collection of many examples of shamanistic art, along with a poetic description of the shaman's work.

Hill, Tom, and Richard W. Hill, Sr., eds. *Creation's Journey: Native American Identity and Belief.* Washington, DC: Smithsonian Press, 1994. A collection of large photographs of native art from both North and South America, with sensitive descriptions of the art objects.

Knudtson, Peter, and David Suzuki. *Wisdom of the Elders.* Toronto: Stoddart, 1993. A collection of ecological worldviews and wisdom from native cultures around the world, arranged by topic, such as plants, animals, sacred space, and the kinship of all living things.

Mbiti, John. *Introduction to African Religion.* London: Heinemann, 1986. A good description of patterns in African religions by an African scholar.

Taylor, Colin, ed. *The Native Americans.* New York: Salamander Books, 1991. A well-illustrated study of the native peoples of North America, divided according to region.

Tucker, Michael. *Dreaming with Open Eyes: The Shamanic Spirit in Twentieth Century Art and Culture.* London: HarperSanFrancisco/Aquarian, 1992. A book that emphasizes the rebirth in modern art of a magical way of viewing reality, akin to the spirit of oral religions.

Willett, Frank. *African Art.* Rev. ed. London: Thames and Hudson, 1993. A scholarly but readable discussion of African art, with good illustrations, particularly of masks and statues.

KEY TERMS

Calumet: A long-stemmed sacred pipe used primarily by many native peoples of North America; it is smoked as a token of peace.

Divination: A foretelling of the future or a discovery of the unknown by magical means.

Holistic: Organic, integrated; indicating a complete system, greater than the sum of its parts; here, refers to a culture whose various elements (art, music, social behavior) may all have religious meaning.

Libation: The act of pouring a liquid as an offering to a god.

Shaman: A human being who contacts and attempts to manipulate the power of spirits for the tribe or group.

Taboo: A strong social prohibition (Tongan: tabu; Hawaiian: kapu).

Totem: An animal (or image of an animal) that is considered to be related by blood to a family or clan and is its guardian or symbol.

CHAPTER 3

Hinduism

 FIRST ENCOUNTER

The plane that you have taken into India from Nepal circles in preparation for landing at the Varanasi airport, near Benares. Looking down from your window seat, you can see the blue-white Ganges River, quite wide here. Everything else is a thousand shades of brown: beyond the coffee-colored city, the beige fields spread out, seemingly forever.

At the small airport, a dignified customs inspector with a turban and a white beard asks, "Why have you come to India?" Before you can think of an appropriate response, he answers his own question. "I know," he says with a smile and a wave of the hand. "You westerners are all the same." He shakes his head from side to side. "You have come for *spirituality.*" After pausing briefly, he adds, "Haven't you!" which sounds more like a statement than a question. It takes you a second to understand his quick pronunciation of that unexpected word—*spirituality.* In a way, he is right. You *have* come for that. You nod in agreement. He smiles again, writes something down on his form, and lets you through.

As you take the small black taxi to your hotel, you realize that you have just accepted—willingly or not—the ancient role that the customs inspector has bestowed upon you. You are now just one more pilgrim who has come to Mother India for her most famous product: religious insight. You are now a Seeker.

After unpacking at your hotel, you walk out into the streets. It is dusk. Pedicab drivers ring their bells to ask if you want a ride, but you want to walk, to see the life of the streets. Little shops sell tea, and others sell vegetarian foods made of potatoes, wheat, beans, and curried vegetables. Children play in front of their parents' stores. Down the street you see a "gent's tailor" shop, as a thin cow wanders past, chewing on what looks like a paper bag. Another shop sells books and notepaper; and others sell saris and bolts of cloth. From somewhere comes a smell like jasmine. As night falls, the stores are lit by dim bulbs and fluorescent lights, and vendors illuminate their stalls with bright Coleman lanterns. Because you will be rising long before dawn to go down to the Ganges, you return early to your hotel and go to bed.

The telephone rings the following morning, waking you out of a dream. The man at the front desk notifies you that it is four A.M. Being somewhat groggy, you have to remind yourself that you are in Benares. You get up and dress quickly.

At the front of the hotel you wake a driver sleeping in his pedicab. You negotiate the fare, climb onto the seat, and head off to the main crossing of town, near the river, as the sky begins to lighten. The pedicab drops you near the *ghats* (the stairs that descend to the river), which are already full of people, many going down to the river to bathe at dawn. Some are having sandalwood paste applied to their foreheads as a sign of devotion, and others are carrying brass jugs to collect Ganges water.

As you descend to the river, boat owners call to you. You decide to join the passengers in the boat of a man who has a white handlebar mustache and looks like a Victorian patriarch. Off you go, moving slowly upstream. Laughing children jump up and down in the water as men and women wade waist-deep and face the rising sun to pray. Upstream, professional launderers beat clothes on the rocks and lay them out on the stones of the riverbank to dry.

The boat turns back downstream, passing the stairs where you first descended to the river. In the bright morning light you see large umbrellas, under which teachers sit cross-legged, some with disciples around them. Who, you wonder, are these teachers? The area near the shore is crammed with people and boats. On a nearby boat, people shout, *Vijaya Ganga Ma*— "Victory to Mother Ganges!"

The boat continues downstream. On the shore, smoke rises from small pyres, where bodies, wrapped in red and white cloth, are being cremated. The boatman warns, "No photos here, please." The boat pulls in to shore downstream of the pyres, and everyone gets off. Walking up the stairs, you see small groups of people quietly watching the cremations. At the pyres, a man tends the fires with a bamboo pole, and a dog wanders nearby.

Figure 3.1 India

Later, as you make your way back to the center of town, you notice a pedicab with a covered body tied on the back. It cycles past women sitting beside the road selling plastic bracelets and colored powders. The pedicab must be on its way to the pyres, you think. The blend of opposites fills your mind: on the banks of the very same river, laundry is washed and bodies are burned. In the streets, life and death are side by side, yet no one seems to notice the contrast. Here, the two are one.

THE ORIGINS OF HINDUISM

Looking at a map of India (Figure 3.1) you can see that this subcontinent, shaped like a triangle, is isolated. Two sides face oceans, while the north is bounded by the steep Himalaya Mountains. There are few mountain passes, and the only easy land entry is via the narrow corridor in the northwest, in the vicinity of the Indus River, where Pakistan now lies. It is the relative isolation of India that has helped create a culture that is rare and fascinating.

India's climate is warm, which allows people to live outdoors much of the time. Indeed, some may even claim that the climate has helped promote religious values that, at least for some, minimize the importance of material goods such as clothing, housing, and wealth.

Although hot and dry in many parts, India has many rivers and streams. Most important is the Ganges, which flows out of the Himalayas and is enlarged by tributaries as it moves east toward the Bay of Bengal. By the time the Ganges has reached the town of Varanasi, also known as Benares and Kashi, the river is enormous; and after the summer monsoons, the river becomes so wide that often one cannot see to the other side. Because the water of the Ganges is regular and dependable, it has allowed civilization to flourish across much of northern India. It has also given Indian culture a sense of security, protection, and even care, which has led to the popular name for the river, *Ganga Ma* ("Mother Ganges").

The religious life of India is something like the river Ganges. It has flowed along for thousands of years, swirling from its own power but also from the power of new streams that have added to its force. Hinduism, the major religion of India, has been an important part of this flowing energy. Many influences—early indigenous religion and influences from later immigrants—have added to its inherent momentum. It has no one identifiable founder, no strong organizational structure to defend it and spread its influence, nor any creed to define and stabilize its beliefs; and in a way that seems to defy reason, Hinduism unites the worship of many gods with a belief in a single divine reality. In fact, Hinduism is more like a family of related beliefs, and the name *Hinduism,* if used to suggest a unified religion, can be misleading.

But the limitations of Hinduism may also be its strengths. It is like a palace that began as a two-room cottage. Over the centuries, wings have been built on to it, and now it has countless rooms, stairs, corridors, statues, fountains, and gardens. There is something here to please and astonish—and dismay—almost everyone. In fact, its beliefs have been so rich and profound that Hinduism has greatly influenced the larger world, and its influence is growing still. In this chapter we will explore the various elements of this religion's foundation, and the stages in which additions were made to the sprawling house of Hinduism.

The Earliest Stage of Indian Religion

In the early twentieth century, engineers who were building a railroad discovered the ruins of an ancient culture in the Indus River valley. Today, most of the Indus River lies in Pakistan, but it traditionally formed the natural border of northwestern India—in fact, the words *India* and *Hindu* derive from *Indus.* The culture that archeological workers uncovered there

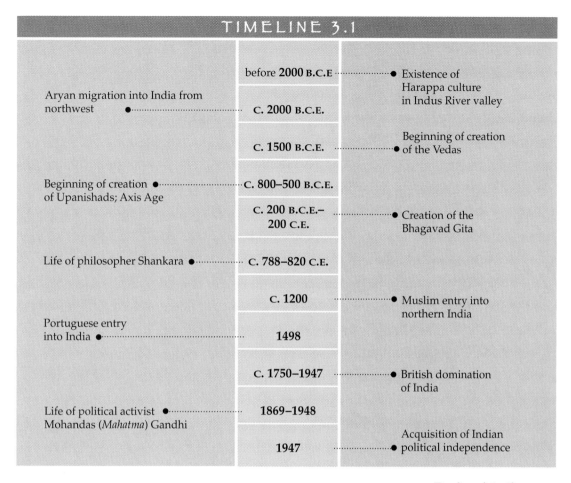

	before **2000 B.C.E** ·········· ● Existence of Harappa culture in Indus River valley
Aryan migration into India from northwest ● ··········	**C. 2000 B.C.E.**
	C. 1500 B.C.E. ·········· ● Beginning of creation of the Vedas
Beginning of creation ● ·········· of Upanishads; Axis Age	**C. 800–500 B.C.E.**
	C. 200 B.C.E.– 200 C.E. ·········· ● Creation of the Bhagavad Gita
Life of philosopher Shankara ● ··········	**C. 788–820 C.E.**
	C. 1200 ·········· ● Muslim entry into northern India
Portuguese entry into India ● ··········	**1498**
	C. 1750–1947 ·········· ● British domination of India
Life of political activist ● ·········· Mohandas (*Mahatma*) Gandhi	**1869–1948**
	1947 ·········· ● Acquisition of Indian political independence

Timeline of significant events in the history of Hinduism.

flourished before 2000 B.C.E. and is named the Harappa culture, after one of its ancient cities (Timeline 3.1).

Archeologists were amazed by the type of civilization they had found. The cities contained regular streets and solid brick houses. Pots and coins were found, as well as evidence that running water was used for toilets and baths. As historian Arthur Basham remarks, "no other ancient civilization until that of the Romans had so efficient a system of drains"[1]—a genuine sign of technical development. This complex culture had also invented a writing system, which scholars are still working to decipher.

Property owners marked their belongings with seals bearing the images of animals, such as the bull, tiger, and rhinoceros, as well as images of men and women. Three seals show a male, sitting in a yogic meditation posture, with horns on his head.[2] Small pillars that suggest male sexuality were also found. Because many of these same symbols still appear in contemporary Indian culture, we can assume that some current religious practices have survived from the distant past. For example, the male with the horns on his head may be a deity and an early form of the god Shiva, and the pillars resemble the low columns that some contemporary Indians worship in honor of Shiva (see page 80). It is also quite possible that the present-day worship of the divine Great Mother and of tree spirits goes back to this early time.

The Aryans and Their Religion

It is widely thought that around 2000 B.C.E. another people entered India from the northwest. They brought with them their own religion, which would make its distinctive contribution to what would later be known as Hinduism. These people called themselves Aryans, their word for *noble,* and they seem to have spread in several directions from their place of origin—probably southeastern Europe. Some settled in Iran (whose name derives from *Aryan*), and others went to western Europe, becoming the ancestors of the Greeks, Romans, and Germans. The "Indo-European" language they spoke, which scholars have reconstructed, is distantly related to the family of languages that includes Sanskrit, Hindi, Greek, Latin, French, Spanish, German, and English.

The Aryans who came to India spread throughout the region of the Harappa culture and changed it. They were an active, warrior-dominated, patriarchal society that herded animals and loved horses. Whether their entry into India was rapid or gradual is not certain. It may have extended over many centuries between approximately about 2500 and 1500 B.C.E. Their advance was certainly helped by their technology, particularly horse-drawn chariots. The Aryans had a social system of three classes—priests, warriors, and commoners. When the Aryans took over the Harappa culture, they generally placed the conquered people, whom they called *dasas* (servants), below their own classes—although some evidence suggests that there was assimilation into higher ranks, as well.

Aryan religion consisted of the worship of mostly male gods who were believed to control the forces of nature. The father of the gods was Dyaüs Pitr, whose name means "shining father." (He is clearly the same god as the Roman god Jupiter and the Greek god Zeus Pater.) The god Indra, god of storm and war, received great attention, because of the strength his worshipers hoped to receive from him. He was possibly the memory of a military ancestor, deified by later generations. The god of fire, Agni (whose name is related to "ignite" and to *ignis,* the Latin word for fire), carried sacrifices up to the world of the gods. Dawn and renewal were the charge of the goddess Ushas, one of the few female deities. The god Rudra brought winds. Varuna was the god of the sky and justice; Vishnu was a god of cosmic order; and Surya was the major sun god. The god Soma was thought to cause altered states of mind and to expand consciousness. He worked through a ritual drink, possibly made from a psychedelic mushroom that had the same name (*soma*) and allowed contact with the realm of the gods. The god Yama ruled the afterlife.

The ancient Vedic fire ceremony is a part of this New Delhi wedding.

Worship of the gods took place at outdoor fire altars. Priestly specialists set apart a square or rectangular space, purified it with water, and constructed one to three low altars inside the space for sacrifice. The usual offerings were milk, melted butter (called *ghee*), grains, and sometimes animals. A special horse sacrifice, believed to confer great power on a king, occurred on rare occasions.

Sacred chants, which the priests knew from memory, were an essential part of the ceremonies; and because they believed that the chants had power of their own, the priestly class protected them and handed them down orally from father to son. It is these chants, in written form, that make up the core of the Aryans' earliest sacred literature, called the **Vedas.** Although many of the Aryan gods are no longer worshiped, elements of the Aryan religion—such as the use of fire and some of the ancient chants by a priestly class—continue to be of great importance to Hindus today.

The Vedas

The Vedas, which originally were preserved only in oral form but eventually were written down, are the earliest sacred books of Hinduism. The name means "knowledge" or "sacred lore," and related words in English are *vision* and *wisdom.* Although scholars date the earliest versions of the Vedas to about 1500 B.C.E., pious Hindus consider them to be far more ancient. They say that the Vedas were revealed to *rishis* (holy men of the distant past), who did not create the Vedas but heard them and transmitted them to later generations. It is also possible that some of the Vedic material may reflect assimilation of pre- and non-Aryan traditions.

There are four basic sacred text collections that constitute the Vedas. The Rig Veda[3] ("hymn knowledge") is a collection of more than a thousand chants to the Aryan gods; the Yajur Veda ("ceremonial knowledge") contains matter for recitation during sacrifice; the Sama Veda ("chant knowledge") is a handbook of musical elaborations of Vedic chants; and the Atharva Veda ("knowledge from [the teacher] Atharva") consists of practical prayers and charms, such as prayers to protect against snakes and sickness.

The Rig Veda, the most important of the Vedas, has an account of the origin of the universe. The universe is said to have emerged from a division and cosmic sacrifice of a primeval superperson, Purusha. But the account includes a touching admission of uncertainty: "Who knows it for certain; who can proclaim it here; namely, out of what it was born and wherefrom his creations issued? The gods appeared only later—after the creation of the world. Who knows, then, out of what it has evolved?"[4]

The term *Vedas* sometimes indicates only these four collections. In its more common use, it also refers to some later material, as well. Detailed ceremonial rules, called Brahmanas and Aranyakas, were added by later generations to each of the four Vedic collections. The Brahmanas, named for the priests who would use them, give details about the proper time and place for ceremonies, the preparation of the ground, ritual objects, and purification rites. The Aranyakas ("forest books") allowed the rituals to be understood and practiced in nonliteral, symbolic ways by men who had left society and become ascetics in the forests. The four Vedas end with even later works, called the **Upanishads,** which express philosophical and religious ideas that arose in introspective and meditative traditions.

THE UPANISHADS AND THE AXIS AGE

Around 500 B.C.E., the Indo-Aryan civilization experienced such widespread and important changes that the period is known as the Axis Age, meaning that everything turned in a new direction at this time. Interestingly, great changes were also taking place in other religions and cultures as well: it was the time of the Buddha, Confucius, major Hebrew prophets, and early Greek philosophers.

After many centuries, the Indo-Aryans became so firmly settled in the Indus and Ganges river valleys that the environment and their own indigenization began to influence their traditional religious practices. The older Aryan religion had been active, optimistic, patriarchal, and polytheistic. Questioning of religious beliefs and practices—perhaps prompted by the settled agricultural lifestyle—began to emerge with strength. It is possible that pre-Aryan religious disciplines reasserted themselves, and there may have been resentment against the Aryan priestly class. Some critics questioned the value of the Vedic sacrifices, and we know from the Aranyakas that certain people abandoned social life to live alone in the forests, giving themselves much time for thought and religious experimentation. Thinkers

An ascetic carries water from the Ganges as cows pursue their own paths.

questioned the ancient belief in many gods, seeking instead a single divine reality that might be the source of everything.[5] Some went even further and saw all things as being mystically united. And a few rejected religious ritual altogether.

During this period there seems to have been interest in all sorts of techniques for altering consciousness, such as sitting for long periods in meditation, breathing deeply, fasting, avoiding sexual activity, practicing long periods of silence, going without sleep, experimenting with psychedelic plants, and living in the darkness of caves. All of these things could be done by people of any social class—not just by priests. Evidence of this intellectual ferment and the practice of spiritual disciplines is recorded in the documents called the Upanishads.

The Origin of the Upanishads

The Upanishads are a collection of about a hundred written works that record insights into external and internal reality. Although several interpretations of the origin of the name *Upanishads* have been proposed, it is commonly thought to be derived from words that mean "sitting near."[6] If

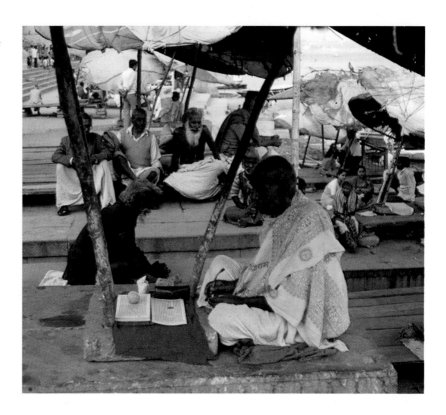

A Brahmin reads
scriptures on the banks of
the Ganges, at Benares.

the term's derivation is correct, it would suggest disciples sitting near a master, learning techniques for achieving religious experience. In any case, primary to the Upanishads is the notion that with spiritual discipline and meditation, both priests and nonpriests can experience the spiritual reality that underlies all seemingly separate realities. Unlike much of the earlier Vedic material, which dictates that only hereditary priests can be religious masters, the Upanishads tell us that a person who has the necessary experience can be a spiritual master. The Upanishads thus possibly continue the religious interest of the "forest dwellers" of the Aranyakas.

The Upanishads are written primarily in dialogue form, appearing both as prose and as poetry. Because they were produced over many hundreds of years, dating them is not easy. It is generally thought that those in prose form (such as the Chandogya, Brihadaranyaka, Taittiriya, and Kena Upanishads) may be earlier works than those in poetic form (such as the Katha and Mandukya Upanishads). About a dozen Upanishads are especially popular.

Important Concepts of the Upanishads

The most important notions in the Upanishads are *Brahman, Atman, maya, karma,* and *moksha.*[7] These primary concepts, which would become essential notions in much later Hindu spirituality, continue to be taught today.

Brahman and Atman   The term **Brahman** originally stood for the cosmic power present in the Vedic sacrifice and chants, over which the priest had control. (The Sanskrit word "Brahman" is neuter and comes from a stem meaning "to be great.") In the Upanishads the word *Brahman* was expanded to mean a divine reality at the heart of things. One of the most famous dialogues appears in the Chandogya Upanishad. It presents a priestly father and his son in discussion. The young man, Shvetaketu, has been away studying and memorizing priestly lore—chants and rituals— with a specialist for many years. The young man's father questions him about what he has learned, and his son proudly recites the many formulas he knows. The father then asks him what he knows about Brahman, the Supreme Spirit; but the young man knows nothing. Trying to assist the son's understanding, the father asks his son to fill a glass with water, put salt in it, and leave it overnight. The next day he asks his son to find the salt:

> "Bring me the salt you put into the water last night."
> Shvetaketu looked into the water, but could not find it, for it had dissolved.
> His father then said: "Taste the water from this side. How is it?"
> "It is salt."
> "Taste it from the middle. How is it?"
> "It is salt."
> "Taste it from that side. How is it?"
> "It is salt."
> "Look for the salt again and come again to me."
> The son did so, saying: "I cannot see the salt. I only see water."
> The father then said: "In the same way, O my son, you cannot
> see the Spirit. But in truth he is here.
> "An invisible and subtle essence is the Spirit of the whole
> universe. That is Reality. That is Truth. Thou art That."[8]

The Upanishads insist that Brahman is something that can be known— not simply believed in. The Shvetasvatara Upanishad, for example, says "I *know* that Spirit whose infinity is in all, who is ever one beyond time."[9] Brahman, the divine Spirit, is so real that it may be known directly, and, as the boy Shvetaketu learned, knowledge of it can be as immediate as tasting a flavor.

What is it to know Brahman? The Upanishads insist that it cannot be put fully into words, but they give hints. Brahman is the lived experience that all things are in some way holy because they come from the same sacred source. It is also the experience that all things are in some way ultimately one, a concept that seems to defy common sense—the world appears to be divided into many objects and types of reality. Nevertheless, when we consider reality more deeply, we recognize many unities: a piece of wood can become a boat or a house or fire or ash; water can turn into a cloud or a plant. So, on closer inspection, all apparent separations and divisions blur. To experience Brahman is to know, firsthand, that every apparently individual reality in the world is actually a wave of the same sacred ocean of energy. Brahman, according to the Upanishads, "is the sun, the moon, and the stars. He is the fire, the waters, and the wind."[10] Brahman is "the God who appears in forms infinite."[11]

Brahman is also referred to by three words that help describe its nature as perceived by the knower: Brahman is *sat,* reality itself; *chit,* pure consciousness; and *ananda,* bliss. And although Brahman can be experienced within our everyday world of time and space, those who speak of their experience say that Brahman is ultimately beyond time and beyond space. Thus the Upanishads often add that experiencing the timelessness of Brahman can bring an end to everyday suffering and to the fear of death.

The term **Atman** originally referred to the whole interior mental world that shows itself in consciousness, thought, imagination, trance, and dream. Although *Atman* is sometimes used interchangeably with the term *self* or *soul,* the notion of Atman in the Upanishads is larger than the notion of an individual self or soul. In Hindu belief, each person has an individual soul (*jiva*), but the Upanishads teach that all human beings share the same Atman. Beneath the surface differences among individuals, all human beings share the same divine spirit. Atman, when experienced fully, is identical with Brahman. Atman, like Brahman, is divine, holy, and timeless. Often the term *Brahman* refers to the experience of the sacred and divine reality within nature and the external universe, while *Atman* refers to the experience of the sacred within oneself. However, the same divine nature simply has two names, and both terms can be used interchangeably.

Maya   The Upanishads speak of the everyday world as **maya,** which is usually translated as "illusion."[12] This translation, though, needs explanation. Its root suggests illusion and mystery (as in "*magic*"), but it also has a more positive, objective connotation that suggests the original stuff of which something is made (as in "*material*"). The word *maya* thus contains both meanings: "magic" and "matter." To say that all reality is "maya" is not to say that the world does not exist or that the world is a totally false perception. The world is real but not in quite the way most people assume. For one thing, human beings view the world as consisting of individual things and people, all separate. In reality, the world is one basic holy reality that takes on many different forms. The Shvetasvatara Upanishad advises us to "know therefore that nature is Maya, but that God is the ruler of Maya; and that all beings in our universe are parts of his infinite splendour."[13]

People also assume that the world is solid and permanent. In reality, the outside world is more like the inner world of thoughts and dreams—it shifts and changes, just as thoughts and dreams do. People assume that time is real, that it advances at a regular rate, and that past, present, and future are distinct divisions. In reality, time is relative.

The model of reality set forth by the Upanishads is less like a machine made of individual, moving parts and more like a great consciousness. This view also produces a sense of amazement at the forms and shifts the universe takes—it is all, ultimately, unexplainable magic.

In the Upanishads, death is not a tragedy. However, as I look out at reality from my own individual standpoint, I may see the end of my life as the end of everything. The Upanishads see things differently. First, individuals are not as individual as they suppose but rather are all the manifestation of the divine spirit, which does not end when the individual dies. They are also the continuation of earlier forms of life that have simply taken new forms. Hinduism, from about 500 B.C.E., generally adopted the belief that everything living has its own life force and that every life force, when it loses one form, is reborn into another. This process is known as reincarnation.

Karma   The general Hindu notion of rebirth assumes that human beings have at one or another time existed as a "lower" form, such as animal, insect, and possibly even plant. Hinduism also recognizes grades of human life, from limited and painful to exceptionally pleasant and free. "Higher" forms of life are also possible beyond the human, such as superhuman beings and demigods. Rebirth can move in either direction, and the human stage is a dangerous one because each human being must make dramatic choices about how to live. If a human being does not live properly, he or she may be reborn into a very poor or cruel human family—or possibly in the form of life that may be even more limited and difficult, such as a dog, a pig, or an ant. A human being can also make a spectacular leap upward beyond the human level to a superhuman existence or even beyond, to complete freedom.

What determines the direction of one's rebirth is **karma.** The word comes from a root that means "to do" and implies the notion of moral consequences that are carried along with every act. Karma is the moral law of cause and effect, and belief in karma is a belief that every action has an automatic moral consequence.

Some teachers say that karma is intrinsically neither good nor bad but only seems so to the person who experiences it. In this conception, karma is like gravity—it works like a force of nature. It is like rain, which can cause a plant to grow just as it can bring a picnic to its end. Karma helps explain why some people are born with great gifts while others are born with no advantages at all.

Moksha   The term **moksha** means "freedom" or "liberation" and comes from a root which means "to be released." In the Upanishads, moksha is the ultimate human goal. It has various connotations. Moksha certainly includes the notion of getting beyond egotistic responses, such as resentment and anger, which limit the individual. Furthermore, unlike the Western ideal of freedom to satisfy one's individuality, moksha implies liberation even from the limitations of being an individual—from being born a particular person at a specific time to a unique pair of parents—a person with distinct physical

Portrayals of Krishna are
popular among his
devotees and frequently
show him as a boy or
young man. Here, however,
Krishna is portrayed in his
divine nature. The many
heads and arms show his
power.   ▶

characteristics, emotions, desires, and memories. One can take action to overcome these restrictions (for example, by leaving home), which is sometimes a means of attaining moksha, but one can also accept the limitations even while living with them, thereby gaining inner peace and mental freedom.

As a person becomes freer, one looks at life less from a selfish and egotistic point of view and more from a perspective that embraces the whole. The unity and sacredness that everything shares becomes a part of everyday experience. Kindness to all—to animals as well as to people—is one natural result of this new insight, and kind actions also generate helpful karma. Detaching oneself from pleasure or pain is another practice that leads to freedom from egotism.

Ultimately, with enough insight and ascetic practice, the individual can go entirely beyond the limited self to know the sacred reality that everything shares. When insight and kindness are perfect, at last the pain of rebirth ends; the limitations of individuality are gone, and only Brahman remains. The Brihadaranyaka Upanishad explains complete freedom: "when all has become Spirit, one's own Self, how and whom could one see?"[14]

The Upanishads, though sometimes obscure, are devoted to promoting an insight into ultimate oneness. But the Upanishads do not give detailed instructions about techniques for creating that kind of insight or for living spiritually in the everyday world. Such guidance would have to be developed by later Hindu commentators and practitioners.

LIVING SPIRITUALLY IN THE EVERYDAY WORLD

The Hinduism that guides people's lives today is a practical mixture of elements, some of which came from the early stages of religious practice, which we've already discussed, and others which developed later. Hindu practice for the ordinary layperson usually involves devotion to at least one deity. It recommends finding one's proper work and then doing it unselfishly. Hindu practice may also include the study of religious texts, meditation, and other specifically religious disciplines. The following section will deal with the elements of this practical synthesis, much of which can be found in the short classic, the Bhagavad Gita.

The Bhagavad Gita

The **Bhagavad Gita** ("divine song" or "song of the Divine One") is part of a very long epic poem called the Mahabharata. The Mahabharata, written sometime between 400 B.C.E. and 400 C.E., tells how the sons of Pandu (Pandavas) conquered their cousins, the Kauravas, with the help of the god Krishna. The Bhagavad Gita was inserted at some time into this poem but has its own identity and is often printed separately from the Mahabharata. The Bhagavad Gita, shaped probably between 200 B.C.E. and 200 C.E., has

become a spiritual classic. It recalls themes from the Upanishads, but it also tries to strike a balance between mysticism and the practical needs of everyday life. Action and adherence to duty are approved and can even be thought of as a spiritual path. As the Bhagavad Gita says, "the wise see knowledge and action as one."[15]

The Bhagavad Gita, like the Upanishads, is written in dialogue form. It occurs almost entirely between two figures: a prince, Arjuna, and his charioteer and advisor, Krishna. Arjuna's royal power is threatened by his hundred cousins, called Kauravas, and he must decide whether to fight with his brothers against them to restore his throne or to accept their rule. He is torn. On the one hand, he knows that his rule is correct, but on the other, he wants to avoid violence. That his enemies are close family members makes the matter even harder. Depressed, Arjuna "[throws] aside his arrows and his bow in the midst of the battlefield. He [sits] down on the seat of the chariot, and his heart [is] overcome with sorrow."[16] In response, Krishna, who later reveals that he is a form of the god Vishnu, explains the need for action. "Now you shall hear how a man may become perfect, if he devotes himself to the work which is natural to him. A man shall reach perfection if he does his duty as an act of worship to the Lord."[17]

Contrary to the teaching of nonviolence that was at the time of this epic's creation growing strong in India in traditions like Buddhism and Jainism, Krishna advises Arjuna to fight to protect his throne and the structure of society—to fight is his duty. At a moment of great revelation, Krishna shows Arjuna that a divine reality is at work within everything in the universe—in living and also in dying. Krishna even says that for the warrior "there is nothing nobler than a righteous war."[18]

The recommendation that Arjuna should fight has posed a moral problem for some followers of Hinduism. Mohandas Gandhi (1869–1948) is typical of those who have solved this problem by saying that the Bhagavad Gita is religious allegory. Gandhi held that the call to arms is not about real war but a call to fight against dangerous moral and psychological forces, such as ignorance, selfishness, and anger. This interpretation, though it seems to go against the literal intent of the text, has been influential.

We should note here the nobility of the personality of Krishna in the Bhagavad Gita. His dignity is a subject that has inspired much art and literature and has been portrayed frequently in film and on television.

The Caste System

When Krishna urges Arjuna to do what his position as a warrior demands, he is reinforcing the division of society into **castes** (social classes that are created by birth or occupation). The caste system was accepted widely by 500 B.C.E. but was mentioned before this time in the Rig Veda: "When they divided Purusha [the first person, a superbeing], in how many different portions did they arrange him? What became of his mouth, what of his two arms? What were his two thighs and his two feet called? His mouth became the brahman [priest]; his two arms were made into the rajanya [warrior-noble]; his two thighs the vaishyas [merchants]; from his two feet the shudra [peasant] was born."[19]

The caste system receives further religious approval in the Bhagavad Gita, which recognizes that there are different types of people and that their ways to perfection will differ, depending on their personality type and role in society.[20] For example, active people will perfect themselves through the unselfishness of their work; and intellectual people will perfect themselves through teaching and study.

Traditionally, the caste system is based on more than one's type of work, and in modern times it does not always indicate the type of work a person does. Castes (as the term is commonly used) are really social classes (*varna*), which are subdivided into hundreds of subcastes.[21] The caste system dissuades members of different castes, and often subcastes, from intermarrying. It remains strongest in the countryside and in the more conservative south of India, but it is weakening in the cities, where people regularly eat together in restaurants and travel together in buses and trains.

Members of society are divided into five main social classes:

The priest (**brahmin**)[22] traditionally performs Vedic rituals and acts as a counselor. In modern times, members of this caste are also in demand as cooks, which is seen as a natural extension of the priestly relationship with fire and sacrifice. This function is practical because brahmins, being of the highest caste, may prepare food for people in all other castes as well as their own.

The warrior-noble (*kshatriya*) has the role of protecting society. This is the traditional caste of the aristocracy.

The merchant (*vaishya*) class includes landowners, moneylenders, and sometimes artisans. Males of the three upper castes receive a sacred cord during a ceremony in their youth and afterward are called "twice-born."

The peasant (*shudra*) does manual labor and is expected to serve the higher castes. The origin of this caste probably goes back to the Aryan subjection of native people, who were forced to do the work of servants. The peasant is called "once-born."

The outcaste (or untouchable, *mlechcha*), as the name indicates, is considered so low as to be outside the caste system. Untouchables traditionally do the dirtiest work—cleaning toilets, sweeping streets, collecting animal carcasses, and tanning animal hides. What was probably an early concern for hygiene led to the exclusion of untouchables from the rest of society. Untouchables have routinely been denied the use of wells used by other social classes and have even been forbidden from entering many temples. They have often been forced to live in ghettos and sometimes been horribly mistreated. Their low status prompted the Indian reformer Mohandas Gandhi to promote another name for the class—*Harijan* ("children of God")—and he urged their inclusion in regular society.[23]

Bride and groom
participate in their
wedding ceremony.

The Stages of Life

Just as the individual's path to "correct action" is suggested by caste and
subcaste, traditional Hinduism holds that each stage of life also has its
proper way of being lived. Every culture recognizes specific life stages
through which each individual passes. In modern secular life the stages
seem to be childhood, the teenage period, the career years, and retirement,
stages that are strongly colored by employment; but in India the notion of
life stages is more religious. The conception was shaped by the ancient ideal
of the development of the upper-caste male, particularly of the priestly
caste:

1. Student (*brahmacharin*): This first stage is spent laying a religious
   foundation for life. The young person, between the ages 8 and 20,
   studies religious works. Celibacy is a necessary part of the training.
2. Householder (*grihashta*): Marriage (traditionally, arranged by the
   parents) occurs at about age 20, and the person fulfills the demands of
   society by raising children.
3. Retiree (*vanaprastha*): When grandchildren arrive, the individual may
   retire somewhat from ordinary life to spend time once again on
   religious matters. The ancient ideal was to go into the forest to live,
   possibly with one's wife, away from society. In reality, retirees often
   continue to live with their children and with other relatives in an
   extended family setting, but they may eat separately from the rest of
   the family and spend time on religious pursuits with friends.
4. Renunciate (*sannyasin*): To enter this last stage is considered to be
   appropriate only after retirement. It is not expected of everyone but is
   simply an option. If one wishes to live entirely free from society, it is

possible to leave home and live as a homeless nomad. A man may leave his wife, although he must ensure that she will be supported. Celibacy is expected, and the sign of this devout, celibate state is an orange robe. The **sannyasin,** considered to be outside the caste system, is free to wander, begging his food along the way, and many temples have endowments to feed such pilgrims. The sannyasin may remain a homeless traveler, making pilgrimage to the sacred sites of India, or he may settle in an **ashram** (religious community) or even live in a cave. The purpose of this kind of life is to hasten mystical insight, to free oneself of all attachments, to end rebirth, and to attain moksha.

The Goals of Life

Although the Hindu spiritual ideal—such as the lifestyle of the sannyasin—is generally world-denying, there is also a respect for more worldly goals. In order of increasing value these goals are: pleasure (*kama*), economic security and power (*artha*), and social and religious duty (*dharma*). These life goals, which may be pursued simultaneously, are acceptable and even virtuous, as long as they are tempered by moderation and social regulation. Considered highest of the goals, however, is moksha—complete freedom.

The Yogas

Although the Bhagavad Gita endorses quiet contemplation, it also recommends active spiritual paths. It not only endorses meditation but also the work demanded by one's caste and individual place in society. The various types of yoga are methods that can be used to help people live spiritually. The word **yoga** means "union" and is related to the English words *join* and *yoke.* A yoga is a way for people to perfect their union with the divine, and because the yogas suggest roads to perfection, they are also called *margas* ("paths"). There is a tolerant recognition in Hinduism that different sorts of people need different spiritual paths, and an individual's caste and personality type will help determine the appropriate yoga to practice. The ancient teaching of yogas is still quite alive in modern Hinduism.

Jnana Yoga ("Knowledge Yoga")   This type of yoga brings insight into one's divine nature by studying the Upanishads and Bhagavad Gita and their commentaries and by learning from gurus who have attained insight. *Jnana yoga* is particularly appropriate for priests and intellectuals.

This yoga was highly refined by a school of philosophy that is still quite vital, the school of Vedanta ("Veda end").[24] The term refers to the Upanishads—which come at the end of the Vedas—and to the fact that the Vedanta school has used the ideas of the Upanishads as its primary inspiration.

The greatest teacher of Vedanta, Shankara (c. 788–820), argued that everything is ultimately one—all is Brahman.[25] According to Shankara, although our ordinary experience may see things as being separate and different, this perception is mistaken. To show that sense perception can be wrong, Shankara used the example of a person who at dusk is frightened by a coil of rope—the observer mistakenly perceives the rope to be a snake. In the same way, Shankara would say, a person who perceives things as being ultimately separate and different from Brahman is mistaken. In his *Crest-Jewel of Discrimination*, the author likened Brahman to gold, which can take many shapes. Brahman "is that one Reality which appears to our ignorance as a manifold universe of names and forms and changes. Like the gold of which many ornaments are made, it remains in itself unchanged. Such is Brahman, and 'That art Thou.' Meditate upon this truth."[26] Similarly, the waves of the ocean and the drops of water in the waves may be considered separate entities; but the larger truth is that they are all just the same ocean in varied, changing forms.

Shankara thought that spiritual liberation was achieved when the individual personally came to understand the unity of all things. Shankara so emphasized monism—the oneness of everything—that his branch of the Vedanta school is called *Advaita*, which, literally translated, means "not-two-ness" (*a-dvai-ta*). The significance of the term is very subtle. If I say that all reality is "one," some "other" reality could also exist—something in contrast to the one. But the term *not-two* makes clear that ultimately there is no other reality.

For Shankara, therefore, any devotion to a god or goddess who is thought to be different from the worshiper is also mistaken. This rejection of devotion, however, posed a great problem for those types of Hinduism that emphasized it. As a result, later thinkers of the Vedanta school, such as Ramanuja (c. 1040–1137) and Madhva (fl. 1240), qualified or denied ultimate monism. They emphasized passages in the Upanishads that seem to speak of Brahman as being separate in some way from the world. They could thereby create dualistic or semidualistic systems that made room for religious devotion.

Karma Yoga ("Action Yoga")   This type of yoga proposes that all useful work, if done unselfishly, can be a way to perfection. (The word *karma* here is used in its basic sense of "activity.") Much of what we ordinarily do is motivated by money or pleasure or praise, but deeds performed without a desire for reward are the heart of **karma yoga.** As the Bhagavad Gita says, "Desire for the fruits of work must never be your motive in working."[27]

Bhakti Yoga ("Devotion Yoga")   Most of us have at one time or another fallen in love, and we know that there is something purifying about the experience, because it forces us to look outward, beyond ourselves, to another object of affection. Religions utilize this purifying power when they promote devotion to a god or saint—who is often made visible in a

Hindu Meditation: More Than Emptying the Mind

Over the last three decades, meditation has become popular in the Western world. From students in elementary schools to executives in corporate offices—all kinds of people take time out to empty the mind, sit quietly, and let stress float away.

Meditation in Eastern religious traditions, however, is more complex, at least theoretically. The Yoga Sutras, often attributed to the grammarian Patanjali[29], list eight steps necessary for perfection of meditation:

- Self-control (*yama*) is the fundamental reorientation of the personality away from selfishness. It involves practicing **ahimsa** (not hurting living beings), exhibiting sexual restraint, shunning greed, refusing to steal, and embracing truthfulness.
- Observance (*niyama*) is the regular practice of the five preceding virtues.
- Posture (*asana*) is an integral aspect of meditation, particularly the "lotus posture" (*padmasana*), in which the legs are crossed and each foot touches the opposite leg.
- Breath control (*pranayama*) involves deep, regular breathing, holding the breath, and breathing in various rhythms.
- Restraint (*pratyahara*) helps the meditator tune out external distractions.
- Steadying of the mind (*dharana*) teaches the meditator to focus on only one object in order to empty the mind of everything else.
- Meditation (**dhyana**) occurs when the mind is focused only on the object of concentration.
- **Samadhi** is the mental state achieved by deep meditation, in which the individual loses the sense of being separate from the rest of the universe.[30]

painting or statue. Hinduism, because of its belief in multiple gods, offers rich possibilities for devotion. In the Bhagavad Gita, Vishnu tells Arjuna, "Regard me as your dearest loved one. Know me to be your only refuge."[28]

Bhakti yoga can involve various forms of devotion—most commonly chants, songs, food offerings, and the anointing of statues. Bhakti yoga can extend also to acts of devotion shown to one's **guru** (spiritual teacher), to one's parents, and to one's spouse. The gods worshiped in bhakti yoga will be described later.

Raja Yoga ("Royal Yoga")   This type of yoga promotes meditation. The term **raja yoga** does not appear in the Bhagavad Gita but was introduced later to refer to the steps of meditation described in the box "Hindu Meditation: More than Emptying the Mind." Nonetheless, Chapter 6 of the Bhagavad Gita describes basic meditation—sitting quietly, turning inward, and calming the mind. Done for short periods of time on a regular basis, meditation lowers stress and brings a sense of peace; done for longer periods of time, it can induce new states of consciousness.

There are many types of meditation. Some involve emptying the mind of thought; others involve focusing on some physical or mental object. Meditation can be done with the eyes closed or open or focused on a point a short distance in front of the face. A word or brief phrase, called a **mantra,** is often recited with each breath to help clear the mind of thought. (The short mantra *Om*—which is sometimes called the sound of creation—is frequently used.) Meditation can be done in silence or to gentle music; it can

The chakras are centers through which energy rises from the base of the spine to the crown of the head.

also be done gazing at a candle, at the moon, or at moving water. Some advanced types of meditation involve techniques taken from additional yogas. They may have the meditator create symbolic mental images (frequently of a deity), contemplate a sacred diagram (called a *yantra*), or repeat complicated sacred phrases.

The many techniques of meditation are called *sadhanas* ("practices"), and Kundalini Yoga offers additional help toward the goal of meditation yoga. It emerged from a tradition, called Tantrism, which focused on use of the body and all its energies to reach higher consciousness. Kundalini Yoga teaches that there are seven psychic centers, called *chakras* ("wheels"), that exist one above the other along the spinal column (Figure 3.2). Meditation and physical exercises (described in the following section) help the meditator lift spiritual energy—called *kundalini* and envisioned as a coiled serpent—from one center to the next. Each chakra is like a gateway through which the kundalini passes, bringing increased insight and joy. When the kundalini reaches the topmost and seventh center of energy at the crown of the head, the practitioner experiences profound bliss. The topmost center of energy (*sahasrara*) appears in imagery as a lotus flower, and reaching it is compared to the opening of a lotus.

Hatha Yoga ("Force Yoga")   When most of us in the West think of yoga, we think of the physical exercises of hatha yoga. These exercises, which were originally developed to help make long periods of meditation easier, mostly involve stretching and balancing. Breathing exercises are sometimes considered a part of **hatha yoga.**

In addition to these five yogas are others. In fact, any set of techniques that leads to greater spirituality can be considered a yoga.

Hatha yoga has spread beyond Hinduism because of its benefit to health and relaxation.

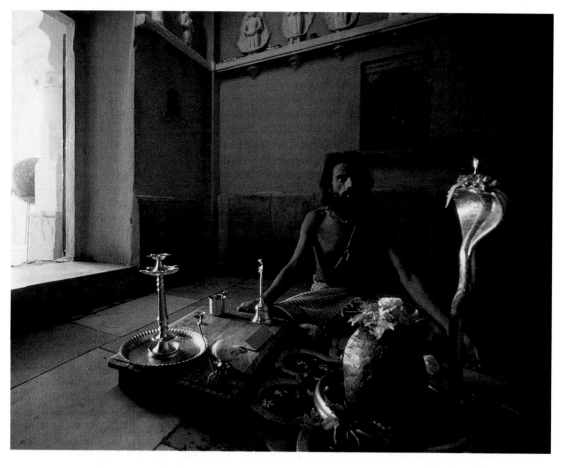

A priest prepares to worship Shiva.

DEVOTIONAL HINDUISM

Indians have been primarily a rural, agricultural people, and even today only about fifteen percent of the population lives in cities. The rest live, as they have for centuries, in more than half a million villages. Men in the villages spend most of their waking hours working as merchants, craftsmen, and farmers, while women marry when young and spend most of their time preparing food, running their households, and caring for their children. The duties of everyday life leave little time to pursue more philosophical paths.

For the majority of Hindus, then, some of the spiritual disciplines just mentioned—study, meditation, and special physical exercises—have had limited appeal. Instead, the great majority of Hindus have followed the path of devotion (**bhakti**) to a god or gods. Hindus worship their gods in village temples and at home altars. Most worship daily, and there are special days dedicated to individual gods. Ritual commonly performed at altars is called **puja,** and includes the offering of flowers, food, fire, and incense to the images, as well as the singing of hymns.

The earliest layer of devotional Hinduism, probably traceable to the pre-Aryan Harappa culture, seems to have involved the anointing of phallic

Morning rituals in the Ganges may include the veneration of the lingam.

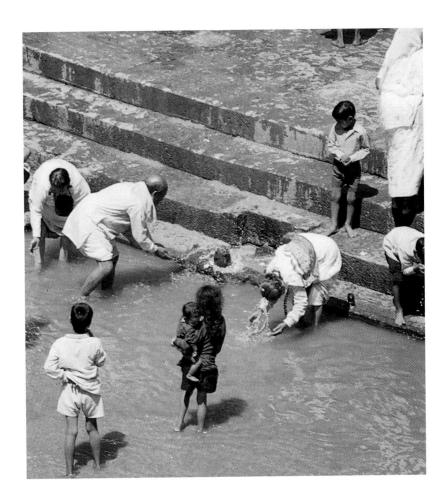

stones, devotion to female divinities of fertility, and the worship of nature spirits. This type of religious devotion continues in India today.

The Aryan religion introduced the Vedic gods as additional objects of worship. Some of these, such as Indra and Agni, were once highly popular, while others, such as Dyaüs Pitr, lost devotees and moved to the background quite early. In this devotional pattern we can see that a certain fluctuation of interest is natural: throughout history, in all religious devotion, the stock of some gods rises while the stock of others falls.

Certain gods and goddesses seem to have emerged separately, not as a part of the Vedic pantheon—of these Krishna is one of the best known. Some animal forms became deified, and all deities were eventually incorporated loosely into what is today a fairly large pantheon.

Although Hinduism is often described as a religion that promotes a belief in many gods, in reality individuals often focus their devotion on only one of the gods. Sometimes that god is considered to be the greatest of all divine manifestations. There is also an underlying monotheistic tendency in Hinduism, since all gods are frequently considered expressions of a single divine reality. Devotion to an individual god or goddess is often justi-

fied by saying that although the divine is ultimately formless, human beings must worship the divine through physical manifestations, giving rise
to much painting, sculpture, music, and ceremony in honor of the gods described in the following sections.

The Trimurti: Brahma, Vishnu, and Shiva

Three major gods are objects of devotion, because they are associated with
the interlinked forces of creation, preservation, and destruction. The three
gods are Brahma, Vishnu, and Shiva, sometimes together called the
Trimurti, which means "triple form."

Brahma represents the creative force that made the universe. The god
Brahma is more commonly the object of collective worship (that is, devotees worship him along with Vishnu and Shiva) than he is of singular worship. This is not to say that he is neglected. Brahma is frequently represented in art, yet only two temples in India are dedicated to him alone.
Brahma is commonly depicted as an ancient, thoughtful king, with four
faces that look in all four directions and four arms. His companion animal
is a white goose.

Vishnu represents the force of preservation in the universe. In the
Vedas he is a god associated with the sun, although his role there appears
to be small. Thought of as light and warmth that destroys darkness, Vishnu
grew in stature until finally becoming a major god of Hinduism. His followers are called Vaishnavites (or Vaishnavas).

In painting and sculpture, Vishnu is shown in many forms, though
usually with a tall crown and a regal manner. Almost always he has four
arms, which hold symbols of power. His companion animal is a great
eaglelike bird, Garuda, on whom he flies through the universe.

Because Vishnu is associated with loving-kindness, it is believed that
he can appear on earth at different times and in various physical forms to
help those in need. Ten major incarnations (or **avatars**) of Vishnu are commonly listed, of which one is still to appear. Some previous incarnations
were in animal form: a fish, a boar, and a tortoise. Another was Siddhartha
Gautama, the Buddha—an intriguing inclusion, which helped Hinduism
partially reabsorb Indian Buddhism (see Chapter 4). The incarnation yet to
come will be a savior figure on horseback who will judge the human race.
Two incarnations of Vishnu are wildly popular—Rama and Krishna.

Rama may have been a historical figure who later took on mythic pro-
portions. He appears in the great epic the Ramayana, whose stories of Rama
have inspired dance as well as art. One of the most commonly told stories
is about the abduction of Rama's wife, Sita, by Ravan (or Ravana), the demon king of Sri Lanka. Rama, a king, gains the help of Hanuman, leader of
the monkeys and a god in his own right. Hanuman helps Rama in killing
Ravan and in locating and returning Sita. Rama and Sita are thought of as
the ideal loving couple.

Surrounded by the flames of destruction, Shiva as Lord of the Dance (Nataraja) is the power at work in all death and regeneration. ▶

Krishna, another incarnation of Vishnu, may have begun as an object of fertility worship and is depicted in several forms, which might indicate that he is a coalescence of traditions. In the long epic the Mahabharata, Krishna appears as a mature and solemn god. In later devotional works, the Puranas ("legends"), he is younger; there he is friends with *gopis* (milkmaids who look after herds of cows), and he steals butter and plays the flute, expressing the playful aspect of the divine. In depictions of Krishna, his face and skin are often blue, the color of the sky and of heaven, indicating his true otherworldly nature. His closest milkmaid companion is Radha, with whom he is romantically linked in the Hindu mind.

Shiva, the third of the Trimurti and the god linked with destruction, is the most complicated of the gods, both in origin and in conception. The horned figure, sitting in yogic meditation posture and found on seals from the Harappa period, may be an early form of Shiva, meaning that some aspects of the present-day god may extend back to pre-Aryan India. Another source is apparently the Vedic god Rudra, a dangerous god of mountains and winds, whom worshipers probably began to call *shiva* ("lucky") in order to neutralize the fear he inspired. In later times, however, his link with destructiveness is often shown in pictures of Shiva appearing at cremation grounds, above a human body that is dissolving in flames.

Shiva's connection with destruction may be hard for many non-Hindus to appreciate. In Western religions, creation is associated with a good God, and destruction comes from what is not God—from sin or evil or Satan. In Hinduism, however, destruction is considered to be simply another part of the divine energy at work in the world. Destruction is a type of recycling, the necessary loss of form, which occurs so that new forms may appear; and death is always thought of as leading to new life. We know that the seed disappears when the tree grows, and the flower must die to make the fruit. Thus Shiva is also associated with re-creation.

The destructive side of Shiva is portrayed in the bronze statues called *Shiva Nataraja* ("ruler of the dance"). As he dances, Shiva is surrounded by a ring of fire (symbolic of destructive and transformative power) and his long yogi's hair flies in the air. He has four arms. In his upper right arm is a drum, symbolizing creation and the beginning of time; and in the upper left arm is a flame, symbolizing destruction. His lower left arm is pointing to his upraised foot, suggesting that everyone should join him in his dance. His lower right arm is extended in blessing, which in a symbolic way says "Don't be afraid." He dances on a dwarf-demon, representing the ignorance of all those who do not understand that death is part of the divine process. The art historian Heinrich Zimmer explains that "conquest of this demon lies in the attainment of true wisdom. Therein is release from the bondages of the world."[31]

The aspect of Shiva that brings re-creation is represented by sexually suggestive forms. (We should note here that in nonindustrial societies, the bearing of children is crucial—both for the economic survival of the family and for the care of the parents in their old age. Parents pray to have many

नटेश

81

Behind half-open doors, the vertical lingam and the circle of the yoni represent the mysterious power of Shiva.

Hindu gods take many forms. This simple statue of Shiva stands in contrast to the image of Shiva as Lord of the Dance, shown on page 80.

healthy children.) A frequent representation of Shiva is a columnar *lingam*—often black, which adds to its mystery. It usually rests on a *yoni*—a circular base that is the female complement to the lingam. The lingam may be a large, natural stone worshiped outdoors; a metal object small enough to be worn around the neck; or a wooden piece of an appropriate size for worship in the home. Shaivites (devotees of Shiva) may pour various liquids, such as milk and rosewater, over the lingam in an act of devotion.

Fertility is further emphasized by Shiva's companion animal Nandi the bull and by Ganesha, the elephant-headed son of Shiva, who has become a symbol of strength and abundance. Both are frequently found in temples dedicated to Shiva. Worship of Shiva is most common in Kashmir and southern India. We should note, too, that Shiva is closely linked with destruction only when he is viewed as part of the Trimurti. Among Shaivites, he is the sole God and is not exclusively related to destruction.

Worship of the Divine Feminine: Devi

The three gods of the Trimurti are usually portrayed as masculine. But of all the great world religions, Hinduism (perhaps most strongly) recognizes the female aspects of divinity. This may come from a practical interest in fertility. Worship of female divinities, too, seems to have been a part of pre-Aryan religion, and elements of that early worship have lived on.

The Great Mother, also called **Devi** ("goddess"), is worshiped throughout India but particularly in the northeast. She is portrayed in many forms and can be both loving and cruel, especially to those who show themselves unworthy of her love. Devi is frequently worshiped with extreme human feeling. The worshiper may take on the emotions and even the clothing of child or spouse of the Great Mother. The mystic Ramakrishna (1836–1886), priest at a temple near Calcutta, spoke of his special devotion to her. "I practised austerities for a long time. I could no longer eat or sleep. My longing for the Divine Mother was so great that I would not eat or sleep. I would lie on the bare ground, placing my head on a lump of earth, and cry out loudly: 'Mother, Mother, why dost thou not come to me?' I did not know how the days and nights passed away. . . .When I reached the state of continuous ecstasy, I gave up all external forms of worship; I could no longer perform them. Then I prayed to my Divine Mother: 'Mother, who will now take care of me? I have no power to take care of myself.' "[33]

The Divine Feminine appears as several goddesses, of which the most popular are Durga and Kali. The goddess **Durga** ("awe inspiring," "distant") is frequently represented with ten arms, full of implements used to destroy evil. Her face is serene, surrounded by a halo, and she wears a crown. She rides a tiger, which helps her conquer all dangerous obstacles.

Kali ("dark") is more fearsome still. She is often shown wearing a necklace of human skulls, and her fanged teeth drip with blood. Her many arms are full of weapons, which are thought to be dangerous to enemies but

> Those who have riches build temples for Thee; what shall I build? I am poor. My legs are the pillars; this body of mine is the temple.
>
> —Basavaraja, in praise of Shiva[32]

protective of her children. Calcutta ("Kali's stairs") is named after her temple in this city.

The important role of the Divine Feminine is also seen in the female consorts who accompany many male deities. They are so much a part of the male god that the god cannot be active without them, and thus they are called *shaktis* ("energies"), because they allow the male gods to be effective in the human world.

The shakti of Vishnu is the goddess Lakshmi, who is commonly dressed as a queen and sits on a lotus. As the consort of Vishnu, she dispenses good luck and protection. Shiva is portrayed with a variety of shaktis, the best known being Parvati and Uma. Sometimes Shiva is himself portrayed as androgynous: half of his body is masculine, while the other side shows a female breast. This androgyny represents the unity that underlies all the apparent opposites of reality—a unity also spoken of in the Upanishads and the Bhagavad Gita.

Divinities of nature are frequently female. The goddess Ganga, who animates the Ganges River, is a good example. Tree spirits, too, are considered female, and frequently it is women who offer them worship.

The Guru as Object of Devotion

Because Hinduism is not organized in a hierarchical fashion, devotion to a guru (spiritual teacher) is a large and ancient component of Hindu spirituality. The etymology of the word *guru* is expressive: "the one who removes darkness." Anyone who seeks spiritual growth—no matter what his or her caste or station in life—may seek a guru, whom the individual can visit regularly to seek advice. Even gurus who have taken vows of silence can offer advice and insight to their disciples by writing on tablets or simply by looking at them with love.

Although the majority of gurus are men, female gurus are not uncommon. All that is necessary is that the guru be recognized as a person of holiness. Because a guru expects to be surrounded by students and devotees, he or she will frequently set up a community, called an *ashram*, for disciples. Usually an ashram is a commune of people living in a single compound, separate from ordinary society, but it may also be in a town and made up of various buildings owned and used by the devotees. Most gurus stay within their communities, but some travel, even outside India, to set up additional ashrams elsewhere. Frequently an aging guru will designate a successor from among his or her closest disciples and those specially trained.

It is common to touch and even kiss the feet of a guru—an act of reverence that is also performed at times for parents and grandparents. To an outsider, such an act may seem excessive. However, many Hindus believe that the guru is both a saint and a living embodiment of the divine. Behind this conception is the recognition that although divine reality exists within all human beings, most people manifest their divine nature inadequately, because their ignorance and self-centeredness restrict its expression. Such

As a man may be blindfolded, and led away, and left in a strange place; and as, having been so dealt with, he turns in every direction and cries out for someone to remove his bandages and show him the way home; and as one thus entreated may loose his bandages and give him comfort; and as thereupon he walks from village to village, asking his way as he goes; and as he arrives home at last—just so does a man who meets with an illumined teacher obtain true knowledge.

—Chandogya Upanishad[34]

people are compared to glass windows that are so dusty that only a little light shines through. However, some people, over many lifetimes of effort, have reached a stage of such achievement that their ego has disappeared and their charity has grown immense. In these rare people the innate divine light shines brilliantly. This view explains why Hindus believe that one need only be in the presence of the guru to benefit—like a plant in sunshine—from that person's spirituality.

It also explains the intriguing practice of *darshan* ("presence"). Because people of spiritual accomplishment are thought to radiate their divine nature, disciples like to be in the presence of the holy person. Sometimes also a holy person will sit or stand silently, allowing devotees to come forward one by one to look into the teacher's eyes and to experience the divine energy that shines out.[35]

Devotion to Animals

Hinduism is distinctive among world religions for its kindness to animals. A devout Hindu does not kill or eat animals. Cows often wander along Indian streets, and cars and taxis take care to drive around them. Furthermore, visitors to some Hindu temples may find monkeys and even mice well fed and running free. Several extremely popular gods, such as Ganesha and Hanuman, have animal features; and gods like Shiva and Vishnu are regularly portrayed in the company of their animal companions. A

In Hinduism, cows are treated with special veneration. They are often fed in public and festooned in garlands at festivals.

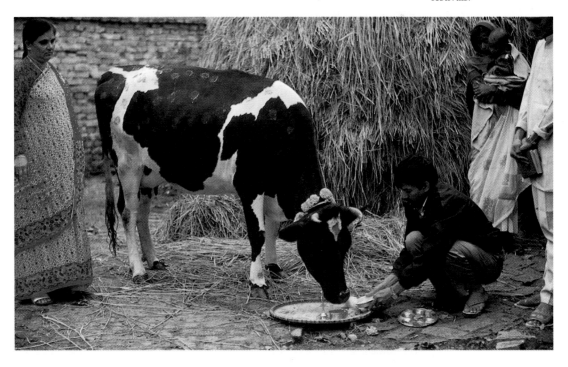

Hindu Celebrations

Religious festivals are frequent and usually joyous. Some are clearly associated with the seasons, such as a springtime fertility festival and a post-monsoon festival. Others are related to events in a god's life, such as the site of his birth or places he traveled to. Some festivals are regional, and some are national.

Although India is hot during most of the year, winters can be cold, especially in the north. The spring is therefore welcomed with the celebration *Holi*. It is traditional for boys and girls to playfully throw colored water on each other (nowadays some even use squirt guns), thus evoking images of Krishna's exploits with the milkmaids.

After the monsoons of the summer months, the land is green, the air is cool, and there is a sense of peacefulness. The season has the feeling of a second spring and a new beginning. People often spend time repairing any damages the rains may have caused. Holidays at this time reenact the power of goodness to conquer evil forces. For example, *Divali*, recalling the return of Rama and Sita, is a time when people clean their houses and illuminate them outside with candles and lights; Ganesha and Lakshmi, who are both associated with good fortune, are particularly honored at this time.

Durga Puja, held in December and particularly popular in northeast India, celebrates the goddess Durga's ability to overcome dangerous powers. People dance in front of her statues in the street, and in Calcutta the festival ends with the immersion of her statues in the river.

Shiva temple would often be thought incomplete without a statue of Nandi, the bull who is Shiva's vehicle.

This animal presence in Hinduism has several possible origins: an ancient deification of certain animals, such as the elephant and tiger; the desire to neutralize dangerous or mischievous animals, such as the snake, rat, and monkey; and even a sense that human beings and animals have the same origin (a belief also common in oral religions). Belief in reincarnation has undoubtedly also played a role. Many Hindus, when they see animals and insects, see prehuman beings who in their spiritual evolution will eventually become human themselves. This brings a feeling of closeness to nonhuman forms of animal life.

Among the animals, cows receive special veneration. This tradition may stem from pre-Aryan worship in the Indus River valley of the bull or cow, a symbol of fertility and economic value. In rural India, to have a cow is to have milk and butter, fuel (dried dung), and the warmth and comfort associated with household pets. With a cow, one is never utterly destitute. Affection for the cow may also arise from the strong thread of ancient devotion to the Divine Feminine and thus may represent a vestige of earlier matriarchal society—hinted at by the commonly used term *gau mata*, "mother cow." (The fact that Muslims butcher cows is a source of terrible friction between the Hindus and Muslims in India.)

Other Forms of Religious Devotion

Indian thought loves multiplicity. "As many as the sands of the Ganges" is a description applied to a variety of subjects. One example of multiplicity is the Hindu recognition of immense numbers of gods. Realizing that each god or goddess may have several forms, and may be accompanied by divine consorts and animal companions, we gain a dizzying sense of the limitlessness of devotional possibilities. In everyday life, every person is expected to have a religious practice involving at least one of these deities, but the exact form generally is not dictated, and virtually no form of devotion is rejected.

Pilgrimage is a common form of religious expression in Hinduism, as it is in many religions. India is dotted with sites that are held to be sacred to the most popular gods and goddesses, and devotees of a particular deity will often try to visit all the important sites associated with that deity. Pilgrimages can also involve listening to a famous guru's sermons and meditating with the guru's followers.

PERSONAL EXPERIENCE: GAZING INTO THE MOTHER'S EYES

During my first trip to India, I heard often of the great writer Sri Aurobindo (originally, Aurobindo Ghose, 1872–1950) and of the woman whom many called his shakti, or female consort. Sri Aurobindo had died long before my visit, but his work was being carried on by his spiritual companion, a Frenchwoman simply called the Mother. I was eager to visit the Aurobindo ashram in Pondicherry, on the southeast coast of India. I wanted to see the European woman who had made her permanent home in India and become a Hindu guru herself. Dr. Sobharani Basu, my teacher at Banaras Hindu University, kindly made arrangements, and I left on the train two nights later.

When I arrived at the neat, whitewashed Indian town, I discovered that the Aurobindo ashram was not a single community located outside the city but rather a collection of buildings scattered around town. This arrangement was meant to be temporary, however, because a utopian city called Auroville was being planned and built nearby. I noticed that in many of the town's restaurants and shops, as well as in private homes, large photos of the Mother hung on the walls.

A mystique surrounds Aurobindo at Pondicherry. Many residents consider him to be one of the greatest thinkers of the last hundred years; and in a country full of philosophers and holy men, he is said to be in a class by himself. I remember a professor in Pondicherry saying, "Westerners would appreciate Hinduism if they would study the thought of Aurobindo."

The core of Aurobindo's teaching, expressed in his work *The Life Divine,* is that Brahman is at the heart of the evolutionary process. Human evolution continues and is aided by all modern inventions that expand consciousness and ability. Human beings, if they understand and embrace the evolutionary process, can evolve into fully divine beings.

At last the day came when I would meet Aurobindo's spiritual successor, the Mother. There would be no talking, however. This was to be a silent audience.

In midmorning I came to the Mother's house and stood patiently outside in line with about twenty others. Almost all the visitors were Indian and held bouquets of flowers to offer her.

Upstairs, in the Mother's reception room, a small, gray-haired lady in Indian dress stood quietly at the far end of the room. It was the Mother. She looked more Indian than European. Each person approached individually and stood for a moment in front of her. A woman attendant took the bouquets.

When my turn came, I approached the Mother. She smiled and bent her head slightly to the right. Her eyes were clear and luminous. To meet someone for the first time and not have to fumble for words was a rare experience for me. We, two strangers in India who were not Indian, could simply look into each other's eyes and wonder at what we found there. In her eyes I sensed the presence of that elusive something—spirituality—that is India's promise. The Mother's gaze was unflinching. Our eyes locked for many seconds. Then I felt the arm of an attendant and was gently pulled away.[36]

HINDUISM AND THE ARTS

Given Hinduism's tendency toward multiplicity, it is not surprising that Hindu temples, particularly in the south of India, are often covered with statues, many with multiple faces and arms. The concept of multiplicity has a purpose. To illustrate, think of a wheel that begins to turn. At first, each spoke of the wheel is visible, but as the wheel turns more quickly, the spokes disappear and dissolve into a unity. The profusion of images in Hindu art can be similarly hypnotic, with the experience of multiplicity frequently leading to an overarching sense of unity. Profusion thus fits in well with the mystical orientation common in Hinduism.

Another characteristic of Hindu artistic sensibility is symbolism. One of the clearest examples is the multiple arms and faces on figures found in painting and sculpture, which are not literal but symbolic representations of power and wisdom. Specific symbols are associated with individuals and allow them to be identified. Krishna, for example, is recognized by his flute.

Hindu painting can sometimes be disappointing. Much of what one sees in India is rather garish devotional art, sold at temple gates. Many fine paintings of the past have undoubtedly vanished because of the fragility of the paper and cloth on which they were done. The murals that remain, however, demonstrate the heights Hindu devotional painting has sometimes attained; and some yantras—geometrical paintings used in meditation—are unforgettable.

Hindu temple exteriors, like the interiors, are often elaborately decorated. (Note in the background the minaret of a nearby Muslim mosque.)

Hindu sculpture, however, far outshines Hindu painting. Fine pieces of sturdy stone and metal are on display in India and in museums around the world. Metal sculpture advanced quite early. The finest generic example of Hindu sculpture is Shiva in his guise as "lord of the dance"—an image that was introduced in southern India more than a thousand years ago but is still produced today. For many, this sculpture represents the perfection of Hindu art, combining visual beauty with a symbolic meaning that intensifies the visual power.

The power of stone sculpture is often quite sensuous. Given the world-denying aspect of some Hindu thought, one might expect that the great stone sculpture of Hinduism would be ascetic—perhaps elongated and otherworldly. The opposite is true, however. Some of the best-known examples of stone sculpture are the figures of sensuous men and women, enjoying life and each other, on the temples of Khajuraho in central India. This sort of sculpture was influenced by Tantrism, the antipuritanical movement that teaches that everything in the world, including sex, can be used to attain higher states of consciousness.

Popular Hinduism has made use of hymns to many gods as expressions of bhakti yoga. Their regular rhythm and repetition help produce a state of altered consciousness in the worshiper, bringing a sense of selflessness and union with the divine. Instrumental music—especially of drums and harmonium, a hand-pumped reed organ—has also been an integral part of religious celebrations for centuries.

Classical Indian instrumental music is less obviously religious, yet much of it has an undeniable mystical quality. It makes use of *ragas*, elements of Indian music that blend features of both scales and melodies. Frequently these ragas are played and musically developed over deep tones that are played as a drone. (The *sitar,* the best known Indian stringed instrument, has drone strings on its side.) The drone suggests the underlying timeless world of Brahman, against which changing melodies—suggestions of the world of time—move. Musical pieces often begin quite tentatively, then gradually speed up to a very quick pace, and suddenly stop, bringing to the listener (and players) an experience of release and peace.

Indian classical dance is more obviously tied to religion. It interprets stories derived from the tales of the gods, such as Krishna and Rama. Much of it also originated as a part of religious ceremony, performed at religious festivals and in or near temples. Dance is meant to produce delicate states of feeling, some of which are thought to assist contact with particular gods.

HINDUISM: MODERN CHALLENGES

European values have gradually posed a major challenge to traditional Hinduism. This process began after 1500 C.E., when European powers took control of parts of India. Goa, on the west coast, became a center of Portuguese culture that lasted until 1960, when Goa was taken over by Indian army forces. Similarly, Pondicherry, on the southeast coast, was at one time a center of French culture. The most significant European influence on India, however, was English. Great Britain controlled most of the subcontinent for about two centuries. Although India became independent of Britain in 1947, British influence is evident in modern India's law, education, architecture, rail transportation, and military life.

Throughout India today one can find former British churches, mostly shuttered and closed, which only hint at both the positive and negative impact of British Christianity on India. The British were not successful in making many converts, but through their schools and colleges British Christian missionaries helped challenge and change some traditional Hindu beliefs and practices. Among those elements that were questioned were untouchability, child marriage, prohibition of the remarriage of widows, polytheism, the content of education, and the role of women.

One of the earliest British-inspired Indian reformers was Ram Mohan Roy (1772–1833). He was typical of the many reformers who grew up in Calcutta, which was for a long time the capital of British India and the center of westernizing thought. While remaining a Hindu and even writing articles in defense of Hinduism, his thinking was influenced by both rationalism and Christianity.[37] He began a movement, the Brahmo Samaj, that adopted Christian-inspired elements: the belief in one god, the rejection of polytheism, congregational worship, and an ethical urgency that sought to better the lot of the oppressed. The Brahmo Samaj later split into three branches—all of which are still active.

Possibly as a result of contact with European values, one practice that was made illegal in the early nineteenth century was that of *sati* (or *suttee,* meaning "good wife"). A woman whose husband had died was expected, as a sign of her wifely devotion, to voluntarily be burnt alive on her husband's funeral pyre, and if she were not willing, her relatives would sometimes force her. Although the British found sati horrible, they were unwilling to intervene at first. Reform-minded Indians, however, worked with the British to abolish the practice. (Instances of sati still happen today, but they are rare.)

Untouchability was also questioned, but legal assistance came only in the twentieth century. Untouchables are now allowed to enter all temples in India and have made strides toward some social equality. For example, there is a system whereby untouchables must be included in governmental hiring. In general, the caste system is weakening, especially in large cities. Nonetheless, a glance at a big-city Sunday newspaper is all it takes to find evidence of the caste system's hold on contemporary life: it is not uncommon for Indian parents to place ads in the newspaper to find a spouse for their child; these ads often detail the child's caste, educational background, and sometimes even complexion.

The role of women has expanded in modern India. In India's distant, pre-Aryan past, it is possible that women played an important public role, but the incoming Aryan culture was thoroughly patriarchal. Just as it has been canonized in other religions, so male domination in India was

Rural women sell powders to decorate hands and feet.

canonized by the law code of Manu (second century B.C.E.). This code made the female subservient to the male and the wife subservient to her husband. A good wife was expected to treat her husband as a god, no matter what his character or treatment of her. Women were not trained to read and write, as this was thought to be unnecessary and even detrimental to their principal roles as wives and mothers. Nowadays, however, Hindu women commonly learn to read and write, and many go on to higher education and important public roles, particularly in education, medicine, and government. This development, however, is also a fairly urban phenomenon, as most Hindu women outside the cities remain in their traditional roles as wives and mothers.

Modern education incorporates many nonreligious subjects—chemistry, physics, engineering, electronics. Among some Hindus, this trend has contributed to the growth of secularism and to an attitude that suggests that Hinduism is old-fashioned. "India is too religious," some say. On the other hand, many Hindus remain ardently religious—despite secular education—and seek to blend Hinduism with science and modern values by emphasizing elements of Hinduism that fit with a contemporary worldview. One approach is to see all modern discoveries and inventions, such as vaccines, electricity, and airplanes, as a continuing expression of the divine spirit within all things. Some emphasize those parts of Hinduism, especially its mysticism, as an antidote to Western materialism. Others make use of the traditional tolerance and diversity of traditional Hinduism in order to embrace newer values.

Mohandas Gandhi

Mohandas Gandhi (1869–1948) was born in the seaside town of Porbandor in western India, north of Bombay. Because Britain then controlled the country, many Indians advocated violence as a response to British domination. This historic turning point became a defining time in Gandhi's life.

As a young man, Gandhi learned basic ideas of nonviolence from Hinduism, and he was a vegetarian because of his religious upbringing. In his day, young Indian boys believed that the British were strong because they ate meat. Young Gandhi tested this theory by eating meat for a year, but he had a dream of a goat crying in his stomach and was compelled to give up his experiment.[38] His marriage at the young age of 13 was arranged by his family to a girl named Kasturbai, also 13.

During his late teen years, family members recommended that Gandhi study law in London. Because his pious Hindu mother feared the bad influences he would be exposed to there, he agreed to take a vow that he would not eat meat, drink wine, or touch a woman while abroad. A Jain monk (see Chapter 5) administered the vow, and Gandhi left for London in the fall of 1888 at the age of 19.

Being a rebel at the time, Gandhi enthusiastically adopted English clothes and manners and even took dancing lessons, but in London he also began serious study. Becoming familiar with the Christian Bible, he was particularly moved by Jesus' call to forgiveness and nonviolence, which he found in the Sermon on the Mount (Matt: 5–7) in the New Testament.

It was in London, too, that he first read the Bhagavad Gita, discovering outside India the wisdom in Hinduism. He took to heart its ideal of the active but selfless human being. Such a person, Gandhi later wrote, is a person who is "without egotism, who is selfless, who treats alike cold and heat, happiness and misery, who is ever forgiving, who is always contented, whose resolutions are firm, who has dedicated mind and soul to God, who causes no dread, who is not afraid of others."[39]

After obtaining his law degree in 1891, Gandhi returned to India but soon decided to accept an offer to practice law in South Africa. There he learned of the inequities of *apartheid* (the official system of racial segregation that endorsed legal restrictions against non-European people, including Indians), and he began to perfect the ideologies that he would later spread in India. His thinking was influenced by writings that advocated simplicity and nonviolence, such as the essay "On Civil Disobedience" by the American author Henry David Thoreau and the book *The Kingdom of God Is Within You* by the Russian writer Leo Tolstoy. A farm that Gandhi bought became something of an ashram, while his law office in Johannesburg became a center for nonviolent political action. He began to employ strikes and marches to publicize his goals and to wear Indian clothing (specifically the dhoti, a type of loincloth) as a way of identifying with the Indian cause.

Gandhi returned to India in 1915 and dedicated his life to seeking Indian independence from Britain. Although he was repeatedly imprisoned, Gandhi insisted that all his followers remain nonviolent. Gandhi called the power of nonviolence *satyagraha* ("reality force"). He made use of every possible nonviolent technique: marches, hunger strikes, talks, demonstrations, and, of course, publicity. He argued that violence only begets further violence and brutalizes those who are violent, whereas nonviolence begets admiration, spiritual greatness, and ultimate freedom.[40]

One brilliant example of his nonviolent techniques was the Salt March of 1930. At that time the British taxed all salt eaten in India and made it illegal to possess salt not bought from the government monopoly. Gandhi cleverly led a three-week march on foot from his ashram to the ocean, nearly 250 miles away. Fewer than a hundred people began the march with him, but thousands joined along the way. Reaching the sea, Gandhi collected the natural salt left on the beach by the waves—thus breaking the

Mohandas Gandhi adopted nonviolent strategies to win Indian independence from Great Britain.

law. In seashore communities all around India, people came to do the same, and thousands were put into jail, along with Gandhi. This march was the turning point. Weakened both by the Indian independence movement and by World War II, the British forces at last agreed to leave India in 1947. Perceiving Gandhi's greatness, the writer Rabindranath Tagore called him *Mahatma* ("great spirit"), which then became his new title.

Gandhi believed so much in loving tolerance that he hoped it could keep a newly independent India free of religious battles. Muslim leaders, however, fearful that the Hindu majority would oppress Muslims, worked to create the new separate Muslim state of Pakistan. Some Hindu militants wanted revenge for what they perceived as wrongs done by Muslims to Hindus in the new Pakistan, and one of these Hindu militants assassinated Gandhi early in 1948.

Gandhi's example was so strong that the idea of satyagraha spread to other countries and was adopted in the 1960s by the Baptist minister Martin Luther King, Jr., to help protest racial segregation in the United States. King insisted that activists march peacefully and sit in restaurants quietly, without responding to threats or cruelty. Their gentle persistence, magnified by publicity, brought success.

Hindu Influence Beyond India

Over the centuries, Hinduism has spread to countries near India and far away, often by way of traders and immigrants. In a few places, it has remained strong, while in others it has surrendered to other religions. Approximately half of the population of Nepal is Hindu, while the other half is Buddhist. Hinduism was once widespread in Southeast Asia, but today only traces of it remain. In Cambodia (Kampuchea) is the great ruin Angkor Wat, originally a Hindu complex. In Thailand, vestiges of a Brahmanical priesthood are particularly active in court ceremony. Some forms of ritualistic Buddhism in northern and eastern Asia have kept alive a few Hindu gods, such as Indra, in art and ceremony. Hinduism, of course, continues wherever Indians have immigrated. It is strongest in South Africa, Malaysia, Fiji, Singapore, and England.

Hinduism was once widespread in Indonesia, where it had been spread by Indian traders. During the Muslim invasions, however, the Hindu court was forced to retreat from the main island of Java and settled to the east on the small island of Bali, where a fascinating example of Hindu culture thrives. Here, Hinduism lives on in a complicated, beautiful form that is mixed with folk religion and Buddhism. Each village has Hindu temples, where dances based on Indian tales (especially about Rama) are performed. Shadow-puppet plays tell Hindu stories, and Balinese wood carvings reproduce images of Hindu gods, goddesses, and heroes. Although the rest of Indonesia is primarily Muslim, some Hindu elements remain in Indonesian dance and puppet plays. Interestingly, the national airline of Indonesia, despite the country's primarily Muslim orientation, is named

Balinese dance retells tales from the Hindu epics.

Garuda Airlines, after the magical bird that carries Vishnu through the skies.

Hinduism has had some influence in the West since the nineteenth century. The earliest impact was intellectual, a result of the translations of the Upanishads and the Bhagavad Gita into Latin, French, German, and English. The translations generated great interest among philosophers, scholars, and poets. In the United States, the New England movement called Transcendentalism owes a good deal to its literary contact with Hinduism. Ralph Waldo Emerson (1803–1882), Henry David Thoreau (1817–1862), and Walt Whitman (1819–1892) all spoke in their writings of a sense of the sacredness of nature and the ultimate unity of all things and sometimes even used terms demonstrating Indian influence, such as *Brahma* and *Oversoul*. This literary trend was expressed in another form in England, where composers such as Gustav Holst (1874–1934) and Ralph Vaughan Williams (1872–1958) put selections from the Rig Veda and Whitman's *Leaves of Grass* to music.

The next wave of influence occurred when Indian gurus began to travel to the West. The first of these gurus was Swami Vivekananda (1863–1902), who represented Hinduism at the first World Parliament of Religions, held in Chicago in 1893. He was the successor to Ramakrishna (mentioned earlier), the noted mystic and devotee of the Great Mother. Vivekananda began the Ramakrishna Mission and set up Vedanta societies and Ramakrishna centers across Europe, India, and the United States. A Vedantist center has existed in Hollywood since the 1930s, and British writers such as Christopher Isherwood (1904–1986), Aldous Huxley (1894–1963), and Gerald Heard (1889–1971) all practiced meditation there. Isherwood, under the influence of his guru, Swami Prabhavananda, became a Vedantist and translated the Bhagavad Gita into English.

The third wave of Hindu influence in the West arose in the late 1960s. The American counterculture embraced India as the fount of wisdom. Commercial air travel was now more open to both Indian teachers to come to the West and to westerners to travel to India. Some westerners, such as the Beatles, studied in India with the guru Maharishi Mahesh Yogi and became enamored of Hinduism. (George Harrison's song "My Sweet Lord" was written to honor Krishna.) The Maharishi eventually came to the United States and established the Transcendental Meditation movement, which promotes regular daily meditation to achieve health and happiness. Some westerners who went to India became disciples of Sai Baba, a contemporary teacher in south-central India, and still others, such as the psychologist Richard Alpert (who took the name Ram Dass), studied with Indian teachers and returned to write about their experiences. Western visitors to India adopted forms of yoga, Hindu vegetarian cuisine, Indian clothing, and Indian music and took them back to Europe, Canada, and the United States, where they entered the Western mainstream.

The movement called the International Society for Krishna Consciousness (ISKCON) was founded in New York in 1967 by Swami Bhaktivedanta Prabhupada (1896–1977) to spread a form of devotional practice among westerners. Commonly known as the Hare Krishna movement, ISKCON has succeeded in attracting westerners to live a traditional form of Hindu religious life. Its practitioners worship Krishna as the highest incarnation of the divine, chant daily, eat a vegetarian diet, and, if celibate, wear the traditional orange robe. The impact of this movement in the West has been

The International Society for Krishna Consciousness is a colorful presence in many cities of the world today.

particularly strong in the area of cuisine, prompting the opening of vegetarian restaurants across Europe, the United States, and Canada.

The largest recent influence of Indian culture has been due to the immigration into North America and Europe of millions of Hindus, ensuring that virtually every major city has a large Hindu population, along with the associated temples, festivals, and art. As Hindus settle around the globe, we can expect the appreciation of Hinduism to grow.

What we have just discussed—the impact of Hinduism on Western thinkers, musicians, and poets—was in large measure achieved by non-Hindus inspired by Hindu culture. Now Hindus themselves, in and out of India, are producing internationally acclaimed works, especially novels and films. Their particular points of view result from experiences accumulated across centuries in one of the world's richest cultures. Those experiences will in time help global citizens, whatever their origins, to see themselves with an understanding that has been enriched by the Hindu worldview.

RELIGION BEYOND THE CLASSROOM

In the United States, Canada, and elsewhere, one can visit centers of the Vedanta Society and temples of the International Society for Krishna Consciousness (ISKCON, also known as the Hare Krishna movement). They exist primarily in major cities, and both organizations welcome all who are interested. Many ISKCON temples hold weekly public services that include chanting, a lecture, and frequently a vegetarian meal. An elaborate temple exists at New Vrindavan, West Virginia. Temples built by immigrant Hindu communities exist in many major cities.

Outside North America, Hinduism can be experienced in four places that are available to the international traveler: India, Bali, Nepal, and Singapore. India, being the home of Hinduism, is filled with important Hindu temples and other religious sites. If the traveler has only a short amount of time, the most important religious sites to visit in conjunction with Hinduism are possibly Benares (Varanasi), to observe religious practices at the Ganges River, and Khajuraho, to see its elaborate temples. Museums with major collections of Hindu art are found in Bombay, New Delhi, and Calcutta.

Bali, as mentioned earlier, is a unique society, derived from the Hindu culture that once existed on Java. Each village has its own gamelan orchestra (consisting primarily of percussion instruments, such as gongs, xylophones, and drums) and regular dance ceremonies, many of whose stories are based on Hindu tales. Balinese painting and wood carving are similarly inspired by Hinduism. The temple complex on Mount Agung is the mother temple of Balinese Hinduism. Called Pura ("temple") Besakih, it is dedicated to Brahma, Vishnu, and Shiva. The offshore temple at Tanah Lot is scenic. Other temples of note exist at Batuan, Mengwi, and Bedugul. Entry to temples is allowed to non-Hindus, but a special waistband must be worn.

Half of the population of Nepal is Hindu. The capital city of Katmandu stands in a high valley that also contains two other towns, Patan and Bhadgaon (Bhaktapur), and all three have interesting temples. The traveler can rent a bicycle in Katmandu for visiting the towns and the rest of the valley.

Singapore, a thoroughly modern city and a financial center of Asia, affords an intriguing view of Hinduism active in an urban environment. Hindu temples to see include Sri Mariamman Temple and Sri Srinivasa Perumal Temple.

FOR FULLER UNDERSTANDING

1. Investigate to see if examples of Hindu practice exist near your home or school. Visit a Hindu temple or center, and attend a service if possible; then write a short description to share with others.
2. Read one of the numerous excellent works by contemporary Indian novelists (such as V. S. Naipaul, Arundhati Roy, Amritava Ghosh, Bikram Seti, and Sashi Tharoor)—works that describe life in today's India or in the communities of Indians who have emigrated to the West. Make notes on the elements of Hinduism you find in the novel.
3. Read various selections from Walt Whitman's powerful group of poems *Leaves of Grass*. Copy three short pieces that seem to suggest Hindu teachings. Read these poems aloud to friends, and then discuss their possible parallels with Hindu teachings.
4. Investigate the life of Martin Luther King, Jr. How and when did he learn about the techniques of nonviolent resistance? Describe specifically how he made use of these techniques. What parallels do you see with the traditions of Hinduism and with the work of Gandhi?
5. As part of a longer project, read some of the books that influenced Gandhi as he was working toward his philosophy of nonviolent resistance. What are the key ideas that you take from your reading? How might these ideas be applied to the problems and issues facing today's world?

RELATED READINGS

Basham, A. L. *The Wonder That Was India*. New York: Grove, 1959. A detailed study of virtually all aspects of early Indian culture, offering insight into the lives of everyday people of the past.

Eck, Diana L. *Benares: City of Light*. Princeton: Princeton University Press, 1983. An introduction to the most sacred city of Hinduism.

Eliade, Mircea. *Yoga: Immortality and Freedom*. Princeton: Princeton University Press, 1973. A detailed summary of many yogic techniques that have been used to defeat the limitations of the physical world.

Fischer, Louis, ed. *The Essential Gandhi*. New York: Random House, 1983. A study of Gandhi by a man who knew him personally.

Harvey, Andrew. *Hidden Journey: A Spiritual Awakening*. New York: Arkana/Penguin, 1992. The author's account of his travel to Pondicherry and his becoming a disciple of Mother Meera.

O'Flaherty, Wendy. *Siva: The Erotic Ascetic*. Oxford: Oxford University Press, 1981. A description of the many strands of meaning to be found in Shiva, possibly the most complex Indian god.

The Song of God: Bhagavad-Gita. Translated by Swami Prabhavananda and Christopher Isherwood. New York: Mentor, 1972. A well-known translation of the Bhagavad Gita with a valuable introduction by Aldous Huxley.

The Upanishads. Translated by Swami Prabhavananda and Frederick Manchester. New York: Mentor, 1970. A readable translation of the basic Upanishads.

KEY TERMS

Ahimsa (*uh-him'-sa*): "Nonharm," "nonviolence."

Atman (*at'-mun*): The spiritual essence of all individual human beings.

Ashram (*ash'-ram*): A spiritual community.

Avatar (*ah'-va-tar*): An earthly embodiment of a deity.

Bhagavad Gita (*bhuh'-guh-vud gee'-ta*): A religious literary work about Krishna.

Bhakti (*bhuk'-ti*): Devotion to a deity or guru.

Bhakti yoga: The spiritual discipline of devotion to a deity or guru.

Brahma (*bruh-mah'*): God of creation.

Brahman (*bruh'-mun*): The spiritual essence of the universe.

Brahmin (*bruh'-min*): Member of the priestly caste.

Caste: One of the four major social classes sanctioned by Hinduism.

Devi (*deh'-vee*): "Goddess"; the Divine Feminine, also called the Great Mother.

Dhyana: Meditation.

Durga: "Awe-inspiring," "distant"; a goddess, a form of Devi.

Guru: Spiritual teacher.

Hatha yoga: The spiritual discipline of postures and bodily exercises.

Jnana yoga: The spiritual discipline of knowledge and insight.

Kali: A form of Devi; a goddess associated with destruction and rebirth.

Karma: The moral law of cause and effect that determines the direction of rebirth.

Karma yoga: The spiritual discipline of selfless action.

Krishna: A god associated with divine playfulness; a form of Vishnu.

Mantra: A short sacred phrase, often chanted or used in meditation.

Maya: "Illusion"; what keeps us from seeing reality correctly; the world, viewed inadequately.

Moksha (*mohk'-shah*): "Liberation" from personal limitation, egotism, and rebirth.

Puja (*poo'-jah*): Offerings and ritual in honor of a deity.

Raja yoga: The "royal" discipline of meditation.

Rama: A god and mythical king; a form of Vishnu.

Samadhi (*suh-mah'-dhee*): A state of complete inner peace resulting from meditation.

Sannyasin (*san-nyas'-in*): A wandering holy man.

Shiva (*shee'-vah*): A god associated with destruction and rebirth.

Trimurti (*tree-mur'-tee*): "Three forms" of the divine—the three gods Brahma, Vishnu, and Shiva.

Upanishads (*oo-pahn'-i-shads*): Written meditations on the spiritual essence of the universe and the self.

Vedas (*vay'-duhs*): Four collections of ancient prayers and rituals.

Vishnu: A god associated with preservation and love.

Yoga: A spiritual discipline; a method for perfecting one's union with the divine.

CHAPTER **4**

Buddhism

 FIRST ENCOUNTER

Caught in the Bangkok city traffic, the taxi you took from your hotel drives slowly, but that allows you to look carefully at all the sidewalk activities. People sit on stools while eating noodles at a small wagon. Next to them vendors sell watches, belts, and shirts. The taxi turns onto a side street, where men covered with soot carry charcoal. In the next block, two men are repairing motorcycles in the middle of the sidewalk, which is scattered with parts. A little girl sits on a wooden crate outside a repair shop, looking through the window at a Bugs Bunny cartoon playing on television.

Although Bangkok is not an old city, like Kyoto or Rome, it was planned on a grand scale as a royal city, with a fine palace and magnificent temples. One of these temples is Wat Benchamabophit, called the Marble Temple, where the taxi at last stops to let you out. Just inside the gate, you see an elderly lady chatting with a young couple. A dog lies beside them in the sun and another dog saunters past. You nod politely to the people and walk to the stairs, leaving your shoes

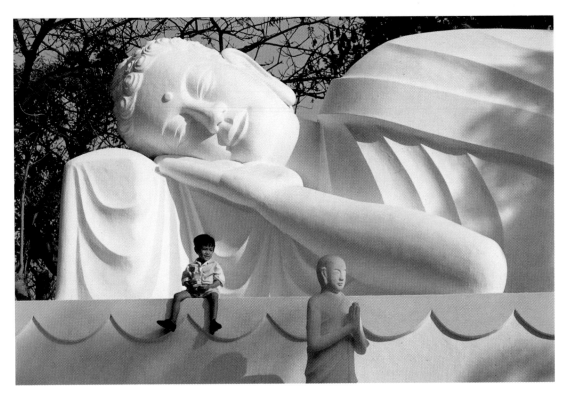

The life history of the Buddha is echoed in this portrait of a young boy sitting in front of an image of the mature, perhaps even dying, Buddha.

next to the many pairs already lined up there. People are crowded in the inner chamber. As you gradually squeeze your way inside, you are struck by the strong fragrance of flowers and incense. Electric fans revolve at each side of the room, moving the humid air.

A young man dressed in white stands facing the statue of the Buddha at the front of the interior. Behind him are two rows of men with shaved heads and bright orange robes. The young man apparently is being accepted into the order of monks. It does not look like an unhappy fate. You ask yourself, Why the shaven heads? Why the color orange? You wonder what kind of life Thai Buddhist monks live, which leads you to be curious about the life of the Buddha, the founder of this religion, and about where all of this began.

THE BEGINNINGS OF BUDDHISM: THE LIFE OF THE BUDDHA

Buddhism is one of the world's oldest and most significant religions. It has spread through almost all of Asia, influencing the many cultures there, and is now gaining followers in the West. But it had its beginnings in India and arose from the experience of one person.

India in the fifth century B.C.E. was in a state of religious ferment. As the caste system hardened and the brahmins (priests) asserted their rights to religious and social power, other classes, particularly the aristocracy, felt threatened. At the same time, there was great enthusiasm for personal religious experience, leading people to experiment with meditation and deep breathing and to study with gurus. A growing number of schools of philosophy taught new ways of thinking, some of which opposed the priestly religion. Into this world came Siddhartha Gautama (c. 563–483 B.C.E.), who would come to be known as the Buddha, or the Awakened One.

Because so many devout legends have grown up around the story of the Buddha's life and teaching, it is sometimes hard to separate fact from fiction.[1] There is no single, authoritative biography of the Buddha, but his legendary life follows these outlines. Siddhartha was born the son of a prince of the Shakya tribe in what is today Nepal, in the lower Himalaya Mountains. Legend says that his mother, Maya, dreamt that a white elephant entered her side—this was the moment of conception of the future Buddha—and that Siddhartha was born miraculously from her side. Siddhartha's mother died a week after childbirth, and the boy was raised by his aunt.

When a sage inspected the child, he saw special marks on Siddhartha's body, indicating that he would be an illustrious person. At his naming ceremony, Vedic priests foretold that his life could go in one of two directions: either he would follow in his father's footsteps, inheriting his position and becoming a great king, a "world ruler"; or, if he were exposed to the sight of suffering, he would become a great spiritual leader, a "world teacher."

Siddhartha's father, wanting his son to succeed him, took measures to keep the boy from exposure to suffering. Kept in a large walled palace compound, Siddhartha grew up in luxury, married at an early age to a young woman his father had chosen, and had a son. He was educated and trained as a warrior because he was, tradition says, born into the kshatriya caste.

All was going according to his father's plan until Siddhartha disobeyed his father's command not to leave the royal grounds. Visiting a nearby town, he soon witnessed the suffering of ordinary life. He saw—and was moved by—what are called the Four Passing Sights. He came across an old man, crooked and toothless; a sick man, wasted by disease; and a corpse being taken for cremation. Then he saw a sannyasin (a wandering holy man, a renunciate) who had no possessions but seemed to be at peace.

The paintings in Buddhist temples retell dramatically Siddhartha's response to what he saw. At 29, he realized that his life up until then had been a pleasant prison, and he saw the same programmed life stretching forward into his old age. The suffering he had just encountered, however, prompted him to question the meaning of human experience and threw him into a depression that kept him from enjoying his luxurious and carefree life any longer.

Siddhartha decided to escape. Legend tells how he took a last look at his sleeping family and attendants and rode to the edge of the palace grounds, where he gave his horse to his servant, removed his jewels, and cut off his long black hair. Putting on simple clothing, he went out into the world with nothing but questions. This event is called the Great Going Forth.

It is common in Indian spirituality to seek a teacher, and Siddhartha did just that. Traveling from teacher to teacher, he learned techniques of meditation and discussed philosophy, but he was ultimately unsatisfied. Begging for food and sleeping outdoors, Siddhartha spent about six years seeking answers to his questions—particularly the troubling facts of suffering and death. His own mother had died young, apparently without meaning. Why, he often asked, is there suffering? Why do people have to grow old and die? Is there a God or unchanging divine reality behind the surface of things? Is there a soul and an afterlife? Are we reborn? Can we avoid suffering? How should we live? (Many of these questions were the common concerns of the period, and we therefore find many of the same topics discussed in the Upanishads of Hinduism [see Chapter 3] and among the Jain doctrines [see Chapter 5].)

Seeking answers to his questions, Siddhartha discovered that his teachers agreed on some issues but not on others. So, in the company of five other nomadic "seekers," he set out to find the answers he needed. To rid himself of distractions and to purify himself spiritually, Siddhartha also practiced great austerity, living on as little food, drink, and sleep as possible in the hope that he would find new insight and even gain spiritual powers.

Images of Siddhartha Gautama weakened by his fasting are often startling, especially when compared to more conventional images of the Buddha.

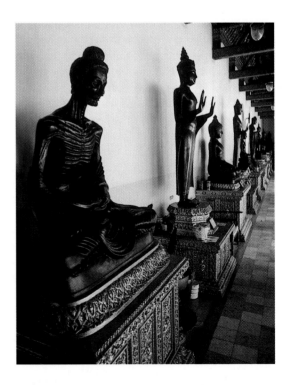

Eventually, Siddhartha collapsed from weakness. He was found resting under a sacred tree by a kind woman who had come from the nearby town of Gaya to worship the spirit of the great tree. (Siddhartha was so emaciated that she may have thought him to be the tree spirit.) She offered him food, which he took gratefully. Once revived, Siddhartha realized that his austerities had not strengthened him or brought him any closer to the answers he sought. Moreover, because he had rejected extreme asceticism by accepting food and had deliberately avoided the hot sun by sitting under a large shade tree, Siddhartha's five companions, when they discovered his apparent backsliding, left him.

Being a practical person, Siddhartha decided to adopt a path of moderation—a middle way between self-indulgence and asceticism. He went to another tree, now called the Bodhi Tree,[2] and sat facing the east, resolving to remain there in meditation until he had the understanding he needed. Various traditions give different details: one says he sat for a week; another says he remained there for forty-nine days—a week of weeks. Nevertheless, every version talks of his struggle with hunger, thirst, doubt, and weakness. Some stories describe the work of an evil spirit, Mara, and his daughters who tempted Siddhartha with sensuality and fear. But Siddhartha resisted all temptation. During one entire night as he sat meditating under a full moon, Siddhartha entered increasingly profound states of awareness. Legend says that he saw his past lives, fathomed the laws of karma that govern everyone, and finally achieved insight into release from suffering and rebirth.

At last, at dawn, he reached a state of profound understanding, called his Awakening or Enlightenment (**bodhi**). He saw suffering, aging, and death in a new way, recognizing them as an inevitable part of life but also seeing the possibility of release. We might wonder about the influence of the tree and the moon on Siddhartha. The tree overhead, with its thousands of leaves and twigs, despite its appearance of permanence, would change, age, and die; and the full moon, with its brilliant light, was a promise of new understanding. Whatever the cause of his enlightenment, Siddhartha arose and said that he was a man who had woken up. From this came his new name: the Buddha, the Awakened One, from a Sanskrit word meaning "to wake up."

From the site of his enlightenment at Gaya, the Buddha traveled west and explained his awakening to his five former companions at a deer park at Sarnath, near Benares. Although they had parted with him earlier for abandoning his ascetic habits, they reconciled with him and became his first disciples.

The Buddha spent the rest of his long life traveling from village to village in northeastern India, teaching his insights and his way of life. He attracted many followers, particularly among the warrior-noble caste, and donors gave land, groves, and buildings to the new movement. The Buddha thus began an order (*sangha*) of monks and later of nuns. The Buddha's way was a path of moderation, a middle path, not only for himself but also

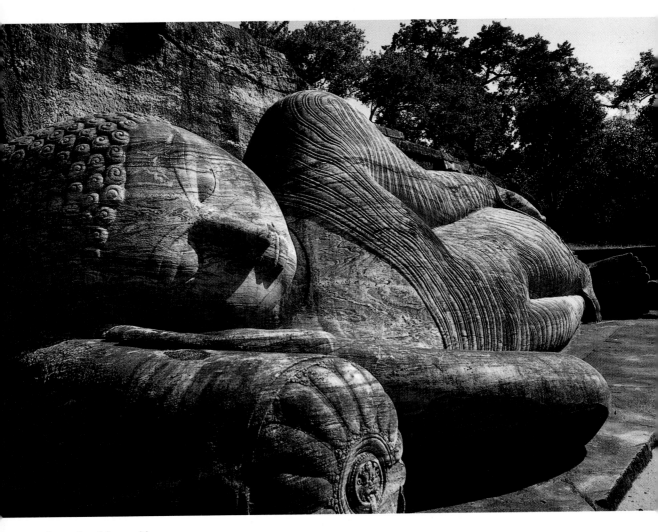

A wonder of the world, this huge statue of the Reclining Buddha in Polonnaruwa, Sri Lanka, may be unsurpassed in conveying the serenity that is the core of Buddhist teaching.

for his disciples. It was midway between the worldly life of the householder that he had lived before leaving home and the ascetic life of social withdrawal that had followed after his departure from home. But the specifics of monastic community life and its relation to the nonmonastic world (on whom the monks relied for food) had to be worked out over time.

Tradition tells of the warm friendship the Buddha shared with his disciples and of their way of life, wandering about begging and teaching. The monks remained in one place during the monsoon months of summer only, when the rains were so heavy that travel was impractical. Looking on the Buddha's lifestyle from a modern vantage point, we can see that it was a healthy one: moderate eating, no alcohol, daily walking, regular meditation, pure air. Probably because of this, the Buddha lived to an old age.

When he was 80, legend says, the Buddha ate food offered by a well-meaning blacksmith named Chunda, but the food was spoiled and the Buddha became terribly sick. Sensing that he was dying, he called his disciples. To those who were crying over his impending death, he reminded them that everything must die—even the Buddha himself. He then offered these final words of advice: "So, Ananda, you must be your own lamps, be your own refuges. Take refuge in nothing outside yourselves. Hold firm to the truth as a lamp and a refuge, and do not look for refuge to anything besides yourselves."[3] In other words, the Buddha's final instruction was this: Trust your own insights, and use self-control to reach perfection and inner peace.

Following this pronouncement, the Buddha turned on his right side and died. The many sculptures and paintings of the so-called Reclining Buddha may be images of his serene moment of death.[4] In any case, Buddhists idealize the Buddha's attitude toward death as a model for everyone.

THE BASIC TEACHINGS OF BUDDHISM

It is impossible to know exactly what the Buddha taught. He did not write down his teachings, nor did his early disciples. The only written versions were recorded several hundred years after his death, following centuries of being passed on orally—and of being interpreted in multiple ways.

The basic teachings have come down to us in a number of written languages, all of which are different from the language (apparently a variation of Magadhi) spoken by the Buddha. One of the most important languages through which Buddhist teachings have been passed down is Pali, a language related to Sanskrit; another is Sanskrit itself—often called the Latin of India because of its widespread use in earlier years for scholarly works.

At the core of what is generally regarded as basic Buddhism are the Three Jewels (Sanskrit: *Triratna*; Pali: *Tiratana*)—that is, the Buddha, the Dharma, and the Sangha. The Buddha is thought of as an ideal whom human beings should imitate, and the image of him, seated in meditation, is a constant model of self-control and mindfulness. He is not usually thought of as being dead but as existing in a timeless dimension beyond the world. The **Dharma** (Sanskrit), or Dhamma (Pali), means the sum total of Buddhist teachings about how to view the world and how to live properly. The **Sangha** is the community of monks and nuns.[5]

The Buddha's teachings are like the Buddha himself—practical. Surrounded in the India of his day by every kind of speculation about the afterlife, the nature of the divine, and other difficult questions, the Buddha concentrated on what was useful. He refused to talk about anything else—a benign neglect which has been called his noble silence. He said that a person who speculated about unanswerable questions was like a man who had been wounded by an arrow but refused to pull it out until he knew everything about the arrow and the person who shot it. Before the wounded man could get all the information he wanted, he would have died.

The Buddha wished to concentrate on the two most important questions about existence: How can we minimize suffering, both our own and that of others? And how can we attain inner peace? The Buddha's conclusions are not just intellectual solutions, but they also provide a practical way of living; and Buddhist doctrines are meant to be accepted not on blind faith but rather only after they have been experienced as truths by the individual.

The Three Marks of Reality

Common to all forms of Buddhism is a way of looking at the world. Although this view may seem pessimistic at first, it is meant to be a realistic assessment of existence that, when understood, helps lead one, ultimately, to inner peace and even joy. According to this view, reality manifests three characteristics: constant change, a lack of permanent identity, and the existence of suffering. This view is the foundation for the Four Noble Truths and the Noble Eightfold Path, which we will discuss shortly.

Change   One of the things the Buddha asked is that we look at life as it really is. When we do, he said, the first thing we notice is life's constant change, or impermanence (Pali: **anichcha;** Sanskrit: *anitya*). We are often surprised by change—and pained by it—because we do not expect it, but the fact is that nothing we experience in life ever remains the same. We get used to things (our own face, family, friends, house, car, neighborhood), and they seem to remain basically the same every time we look at them. But that is an illusion, for they are changing daily, gradually. We usually only notice the changes over time.

Everyone knows the shock of change, such as seeing a friend after a few years of separation or looking at childhood photos. Even old movies on television and old songs on the radio—the performers now aged or even long gone—clearly convey the Buddhist sense of the inevitability of change. A family gathering can have the same effect: the death of a dear grandparent may be contrasted by the sight of a little child playing in a playpen in the corner.

People also change. Think of what the word *love* means to a five-year-old, a teenager, a new parent, or a person who has lost a spouse. Or imagine hearing the news of a divorce between two people you thought were happy and well suited.

When we truly experience impermanence, we see that all reality is in motion all the time, that the universe is in flux. As the kaleidoscope of reality slowly turns, its patterns change, and while old patterns disappear, new patterns are born, all of them interesting. As the Buddha taught, the wise person expects change, accepts it, and even savors it. The wise person might also reflect that just as pleasures do not last forever, neither do sorrows.

No Permanent Identity   We know that the Buddha urged people to abandon egotism and a fixation on material objects. Related to this, it is commonly thought that he denied the existence of the permanent identity of anything. Thus, the second mark of reality is that each person and each thing is not only changing but is also made up of parts that are also constantly changing, a concept referred to as the fact of "no permanent identity." In the case of people, it is called "no permanent soul" or "no self." The Pali term is **anatta;** in Sanskrit it is *anatman* ("no *Atman*"), because of the Buddha's refusal to accept the Hindu notion of a timeless, unchanging reality (*Atman*) underlying everything—people, things, essences, and gods.

For the sake of logical convenience, we often talk about each person or thing as if it were a single unified reality. Let us first consider something nonhuman, say, a car. We call it *a car* as if it were one single reality, but actually it is made up of many things—glass, aluminum, rubber, paint, headlights, belts, pistons, wires, and liquids—all of which are either going wrong right now or probably soon will be.

Then think of how each human being, though called by a single name, is actually made up of organs, body parts, instincts, memories, ideas, and hopes—all of which are constantly changing. Consider also one's self-perception. I naively think I am the same person from day to day, even if I get a haircut or lose weight or see a film. But if I recall myself at age 10 and then compare that person with who I am now, I seem now to be someone different.

To the Buddha, to believe that a person has some unchanging identity or soul is as mistaken as believing that a car has an unchanging essence. The car is not a car because it has a "car soul"; rather, it is a car because of a social convention that refers to its many related parts by a single word. This tendency is so strong that we sometimes think that a label (*car*) is the reality. Although the Buddhist view may seem strange at first, it is quite rational—and it helps eliminate surprise when the car won't start, when a friend becomes spiteful, or when a photo reveals the inevitability of aging. All these changes show the same process at work.[6]

Suffering   The third characteristic of reality, known as **dukkha** (Pali), or *duhkha* (Sanskrit), is usually translated as "suffering" or "sorrow," but it also means "dissatisfaction" or "dis-ease." It refers to the fact that life, when lived conventionally, can never be fully satisfying because of its inescapable change. Even in the midst of pleasure, we often recognize that pleasure is fleeting. Even when all the bills are paid, we know that in a few days there will be more. Try as we might to put everything in our lives in order, disorder soon reasserts itself. In the midst of happy experiences, we may worry about the people we love. And there are times when ever-changing life brings misery: the death of a parent or spouse or child, divorce, sickness, fire, flood, earthquake, war, the loss of job or home.

Dukkha encompasses the whole range, from horrible suffering to everyday frustration. Someone once amusingly compared dukkha to buying a new car. It brings the pleasures of mobility and pride of owner-ship, but as you go for your first ride you know what lies ahead: insurance premiums, routine maintenance, and costly repairs.

The Buddha concluded that to live means to experience sorrow and dissatisfaction. But he analyzed the nature and causes of suffering much like a doctor would diagnose an illness—in order to understand and over-come them. Those who say that Buddhism pessimistically focuses on suf-fering do not see the hopeful purpose behind that focus. Indeed, no one can escape suffering, but each person can decide how to respond to it, as indi-cated in the Four Noble Truths.

The Four Noble Truths and the Noble Eightfold Path

Perhaps to aid in their memorization, some Buddhist teachings were grouped into fours and eights. The Four Noble Truths are a linked chain of truths about life: (1) suffering exists; (2) it has a cause; (3) it has an end; and (4) there is a way to attain release from suffering—namely, by following the Noble Eightfold Path. Let's look at each concept more closely.

The First Noble Truth: To Live Is to Suffer To say it perhaps more descriptively, "birth is attended with pain, decay is painful, disease is painful, death is painful."[7] In other words, "Living means sorrow." Although the message sounds dark, this truth urges us to be realistic, not melancholy; it is also hopeful in the sense that if we recognize why suffering comes about, then we can lessen it.

The Second Noble Truth: Suffering Comes from Desire When he analyzed suffering, the Buddha saw that it comes from wanting what we cannot have, and from never being satisfied with what we do have. The word *trishna* (Sanskrit), or *tanha* (Pali), which is often translated as "desire," might better be translated as "thirst"; it can also be translated as "craving," sug-gesting both an addiction and a fear of loss. Some of our desires are obvious: food, sleep, clothing, housing, health. Some desires are more subtle: privacy, respect, friendship, quiet, stresslessness, security, variety, beauty. And some desires are simply "wants" that are cultivated by our society: alcohol, designer clothes, tobacco, entertainment, fine food. We all have desires, and because life around us is always changing, no matter how much we acquire we can-not be permanently satisfied. Desire is insatiable, and the result is discontent, dissatisfaction, and sometimes mis-ery. But is there a way to be free of suffering?

The eight-spoked wheel is an ancient symbol of Buddhist teachings.

The Third Noble Truth: To End Suffering, End Desire   It is hard to argue with the reasonableness of this truth, yet it goes against modern Western notions. The Western tendency is to strain to achieve every imaginable desire. This tendency seems to grow out of cultures (such as many modern ones) that emphasize individual legal and moral rights, competition between individuals, and individual success in school, in one's job, and in sports. Belief in a distinct and permanent self or an immortal soul may be the origin of such individualism. This tendency is rather different from the sense of self that comes from a worldview that values the individual's membership in the group—a view of self more common, traditionally, in tribal and Asian cultures.

To our modern way of thinking, the Buddha may seem to have been rather stark in his recommendations. Nevertheless, he himself left home and family and possessions, because he believed—and taught—that *any* kind of attachment will bring inevitable suffering. The shaven head and special clothing of monks and nuns symbolize their radical detachment from worldly concerns.

Buddhists themselves recognize, though, that not everyone can be a monk. Consequently, this third truth is moderated for laypeople. It is commonly interpreted as a recommendation that everyone accept peacefully whatever occurs, aiming less for happiness and more for inner peace. The individual should concentrate on the present moment, not on the past or the future or one's desires for them. Because times of happiness are always paid for by times of unhappiness (the pendulum swings in both directions), a certain emotional neutrality is the best path.

Acceptance is a step to inner peace if I recognize that what I have right now is actually enough. Ultimately, I have to accept my body, my talents, my family, and even my relatives. Of course, some adjustments can be made: I can move, have plastic surgery, change my job, or get a divorce. Ultimately, though, much of life simply has to be accepted—and appreciated when possible.

The essence of the Third Noble Truth is this: I cannot change the outside world, but I can change myself and the way I experience the world.

The Fourth Noble Truth: Release from Suffering Is Possible and Can Be Attained by Following the Noble Eightfold Path   **Nirvana** (Sanskrit; Pali: *nibbana*) is the ultimate goal in Buddhism. The term *nirvana* suggests many things: end of suffering, inner peace, and liberation from the limitations of the world. The word *nirvana* seems to mean "blown out," or "cool," suggesting that the fires of desire have been extinguished. Upon attaining nirvana, the individual has self-control and is no longer driven from inside by raging emotional forces or from outside by the unpredictable events of life. It may not necessarily imply the elimination of anger (stories tell of the Buddha's getting angry at disputes within the monastic community), but it does suggest a general inner quiet. Nirvana is also believed to end karma and rebirth after the present life. (More will

> Look within.
> Be still.
> Free from fear and attachment,
> Know the sweet joy of the way.
> —The Dhammapada[8]

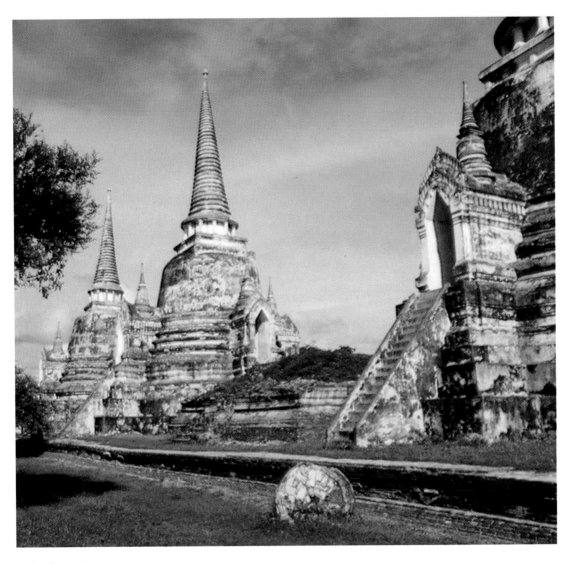

In Buddhism, the movement toward liberation is often symbolized by a rising architectural form. Although the pagoda is the most familiar example, the stupa (shown here) is an earlier version.

be said about nirvana later in this chapter.) To reach nirvana, Buddhism recommends following the Noble Eightfold Path.

The Noble Eightfold Path: The Way to Inner Peace The eight "steps" of the path actually form a program that the Buddha taught will lead us toward liberation from the impermanence and suffering of reality. Together, they describe three main goals: to face life objectively, to live kindly, and to cultivate inner peace. Although they are often called "steps," the eight recommendations are not to be practiced sequentially but rather all together. As it is usually translated, the Noble Eightfold Path sounds so old-fashioned that readers may not immediately perceive its practicality. (Keep in mind that the word *right* is a translation of a word that might better be translated as "correct" or "complete.")

1. *Right understanding* I recognize the impermanence of life, the mechanism of desire, and the cause of suffering.
2. *Right intention* My thoughts and motives are pure, not tainted by my emotions and selfish desires.
3. *Right speech* I speak honestly and kindly, in positive ways, avoiding lies, exaggeration, harsh words.
4. *Right action* My actions do not hurt any other being that can feel hurt, including animals; I avoid stealing and sexual conduct that would bring hurt.
5. *Right work* My livelihood does no harm.
6. *Right effort* With moderation, I consistently strive to improve.
7. *Right meditation* I use the disciplines of meditation (**dhyana**) and focused awareness to contemplate the nature of reality more deeply.
8. *Right contemplation* I cultivate states of blissful inner peace (**samadhi**).

THE INFLUENCE OF INDIAN THOUGHT ON EARLY BUDDHIST TEACHINGS

It is uncertain whether the Buddha intended to begin an entirely new religion. Early Buddhist literature rejects certain elements of the common Vedic practice of the time, particularly its ritualism, its reliance on priests, its caste system, and its belief in any permanent spiritual reality. Non-Buddhists responded argumentatively when women and slaves entered the Buddhist monastic order. Such evidence leads us to think that early Buddhists saw themselves as outside of the mainstream priestly Vedic culture—a fact that may have assisted them in developing their own statements of belief and practice. Nevertheless, we do know that early Buddhist teachings accepted some elements of Indian thought that are today shared to some extent by Hinduism, Jainism, and Buddhism.

Ahimsa: "Do No Harm"

Foremost among the elements adopted from the Indian worldview of the Buddha's day was the ideal of *ahimsa* "nonharm"; see Chapter 3). It is not clear how old this ideal is, and it has not always been followed. We do know that Vedic sacrifice at the time of the Buddha sometimes included animal sacrifice (and animal sacrifice in Hindu practice can still be found—though it is rare—particularly in Nepal and Bali). But we also know that the ideal of ahimsa was already prominent in India before the time of the Buddha and may have had ancient and pre-Aryan origins.

For Buddhism, ahimsa is fundamental. The ideal holds that to cause suffering to any being is cruel and unnecessary—life is already hard enough for each of us. Ahimsa discourages not only causing physical pain but also psychological hurt or the exploitation of another. Upon reaching a real understanding that every being that feels can suffer, the individual gains wider sympathy. It is then natural and satisfying for the individual to live with gentleness.

Ahimsa is a high ideal and not always easy to achieve. Furthermore, we must recognize that there will always be a gap between the ideal and actual practice in different Buddhist cultures and among individuals. Nevertheless, however murky the definition of the "best action" may be, the ideal is fairly clear. A compassionate person does everything possible to avoid causing suffering: "ashamed of roughness, and full of mercy, he dwells compassionate and kind to all creatures that have life."[9] This empathetic ideal has been interpreted as recommending, when possible, a vegetarian diet, and it warns against involvement in any jobs or sports that would hurt others, such as being a butcher, hunter, fisherman, soldier, or weapon maker. The result is a way of life that is harmonious and free of remorse.

The Soul and Karma

The Buddha seems to have rejected the notion of a soul (an unchanging spiritual reality), but he apparently accepted some notion of rebirth. How, we might then ask, can an individual be reborn if there is no soul? Buddhism holds that while there is no individual soul, the elements of personality that make up an individual can recombine and thus continue from one lifetime to another. Buddhism offers the examples of a flame passing from one candle to another and the pattern caused by a breeze that passes over many blades of grass. The candles are separate, but the flame that passes between each is one; the blades of grass are rooted to separate places, but the pattern of the breeze travels across them and "unites" them in movement.

Closely related to the notion of rebirth is *karma*. As we discussed in Chapter 3, karma determines how one will be reborn. In Hinduism and Jainism, karma is like something that clings to the soul as it passes from life to life in reincarnation. It works automatically: good actions produce karma that brings good effects, such as intelligence, high birth, and wealth; bad actions produce karma that brings the opposite, including rebirth into animal and insect life-forms. Because the Buddha seems to have rejected the existence of a soul, explaining how karma works is more difficult in Buddhism. It is thought to accompany and affect the elements of personality that reappear in later lifetimes. Regardless of their specific manner of functioning, karma and rebirth were already such powerful ideas in the India of the Buddha's time that they continued in early Buddhism and from there have spread well beyond India. They remain highly influential concepts in Buddhist countries today.

Nirvana

In Buddhism, the everyday world of change is called **samsara,** a term that suggests decay and pain. Liberation from samsara, however, is attained in nirvana. The notion has many similarities with the Hindu goal of *moksha*

Was the Buddha an Atheist?

Philosophers often ask questions about the nature of reality. Is there a Creator? Is the universe eternal? Is the extent of the universe infinite?

The Buddha witnessed intense wrangling over such questions in the India of his day and apparently disliked the tendency of debate to inflame anger. He thus avoided paying too much attention to the "unanswerable questions." His teachings and the earliest monastic rules do, however, clearly use reason to address such questions.

What, then, did the Buddha believe and teach about the existence of God? To answer this requires two more questions.

- Is there a Creator God? Early Buddhism explicitly rejects such a belief, as did other religious movements in India at that time. For example, we know that Jainism was explicitly atheistic (the reasons for its atheism are discussed in Chapter 5). We also know that a philosophical school of the time, the Lokayata, was also explicitly atheistic.

- Is there an Unchanging Divine Reality? Regarding such a belief—called Brahman in the Upanishads and elsewhere—early Buddhism exhibited a similar skepticism. Apparently the Buddha saw *everything* to be in constant change, and his experience did not recognize anything whatsoever that was unchanging, thereby precluding a belief in Brahman.

Perhaps the Buddha would best be called a nontheist. Although details of the Buddha's thought are not entirely clear, what is obvious is the extreme practicality of his focus. He opposed religious dogmatism, blind devotion to a guru, and the power of a priestly caste. From his point of view, rebirth as a human being was a rare opportunity and one's focus in life should be on living in such a way as to bring enlightenment. Regarding all questions, the Buddha asked disciples to experience things for themselves and then to trust their own judgment.

("liberation"; discussed in Chapter 3). Nirvana is thought of as existence beyond limitation. Many people in the West associate nirvana with a psychological state because it is described as evoking joy and peace, but perhaps it is better to see nirvana as being indescribable and beyond all psychological states. Although reaching nirvana occurs rarely, it is theoretically possible to attain during one's lifetime; the Buddha is said to have "entered nirvana" at the time of his enlightenment. Once a person has reached nirvana, rebirth is finished, and in a culture that believes that individuals have already been born many times before this current life, an end to rebirth can be a welcome thought.

THE EARLY DEVELOPMENT OF BUDDHISM

Buddhism might have remained an entirely Indian religion, much as Jainism has, if it were not for an energetic king named Ashoka, who flourished about 250 B.C.E. (Timeline 4.1). Ashoka's plan to expand his rule over a large part of India naturally entailed much fighting. After a particularly bloody battle in eastern India, as Ashoka was inspecting the battlefield, he saw the scene very differently than he had before. The whole experience was so horrifying that Ashoka converted to the ideal of nonviolence. Although it is uncertain whether Ashoka became a Buddhist, he did make political use of

Left	Date	Right
	C. 563–483 B.C.E	Life of Siddhartha Gautama, the Buddha
Life of Ashoka, Indian king who spread Buddhist values	C. 273–232 B.C.E.	
	C. 50 C.E.	Entry of Buddhism into China
Creation of the Lotus Sutra	C. 100 C.E.	
	C. 300 C.E.	Beginning of the spread of Buddhism in Southeast Asia
Entry of Buddhism into Korea	C. 400 C.E.	
	C. 520 C.E.	Introduction of Bodhidharma's Meditation School of Buddhism to China
Acceptance of Buddhism in Japan	C. 552 C.E.	
	C. 630 C.E.	Entry of Buddhism into Tibet
Founding of Tendai and Shingon Buddhism in Japan by Saicho (767–822) and Kukai (774–835), respectively	C. 820 C.E.	
	845 C.E.	Third great persecution of Buddhism in China, which permanently weakened Chinese Buddhism
Revival of Theravada Buddhism in Sri Lanka and Southeast Asia	C. 1000 C.E.	
	C. 1100–1500	Decline of Buddhism in India
Life of Honen, founder of the Pure Land sect in Japan	1133–1212	
	1158–1210	Life of Chinul, founder of Korean Chogye order
Beginning of growth of Zen in Japan	C. 1200	
	1222–1282	Life of Nichiren, founder of Nichiren Buddhism in Japan
Life of Tsong Kha-pa Tibetan Buddhist reformer	1357–1419	
	1952	Beginning of World Fellowship of Buddhists

FIGURE 4.1

The birthplace and home of Buddhism: India, China, Japan, and Southeast Asia.

Buddhist moral values. A cynic might note that forbidding violence is a practical move for any ruler who wishes to remain on the throne. In any case, the principle of nonviolence is most effective when it is embraced widely; otherwise, the few people who are nonviolent will be preyed upon by the violent.

To bring a large number of the population around to his new nonviolent way of thinking and acting, Ashoka, it is thought, decided to spread the principles of nonviolence throughout India and possibly even beyond. To do this, he erected many stone columns inscribed with his principles, placing some at sites important in the Buddha's life. A number of these columns still exist today.

Our historical knowledge of Ashoka is quite limited, but Ashoka looms large in Buddhist legend. One story tells us that Ashoka sent as a missionary to Sri Lanka a son or nephew named Mahinda (also called Melinda, Mahendra, and Menander). Whatever the truth of this story, it is a fact that Sri Lanka is largely Buddhist today. Indeed, it may have been Ashoka who gave Buddhism its urge to spread and helped to make it one of the world's great missionary religions (Figure 4.1).

In the first centuries after the Buddha's death, in response to widespread and long-standing disagreements over the Buddha's teachings, many Buddhist schools and splinter groups arose. Most of these ultimately

◀ Timeline of significant events in the history of Buddhism.

died out and are only names to us today. A few survived and crystallized into the great branches of Buddhism that we now recognize: Theravada, Mahayana, and Vajrayana.

THERAVADA BUDDHISM: THE WAY OF THE ELDERS

In the early centuries of Buddhism, several schools claimed to adhere to the original, unchanged teachings of the Buddha. All of them shared the Buddha's opposition to Vedic ritual and the brahmin priesthood, as well as his appreciation for simplicity, meditation, and detachment. They took a conservative approach, hoping to protect the Buddha's rather stark teachings and simple practice from being altered. Of all the conservative schools, one has survived to the present day: Theravada. Its name is often used today to refer to the entire conservative movement.

The Theravada school takes its name from its goal of passing on the Buddha's teachings unchanged. Its name means "the way (*vada*) of the elders (*thera*)." Theravada monks originally passed on the teachings in oral form, but they eventually wrote them down. Although the school's claim to have kept its teachings relatively unchanged over time is doubtful, it is true that Theravada has a deliberately conservative orientation. Furthermore, the fact that its home in Sri Lanka was somewhat isolated from the changes occurring within Buddhism in India may have protected the original Theravada teachings from altering greatly.

The heart of Theravada Buddhism is its community of monks. As a school, it has always stressed the ideal of reaching nirvana through detachment and desirelessness achieved through meditation. (This of course is an ideal that some would point out has been contradicted by the Sangha's having courted wealth and temporal power.) Although Theravada does accept that laypeople can attain nirvana, the life of the monk offers a surer path. The notion is enshrined in the ideal of the **arhat** (Sanskrit; Pali: *arahat* meaning "perfect being," "worthy"), a person who has reached nirvana.

The Theravada monastic community had its distant origins in the wandering sannyasins and in the groups of Hindu ascetics who lived in the forests. A sign of this connection is the orange robe of the Theravada Buddhist monk, also worn today by Hindu monks and ascetics. But even during the Buddha's lifetime, his monks began to live a settled life during the summertime monsoon season, giving their time to discussion and inhabiting caves or groves and parks donated by lay followers.

Note: In the discussion of Theravada Buddhism, it would be more accurate to use the Pali terms *nibbana, sutta, arahat,* and *Tiratana* as opposed to the Sanskrit terms *nirvana, sutra, arhat,* and *Triratna*; however, for the sake of consistency, the text throughout this chapter will reflect the terminology (whether Pali or Sanskrit) that is most familiar in the West.

In Theravada, the life of the monk offers the best hope of attaining nirvana.

In Theravada countries such as Thailand, monks' robes hung out to dry are a common sight in the neighborhoods of temples.

Theravada had spread very early from India to Sri Lanka, where it co-existed for centuries with other forms of Buddhism before becoming dominant in the twelfth century of the common era. It was then carried to Myanmar (formerly Burma) and Thailand, along with other elements of Indian culture, by traders by the fourth century. Theravada did not become predominant in Myanmar until the mid-eleventh century, when Pagan began to flourish as a great Buddhist city and center of Theravada under King Aniruddha. Fourteenth-century Thailand, having freed itself of Khmer domination, also adopted Theravada Buddhism. The conservatism of Theravada was politically appealing to rulers for its moral rigorousness. Today it is the dominant religion in Sri Lanka, Myanmar, Thailand, Laos, and Cambodia (Kampuchea).

Theravada monks must beg daily for their food, which has meant that they, like the Buddha's early followers, have to live close to laypeople. In fact, Theravada monasteries are often in the middle of towns. When Theravada monks go out on their begging rounds, people who wish to donate food freely give them cooked rice and vegetables. Donors believe they are receiving beneficial karma from their acts of generosity, and people support the monasteries much like other societies give to libraries and other social agencies. In return for donations of food and clothing, many monasteries run schools, meditation centers, and medical clinics, as well as care for stray animals. Monks are honored guests at both civic and family occasions. They are role models of gentleness and insight and are often consulted for advice.

Theravada Teachings and Literature

The Theravada collection of the Buddha's teachings is called the Pali Canon. As a whole, this mass of material is called *Tipitaka* (Pali), or **Tripitaka** (Sanskrit), which means "three baskets." The name comes from the fact that the writings were divided according to their subject matter into three groups.

The first collection comprises sayings of the Buddha, in the form of sermons or dialogues. This type of material is called *sutta* (Pali), or **sutra** (Sanskrit), and it is subdivided into five groups: Digha Nikaya ("long teachings"), Majjhima Nikaya ("middle-length teachings"), Samyutta Nikaya ("connected teachings"), Anguttara Nikaya ("graduated teachings"), and Khuddaka Nikaya ("small book collection"), which includes the Dhammapada.

The second collection (called *vinaya*; Pali and Sanskrit) outlines the procedural rules for monastic life. These include rules on begging, eating, relations with monks and nonmonks, and other disciplines.[10]

A third collection, developed later, is called *abhidhamma* (Pali), or *abhidharma* (Sanskrit), meaning "the works that go beyond the elementary teachings." It systematized the doctrine presented more or less randomly in the sutras.

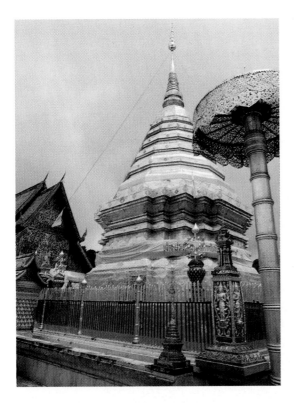

The umbrella has often symbolized the Buddha's authority, and stupas—another important symbol of the Buddha's teachings—have been built over the remains of Buddhist monks.

Theravada Art and Architecture

Images of the Buddha did not appear in the earliest centuries of Buddhism; instead, artists used symbols to represent him and his teachings. One symbol was the eight-spoked wheel, which derived from the Noble Eightfold Path and represented all the basic Buddhist teachings, the Dharma. The umbrella, often carried to protect an important person from the hot sun, symbolized the Buddha's authority. Other common symbols included a set of footprints, a lotus flower, and an empty throne. Many types of **stupa,** or large mound, arose over the remains of Buddhist monks and at important Buddhist sites. Symbols may have been used at first, as artists struggled with the basic challenge of depicting simultaneously the humanity of the Buddha and his great spiritual attainment, his enlightenment.

By the first century of the common era, however, images of the Buddha began to appear. (Scholars debate the possible influence of Greek sculptural traditions.[11]) In Theravada countries we now frequently see statues of the Buddha meditating, standing (with hand outstretched in blessing), walking, or reclining. Although there are exceptions, in Theravada countries, the images of the Buddha (even those that are large) are not overwhelming. In the temples of Sri Lanka, Thailand, Myanmar, and elsewhere, they are

This Reclining Buddha in Bangkok is one of the most visited images in Thailand.

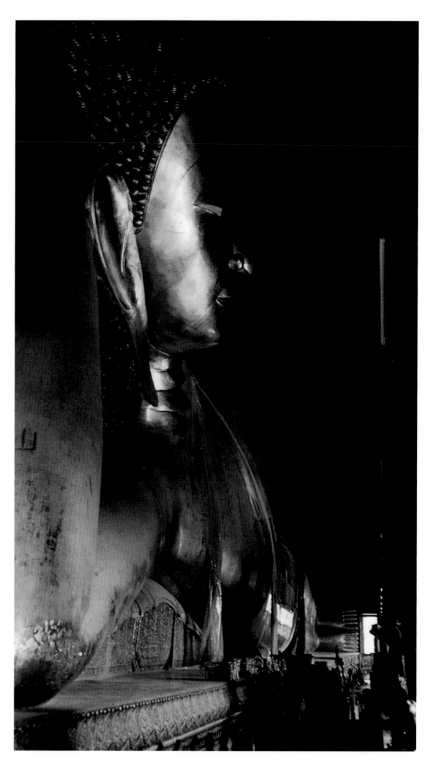

usually about two to three times human size and rarely reach the vast height and scale that we occasionally find in the Mahayana Buddhist sculpture of China, Korea, and Japan. Some of the most beautiful sculptures are the Reclining Buddhas of Sri Lanka and Thailand.

MAHAYANA BUDDHISM: THE "BIG VEHICLE"

The second great branch of Buddhism is called Mahayana, a word that is usually translated as "big vehicle." It suggests a large ferryboat in which all types of people can be carried across a river and hints at the broad scope of the Mahayana vision, which can accommodate a wide variety of people seeking enlightenment. Mahayana emphasizes that nirvana is not only attainable by monks but is a possibility for everyone. Mahayana also stresses that enlightenment is a call to compassion, for "the Mahayana tradition maintains that a person must save himself by saving others."[12]

Some critics of Mahayana Buddhism claim that it has allowed ritualistic and speculative tendencies (which had been deemphasized by the Buddha) to creep back in. It is possible that the Indian love of ritual and imagery remains alive in a new form in Mahayana. For example, the fire ceremony of some Mahayana sects certainly derives from Vedic practice. But this is really to say that Mahayana initially was thoroughly Indian and sought to express its truths in very Indian ways.[13]

It is possible that some practices or attitudes of early Buddhism do not always fulfill the religious needs of many ordinary people who appreciate ritual. Mahayana Buddhism, however, abundantly meets almost every religious and philosophical need.[14] It is the source of some of the most extraordinary creations of the human mind—in its art, architecture, philosophy, psychology, and ceremony.

Mahayana Teachings and Practice

In Mahayana Buddhism, the religious ideal broadened: from the exemplar of the monastic person, fairly detached from family life, it expanded to include nonmonks, women, and the married. Mahayana began to explore the possibilities of following a religious path that was active in the world. This difference signals a shift in the notion of what is virtuous. This change might have represented a reaction against Indian asceticism and the cult of the sannyasin, or it might have indicated a new form of devotionalism and love of ritual. It might also have come from a widening of the concept of nirvana, in which nirvana was thought to be found within samsara, the everyday world of change. This devotional shift began in India and in central Asia, but it grew in strength when Mahayana entered China, a culture that has long valued nature and the physical world in general. In Mahayana, the human body and the material realm are viewed positively, and there is a great openness toward art and music. Mahayana grew as the senses and emotions were increasingly viewed as means of spiritual transformation and as the gulf between sacred and nonsacred (typical of Vedic practice) was bridged.

In Mahayana, wisdom remained an important goal, but the pairing of wisdom and compassion was central to its teachings. Compassion became an essential virtue and the preeminent expression of wisdom. The term for this compassion is **karuna,** which may also be translated as "empathy," "sympathy," or "kindness." Karuna is somewhat different from the Western notion of kindness, in which one separate human being, out of an abundance of individual generosity, gives to another separate human being. Rather, karuna implies that we all are part of the same ever changing universe. Deep down, the individual is not really different from anyone or anything else. To be kind to others is actually to be kind to oneself. Karuna in action simply means living out this awareness of the oneness of the universe. With this perception of the interrelatedness of all beings, including animals, compassion comes naturally: if I am kind, my kindness must be

The Hindu ritual of anointing sacred objects became a part of Mahayana devotional practice.

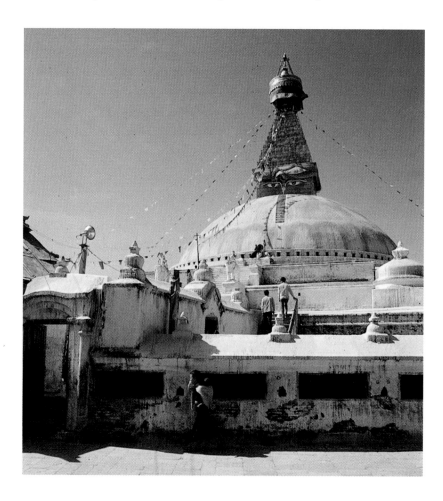

shown toward anything that can feel pain. The great prayer of Buddhist compassion is this: May all creatures be well and happy. It is a common Mahayana practice to mentally project this wish to the world every day.

The esteem for karuna influences the human ideal in Mahayana. Instead of the Theravada ideal of arhat, who is esteemed for detached wisdom and unworldly living, the ideal in Mahayana Buddhism is the person of deep compassion, the **bodhisattva** ("enlightenment being"). Because the bodhisattva embodies compassion, it is often said that the bodhisattva will refuse to fully enter nirvana, in order to be reborn on earth to help others. A person may take the "bodhisattva vow" to be constantly reborn until all are enlightened.

The same kind of openness to a variety of religious paths that we saw in Hinduism is also typical of Mahayana Buddhism. Mahayana recognizes that people differ greatly and find themselves at different stages of spiritual development. For example, a person who would not benefit from study or meditation might be able to achieve a new level of understanding through the use of ritual, imagery, and religious objects. It is possible that Hindu bhakti yoga (see Chapter 3) returns in Mahayana, because Mahayana even endorses devotion to deities. Some critics who appreciate the historical Buddha's rejection of such religious practices may label them as superstition. Regardless, Mahayana is open to anything that can lead to greater spiritual awareness, a concept known as "skillful means" (Sanskrit: *upaya*).

Mahayana Thought and Worldview

Mahayana has encouraged a vision of reality that is imaginative, wide, and often profound. An old story, whether true or not, tells of a Chinese emperor who began reading certain Mahayana sutras and then said in astonishment that the experience was like looking out over the ocean. He sensed the vastness of the Mahayana vision as he experienced both the quantity and the quality of the sutras (and possibly the art, as well) that he was attempting to understand.

Several key notions must be introduced here. They show a worldview that sees the universe as being full of the divine and populated by holy personalities. These notions can seem dry to the beginner, but they underlie Mahayana doctrine and have inspired its art.

The Three-Body Doctrine (Trikaya Doctrine)   In Mahayana, the Buddha nature can express itself in three ways. This is called the **trikaya** ("three-body") doctrine. The historical Buddha who lived in India came to be considered the manifestation of a divine reality, "the cosmic Buddha nature." The Sanskrit term for this is *Dharmakaya* (often translated as "law body," "form body," or "body of reality"). According to Mahayana Buddhism, the cosmic Buddha nature, although invisible, permeates all things. In people it frequently presents itself as potential. In fact, it is our true nature that we need to recognize and realize. Dharmakaya also exists

At Boudhanath in Katmandu, Nepal, these eyes represent the omnipresent Buddha nature.

in the natural world, too, for all things are a sacred manifestation of the cosmic Buddha nature. When we experience the mystery of the natural world, we experience the Dharmakaya.

Siddhartha Gautama's physical body, because it is considered an incarnation of this divine reality, is called Nirmanakaya ("transformation body"). The notion that the historical Buddha was a divine manifestation reminds us of the Hindu notion of the many incarnations of Vishnu, and it may have been influenced by that belief.

In keeping with the notion of many incarnations, many Mahayana schools believe in more than one transformation body of the Buddha. We might recall that both Theravada and Mahayana schools describe the Buddha's knowledge of his past lives. Both branches of Buddhism also believe that another historical Buddha, **Maitreya** (Sanskrit; Pali: *Metteya*), will appear on earth in the future to inaugurate a golden age. In several Mahayana cultures, this belief has taken on great importance: in China the Buddha who will come is called Mi-lo-fo and in Japan, Miroku. In Korea, the notion of Miruk (as Maitreya is known there) has been especially influential in generating belief in a messianic future, which has prompted the creation of many beautiful statues in his honor. He is often shown seated on a stool or raised platform in the so-called Western style, with one leg down on the floor and the other crossed over it, his head resting thoughtfully on one hand as he contemplates the future.

In Mahayana philosophy, the cosmic Buddha nature has also taken bodily shape in supernatural Buddhas who live in the heavens beyond our earth. These Buddhas have radiant, invulnerable bodies and live in

Mahayana supported the creation of immense Buddha images, some of the largest of which are found in the Datong Caves of western China.

constant happiness. In Sanskrit, they are called Sambhogakaya Buddhas ("perfect-bliss-body" Buddhas). Because Mahayana Buddhism envisions heavenly realms spreading in all directions, followers came to think that each of the directions must have its own reigning bliss-body Buddha. Particularly important is the bliss-body Buddha who rules the Western Paradise, the direction toward which the sun moves. His name in India was **Amitabha Buddha** (Chinese: Amito-fo; Japanese: Amida Butsu). Many devout Buddhists have hoped to be reborn in his paradise. Their devotion to Amitabha Buddha has inspired a great body of fine painting and sculpture, in which a large Buddha is seated on a lotus flower surrounded by peaceful disciples in pavilions with gardens full of flowers.

Heavenly Bodhisattvas We have already discussed the focus of Mahayana on· the earthly bodhisattva, a saintly person of great compassion. But Mahayana Buddhism also holds that many bodhisattvas who are eager to help human beings also exist in other dimensions beyond the earth. They, too, are beings of great compassion. Some once lived on earth and have been reborn beyond this world but retain an interest in it. They may appear miraculously on earth when needed or possibly even be reborn to help others.

The most significant of the heavenly bodhisattvas has been Avalokiteshvara, who looks down "from a location above" (as his name indicates) in order to give help. In India, Avalokiteshvara was portrayed as male, but in China this bodhisattva was conceived to be feminine, because of her association with compassion and mercy. Under the name of **Guanyin** (Kuan-yin, "hears all cries"), this bodhisattva was shown in early depictions as having both male and female characteristics; eventually, though, the bodhisattva became entirely feminine. East Asian paintings and sculpture frequently show her with a very sweet face, dressed all in white, holding the jewel of wisdom, with the moon in the sky behind her or under her feet. Other artistic renderings of her, particularly in temple sculpture, show her with a halo of many arms (she is said to have at least a thousand), representing her many powers to help. In the palm of each hand is an eye, symbolizing her ability to see everyone in need. In temples, Guanyin is fre-

In Mahayana, compassion is especially manifested in the many-armed form of Guanyin (Kuan-yin).

quently paired with the Buddha. He is often in the front and center of the sanctuary, and she is located immediately behind him; or she may be a member of a triad, sitting to one side of the Buddha, with another bodhisattva or disciple of the Buddha on the other side. In Japan, where this bodhisattva became popularly known as Kannon, many temples were dedicated to her alone.

Shunyata   One Mahayana doctrine asserts that all reality is *shunya* ("empty"; that is, empty of permanent essence). Literally, **shunyata** can be translated as "emptiness" or "zeroness." But what does this mean? The notion is an outgrowth of the basic Buddhist view of reality that everything is constantly shifting, changing, taking new form. If we consider an individual person, we can say the "individual" is a pattern, made of parts in continuous change. If we broaden our scope, larger patterns appear, such as the patterns of a family, a city, or a society. Similarly, nature is a combination of smaller patterns making larger patterns, like wheels within wheels. And even the parts themselves ultimately disintegrate as new parts are born. To better understand this concept, think of clouds, which look large and substantial but are forever appearing and disappearing, moving past each other and changing shape and size. Because everything is in constant change, each apparently individual person and thing is actually "empty" of permanent individual identity.

Tathata   Literally translated, the word **tathata** means "thatness," "thusness," or "suchness." This is a rich notion that invites each person's experience and interpretation. Tathata represents a view of experience that says that reality is revealed in each moment, as we savor patterns, relationships, and change. Because no moment is exactly the same, each one can be observed and appreciated as it passes. Thus, simple, everyday events reveal the nature of reality. We may experience "thatness" when two elements come together in an unexpected way—for example, when a small child says something wise beyond her years. Sometimes it comes when we notice a moment of change, such as when, after a long string of muggy summer days, we get up to add a blanket to the bed on the first crisp autumn night. Or it might be when we notice random elements coming together—for example, when a bird drinks from a water fountain or a dog sticks its nose out of the window of a passing car. It might be the beauty of an apple in a supermarket or the way a tree's shadow falls on a building. It could even be something funny or sad. Although tathata involves the mundane, it is also a poetic moment that will never return in exactly the same way.

The Mahayana teaching of tathata tells that all reality, like a drop of water, is transitory.

The wonder that can be seen in everyday life is what the term *tathata* suggests. We know we are experiencing the "thatness" of reality when we experience something and say to ourselves, "Yes, that's it; that is the way things are." In the moment, we recognize that reality is wondrously beautiful but also that its patterns are fragile and passing.

Mahayana Literature

Mahayana Buddhism in India used a Sanskrit version of the Tripitaka, but to these works it added a host of other materials. (Consequently, the Mahayana Tripitaka is longer than that of Theravada.) Many of the new Mahayana works were called sutras because they purported to be the words of the Buddha, but in reality they were imaginative, colorful creations written at least several centuries after the Buddha lived, from about 100 B.C.E. to about 600 C.E. The teachings of these sutras, however, may be seen as a natural development of basic Buddhist insights.

Primary among these texts are the Prajnaparamita Sutras ("sutras on the perfection of wisdom"), the earliest of which may have been written about 100 B.C.E. These sutras attempt to contrast ordinary understanding with the enlightened understanding that everything in the universe is interdependent.

The influential Vimalakirti Sutra teaches that it is possible to live a devout Buddhist life without necessarily becoming a monk. The hero of the sutra is the man Vimalakirti, who was, as historian Kenneth Ch'en describes him, "a layman rich and powerful, a brilliant conversationalist, a respected householder who surrounded himself with the pleasures of life, but was also a faithful and wise disciple of the Buddha, a man full of wisdom and thoroughly disciplined in his conduct."[15] Because the main figure is not a monk but more like a devout gentleman, we can see why this sutra became popular with laypeople. Its purpose, though, was serious—to show that an individual can work successfully amidst the dangers of worldly life and can avoid hurting (and actually help) oneself and others.

One of the most widely loved works of Mahayana was the Saddharma Pundarika Sutra ("lotus sutra of the good law"), known simply as the Lotus Sutra. In this sutra, the Buddha shows his transcendent, cosmic nature. As he preaches to thousands of his disciples, his light and wisdom extend throughout the universe. Using parables, the sutra insists rather democratically that all people have the Buddha nature and that all, therefore, can become Buddhas. Many of its parables talk of the "skillful means" that can lead people of differing types and mentalities to enlightenment.

Mahayana in China

Mahayana Buddhism spread out of India to central Asia and to China, which it entered in the first century of the common era. As Buddhism spread to China and its neighboring regions, the Sanskrit canon was trans-

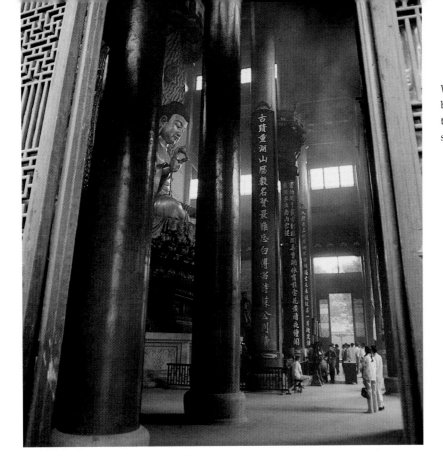

Worshipers are dwarfed by the Buddha image in this Mahayana temple of southern China.

lated bit by bit, into at least thirteen central Asian languages. In China, several language versions were made of most of the major works. At first the translations were rough, but later versions were more exact, once translators had a better knowledge of Buddhist ideas and how to convey them in the Chinese idiom. By the eighth century, an enormous number of Buddhist works had been translated into Chinese.[16]

The appeal of Mahayana Buddhism in ancient China is worth considering. In some ways, the Buddhist ideal of monastic celibacy went against the grain of the Chinese Confucian culture, which (1) saw moral demands existing within family relationships, (2) venerated ancestors, and (3) valued continuity of the family line (see Chapter 6). Yet Mahayana Buddhism had virtues that would appeal to a wide spectrum of the population: it accepted local cults and continued their practice of using rituals that promised magic, healing, and fertility for the masses of ordinary people. It created great temples with beautiful art and ceremony. It promoted peace and family harmony. It answered questions about the afterlife and performed funeral and memorial services for the dead. It provided a secure way of community life for people not interested in having children or creating their own families. It offered philosophical insights not already present in Chinese culture. And it provided many rulers with prayers and rituals that would help protect the nation and the rulers themselves.

The monastery of Hengshan hangs on a hillside in Shanxi Province in China, a witness to the Buddhist desire for detachment from the world.

Mahayana Buddhism had great success in China in the four centuries after its introduction but repeatedly clashed with Taoists and Confucianists over issues of government influence and social values. As a result, Buddhism in China suffered three major persecutions (in 446 C.E., 574 C.E., and 845 C.E.). There were several reasons. Buddhism was sometimes considered a dangerous foreign import, teaching antisocial thought and practice. Because monks and nuns had no children, they were thought to be neglecting a necessary religious role as parents, and their monastic life did not allow them to take care of their own aged parents—a fact that seemed unfilial. Furthermore, monks and nuns were not taxed and could not be employed in public work projects. And because so much metal (especially copper) was used for statues and religious implements, there was sometimes not enough to mint coins.

After the third great persecution, Buddhism never entirely recovered its strength in China. The beliefs and practices of some Mahayana schools that had begun in China were transmitted to Japan and continue to some extent there (as we will see in the following section). Ultimately, especially after later Mongol and Manchu control, Buddhism would become (along with Confucianism and Taoism) one of the "Three Religions"—a strand in a Chinese religious mixture of the "three religions" and folk belief.

Mahayana in Korea

Buddhism and its literature were carried into Korea from central Asia and China as early as 372 C.E.[17] Buddhism was adopted widely for its supposed powers to protect the three kingdoms then ruling the peninsula. Monasteries were thought of as powerhouses, sending monks' prayers to powerful Buddhas and bodhisattvas and receiving their celestial care in return. Korea was unified by the Silla kingdom, producing the Unified Silla dynasty (668–918 C.E.), and this unification led to a blending of religious elements from Taoism, Confucianism, shamanism, and Buddhism, which became the state religion and primary practitioner of official ritual.

Buddhism in Korea reached its apogee during the Koryo dynasty (918–1392 C.E.). During this time, 80,000 wooden blocks were carved for the printing of all Korean and Chinese Buddhist texts of the Korean Tripitaka. After the first set of blocks was burned during a Mongol invasion, another set, which still exists, was finished in 1251. One of the greatest exponents of Korean Buddhism at this time was the monk Chinul (1158–1210). Given to a monastery as a young boy, he began meditation and textual study early. He had three great experiences of insight, all prompted by his reading of Mahayana materials. He founded the Chogye order, which combines textual study with regular meditation and which is still influential today.

Buddhism was supplanted by Confucianism as the state religion in the Yi dynasty (1392–1910). Nevertheless, although the aristocracy identified with Confucianism, the common people remained Buddhist. The Japanese takeover of Korea, beginning in 1910, was marked by efforts to force monks to marry. After the Japanese occupation ended in 1945, the Chogye order reverted to complete celibacy, and married monks entered the T'aego order.

Mahayana in Japan

Buddhism entered Japan in the sixth century C.E., where it began to grow after some initial resistance. It became so powerful in the early capital of Nara that in 794 the new capital city of Kyoto (then called Heian-kyo) was founded partly in order to be free from the influence of Buddhist clergy. The new capital was designed on a grid pattern, after Chinese models, and Japanese culture imported many elements of the Chinese culture of the time. Because the founding of the new capital coincided with a vibrant period of Mahayana Buddhism in China, Japanese Buddhism also imported Chinese Buddhist schools.

The history of Buddhism in Japan shows a movement of increasing laicization. The first period, when the capital was at Nara, was dominated by essentially monastic Buddhist schools. In the second period, after the capital moved, the dominant schools (Shingon and Tendai) were ritualistic and appealed to the aristocracy. Their prominence lasted for about four hundred years. In the thirteenth century, however, two schools (Pure Land and

Zen) emerged that appealed to commoners and the military. Because Zen was adopted by many in the military, which controlled Japan until 1868, it became enormously influential in Japanese culture in general. (The separate schools are described in the following section.)

Some Major Schools of Mahayana

The many ideals of Mahayana Buddhism contain the seeds for a variety of schools of intellectual interpretation and practice. One such ideal—the notion that kindness is the supreme sign of enlightened awareness—has allowed many pre-Buddhist beliefs and practices to continue within Mahayana Buddhism: old gods receive new names, making them into heavenly Buddhas and bodhisattvas; old beliefs are absorbed; and old practices persist with new meanings. As we discussed earlier, Mahayana Buddhism (as well as other religions) also recognizes that people find themselves at different stages of spiritual evolution. Thus, whatever helps a person move to the next stage of awareness may be religiously acceptable. This is the notion of "skillful means": some people need images to look at and gods to pray to; other people need a community of friends; and a very few need

Mahayana often absorbed pre-Buddhist gods. Here, at the entrance to a Japanese temple, we see wooden sculptures of such deities, intended to ward off evil spirits.

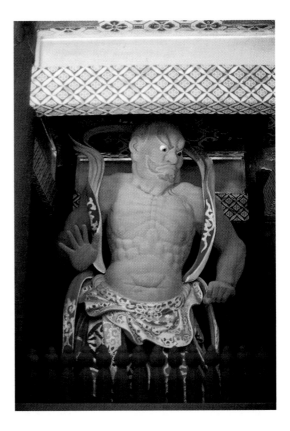

only silence and emptiness. Finally, the multiplicity of Mahayana texts invites many philosophical and practical approaches, as one Buddhist group focuses on one text and another Buddhist group focuses on another. The sects of Mahayana Buddhism thus show a wide variety in attitudes toward the use of art and ritual, toward the acceptance of pleasure, and toward worldly success.

These interesting differences are exhibited in the major sects of Japan, described in the following pages. Only one of the Japanese sects we will cover did not come originally from China. Most of the others, though, began in China and were then carried to Korea and Japan, both by missionaries from China and by students from Korea and Japan who traveled to China to study. Looking at the sects that came from China to Japan suggests what the separate sects were once like in China. Over time, Buddhist sects in China and Korea tended to borrow from each other and to blend. In Japan, however, the sects have remained fairly separate. Their Japanese names, being well known, are given in the following headings.

Shingon   The name of this school, *Shingon* (Chinese: *Zhen-yan, Chen-yen*), which means "true word," refers to the use of sacred chants, called *mantras.* We might recall that the spread of Mahayana Buddhism in China was due in part to the magical effects that were thought to come from Buddhist ritual. People believed that Buddhist ritual, if carefully performed, would provide security for rulers, children for married couples, and more favorable agricultural conditions for farmers.

Behind Shingon ritual is a focus on experiencing union with the cosmic Buddha nature. This can be accomplished through chanting mantras, accompanied by a multitude of rituals and ritual objects. Foremost among these rituals is a fire ceremony, the *Goma,* a continuation of the Vedic fire ceremony. In this ceremony, the priest builds a fire within a square sacred space bounded by colored cords. The priest throws wood and leaves slowly into the fire, symbolically destroying all egotistic hindrances to mystical union.

Shingon uses two **mandalas,** which are geometrical designs, usually painted on cloth, that present reality in symbolic form. One mandala, the Kongo-kai ("diamond-world") mandala, shows the universe from the point of view of wisdom. The other, the Tai-zo ("womb") mandala, represents the universe from the point of view of compassion.

Shingon was brought to Japan from China by Kukai (774–835 C.E.), a Japanese monk who studied in China and returned to Japan with a knowledge of ritual and with books, mandalas, and altar implements. As Kukai became influential among the aristocrats of the new capital of Japan, he instituted a network of Shingon temples, which spread his sect across southern Honshu and the island of Shikoku. The monastic center that he founded is located at Mount Koya, near Osaka. After his death, he received the name Kobo Daishi ("the Great Master who broadly spreads the Dharma"), and under that name he has become a venerated cultural hero in Japan.

An image of the bodhisattva Jizo is backed by a painting of the Shingon Kongo-kai mandala.

Shingon, because of its love of ritual, has inspired many arts, particularly sculpture and painting. It has similarities with Tibetan Buddhism, and it thus contains some elements of Vajrayana Buddhism (discussed later in this chapter).

Tendai The Tendai (Chinese: Tiantai, T'ien-t'ai) sect is named for the greatest Chinese monastic mountain institution at Mount Tiantai ("heavenly terrace"), where the sect began in eastern China. A large complex of monasteries arose there.[18] The Tendai school has focused on ritual, much like Shingon. In Japan, this sect was favored by the emperor and his court for the expected benefits and protection it would bring to the country. The Japanese monk who went to China and returned with skills in Tendai Buddhism was Saicho (767–822), who later received the honorary title Dengyo Daishi ("the Great Master who transmits the teachings"). Tendai's center, Enryaku-ji, is located on Mount Hiei, north of Kyoto. Although the earlier complex of more than 1,200 monastery buildings was burned in the late sixteenth century, what has been rebuilt is quite extensive.

Saicho borrowed from many sources. In addition to his use of ritual, he and his followers accepted various devotional practices, such as regularly chanting the name of Amitabha (Amida), the Buddha of the Western Paradise. Another practice was to take walks that lasted many days, a tradition that grew out of the austerities of Japanese ascetics living in the mountains.

Jodo, or Pure Land   The Pure Land (Chinese: Jingtu, Ching-t'u) school created a devotional form of Buddhism that could be practiced by laypeople as well as monks. The cult of bodhisattvas already existed in India and central Asia, but it had great appeal in China, too. Pure Land Buddhism in China can be traced back to the monk Tan Luan (T'an Luan, c. 476–542). Legend says that he instituted the devotion to Amitabha Buddha as the result of a vision. Complete devotion to this Buddha, the monk thought, would result in the believer's rebirth in Amitabha's "Pure Land," the Western Paradise. Devotees regularly repeated a short phrase, derived from early Mahayana scriptures and praising Amitabha Buddha. At first the repetition of the Buddha's name was a monastic practice, but it then spread to the laity. In Chinese, the phrase is *Namo Amito-fo*; in Japanese, it is *Namu Amida Butsu*. Both mean "Praise to Amitabha Buddha." Daily repetition and recitation at the moment of death were thought to ensure the believer's rebirth in the Western Paradise.

In Japan, the Pure Land movement was spread by the monk Honen (1133–1212), who was originally a Tendai monk at Mount Hiei. His movement became a separate sect called Jodo Shu ("Pure Land sect"). Shinran (1173–1262), a disciple of Honen, continued the laicization of the *nembutsu*, as the chant is called in Japanese. He taught that human actions to attain salvation were unimportant in comparison to the saving power of the Buddha. The movement that Shinran began eventually grew into the Jodo Shin Shu ("True Pure Land sect"), which is now the largest Buddhist sect in Japan.

Pure Land Buddhism has inspired—and continues to inspire—the arts. In sculpture and painting, Amida (Amitabha) is often shown at the center of a triad. At his left is Kannon (the bodhisattva Avalokiteshvara) and at his right is Seishi (the bodhisattva Mahasthama-prapa). The same images, sometimes drawn in gold on indigo paper, often appear in manuscripts of the Lotus Sutra.

Nichiren   Unlike the other sects discussed thus far, Nichiren began in Japan. Its founder was a Tendai monk, Nichiren (1222–1282). After being trained at Mount Hiei, Nichiren sought a simpler path than Tendai, which used many sutras and practices in the search for enlightenment. Out of the thousands of Mahayana texts, Nichiren wanted to find one that contained all the essential teachings of Buddhism. Following the lead of the Tendai tradition, which had already given much attention to the Lotus Sutra, Nichiren asserted that the Lotus Sutra was indeed the embodiment of all essential religious teaching. He thought of himself as a reincarnation of a minor Buddha in the Lotus Sutra (his monastic name *Nichiren* means "sun lotus"). His sect uses a chant that honors this sutra: *Namu Myoho Renge Kyo,* meaning "Praise to the mystic law of the Lotus Sutra." Devout followers repeat the mantra many times a day, especially in the morning and evening. They believe that doing so will connect them with the divine power of the universe.

Of the many sects of Buddhism, Nichiren is perhaps the most materially oriented, the offshoot called Nichiren Sho-shu is especially so. It values the material world and earthly success and aims at the creation of a peaceful, abundant society here on earth. A secular organization of Nichiren Sho-shu, called Soka Gakkai, works to reform society through political means, and some of its members have run as political candidates and been elected to the Japanese Diet (parliament). The political interest is in keeping with the nationalism of the founder, the monk Nichiren.

Nichiren Buddhism was virtually unknown outside Japan until after World War II, when American military personnel stationed there married Nichiren Buddhist women, who then brought their belief to the United States. Nichiren Sho-shu of America (NSA) has a center in Los Angeles. Its goal-oriented practice has been attractive to some westerners, and several celebrities practice this faith.

ZEN BUDDHISM: ENLIGHTENMENT THROUGH EXPERIENCE

Zen Buddhism, a school of Mahayana Buddhism, began in China and was carried to Japan, like most of the schools just mentioned. Its influence is so significant that it needs to be discussed apart from the other schools of Mahayana Buddhism. Zen takes its name from the seventh step of the Noble Eightfold Path—*dhyana* ("meditation"). In Chinese the word is *chan (ch'an),* and in Japanese it is *zen.* (In the discussion here, *Chan* refers to the sect in China, and *Zen* refers to the sect as it developed in Japan.) The complexity that had overtaken Chinese Buddhism helped create a counterbalancing movement toward simplification. For the Chan sect in China, simplification came from looking directly to the enlightenment experience of Siddhartha Gautama. Siddhartha had become the Buddha, the Enlightened One, through his practice of meditation. Although he did not deny the value of ritual, the Buddha did not think that it led to enlightenment. Taking after the Buddha, the members of the Chan movement, in their desire for enlightenment, favored the technique of seated meditation, just as Siddhartha Gautama had.

Chan Buddhism traces itself back to a Buddhist monk named Bodhidharma, who is said to have come to China (about 470 C.E.) from India or cen-

Although Zen monks spend much time in the practice of meditation, they also teach techniques that lead to enlightenment.

tral Asia and in China began his Meditation school. Bodhidharma is often shown sitting in meditation, with Western facial features, swarthy skin, a light beard, and an earring. In paintings, he faces a wall to indicate his strong desire to block out anything that would distract him from his meditation. It has been said that he meditated for so long that his legs became withered. He is the embodiment of patience and persistence.

The native Chinese religious and philosophical movement called Taoism (see Chapter 6) undoubtedly paved the way for Chan Buddhism and influenced it. Taoism had similar ideals: silence, detachment, acceptance, distrust of symbolization, and union with the universe. Taoism also practiced meditation. Taoism may have added to Buddhism its own esteem for the natural world and its appreciation for humor, although exactly how Taoism influenced Chan is debated. There are also Confucian elements in Chan and Zen, such as the communal nature of monastery life and the transmission of realization from master to disciple.

In the long history of Buddhism, some teachers have emphasized the importance of regular meditation and the effectiveness of meditative techniques, saying that they produce enlightenment gradually but inevitably, like the coming of dawn. Others have stressed that enlightenment can occur as a sudden awakening to one's true nature, like a flash of lightning, anywhere and at any time. One Chinese school, the "northern school," is thought to have taught a gradual method of attaining enlightenment, while the "southern school" advocated methods aiming at a sudden experience of enlightenment. In China, the "northern school" eventually died out, and Chan and Zen later assumed the possibility of sudden enlightenment. Both of the two main Zen schools of Japan today—Rinzai and Soto—descend from the "southern school" of Chan Buddhism. The Soto school values meditation, which it calls "just sitting." Consequently it is considered to be a bit more relaxed than the stricter Rinzai school, which focuses on the ideal

Manual labor, here ▶
practiced in a Korean
temple, is a Zen technique
for emptying the mind.

of sudden enlightenment and makes use of additional techniques for enlightenment (discussed in the following section).

The enlightenment experience (called **satori,** or *kensho*) brings an awareness of the unity of oneself with the rest of the universe. The enlightened person knows that human distinctions and separations—mine, yours; this, that; one, many—are distinctions that societies and individuals' minds create and then project onto other people and things. Such distinctions are not ultimate, though, for all human beings consist of the same basic energy of the universe, appearing in many varied shapes. This experience of ultimate oneness brings new insights and emotions to the art of living: less anxiety over attaining goals, less concern about death, and an appreciation for the preciousness of everyday life.

Zen Techniques for Enlightenment

The most fundamental Zen technique for reaching enlightenment is regular "sitting meditation," called *zazen.* In Zen monasteries, zazen is normally done for several hours in the morning and evening. It involves sitting in silence with one's back straight and centered, keeping the body still, and taking deep and regular breaths. (In traditional practice, the meditator sits with crossed legs on a cushion on the floor; but sitting meditation outside a monastery can also be done in a chair.) The surroundings should be as peaceful as possible. As a beginner, the meditator is taught just to focus on his or her inhalation and exhalation, to mentally repeat a word, or to count each breath up to ten and then exhale and begin the count again on the following inhalation. These are just simple techniques for quieting the mind and focusing on the moment. The mind becomes more peaceful, and ideally, with long practice, a state of simple awareness takes over as one's "true nature" is revealed.[19]

A question, called a **koan,** is another technique for attaining awareness. Its origin is uncertain, but the name derives from the Chinese *gong-an* (*kung-an*), translated as "public discussion." The koan is not a question that can be easily answered using logic. It demands pondering. Consider, for example, the question, Why did the monk Bodhidharma come from the West? An appropriate answer could be, "the bush in the garden"—or any response that mentions an ordinary object. The meaning of this apparently odd answer is that Bodhidharma's whole purpose was to make people wake up to the wondrous nature of even simple objects in everyday life. Sometimes a good answer to a koan need not be a verbal response, but rather an appropriate action, such as lifting up a hand, taking off a shoe, holding up a flower, or even raising an eyebrow.[20]

Manual labor is also essential to Zen training. In a Zen monastery, work in the garden and kitchen and the repair and cleaning of the monastery are techniques to combat the inadequacy of words to describe reality. Zen, influenced here by Taoism, maintains that words are often barriers that keep us from immediate contact with the true nature of things. Silent meditation

blended with direct experience of the physical world can take us beyond words and thoughts to experience reality itself.

Buddhism and the Arts of Japan

Many people assume that Buddhism has had a role in shaping the arts of Japan. As a matter of fact, what we think of as "Japanese style" is a mixture of Shinto (Chapter 7), Buddhist influences (especially Zen), and traditional Japanese attitudes toward nature. Although Zen has indeed influenced Japanese arts, the extent of its influence will always be debated. After all, the various arts were developed not only by monks but more often by craftsmen and talented amateurs under the influence of Buddhism. And in the last three hundred years, these arts have taken on a life of their own, carried on by laypeople and organized by hereditary teaching institutions.

Haiku   A *haiku* is an extremely short poem. In Japan, longer Chinese poetic forms were telescoped and refined. The model haiku is a 17-syllable poem written in three lines (the first in five syllables, the second in seven, and the third, again, in five). The ideal traditional haiku should mention or suggest the season, and, like a good photograph, it should capture the essence of a moment before it passes.

Basho (1644–1694) is considered the greatest of Japan's haiku writers. The following poem is widely quoted and considered to be his masterpiece:

Old pond:
A frog jumps in.
Sound of water.

Why, we may wonder, is this poem held in such esteem? On first reading, it seems simple, insignificant. But at closer inspection, it reveals intriguing balance and contrast. There are many possible interpretations. The old pond suggests timelessness, but the splash is momentary, representing every daily event when seen against the backdrop of eternity. Or the frog could represent a human being; the pond, the mind; and the splash, the sudden breakthrough to enlightenment. Perhaps the frog signifies the Buddhist monk in meditation, while the pond suggests all of Buddhist teaching. Or maybe the frog symbolizes the poet himself and the splash the poet's insight. Thus, the imagery can be taken both literally and in several equally valid symbolic ways.

Tea Ceremony   The making, drinking, and offering of tea to guests has developed into a fine art in Japan, called *chado* (or *sado*, "the way of tea"). Bringing guests together for a ritual tea ceremony in Japanese is called *cha no yu* ("hot water for tea"). The drinking of tea had first been used in Chinese monasteries for medicinal purposes and as an aid for staying awake during meditation. There, tea drinking also developed some ritual elements. Tea drinking was then carried to Japan and was practiced assiduously both by Zen monks and lay disciples. Under the tea master

The tea ceremony, which grew out of Buddhist practice, has become a fine art in Japan.

Sen no Rikyu (1522–1591), the tea ceremony took on its highly stylized current form.[21]

The essence of the Japanese tea ceremony is the gathering of a few guests, the preparation of green tea, and the offering of tea and sweets. The tea ceremony normally takes place in a tea pavilion, whose design is inspired by a rustic country hut, often mentioned in Chinese poetry. Today, these pavilions may look deliberately small and rustic but often cost far more to build in a traditional style than in a more contemporary manner. (Tea ceremonies can also be given for many people in a large room, often involving costly displays.)

Guests approach the tea pavilion along a garden path of stones and wash their hands at a stone basin with a bamboo ladle. They enter the room and kneel before the *tokonoma,* an alcove at the front of the room adorned by a hanging scroll and a flower arrangement. After pausing to appreciate the scroll and flower arrangement, the guests proceed to cushions on one side of the room. At the other side of the room, the host kneels in front of a lighted charcoal brazier and ritually cleanses the tea bowl and serving implements. A plate of sweet cakes is then offered, to balance the taste of the green tea. Next, the host stirs boiling water into the powdered green tea and offers some to each guest. Conversation is usually limited to appreciative remarks and questions about the scroll, the tea, the tea bowl, and other objects in the room. The purpose of the ceremony is to create and enjoy together an atmosphere of harmony and beauty, where each object, action, and word contributes to the tranquil experience.

Ceramics   Bowls used in the tea ceremony look deliberately natural, almost as if they were dug up out of the ground. They often look rough and unfinished, with earth-colored glazes dripping down their sides. The rims sometimes are not quite even, and colors are not always uniform. Sometimes there are even bubbles and cracks in the ceramic. All this is deliberate. The accidents of firing the bowls in the kiln are appreciated, as are the subtle shades of earth tones that are produced. The aim is, paradoxically, to create pieces that exhibit deliberate naturalness and a calculated spontaneity.

Ikebana   The word for Japanese-style flower arrangement—*ikebana*—means "living flower." Each arrangement is designed to suggest flowers in their natural state, as if a piece of garden were brought inside a home—even if the suggestion of "natural state" is artfully accomplished with clippers and wire!

Flower arrangement can be traced back to the offerings of flowers placed on altars in the temples of China and Japan. But ikebana grew into a unique art form of its own, and examples of ikebana now are found in restaurants, offices, and homes.

Ikebana is quite different from Western flower arrangement, which tends to be dense, symmetrical, and colorful. Ikebana is the opposite. The arrangements are airy, asymmetrical, and generally of no more than two colors. Effective ikebana is temporary sculpture, lasting but a few days and changing every day. Thus, some see ikebana as a manifestation of Buddhist insight into impermanence.

Garden Design   In China and Japan, gardens have long been an essential part of architecture, planned along with the buildings they complement. Garden designers are ranked as highly as poets and artists. Some gardens are created for strolling, others for seated contemplation from under an eave. They are not essentially Buddhist, of course, and not all monasteries have a garden. But they are found frequently enough in Buddhist environs for us to say that gardens have been used to present Buddhist ideals.

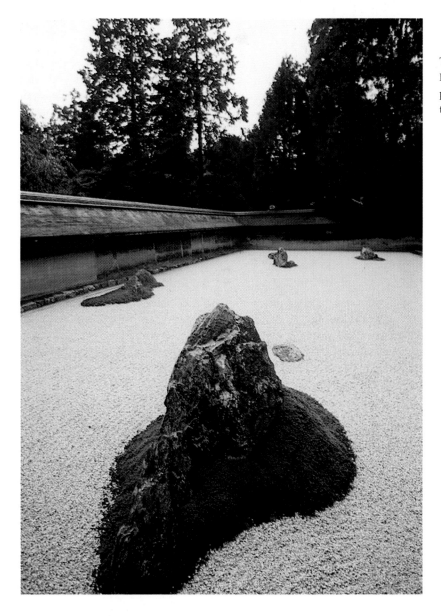

The monastery garden of Ryoan-ji expresses the peaceful simplicity that is the hallmark of Zen.

A famous example is the rock garden at Ryoan-ji, in northwest Kyoto. Ryoan-ji garden, enclosed on two sides by a low earthen wall, consists of five clusters of large boulders set in raked white gravel. The rocks and gravel suggest mountain peaks rising through clouds or islands in a river. The fascination of the garden is the relation between the clusters of boulders. Viewed this way, the boulders seem more like ideas in a great mind. The only vegetation in the garden is the moss at the base of the stones and the trees beyond the wall. Really more like an x-ray of an ideal garden, Ryoan-ji would seem to be unchanging because of its stony nature; but it changes a great deal, depending on the season, the weather, the light, and the time of day.

Calligraphy and Painting Calligraphy (Greek: "beautiful writing") is a highly prized art form in China and Japan. Because the characters used in Japanese and Chinese writing are closer to pictures and to drawing than they are to alphabet letters, they have a great range of vitality and beauty. The Zen ideal is to produce what is spontaneous but also profound, and because writing is done with an inkbrush, great expressiveness in darkness, weight, movement, and style of characters is possible. Furthermore, the ink cannot be erased, and the result is thought to be the immediate expression of the writer's personality and level of awareness. When fine calligraphic talent is employed to write a striking phrase or poem, the result is doubly powerful.

Painting is closely related to calligraphy, because both are done with the same type of brush. Frequently, calligraphy and pictures are combined in the same work, so that one reinforces the other. Zen-style painting is done quickly, often taking nature as its subject and ordinarily using black, white, and intermediate shades of gray. Some Zen-inspired painting is almost cartoonlike, as exhibited in satirical drawings of Zen personages and quick sketches of everyday objects, such as brooms and buckets.

The epitome of Zen simplicity in art is the *enso,* a black circle, almost always done in a single, quick stroke on paper or a piece of wood. The empty circle represents the emptiness of all reality.

VAJRAYANA BUDDHISM: THE "DIAMOND VEHICLE"

Mahayana Buddhism in India developed practices and beliefs that have sometimes been called esoteric (hidden, not openly taught), such as the use of special chants and rituals to gain supranormal powers. When some of these traditions entered Tibet, Indian Mahayana Buddhism joined with Tibetan shamanism to create Tibetan Buddhism, a complex system of belief, art, and ritual. Although Vajrayana actually includes other forms of esoteric Buddhism, Tibetan Buddhism is its most prominent expression.

The name *Vajrayana* means the "vehicle of the diamond" or "vehicle of the lightning bolt." The name suggests strength, clarity, wisdom, and flashes of light, all of which are associated with the enlightened awareness that this vehicle seeks to transmit. Vajrayana Buddhism is sometimes considered a third branch of Buddhism because of its complexity and unique elements. Many, however, see Vajrayana as a special form of Mahayana.

Origins, Practice, and Literature of Tibetan Buddhism

The pre-Buddhist Tibetan religion worshiped the powers of nature. As was the case with many native religions, these powers were often envisioned as demons that had to be appeased. Shamanistic rituals involving animal sacrifice and the use of bones, dance, and magical incantations were intended to control the demonic powers.

Buddhist Festivals

The most important Buddhist festivals focus on the birth of the Buddha, his enlightenment, his death, the celebration of the New Year, and sometimes the commemoration of the dead. The exact dates for these celebrations and memorials differ from culture to culture.

In Theravada Buddhist countries, one great celebration (Vesak) recalls the birth, the enlightenment, and the death of the Buddha. It is celebrated at the time of the full moon in May.

In Mahayana Buddhism, the three festivals of the Buddha's life are separate. His birth is celebrated on the eighth day of the fourth month; his enlightenment is commemorated in winter on Bodhi Day, the eighth day of the twelfth month; and his death is recalled in early spring on the fifteenth day of the second month. (Chinese and Korean Buddhists follow the lunar calendar, while Japanese Buddhists use the Western calendar.)

Celebration of the New Year often includes a visit to a temple to end the old year and the sharing of a vegetarian meal to welcome the new year. (The Japanese keep the Western New Year, while the Chinese celebrate their lunar New Year in February.)

In Japan the dead are remembered in a midsummer festival called O-Bon, derived from older Chinese practice. It has blended with Shinto elements and a belief in the Mahayana bodhisattva Jizo, who guides the dead back to the spirit world. If possible, the spirits' return is lighted with candles that drift down a stream or out into the ocean.

Festive lanterns are part of the Buddha's birthday celebration in Seoul.

In the summertime, circular O-Bon dances are performed in Japan to welcome the temporary return of ancestors to homes.

This Tibetan religion was challenged by a new religion, a special type of Buddhism practiced in northeast India, named "Tantric Buddhism" for its scriptures, the *Tantras* ("spread out"). Tantric Buddhism opposed the original Buddhist detachment from the world and its negative attitude toward bodily pleasure. The Tantras taught that the body and all its energies could be used to reach enlightenment. For Tantric Buddhism, enlightenment is an experience of ultimate oneness that occurs when a practitioner unites all opposites. Sexual union is a powerful experience of unity, and Tantric Buddhism uses the imagery and (rarely) the practice of sexual union to help attain enlightenment. In its imagery and belief system, Tantric Buddhism shows influence from Hinduism—particularly the Hindu tendency to pair a male and a female deity and the love of multiple deities. Vajrayana believes the divine Buddha nature expresses itself in a multitude of male and female deities.

A form of Tantric Buddhism first entered Tibet in the seventh century and was spread by Indian missionaries. Tradition holds that a king named Song-tsen-gam-po (fl. c. 630) became its patron and made it the national religion. In the beginning, native priests fought against this new religion, but a legendary Buddhist monk named Padmasambhava, who came from India in the late eighth century, reconciled the two religions and turned the native demonic gods of Tibet into guardian deities of Buddhism.

The resulting religion blended shamanistic interests, the sexual imagery of Tantric Buddhism, and traditional Buddhist elements, such as the chanting of sutras, meditation, the ideal of nonviolence, and the search for enlightenment. Monks thus were called upon not only as teachers but also as doctors and shamans; they were expected to bring health, control weather, and magically protect worshipers from death. A Tibetan teacher is often called **lama,** a Tibetan translation of the word *guru.*

Although the Indian ideals of the wandering holy man and cave-dwelling solitary did not die out in Tibetan Buddhism, they were not well suited for a climate as severe as that of the cold and barren Tibetan plateau. More compatible, it seemed, were the large monastic complexes that had grown up in late Indian Buddhism. The Tibetan version of such a complex often looked like a fortified hilltop castle, and was in effect a complete city for sometimes thousands of monks, containing libraries, prayer halls, kitchens, storage areas, and large courtyards for public performances. A written form of the Tibetan language was created for the translation of Buddhist scriptures from India. It also made possible the writing of scriptural commentaries and other treatises.

Over time, the practice of celibacy declined, and the heads of Tibetan monasteries frequently passed on their control to their sons. The consumption of meat and alcohol was common, as well. A reform movement, however, emerged under the monk Tsong Kha-pa (1357–1419), demanding that monks be unmarried and that strict monastic practice be reinstituted. His sect, as a result, came to be known as Gelug-pa, meaning "party of virtue." (It is also commonly called the Yellow Hat sect because of the tall, crested yellow hats that the monks wear during religious services.) This sect grew powerful. It helped create many of the greatest monasteries, full of art and complete sets of Buddhist scriptures, and it provided Tibet with its political leadership for several centuries. The executive head of the Gelug-pa is called the Dalai Lama ("great ocean superior one").

It became a common belief in Tibetan Buddhism that certain major lamas are reincarnations of earlier lamas, who in turn are considered emanations of Buddhas and bodhisattvas. (A belief in reincarnation thus solved

The Potala in Lhasa, the residence of the Dalai Lama until 1959, is the symbolic center of Tibetan Buddhism.

the problem of transmission of leadership, which in a celibate monastic order cannot pass to a son.) The lineage of the Dalai Lama, for example, traces itself back to a nephew of Tsong Kha-pa, the first of the line of succession. Each Dalai Lama is considered to be an emanation of Avalokiteshvara, the heavenly bodhisattva of compassion. When a major lama dies, his reincarnation is sought, found, and trained. The current Dalai Lama, for example, was found in eastern Tibet. A delegation of monks, after consulting a state oracle about the place of rebirth, took objects (such as prayer beads) that had been used by the previous Dalai Lama and mixed them with similar objects. The boy who was recognized as the current Dalai Lama selected only those objects used by the previous Dalai Lama, helping to prove his identity.

The literature of Tibetan Buddhism consists of two large collections of writings. The Kanjur is the core, made up of works from the Tripitaka (mostly Mahayana sutras and the vinaya with Tantric texts). The second part, the Tenjur, comprises commentaries on scripture and treatises on a wide variety of disciplines, such as medicine and grammar. The collection exceeds four thousand works.

Ritual and the Arts

Vajrayana Buddhism is interested in the acquisition of both internal and external powers and holds that such powers may be attained through proper ritual. The ritual allows the individual to become identified with a particular

Prayer wheels, which contain sacred chants in written form, are turned by Tibetan Buddhists as an act of devotion.

Buddha or heavenly bodhisattva, thus giving the individual the power and protection of that heavenly being.

Because correctly performed ceremony brings identification with a powerful deity, ceremonial objects play significant roles. We have noted some devices (the mantra and mandala) used in earlier Mahayana practices that were subsequently adopted by Vajrayana, but in Vajrayana, these devices take on special importance.

Among the significant ritual objects is the **vajra,** a metal object somewhat like a divining rod or scepter that represents a stylized bolt of lightning. The vajra is associated with diamond-hardness, power, and insight. It is held in the right hand and suggests kind action. It is used with the bell, which is held in the left hand and symbolizes wisdom. When used together, one in each hand, they represent the union of wisdom and compassion. The vajra and bell are essential to Tibetan Vajrayana ritual in a way that other religious objects (mentioned in the following paragraphs) are not.

Another important Tibetan Buddhist object is the prayer wheel, which comes in all sizes—from very tiny to as tall as a two-story building. A prayer wheel is a cylinder that revolves around a central pole. Inside the cylinder are pieces of paper inscribed with sacred phrases. It is believed that the turning of the written prayers creates as much good karma as if one were to recite them. Believers often carry small prayer wheels and turn them as they walk, while the devout push or pull large prayer wheels at temples and in public places. Some prayer wheels are placed in streams, where the flowing water turns them. The same principle applies to the wind blowing through prayer flags, which consist of square or triangular pieces of cloth containing inscriptions.

Certain ritual objects evoke awe at first because of their connection with death. They are meant to inoculate the believer against the fear of death by forcing the individual to accept death long before it comes. For example, human thighbones are used to make small trumpets, and half of a human skull, decorated with gold or silver, might be used as a ceremonial bowl. Paintings and statues of fierce deities often have a similar function.

Music and dance, used by shamans to protect against demons, also play an important role in Tibetan Vajrayana. Drums, long trumpets, bells, and cymbals are used to accompany a deep, slow droning chant. The effect is hypnotic and evokes the sacredness that underlies reality.

In Vajrayana as well as Mahayana, a mantra is chanted or written to bring power and wisdom through repetition. The most highly revered mantra in Tibetan Vajrayana is *Om mani padme hum!* (literally translated, "Om—the jewel—-oh lotus—-ah!"). One translation employs Tantric sexual symbolism: "The jewel is in the lotus." The jewel and lotus represent sexual opposites, and the mantra represents sexual union—symbolic of enlightenment. In yet another symbolic translation—"The jewel *is* the lotus."—the jewel represents the divine Buddha nature, and the lotus represents the everyday world of birth and death. Hence, the mantra means that this world of suffering is the same as the Buddha nature and that the enlightened person sees that they are the same. Both symbolic translations and their messages are valid. In addition to this mantra, there are many others, each of which is believed to be sacred to a particular Buddha or bodhisattva or which is valuable for obtaining a certain result.

Symbolic hand gestures (**mudras**) on statues of the Buddha are common throughout all forms of Buddhism. For example, the right hand extended with the palm outward and the fingers pointing up is a mudra of blessing; if the palm is open but the hand is turned downward, the mudra symbolizes generosity. In Vajrayana, a large number of mudras have evolved to convey more esoteric meanings, such as the unity of opposites. Mudras also help distinguish individual Buddhas and bodhisattvas within the large pantheon of deities. Moreover, mudras can be performed to a chant, with the two hands simultaneously forming mudra after mudra to create a harmonious balance of opposites.

The mandala (geometrical art form) that is used in some forms of Mahayana takes on great variety and complexity in Tibetan Buddhism. We might recall that a mandala is a sacred cosmic diagram, often used in meditation. It may represent in symbolic form the entire universe, the palace of a deity, or even the self. A common form is a circle within or enclosing a square or a series of circles and squares that grow smaller and smaller as they come closer to the center of the design; another form looks like a checkerboard of many squares. A mandala usually appears as a painting on cloth, but it may take many forms. For some ceremonies, monks create a mandala in sand and then destroy it at the end of the ritual, expressing vividly the Buddhist teaching that everything must change.

Any painting on cloth is called a *thangka* (pronounced *tan'-ka*). In addition to mandala designs, a wide variety of subjects can appear on thangkas. Common images are Buddhas, bodhisattvas, and guardian deities, painted in both benevolent and terrifying forms (the terrifying forms both frighten away demons and chasten the believer). The female deity Tara, who represents mercy, appears in two major forms (white and green) and in several minor forms. We also find frequent representations of the monk Padmasambhava and other noted teachers. The existence of so many celestial beings and saints—with their attendants and symbolic objects—provides artists with a multitude of subjects to paint and sculpt.

PERSONAL EXPERIENCE: VISITING THE DALAI LAMA

For many in the West, a visit to the Dalai Lama means a visit with the most renowned teacher of Buddhism alive. As the religious leader of Tibetan Buddhism, the current Dalai Lama is fourteenth in the line. Until 1959, when he fled to escape advancing Chinese Communist soldiers, he was also the political leader of Tibet. With the permission of the Indian government, he and his advisors settled in Dharamsala, a hill town in northern India, where he continues to live today. He received the Nobel Peace Prize in 1989 for his promulgation of nonviolence and peace.

Through the kindness of a friend, I got a letter of introduction so that I could visit the Dalai Lama at his home. It was late spring when a colleague and I traveled on a packed and noisy bus into the foothills of the still-snowy Himalayas to Dharamsala. Dharamsala is actually two towns, Upper and Lower, and was once an English hill station where British colonials relaxed

The Dalai Lama's complex in Dharamsala offers views of the Himalayan foothills.

The Dalai Lama, the head of Tibetan Buddhism and Nobel Peace Prize Laureate, speaks frequently to both followers and the world community.

in the hot summer months. Now the English are mostly gone; Lower Dharamsala is inhabited by Indians; and Upper Dharamsala is primarily Tibetan.

After arriving, I called the monk-secretary of the Dalai Lama to confirm my appointment and then went out for a walk around Upper Dharamsala. In the center of the town, a group of large prayer wheels drew a small crowd of men and women in bright Tibetan clothing, moving from one wheel to the next. I stopped in a store, where I bought a white scarf to present to the Dalai Lama the next day. This is a traditional offering in high-altitude Tibet, where flowers are not easily obtainable.

The Dalai Lama lives in a modest villa near a large, modern Tibetan temple. At 2:00 P.M. we were ushered into a reception room. After five minutes, the Dalai Lama and his secretary entered. Both wore dark Tibetan monks' robes.

The Dalai Lama seemed a mixture of opposites. His handshake was firm but his manner gentle. His voice was deep, but his frequent laugh was high and bell-like. He seemed reserved behind his lively eyes. His accented English was good, but he would often speak to his secretary in Tibetan, checking on the proper translation of a word into English.

Our conversation was almost entirely about religion. We spent nearly an hour discussing the role of religion in the modern world. "Why does religion exist?" I asked. He said that religion was only a means to an end, which is human goodness.

"Is there any difference between a good person and a holy person?" "There is no such difference," he declared.

He said that it is quite possible to become trapped by the forms of religion, which should really lead beyond themselves to kindness and insight. "It is necessary to go further, beyond individual religions, and not be limited by the forms themselves. It may also be necessary to find new forms for religion," he said.

I began to ask him which of his teachers had been most influential. "I have been influenced by great pundits [sages]," he said. I nodded, thinking he was referring to special teachers he had encountered in his youth as a student. "The great pundits of the last few centuries," he added. I nodded again, now thinking he meant the great teachers discussed in books that he had read. But when he explained further, it was clear to me that these pundits who had personally influenced him were the teachers who had taught the previous Dalai Lamas, his earlier incarnations. I continued to nod but suddenly was aware that we had two very different ways of looking at existence.

We talked about the symbolism of colors and their use in Tibetan Buddhism. He pointed to my shirt, which was turquoise. "That is my favorite color," he exclaimed with a sharp laugh.

At the end of the interview, we went out into the garden. I left with the scarf I had brought—returned to me by the Dalai Lama as a memento of the visit. I also left with the feeling that I had met a good man who was indeed a holy man, too.

BUDDHISM, THE WEST, AND MODERN CHALLENGES

Buddhism has been attractive to people in the West for a long time. They appreciate its basically rational approach to understanding reality, which fits in well with a scientific orientation. Some appreciate what they see as its emphasis on awareness, self-reliance, and psychological development (even if, as critics argue, "using" Buddhism this way turns it into just another form of ego gratification). Many in the West are also attracted to the Buddhist ideal of nonviolence as a standard for civilized behavior in a multicultural world—an attraction that has been magnified by the Dalai Lama's selection for the Nobel Peace Prize in 1989.

Buddhism's first contact with the West occurred in the late eighteenth century, when translations of primarily Theravada material were brought back to Europe from Sri Lanka and Myanmar by English colonials and missionaries.

The opening of Japan to foreigners in the second half of the nineteenth century created a second wave of interest in Buddhism. French, English, and American people began to read about Japanese culture and to see photos of early Buddhist temples and examples of Buddhist-inspired art. Foreign interest dovetailed with anti-Buddhist government actions in Japan after 1868, which forced many Buddhist temples to sell some of their art. Japanese art was then collected widely in Europe and America, both by private collectors and by museums.

Exactly how much Buddhist influence a person sees in various forms of Japanese art is directly related to how much that person sees Buddhism's influence via Japan on the West. There is no doubt that the Japanese influence on Western art has been extraordinary since Japan opened to the West. French art of the late nineteenth century was invigorated by the discovery of Japanese prints and scrolls, which flooded into France after 1880. Asymmetry, a love of nature, and an appreciation for the passing moment—features of much Japanese art—began to appear in the work of the Impressionists and Postimpressionists, particularly Vincent van Gogh (1853–1890), Henri de Toulouse–Lautrec (1864–1901), and Claude Monet (1840–1926). (One of van Gogh's self-portraits was almost certainly influenced by pictures of Buddhist monks that he had seen.) Monet's Japanese-style water garden, with its pond of water lilies, at Giverny near Paris is a good example of the influence Japan had at the turn of the century in France.

Haiku and other forms of Japanese poetry began to influence Western poetry at the same time. We see this particularly in the Imagist school, which produced short poems that depended on a few strong images presented in simple language. Poets who exemplified this style include Ezra Pound (1885–1972), e. e. cummings (1894–1962), H. D. (Hilda Doolittle, 1886–1961), and William Carlos Williams (1883–1963).

A third wave of Buddhist influence came in the decades just after World War II, when U.S. soldiers returned from the American occupation of Japan. The great interest of the time was Zen (perhaps only loosely understood), which influenced the poetry of the Beat movement and the lifestyle of the counterculture. A Zenlike love of the spontaneous appears in the writing of Lawrence Ferlinghetti (b. 1919), Allen Ginsberg (1926–1997), Gary Snyder (b. 1930), and Jack Kerouac (1922–1969).

Zen centers, often under lay leadership, were established at this time in major cities in North and South America and Europe. These centers have allowed westerners to learn directly about Zen through both instruction and meditation. Some centers have also opened bookstores, vegetarian restaurants, and retreat centers.

A fourth wave of Buddhist influence is more recent and involves several types of Buddhism. Tibetan Buddhism has established communities of immigrant Tibetans and converts in many places in the United States

(California, Colorado, New York, Hawaii) and in Europe (Switzerland, France, Great Britain); and Tibetan Buddhist art is now regularly acquired and exhibited by museums. Nichiren Buddhism, from its new-world base in Los Angeles, has made many converts in California and in some large cities of the United States. And Asian immigrants from Taiwan, Hong Kong, and Southeast Asia have all begun their own temples and celebrations in major cities of North America, particularly Vancouver, Seattle, San Francisco, and Los Angeles.

In the past, Buddhism was spread by monks who taught, formed communities, and carried on Buddhist rituals for the laity. But much of the Buddhist influence in the West has come through books and art rather than through contact with monks. Western Buddhism has thus been somewhat more philosophical and academic than devotional. Much of it is practiced without ritual or even meditation. In addition, many centers are run not by monks but by married couples and other lay leaders. For those reasons, Buddhism in the West has lost some traditional monastic contact and some of the appreciation for rituals that thrives when religion and culture are closely connected.

Ironically, even as it gains followers in the West, Buddhism is under siege in many countries and regions that have been its traditional home. When Tibet was taken over by the Chinese government in 1959, the Dalai Lama fled and Tibetan Buddhism was severely repressed. At least a million Tibetans are thought to have died in the ensuing persecution, and several thousand monasteries were destroyed, particularly during the Cultural Revolution (1966–1976). In Korea, Christianity is making inroads, and now almost a quarter of the population is Christian. In Sri Lanka, the separatist movement in the north of the country leads Hindus and Buddhists to fight against each other, severely straining the tradition of nonviolence in both religious traditions. In Myanmar, Buddhist human rights activists have been jailed.

On the other hand, relations with the non-Buddhist world have brought new vigor to Buddhism in its traditional areas. For example, we now see Buddhist environmental groups in Thailand. (Members of one group place monks' orange robes around trees they hope to save.) There is growing interest in Buddhist monastic life for women and in female leadership roles. And although Buddhists have long been associated with certain types of compassionate work, they are now in some quarters turning their attention to newly perceived areas of injustice and inequality and sometimes even reconsidering cherished understandings of basic Buddhist teaching.

Buddhism is clearly entering a new phase in its long journey. In part, Buddhism can predict what that phase will bring: the one constant, as always, is change.

A monk in China offers the universal ▶
Buddhist gesture of greeting.

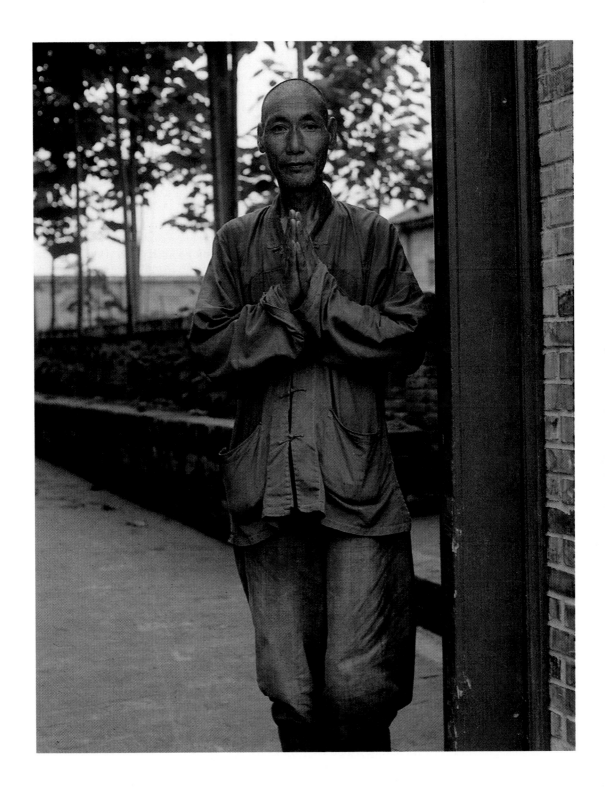

RELIGION BEYOND THE CLASSROOM

Buddhism has now spread widely enough in North America that it is easily accessible to those interested in experiencing it, and non-Buddhists are welcomed. (A directory at the back of the popular Buddhist magazine *Tricycle* lists monastic and practice centers across the continent.) Almost every large city has a Zen center, as well as temples for Chinese, Japanese, Thai, and Tibetan Buddhist practice. The West Coast and Hawai`i are particularly rich with people and places to visit. Japanese gardens are open to the public in such places as the Golden Gate Park in San Francisco and the Butchart Gardens in Victoria, British Columbia.

Travel in Asia allows the visitor to see Buddhist art in its traditional environs, where monks reside and hold services. Five countries in Asia offer westerners particularly rich experiences of Buddhism: Thailand and Sri Lanka for Theravada, Japan and South Korea for Mahayana, and China for both Mahayana and Vajrayana.

Thailand is easily accessible, because Bangkok is an airline hub for all of Southeast Asia. Although Bangkok is not an old city, it has several temples on a grand scale. At Wat Po, one can walk around a large but charming Reclining Buddha. Wat Phra Keo houses the famous Jade Buddha statue. And visitors can take an easy day trip by boat from Bangkok upriver to Ayutthaya, an old capital full of temples and sculpture in various states of preservation.

Sri Lanka is a tropical island south of India. One of the most moving statues of the Buddha anywhere is at Polonnaruwa. The statue, cut from the rock of a cliff, depicts the Buddha lying peacefully on his right side. The Buddha's face—certainly not the face of an 80-year-old—is serene. The serenity is reinforced by the drapery of his robe, which looks like sheets of water smoothly cascading over the Buddha's body. The delicacy of the face and clothing contrasts with the large, squarish feet, placed firmly together, which convey a sense of determination and strength. The other major sight in Sri Lanka is the ancient, great white stupa at Anuradhapura, a monument that exhibits the origins of the stupa shape.

Japan is dotted with thousands of Buddhist temples. The greatest concentration of historic temples is in the former capital cities Kyoto and nearby Nara. In Kyoto, essential sights include Ryoan-ji, the most famous Zen garden in the world; Kiyomizu-dera, a temple set on wooden pillars high on a hillside; and Kinkaku-ji, the Gold Pavilion. But this is only a small sample. Nara contains one of Japan's largest statues of the Buddha, the Daibutsu, housed in the largest wooden building in Japan.

South Korea is not well known to tourists but should be because of the exceptional natural beauty of this country's mountains and forests. South Korea's east coast has fine temples, many of which are located in the scenic national parks of Odae-san and Sorak-san. The greatest temple complex is Pulguk-sa, at Kyongju, in the southeast.

China has so much Buddhist art and architecture that one could spend years visiting its sights. Because most visitors arrive in Beijing, they can easily visit the Lama Temple (Yonghegong, a Vajrayana temple) in the city and hire a taxi to visit two temples in the Fragrant Hills (Xiangshan): Reclining Buddha Temple (Wofusi) and the Temple of the Azure Cloud (Biyunsi). Major cities all contain Buddhist temples, and cave art is featured at Datong and Dunhuang. A visit to the city of Lhasa in Tibet offers a melancholy glimpse into the formerly vibrant center of Tibetan Buddhism. The Dalai Lama once lived at the Potala, part of which is open to the public. The Jokhang, the former "cathedral" of Lhasa, can also be visited. More hopeful examples of Tibetan Buddhism can be experienced in Tibetan refugee communities in Nepal (such as at Patan in the Katmandu Valley) and in India (such as at Dharamsala).

In Asia, although Buddhist art can usually be seen in a religious setting, some of the most important Buddhist works are now displayed in museums—in Tokyo, Bangkok, Seoul, Taipei, New Delhi, and Beijing. Outside Asia, museums in large cities often have collections of Buddhist art. In North America, major museums are located in New York (Metropolitan Museum), Washington D.C. (Freer Gallery), Kansas City (Nelson Gallery–Atkins Museum), Boston (Museum of Fine Arts), Cleveland (Cleveland Museum of Art), Chicago (Art Institute), San Francisco (Asian Art Museum), Los Angeles (Los Angeles County Museum of Art), Seattle (Seattle Art Museum), Honolulu (Honolulu Academy of Arts), and Toronto (Ontario Art Museum). Museums in many European cities also have significant collections of Buddhist art, particularly in London (British Museum, Victoria and Albert Museum) and in Paris (Musée Guimet).

FOR FULLER UNDERSTANDING

1. Many immigrants to the United States from traditionally Buddhist countries continue to celebrate their cultural festivals and are usually quite welcoming of visitors. If your area has such festivals, participate and make notes on (or photograph or videotape) examples of Buddhist influences on the festivities.

2. Do a virtual journey over the world wide web of Buddhist sites, which range from semiprivate devotional websites to museum-based libraries of Buddhist art. Prepare an annotated bibliography of the websites you found most valuable, and describe some of the insights and questions that occurred to you as you explored.

3. Read a biography of the Dalai Lama and other books about Tibetan Buddhism. Prepare a written report on how the Dalai Lama's beliefs and actions earned him the Nobel Peace Prize.

4. Find out if there is a Buddhist meditation center in your area. Visit it, gather information, even take a classmate, and then make a report to your class.

5. Do some library research on American architect Frank Lloyd Wright (1867–1959) and his connections with Japan. Is there any evidence to suggest that Wright was influenced by Buddhist ideas or forms?

6. Around New Year's, phone Chinese restaurants in your area to see if any of them serves the seasonal meal *jai* ("monk's food"). If you find such a restaurant, go with a group of classmates or friends for the feast. Ask the manager or waiter about the tradition's origins, and report (perhaps after additional library research) on what you learned.

RELATED READINGS

Batchelor, Stephen. *The Tibet Guide*. London: Wisdom Publications, 1987. A thorough travel guide to Buddhist sites in Tibet.

Blofeld, John. *The Chinese Art of Tea*. London: Allen & Unwin, 1985. A first-person account of the author's direct experience of Buddhist practice. Blofeld, who lived in China before the Communist Revolution, provides in his book an interesting contrast to the better-known ritual of the Japanese tea ceremony.

Boucher, Sandy. *Turning the Wheel: American Women Creating the New Buddhism*. San Francisco: Harper & Row, 1985. A good witness to the growing role of women in Buddhism.

Ch'en, Kenneth. *Buddhism in China: A Historical Survey*. Princeton, NJ: Princeton University Press, 1970. A respected historical treatment of Chinese Buddhism.

deBary, William Theodore, ed. *The Buddhist Tradition in India, China, & Japan*. New York: Random House, 1972. A collection of readings from all traditions of Buddhist literature, with introductory commentary.

Jones, Ken. *The Social Face of Buddhism: An Approach to Social and Political Activity*. London: Wisdom, 1989. A description of the emerging activism in Buddhism.

Morrale, Don, ed. *Buddhist America: Centers, Retreats, Practices*. Santa Fe: John Muir Publications, 1988. A comprehensive listing of Buddhist centers in the United States.

Mosher, Gouverneur. *Kyoto: A Contemplative Guide*. Tokyo: Tuttle, 1964. A classic guidebook to carry and consult when visiting the major temples of Kyoto.

Rahula, Walpola. *What the Buddha Taught*. New York: Grove Press, 1959. A brief but philosophical approach to Buddhist teaching.

Ryokan. *One Robe, One Bowl: The Zen Poetry of Ryokan*. Edited by John Stevens. New York: Weatherhill, 1987. A collection of extremely beautiful short poems by a Zen wanderer who is only recently gaining acclaim.

Snelling, John. *The Buddhist Handbook: A Complete Guide to Buddhist Schools, Teaching, Practice, and History*. Rochester, VT: Inner Traditions, 1991. A knowledgeable summary of essential Buddhist information.

Statler, Oliver. *Japanese Pilgrimage*. New York: Morrow, 1983. A colorful and descriptive account of the author's pilgrimage to the Shingon Buddhist temples on the island of Shikoku in southern Japan.

Suzuki, D. T. *Zen and Japanese Culture*. Princeton, NJ: Princeton University Press, 1973. One of Suzuki's many books in English on Zen. Suzuki's writings were a major stimulus to the spread of Zen in English-speaking countries.

Tiyavanich, Kamala. *Forest Recollections*. Honolulu: University of Hawaii Press, 1997. A fascinating study of wandering monks of Thailand in the twentieth century, with many personal descriptions of individual monks.

Tonkinson, Carole, ed. *Big Sky Mind: Buddhism and the Beat Generation*. New York: Riverhead Books, 1995. A large collection of Buddhist-inspired writing by (and about) Beat writers, including Allen Ginsberg, Lawrence Ferlinghetti, Gary Snyder, and Jack Kerouac.

KEY TERMS

Amitabha Buddha (*ah-mee-tah'-buh*): The Buddha of the Western Paradise, a bliss-body Buddha in Mahayana.

Anatta (*un-nah'-tuh*): "No self"; the doctrine that there is no soul or permanent essence in people and things.

Anichcha (*uh-nee'-chuh*): Impermanence, constant change.

Arhat (*ahr'-hut*): In Theravada, a person who has practiced monastic disciplines and reached nirvana, the ideal.

Bodhi (*boh'-dee*): Enlightenment.

Bodhisattva (*boh'-dee-suh'-tvah*): "Enlightenment being"; in Mahayana, a person of deep compassion, especially one who does not enter nirvana but is constantly reborn to help others; a heavenly being of compassion.

Dharma (*dhur'-mah*): The totality of Buddhist teaching.

Dhyana (*dee-yah'-nuh*): "Meditation"; focusing of the mind; sometimes, stages of trance.

Dukkha (*doo'-kuh*): Sorrow, misery.

Guanyin: A popular bodhisattva of compassion in Mahayana.

Karuna (*kuh-roo'-nuh*): Compassion, empathy.

Koan (*koh'-ahn*): In Chan and Zen Buddhism, a question that cannot be answered logically; a technique used to test consciousness and bring awakening.

Lama: A Tibetan Buddhist monk.

Maitreya (*mai-tray'-yuh*): A Buddha (or bodhisattva) expected to appear on earth in the future.

Mandala (*mun'-duh-luh*): A circular design containing deities, geometrical forms, symbols, and so on that represent totality, the self, or the universe.

Mudra (*moo'-druh*): A symbolic hand gesture.

Nirvana (*nir-vah'-nuh*): The release from suffering and rebirth that brings inner peace.

Samadhi (*suh-mah'-dee*): A state of deep awareness, the result of intensive meditation.

Samsara (*suhm-sah'-ruh*): Constant rebirth and the attendant suffering; the everyday world of change.

Sangha (*suhng'-huh*): The community of monks and nuns; lowercased, *sangha* refers to an individual monastic community.

Satori (*sah-toh'-ree*): In Zen, the enlightened awareness.

Shunyata (*shoon'-ya-tah*): The Mahayana notion of emptiness, meaning that the universe is empty of permanent reality.

Stupa (*stoo'-puh*): A shrine, usually in the shape of a dome, used to mark Buddhist relics or sacred sites.

Sutra (*soo'-truh*): A sacred text, especially one said to record the words of the Buddha.

Tathata (*taht-ha-tah'*): "Thatness," "thusness," "suchness"; the uniqueness of each changing reality.

Trikaya (*trih-kah'-yuh*): The three "bodies" of the Buddha—the Dharmakaya (cosmic Buddha nature), the Sambhogakaya (celestial Buddhas), and the Nirmanakaya (historical Buddhas).

Tripitaka (*trih-pih'-tuh-kuh*): The three "baskets," or collections, of Buddhist texts.

Vajra (*vuhj'-ruh*): The "diamond" scepter used in Tibetan and other types of Buddhist ritual, symbolizing compassion.

CHAPTER 5

Jainism and Sikhism

 FIRST ENCOUNTER

While you are traveling from Delhi to Bombay, you cannot help overhearing a conversation in your train compartment. Two young Americans are explaining to a middle-aged Indian gentleman that they are traveling to the ashram of a Hindu guru just outside Bombay.

"She has many disciples in California, where we live. We'll stay in her ashram for six months, practicing hatha yoga and meditation," says the young woman, "then we'll travel. We'll be in India for almost a year. What do you recommend we see here in western India?"

"Let me think," says the gentleman. "Well, you might enjoy Elephanta Island near Bombay, known for its statue of Shiva. You would enjoy Goa, too; it's like a bit of Portugal on the Indian coast, with large old churches and fine beaches. And there are the caves of Ajanta and Ellora, famous for their sculpture." He tells the couple about the ferry boat that goes to the island and the bus transportation to the caves.

"Have you been yet to Amritsar, the sacred city of the Sikhs?" the gentleman asks. It is to the north of here. The Golden Temple there is lovely and sits in the middle of its own small lake." The couple responds that they have not been there but that they've heard of the Sikhs. "Sikh men let their hair grow long and wear turbans, I think," says the young man. The older gentleman confirms this.

The conversation then turns to the Jains. "Some live in the south, but there are also a good number in west and northwest India, with some beautiful temples and fine statues," the gentleman says. "The Jains, you know, were a big influence on Mahatma Gandhi, who came from Gujarat, north of Bombay. Jains teach strict nonviolence and are vegetarian, like the Hindus. In fact, I am a Jain myself," says the gentleman.

"Wasn't it hard for you to give up meat?" asks the young man.

"My dear sir, not at all," exclaims the man with shock. "You see, I have never even tasted it!"

The train arrives at the couple's station on the outskirts of Bombay, and the conversation closes abruptly. "Here is my card, with my address and business number in Bombay," says the gentleman. "Call me if I can be of further help. I would be happy to give you a tour of Bombay."

"Thank you very much. We'll be in touch with you after our stay at the ashram," says the young woman. They scramble to gather their backpacks and other things. When they are gone, the gentleman raises his eyes in wonder, and your eyes meet. He smiles beatifically.

SHARED ORIGINS

India is now home to two religions that are not well known in the West: Jainism and Sikhism. The first is ancient, and the other is relatively young. Adherents of the two religions can be found in limited numbers around the world, but the majority live in India.

Both religions have some connection with Hinduism, sharing with it certain characteristics, such as a belief in karma and rebirth. Furthermore, both of them, having developed in opposition to Hindu polytheism and ritualism, strive toward greater religious simplicity. In spite of their similarities, however, Jainism and Sikhism differ in their views of reality and in their emotional tones. Jainism is atheistic and sees the universe simply as natural forces in motion, yet it also recognizes the spiritual potential of each person. Like early Buddhism, Jainism emphasizes the ideals of extreme nonattachment and nonharm (*ahimsa*). Sikhism, to the contrary, embraces a devout monotheism and accepts meat eating and military self-defense. Regardless of their differences, both religions stress the importance of the individual's struggle to purify the self, to act morally, and to do good to others.

JAINISM

BACKGROUND

As the Aryans and their Vedic religion expanded eastward into the Ganges River valley, they naturally created opposition. As we saw in Chapter 4, some people rebelled against the growing strength of the caste system, and non-brahmins, especially the aristocrats, felt threatened by the power of the priests. Moved by compassion, some people opposed the animal sacrifices that were often a part of the Vedic ritual.

Two great religious movements grew out of this opposition. One—Buddhism—which we studied in Chapter 4, is well known because it spread beyond India. The other movement—Jainism—has remained less well known because, until recently, it has not sought converts in other lands. When they arose, both Buddhism and Jainism were influenced by some early Hindu ideas, but they may have also practiced much older ascetic traditions.

It is possible that Jainism has not spread widely because it is uncompromising: in it we find an extremist quality that is fascinating, thought provoking, and often noble. Tendencies toward nonviolence and austerity apparent in Hinduism and Buddhism are carried to their logical endpoint in Jainism, and the skepticism of early Buddhism is practiced rigorously. The study of Jainism, in fact, gives greater clarity to our understanding of those other Indian religions.

Although Jainism did not spread widely, its strong ideal of nonviolence has attracted interest throughout the world. We see its influence directly in the thought and work of Mahatma Gandhi and, indirectly, in the thought and work of Martin Luther King, Jr.

MAHAVIRA AND THE ORIGINS OF JAINISM

Jains date the origins of their religion to the distant past. They believe that in the present cycle of the universe, twenty-four great people have reached perfection; and though living in quite different centuries, these saints have been role models and guides who have shown the way to others. These saints are called **tirthankaras,** which can be translated as "crossing makers" or "ford finders"—a "ford" being a section of a river that allows people to cross through the moving stream to the other side. It is notable that the term does not convey the image of a bridge. The point is, people cannot cross to the other side without getting wet and going through the river itself. The historical existence of most of these tirthankaras cannot be proven, but the twenty-third one, Parshva, may have been a real person who lived in India, possibly about 800 B.C.E.

TIMELINE 5.1

	C. 850–800 B.C.E	● Life of Parshva, the legendary twenty-third tirthankara
Life of Mahavira, the ● twenty-fourth and most recent tirthankara	C. 599–527 B.C.E.	
	C. 350 B.C.E.	● Split between Digambara and Shvetambara sects
Life of Nanak ●	1469–1539 C.E.	
	1563–1606	● Life of Arjan
Life of Gobind Singh ●	1666–1708	

Timeline of significant events in the history of Jainism and Sikhism.

The most recent tirthankara is considered to be the greatest of them all and is often thought of by outsiders to be the founder of Jainism. His name was Nataputta Vardhamana, but he is usually referred to by an honorary title: Mahavira, meaning "great man" or "hero." When he lived is not entirely certain. An older dating, accepted by Jains, puts his life entirely in the sixth century B.C.E. (c. 599–527 B.C.E.; Timeline 5.1), but some scholars believe he lived a bit later (540–468 B.C.E.), almost as a contemporary of the Buddha.

Mahavira's life story is surrounded by legend, although the basic outline—which somewhat resembles the story of the Buddha—seems clear. He was born into an aristocratic family of the warrior-noble (*kshatriya*) caste. Luckily, he was the second son and thus had fewer responsibilities to care for his parents than did his older brother. One branch of Jains holds that he never married; another says that he married and had a child; but all agree that he left home at about age 30 to live the life of a wandering holy man.

After leaving home, Mahavira embraced extreme asceticism, and legend tells of his harshness toward himself and of the harshness received from others. He is said to have pulled out his hair when he renounced the world, and villagers taunted him during his meditations by hurting him with fire and with pins that they pushed into his skin. Dogs attacked him, but he did not resist. In order to avoid all attachments to people and places, he moved to another place every day; and after losing his loincloth, he went entirely naked for the rest of his life. He lived as a wandering holy man, begging for his food along the way. He was so gentle that to avoid causing injury to any living thing, he strained whatever he drank to keep from swallowing any insect that might have fallen into his cup, and he stepped carefully as he walked down a road to prevent himself from crushing even an ant.

After twelve years of meditation, wandering, and extreme mortification, Mahavira, at the age of 42, had an experience of great liberation. He felt completely free of all bondage to the ordinary world—no longer being

166

troubled by pain, suffering, shame, or loss. He now felt fully in control of himself, sensing that he had won out over all the forces that bind a person to the world. As a result of his liberating experience, Mahavira is called a **jina** ("conqueror"). It is from this title that the religion Jainism takes its name.

Mahavira spent the next thirty years of his life teaching his doctrines and organizing an order of naked monks. He died at about 72 at the village of Pava, near present-day Patna, in northeastern India.

WORLDVIEW

Jainism is unusual among world religions for the explicitness of its atheism. While Theravada Buddhism and philosophical Taoism are nontheistic, Jainism rather starkly rejects belief in a Creator God. The Mahapurana, a long Jain poem of the ninth century C.E., states that "foolish men declare that Creator made the world. The doctrine that the world was created is ill-advised and should be rejected."[1] Jainism offers the following philosophical arguments: If God is perfect, why did God create a universe that is imperfect? If God made the universe because of love, why is the world so full of suffering beings? If the universe had to be created, did not God also need to be created? And where did God come from in the beginning?

Jains respond to these questions by denying any beginning and asserting instead that the universe is eternal. Although the universe has always existed, it must continually change, and in the process of eternal change, structure arises on its own. Jainism (like Hinduism) teaches that the universe goes through regular great cycles of rise and fall. During the periods when human beings exist, there is first moral integrity, followed by inevitable moral decay; luckily, however, in each human age, tirthankaras appear to point the way to freedom.

According to Jainism, everything is full of life and is capable of suffering—a view (called **hylozoism,** "matter alive") of reality that may be quite ancient. In addition, Jain philosophy is dualistic, for Jains teach that all parts of the universe are composed of two types of reality, which are intermixed. There is spirit, which senses and feels, and there is matter, which is not alive and has no consciousness. Jainism calls these two principles **jiva** ("soul," "spirit," "life") and **ajiva** ("nonsoul," "nonlife"). Jains, however, see life and consciousness where others do not—even in fire, rocks, and water. Thus they extend the notion of spirit and feeling beyond human beings, animals, and insects. They are also aware of the miniscule life forms that live in earth, water, and wood. Their way of looking at reality makes Jains cautious about injuring anything—even that which does not at first appear to have the capacity to suffer.

Jainism sees the human being as composed of two opposing parts. The material side of the human being seeks pleasure, escape from pain, and self-interest, while the spiritual side seeks freedom and escape from all bondage to the material world and from the limitation of ego. Because other forms of reality are not aware of their two opposing aspects, they can do nothing about the essential incompatibility of the two parts. Human beings, however, have the ability to understand their dual nature and to overcome their limitations. With discipline, human beings can overcome the bondage of the material world and the body, liberating their spirits through insight, austerity, and kindness.

Enriching this vision of the human situation are the Jain beliefs in karma and reincarnation. Like Hindus, Jains believe that spirits are constantly being reborn in various forms. A spirit can move up or down the scale of rebirth, as well as free itself entirely from the chain of rebirths.

What controls the direction of rebirth is karma, which is produced by every action. As discussed earlier, karma is an important notion in Hinduism and Buddhism, but for Jains, karma has a physical quality: it is like a powder or grime that settles on and clings to the spirit. The level of rebirth is determined automatically, according to one's state of karma at the time of the death of one's current body.

The Jain goal is to reach a state of superhuman freedom. Liberated spirits, at last freed of their imprisoning material bodies, live on in a higher realm, which is thought to be at the top of the universe. Mahavira and other tirthankaras dwell there, and although they cannot assist human beings (as deities might), they are role models whom human beings devoutly recall in order to gain strength and courage.

JAIN ETHICS

Jainism has five ethical recommendations, which monks and nuns are expected to keep quite strictly. Laypeople, however, have the flexibility to adjust their practice to their particular life situations. (We must also recall that these are ideals that are not always lived out perfectly by individuals.)

Nonviolence (ahimsa) A more accurate English translation of *ahimsa* might be "gentleness" or "harmlessness." Ahimsa is the foundation of Jain ethics, and Jains are best known for their extreme measures in this regard. Believing that Mahavira swept the ground in front of him as he walked and before he sat down, Jain monks sometimes use a small, soft brush to move ants and other insects out of the way so that no life-form—even the tiniest—will be crushed. Feeling a kinship with the animal world as well, Jains have established hospitals to care for sick animals. They have been known to buy caged animals and set them free. Jains are also strict vegetarians, and some reject the use of animal products such as leather, feathers, and fur.

Because Jain laypeople avoid occupations that would harm insects or animals, hunting and fishing are forbidden, as are slaughtering or selling animal flesh. And although some Jains are

> The saint, with true vision, conceives compassion for all the world. . . . The great sage becomes a refuge for injured creatures, like an island which the waters cannot overwhelm.
>
> —Acaranga Sutra 1:6, 5[2]

Jain nuns carry begging bowls and whisks.

farmers, farming is often avoided because a plow could hurt small animals and insects living in the fields. Jains, instead, have gravitated to jobs that ideally cause no hurt, such as being doctors, teachers, lawyers, accountants, and business people. As an indirect result, the Jains in India make up a powerful business class whose reputation for virtue earns them the trust of others.

Nonlying Jainism discourages the telling of any falsehood and avoids exaggeration, even when meant humorously. Lying and exaggeration are dangerous, Jains think, because they often cause hurt. Although these ideals are not always followed, Jains' general care about speech and their reputation for honesty in their contractual agreements have earned them great respect.

At the same time, Jainism teaches that "absolute truth" is impossible to find or express, because everyone sees a situation from a

Jains and Gentle Suicide

Because it so values nonattachment, Jainism defends a person's right to end his or her own life. (This is also true of Hinduism but not so for many other religions—although most religions are indeed concerned with a good and holy death.) Jain scriptures even teach that Mahavira and his parents died by self-starvation. We must be cautious here, however, in using the word *suicide*. Jains do accept ending one's own life, but we must understand the practice from the Jain point of view and within that context. Jains see all life as a preparation for the liberation of the spirit (jiva) from the body, and when a person is sufficiently evolved spiritually, that person can make the final choice to no longer create more karma.

The Jain ideal thus allows and esteems ending one's life only after a long life of virtue and detachment, and it must be done with consideration for others. Gentle methods of ending one's life are the best, such as walking into an ocean or lake. The most highly esteemed method, however, is self-starvation, called **sallekhana,** "holy death." Jains prepare for sallekhana over the years by practicing fasting. When a person is old and growing weak, eating less and less is seen as an appropriate way to hasten the end. Self-starvation, or "the final fast," involves giving up food but continuing to drink liquids; death comes in about a month. This kind of death by self-starvation is considered an ultimate, noble expression of nonattachment and freedom.

unique point of view. A famous story illustrates the relativity of truth. In this story, three blind men touch the same elephant but experience it quite differently. The first man touches the ear and says it is a fan; the second man touches the leg and says it is a tree trunk; and the third man touches the tail and says it is a rope. (This story is popular among Jains, although it is doubtlessly older than Jainism itself.)

Nonstealing Jains may not take from others that which is not given. Stealing arises from improper desire and causes pain to others.

Chastity For the monk or nun, this means complete celibacy, and for the married individual, this means sexual fidelity to one's spouse. Mahavira saw sex as a danger, because it strongly binds a person to the physical world, strengthens desires, and can create passions that harm others. For those who are sexually active, improper sex is that which hurts others.

Nonattachment Human beings form attachments easily—to family, to home, to familiar territory, to clothes, to money, and to possessions. Jainism asserts that all attachments bring a certain bondage and that some attachments, especially to money and to possessions, can take complete control of a person. For laypeople, the ethical requirement of nonattachment suggests cultivating a spirit of generosity and detachment and limiting one's possessions to what is truly necessary. For monks and nuns, this requirement is interpreted more severely. Jainism teaches that Mahavira abandoned all attachments—family, possessions, even his clothing—and that monks and nuns must imitate him to the best of their capacity.

THE DEVELOPMENT OF JAINISM AND ITS BRANCHES

Jainism first developed in northeast India, in the same area that gave rise to Buddhism. Both Mahavira and the Buddha rebelled against aspects of Vedic religion: they refused to accept the authority of the Vedas, the Vedic gods, or the brahmins, and they placed emphasis, instead, on meditation and self-purification.

Although Buddhism followed a deliberate path of moderation—a "middle way"—Jainism gloried in austerity. While the Buddha rejected both nakedness and suicide as well as all extreme austerity, Mahavira's breakthrough experience of liberation, most Jains believe, was due to his extreme harshness with himself. He was successful precisely because he accepted—and even sought—cold, heat, poverty, nakedness, and humiliation.

The way of extreme austerity, however, is for rare individuals only. For most people, even for monks and nuns, the harshness must be softened according to life's circumstances. Because Jainism spread to different parts of India, with their differences in culture and climate, several branches of Jainism arose, which interpret the basic principles and teachings with some variations.

Digambaras

The name of this sect is beautiful and means "clothed in sky" or "atmosphere-clad." It is a pleasant way of referring to the monks' ideal of going completely naked, even in public. The **Digambara** branch holds that everything must be renounced, including the last scrap of clothing and the consequent shame of nakedness.

Most members of this branch live in southern India today. As tradition explains, a famine that occurred in the north drove many Jains southward. Divergences developed between those who remained in the north and those who had moved south. Thinking that northern followers had lost an essential seriousness, the southern branch became conservative, continuing to insist on renunciation of the most literal type. Its conservatism shows itself in many ways. For example, Digambara Jainism does not accept women into monastic life, holding that they may become monks only when they have been reborn as men. Possibly because of its high regard for celibacy, it also rejects the tradition that Mahavira was ever married.

Shvetambaras

The name of this sect means "clothed in white" and comes from the fact that its monks are allowed to dress in white robes. The **Shvetambara** branch allows women to enter monastic life as nuns and to dress in white as well.

(Being clothed was allowed not only in deference to modesty but also because it was demanded by the colder climate of northern India.) Shvetambara Jainism teaches that Mahavira was indeed married at one time but left home to find liberation. Nowadays this branch has members not only in the northeast but also in western and northwestern India.

Sthanakavasis

By the standards of India, the **Sthanakavasi** branch is fairly young, having grown up within the last few hundred years. It is a reform movement that emerged from the Shvetambara branch in the early eighteenth century. Popular Jainism had increasingly developed the practice of venerating statues of Mahavira and other tirthankaras, influenced by the Hindu practice of **puja** (devotional ritual performed in front of statues and at altars). Some Jain reformers opposed this practice because it seemed to turn the tirthankaras into saints to be prayed to for help. The Sthanakavasis, therefore, do not make use of either temples or images. (Their name comes from the simple buildings—*sthanakas*—in which they meet.) Rather than concentrate on temple ceremony, Sthanakavasis focus on meditation and individual austerities.

JAIN PRACTICES

Because they emphasize the ability of individuals to purify themselves and to perfect their own characters, Jains do not believe that devotional acts, directed toward gods or deceased leaders, bring help. Nonetheless, the Hindu practice of puja has been adopted by most Jains, with the exception of the Sthanakavasis. There is a general feeling that the devotional acts have a good effect on one's state of karma and that they focus the mind on saintly behavior. Jain temples therefore contain statues of the tirthankaras, especially Rishaba (the first tirthankara), Nemi (the twenty-second), Parshva, and Mahavira. The temple statues often look the same. In Digambara temples, the statues are unclothed and simple; in Shvetambara temples, they may be clothed and more ornate. Puja is performed before statues regularly, both by Jains and (in some places) by brahmin Hindus employed for the task. Puja ordinarily involves the offering of food, incense, the flames of oil lamps, and flowers, and sometimes the statues are bathed and devotees circumambulate (walk around) the statues. In some areas, there are large outdoor statues, which are bathed in milk and other liquids on special occasions. Many Jains also maintain home altars where they perform puja.

Fasting is regularly practiced by monks and nuns, particularly at the times of full and new moons. Laypeople join the monks in fasting on the last days of the Jain year in late summer, before the celebration of the New Year begins (in August or September). This period of fasting (*paryusana*) lasts fifteen days for the Digambaras and eight days for the Shvetambaras. The re-

A devotee anoints the feet of a Jain statue. The vines on each side hint at the immobility and perseverance of the tirthankara.

ligious year ends with a confession of wrongdoing and a plea for pardon from anyone the devotee might have offended.

Pilgrimage is an important part of Jain spirituality, and the village near Patna where Mahavira died, is a great pilgrimage center. Jains also visit the great temple complexes (some of which are on mountaintops in west India) and attend the bathing of large statues. Jains celebrate the birthday of Mahavira in the spring and his experience of liberation in the autumn.

JAIN SCRIPTURES

Jains speak of ancient scriptures, the Purvas, that exist no longer in their entirety, but only as limited quotations in later scripture. Disagreement exists among the sects over what is to be accepted as canonical. The literature preserved by the Shvetambara sect consists of forty-five works, divided into the canonical scriptures and later noncanonical works. At the heart of the canonical material are the eleven Angas ("limbs"). (A twelfth is said to have existed at one time.) Jainism holds the Angas to be the teachings of Mahavira, although they were not given final form until two centuries after his

The carvings of the Jain temple complex at Mount Abu in western India are world-famous. While Jainism emphasizes simplicity, some of its most noted architecture is quite elaborate. ▶

death. There are also twelve Upangas ("lesser limbs"), a collection of laws, rituals (particularly associated with assistance in dying), and other miscellaneous texts. Later noncanonical works include biographies of holy persons, commentaries on canonical works, and books of philosophy and science.[3] The Digambara sect does not fully accept the authenticity of the Angas, maintaining that the words of Mahavira were remembered and transmitted imperfectly after the first division of the Jains had taken place. The Sthanakavasis do not recognize any literature as scripture.

JAIN ART AND ARCHITECTURE

The most striking examples of Jain art are the statues of Mahavira and other tirthankaras. Although the seated statues resemble Buddhist sculpture, other sculptural forms contrast greatly with their Buddhist counterparts. Buddha figures are often gentle looking, with a preternatural sweetness in the faces; Jain figures, however, tend to be bold, powerful, and imposing. This is particularly true of statues of tirthankaras shown naked and standing: their nakedness somehow adds to their strength, and the standing figures are often presented with their legs and arms surrounded by vines, their immobility suggesting persistence and strength of character. The tirthankara seems to dare the viewer to be equally as strong.

Jain temple architecture does not echo the simplicity of the sculpture. Some Jain temples (such as the temple complex on Mount Abu, in western India, famous for its carved ceilings) show as much love for richness and decoration as some Hindu temples do. Sometimes, as in Calcutta, the temples also feature exuberant elements borrowed from European architecture, such as Corinthian columns.

SIKHISM

BACKGROUND

Sikhism grew up in an area called the Punjab, which today is part of northwest India and eastern Pakistan. Although the region has a long history of religious conflict between Hindus and Muslims, it is also an area in which significant attempts have been made to bridge division and misunderstanding. It is not surprising, then, that Sikhism, nurtured in the midst of conflict and resolution, exhibits elements reminiscent of both groups.

It is hard to imagine two religions more divergent than Hinduism and Islam. Hinduism recognizes many gods, while Islam recognizes only one; Hinduism cherishes religious images, whereas Islam prohibits them; and Hinduism promotes vegetarianism, but Islam, though it has dietary restrictions, allows the killing and eating of many animals, including cows.

Both religions, though, share an appreciation for religious devotion and value the attainment of mystical consciousness. In Hinduism, these traditions have been cultivated by the devotees of bhakti yoga, and in Islam they have been cultivated by Sufis. (Some scholars maintain that Sufism in fact derived much early inspiration from Hinduism.) Both religions also recognize the important role of a spiritual master—a *guru* or a *shaykh*. And while Islam is known for its rejection of images, Hinduism has also had some members who have similarly spoken against an exaggerated love of images. It was in the Punjab, where these two often-opposing religions collided, that the founder of a new religion was born.

NANAK AND THE ORIGINS OF SIKHISM

The founder of Sikhism, Nanak, was born in 1469 in what is today Pakistan. He was raised in a Hindu family, married, had two children, and held several jobs—first as a herder and then as a clerical assistant to a sultan. Because Nanak's life as a householder was accompanied by a strong religious interest, he and a Muslim friend named Mardana created a devotional association and met in the evenings to sing hymns and to discuss religious ideas.

One day Nanak had an experience so powerful that he saw it as a revelation. After bathing and performing religious ablutions in a nearby river, Nanak went into the adjacent forest and did not reemerge for three days. During that time, he felt himself taken into the divine presence. He would later say that he had experienced God directly. This shattering experience revealed to him that there is but one God, beyond all human names and conceptions.

Nanak referred to the fundamental divine reality as the "True Name"—signifying that all names and terms that are applied to God are limited, because the divine is beyond all human conception. Nanak now understood that Hindus and Muslims worshiped the same God and that a distinction between the two religions was mistaken. Nanak became famous for insisting that when the "True Name" of God is experienced rather than just talked about, there is no "Hindu" and there is no "Muslim."

Nanak's revelation is similar to stories of the life-changing prophetic calls of Zarathustra, Isaiah, and Muhammad (as we will see in later chapters). His revelatory experience resolved his earlier doubts and was the great turning point of his life. Having decided to spread his new understanding, Nanak left his family and home, accompanied by his friend Mardana. As homeless wanderers, they visited holy sites throughout northern India. Wherever they went, Nanak preached and sought disciples, which is the meaning of the word **Sikh.** As a part of his preaching, Nanak sang devotional songs while Mardana, who was from a social class of musicians, played musical accompaniment.

Particularly startling was Nanak's style of clothing, which deliberately blended Hindu and Muslim elements. He wore the Hindu *dhoti* (a cloth drawn up between the legs to form pants) as well as an orange Muslim coat and Muslim cap. He adorned his forehead with Hindu religious markings. The combination of elements was an important prophetic statement, predictably causing consternation among Hindus and Muslims.

Nanak and Mardana continued their devotional teaching together until Mardana's death in his late 60s. Not long after, when Nanak sensed his own end approaching, he passed on his authority and work to a chosen disciple. He died in 1539 at age 70. Nanak is commonly called Guru ("spiritual teacher") Nanak and is recognized as the first of a line of ten Sikh gurus.

THE WORLDVIEW AND TEACHINGS OF NANAK

Just as Nanak's clothing combined elements of Hinduism and Islam, so too did his worldview, at least on the surface. Earlier commentators spoke of Sikhism merely as a combination of Hindu and Muslim elements, yet Sikhs themselves—and more recent scholars—see Sikhism as an entirely unique religion. They speak of Nanak as having rejected both Islam and Hinduism, and they hold that Sikhism comes from a totally new revelation.

Nanak accepted—as does Hinduism—a belief in reincarnation and karma. His view of the human being was similar to that of the Sankhya school of philosophy, which views the human being as a composite of body and spirit. Because the body and physical world by nature bind and limit the spirit, the spirit must overcome physicality as it seeks freedom and absorption in the divine. This process may take many lifetimes to accomplish.

In spite of Nanak's acceptance of reincarnation and karma, there were other elements of Hinduism that he rejected. From a very early age, for example, he resisted Hindu love of ritual, criticizing it for taking human attention away from God. Similarly, he disdained Hindu polytheism, particularly Hindu devotion to images of various gods and goddesses. It is possible that Nanak's views in this regard were influenced by Islam. Islamic practice also supports Nanak's acceptance of meat eating. (Nanak thought of the animal world as having been created for the use of human beings.)

According to Nanak's view of God, although God is ultimately beyond personhood, God does have personal qualities, such as knowledge, love, a sense of justice, and compassion. As such, God can be approached personally by the individual. God, according to Nanak, is the primary Guru; and although Nanak saw himself as God's mouthpiece, he preached that God dwells within each individual and can be contacted within the human heart.

Despite his emphasis on finding the divine within the individual, Nanak held that true religion has a strong social responsibility. He criticized

The "Five K's" of the Sikhs

In India and in big cities of the West, Sikhs today are often associated with turbans. Actually, though, their characteristic dress reflects not one but five practices. The five practices were originally adopted by members of the Khalsa to promote strength and self-identity.* Because the names of the practices each begin with *k*, they are called the Five K's:

- *Kesh:* uncut hair and beard—in association with the lion and its power; the hair on the head is usually worn in a topknot and covered with a turban or cloth.

- *Khanga:* hair comb—to hold the long hair in place.
- *Kach:* special underwear—indicating alertness and readiness to fight.
- *Kirpan:* sword—for defense.
- *Kara:* bracelet of steel—a symbol of strength.

---

*In addition, members of the Khalsa were required to avoid all intoxicants. For a long time, the Khalsa was open only to men, but eventually it was opened also to women.

---

both Islam and Hinduism for their deficiencies in helping the poor and the oppressed. In response to his convictions, Nanak organized religious groups, called *sangats,* which were to offer both worship to God and assistance to fellow human beings.

THE DEVELOPMENT OF SIKHISM

Sikhism has gone through several stages of development. In its earliest stage, Sikhism was not defined as a separate religion. It was simply a religious movement that sought to coexist peacefully with other religions. In the next stage, Sikhism was forced to adopt a militant, self-protective stance toward the world, and it took on some of the elements of a more formalized religion—a sacred book, a sacred city, and clearly defined religious practices. After that period of self-definition and consolidation, Sikhism, in its third and final stage, was able to move beyond its land of origin and to make converts elsewhere.

The earliest stage was that of the first four gurus—Nanak, Angad, Amar Das, and Ram Das. During this period, hymns were written, numerous communities were organized, and a village headquarters was created at Amritsar, in northern India.

The next stage, of consolidation and religious definition, began with Guru Arjan (1563–1606), a son of Ram Das. In his role as fifth guru, Arjan built the Golden Temple and its surrounding pond at Amritsar. Collecting about three thousand hymns—written by himself and earlier gurus and saints—Arjan created the sacred book of the Sikhs, the **Adi Granth** ("original collection"). Because he resolutely resisted attempts by the Muslim emperor Jahangir to make him adopt Islamic practice, Arjan died of torture.

The Golden Temple at Amritsar enshrines the Adi Granth and is the spiritual center of the Sikh faith.

Arjan's son, Har Gobind, steered Sikhism in a more self-defensive direction. As a result of the persecution of his father, Har Gobind enlisted a bodyguard and an army to protect him and his followers. He adopted the practice of wearing a sword and thus abandoned the Hindu ideal of ahimsa. The growing militancy of evolving Sikhism was successful in averting persecution during the tenure of the next gurus, Har Rai and Harkishan.

The ninth guru, Tegh Bahadur, however, was imprisoned and decapitated by the Muslim emperor Aurangzeb, who saw Sikhism as a serious threat to his control. In response, the tenth guru, Gobind Rai (1666–1708) idealized the sword. Because of his military power, Gobind Rai came to be known as Gobind Singh ("Gobind the lion"). He inaugurated a special military order for men, called the Khalsa, and devised a ceremony of initiation, called the baptism of the sword, which involved sprinkling initiates with water that had been stirred with a sword. The Khalsa was open to all castes, for Gobind Singh ended all caste distinctions among Sikhs. Every male within the Khalsa took the name Singh ("lion").

Over time, Gobind Singh suffered the deaths of his four sons and was left without a successor. Possibly foreseeing his own assassination, he declared that the Adi Granth was to be considered both his successor and the final, permanent Guru. The sacred book, both in Amritsar and in Sikh temples (**gurdwaras**), is therefore treated with the same reverence that would be shown a living guru. As such, it is called "Guru Granth." At the death of Gobind Singh, Sikhism was now clearly defined as a religion, with the means to spread beyond its place of origin.

SIKH SCRIPTURES

The primary book of Sikh scripture, the Adi Granth, is divided into three parts. The first and most important part is the **Japji,** a moderately long poem by Guru Nanak that summarizes the religion. It speaks of the indescribability of God and the joy of union with him. Its opening words declare, "There is only one God whose name is true, the Creator, devoid of fear and enmity, immortal, unborn, self-existent."[4] The second part consists of thirty-nine *rags* ("tunes") by Guru Nanak and later gurus. The third part is a collection of varied works, including poems and hymns from Hindu, Muslim, and Sikh gurus and saints. Because the Adi Granth is believed to contain the living spirit of Nanak and his successors, it is treated with utmost reverence and given personal honors as the embodiment of the gurus. At the Golden Temple in Amritsar, it is brought out in the early morning by a gloved attendant, set on a cushion under a canopy, read from aloud by professional readers, fanned throughout the day, and then "put to bed" at night. In gurdwaras, copies of the Adi Granth are enshrined and read. It is consulted for solutions to problems by opening it freely and reading from the top of the left-hand page. (Even children are named by this method, being given names corresponding to the first letter read at the top of the left-hand page when the Adi Granth is opened randomly.) Sikh homes may have a room to enshrine the Adi Granth, and devout Sikhs daily read or recite its passages from memory.

Sikhs eat a meal in a
gurdwara in Los Angeles.

Wonderful Your word, wonderful Your knowledge;
Wonderful Your creatures, wonderful their species;
Wonderful their forms, wonderful their colors;
Wonderful the animals which wander naked;
Wonderful Your wind; wonderful Your water;
Wonderful Your fire which sports wondrously;
Wonderful the earth . . . ;
Wonderful the desert, wonderful the road;
Wonderful Your nearness, wonderful Your remoteness;
Wonderful to behold You present.

—Guru Nanak[5]

SIKHISM AND THE MODERN WORLD

Because of their military training, Sikhs were employed by the British as
soldiers. After the British left the Indian subcontinent in 1947, however, the
Sikhs experienced painful dislocation. More than two million left Pakistan

to avoid conflict with the Muslim majority, most settling in northwest India, where today some Sikhs hope to create an independent state. Antagonism has flared up between the Sikhs and the Indian government over this matter, and Sikh separatists twice have taken over the Golden Temple at Amritsar, although Indian government forces have both times taken it back. In retaliation for her support of Indian government troops during the first of these takeovers, Prime Minister Indira Gandhi was assassinated in 1984 by Sikhs within her bodyguard.

Sikhs have begun to settle widely outside India, particularly in countries open to Indian immigration, such as in England and former British territories. (There is a considerable community, for example, in Vancouver, British Columbia.) They have established gurdwaras, which serve as daily prayer centers as well as charitable kitchens and social meeting places. Although Sikhs do not have a tradition of making converts, their simple and self-reliant lifestyle has attracted many new members. Their success and continued growth is likely.

 ## PERSONAL EXPERIENCE: A VISIT TO THE GOLDEN TEMPLE

The Golden Temple of Amritsar sits in the midst of a busy Indian city on an island in an artificial lake. The day that I visited, however, the water of the lake had been drained and about thirty workers were moving about and chatting down below, as they cleaned and made repairs. While I surveyed the scene, I overheard what sounded like American English being spoken nearby. A man with a short black beard, his blond wife, and his daughter were taking photos and discussing the restoration work. I offered to take their photo against the backdrop of the Golden Temple, and then we fell into conversation. The man introduced himself and his family. Mr. Singh and his wife Marianne were not American, he said, but Canadian.

"I was born in Vancouver just after my parents immigrated to Canada from India. We've come here to visit my grandparents and to see the Golden Temple," he explained. "And I'm from Alberta, originally," added Mrs. Singh. "I'm not a Sikh—at least not yet. I was raised Catholic. My parents immigrated to Canada from Poland and have a farm north of Calgary. My husband and I met in college at the University of British Columbia." She turned to the girl, "This is our daughter June." After shaking hands, we went across the walkway together into the Golden Temple.

The interior was hot and muggy, but a feeling of devotion overcame my discomfort. A venerable-looking man with a long white beard was reading from the Adi Granth, while an attendant waved a large feather fan overhead. People moved very slowly in line, but our time there was actually short, because the crowds kept us from staying inside too long. Outside, we decided to have lunch together and found a small restaurant not far away, where we ate and talked.

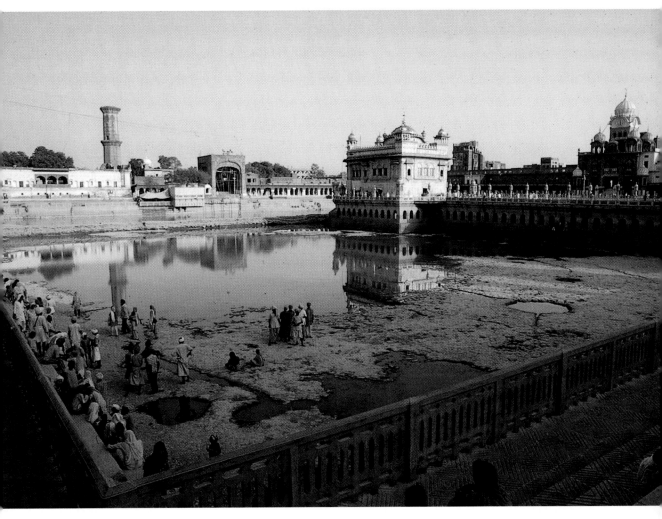

Workers regularly clean and restore the Golden Temple and its pond.

Mr. Singh pointed to his short hair and neatly clipped beard. "As you can see, I do not practice all the traditions of my religion. I am proud of my religion, though, and particularly proud of the emphasis it puts on strength and endurance."

Mrs. Singh nodded. "Being in a mixed marriage, we've certainly needed strength at times, and we've found elements in both our religions that help us. I think, though, that we are typical of many Canadian couples, and our mixed marriage has been a rich experience for both of us."

"For our parents, too," Mr. Singh added, and both laughed and shook their heads knowingly. "My name means 'lion,'" he continued. "I want to use my strength to be a strong individual, not just a representative of a single religious path. Where I live, there's a large Sikh community, and you can deal almost entirely with people of your own religion and ethnic background. But I want to be more universal, while keeping my religion in my heart."

As we got up to leave and were saying our good-byes, Mr. Singh lifted his arm. "Though I cut my hair and beard, I always wear this." He pulled back his shirtsleeve and proudly showed me his kara—his steel Sikh bracelet.

RELIGION BEYOND THE CLASSROOM

Jainism The great sites of Jainism are in India. Elaborate temples are located in several cities, particularly Calcutta, Ajmer, and Bombay. There are temple complexes on several mountains, the most famous of which are on Mount Shatrunjaya near Palitana and on Mount Abu (in western India). The place of Mahavira's death, at Pava near the city of Patna (in northeastern India), is a center of pilgrimage.

Sikhism The greatest site of Sikhism is its religious center, the Golden Temple, set in a large artificial pond in the city of Amritsar, in the Punjab region of northwestern India. Sikh temples can be found in many cities throughout the world and may be visited by non-Sikhs.

FOR FULLER UNDERSTANDING

1. Study present-day India, and mark on a map the places where Jains are to be found.
2. Construct arguments for and against the Jain acceptance of religiously inspired self-starvation.

3. Find out where Sikh communities exist in North America. If there is a Sikh community in your area, learn more about it, visit its temple, and give a report.

RELATED READINGS

Dundas, Paul. *The Jains.* London: Routledge, 1993. A fine modern introduction to Jainism.

Jacobi, Hermann, trans. *The Gaina Sutras. The Sacred Books of the East,* vols. 22 and 45. London: Oxford University Press, 1884. A classical selection of material from two Angas and other works.

Jaini, P. S. *The Jaina Path of Purification.* Berkeley: University of California Press, 1979. An explanation of Jain belief and practice by a foremost Jain scholar.

Koller, John. *The Indian Way.* New York: Macmillan, 1982. A philosophical discussion of Indian schools of thought, including Jainism.

McLeod, W. H. *Guru Nanak and the Sikh Religion.* New York: Oxford University Press, 1969.

———. *Textual Sources for the Study of Sikhism.* Totowa, NJ: Barnes & Noble, 1984. A good selection of Sikh scripture and more recent writing.

Pal, P. *The Peaceful Liberators: Jain Art from India.* London: Thames & Hudson and the Los Angeles County Museum of Art, 1994. A well-illustrated presentation of Jain art, particularly sculpture and manuscript illumination.

Singh, Khushwant. *A History of the Sikhs.* Princeton, NJ: Princeton University Press, 1963. An introduction to the religion by a foremost Sikh, well known in India as a journalist and writer.

KEY TERMS

Adi Granth (*ah'-dee grahnth*): "Original collection"; the primary scripture of the Sikhs.

Ajiva (*uh-jee'-va*): Matter without soul or life.

Digambara (*di-gam'-ba-ra*): "Clothed in sky"; a member of the Jain sect in which monks do not wear clothing.

Gurdwara (*gur-dwa'-rah*): A Sikh temple.

Guru (*goo'-rooh*): A spiritual teacher, such as Guru Nanak (the founder of Sikhism) and his nine successors, who are the mouthpiece of God, the fundamental Guru.

Hylozoism: The belief that all physical matter has life and feeling.

Japji (*jahp'-jee*): A poem by Guru Nanak that begins the Adi Granth; the poem is recited daily by pious Sikhs.

Jina (*jee'-na*): "Conquerer"; the Jain term for a perfected person who will not be reborn.

Jiva (*jee'-va*): Spirit, soul, which enlivens matter.

Puja (*poo'-ja*): Ritual in honor of a tirthankara.

Sallekhana (*sahl-lek-hah'-nuh*): "Holy death"; death by self-starvation, valued in Jainism as a noble end of a long life of virtue and detachment.

Shvetambara (*shvet-am'-ba-ra*): "Clothed in white"; a member of the Jain sect in which monks and nuns wear white clothing.

Sikh (*seek*): "Disciple"; a follower of the Sikh religion.

Sthanakavasi (*stun-uk-uh-vuh'-see*): "Building person"; a member of the youngest Jain sect, which rejects the use of statues and temples.

Tirthankara (*tihr-tahn'-kah-ruh*): "Crossing maker"; in Jainism, one of the twenty-four ideal human beings of the past, Mahavira being the most recent.

CHAPTER 6

Taoism and Confucianism

 FIRST ENCOUNTER

You have gone to Taipei to see one of the world's greatest collections of Chinese art at the National Palace Museum and to experience the color and complexity of Chinese culture. City life is indeed as colorful as you hoped it would be. Taipei is a jumble of sights and sounds. Half the city's population seems to be riding motorbikes. More than once you've seen a whole family—father in front, mother and child in the middle, grandmother at the rear—balanced on a single scooter.

Wandering alternately along bustling boulevards and back streets, you come upon a large Taoist temple, seeing first its walls and then behind them its tall, sloping tile roofs, with ceramic dragons and other figures at the corners. You know you are approaching the entrance when you reach sidewalk stalls selling temple offerings: oranges, grapefruit, red candles, flowers, and long sticks of incense bunched in red-and-gold paper packets. You decide to buy some incense.

Inside the gates, you feel as if you have just walked into a fair. People cluster to talk and then break off, walking in random directions. Near you someone is taking a plate with fruit to a large table, one of several in the center of the big open courtyard. Standing next to the table, a man with a boat-shaped red hat blows on an animal horn. Around a great central brazier, smoke rises in clouds. The smell of incense is so overpowering you have to move away to breathe some fresh air.

At each side of the central courtyard are two lines of people who seem to be waiting for some sort of medical treatment. A woman in a blue smock stands at the front of each line and pats and rubs people on the shoulders and arms and back as they come forward. You stop to watch. A friendly gentleman nearby, happy to practice his English with you, turns and explains, "These women are healing. They used to suffer themselves but were healed, and now they pass on the healing to others."

You notice a young couple putting a few sticks of incense in each of several braziers that front different altars. The gentleman, who is now walking along with you, explains, "They are going to get married and are seeking help from all the gods here in the temple."

A group of elderly people, each carrying incense sticks and fruit, follows a shirtless young man who appears to be in some kind of trance. He leads the group around to the rear of the temple. "They are here from the south to ask advice," the gentleman says. "The young man has special gifts: he can speak with the main god of this place."

You and your companion walk around together, talking about the images and placing your lighted incense sticks at several altars. In front of a small altar, a bent old woman throws what look like two large, wooden, crescent-shaped beans on the floor in front of her. "She is seeking help with her future," says your friend. Behind the scenes, along side corridors, you notice men stretched out asleep, some propped against bright red pillars. Near the exit, you say good-bye and offer thanks to your kind guide. He bows and shakes your hand at the same time.

As you exit through the large gates, you see someone burning silver paper money on the sidewalk. No one else seems to take notice. The vendor from whom you bought your incense smiles and nods, and you smile back as you turn to walk down another crowded, noisy street.

Note: Two systems are currently used for transcribing Chinese words into English: the *pinyin* and Wade-Giles systems. Because the mainland Chinese government and United Nations have adopted pinyin, it has become the most commonly used system. The older Wade-Giles system was the standard transcription system in English until pinyin was adopted and is still frequently encountered (as in the spelling of *Taoism*).

For major Chinese terms in this book, the pinyin spelling is given first and the Wade-Giles spelling second, in parentheses. (Pinyin pronunciation is generally similar to English usage, except that the pronunciation of c is "ts," q is "ch," and x is "sh.") For the words *Taoism, Tao,* and *Tao Te Ching,* however, the Wade-Giles spellings have been used so widely in English publications that they have in effect become standard English and are thus retained here.

BASIC ELEMENTS OF TRADITIONAL CHINESE BELIEFS

Confucianism, Taoism, and Buddhism have been collectively called the Three Doctrines and together have had a profound influence on Chinese culture and history. Buddhism, as we saw in Chapter 4, was an import to China, with roots in Indian belief. Confucianism and Taoism, on the other hand, sprouted and grew in the soil of indigenous Chinese belief. We thus begin our study of these two Chinese religious systems by considering some of the features of traditional Chinese belief and practice.

Early Chinese belief was a blend of several elements. Some of them, such as a belief in spirits, can be traced back more than three thousand years. The following elements provided a basis for later developments in Chinese religion and were especially important to the development of Confucianism and Taoism.

Spirits Early Chinese belief seems to have been polytheistic and animistic, that is, spirits were thought to be active in every aspect of nature and the human world. Good spirits brought health, wealth, long life, and fertility. Bad spirits caused accidents and disease. Disturbances of nature, such as droughts and earthquakes, were punishments from spirits for human failings, but harmony could be restored through rituals and sacrifice.

Tian During the Shang dynasty (c. 1766 – c. 1122 B.C.E.) the omnipotent power that was believed to rule the world was called Shang Di (Shang Ti) and was thought of as a personal god, capable of being contacted by diviners. Perhaps Shang Di was the memory of an ancestor, and veneration of him was part of the ancient practice of honoring ancestors. In the Zhou (Chou) dynasty (c. 1122–256 B.C.E.), a new political regime (the Zhou kings) ignored the Shang belief and began explaining life in terms of a different conception, Tian (T'ien), which is usually translated as "Heaven." It appears that Tian was envisioned as both an impersonal divine force that controls events on earth and as a cosmic moral principle that determines right and wrong.

Veneration of ancestors The same cautious reverence that was shown to spirits was also naturally felt for ancestors. Ancestors at death became spirits and needed to be placated to ensure their positive influence on living family members.

Seeing patterns in nature China's long and mighty rivers, high mountain chains, distinct seasons, and frequent floods, droughts, and earthquakes all influenced the Chinese view of the natural world. To survive, the Chinese people had to learn that while they could not often control nature, they could learn to work with it when they understood its underlying patterns. Some of the patterns were quite easy to discern, such as the progression of the seasons, the paths of

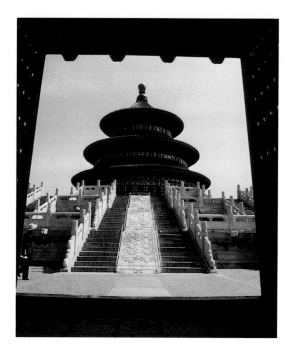

At the Temple of Heaven, in Beijing, the emperor performed ceremonies to honor Tian (Heaven).

the sun and moon, and the cycle of birth and death. Others were more subtle, like the motion of waves and the ripple of mountain ranges, as well as the Tao (which we will discuss shortly), and yang and yin.

Yang and yin After about 1000 B.C.E. the Chinese commonly thought that the universe expressed itself in opposite but complementary principles: light and dark, day and night, hot and cold, sky and earth, summer and winter. The list was virtually infinite: male and female, right and left, front and back, up and down, out and in, sound and silence, birth and death, "strong" foods (meat and ginger) and "weak" foods (fish and rice), and "dynamic" (odd) numbers and "stable" (even) numbers. The names for the two complementary principles are **yang** and **yin.**

These principles are not the same as good and evil. Yang is not expected to win over the force of yin, or vice versa; rather, the ideal is a dynamic balance between the forces. In fact, the emblem of balance is the yin-yang circle, divided into what looks like two intertwined commas. One half is light, representing yang; the other is dark, representing yin. Inside each division is a small dot of the contrasting color that represents the seed of the opposite. The dot suggests that everything contains its opposite and will eventually become its opposite. Both forces are dynamic and in perfect balance as they change, just as day and night are in balance as they progress. We can think of yang and yin as pulsations or waves of energy, like a heartbeat or like breathing in and out.

Yang and yin, symbolized by a circle of light and dark, represent the complementary but opposing forces of the universe that generate all forms of reality.

Divination Divination (methods for knowing more about the future) was an integral part of early Chinese tradition. The oldest technique involved the reading of lines in bones and tortoise shells. Later, an elaborate practice was developed that involves the **Yi Jing (I Ching**, The Book of Changes; discussed later in this chapter), an ancient book that interprets life through an analysis of hexagrams. A hexagram is a figure of six horizontal lines. There are two kinds of lines: divided (yin) and undivided (yang). A hexagram is made of two trigrams and is "constructed" by tossing sticks or coins and writing down the result, beginning with the bottom line. Thus sixty-four different hexagrams are possible. The hexagrams are thought to represent patterns that can develop in one's life, and the Yi Jing gives an interpretation of each hexagram. With the help of the Yi Jing, a person can interpret a hexagram as an aid in making decisions about the future.

We now turn to two great systems of Chinese religious thought, Taoism and Confucianism, which many consider to be complementary traditions. Taoism is often thought to emphasize the yin aspects of reality and Confucianism the yang. Together they form a unity of opposites.

TAOISM

Because Taoism incorporated some of the previously mentioned elements and many others from traditional Chinese belief and practice, the category Taoism is really like a shopping cart filled with a variety of items: observations about nature, philosophical insights, guidelines for living, exercises for health, rituals of protection, and practices for attaining longevity and inner purity. We should note, however, that Taoism and Chinese folk religion are not exactly the same thing (although the terms are often used interchangeably, and in some cases the border between the two is not always clear).

Taoism as we know it today includes ideas and practices both from the early philosophical phase of Taoism and from the later development of Taoism as a religion. It is common to differentiate between the philosophical Taoism that we find in the Tao Te Ching (which we will discuss in the following section) of about 300 B.C.E. and the later ritualized Taoism that arose after 100 C.E. We will do that here for purposes of discussion, though without making too strong a distinction between the two. It is now thought that philosophical Taoism may have emerged, at least in part, from ritualistic origins; and later ritualistic Taoism is now commonly seen as an expression in ritual of the philosophical insights of Taoism. Thus a strong separation of the two is incorrect.

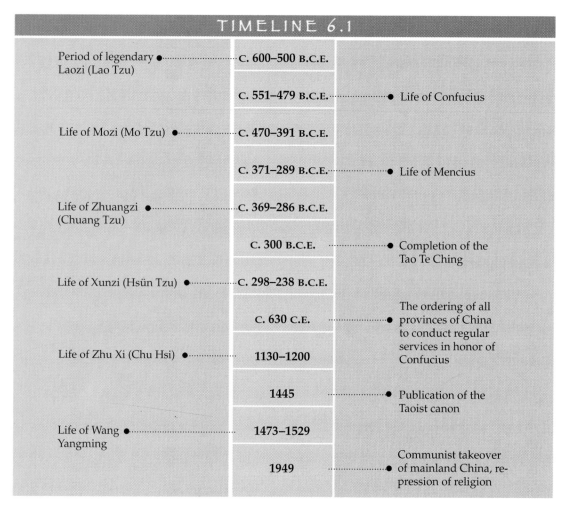

Period of legendary Laozi (Lao Tzu) ●	**C. 600–500 B.C.E.**	
	C. 551–479 B.C.E.	● Life of Confucius
Life of Mozi (Mo Tzu) ●	**C. 470–391 B.C.E.**	
	C. 371–289 B.C.E.	● Life of Mencius
Life of Zhuangzi (Chuang Tzu) ●	**C. 369–286 B.C.E.**	
	C. 300 B.C.E.	● Completion of the Tao Te Ching
Life of Xunzi (Hsün Tzu) ●	**C. 298–238 B.C.E.**	
	C. 630 C.E.	● The ordering of all provinces of China to conduct regular services in honor of Confucius
Life of Zhu Xi (Chu Hsi) ●	**1130–1200**	
	1445	● Publication of the Taoist canon
Life of Wang Yangming ●	**1473–1529**	
	1949	● Communist takeover of mainland China, repression of religion

Timeline of significant events in the history of Taoism and Confucianism.

THE ORIGINS OF PHILOSOPHICAL TAOISM

Early Taoism, while possibly influenced by shamanism, created literature that was philosophically oriented. Later, an organized religion emerged. Here we look at some early thinkers and writings.

Laozi (Lao Tzu)

Taoism as a body of teachings is often traced back to a legendary figure named **Laozi (Lao Tzu),** whose name means "old master" or "old child." In the traditional story, Laozi's birth (c. 600 B.C.E.; Timeline 6.1) resulted from a virginal conception. According to legend, the child was born old—hence the name, "old child." Laozi became a state archivist, or librarian, in the royal city of Loyang for many years. Tiring of his job, he left his post and, carried by an ox, traveled to the far west of China. At the western border,

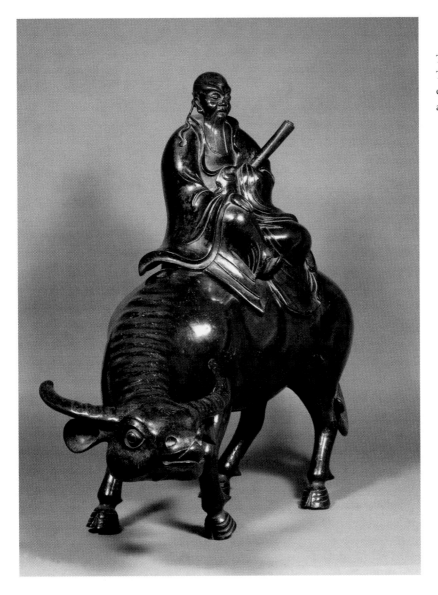

Tradition says that Lao Tzu, when leaving China, disappeared on the back of an ox.

Laozi was recognized as an esteemed scholar and prohibited from crossing until he had written down his teachings. The result was the Tao Te Ching, a short book of about five thousand Chinese characters. After Laozi was finished with the book, he left China, never to be seen again.

The Tao Te Ching

The **Tao Te Ching** is the great classic of Taoism, accepted by most Taoists as a central scripture and one of the world's greatest books. Its title can be translated as "the classical book about the Way and its power." Sometimes the book is also called the Laozi (Lao Tzu), after its legendary author. Possibly because of its brevity, it has had an enormous impact on Chinese culture.

The eighty-one short chapters of the Tao Te Ching are probably a compilation of the work of many people, rather than a single author. The book shows some repetition, has no clear order, and exhibits a deliberate lack of clarity. In form, each chapter is more poetry than prose.

What was the original purpose of the book? One theory holds that its overall purpose was political, that it was meant as a handbook for rulers; another sees it as primarily a religious guidebook, meant to lead adherents to spiritual insight; and still another views it as a practical guide for living in harmony with the universe. It is possible that the Tao Te Ching fulfilled all these purposes and that its passages can have several meanings at the same time. Part of the genius of the book is its brevity and use of paradox: its meaning depends on who is interpreting it.

Throughout the Tao Te Ching are references to the **Tao.** The book speaks of its nature and operation; it describes the manner in which people will live if they are in harmony with the Tao; and it gives suggestions for experiencing the Tao. The book also provides images to help describe all of these things. What, though, is "the Tao"?

The first chapter of the Tao Te Ching begins by saying, "The Tao that can be told is not the eternal Tao."[1] In other words, we cannot really put into words exactly what the Tao is, which is ironic since the book itself uses words. Yet the book goes on to tell us that the Tao is "nameless," that is, it is not any individual thing that has a name—such as a *door,* a *tree,* a *bird,* a *person.* The Tao cannot be named because it has no form. But the Tao *can* be experienced and followed by every individual thing that has a name. The Tao Te Ching says the Tao is the origin of everything and that all individual things are "manifestations" of the Tao.

Although the Tao is the origin of nature, it is not "God," because it does not have personality. It neither cares about human beings nor dislikes them—it only produces them, along with the rest of nature. Because the Tao makes nature move the way it does, it can be called the way or the rhythm of nature.

To experience the Tao, we must leave behind our desires for individual things, a concept that runs counter to everyday concerns—how much something costs, what time it is now, whether something is big or small. In fact, the Taoist way of seeing things is so odd to some people that at first it seems like trying to see in the dark, as the end of the first chapter describes:

Darkness within darkness.
The gate to all mystery.

The Taoist sees things differently. To illustrate, there is an intriguing example in the twentieth chapter of the Tao Te Ching: A Taoist is observing a group of people in a park celebrating a holiday. They all seem happy as they climb up to the top of a terrace where a ceremony will occur. They appear to know what they are doing and where they are going. Not the Taoist, though, who feels "formless" and "like the ocean"—adrift.[2] The Taoist is troubled by the contrast between "self" and "others." They seem happy and sure of themselves, but the Taoist can only watch and feels like an outsider. Then the chapter ends with an extraordinary affirmation. The Taoist recognizes something intensely personal and difficult, but willingly accepts the sense of separateness from the others and from their way of seeing things. The Taoist accepts, and concludes,

> I am different.
> I am nourished by the great mother.

Thus, the Tao cannot be "known" in the same way that we see a car or hear a song, for example. It cannot be perceived directly but rather by intuition. The Tao Te Ching presents several powerful images wherein the Tao seems most active and visible. Contemplating them can help us experience the Tao, and by taking on some of the qualities of these images, we begin to live in harmony with the Tao that inhabits them. Several common images follow:

Water Water is gentle, ordinary, and lowly, but strong and necessary. It flows around every obstacle. Chapter eight praises it: "The highest good is like water."[3] It assists all things "and does not compete with them."[4]

Woman The female is sensitive, receptive, yet effective and powerful.

Child The child is full of energy, wonder, and naturalness.

Valley The valley is yin, and it is mystery.

Darkness Darkness can be safe, full of silence and possibility.

Zhuangzi (Chuang Tzu)

Taoism was enriched by the work of **Zhuangzi (Chuang Tzu),** who was active about 300 B.C.E. What we know of him comes from the writings he left behind. His personality seems playful, independent, and in love with the fantastic. The book of his writings, called the Zhuangzi (Chuang Tzu), is composed of seven "inner chapters," which are thought to be by the author himself, and twenty-six "outer chapters," whose authorship is less certain.

The Zhuangzi, unlike the poetry of the Tao Te Ching, contains many whimsical stories. It continues the themes of early Taoist thought, such as the need for harmony with nature, the movement of the Tao in all that happens, and the pleasure that we can gain from simplicity. But it moves further, particularly underscoring the inevitability of change and the relativity of all human judgments. It also adds to Taoism an appreciation for humor—something quite rare in the scriptures of the world.

The Seasons of Life

A famous story illustrates what it means to live in harmony with nature: Upon hearing of the death of Zhuangzi's wife, a friend, Huizi (Hui Tzu), goes to offer sympathy. Although he expects to find Zhuangzi crying and in ritual mourning, Huizi finds Zhuangzi instead singing and drumming on a bowl. Huizi is shocked—and says so. Responding in a thoughtful way, Zhuangzi says that at first his wife's death saddened him terribly, but then he reflected on the whole cycle of her existence. Before his wife was a human being, she was without shape or life, and her original self was a part of the formless substance of the universe. Then she became a human being. "Now there's been another change, and she's dead. It's just like the progression of the four seasons, spring, summer, fall, winter."[6] When winter comes, we do not mourn. That would be ungrateful. Similarly, a human being goes through seasons. Zhuangzi describes his wife as now being like someone asleep in a vast room. "If I were to follow after her bawling and sobbing, it would show that I don't know anything about fate. So I stopped."[7]

In this story, note that Zhuangzi is singing and playing on a bowl. Rather than mourn passively, he does something to counteract his sorrow. His singing is a profound human response, quite believable. And Zhuangzi does not say that as a result of his insight he no longer feels sad. Rather, he says that as far as mourning is concerned, "I stopped." In other words, despite his feelings, he deliberately behaves in a way that seems more grateful to the universe and therefore more appropriate than mourning.

This tale suggests that to live in harmony with nature means to accept all its transformations. The great Tao produces both yang and yin, which alternate perpetually. The story says that yin and yang are our parents and we must obey them. If we cannot embrace the changes, we should at least observe them with an accepting heart.

Perhaps the most famous of all the stories in the book tells of Zhuangzi's dream of being a butterfly. In his dream he was flying around and enjoying life, but he did not know that he was Zhuangzi. When he woke up he was struck by a question: Am I Zhuangzi dreaming that I am a butterfly, or am I a butterfly dreaming I am Zhuangzi? This story hints that the boundary between reality and the imaginary is not really as clear as we might think.

Another story makes fun of people's judgments and the arbitrariness of their joy and anger. A trainer gives his monkeys three acorns in the morning and four at night. When the monkeys convey their dissatisfaction with receiving too few acorns in the morning, the trainer obliges, giving them four acorns in the morning and three at night. As a result, "the monkeys were all delighted."[7]

The Zhuangzi rejects all barriers, including that between the ordinary and the fantastic, between the normal and the paranormal, as hinted by the story of the butterfly dream. But the love of the marvelous really shows itself best in some stories that talk of the supernatural powers that a wise person can attain. The Zhuangzi tells of an exceptional person who could tell everything about one's past and future, another who could ride on the wind, and another who was invulnerable to heat or pain. The Zhuangzi thus elaborates the potential results of being one with the Tao.

THE BASIC TEACHINGS OF PHILOSOPHICAL TAOISM

The main teachings of the Tao Te Ching and the Zhuangzi can be summarized as follows:

Tao This is the name for whatever mysterious reality makes nature to be what it is and to act the way it does. The Chinese character for *Tao* is commonly translated as "way," but it has also been translated as "existence," "pattern," and "process." Primarily, the Tao is the way that nature expresses itself—the natural way. Human beings can unite themselves with the Tao in the way they live.

Wu wei: The ideal of effortlessness To have commandments would go against the nature of Taoism; but it does offer recommendations about how to live, recommendations that do not come from a divine voice but from nature, the model of balance and harmony. The suggestion most often mentioned in the Tao Te Ching is **wu wei,** which literally means "no action." Perhaps a better translation is "no strain" or "effortlessness." The ideal implies the avoidance of unnecessary action and action that is not spontaneous. If we look at nature, we see

The boatman who goes with the river's flow is an example of wu wei in practice.

that a great deal happens quietly, effortlessly: plants grow, birds and animals are born, and nature repairs itself after a storm. Nature works to accomplish only what is necessary, but no more. Consider the plain strength of the ordinary bird nest. Birds build homes according to their needs, and what they make is simple and beautiful; they don't require circular driveways, pillars, or marbled entryways. The ideal of "no strain" is the antithesis of all those sweat-loving mottoes like "No pain, no gain" and "Onward and upward."

Simplicity Taoism urges its followers to eliminate whatever is unnecessary and artificial and to appreciate the simple and the apparently ordinary. In this regard, Taoists distrust formal education because of its inherent complexity and artificiality. The Tao Te Ching—in the twentieth chapter—states its opinion: "Give up learning, and put an end to your troubles."

Gentleness Because Taoists pursue the gentle way, they hate weapons and war. The wise person loves peace and restraint and avoids all unnecessary violence. The wise person "does not regard weapons as lovely things. For to think them lovely means to delight in them, and to delight in them means to delight in the slaughter of men."[8]

Relativity People see things from a limited point of view that is based on their own concerns. They see things in terms of divisions: I-you, good-bad, valuable-worthless, beautiful-ugly, and so forth. Taoists believe that it is necessary to attain a vision of things that sees beyond these apparent opposites.

TAOISM AND THE QUEST FOR LONGEVITY

Taoism has absorbed many practices that are thought to bring a person into union with the Tao. These practices help the person feel the flow of nature, attain spiritual purity, and live a long life.

To use the word *yoga* to describe Taoist exercises would be misleading, because *yoga* is a Sanskrit word. But this word is useful for conveying to nonspecialists the physical aspect of Taoism. The canon of Taoist literature includes recommendations for many types of arm and body movements, breathing regulation, diet, and massage.

One "yogic" practice is called internal alchemy. It aims at transforming and spiritualizing the life force (**qi, ch'i**) of the practitioner. Some later forms of internal alchemy teach exercises that move the life force from its origin at the base of the spine upward to the head. From there it circles back, via the heart, to its origin. This movement is accomplished through certain postures, muscular exercises, and practices of mental imagery. Some Taoists have held that these practices of internal alchemy can create an entity—the "immortal embryo"—that can survive the death of the body.

Another internal alchemy technique is the cultivation of a new way of breathing, the ideal being the gentle breathing of a sleeping child. To achieve this ideal, breathing can be adjusted to the heartbeats and slowed down by taking fewer and fewer breaths in relation to number of heartbeats.

In ancient China, some people experimented with physical alchemy, hoping to create an elixir that could extend life and even make a person immortal. Because gold did not rust, individuals attempted to make gold either into a liquid that could be drunk or into a vessel from which an elixir could be drunk. Jade, pearl, mother-of-pearl, and compounds of mercury were also utilized. Some people undoubtedly died as a result of these experiments. When there seemed to be little success in this direction, the alchemical search became a metaphor for the development of the type of internal alchemy just described. In Chinese culture, there has remained, however, a great interest in pills, foods, and medicines that are believed to prolong life. Some of these (such as ginseng, garlic, and ginger) seem to have genuine medical benefits.

RELIGIOUS TAOISM

Early Taoism was not an "organized religion." Many of its earliest practitioners lived alone, as some still do today. The eremitical (reclusive) way of life dates back to ancient China, and the Tao Te Ching may have emerged from it.

As time went on, however, the movement became more organized. At first, groups of like-minded individuals came together to pool their experience in the search for longevity and special powers. From these groups sprang organizations headed by charismatic individuals—something like religious orders. One group, called the Yellow Turbans, was led by a man named Zhang Jue (Chang Chüeh, who lived during the first century C.E.) but it eventually died out. Another, led by Zhang Daoling (Chang Tao-ling, c. 150 C.E.), developed an organization that allegedly helped Taoism survive into the present. The organization created a hierarchical structure, based on the son, grandson, and successors of the founder, and set up a system of parishes. Because the successors of Zhang Daoling carry the title "heavenly master," the sect is called the "way of the heavenly masters." It is most active in Taiwan. Taoism also produced monasteries and orders of monks, although this form of Taoism has, for the time being, virtually ended.

One of the stimuli that influenced Taoism to take an organizational path was Buddhism, which entered China by the first century C.E. Buddhism was brought by a monastic clergy who imported and translated a large number of written works and set up monasteries and temples that had impressive rites. In order to survive, Taoism began to imitate these elements. By the fifth century C.E., religious Taoism had grown into an organization with significant political influence.

Although Taoist ritual is rare today in mainland China, some Taoist monastery buildings remain, such as this example in Xi'an.

Taoism also imitated Buddhism in its production of a vast number of sacred books. The range of topics was wide: guidebooks on meditation, breathing exercises, and sexual yoga; stories of ecstatic excursions made to the stars and of wonder workers; recipes for longevity and magical powers; manuals of alchemy; and descriptions of ritual. Collectively, these works form the Taoist canon—a collection of more than a thousand books, similar in authority to the multiple sutras of Buddhism. Publication of the canon took place in 1445, but supplements continued to be added later.

There is consensus among scholars that religious Taoism absorbed many of the elements of the Chinese worldview and brought together various strands and schools interested in philosophy, meditation, and immortality. Ultimately, Taoism embraced everything that is believed to bring physical health and spiritual elevation.

Religious Taoism also developed a pantheon. It honors Laozi and other great people of the past who are thought to be immortal and part of a heavenly court—based on the Chinese imperial bureaucracy—that is ruled by the mythic Jade Emperor.

Religious Taoism is far stronger in Taiwan than in mainland China. This is partly due to the severe repression of all religion in mainland

China by the Communist regime. It is partly due, too, to the fact that the thirty-seventh heavenly master moved to Taiwan after the Communist takeover of the mainland. In Taiwan, Taoist specialists perform esoteric rites, such as the Jiao (Chiao) rite of cosmic renewal. The Jiao lasts at least three days and combines ritual (closed to the laity) and a public celebration outdoors.

Many Taoist clergy do ministerial work, attending to the needs of the public. Exorcists—called Red Heads because of their red hats or scarves—work to heal and restore harmony. Taoist priests—called Black Heads because of their black caps—are also able to perform exorcisms, but they are primarily involved in performing blessings, funerals, the Jiao, and other rites.

Taoist gods and beliefs are kept alive in part by the Chinese tendency to blend beliefs of several systems. It is common, for example, to find Taoist images in Chinese Buddhist temples. In the mind of most Chinese, there need be no argument. In ordinary practice, elements from folk religion, Taoism, Confucianism, and Buddhism are combined. They are mutually supportive—as members of all Three Doctrines have generally agreed.

TAOISM AND THE ARTS

It is possible to see Taoist influences in many Chinese art forms, although the extent of the influence is impossible to determine with precision. Paintings of Laozi riding on an ox are clear examples of Taoist influence, as are references to Zhuangzi in poetry, but beyond that it is perhaps more accurate to say that poetry and the arts share many of the same concerns of Taoist thought—just as they do of Chinese Buddhist and Confucian thought.

As we know, the immensity, flow, and mystery of nature are common themes in the Tao Te Ching, and some of its most important images are flowing water, the valley, and the uncarved block of stone. These themes and images are abundant in Chinese painting.

In Chinese nature painting, perspective is important. Images drawn from nature are often presented either very close up or at a great distance. Paintings of a bird or a stalk of bamboo seen close-up help the viewer see the mysterious energy at work in these nonhuman forms of life: a bird perches in a certain way on a branch, and a stalk of bamboo emerges in its own special way into the sunshine. (The Song dynasty [960–1279 C.E.] produced a great number of these works, although the names of the painters of some of the finest works are not known.) These paintings make us look more closely at the humbler elements of nature—cats, rabbits, deer, birds—and recognize that they, too, have their own interests and patterns of living, and that our human patterns are only a small part of the much wider repertoire of nature.

Taoism influenced Chinese landscape painting in its portrayal of nature's grandeur and of the limited role that human beings have within nature.

The great genius of Chinese nature painting is particularly evident in the paintings of landscapes seen at a distance. These paintings often depict hints of mountains far away and, beyond them, infinite space. Some portray a person gazing far into the distance, even beyond the painting itself. What we most notice in these works is the fascinating use of empty space. Some of the paintings are almost half empty, but they do not feel unfinished, as if something were missing. Ma Yuan (fl. c. 1190–1230) was a master of this effect. In his painting entitled *A Scholar and His Servant on a Terrace,* a gentleman looks out past pine branches into the distance; the upper left half of the painting, in the direction of the man's gaze, is entirely empty. In his painting called *Walking on a Mountain Path in Spring,* a man strolls into an emptiness—virtually the entire right side of the painting—that is inhabited only by one small bird. The space of the paintings is the positive emptiness to which the Tao Te Ching draws our attention.

Chinese poetry frequently praises themes also found in the Tao Te Ching and the Zhuangzi: the joy of life in the countryside, away from the complications of the city; the change of seasons; simplicity; and harmony with nature. The poet who is often praised for his fine expression of Taoist ideals is Li Bo (Li Po), who lived during the Tang dynasty and died about 762 C.E. Little is known about his life, but his death is famous. According to tradition, he died as the result of a poetic accident. Sitting drunk in a boat one night, Li Bo reached out to embrace the moon's reflection on the water but fell in and disappeared beneath the surface. One of his poems is about Zhuangzi's dream of being a butterfly. Another is about being so absorbed in nature that he did not notice dusk coming on; when he stood up at last, flower petals fell off his clothes. His poems are so highly regarded that they have been memorized and recited by Chinese for centuries to express their own feelings.

Chinese garden design is an art form that complements and completes Chinese architecture. The house is yang, the realm of the square and the straight line; the garden is yin, the realm of the circle and the curve. Inside is family harmony; outside is harmony with nature. One realm supports the other.

The importance of nature requires that traditional house design include and even incorporate the garden in its creation. At a minimum, if the family can afford it, the traditional Chinese house features one or several courtyards, with trees, plants, rocks, and possibly even a small pond. In the case of larger constructions, such as palaces and villas, the designs might also include natural or artificial lakes, waterfalls, streams, hills, and grottoes. Chinese garden design differs from that of common Western design. Instead of straight lines and symmetry, walkways meander, and bridges may zigzag. Gates, in imitation of the moon, may be round. And water moves only in its natural manner—that is, flowing downward, not upward, as in a fountain.

In the house man is in the society of his fellow beings, but in the garden he is in the society of nature. Inside the house he is a Confucian with all his moral codes, conventions, and a prescribed way of life, whereas in the garden he is a Taoist, a romantic, primitivistic, carefree "new-born child." . . . But the garden is more than the supplement to the house. It fulfills a higher function of life, the function that only art can fulfill. . . . It is here that man becomes natural, spontaneous, and sincere.

—Wing-Tsit Chan[9]

This garden manifests the harmonies that result from following the Tao.

TAOISM AND
THE MODERN WORLD

Religious Taoism will continue for the foreseeable future in Taiwan and in overseas communities of Chinese. If the government of mainland China continues to relax its antireligious stance, we might expect Taoist ritual to revive there and take the same form we see in Taiwan. There are a few indications of such a trend (although the Communist government strictly controls religion and treats clergy and other religious practitioners primarily as custodians of historical sites that are important to tourism). In mainland China, Taoist ritual is now allowed on some traditionally Taoist mountain sites, such as Mount Tai, and also in a few urban Taoist temples. Other Taoist practices live on as well: in his charming book *Road to Heaven: Encounters with Chinese Hermits,* Bill Porter recounts in photographs and writing his recent meetings with some Taoist hermits living in mainland China.

In world culture, Taoism as a philosophy continues to spread its influence. Or, to be more precise, we might say that popularized Taoist notions—conveyed in the many English translations (and mistranslations) of its classical books—are invoked by a spectrum of the world's citizens, from members of the environmental movement to producers of science-fiction movies. Fans—new and old—of the rereleased Star Wars trilogy who can also quote from the Tao Te Ching may see Taoist thought in the line from the movie: "May the Force be with you." For many, "the Force" is yet another way of referring to the unnamed Tao.

The Chinese Garden—Bridge to the Infinite

The philosopher Wing-Tsit Chan has written of the union of house and garden and of the semireligious role that a Chinese garden can play:

> Nature is never looked upon by the Chinese as chaotic or disorganized. Heaven and earth co-exist in harmony, and the four seasons run their course regularly. Thus the Confucians and the Taoists unite in reminding the Chinese that there is a universal principle pervading all things, whether in the realm of physical nature or in the sphere of human life. This universal principle expresses itself in two aspects, the Yin and the Yang, or the negative and the positive forces. In casting away regularity in favor of irregularity for his garden, the Chinese never violates the regularity of nature. Natural order is religiously preserved. . . . Over and above irregularity and informality, there reigns a higher order, the order of nature. . . .
>
> This harmony of man and nature in the flow of the great stream of rhythm makes the Chinese garden more than something merely secular. It is true that no one would look upon the Chinese garden as a religious structure. . . . But in spite of all this, we cannot deny the fact that the garden is regarded as an ideal place for meditation. Meditation may be purely moral, an effort at self-introspection. Intense and sincere meditation, however, inevitably leads to the absorption in the Infinite.[10]

Roofline of a Taoist temple in Taiwan.

CONFUCIANISM

Taoism, as we just saw, seeks to bring human beings into union with the Tao, particularly through imitating certain qualities in nature—its harmony, lack of strain, and flowing mystery. The complex of ideals and beliefs that helped give shape to Laozi's teachings also influenced Confucius, the major teacher of the second great Chinese school of thought. Thus, it is not surprising to find Confucianism as concerned with the Tao as Taoism is; as one Confucian classic says, "He is the sage who naturally and easily embodies the right *way*."[11] This "way" is the cosmic Tao that permeates the entire universe—the Tao that we see in the everyday life of the noble person also "in its utmost reaches, . . . shines brightly through heaven and earth."[12]

THE TAO IN CONFUCIANISM

There is a difference, however, between Taoist and Confucian notions of the Tao. For Confucians, the Tao of primary interest is the Tao within the *human* world, manifested in "right" relationships and in a harmonious society. It was social harmony Confucius described when he listed his particular wishes: "[In] regard to the aged, to give them rest; in regard to friends, to show them sincerity; in regard to the young, to treat them tenderly."[13]

In Taoism, everything is a part of the rhythm of nature—the Tao. In Confucianism, however, although birds and clouds and trees are what they should be, human beings do not automatically become or remain what they should be. The sweet, spontaneous infant can quickly turn into the selfish child. The Confucian would say that training in virtue is necessary to enable the Tao to manifest itself clearly in the human being.

The Doctrine of the Mean, an important Confucian text (discussed later in this chapter), recommends several types of training, including training in the cultivation of personal equilibrium and harmony. We should recall that Taoists avoid such "training," feeling that formal education has a potential for distorting one's originally pure state. Confucians, however, hold that the best training does not contaminate character but, by cultivating virtues, gives it definition and clarity.

The Master said, "At fifteen, I had my mind bent on learning. At thirty, I stood firm. At forty, I had no doubts. At fifty, I knew the decrees of Heaven. At sixty, my ear was an obedient organ for the reception of truth. At seventy, I could follow what my heart desired, without transgressing what was right."

—from the Confucian Analects[14]

THE LIFE OF CONFUCIUS

Confucius was born in 551 B.C.E., at a time when China was not a single empire but a group of small kingdoms. His name was Kong Qiu (K'ung Ch'iu). He later became known by the title of Kong Fuzi (K'ung Fu Tzu), meaning "Master Kong," but he is known in the West by the Latin version of his name which was created and spread by European Catholic missionaries.

許真人

The ideal of Confucius, pictured here, was the cultivation of human nobility.

Tradition relates that Confucius was from a once-noble family which had fled at a time of political danger to the state of Lu (south of present-day Beijing). His father died when he was a child, and despite their poverty, his mother raised him as an educated gentleman. He enjoyed chariot riding, archery, and playing the lute. In his teens, he became seriously interested in pursuing scholarship. He is said to have held a minor government post as tax collector, probably to support his mother and his studies. His mother died when he was in his late teens, and he entered into a state of mourning. When the period of mourning was over, he began his public life as a teacher.

Despite his eventual success as a teacher, Confucius had always wanted to play an influential part in government; and it is possible that for a time (from about 500–496 B.C.E.) he became a government minister. Confucius married and is believed to have had a son and a daughter. He wandered for about fifteen years outside of his home state but eventually returned to Lu to take a somewhat ceremonial post as senior advisor. He died about 479 B.C.E.

Confucianism: Philosophy or Religion?

Should Confucianism be treated as a philosophy or as a religion? Those who wish to call it a philosophy point out its lack of interest in a God or gods and its lack of focus on any world beyond this one. And although they recognize that some Confucian religious ritual exists, they argue that ritual is not essential and has been largely abandoned in public life.

It is possible, though, that the particular standards some people use to downplay Confucianism as a religion have been taken unconsciously from Western notions of religion and then applied to all systems, Western and non-Western alike. Other people, applying different standards, point out that Confucianism is more than simply a philosophy. If Theravada Buddhism can be treated as a religion, they argue, so too can Confucianism. Like Theravada Buddhism, Confucianism is a moral system that functions as a religion in providing meaning and order in people's lives. Confucianism can also be said to have its scriptures (the Confucian classics, as we will discuss a little later) as well as a mystical dimension that enables people to experience their unity with the universe through inner equilibrium and harmony with society. These facts invite us to treat Confucianism from a religious point of view, as we do in this book.

LIVING ACCORDING TO CONFUCIAN VALUES

The period in which Confucius was born was a time of social turmoil because of the disintegration of the feudal system. Seeing families and individuals suffering from the social disorder, Confucius concluded that society would function properly only if virtues were taught and lived.

The ideals of Confucius were two: he wanted to produce "excellent" individuals who could be social leaders, and he wanted to create a harmonious society. He believed that these ideals were complementary: excellent individuals would keep society harmonious, and a harmonious society would nurture excellent individuals.

Confucius believed that each human being is capable of being good, refined, and even great; but he differed from the Taoists because he was convinced that a human being cannot achieve those qualities in isolation. In his view, a human being becomes a full person only through the contributions of other people and through fulfilling one's obligations to them. These other people include parents, teachers, friends, aunts and uncles, grandparents, ancestors, and even government ministers.

Confucius also believed that more than social interaction (which even animals have) is needed. For Confucius, that "more" is what makes *ordinary* human beings into *excellent* human beings, "superior persons." What constitutes that "more"? What are the sources of human excellence?

Excellence comes partly from the cultivation of an individual's virtues and intellect. Thus, education is essential. We should recognize, though, that for Confucius education meant more than knowledge; it also involved the development of skills in poetry, music, artistic appreciation, manners, and religious ritual. Confucius valued education because it transmitted the lessons of the past into the present. He believed that much of the wisdom

Today, as in past centuries, the Chinese devote themselves to study—here in a study hall of the former Confucian Imperial Academy in Beijing.

required to produce excellent human beings is already expressed in the teachings of the great leaders of the past. Convinced that the past provides fine models for the present, Confucius thought that education could show the way to wise and happy living.

Civilization is a complicated and fragile creation, and as such, civilized human beings must be full of respect and care. Care must be given to the young, who will continue human life on earth, and to the elders, who teach and pass on the traditions. There should be reverence for everything valuable that has been brought from earlier generations.

Confucius believed that social harmony is established when people play their social roles properly. This sense of social responsibility was codified in five great relationships.

The Five Great Relationships

In Confucianism, relationships are just as real as any visible object. Human beings are not individuals but interwoven threads of relationships with many people. To a great extent, in Confucian thinking human beings *are* their relationships.

All relationships, however, are not equal. The level of a relationship may be determined by personal factors, such as friendship or family connection, or by more formal social factors, such as age or socioeconomic status. Confucianism recognizes this inequality and actually lists relationships according to a hierarchy, beginning with the most important:

1. *Father-son* Family is the foundation of society for Confucians, with the relationship between father and son at its core. (This relationship also represents all parent-child relationships.) The father must be

responsible for the education and moral formation of the son, and the son must be respectful and obedient and must care for the father in his old age. Confucians have extended this ideal in ways that some people in more individualistic societies today might not appreciate; for example, the father must help in the selection of a vocation and a marriage partner for his son. Also, the relationship of obligation is mutual and does not end until the death of the father. The parent-child relationship is so fundamental that it can function as the model for similar relationships, such as that between employer and employee.

2. *Elder brother-younger brother* Languages such as English, French, and Spanish do not distinguish between an elder brother and a younger brother. But the Chinese, Korean, Vietnamese, and Japanese languages—which all have been strongly influenced by Confucian thought—have different words for the two kinds of brothers. In their cultures, the distinction is important. An elder brother must assume responsibility for raising the younger siblings, and the younger siblings must be compliant. The practicality of this arrangement becomes clear when we appreciate the possibility of an elderly father dying before all his children have been raised. The paternal responsibility then would shift to the eldest son, who has a unique status in the family.

3. *Husband-wife* Each person in this relationship is responsible for the other's care. In Confucian thought, the relationship is hierarchical. The husband is an authoritative protector, and the wife is a protected homemaker and mother. The Confucian notion of marriage also

The hierarchy of human relationships determines the roles of spouses, parents, and offspring.

implies much less romantic expectation than does the modern Western notion.

4. *Friend-friend* The relationship between friends, especially male friends, has meant to China what romantic love has meant to post-Renaissance Europe and to America. In Confucian culture, a friendship entails serious obligations, and a friendship made in youth is expected to last a lifetime. In some Confucian lists of the Five Great Relationships, this item is described as a friend-friend relationship; in other lists, however, it is described as the relationship between any elder person and any younger person (usually of the same gender). The two types of relationships are actually quite close, however. In friendship there is often a certain hierarchy: the friends may differ in age or rank or health or wealth or knowledge. And the state of friends' welfare can reverse itself over time. In the case of a friend who is wealthier or stronger, that friend has a responsibility to assist the other friend who is in need. The mentor relationship—which implies a difference in age between the two—is common in Confucian cultures, too. This type of relationship might be, for example, that between a teacher and a student, which in Confucian cultures entails serious mutual responsibilities.

5. *Ruler-subject* It might seem that this relationship should be listed first, and sometimes it is.[15] However, more often it appears last in the lists, reflecting the Confucian perspective on the role of the ruler: above all, a ruler must act like a father, assuming responsibility and care for the subjects who are like his children. Thus, the father-son relationship is primary in that it is the model for most other relationships. Confucianism holds that social order begins in a harmonious home and then extends outward—to town, province, and country. The last item then brings the list full circle, back to the smallest unit of society—the family.

The Five Great Relationships signify that each person must live up to his or her social role and social status. This has been called the rectification of names. I have only to consult my social role and title to know my duty. For example, a father must be a caring father, a ruler must be a responsible ruler, and a friend must be a good friend.

In Confucian societies, consequently, people see each other quite strongly in terms of their relationships and social roles, and because the family is the primary model for all groups, age determines position. We see interesting implications of the Five Great Relationships in Confucian countries today. For example, modern Japanese and Korean companies often act like large families, and management plays a fatherly role. Similarly, an employee's identity comes largely from his or her place in a company, and job titles are significant. The exchange of business cards—on which the person's title is prominently featured—is a careful ritual. Seniors have responsibility for juniors, and one's pay and role are largely based on seniority.

Privacy and individual rights are not highly emphasized, and there is more togetherness. Harmony is all-important.

Just as social harmony comes from the living out of the Five Great Relationships, so personal excellence comes from the manifestation of five virtues.

The Confucian Virtues

Although they emphasize harmony between people, the Confucian virtues do not lead to antlike conformity. Some Confucian virtues, such as love of education and the arts, help individuals develop their unique talents. But the virtues most prized by Confucianism are indeed largely social virtues. Individual uniqueness, although valued by Confucianism, is expected to be muted, subtle, and considerate of others.

Ren (jen) The Chinese character for **ren (jen)** illustrates the word's meaning by blending two simpler pictographs—for "person" and "two." When we look at the Chinese ideogram for the virtue of ren, we understand its meaning: to think of the other. It is translated in many ways: "sympathy," "empathy," "benevolence," "humaneness," "kindness," "consideration," "thoughtfulness," and "human-heartedness." It does not mean to drop one's own self-interest or to be mindlessly generous. It simply means that one must be considerate of the other person through one's actions and words.
Some people, though, do not know how to be kind or have difficulty in certain situations being kind spontaneously. In Confucian thinking, following social conventions is an important way for such people to show ren. After all, underlying all worthy social conventions is consideration. A motto that reflects the essence of ren is, "If you can't be kind, then be polite."

Li This word is often translated as "propriety," which means "doing what is appropriate" or "doing what is proper to the situation." Originally, **li** referred to carrying out rites correctly. More generally, it means knowing and using the proper words and actions for social life. For each situation, there are appropriate words to say, proper ways to dress, and correct things to do. Sometimes propriety entails the control of one's own desires. The **Analects,** which record the sayings of Confucius, assert, "To subdue one's self and return to propriety, is perfect virtue."[16] In Western culture, which values what is different and individualistic, the notion of li may seem oppressive and suggest personal weakness. Confucianism, on the contrary, sees self-control as a sign of strength—and practicality. We all recognize that every social situation has its hidden structure. Chew gum at a job interview and you will not get the job; wear shorts to a funeral and you will probably cause hurt to the mourners. Li means good manners. It is putting ren into practice.

Shu The usual translation of **shu** is "reciprocity," but its essence addresses the question, How will my action affect the other person? It is another form of ren. It is also another version of the Golden Rule: Do unto others as you would have them do unto you. The Confucian version, interestingly, is stated in negative terms: "Do not do unto others what you would not wish done to yourself."[17] It is therefore often called the Silver Rule. Logically, we may argue that the two formulations mean the same thing. But there is something gentler about the Confucian version. The Golden Rule can be misleading. For example, I may love wine, but this does not mean that I should "do unto others" by serving wine to everyone who comes to my home. The Silver Rule helps me consider my actions from the other person's viewpoint .

Xiao (hsiao) The word **xiao (hsiao)** is usually translated as "filial piety" (devotion of a son or daughter to a parent). It also means the devotion that all members have to their entire family's welfare. It encompasses several notions: remembrance of ancestors, respect for parents and elders, and care for children in the family. Xiao means doing what would please one's parents and bring them respect, such as getting a good education. It means caring for siblings. It can also mean feeling a sense of responsibility to marry in order to continue the family line. Ideally, it means valuing the entire extended family— of past, present, and future.

Wen The term **wen** means "culture" and includes all the arts that are associated with civilization. Confucianism has a special love for

This shop window displays writing brushes and, to the left, stones into which are to be incised with owners' personal seals. Proper use of these materials exhibits cultivation.

The Ideal Human Being

Confucianism is often thought of as a system for the regulation of social groups. Yet Confucianism is also a system for the transformation of the individual. Undergirding Confucianism is not just the ideal of an orderly society but also the ideal of a perfect human being.

This perfect person is the **junzi (chün tzu)**—a term usually translated as "superior person," although a better translation may be "noble person." The following quotations give a sense of the virtue that guides the junzi—the person who shows humanity at its best. In such a noble human being the Confucian ideals have been inculcated since childhood, and the virtues have been practiced for so long that the whole Confucian manner of relating to the world has become completely natural. The "noble person," as Alfred Bloom nicely describes, is

> distinguished by his faithfulness, diligence, and modesty. He neither overpowers with his knowledge, nor is afraid to admit error. He looks at all sides of any issue, is cautious and not concerned for personal recognition. Carrying himself with dignity, he appears imperturbable, resolute, and simple. He is exemplary in filial piety and generous with his kin. In his relations with others he looks for good points, though he is not uncritical. As a leader, he knows how to delegate responsibility and when to pardon or promote. He is sensitive to the feelings and expressions of others.[18]

A subtle portrait of such a person has been given by George Kates, who describes the man who became his personal tutor in China. Kates describes the civilized manner that manifested itself in all his tutor's actions, even in the cultivated way the tutor entered a room and sat in a chair. The tutor, Mr. Wang,

> had contrived to make his humdrum life, composed of a daily routine of monotonous teaching and domestic privation, symmetrical and reasonable indeed. . . . His eyes were kind; and his glance could at times glow when some new thought would catch and hold him. His side-face made you like him. . . . He . . . remained closed and therefore secure, if only because he knew so well by indirection how to turn aside effectively any indiscreet remark or lolloping conduct on the part of some new and immature pupil. . . . When Mr. Wang became assured that we thus had the same sense of decorum, barriers fell. Yet I remained more unwilling than ever now to press in upon his carefully guarded privacies; and upon this base we built a tranquil relation, partial it is true, but one that lasted us peaceably through many years. He became my formal teacher.[19]

poetry and literature, as well as a fondness for calligraphy, painting, and music. The educated person is expected to not only have a knowledge of these arts but to have an amateur skill in them as well. Wen can also entail the general notion of art appreciation, or connoisseurship. A connoisseur has a highly developed aesthetic sense and is able to know and appreciate beauty in its many forms.

Confucianism stresses other virtues, too, particularly loyalty, consensus, hard work, thrift, and emotional control. One virtue frequently mentioned is sincerity, although the Confucian notion of sincerity is not the same as the Western notion, in which an individual says or does something personal and "from the heart." Instead, the Confucian sense of sincerity means to choose naturally and automatically to do what is right, particularly in fulfilling one's job duties and social obligations properly. Through sincerity, the noble person unites with the force of the universe, which is already—according to Confucian thought—sincere. "Sincerity is the way of

Heaven. . . . He who possesses sincerity is he who, without an effort, hits what is right. . . . He who attains to sincerity is he who chooses what is good, and firmly holds it fast."[20]

CONFUCIAN LITERATURE

Confucius considered himself primarily a transmitter of wisdom. Consequently, much of what is called the literature of Confucianism actually preceded him and was subsequently edited and added to by Confucian scholars. Thus, it is not always possible to separate with certainty the teachings of Confucius, his predecessors, and his followers.

Confucian literature, divided into the **Five Classics** and the **Four Books,** includes pre-Confucian works of poetry, history, and divination; the sayings of Confucius and his disciples; and the sayings of Mencius, a later Confucian teacher. The canon of Confucian literature has varied, but became settled during the Song dynasty (960–1279).

Confucian literature became the "core curriculum" for almost six hundred years in China, from 1313 until 1912. China was the first country in the world to have regular examinations to enter the civil service; but these were based on the Confucian books and their commentaries. Any male could take the examinations, and success in them often guaranteed a post with the government. The common practice in families who could afford it was to select at least one boy in the family to receive a Confucian education and to prepare him for the examinations. In aristocratic families, all boys were given a Confucian education.

Because the Confucian books were part of the established educational system, the sayings of Confucius and Mencius came to pervade Chinese culture. They have been quoted as authoritatively in China as the Bible is quoted in the West or the Qur'an is quoted in Muslim societies. They also have put a heavy stamp on the neighboring cultures of Korea, Japan, and Vietnam, as well as overseas Chinese communities everywhere. Although the literature is no longer an essential part of the educational curriculum in Asia, Confucian values continue to be taught both formally in school and less formally in the family and surrounding culture.

The Five Classics

The Book of History (Shu Jing, Shu Ching) is an anthology of historical material about kings from earliest times up until the early Zhou (Chou) period (c. 1122–256 B.C.E.).

The Book of Poetry (Shi Jing, Shih Ching) is a collection of three hundred poems of the Zhou period, some with a moral intent.

The Book of Changes (Yi Jing, I Ching) speaks of the basic patterns of the universe. It is used to understand future events and to work with

them properly. It is also an important Confucian document because it tells how the noble person will act in the face of life's events.

The Book of Rites (Li Ji, Li Chi) lists ancient ceremonies and their meaning. Another classical book, The Book of Music, is said to have once been a part of the classics but no longer exists separately. Part of it may perhaps survive, embedded in The Book of Rites.

The Spring and Autumn Annals (Chun Qiu, Ch'un Ch'iu) comprises historical records of the state of Lu, where Confucius lived, and ends with a later commentary.

The sayings attributed to Confucius are frequently carved into hard stone. Here, words carved on a pillar rest on the back of a tortoise.   ◄

The Four Books

The Analects (Lun Yu, Lun Yü) are the sayings of Confucius and his conversations with followers. Tradition holds that his followers collected his sayings and wrote them down, but this work may better be attributed to the disciples of his followers. It is possible that some sayings are much later additions. The twenty sections of the Analects contain little stories and short sayings—sometimes only a sentence or two long—that often begin with the phrase "The Master said." They cover a wide variety of topics but often relate to the character of the noble person. Here are two typical sayings: "The Master said, a gentleman takes as much trouble to discover what is right as lesser men take to discover what will pay"[21]; and "a gentleman covets the reputation of being slow in word but prompt in deed."[22]

For centuries, the Chinese have acquired personal copies of Confucian sayings by making rubbings of stone columns into which the sayings have been carved.

The Great Learning (Da Xue, Ta Hsüeh) is a short discussion of the character and influence of the noble person. Its introductory section is traditionally attributed to Confucius and the remainder to a disciple, but this attribution is dubious. It contains many quotations from the Book of Poetry, which are given a moral interpretation. Although it was at one time added to the Book of Rites, The Great Learning has been printed separately since the thirteenth century C.E. It was the very first book to be memorized and studied by Chinese students. This book stresses that one must begin with self-cultivation and personal virtue if one wishes to produce order in the family and state. "From the Son of Heaven [the emperor] down to the mass of the people, all must consider the cultivation of the person the root of everything besides."[23]

The Doctrine of the Mean (Zhong Yong, Chung Yung), another work once added to the Book of Rites, speaks in praise of "the mean," or equilibrium. Its beginning—with its references to "Heaven" and the "way"—hints at the mystical side of Confucianism. "What Heaven has conferred is called the nature [of humanity]; an accordance with this nature is called the path of duty; the regulation of this path is called instruction. The path may not be left for an instant."[24] A human being who follows "the way of Heaven" avoids extremes and remains in harmony. This balance unites the individual with the balance of the universe. "Let the states of equilibrium and harmony exist in perfection, and a happy order will prevail throughout heaven and earth, and all things will be nourished and flourish."[25]

The Mencius (Mengzi, Meng Tzu) is a long collection of the teachings of Mencius, a Confucian who lived several centuries after Confucius. (More will be said about him later in this chapter). Like the Analects, the sayings of the Mencius frequently begin with the phrase "Mencius said." Sometimes the tone seems quite gentle, such as in this saying: "Mencius said, The great man is he who does not lose his child's-heart."[26]

THE DEVELOPMENT OF CONFUCIANISM

Schools of Philosophy

The basic nature of human beings has been one of the great topics of discussion throughout the history of China. Is human nature good or bad or somewhere in between? This is not a theoretical question at all, because how one answers this question has crucial practical results. If human nature is basically good, it should be left on its own and trusted, and moral training, laws, and punishments are of little importance. If human nature is basically evil, human beings need strict moral education, stern laws, harsh punishments, and a strong ruler. A middle position is also possible: if human nature is neutral, human beings need education that is not necessarily coercive and a ruler who governs primarily through example.

Before Confucianism was adopted as official state policy in the Han dynasty (206 B.C.E.–220 C.E.), major schools of thought on this topic already had emerged, reflecting a full spectrum of opinion. The Confucian schools took a middle course between extremes, recognizing both the great abilities of human beings and the need for their formation.

The most liberal of the thinkers were the Taoists, who were so optimistic about the natural goodness of human beings that they rejected moral or intellectual education of any kind. The Tao Te Ching shows clearly the Taoist rejection of Confucian education.[27] The entire book presents instead a vision of people living simple lives in small villages, governing themselves with natural good sense.[28] Laws should be few, because if life is lived simply, order will arise spontaneously.

Closer to the center, but still to the left, was the teaching of Mencius, a Confucian who flourished about 300 B.C.E. (His name is the Latin version of his Chinese name, Mengzi, or Meng Tzu.) The teachings of Mencius were ultimately so acceptable to many that his writings, named after him, became one of the Four Books.

Mencius did not merely repeat the thoughts and values of Confucius; it seems he was a bit more optimistic about human nature, perhaps because of his contact with Taoism. There are innumerable Taoist-sounding passages among his sayings (such as the quote on page 218). Another of his sayings uses a different image loved by the Taoist: "The people turn to a benevolent rule as water flows downward."[29]

Mencius was struck by the many virtues that could be found in ordinary people: mercy, kindness, conscience. "The feeling of commiseration belongs to all men; so does that of shame and dislike; and that of reverence and respect. . . ."[30] In human beings, he thought, there is an "innate goodness," and virtues exist in everyone, at least in seedling form. The sprouts need only the proper nurturing, which education can provide by helping naturally good tendencies in a child to grow properly and to flower. Education does not radically redirect human nature, but helps it to become what it already potentially is.

Mencius was aware of the ideal of universal love but thought that such an ideal was impossible and unwise. According to Mencius, in society there is a hierarchy of love and responsibility: we must love our families first, then our friends and neighbors, and then the rest of society; and to reject that structure would bring about social disorder. Education is valuable in making the natural order clear and in helping individuals live with it dutifully.

Confucius's position on human nature seems to have been fairly close to the center of the spectrum. We have already seen this in his view on the importance of education. Confucius was also optimistic; he believed that human beings respond to kindness and good example.

A darker view of human nature was held by Xunzi (Hsün Tzu), who was active about 250 B.C.E. He is also considered a Confucian, but because of his pessimism about human nature his thought did not ultimately receive the official support that was eventually given to Mencius. Mencius and Confucius tended to view Heaven, the power which rules the universe, as ultimately benevolent. But for Xunzi (as for the Taoists), the universe is totally uncaring; it works according to its own nature and patterns.

Xunzi viewed human nature and human beings as functioning in a similarly mechanistic way. Human beings will veer toward self-interest unless they are taught differently. Consequently, education is not social refinement of an already good person; instead, it must be a radical moral and social reformation of human tendencies that are primarily selfish and individualistic. Education must inculcate proper ceremonies, manners, laws, and customs, for these artificial rules help transcend individual interest and make civilization possible. "All propriety and righteousness are the artificial production of the sages, and are not to be considered as growing out of the nature of man. It is just as when a potter makes a vessel from the clay . . . or when another workman cuts and hews a vessel out of wood. . . ."[31]

Holding a view of human nature similar to Xunzi's was the **Mohist** school, although its exact position is not easy to categorize. Mozi (Mo Tzu, c. 470–391 B.C.E.) was known as a self-disciplined, idealistic person, who lived simply and worked actively against war and for the betterment of common people. He thought that without laws, people were predatory; and with laws, there was order, but it was often inequitable. He held that social problems arise because people's love is graded and therefore partial, and the answer was to practice universal love for all. "Who is the most wise? Heaven is the most wise. And so righteousness assuredly issues from Heaven. Then the gentlemen of the world who desire to do righteousness cannot but obey the will of Heaven. What is the will of Heaven that we should all obey? It is to love all men universally."[32]

The **Legalists,** who were influential from about 400–200 B.C.E., also had a view of human nature like Xunzi's and Mozi's but possibly even starker. For the Legalists, human beings are fundamentally selfish and lazy. They will lie, cheat, steal, and kill whenever it is in their interest. "Civilization" is just a very thin veneer, easily shattered; and without stern laws and punishments, people will destroy one another. According to the Legalists, the education of children should consist mainly of warning and punishment, and society must continue these sanctions with adults, because adults are really just children in disguise.

For several centuries after the time of Confucius, the various philosophical schools strove for influence. Legalism triumphed for a time in the third century B.C.E. The foundation of the Han dynasty (206 B.C.E.–220 C.E.), however, provided an opportunity to find a school of thought that could make the greatest contribution to social order. Around 135 B.C.E., a scholar proposed to the emperor that Confucianism would help unite the country.

This scholar, Dong Zhongshu (Tung Chung-shu), also recommended that the emperor set up a Confucian school for the education of government officials. The emperor followed his advice, and Confucian thought began to gain recognition as an important political philosophy.

The Development of Confucianism as a Religious System

Confucianism grew in response to many needs and interests. In its first phase, as we have just seen, it was challenged by rival philosophies. Next, it was challenged by religion.

When Buddhism entered China in the first century C.E., it brought new ideas and practices (as we saw in Chapter 4). One radical idea was its general deemphasis of worldly human concerns and duties, as exemplified by unmarried Buddhist monks. Monks did not have children to continue the family line, nor could they take care of their parents in old age—another deficiency which seemed to counter the virtue of filial piety (xiao). Buddhism appeared to focus on the topics of death, karma, nirvana, past lives, and future lives, and it created expensive temples and ceremonies. It is important not to overstate the case, but to some Confucians these tendencies were socially deficient.

Of course, the aspects of Buddhism that some Confucians discounted were what made it so appealing to many people. Buddhism was colorful, imaginative, and ritualistic, and it gave people hope that there were supernatural beings who could help them. Chinese who became monks and nuns also benefited because they had a fairly secure life and paid no taxes.

Partially in response to Buddhism's success, Confucianism entered a second phase and took on explicitly religious characteristics. The family of Confucius had made sacrifices to the spirit of Confucius at his tomb long before Buddhism entered China. Several Han emperors did likewise. But in succeeding centuries, Confucius received posthumous titles, and in the seventh century, every province of China was expected to establish a Confucian temple and to support regular ceremonies. Statues of Confucius were set up, along with pictures of his disciples; and elaborate ceremonies, with sacrifice, music, and dance, were offered in spring and autumn. Authorities began to place Confucianism on a par with Buddhism and Taoism; and the three traditions were viewed as a religious triad. The three systems (which, many agreed, complemented each other) were compared to the sun, the moon, and the planets, each one a necessary part of a complete religious cosmos. Pictures and statues of the three founders—Laozi, Confucius, and the Buddha—began to appear, with the three figures side-by-side in friendly poses. This practice continues today.

In its third phase, after 1000 C.E., Confucianism was enriched by scholarship and philosophy. The movement, called Neo-Confucianism, clarified texts and codified the elements of Confucian thought. It attempted to determine which Confucian schools taught doctrine that was consistent with

Laozi, the Buddha, and Confucius are frequently pictured together in harmony.

the vision of Confucius. It also sought to provide a metaphysical vision of all reality for Confucianism, akin to that found in Taoism and Buddhism.

The greatest exponent of Neo-Confucianism was Zhu Xi (Chu Hsi, 1130–1200 C.E.), a scholar who gave Confucianism its mature shape as a complete system of thought and action. In judging the teachings of Confucian thinkers after Confucius, Zhu Xi concluded that Mencius belonged among the orthodox but that Xunzi did not because of his notion that human nature was inherently bad. The prestige of Zhu Xi's commentaries on the Four Books helped the Four Books and his commentaries on them to become the basis for the civil service examinations.

Zhu Xi attempted to formulate a general vision of reality using notions found in the teachings of Confucius and Mencius. He rejected the Mahayana Buddhist notion of ultimate emptiness and instead adopted a view of reality that was closer to the Taoist notion of the constant generation of reality. His view, though not scientific in the modern sense, was positivistic and stressed the natural order of things. Trying to discover the source of change, Zhu Xi spoke of two fundamental principles: qi (ch'i), "vital force" or "material force"; and li, "law" or "rational principle." Although they are distinct, the two principles work together. Li impels qi to generate the permutations of yang and yin. Zhu Xi called li the Great Ultimate (Tai

Ji, T'ai Chi), because he saw the one principle of li working everywhere in the world. In human beings, it is "the mind," which is one with the mind of the universe. "Fundamentally there is only one Great Ultimate, yet each of the myriad things has been endowed with it and each in itself possesses the Great Ultimate in its entirety. This is similar to the fact that there is only one moon in the sky but when its light is scattered upon rivers and lakes, it can be seen everywhere."[33]

Another Neo-Confucian of importance was Wang Yangming (1473–1529). Unlike Zhu Xi, he did not stress the need to look outward. Rather, he believed that truth could be discovered through intuition (whether this was mystical insight or conscience or something different is not entirely clear). Wang Yangming compared the mind to a mirror, which had the native ability to reflect but needed polishing and cleaning to keep it working properly. He saw a close connection between knowledge and virtue, holding that innate insight gives a person not only an understanding of fact but also an appreciation for virtue. Those who know about goodness, he said, will practice it.

An attempt to purify Confucian ceremony came during the Ming dynasty (1368–1644), when an imperial command dictated a simplification of Confucian temples and their ritual. Statues of Confucius and his disciples were replaced by tablets inscribed with their names and titles. Ritual became simpler in order to conform to what were considered ancient patterns, and the Confucian temples took on an archaic spareness that seemed truer to the spirit of Confucius. This spareness is still quite moving today.

If we look back at the 2,500-year history of Confucianism, we can see general patterns and turning points. In the first 500 years after Confucius, Confucianism began to emerge as an officially endorsed philosophy. In the next 1,000 years, state temples and ritual were organized. In the succeeding millennium, Confucianism absorbed philosophical elements from Taoism and Buddhism but moved toward greater simplicity in its ceremonial life. And in the twentieth century, formal Confucian education and ritual lost most of its governmental support. However, as we shall see later, many of its values live on in family, corporate, and government life.

CONFUCIANISM AND THE ARTS

Confucianism has been a great patron of the Chinese arts. The ideal human being, the junzi, does not need to be rich, but he or she must be a well-rounded lover of history, art, poetry, and music. Because of Confucianism's high esteem for education and books, the noble person must cultivate in particular all aspects of writing—the premier art form of Confucianism.

Confucianism so values the written word that the greatest influence of Confucianism on the arts has been in calligraphy. In the West, calligraphy is not valued in the same way that it is in China and the countries China has

Friends from Far Away

A colleague who specializes in calligraphy related the following experience: One winter she made a visit to the home of a Confucian scholar and calligrapher in rural Korea—there, old Chinese traditions are still miraculously alive. She described the entry hall, where a Chinese scroll hung with a passage from the Analects: "How delightful when friends come from far away" (1:1). The hall was cold, though, and luckily she did not have to wait long.

She was soon led into the scholar's study, which was heated from below the floor. Above the desk was a wide scroll with thick black Chinese characters. Its message: "The virtuous person is never alone." The scholar's wife brought in tea but did not stay. The gentleman asked his visitor questions about her stay in Korea and her family—a necessary polite preamble, before they could talk about their mutual interest, calligraphy. Soon they moved to the far side of the room, where the scholar did his calligraphy. They examined the scholar's collection of inkstones, wondrously carved brush rests, ceramic water pots and brush holders, thick and thin brushes, and blocks of solid inks, some quite old and still in wrappers. They talked of red and black inks, sable brushes, and the best kinds of paper. At last the scholar prepared fresh wet ink and selected a piece of heavy paper and a brush. Then, with beautiful deliberateness, he wrote this message: "In dark night, one light shines." He gave her this work as a parting gift.

influenced. The importance of artistic writing is easily apparent to any visitor of a country in east Asia.

(Calligraphy can appear in unexpected places. I remember a bus driver in China who was deeply pleased with a purchase he had made. We had stopped for lunch in a small, dusty town in western China. After lunch, as the passengers climbed back on board, the bus driver held a rolled-up scroll he had just bought at a tiny shop. With just the faintest urging, he unrolled the scroll carefully. The Chinese passengers were hot, tired, and ready to sleep, but everyone at the front of the bus strained to look over each other's shoulders at the scroll. The Chinese characters were solid but lively, with fine balance between the heavy black ink of the characters and the white paper. On the narrow scroll the vertical Chinese message was this: "To see the view, climb higher." A similar event could have happened a thousand years before, only in an ox cart.)

The tendency to place Chinese calligraphy on the walls of homes, restaurants, and hotels is still strong wherever Chinese culture has penetrated, both in and out of China. It is sometimes even done where ordinary laypeople (such as in Korea) can no longer read many of the Chinese ideograms.

Calligraphy came to be considered one of the greatest of the Chinese arts because it combines so many elements of value. A work of calligraphy can show physical beauty, as well as intellectual and moral beauty. It manifests the cultivated nature of the person who wrote it, shows respect for poets and thinkers of the past, and inspires the viewer to scholarship and virtue.

Confucian influence might also be seen in the common practice of adding written material to a painting. We should recall that the same kind of brush is used for both painting and calligraphy. Consequently, the artist might include a poem at the side of the painting—a later owner might even add an appropriate poem to indicate his or her appreciation for the painting.

Just as Taoism has considerably influenced Chinese art—particularly in nature painting—so too has Confucianism, most notably in its portraiture of ancestors. It was common in the past for Chinese families to commission paintings of parents and immediate ancestors and to keep these in the home to represent the presence of the deceased person. (Nowadays a photo is used, and sometimes a wooden plaque with the ancestor's name is a suitable substitute.) Other genres of painting that were influenced by Confucianism were the court paintings of honored officials, which show both artistic skill and psychological insight. Paintings that under Taoist influence might have shown only mountains, mists, and streams may depict central groups of people performing activities in houses and pavilions, the ideal being a harmonious blending of the three essential elements—Heaven, earth, and humanity.

Not only did Confucianism influence the arts, it seems the sensual nature of the arts may have softened the sharp edges of Confucianism. One cannot love the arts and hate the physical world, because the arts celebrate its beauty. But Confucianism has recognized that all artworks have a moral aspect. At the lowest level, the morality of an artwork can be judged in a way that depends on the obvious. A simple person, for example, may think

Ancestors' names are frequently inscribed on small tablets that are displayed on an altar, in keeping with Confucian values. This memorial is in Korea, a country still very much under the influence of Confucianism.

225

that an art object is automatically moral if it has a proverb written on it. At a more sophisticated level, however, we recognize that an artwork conveys morality by its quality. Thus we say that there is "bad" art and "good" art. It is interesting that we use the terms "bad" and "good" to describe both art and human behavior. Confucians would say that this usage is quite correct and that good art makes good people.

PERSONAL EXPERIENCE: AT A CONFUCIAN TEMPLE

In my visits to Confucian temples in Korea and Taiwan, I was struck by their austere beauty. They are quite different from many Taoist and Buddhist temples, which have fantastic numbers of statues, throngs of visitors, and enough incense rising from huge braziers to turn the air blue.

In Confucian temples, I would find peaceful courtyards with ponds and old trees enclosed by red-pillared colonnades. As I entered the temples, the noise of the street would give way to deep silence. Few other people would be there. Walking along the covered porches, I could peer in windows and see the old-fashioned musical instruments still used in Confucian ceremonies. In other windows I would see yellowing photos of celebrations held in years past, in which people in robes and antique hats stood in rows, some holding long feathers and others playing musical instruments. After going through smaller courtyards and walkways, at last I would arrive at the main temple building, far in the back. Inside, on top of tall dark tables would be wooden tablets inscribed with the names of Confucius (in the very center) and his disciples. A few sticks of incense would be burning in a single small incense holder. The deliberate simplicity, along with the absence of even one statue, provoked much thought about the values of that teacher who had lived more than two thousand years ago.

I was eager, on my first trip to China, to see the Confucian Temple (Kongmiao) and former Confucian Imperial Academy (Guozijian) of Beijing. Maps showed them close to the Vajrayana Buddhist Lama Temple in an old section of the city. I was told that services were not held there and that the current government on the mainland does not generally promote services in honor of Confucius, except at the place of his birth. The Confucian temples and ancestral temples that survive have been given new uses as storehouses, community centers, and small factories. But I was hopeful.

I took a taxi, choosing one among the many that were waiting for foreign customers at the entrance to my hotel. The Confucian Temple stood behind walls on a narrow street in an old-fashioned residential area of one-story houses. There were lovely trees and no traffic. Beyond the entrance, the garden looked overgrown.[34] Just inside the garden stood tall, wide columns of stone—carved with Chinese characters—that had once been

The entrance to Beijing's Confucian temple Kongmiao.   ▶

white but were now gray-green. These columns were among the many tablets in the complex that contained the names of Confucian scholars, the texts of Confucian classics, and records of Chinese history. They had been placed there long ago as a public service for anyone who wished to read and copy them. Some of the columns had obvious cracks through the middle. Although once broken, they appeared to have been repaired and set up again.

Looking at the cracks, one imagined the angry young people who may have felt virtuous in knocking them over during the Cultural Revolution that began in the 1960s. I noticed the barbed wire that now sat on top of the wall around the enclosure—perhaps to protect the tablets should trouble arise again. I walked up the stairs to the wide uneven stone platform in front of a main building. I tried to look inside, but the old wooden doors were locked with a chain and rusty padlock. I couldn't even find a crack wide enough to look through. On the platform in front of the building a volleyball net had been set up some time ago, its posts leaning crookedly.

The building that housed the old Confucian Imperial Academy was nearby, and I made my way there, wondering about its state of repair. How had it survived the Cultural Revolution? Would it even be open? As I came close, I could hear the sound of electric fans, but otherwise there was complete silence. Doors were open, and the large room was illuminated by dim, bluish fluorescent lights. It was absolutely packed full of students—all studying at long desks. Every seat was taken, but the room was so quiet that I wondered if the students were taking an examination. I ascertained that they were not. Not a person moved or coughed, and no one came in or out. Not wanting to disturb the students, I retraced my steps toward the temple grounds. It was clear that Confucianism as temple ritual here had been abandoned, but Confucianism as a value system and a way of life in many ways seemed quite alive.

I walked again around the marble tablets. While I had been in the academy, a student had entered the grounds. He stood on a short stepladder next to one of the columns. Placing a large piece of white paper on the carved Chinese characters, he began to do a rubbing. He was so intent in making his copy of the characters that he did not see or hear me as I quietly went out the gate.

CONFUCIANISM AND THE MODERN WORLD

The modern world has been hard on government-sponsored Confucianism. In 1911 the Qing dynasty collapsed and with it also collapsed the public system of Confucian ceremony and education. When faced with the new scientific knowledge introduced to China by European countries, Confucianism as a total educational curriculum seemed desperately inadequate.

As young Chinese sought a whole new form of education, traditional Confucianism could not compete. Confucian temple ritual also came to an end in China, having always relied on support from the state.

Early attacks on Confucianism were made by the New Culture Movement, beginning in 1916. While some members wished to hold on to basic Confucian ethics, others thought that all vestiges of Confucianism should be destroyed. Some of the leaders of the movement had studied in the West. Among these was Hu Shih (1891–1962), who studied at Columbia University under the philosopher John Dewey (1859–1952) and returned to China to teach and write. The movement looked to pragmatic thinkers, such as William James (1842–1910), John Dewey, and Bertrand Russell (1872–1970), and criticized Confucianism on many counts. Confucianism was accused of enslaving women to their fathers and husbands; of subjugating sons to tyrannical fathers; and of keeping alive a culture and literature that only looked to the past.

The Communist takeover of mainland China in 1949 further weakened Confucianism as a belief system. Continuing the earlier anti-Confucian themes, Communism has been highly critical of Confucianism for several reasons. First, Confucianism preaches elitism rather than egalitarianism. Although Confucianism maintains that anyone can become a junzi (noble person) through training, in fact Confucian education has often been limited to those whose parents could afford it. Communism, in contrast, proposed to educate all equally.

Secondly, the Communists accused Confucianism of valuing males over females, reserving education and power for males, and providing no official power to wives and daughters. With only one exception in all of Chinese history (the empress Wu, who ruled from 683 to 705 C.E.), the official role of emperor has been confined to males. Women's roles have been traditionally concerned with childbearing, and women have derived much of their social identity from men. Communism has preached (at least in theory) that Confucianism's sexist tendencies have created oppression and a loss of talent for society.

Thirdly, the Communists criticized Confucianism for focusing on the old rather than the new and on the humanities rather than the sciences. To Communism this focus on the past reflects a backward vision, like driving a car by looking at a rearview mirror.

Many Communists thought that only when Confucianism was destroyed could China move forward. On the mainland, these views led to either the destruction of Confucian temples or their use for other purposes, and to the development of a Western-based curriculum for education and government jobs. Mao Zedong (Mao Tse-Tung), the leader of the Communist Revolution, hated the rigidity and old-fashioned thinking that he saw in Confucianism. Mao's anti-Confucian ideals were particularly destructive during the Cultural Revolution (1966–1976), when students reviled their teachers and destroyed much that was considered to be antiquated. On the other hand, Mao also cultivated the image of himself as a benevolent

Confucian ruler and father figure; he was a poet and writer; and many of the virtues he encouraged in his people are reminiscent of Confucian ideals—particularly duty, sacrifice, and self-cultivation.

The system of Confucianism has fared better in neighboring Asian countries and regions, such as South Korea and the island of Taiwan, where Confucian temples and ritual are maintained, although in diminished form, by the government or private families. But in every country influenced by China, such as Japan and Singapore, we find the Confucian system of virtues and behaviors still very much alive. Although these countries have adopted Western science into their curriculums, their cultures maintain an ethic that is Confucian. They highly value the extended family, education, personal discipline, and public order.

Ironically, according to many scholars, Confucian virtues may have helped lead many Confucian countries to modern economic development. This fact has not been lost on the government of mainland China, which has begun to soften its earlier anti-Confucian stance. What will probably become more common there is a growing public respect for Confucius, a restoration of some Confucian materials to the curriculum, and the teaching of Confucian virtues in modified form—all blended with a Western interest in science, mathematics, and computer technology.

The leaders of Confucian countries are horrified by what they have seen of the chaotic individualism and violence in some Western countries. They see the Confucian ethic as an antidote to social ills and therefore continue to view education as character-building, not merely as intellectual formation. Singapore has already developed a national educational curriculum that teaches Confucian virtues, and this may become a model elsewhere. Confucian virtues continue to be promulgated in schools, companies, and government work in many east Asian countries. It is also intriguing to see how much Confucian instruction appears on television in east Asian countries. There, behavior expressing the values of harmony, loyalty, and filial piety is visible both in historical dramas and in many stories of modern life. Television instruction in Confucian virtues may become a deliberate technique used by some Asian governments to attain their goals.

Confucian teaching is, in practice, being modified for modern life. The lesser status of the female is being abandoned widely as women are beginning to demand equal opportunity. Confucian societies everywhere now offer curriculums that blend science and a focus on the future with studies of the past. Greater latitude is gradually being given to individual needs and personalities. With these modifications, Confucianism is gaining a renewed attractiveness.

Rather than dying, Confucianism is possibly beginning a new stage in its long life. The core of Confucianism is unassailable. It is primarily ethical, because it focuses on correct behavior. Yet it is more, because it rests on a vision of human unity and a connection with the harmony of the universe.

RELIGION BEYOND THE CLASSROOM

For a view of popular Taoist religion the temples of Hong Kong and Taiwan offer a mixture of Taoist and folk elements. In mainland China, two Taoist temples in Beijing are open to the public: White Cloud Temple (Baiyunguan) and the temple of the god of Taishan (Dongyuemiao).

A location that has been influential in Chinese landscape painting is Guilin (Kwei-lin). A boat trip on the River Lu is a good way to experience this surreal landscape of high mountains. Places of Taoist interest in the vicinity are the White Cloud Temple (Baiyunguan) and Reed Pipe Cave (Ludiyan). Chinese gardens of special beauty are located in southern China in Hangzhou, Suzhou, and Shanghai.

For a view of Confucianism, visitors can go to the Confucian Temple (Kongmiao) and former Confucian Imperial Academy (Guozijian) in Beijing. Traditional Confucian ritual has been restored at the Temple of Confucius in the town of Qufu, which also contains the tomb of Confucius and the Confucian Family Mansion.

Although Confucianism as a value system is alive throughout much of east Asia, traditional Confucian ritual and training are most visible in South Korea and Taiwan. Rituals are common in September or October, in honor of Confucius's birthday (often marked on or near September 28). Some places also have festivities in springtime, particularly at the spring equinox.

Traditional Confucianism is still influential in South Korea. In Seoul, one should visit the impressive Chongmyo Royal Ancestors' Shrine. A Confucian ceremony (called Cherye) occurs there each year on the first Sunday of May. Songgyun'gwan University contains a Confucian shrine, and Confucian music and ritual are performed there in spring and autumn.

Beyond Seoul, Confucian academies are located throughout South Korea, although nowadays they are used for a variety of educational purposes. In Andong there is the Tosan Sowon, and near Angang is the Oksan Sowon. In Kangnung, visitors can visit the Hyangkyo and Taesungjon Confucian Academy and Shrine at Myungnung School. Six miles from Kangnung is the Ojuk-hon Confucian Shrine, with a festival on October 26. Chunghakdong, in the hills near Chinju, is a Confucian village where the Confucian classics are taught in traditional style. Some families also maintain private Confucian shrines for the veneration of Confucius and their ancestors.

In Taiwan, sizable Confucian temples can be found in major urban areas. The Confucian temples in Taipei and Tainan are especially beautiful. Ceremonies are conducted at most Confucian temples early on the morning of Confucius's birthday (September 28).

FOR FULLER UNDERSTANDING

1. Try to describe the personality of Confucius. Can you think of any recent historical figure who displays a similar character and values? Compare the two.
2. Describe how Taoism and Confucianism complement each other.
3. List the differences that you see between the Confucian "noble person" (junzi) and the Theravada Buddhist monk.
4. Do you see any contradiction between the Taoist ideal of gracefully accepting death, suggested by the Tao Te Ching, and the Taoist search for long life and immortality? Can the two goals be reconciled? Explain your answer.
5. Do some research on contemporary life in Korea and Japan. Look particularly for evidence of Confucian virtues that seem to contribute to their economic growth.
6. Consider your own "home culture." If Confucianism became an influence there, how would its principles or rules be expressed in everyday language and activity?

7. Investigate whether your area has a Chinese garden and visit it if you can. Find books in the library with photographs of Chinese gardens. What common Taoist themes and images do you find there?

RELATED READINGS

Confucius. *The Analects.* Translated by D. C. Lau. New York: Penguin, 1979. A clear translation of the sayings of Confucius.

Kates, George. *The Years That Were Fat.* Cambridge, MA: MIT Press, 1960. A beautifully written appreciation of the elements of traditional Chinese life.

Kidd, David. *Peking Story.* New York: Clarkson Potter, 1988. Originally sketches in the *New Yorker,* this is a description by a unique individual of life in an aristocratic family at the time of the Communist Revolution.

Kohn, Livia. *The Taoist Experience: An Anthology.* Albany: State University of New York, 1993. A wide selection from about fifty texts of the Taoist canon and other Taoist sources.

Liu I-Ming. *Awakening to the Tao.* Translated by Thomas Cleary. Boston: Shambala, 1988. Meditations on seeing and living the Tao, written in 1816 by a Taoist sage at the age of 80.

Louie, Kam. *Critiques of Confucius in Contemporary China.* New York: St. Martin's Press, 1980. A study of anti-Confucian thought in modern China.

Moore, Charles, ed. *The Chinese Mind.* Honolulu: University Press of Hawaii, 1974. A collection of scholarly essays on Chinese thought.

Nosco, Peter, ed. *Confucianism and Tokugawa Culture.* Honolulu: University of Hawaii Press, 1984. Essays on the influence of Confucianism in Japan from the seventeenth to the nineteenth centuries.

Porter, Bill. *Road to Heaven: Encounters with Chinese Hermits.* San Francisco: Mercury House, 1993. The journal of a search for and conversations with Taoist and Buddhist hermits in modern China.

Schipper, Kristofer. *The Taoist Body.* Berkeley: University of California Press, 1993. A detailed description of Taoist religious thought and practice by a European scholar who was ordained a Taoist priest.

KEY TERMS

Analects: The book of the sayings of Confucius.

Five Classics: The classical literature of the time preceding Confucius, including poetry, history, and divination.

Four Books: The major Confucian books, which include the sayings of Confucius and Mencius.

Junzi (chün-tzu; *joon'-dzuh*): "Noble person," the refined human ideal of Confucianism.

Laozi (Lao Tzu; *lau'-dzuh*): The legendary founder of Taoism.

Legalists: The strictest of the Chinese philosophical schools, which advocated strong laws and punishments.

Li (*lee*): Appropriate action, ritual, propriety, etiquette.

Mohists: A Chinese school of philosophy that taught universal love.

Qi (ch'i; chee): The life force.

Ren (jen; *ren*): Empathy, consideration for others, humaneness; a Confucian virtue.

Shu (*shoo*): Reciprocity; a Confucian virtue.

Tao (*dau*): The mysterious origin of the universe which is present and visible in everything.

Tao Te Ching (*dau-duh-jing*): The classic scripture of Taoism.

Wen: Cultural refinement; a Confucian virtue.

Wu wei (*woo'-way'*): "No action," "no strain"; doing only what comes spontaneously and naturally; effortlessness.

Xiao (**hsiao;** *shyau*): Family devotion, filial piety; a Confucian virtue.

Yang (*yang*): The active aspect of reality that expresses itself in speech, light, and heat.

Yi Jing (**I Ching;** *ee jing*): An ancient Confucian book of divination, one of the Five Classics, still in use today.

Yin: The receptive aspect of the universe that expresses itself in silence, darkness, coolness, and rest.

Zhuangzi (**Chuang Tzu;** *jwang'-dzuh*): Author of the Zhuangzi, a book of whimsical stories that express themes of early Taoist thought.

CHAPTER **7**

Shinto

 FIRST ENCOUNTER

In a lush park of Tokyo stands Meiji Shrine, a Shinto shrine created in the early twentieth century to honor the spirit of the emperor who had opened Japan to the rest of the world. After the Emperor Meiji died in 1912, schoolchildren all over Japan contributed trees for the grounds. The trees, which have since grown very tall, surround spacious beds of purple and white Japanese iris that bloom thickly in the summer.

You enter the shrine by walking through a **torii,** a simple tall wooden portal. As you move toward the compound of shrine buildings, you see large stone basins of flowing water. You stand in line and watch visitors dip bamboo ladles into the basins, pour a bit of water over their hands, touch their faces, and then dry their hands with white handkerchiefs before proceeding. The worshipers walk quietly along the gravel path toward the main building. They climb the steep stone stairs, stand reverently on the landing before the entrance to the shrine hall, pull a thick rope attached to a large round bell, and clap their hands several times. They bow their heads silently before descending the stairs. Off to the side, two women attach small pieces of white paper to a tree, while other visitors crowd in front of booths that sell what look like amulets and other mementos. Meanwhile, five men in white robes, wearing stiff black hats and large, oddly shaped black shoes, stride silently across the courtyard single file.

You wander slowly to the iris garden. It is so full of people admiring the flowers that you must inch your way along the gravel and stone paths that wind between the gardens and ponds. Several people, to your amazement, have set up easels in front of the irises and are actually painting, despite the crush of people trying to take photos behind them.

You take a vacant seat on a stone bench and pause to look at the flowers and the people. What was meant by the jingling bell and the clapping of hands? Why did people pour water over their hands at the entrance to the courtyard? Who were the men in the white robes? What does all this have to do with the spirit of an emperor? Why does the complex look more like a park than a church or temple?

THE ORIGINS OF SHINTO

Unlike many religions, Shinto has no known person or group as its founder. In fact, its mysterious origins date back to the ancient people of Japan and their stories of how the world came into being. Like many people long ago, the people of the Japanese islands (Figure 7.1) lived close to nature, and Shinto as a religion reflects that reality in its worship of the spirits who are believed to inhabit the natural world. Shinto seems to have arisen from a human awareness of the power of nature and the need to be in harmony with it. Shinto retains elements of shamanism, contact with nature spirits, and mysterious healing. While most of the world's old religions of nature have disappeared, Shinto still exists in modern Japan, a fact that is sometimes marked by a shrine tucked between concrete skyscrapers.

Shinto is more, however, than a nature religion. It also has ethnic and family dimensions. The spirits that are worshiped include the spirits of departed family members, distant ancestors of one's clan, and great leaders—such as the Emperor Meiji.

The name *Shinto* emerged when Buddhism came from China to Japan. Before that time, there was no need to name the native religion—it was simply what everyone did. In fact, the Japanese name for Buddhism, *Butsu-do* ("the way of the Buddha"), helped give a name to the native religion. The indigenous Japanese religion came to be called the *shen-dao* ("the way of the gods") in Chinese, pronounced *shin-to* in Japanese. ("The way of the gods" is also expressed in the Japanese language by the phrase *kami-no-michi*.)

Like the origin of Shinto, the origin of the Japanese people is also mysterious. Although Japanese often think of themselves as a single "race," they apparently descended from at least two immigrant groups, one from the northwest, possibly Siberia, and the other from the south, possibly from

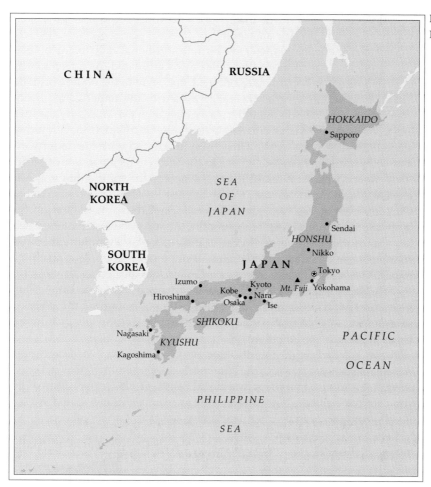

FIGURE 7.1
Islands of Japan.

the Malay Peninsula. Although these two immigrant groups may have focused their primary worship on different natural forces (such as the sun and the moon), it seems their traditions eventually mixed, ultimately blending a large number of gods into a pantheon and yielding a single creation myth.

In the beginning, as the creation myth relates, there was primeval chaos, which came to be populated by several generations of deities, or spirits, called **kami** (meaning "above," "superior").[1] Two of these kami—**Izanami** ("female who invites") and **Izanagi** ("male who invites")—became the cosmic parents who created the first islands of Japan. According to an ancient chronicle, the Kojiki: " Hereupon all the Heavenly Deities commanded the two Deities His Augustness the Male-Who-Invites and Her Augustness the Female-Who-Invites, ordering them to 'make, consolidate, and give birth to this drifting land.' Granting to them an heavenly jeweled spear, they deigned to charge them. So the two Deities, standing upon the Floating Bridge of Heaven, pushed down the jeweled spear and stirred [the ocean] with it . . . ; the brine that dripped down from the end of the spear was piled up and became an island."[2]

Izanagi and Izanami then gave birth to additional kami, many of them nature deities. One of the nature deities was a fire god. As a result of his birth, Izanami was horribly burned, died, and went to the underworld. Because of his immense grief, Izanagi traveled to the underworld to find Izanami, but she rebuffed him because of her ugliness caused by the burn and decay—maggots even crawled in her body. Horrified, Izanagi returned alone to the everyday world. Dirty from his contact with the underworld and with death, he cleansed himself in the ocean to regain a state of purity. As he washed, from his tear-filled eyes emerged the spirit of the sun, **Amaterasu** ("shining in heaven"), and the spirit of the moon, Tsukiyomi ("moon night possessor"). From his nostrils came the spirit of the wind, Susanowo ("impetuous male").[3] Eventually, the sun goddess Amaterasu sent her grandson to bring order to the islands of Japan. From him, the myth continues, came Jimmu, the first human emperor of Japan. As a result, the imperial house mythically traces its origin back to the goddess of the sun.

This story is intriguing for a number of reasons. It puts the kami of sun, moon, and wind into a family relationship, thus harmonizing the stories of several kami who might have once been worshiped separately by different tribes. It declares the emperors of Japan to be divine in origin (which, as we shall see, has had serious ramifications in Japan's history). It also portrays Amaterasu as female, while the kami of the moon, Tsukiyomi, is male. Although it is more common in traditional belief systems for the deity of the sun to be male and the deity of the moon to be female, Shinto belief in a sun goddess may reflect an earlier matriarchal society.

The sun, here shining above the rooflines of a Shinto shrine, is associated with the goddess Amaterasu.

This story also expresses a concern with purity—a major focus of Shinto. Pollution (*tsumi*) comes especially from contact with death, but purity can be restored by washing and ritual expiation (*harai*).

Another significant aspect of this creation story is that the islands of Japan are believed to be the creation and the home of divine spirits. Japan is thus a sort of "this-worldly" heaven, which human beings share with divine beings. (Traditional Japanese belief maintains that the spirits live in an "upper world" but that their realm is not separate from this world and thus can exist and appear in this world.) Such a view differs significantly from those religions that see this world not as a paradise but as a place of suffering—a prelude to a heaven that can be reached only after death. In the more optimistic Japanese view, the task of human beings is to live up to the heavenlike world into which they have been born.

THE HISTORICAL DEVELOPMENT OF SHINTO

As we have already mentioned, the entry of Buddhism into Japan in the sixth century (Timeline 7.1) forced Shinto to define itself. It was a process that was complicated by the tendency of Mahayana Buddhism not only to tolerate but also to absorb native religious elements. Buddhist monks viewed Shinto kami simply as different forms of Mahayana buddhas, bodhisattvas, and other heavenly beings, and they preached that the Buddhist deities were already being worshiped in Japan under Shinto names. This approach made the introduction of Buddhism fairly easy. At first there was some resistance, and the new religion was viewed as dangerous and foreign. But over time elements from both religions were drawn upon, and a certain blending of religious practice occurred.

Along with Buddhism came a torrent of cultural elements from China. Before contact with the mainland, Japan already had a culture of its own, but it was fairly simple in comparison to that of China. Contact with China introduced a system of writing, which the Japanese began to adapt for their own use. It also introduced Chinese architecture, poetry, ceramics, art, and all sorts of new ideas in everything from philosophy to cuisine, from clothing design to city planning. The Japanese were fascinated by all these novelties, and the importation of Chinese culture continued, with some interruptions, for a thousand years.

Accommodation with Buddhism and Confucianism

Despite the enthusiasm for Buddhism and the accompanying aspects of Chinese culture, Shinto did not disappear. Instead, the two religions reached an accommodation. Although there were many exceptions, several patterns emerged: Shinto was often associated with agriculture, fertility, and birth, while Buddhism was called on for philosophy, help with serious sickness, funerals, and the afterlife.

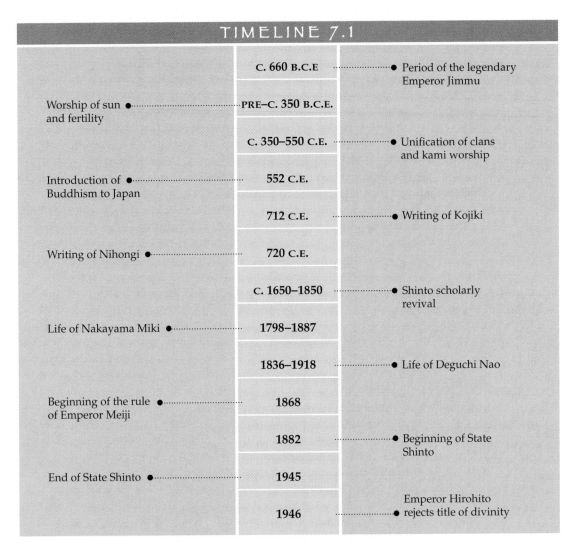

TIMELINE 7.1

	C. 660 B.C.E ·········· ● Period of the legendary Emperor Jimmu
Worship of sun ● ········· and fertility	PRE–C. 350 B.C.E.
	C. 350–550 C.E. ·········· ● Unification of clans and kami worship
Introduction of ● ········· Buddhism to Japan	552 C.E.
	712 C.E. ·········· ● Writing of Kojiki
Writing of Nihongi ● ·········	720 C.E.
	C. 1650–1850 ·········· ● Shinto scholarly revival
Life of Nakayama Miki ● ·········	1798–1887
	1836–1918 ·········· ● Life of Deguchi Nao
Beginning of the rule ● ········· of Emperor Meiji	1868
	1882 ·········· ● Beginning of State Shinto
End of State Shinto ● ·········	1945
	1946 ·········· ● Emperor Hirohito rejects title of divinity

Timeline of significant events in the history of Shinto.

The accommodation was signaled in various ways. Shinto shrines frequently contained a Buddhist place of worship or had some Buddhist rites for the kami, while Buddhist temples often had a Shinto shrine on their grounds. Shinto also adopted the Buddhist practices of preaching sermons, venerating statues, and using incense. Furthermore, Shinto shrines featured Chinese architectural details, such as tile roofs and red paint. Often the mixture was so thorough that a place of worship was neither exclusively Shinto nor Buddhist. Although the two religions were forced in the nineteenth century to disentangle themselves, one can still see many examples of their mutual influence.

Confucianism was also introduced to Japan along with Chinese culture. It meshed nicely with Japanese practices such as the veneration of ancestors, who were thought of as kami, and the loyalty given to family and clan. As it had in China, Confucianism in Japan began to play the role of an

Even this simple neighborhood shrine shows Chinese influence in its red curving roofline.

ethical system that supported education, family, and government. The whole nation began to view itself as being joined in a family relationship, with the emperor as father and the government ministers as elder brothers. Family and school instilled the Confucian virtues of respect for the emperor, reverence for ancestors and elders, care for juniors, loyalty, discipline, and love of learning. Many of these values were subsequently reinforced by Shinto.

Shinto and Japanese National Identity

Japan tends to swing back and forth between a great enthusiasm for outside cultures and a strong desire to assert Japanese uniqueness. Chinese cultural imports, which were strong in the seventh and eighth centuries, weakened but then returned again in another wave in the thirteenth century. Western influence, which arrived with the Portuguese in the sixteenth century, was considered so dangerous that Japan largely sealed itself off from the outside world until the mid-1800s. After that came a great wave of Western influence that strengthened over the rest of the nineteenth century. Except for the years just before and during World War II, direct Western influence has continued until the present.

Emperor Akihito wore Shinto robes at his investiture ceremony.

In the face of these strong influences from other shores, the Japanese have relied on Shinto to help give them a sense of identity. When Buddhism threatened to nearly swallow up Shinto, priests at the shrine of **Ise** in the fourteenth century demanded an independent Shinto, separated from Buddhist influence. They argued that the "original" gods of Japan were Shinto and that the Buddhist deities associated with them were at best only later manifestations of the Shinto kami.

The movement for an independent Shinto grew stronger from the seventeenth to the end of the nineteenth centuries. Thinkers and writers such

Kamikaze Pilots and Shinto

During World War II, Japanese pilots who made suicidal crash attacks achieved such notoriety in the West that the Japanese word **kamikaze** ("spirit wind") entered the English language. The kamikaze pilots were practitioners of the cult **bushido** ("warrior knight way"), a cult promoted by State Shinto. For centuries, the Japanese have idealized the role of the loyal **samurai** and noble warrior, and bushido came to be treated as a spiritual path that soldiers should follow. As a warrior code, bushido demands courtesy, utter loyalty to one's lord, honor, and willingness to commit suicide for a cause. The ideal of the kamikaze spread this code widely.

Although Shinto was allied with this warrior ideal, bushido is actually an amalgam of elements from several religions. From Zen Buddhism it derived its sense of the transiency of all life. From Confucianism it derived its stress on loyalty to one's superior. And from Shinto it derived an identification with the Japanese state.

Shinto is not a military religion, but during certain periods it has been manipulated to promote war. Actually, in its essence it idealizes harmony and peace. In fairness, we should note that Buddhism, in addition to State Shinto, also generally supported Japan's role in the war effort.

as Motoori Norinaga (1730–1801) and Kamo Mabuchi (1697–1769) wrote about the early myths and kami of Shinto, hoping to divest it of later additions. They wanted to restore a purified, original Shinto separate from the ritual and beliefs of Buddhism and the ethics of Confucianism.

When the West challenged Japan to modernize in the late nineteenth century, Shinto was enlisted as a cultural counterweight that would preserve the "Japanese spirit." In 1868, the Emperor Meiji came to the throne, assuming real rather than symbolic power, thus beginning the deliberate modernization of Japan—a turning point in Japanese history that is called the Meiji Restoration. Shinto was forced to separate from Buddhism, and places of worship had to decide whether to declare themselves Shinto or Buddhist. For a short time Buddhism even suffered persecution, as Japan's leaders emphasized the divine origins of the emperor and began to tie Shinto to a growing spirit of nationalism.

Shinto was now a tool in the national buildup, and in 1882 a national religion called State Shinto was set up. Thousands of shrines received a special national status, with government financial support and control by the Home Ministry. Priests at these shrines were official government employees, and in return for financial support, they were supposed to represent the imperial household and maintain traditional values. All other nongovernmental Shinto shrines and organizations were treated as independent, self-supporting institutions and together were called Sect Shinto.[4]

Unfortunately, these developments set the stage for the exploitation of Shinto during the militaristic expansion that occurred after Japan's victory (1905) in the Russo-Japanese war. The government increasingly used State Shinto to generate patriotism, both during the military buildup of the 1930s and then during World War II. The divinity of the emperor—the descendant of Amaterasu—was officially taught in schools, and schoolchildren memorized and recited daily a special statement endorsing this view, the Imperial Rescript on Education.

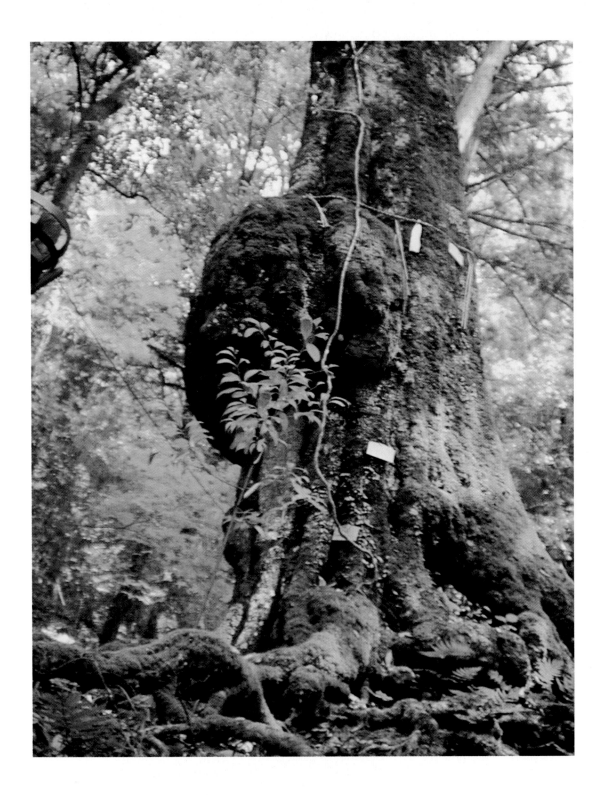

When World War II ended, the Occupation forces demanded that Japan become a secular country. State Shinto was abolished by the government, Shinto shrines were returned to private religious practice, and all religions were placed on an equal footing. In theory, Shinto became a strictly private religion, but in reality Shinto retains a special place in national life.

Folded white paper on twisted rope often marks venerated trees, rocks, and sites.   ◄

ESSENTIALS OF SHINTO BELIEF

The heart of Shinto is a sensitivity to the mysterious powers of nature. Kami are not thought of so much as beings living in another, distant realm, but rather as powers in or near this world whose presence might be felt, for example, when we are standing in a grove of trees or looking at a waterfall or contemplating a distant mountain. The kami can also cause dread, such as one might feel in the midst of a terrible storm or being lost on an ocean. The kami are the energies that animate nature: they cause rice to grow and wind to blow; they cause volcanoes to spew lava and earthquakes to split the land. The kami of nature especially love to dwell and be active in places of power and beauty.

Kami are treated as persons and are given names—a fact that allows human beings to approach them and feel closely related to them. We have already learned the names of the major kami: Izanagi, Izanami, Amaterasu, Tsukiyomi, and Susanowo. In addition there are lesser kami. Among them are the god of fire, the goddess of grain, ocean spirits, mountain spirits (among whom the god of Mount Fuji is preeminent), and spirits of great trees, rivers, and waterfalls. There are also animal spirits, particularly of animals thought to have mysterious cunning, such as the badger, the fox, and the snake.

Ancestors—who have also become kami—live close by, ready to return to see how their descendants are faring.[5] Shinto is thus a way of maintaining a connection with family and clan members. Respect for the dead comes both from a love of deceased family members and from the natural fear of the unknown. In Shinto, ancestors are believed to be capable of influencing a family's earthly life. The spirits of great leaders—especially past emperors, artists, teachers, and scholars—are particularly venerated; and Confucianism, as we have seen, strengthened this Shinto respect for ancestors and for other great people of the past.

After Buddhism entered Japan, influential members of the court feared that the early myths might be lost. In the early eighth century, at imperial request, the myths were written down, using the new script that had come from China. The ancient myths appear in the beginnings of two core works, the **Kojiki** ("chronicle of ancient events," 712 C.E.) and the **Nihongi** ("chronicle of Japan," 720 C.E.).[6] These works also contain genuinely historical material. Ancient Shinto ritual and prayers (*norito*) were recorded in the tenth century.

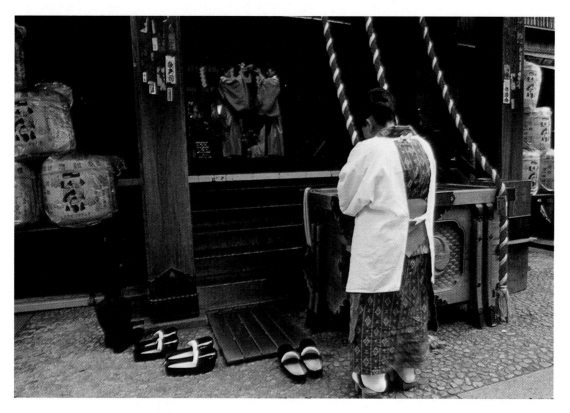

A woman prays at a small Shinto shrine in the Tsukiji fish market in Tokyo.

Although Shinto has no clearly defined code of ethics, a type of morality does flow from the Shinto system of values and its way of looking at life. The Western notion of internal guilt is not found in Shinto. There is no moralistic God who gives commands or judges a person, nor is there a sense of original sin or of any basic sinful tendency. Instead, human beings are fundamentally good, the body is good, and this earthly life is good. Shinto worships fertility and new life, and sex is viewed positively, without guilt. Sexual imagery—particularly phallic rocks and wood carvings—can be seen at many shrines.[7]

Unlike many other religions, Shinto tends to turn its focus away from death, which is thought of as the opposite of life and growth.[8] Because Shinto worships the life force, it works to counteract whatever brings sickness or death. Just as dirt is removable, so too are all other pollutants. According to Shinto, we must keep our bodies, houses, and clothes clean and bright; and when they become dirty or contaminated, we must wash them, get rid of the dirt, and purify them with blessings. In Japan, washing, sweeping, and cleaning—seen everywhere daily—have religious implications. One's character must be unstained, too, and human relations must be kept healthy. Similarly, the human character must have "sincerity" (*makoto*)—it must be pure, without egotism, committed. (Many of the em-

Shinto Ethics: Basic Rules for the Twenty-First Century?

The moral philosophy of Shinto can be summarized in two guidelines:

- Engage in respectful behavior toward spirits, human beings, and nature.
- Practice appropriate rituals of purification and reverence.

On other moral questions about human behavior, Shinto is silent. There is, for example, no official Shinto position on the morality of birth control, divorce, genetic engineering, and other such issues that preoccupy many today. The individual is free to decide.

peror Meiji's poems, available for sale at Meiji Shrine, are about the importance of sincerity.) Human beings conserve and restore their purity by fulfilling all obligations, repaying debts, and apologizing for misdeeds.

Because kami are everywhere, living with them demands that we show them reverence. One way is to visit them at their shrines, which are their homes. Another way is to show respect for nature, which is one reason for Japan's high esteem for farming and carpentry and for the architectural use of elements like wood and stone in their natural state. Respect for nature also means maintaining a harmony with nature and all its processes.

SHINTO RELIGIOUS PRACTICE

Shinto practice occurs at several levels. It encompasses formal worship and blessings by priests at shrines, blessings by priests away from the shrine, Shinto observances of holidays, the seasons, and nature, everyday practice by individuals in their homes, and the ceremonial practice of Shinto by the emperor and other authorities. Active shrines have a priest—a job that is frequently hereditary.

Worship at Shrines

People visit shrines to pray for health, for success in school and career, and for the well-being of those they love. A visit begins by passing under the torii, which looks like a ceremonial entrance or gateway and is sometimes tall and magnificent.[9] Worshipers wash their hands and mouth at a water basin just inside the entrance. They proceed through an open courtyard to the building—the *haiden*—where the kami is worshiped. Behind the haiden (and often visible from it) is a small hall or cabinet where the kami is enshrined. In smaller shrines, there may be no front worship hall but only a small place where the kami is enshrined. (It is possible that the earliest shrines had no buildings at all.[10]) Worshipers ascend the stairs to the haiden or to the space in front of the room where the kami is enshrined. They bow, donate a coin, then ring a bell

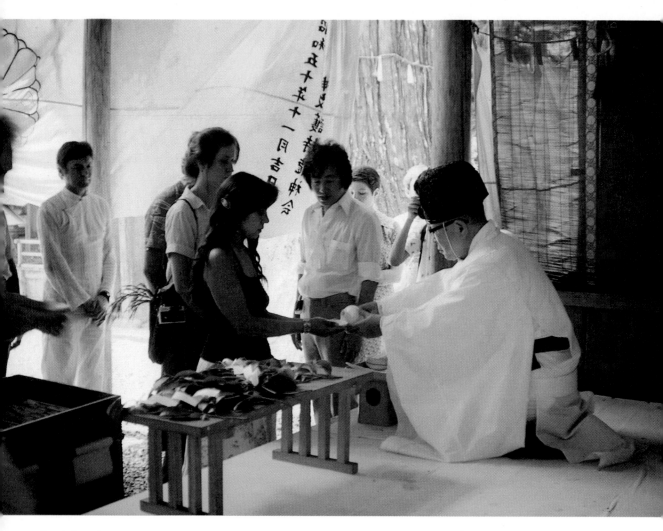

A priest receives a symbolic offering of pine at the entrance to a haiden.

and clap several times to gain the kami's attention. They bow again and pray, either silently or by chanting. Then they bow again and leave. Sometimes they tie small wooden plaques (*ema*) or pieces of paper, with their requests written on them, to the branches of a nearby sacred tree.

When worshipers visit a shrine for a blessing, a priest waves over them a branch or wand adorned with paper streamers. This implement is used to purify the devotee and the surrounding area.

Shrines sometimes have shrine "treasures," which possibly originated as gifts from visiting dignitaries. Most commonly these are antique metal mirrors, swords, and symbolic jewels—mirrors are considered particularly important. It is believed that kami sometimes present themselves in these treasures. The treasures are not shown publicly, however, and many shrines do not have them.

Each shrine has its special festival days (*matsuri*). These may be celebrated with grand processions and various types of entertainment. Sometimes, to honor the kami, celebrants parade the kami in a hand-carried litter (*o-mikoshi*). On festival days, temporary booths are set up to sell foods and religious souvenirs. (Large shrines, such as Meiji Shrine, have permanent booths.) Among the souvenirs are amulets of various kinds, some in brocade bags, which are thought to bring good luck. Some amulets are kept in the home, and small ones are kept in a car for protection.

People visit shrines for blessings at important times in their lives. Babies are brought for a blessing a month after birth. Children are brought for additional blessings when they are young, when special protection is thought to be valuable. This practice is known as "7-5-3"; girls are brought at ages 3 and 7, and boys at age 5.

(Shinto priests also perform ceremonies, such as weddings, away from the shrine. Once held in homes, weddings nowadays often occur in large hotels or reception rooms, because they are usually followed by a banquet. Priests also bless construction sites, houses, and cars, as well as perform exorcisms at locations that have come to be associated with misfortune, in order to make people feel comfortable there again.)

Shinto priests wear long robes (usually white—symbolizing purity—or perhaps light shades of pink, turquoise, and gray) that are based on old Chinese aristocratic design. Their shoes are made of strong, black, multilayered lacquered paper (resembling Dutch wooden shoes), and they wear high caps of black lacquered horsehair. The hats of dignitaries have a long flexible extension, which is attached at the top or back of the hat. The extension, created in China, is believed to represent the tail of the horse. (Thought of as a symbol of energy and strength, the horse came to be considered a sacred animal. A few Shinto shrines have even kept stables of horses.)

Symbolic purification may mark entrance to ceremonial hall.

Some shrines also have female attendants (*miko*) who wear bright red robes. They assist in ritual, play a short metal musical instrument covered with bells, and represent a vestige of early shamanism.

Celebration of the New Year

New Year's is a very special time in Shinto practice. The home must be thoroughly cleaned before New Year's in order to make it attractive to the spirits, who are invited to visit. The main gate or door is decorated with a special arrangement called the *kadomatsu* ("door pine"), which is made up of three pieces of cut green bamboo, a small branch of pine and, if possible, a sprig of plum. The bamboo signifies persistence; the pine, freshness and life throughout the winter; and the plum, the first sign of life in early spring. Together, the branches of greenery in the kadomatsu symbolize human virtue.

During New Year's, rice is pounded into a soft dough called *mochi,* then made into round shapes that are piled on top of each other and topped with a tangerine. Rice signifies wealth and fertility, and the mochi anticipates the planting of rice in the spring. On New Year's eve, the family gathers to eat a special soup made of vegetables and mochi, called *ozoni,* which is thought to promote health. On New Year's day, men and women dress in kimono, take offerings to Shinto shrines, and pray there for success in the coming year. In days after that they make formal visits to relatives and friends and renew relationships. The themes of the whole holiday season are cleansing and the renewal of life.

Observances of the Seasons and Nature

Traditionally, Shinto has marked the seasons with special practices, particularly for planting and harvesting rice. In the industrial nation of Japan today, however, these rituals are becoming less important.

Because respect for nature is at the heart of Shinto, reverential objects and small shrines are sometimes placed in the midst of forests, in fields, or on mountains. Among these are torii (which can even be found in the ocean), a pile of stones (possibly phallic in origin), or a sacred rope. Respect for the spirits of ancestors is shown by pouring water or tea over gravestones and by leaving offerings of food and flowers.

One noteworthy Shinto practice is purification with water, a practice that must be very ancient because it appears in several myths about the kami. As we have already mentioned, devotees always wash their hands with water at the entrance to a shrine. A related ritual, called **misogi,** involves standing under a waterfall as a ritual act of purification. Before entering the water, the devotee does calisthenics and deep-breathing exercises. The practitioner is then cleansed with a bit of salt. Backing into the water, the person stands for some time as the water falls full-force on his or her shoulders. The practitioner may shout and cut the air with a hand to enhance the experience of purification. The ritual ends with a drink of *sake*

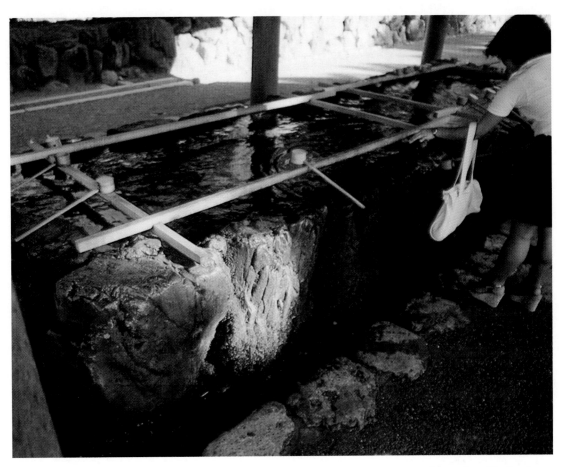

Personal purification is necessary when entering a shrine.

(rice wine) and possibly a meal, if it is performed with others. Misogi combines the ritual of cleansing with the ideal of self-discipline and probably began in the practices of ascetics who lived in the mountains.

Another Shinto practice is the climbing of a sacred mountain to gain union with the spirit of that mountain. The climb up Mount Fuji, for example, is something that many Japanese hope to accomplish at least once in their lifetime, and several Shinto sects specifically worship the kami of Mount Fuji.

Other Practices

Daily worship occurs in the home, where a small Shinto shrine called the *kamidan* is maintained, often on a high shelf. It may contain a mirror, and offerings are made there, especially of rice and water. It is common to offer prayers there at the beginning of each day. Some homes also maintain an outdoor shrine in the garden.

Mount Fuji, a volcanic cone, is the most sacred mountain in Japan and a frequent site of pilgrimage.

A semiofficial form of Shinto, practiced by the emperor and his household, is also still part of the religion. The emperor has traditionally been considered the high priest of Shinto, and his reign is inaugurated with Shinto rites. He participates every spring in Tokyo in a ceremonial rice-planting on the palace grounds in order to guarantee the fertility of the rice harvest for the entire nation. He and his family also visit the shrine of Ise annually to pray for the country. An emperor, when he dies, is buried with Shinto rites—something quite rare, because among ordinary Japanese people funeral services are conducted by Buddhist priests.

 ## PERSONAL EXPERIENCE: A TEMPLE HIGH ABOVE KYOTO

On my first trip to Kyoto, I had planned to spend a full day walking in its beautiful eastern hills. My ambitious plan was to begin at the north end, to continue south through the eastern part of the city, and to end finally at the Buddhist "mother temple" of Kyoto, Kiyomizu-dera ("clear water temple"). I had heard that it was a wonderful spot for watching the sun set.

Kiyomizu-dera (clear water temple) stands on a hillside in Kyoto. It is primarily known as a Buddhist temple, but is also the site of a Shinto shrine and a waterfall used for misogi.

As sunset grew near, I arrived at the stairs that lead up to the temple. To call the place a single "temple" is misleading. It is really a large complex of wooden buildings scattered across a wooded hill. The main part of the temple is built on top of an enormous deck that extends far out over the hillside, supported by wooden pillars that rise high above the treetops.

Standing on the deck, I could see across all Kyoto. Other people were there, too, standing patiently at the railing waiting for the sunset. All of us watched reverently as the sun slipped beneath the horizon; then the clouds turned pink and the city was engulfed in an orange haze. As daylight faded and the gray city turned blue, nighttime Kyoto was being born. It was easy to imagine, down below, the dinner restaurants, noodle shops, and tiny bars all coming to life. Up here, however, the antique atmosphere of Kiyomizu-dera embraced us with its distance from the world.

On the way out was a triple stream—the "clear water" that gave the temple its name—and three long bamboo ladles lay there for visitors who wanted a drink. Leaning over to catch water in my ladle, I could see the water cascading below. After I took my drink, I looked again. There at the base of the waterfall, obscure in the dimness and the plunging water, was a man in a white robe, knee-deep in the stream. I could make out his palms, pushed together in a gesture of prayer. I put the ladle down and continued walking to the stairs that led out into the valley below the temple. I looked back one last time at the water falling. The man had not moved.

Later, I learned that a Shinto shrine dedicated to fertility and childbirth is located next to Kiyomizu-dera—another sign of the intermingling of Shinto and Buddhism. The shrine, Jishu Jinja, is a place for worship of the protective kami that guards the temple.

I'd gone to Kiyomizu-dera expecting a beautiful sunset, perhaps the scent of incense and the sound of a Buddhist chant. What I hadn't expected to find, near the temple's base, was the practice of the Shinto ritual misogi. Yet how fitting, I thought, that a religion in Japan built upon the shoulders of the earlier native religion should today have, as the basis for its name and at the base of this grand temple's frame, waters sacred to a Shinto kami.

SHINTO AND THE ARTS

Shinto worships beauty, but the influence of Shinto on art is not immediately clear. There is no strong Shinto tradition of figurative art, in which gods are portrayed in paintings and sculpture. There are some exceptions, but kami are thought of almost universally as invisible presences, not to be portrayed. Instead, the defining features of Shinto art are openness, a use of natural elements, and a deliberate simplicity.

It can be argued that Shinto's high esteem for nature has had a profound influence on Japanese art and architecture. The Japanese screens and scrolls that portray nature that are often said to be the product of Zen are equally the product of Shinto. This can also be said of all the fine and decorative art forms, such as ceramics and kimono design, in which elements of nature are a primary inspiration. Traditional Japanese architecture, with its floor of rice matting and its unpainted wooden walls, also shows Shinto influence.

Perhaps because Shinto places almost no emphasis on doctrines and ethical demands, it has focused instead on the beauty of ritual, giving Shinto an important relationship with the arts. Its love of ceremony has demanded that attention be paid to all objects and clothing used in its sacred ritual, to the places where the ritual takes place, and to the exact way the ritual is performed.

Architecture

The traditional architecture of shrines (**jinja**) is a primary expression of Shinto artistic expression. These structures seem to have begun as storehouses for grain and other foods that were raised off the ground for protection from water and insects. These granaries functioned as the natural and comfortable homes of the gods who served as protectors of the stored foods. The original pattern of the shrine called for walls made of wood and roofs made of thatch, which would be renewed regularly. Roof beams often extended high above the roof, in a style that is also found in South Pacific island architecture. This feature of extended roof beams (*chigi*) and the fact that the construction materials seem to be appropriate for a warm climate, lead many to think that the Shinto shrine originated possibly in Malaysia and islands farther south.

As discussed earlier, Shinto architecture today reflects Japan's history. The Chinese influence, a force since 500 C.E., is evident in symmetrical compound design, curving roofs, and roof tiles. The Shinto scholarly revival of the seventeenth century, as well as the nationalistic Meiji Restoration of the later nineteenth century, produced efforts to rid Shinto of Buddhist (and therefore Chinese) influences. These efforts were only partially successful. "Pure" Shinto style, with uncurving gabled thatch roofs, unpainted and uncarved wooden walls, and nailless construction, is most evident at Ise. Because the wood and thatch need to be replaced regularly in order to keep them bright and fresh, the maintenance of this style can be afforded at only a few sites.

The shrines of Ise, which are rebuilt every twenty years, are striking because of their extreme simplicity. They sit on a ground of white stones in the midst of tall cedar trees, and to reach the inner shrine, the visitor must cross a river. In the summer, the cicadas fill the air with chirping sounds, adding to the sense of primordial mystery.

The earliest torii, or ceremonial entryway, was probably made of three logs lashed together, though we don't know its exact origin. From this basic shape, many graceful variations emerged. The original torii were certainly unpainted wood, although today many are painted white, red, or orange. The torii usually signify sacred landmarks, but they can also be set in water. (The enormous orange torii standing in the ocean at Miyajima island near Hiroshima is the best-known example.)

At some shrines, so many torii are set up as thanksgiving offerings that over many years they create a tunnel (as seen at Fushimi Inari Shrine, near Kyoto). Tied to the torii or to the front of a shrine is often a ceremonial rope (**shimenawa**), from which may be hung white paper streamers, particularly on festival days. Special shimenawa, occasionally very thick and elaborate, are created for New Year's celebrations. These shimenawa have become an art form in their own right, appearing at New Year's time not only on shrines but also over the doors of shops and homes. Because kami are considered to reside in any place in nature that is awe-inspiring, shimenawa may also adorn exceptional trees and rocks.

Music and Dance

Shinto is also known for its distinctive music called **gagaku.** Originally played in the Chinese imperial court of the Tang and Song dynasties, gagaku was adapted by Shinto and so slowed down that it creates an impression of ancient solemnity. The instruments used make a flutelike, reedy

A simple form of torii built of logs in the middle of a forest.

sound that sounds close yet far away, fresh and new, but also timeless. Gagaku is a perfect accompaniment to Shinto ritual.

One story in the Kojiki tells of how Amaterasu was lured out of a rock cave by music and dance. Shinto shrines often include dance at festival times to entertain the resident kami. From this shrine dance evolved the stately **Noh** dance dramas, which tell the stories of people and their contacts with the spirits. The making of masks and exquisite robes for Noh performers has become a fine art.

SHINTO OFFSHOOTS: THE NEW RELIGIONS

The fact that Shinto is not a strongly institutionalized religion is both a weakness and a strength. It is a strength because anyone can set up a Shinto shrine and even begin a Shinto-inspired movement; it is a weakness, however, because Shinto generally has not had the organizational structure necessary to make converts or spread the religion beyond Japan. Shinto shrines do belong to confederations, however, which help them with staffing, and many smaller shrines are affiliated with one of the old and large national shrines.

Shinto, possibly helped by its lack of institutional structure, has produced (and still produces) an amazing variety of sects, especially over the last two centuries. Some are more traditional than others. Some worship all the major kami or focus on just one of them. Some borrow from Confucianism, Buddhism, or Christianity and speak of a divine parent (or parents) and of the human race as a single family. Some utilize traditions derived from mountain asceticism. Some emphasize healing. Some venerate a charismatic founder who is thought to be a kami and the recipient of a divine revelation.

It is possible to group Shinto sects and offshoots into those that are the most traditional, those that emphasize mountain spirituality, those that stress purification, and those that have emerged from shamanistic revelations. The last group is especially prominent. Offshoots that consider themselves separate religions are sometimes called the New Religions.

Japan, like Korea, has had a long history of shamanism; and in both countries the shamans are often female. We might recall that the shaman acts as an intermediary between the gods and human beings. The shaman helps bring physical and emotional healing. This openness to shamanism has helped produce the offshoots of Shinto that revere an inspired leader who was the recipient of a divine revelation. These offshoots illustrate the ability of Japanese religious traditions to take on new forms.

One of the New Religions is **Tenrikyo** ("heavenly reason teaching"), founded by Nakayama Miki (1798–1887), who discovered her religious abilities by accident. When Miki called in a shaman to perform rites to improve her unhappy life and miserable marriage, she intended only to act as

Noh dancing is sometimes performed independently of the ritualistic plays in which it originated.

the shaman's assistant but instead went into a trance that lasted several days. During the trance a kami spoke through her, saying "I am the True and Original God. . . . I have descended from Heaven to save all human beings, and I want to take Miki as the Shrine of God. . . ."[11] When Miki came out of the trance, she explained that many kami had spoken to her. The greatest, she said, was the parent kami (*Oya-gami*) of all human beings. The name of the kami was Tenri-o-no-mikoto ("Lord of divine wisdom"). This kami wished her to disseminate teachings to people about how to live properly so that they might have health and long life.

The notion that physical health comes from mental health is strong in Tenrikyo, which preaches healing by faith. This religion is exceptional for its institutional structure and other traditional religious elements that allow it to spread beyond Japan. It has sacred scripture—the poetry that Nakayama Miki wrote as a result of her revelations.[12] The sect has even created a city near Nara, called Tenri City, where its ideals are put into practice. Tenri City contains a university, library, and museum; religious services are offered twice daily in the main hall.

Another New Religion is called *Omotokyo* ("great origin teaching"), or simply **Omoto.** It was founded by Deguchi Nao (1836–1918), who suffered terrible poverty and misfortune. Of her eight children, three died and two suffered mental illness. Nao's husband died when she was 30 and she was reduced to selling rags. In her despair, she experienced a vision of the creation of a new, perfect world. Working with a man she adopted as her son, Deguchi Onisaburo, Nao established a religion that she hoped would begin the transformation of society.

Nao's vision grew out of the traditional Shinto view of earth as a heavenly realm of the spirits and its shamanistic trust in the spirits to bring healing to human life. Like many other New Religions, Omoto aims to better *this* world rather than accumulate rewards for an afterlife. It wishes to bring happiness to the individual and peace to society.

Omoto is of particular interest because it sees in the creation of art the essence of religious manifestation. For Omoto, all art is religious. To spread its belief about the connection between art and religion, Omoto began a school at its headquarters at Kameoka, near Kyoto, to teach traditional Japanese arts to non-Japanese. There, students learn ceramics, calligraphy, and other arts that they are urged to spread in their home countries. To encourage world peace, Omoto has promoted the study of Esperanto (a universal language) and sponsored contacts with members of other religions, such as Muslims and Christians. Omoto has even held services in New York's Cathedral of Saint John the Divine, where Shinto ritual objects remain on display.

These Shinto offshoots have themselves produced offshoots: for example, from Tenrikyo has come *Honmichi* ("true road"), and from Omoto *Seicho-no-Ie* ("house of growth") and *P.L.Kyodan* ("perfect liberty community"). Their goals are similar: beauty, happiness, and the creation of paradise on earth.

This shrine and torii, set amid modern office buildings in Tokyo, stand as testimony to the robust nature of Shinto.

The New Religions are the object of some interest for what they may foretell about the direction of religions in the future. They tend to be practical, peace-oriented, and "this-worldly." Many value the contributions of women, and many esteem the arts. Borrowing valuable elements from other religions, they are moving in new directions.

SHINTO AND THE MODERN WORLD

Shinto could have died out under the onslaught of Buddhism, or it could have easily faded away when Japan adopted Western science and technology. Yet Shinto is a unique example of an early nature religion that is still vital in the modern world.

Why does Shinto seem to maintain its relevance in modern life? Four of its elements have particular modern significance:

An esteem for nature Because much of our natural world is threatened by overpopulation, pollution, and exploitation, we may have something to learn from the Shinto attitude toward nature.

The stance of benevolent silence about most moral and doctrinal questions For modern democracies that attempt to blend many viewpoints, Shinto provides a religion that does not fragment society over doctrinal and moral issues.

Aesthetically pleasing ritual Some religions have downplayed the importance of ritual, ranking it below doctrine and morality. But for

> Art is the mother of religion.
> —Omoto saying

many people who question traditional ethics and doctrines, the nonjudgmental ritual of Shinto appears all the more valuable.

Eclecticism Shinto does not exclude other religions, but allows their practice and sometimes absorbs their teachings and various elements. The eclecticism of Shinto reflects its inclusive viewpoint.

Shinto has gone wherever Japanese people have settled: Brazil, Peru, the United States (particularly Hawai`i and California). Some believers in Shinto see its potential as a universal religion of nature and would like to see it spread to non-Japanese. But Shinto is not a missionary religion, nor does it generally have the institutional structure to do missionary work. It is possible, however, that some well-organized Shinto offshoot, such as Ten-rikyo, will spread far beyond its country of origin.

It may be that traditional Shinto derives much of its vitality from the specific terrain, climate, and geographical isolation of Japan—from its mountains, waterfalls, thick forests, and myriad islands, all in continual change from the procession of the seasons. If so, then Shinto will remain restricted to that country. Nonetheless, it is easy at least to imagine the spread of traditional Shinto, especially to areas in which its special elements might take root in a welcoming, supportive community.

RELIGION BEYOND THE CLASSROOM

Every town and village in Japan has at least one shrine, and most have many more. The neighborhood shrines are full of charm and worth visiting, particularly during a fair or festival (*matsuri*). (Check guidebooks and local English-language newspapers in Japan for dates and times.)

In Tokyo, Meiji Jingu is the preeminent shrine. Sundays, New Year's, and midsummer are especially good times to visit. Yasukuni Jinja is another large shrine in Tokyo. (Because it is dedicated to military personnel who died in war, it is sometimes a center of controversy for those who fear a resurgence of militarism.) Both shrines are in traditional Shinto style. An example of "baroque" Shinto style can be seen just outside Tokyo; located at Nikko (an easy day trip from Tokyo), Toshogu Shrine is a large complex of elaborate buildings.

Kyoto, the ancient capital, has several shrines of beauty and interest. The most imposing is Heian Jingu, painted red in the Chinese style. Gion Jinja, Kitano Jinja, and Yasaka Jinja are also located in Kyoto.

Ise, in eastern Honshu, is not easily accessible to the foreign visitor because it is off the usual tourist route, but it can be reached by train from Tokyo, Osaka, or Kyoto. In pure Shinto style, its shrine is one of the greatest architectural sights in the world.

Mount Fuji is the most important and possibly most beautiful mountain of Japan. Several Shinto sects worship its kami, and many Japanese climb Mount Fuji once in their lives as a semireligious pilgrimage. Visitors commonly travel to Mount Fuji, stay overnight, and walk up to experience dawn from a lookout spot near the top of the mountain. (Consult the Japan National Tourist Association for help in making all travel plans and reservations.)

Because of the immigration of Japanese to Hawai`i, Shinto is quite evident there. The main shrine of Honolulu is Izumo-Taisha-kyo, near the downtown area and Chinatown. It is in fairly pure Shinto style. Another is Kotohira-Jinsha, near the Bishop Museum in Kalihi. Wakamiya Inari Shrine is located in the Plantation Village at Waipahu Cultural Garden Park. This red shrine is typical of a small, local shrine; it is dedicated to Inari, goddess of rice, and to the fox god.

FOR FULLER UNDERSTANDING

1. Design a "new"religion that builds upon some of the elements of Shinto and perhaps incorporates traditions from other religions and institutions.
2. Research one of the Shinto New Religions. Look into its origins, its current status, and its spread. Use your research to predict its future course.
3. Most of the New Religions, such as Omoto and Tenrikyo, have offices dedicated to international outreach. At a library, find out the address of the Japanese headquarters of one of these religions, and send a written request for information in English. Share the information with your class.
4. Using a library, an architects' association, and/or the world wide web, research recent trends in Japanese architecture, both grand (public spaces) and small (private homes). Write a report that highlights the connections between recent trends and traditional Shinto attitudes and arts.

RELATED READINGS

Blacker, Carmen. *The Catalpa Bow.* London: Allen & Unwin, 1975. A literate study of Japanese shamanism.

Kitagawa, Joseph. *On Understanding Japanese Religion.* Princeton, NJ: Princeton University Press, 1987. A good introduction to Japanese religions, including the New Religions, by a major scholar.

Moore, Charles, ed. *The Japanese Mind.* Honolulu: University Press, 1971. A collection of scholarly essays on patterns in Japanese philosophy, religion, and culture.

Picken, Stuart. *Shinto: Japan's Spiritual Roots.* Tokyo: Kodansha, 1980. An explanation of the essentials of Shinto, accompanied by excellent photographs.

Tanaka, Ikko, and Kazuko Koike. *Japanese Coloring.* Tokyo: Libro, 1982. A photographic presentation of everyday objects in Japan, many of which show Shinto influence.

KEY TERMS

Amaterasu (*ah'-mah-te-rah'-soo*): "Shining in heaven"; goddess of the sun.

Bushido (*boo'-shee-doh*): "Warrior knight way"; military devotion to a ruler, demanding loyalty, duty, and self-sacrifice; an ideal promoted by State Shinto.

Gagaku: The stately ceremonial music of Shinto.

Ise (*ee'-say*): Location in eastern Honshu of a major shrine to Amaterasu.

Izanagi (*ee-za-nah'-gee*): "Male who invites"; primordial male parent god.

Izanami (*ee-za-nah'-mee*): "Female who invites"; primordial female parent god.

Jinja (*jin'-ja*): A Shinto shrine.

Kami (*kah'-mee*): A spirit, god, or goddess of Shinto.

Kamidan (*kah'-mee-dan*): A shelf or home altar for the veneration of kami.

Kamikaze (*kah'-mee-kah'-zay*): "Spirit wind"; suicide fighter pilots of World War II.

Kojiki (*koh'-jee-kee*): The earliest chronicle of Japanese history.

Misogi (*mee-soh'-gee*): A ritual of purification that involves standing under a waterfall.

Nihongi (*nee-hohn'-gee*): The second chronicle of Japanese history.

Noh: Dramas performed in mask and costume, associated with Shinto.

Omoto (*oh'-mo-to*): A New Religion, which stresses art and beauty.

Samurai (*sah'-moo-rai*): Feudal soldier.

Shimenawa (*shee-may-nah'-wa*): Twisted rope, marking a sacred spot.

Tenrikyo (*ten'-ree-kyoh*): A New Religion devoted to human betterment.

Torii (*to-ree'*): A gatelike structure that marks a Shinto sacred place.

CHAPTER 8

Judaism

 FIRST ENCOUNTER

After spending two days in Tel Aviv, you leave for Jerusalem and arrive at your hotel near the old part of the city. Once there, you can't wait to begin exploring. The Old City is a place for walking and wandering, with wonderful sights in its narrow streets.

Drawing you like a magnet is the site of the ancient temple, destroyed by Roman soldiers nearly two thousand years ago. Only its foundation stones remain. On the mount where the temple once stood is now a glittering golden dome. Built by Muslims, the Dome of the Rock covers the great stone beneath it, which is venerated by Muslims and Jews alike, who hold that their ancestor Abraham came to this spot.

You decide to walk down from the city, to view the mount from below, after which you plan to turn back and travel, like a true pilgrim, "up to Jerusalem." You buy food for a picnic lunch at stalls as you walk inside the city. Soon you are beyond the Old City gate. Luckily, the day is sunny but not hot. You see a large stone tomb in the valley below and beyond it, in the east, Mount Scopus.

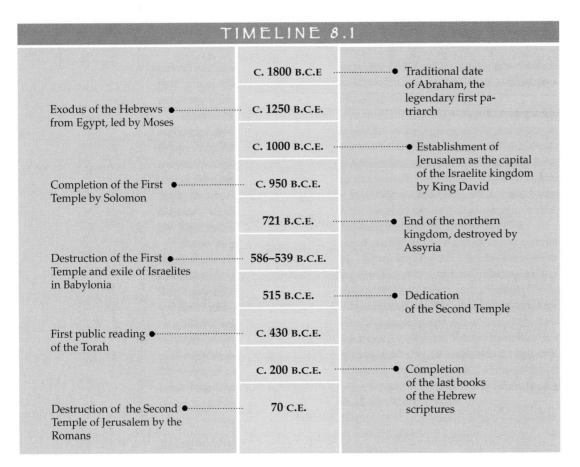

TIMELINE 8.1

	C. 1800 B.C.E	Traditional date of Abraham, the legendary first patriarch
Exodus of the Hebrews from Egypt, led by Moses	C. 1250 B.C.E.	
	C. 1000 B.C.E.	Establishment of Jerusalem as the capital of the Israelite kingdom by King David
Completion of the First Temple by Solomon	C. 950 B.C.E.	
	721 B.C.E	End of the northern kingdom, destroyed by Assyria
Destruction of the First Temple and exile of Israelites in Babylonia	586–539 B.C.E.	
	515 B.C.E.	Dedication of the Second Temple
First public reading of the Torah	C. 430 B.C.E.	
	C. 200 B.C.E.	Completion of the last books of the Hebrew scriptures
Destruction of the Second Temple of Jerusalem by the Romans	70 C.E.	

Timeline of significant events in the history of Judaism.

At last it is time to stop for a rest and to eat your lunch. You sit under a tree and look back, thinking to yourself about the events this site has witnessed. Your mind becomes crowded with the names of biblical kings, prophets, and priests associated with Jerusalem: David, Solomon, Melchizedek, Isaiah, Jeremiah. As the sounds of everyday traffic filter through your thoughts, you imagine the many battles over this holy city and the successive waves of conquerors—Babylonians, Greeks, Romans, Arabs, and European Crusaders—who took possession of it in the past, and you think of the more recent battles here, after the emergence of the new state of Israel. You are grateful to be here when there is peace, recalling that the root of the city's name—*salem*, like *shalom*—means "peace" and "wholeness."

You start back, walking uphill thoughtfully. You see the small tombstones in front of the walls, the high walls themselves, and a beautiful double stone gate, now sealed. Slowly, you make your way back through the city streets around to the western side, to what is left of the great temple. The immense foundation stones, set there during an enlargement ordered by King Herod the Great, were too solid to be knocked down and too big to be carted off. An open area at their base, the **Western Wall,** is now used for contemplation and prayer—on the left stand men, and on the right,

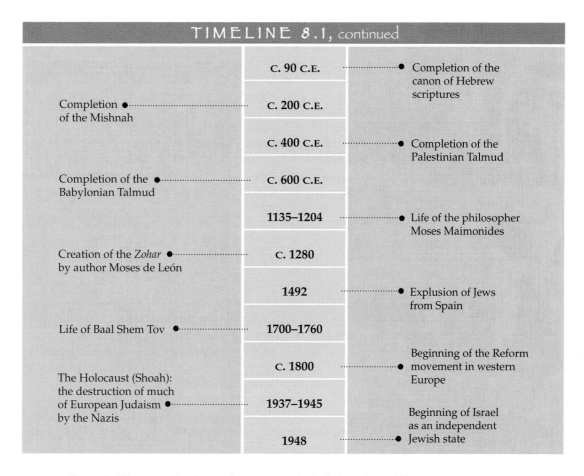

	C. 90 C.E.	Completion of the canon of Hebrew scriptures
Completion of the Mishnah	C. 200 C.E.	
	C. 400 C.E.	Completion of the Palestinian Talmud
Completion of the Babylonian Talmud	C. 600 C.E.	
	1135–1204	Life of the philosopher Moses Maimonides
Creation of the *Zohar* by author Moses de León	C. 1280	
	1492	Explusion of Jews from Spain
Life of Baal Shem Tov	1700–1760	
	C. 1800	Beginning of the Reform movement in western Europe
The Holocaust (Shoah): the destruction of much of European Judaism by the Nazis	1937–1945	
	1948	Beginning of Israel as an independent Jewish state

women. Some hold prayer books, and many touch their hands and fore-heads to the wall. You see little pieces of paper, which have prayers writ-ten on them, rolled up or folded and placed in the cracks between the stones, left here by people who have come to speak with God and to re-member their family members in prayer. You reflect on the historical events that led up to the building of the temple, whose foundation stones are all that remain. You think of the long and great history of the Jews, who developed and flourished in spite of persecution in lands far away. You re-flect on the re-creation of a Jewish homeland and the revival of the Hebrew language, which you now experience all around you. It is deeply moving to be here, and you stay a long time in silent contemplation.

AN OVERVIEW OF JEWISH HISTORY

Jewish history goes back two thousand or four thousand years, depending on one's point of view. This difference of opinion revolves around a major historical event—the destruction of the Second Temple of Jerusalem by the Romans in 70 C.E. (Timeline 8.1), which brought about the end of the temple-based ceremonial religion of that region and the widespread dispersion of its people to lands far away from Israel. Following the calamity of the temple's destruction, the earlier religion had to develop in new ways to survive. From the centralized, ritualistic religion based in Israel and focused on the temple arose another form of religion that could be practiced largely in the home and synagogue and could be lived out anywhere in the world. In recognition of this fundamental religious reorientation, a distinction is often made between **biblical Judaism** and **rabbinical Judaism.** When we study the Judaism of today what we are really studying are the forms of Jewish belief and religious practice that largely came into existence after the destruction of the Second Temple.

The two great spans of time—before and after the destruction of the Second Temple—are also commonly subdivided into two periods each. Over the first great span of time, a homeless people established a homeland in Israel and made Jerusalem the capital of its kingdom. Great change occurred and another period began, however, when the kingdom of Judah and its First Temple were destroyed by the Babylonians (586 B.C.E.), forcing the Israelite people into exile in Babylonia (present-day Iraq) for nearly fifty years. These events made clear to the exiled people that religious law and history had to be put in written form to guarantee their survival. As a result, the Hebrew Bible was created, and study of the scriptures and prayer in synagogues became important, even after the temple was rebuilt.

The second great time span comprises the two thousand years of the development of Judaism in the common era. It also can be subdivided into two periods. The first period marks the evolution of Judaism and traditional Jewish life, from about 100 C.E. to approximately 1800 C.E., the beginning of the modern period. About two hundred years ago, a movement began in Judaism as a response to the new thinking of the European Enlightenment, the liberal thought of the American and French Revolutions, and the laws of Napoleon, which were carried widely beyond France. The movement, called the **Reform,** questioned and modernized traditional Judaism and helped produce the diverse branches within Judaism that exist today. The Reform also raised the issue of Jewish identity. Who is a Jew? What is essential to Judaism? These are two questions to which we will return later.

The Hebrew Bible records that the roots of Judaism go back far into the past, to a landless people sometimes called Hebrews and more commonly called Israelites, who traced themselves to an ancestor named Abraham. Because much of what we know of the first two-thousand-year span of Hebrew history comes from the Hebrew Bible, we will examine it first. We should note, however, that the Hebrew Bible is significant not only in terms of the history of the Hebrews but also because of its role in the development of Judaism over the last two thousand years. When the ceremonial religion of the Jerusalem Temple ended in the first century C.E., it was the Hebrew scriptures that provided a foundation for the development of rabbinical Judaism. The scriptures offered a firm basis for Jewish **rabbis** (teachers) to offer their interpretation (*midrash*) of biblical laws and practices: the books gave the Ten Commandments and other ethical teachings; they established the major yearly festivals that would guide and sanctify the lives of Jews; and they contained the psalms that became the everyday prayers of Jews everywhere.

Thus, we turn first to the Hebrew Bible, to understand its structure and to examine the laws and history of the Hebrew people. After looking at the Hebrew Bible and at Hebrew and Jewish history, we will then consider Jewish belief, practice, and influence.

THE HEBREW BIBLE

Judaism is often associated with the land of Israel, but Judaism is perhaps better associated with its most important book, the Hebrew Bible. Although nowadays the Hebrew Bible is published as a single volume, it is made up of individual "books," which were once separate written scrolls. The word *Bible*, in fact, comes from the Greek term *biblia*, which means "little books." The individual books were originally oral material that was subsequently written down in some form perhaps as early as 800 B.C.E., although the final form was not achieved until about 200 B.C.E. It was once thought that

Traditional Jews open a Torah scroll in Jerusalem.

Books of the Hebrew Bible

Torah

Genesis (Bereshit)

Exodus (Shemot)

Leviticus (Vayiqra)

Numbers (Bemidbar)

Deuteronomy (Devarim)

Nevi'im (the Prophets)

Joshua (Yehoshua)

Judges (Shofetim)

Samuel (Shemuel)

Kings (Melakhim)

Isaiah (Yeshayahu)

Jeremiah (Yirmeyahu)

Ezekiel (Yehezaqel)

Book of the Twelve (Tere Asar): Hosea, Joel, Amos, Obadiah, Jonah, Micah, Nahum,

Habakkuk, Zephaniah, Haggai, Zechariah, Malachi

Kethuvim (the Writings)

Psalms (Tehillim)

Proverbs (Mishle)

Job (Iyyov)

Song of Songs (Shir Hashirim)

Ruth (Ruth)

Lamentations (Ekhah)

Ecclesiastes (Qohelet)

Esther (Ester)

Daniel (Daniel)

Ezra-Nehemiah (Ezra-Nehemyah)

Chronicles (Divre Hayamim)

Moses wrote the first five books of the Bible, but this is no longer commonly held.

The Hebrew Bible is divided into three sections: the **Torah** (the teaching), the Prophets (in Hebrew, **Nevi'im**), and the Writings (**Kethuvim**). Considered as a whole, it is often called **Tanakh** (or Tanak), which is an acronym (like *sonar*, *s*ound *n*avigation *r*anging) made up of the introductory letters of the Hebrew names for the three sections: *t, n, k*.

The Torah is the sacred core of the Hebrew Bible, with its stories of the creation, Adam and Eve, Noah, and the Hebrew patriarchs and matriarchs—the early ancestors of the Hebrew people. It introduces Moses, the great liberator and lawgiver, and his brother Aaron, the founder of the priesthood. It includes laws about daily conduct and religious ritual—material which would be of great importance to the later development of Judaism.[1] Because the Torah comprises five books, it is sometimes called the Pentateuch (Greek: "five scrolls"). (We should also recognize that the term *Torah* is also used more widely to refer to all teachings, both written and those that were orally transmitted, that are thought of as having been revealed by God.)

The second part of the Tanakh is called the Prophets, named for those individuals who spoke in God's name to the Jewish people. The books that concentrate on the history of the Israelite kingdom are called the Former Prophets, followed by additional books, which are more strongly visionary and moral in tone, called the Latter (or Later) Prophets. In the Latter Prophets, the voices of the individual prophets tend to predominate.

The third part of the Tanakh, called the Writings, is closer to what we think of as imaginative literature. It includes some late historical books, but it contains primarily short stories, proverbs, reflections on life, hymn (psalm) lyrics, and poetry.

We will use the term Hebrew Bible (or Hebrew scriptures) for all of this material. (Jews do not refer to the Hebrew scriptures as the Old Testament, as do Christians, because the title implies that the Jewish books have meaning relative to the Christian books, collectively called the New Testament. Also, the order of books in the Hebrew Bible, in the format that it assumed by the end of the tenth century C.E., differs somewhat from the general order that is found in Christian Bibles.) The commonly used titles of the books are Greek, based on early Greek translations.[2]

The historical accuracy of the Hebrew Bible is not always certain, because not all biblical accounts can be verified by archeological finds or references in other historical records. (No archeological evidence, for example, has yet been found that proves the existence of Abraham or Moses, and their historicity is debated.) Although we can presume that many of the accounts (particularly those of events after the Jewish kingdom was established) are based on historical fact, we must also recognize that they were recorded by the Jews themselves, who naturally viewed historical events from their own special perspective. Furthermore, many accounts were transmitted orally long before they were written down or assembled in final form, thus affecting the way they were recounted.

BIBLICAL HISTORY

Whatever its historical accuracy, the heroic and mythic power of the Hebrew Bible cannot be denied. It is filled with astonishing people and powerful images. Adam and Eve, for example, stand naked and suddenly aware among the trees and streams of the Garden of Eden. Noah and his wife are surrounded by animals in their big wooden boat, riding out a long flood. Moses climbs to the top of cloud-covered Mount Sinai to speak with God and receive the Ten Commandments. These images and ideas are not only unforgettable, but are part of Western culture, and have influenced its laws, art, literature, and ways of living.

In the Beginning: Stories of Origins

The earliest stories of the Hebrew Bible, given in Genesis 1–11, have a mythic quality that is universally appealing. The story of the origin of the world presents God as an intelligent, active, masculine power who overcomes primeval chaos. To create order, God imposes separations—separating light from darkness and land from water—and completes his work of creation in stages, spread over six days. At the end of each day, God views what he has done and sees that it is good. Finally, satisfied with the result of all his labor, God rests on the seventh day.

Paradise, by Marc Chagall, (1962) captures Adam and Eve, caretakers of the Garden of Eden, just before they partake of the apple.

This account (which shows parallels with the creation story in the Babylonian epic poem *Enuma Elish*) appears in the first chapter of Genesis, the first book of the Bible. This first account is cosmic and measured—possibly written that way in order to be read out solemnly by a priest at temple ceremonies. The second account (perhaps written earlier than the first) begins in the second chapter of Genesis. This account is more human, utilizes colorful dialogue, and focuses on the first human parents, Adam and Eve, and on their moral dilemma.

The Garden of Eden, which God has created for his refreshment, is based on the pattern of a walled garden, complete with fruit trees, birds, exotic animals, a central fountain, and streams to cool the air. God creates Adam to live in the garden (presumably as its gardener and protector), forming his body from the dust of the earth and breathing life into Adam with his own breath. In some way, Adam is a copy of God himself, for the human being, the Bible says, is made "in the image of God"[3] (Gen. 1:27), bearing some of the dignity of God. Soon, though, because Adam is lonely, God decides to give him a companion. Taking a rib from Adam while he is in a deep sleep, God forms Eve around that rib. In the first account of creation, male and female were created simultaneously; but in the second account, the male is created first and the female afterward—leading to the unfortunate interpretation that while the male is a copy of God, the female is only a copy of the male. Interestingly, the conception of God in the creation stories is somewhat different from many later views. For one thing, although the biblical God has no apparent rivals, he does not appear to be alone, and when he declares "Let *us* make man" (Gen. 1:26),[4] he is most likely addressing his heavenly counselors, some of whom are identified in later texts (such as Psalms and Job). In addition, God is not represented as pure spirit. The account in chapter two of Genesis says that God walks and eats; and having made the garden to enjoy, he strolls in it when he wants to enjoy its cool breezes. God allows Adam and Eve to eat from almost all the trees but forbids them to eat fruit from the two trees that he especially needs to nourish his supernatural life and insight. Eve, tempted to eat from one of the trees, does so, then urges Adam to do the same. For their disobedient act, they are exiled from God's garden. God can no longer trust them, knowing that if they were to remain they might become his rivals. Now they must live outside the garden, work, and suffer for the rest of their amazingly long lives.

To some, the portrait of Eve—a temptress who brings down punishment on Adam and herself—is distressing. But it should be pointed out that Eve is the one with ambition and personality, while Adam seems far less colorful. Whatever the interpretation—and there have been many—the story of Adam and Eve has influenced Western views of women and marriage for several thousand years.

Next is the story of Adam and Eve's children, Cain and Abel (Gen. 4:1–16), whose sibling rivalry ends in Cain's murder of Abel. This tale may reflect ancient rivalries between farmers and herders.

Following this is the story of the Great Flood (Gen. 6–9), which echoes a Mesopotamian tale, the *Epic of Gilgamesh*. Disgusted with the rapidly growing, immoral human population, God sends a flood to do away with humanity—all of humanity, that is, except the righteous Noah and his family. He warns Noah to build a large wooden boat (an ark) and fill it with animals, because only those in the boat will survive the coming downpour. At the end of the flood, God makes a pact with Noah never again to destroy the earth by water. As a sign of this promise, God places his "bow" (perhaps an archer's bow) into the sky. The "rainbow" is a reminder of his solemn promise. Like several of the early stories, this account gives an explanation for a natural phenomenon. This story also explains how, from the three sons of Noah, different races arise.

Chapter eleven of Genesis tells the story of the tower of Babel (or Babylonia). Wanting to reach the heavenly realm that was believed to exist above the skies, people began building a very tall tower. God, not willing to have his private world invaded, stopped the building by making the builders speak different languages. Because they could no longer understand each other, they could not finish their tower. This story also gives a convenient answer to the question, Why are there different languages in the world?

The World of the Patriarchs and Matriarchs

The first Hebrew patriarch (or "father") is Abraham, who is introduced in chapter twelve of Genesis, the point at which the book becomes more seemingly historical. Abraham, first known as Abram, is called by God to leave his home for another land. Originally from Ur (in present-day Iraq), Abraham migrates via Haran (in Turkey) to the land of **Canaan.** "Now the Lord said to Abram, 'Go from your father's house to the land that I will show you. I will make of you a great nation.'" (Gen. 12:1–2a).[5] This passage is significant to Judaism because it establishes a claim to the region now called Israel. Abraham's migration becomes a pilgrimage of great importance, making him, his son Isaac, and his grandson Jacob the patriarchs of Judaism.

After assuring Abraham of land and many descendants, God enters into a solemn **covenant,** a contract, with Abraham. God promises to provide land, protection, and descendants, but in return Abraham and his male descendants must be circumcised as a sign of their exclusive relationship with God (Gen. 17).

The most famous story of Abraham concerns his son Isaac. Abraham had long been unable to have a son by his wife, Sarah. At Sarah's urging, he fathers by her maid, Hagar, a son named Ishmael. But then at last, to the amazement of all, Sarah herself has a son (Gen. 19). Shockingly, God then asks (in Gen. 22) that Abraham offer Isaac, the beloved son of his old age, as a sacrifice. (Perhaps this is a vestige of an earlier practice of human sacrifice.) Abraham agrees and sets out with his son to Mount Moriah, believed by Jews to be the hill on which Jerusalem now rests. Just before the boy is to die, God stops Abraham, and a ram, whose horns had become tangled in a bush nearby, is used as the sacrifice instead. God has thus tested Abraham's devotion, and in so proving his absolute loyalty to God, Abraham has shown himself worthy of land, wealth, fame, and the joy of knowing he will have innumerable descendants. (This passage may show the replacement of human sacrifice with the sacrifice of animals.)

Genesis also contains stories about some extremely memorable women, the matriarchs of the Hebrew people: Sarah, Rebecca, Rachel, and Leah. Although these women are always linked with their husbands, they all have strong and carefully drawn personalities. Sarah, for example, stays modestly inside the tent when strangers arrive but laughs so loudly that they hear her and then question her (Gen. 18:10–15).

The stories in Genesis also tell of mysterious contacts with God—called **theophanies**—which are sometimes friendly in nature but at other times fierce and frightening. God appears to Isaac, for example, and promises him protection and many descendants (Gen. 26:24). Isaac's son, Jacob, has a vision of God in a dream (Gen. 28). He sees a stairway leading from earth into the sky. God is at the top, and angels are ascending and descending, linking heaven and earth. A more unusual theophany occurs when Jacob wrestles all night long with a mysterious stranger—God or God's angel. At dawn the fight is over, and Jacob receives from the stranger a new name: Israel

Marc Chagall, *Abraham Preparing to Sacrifice His Son*, 1931. Just as Abraham is on the point of offering his son as a sacrifice, an angel stops his hand and a ram becomes the substitute.

("wrestles with God"). Because Jacob and his sons would settle the land of Canaan, it came to be called Israel after his new name. Jacob, with his two wives and two concubines, has many sons, who would become the ancestors of the twelve tribes of Israel.

Joseph, Jacob's next-to-last son, is the focus of the final section of Genesis. Because Joseph's brothers sense that his father loves him best, they scheme to have him killed. Ultimately, though, they sell him as a slave, and he is taken to Egypt (Figure 8.1). There, through his special gifts, he rises in importance to become a government minister. When a famine in Israel brings his brothers down to Egypt to look for grain, Joseph is not vengeful but invites his brothers to bring their father to Egypt and to settle there permanently. They do so and settle in the land of Goshen in northeast Egypt. The book of Genesis ends with the death of Jacob.

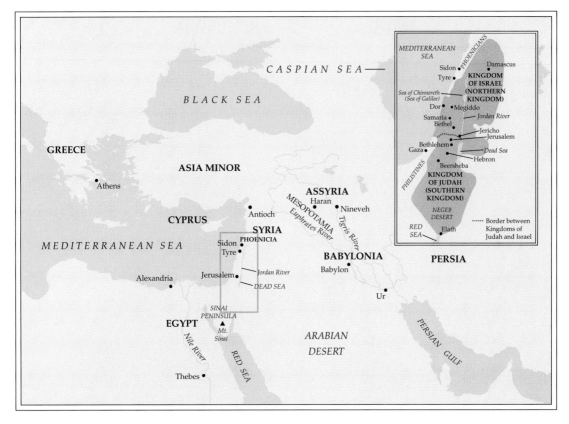

FIGURE 8.1

The eastern Mediterranean with inset of the two kingdoms (c. 900 B.C.E.)

Moses and the Law

After several centuries, the population of Hebrews in Egypt had grown so large that the Egyptians saw them as a danger. The Book of Exodus tells about the proposed solution, in which Hebrew midwives are commanded to kill all baby boys right after birth. The baby Moses (the name is probably Egyptian), however, is spared by being hidden. After three months, when his Hebrew mother is afraid to keep him any longer, she and her daughter fashion a watertight basket, put him inside, and place the basket in the Nile River, where he is discovered by an Egyptian princess who raises him as her own. As a young adult, Moses sees an Egyptian foreman badly mistreating an Israelite slave. In trying to put an end to the cruelty, Moses kills the foreman. Moses then flees from Egypt.

Our next glimpse of Moses comes when he has found a new life beyond the borders of Egypt, where he is now a herdsman for a Midianite priest named Jethro, whose daughter he has married. One day, when Moses is out with his father-in-law's herds, he sees a strange sight: a large bush appears to be burning, but is not consumed. As Moses approaches the bush, he hears the voice of God, who commands Moses to return to Egypt to help free the Hebrews.

This manuscript page illustrates the parting of the Red Sea during the Exodus from Egypt.

Living in a world that believes in many gods, Moses is curious to know the name of the divine spirit speaking to him. The deity, however, refuses to give a clear name and says mysteriously, "I will be who I will be," and then commands Moses to tell the Hebrews "that 'I will be' sent you" (Exod. 3:14).[6] In Hebrew the mysterious answer provides an etymological clue to *the* name for God. The name for God, usually associated with the verb *hayah* ("to be"), is Yhwh. The name is usually written Yahweh, but the exact pronunciation is unknown.

As mentioned, Moses lived in an age when people believed in many gods, and he had grown up in the polytheistic culture of Egypt. People everywhere believed in multiple gods who were thought of as guardian deities of particular groups and regions. Could Moses—or the patriarchs and matriarchs before him—have really been monotheistic? Probably not. A strong possibility is that Moses and the Hebrew patriarchs and matriarchs believed in the existence of many gods, of whom one, possibly a major deity, declared himself the special protector of the Israelites. If this is true, monotheism was not the original belief system of the Israelites but evolved over time. Ultimately, however, the god of the Jews would come to be proclaimed "the one true God."

We see two traditions in the Torah. In one (possibly older) tradition, Yahweh is embodied and appears directly to human beings. In another (possibly later) tradition, Yahweh exists as a spirit, existing apart from human beings. The notion of God as being transcendent and distant strengthened over time, and the transformation was complete when Yahweh came to be considered pure spirit and any reference to his body was considered to be metaphorical. In addition, God's name eventually was thought of as being too sacred to be pronounced; instead of speaking the name "Yahweh," priests and lectors substituted the Hebrew word *Adonay* ("the Lord").[7] Ultimately, all other gods were considered false gods; images of anything that could be construed as a god were prohibited, and Yahweh at last was considered the one God of the entire universe.

But these changes would all occur after the time of Moses. In the book of Exodus, Yahweh, the god of the Hebrews, simply needs to show himself to be more powerful than any of the gods of the Egyptians (Exod. 12:12). It is by his power that ten plagues strike the Egyptians and convince the pharaoh (possibly the great builder Ramses II, c. 1292–1225 B.C.E.) to let his Israelite slaves leave.

The last and greatest of the plagues is the death of the first-born sons of the Egyptians. The Israelites' sons are spared because they have followed Yahweh's warning and have marked the doors of their homes with the blood of a substitute—a sacrificial lamb (Exod. 12:13). Because God has "passed over" Egypt, the event is thereafter called the **Passover** (*Pesach*), and its yearly memorial has become one of the major Jewish festivals (which we will discuss later).

The Bible tells of the Hebrews' journey out of Egypt through a large body of water, the Red (or Reed) Sea, on their way to the Sinai Peninsula. Movies have dramatized the event, showing two walls of water, held back, as the Hebrews marched between them. But the reality was possibly less dramatic. Although Egyptian records do not mention it, the exodus from Egypt has become a central theme of Judaism. A whole people, protected by God, leaves a land of oppression and begins the march toward freedom.

The Books of Exodus and Numbers describe in detail the migration back to Israel—a migration that lasted a full generation, about forty years.

The most significant event during this period of passage is God's encounter with Moses at Mount Sinai. (The location of the mountain, also called Mount Horeb, is unknown, although tradition has placed it in the southern part of the Sinai Peninsula.) The Book of Exodus (chap. 19) paints a terrifying picture: the mountain is covered with cloud and smoke; lightning and thunder come from the cloud; and the sound of a trumpet splits the air. The people are warned to keep their distance, for only Moses may go to meet God at the top of the mountain. Moses enters the cloud and speaks with God.

When Moses descends, he returns to his people with rules for living—the Ten Commandments (Exod. 20). The strong moral orientation of Judaism is apparent here, for Moses does not return with an explanation of the universe, with science, or with art, but rather with ethical precepts. Parallels have been drawn to several other early codes, particularly that of the Babylonian King Hammurabi (c. 1792–1750 B.C.E.).

Undergirding the commandments is the conviction that a covenant—a contract—exists between Yahweh and his people. He will care for them, but they must fulfill their half of the bargain by following his laws and giving him sole worship. Such an agreement had already been made between God and Noah and later with Abraham. The covenant is reaffirmed with Moses and solidified by the laws and commandments, which give it legal form.

Following the Ten Commandments, the Book of Exodus outlines obligations regarding the treatment of slaves, animals, and property. (These instructions were probably deliberately placed here to share in the respect given the Ten Commandments.) We see here important texts that were mined by later teachers for their insight into fairness, justice, and compassion. They take up quite specific cases. In one story, for example, when a landowner begins a fire in his field that spreads to and destroys another landowner's field, the first landowner must pay damages to the second landowner (Exod. 22:6). In another situation, a neighbor's cow or donkey has run loose and the person who sees the animal is obligated to take it back to its owner (Exod. 23:4).

The Book of Leviticus begins with detailed laws about animal sacrifice (chaps. 1–7) and then takes up the complexities of ritual purity. In addition to laws about general honesty and humaneness, Leviticus outlines many special laws that would be important to the later development of Judaism: laws specifying which animals may and may not be eaten (chap. 11), laws prohibiting the consumption of meat with blood in it (17:10) and the cutting of one's beard (19:27), and laws governing the observance of the major religious festivals (chap. 23). The Book of Numbers returns to historical themes, recounting specifically the years of wandering before the Hebrews entered Canaan but also spelling out laws about ritual purity and the keeping of vows. The Torah ends with the Book of Deuteronomy, which repeats the Ten Commandments and describes the death of Moses, an event that occurs just before the Hebrews enter the Promised Land of Canaan.[8]

The Ten Commandments[9]

I am the Lord your God who brought you out of Egypt, out of the land of slavery. You shall have no other god to set against me.

The Ten Commandments begin with a reminder that Yahweh is the protector of the Hebrews and that because of his help they owe him their obedience. There seems to be an understanding, however, that other peoples have their own gods.

You shall not make a carved image for yourself nor the likeness of anything in the heavens above, or on the earth below, or in the waters under the earth. You shall not bow down to them or worship them; for I, the Lord your God, am a jealous god. I punish the children for the sins of their fathers to the third and fourth generations of those who hate me. But I keep faith with thousands, with those who love me and keep my commandments.

The commandment not to make images was meant to prevent worship of any deity but Yahweh, and it has been observed quite strictly over the centuries. Although a few early synagogue paintings of human figures have been found,[10] the prohibition has restrained in general the development of Jewish painting and sculpture. Only in the last hundred years have Jewish artists emerged, and many have been nonrepresentational artists.

You shall not make wrong use of the name of the Lord your God; the Lord will not leave unpunished the man who misuses his name.

The commandment against misuse of Yahweh's name opposes using God's name to bring misfortune on people, as by curses and black magic. Eventually, it was considered unacceptable to pronounce the name of Yahweh for any purpose whatsoever. Only the high priest had this privilege and did this but once a year.

Remember to keep the Sabbath day holy. You have six days to labor and do all your work. But the seventh day is a Sabbath of the Lord your God; that day you shall not do any work, you, your son or your daughter, your slave or your slave-girl, your cattle or the alien within your gates; for in six days the Lord made heaven and earth, the sea, and all that is in them, and on the seventh day He rested. Therefore the Lord blessed the Sabbath day and declared it holy.

The commandment to keep the Sabbath was a humane commandment, intended to give regular rest to servants, slaves, children, workers, and animals.

Honor your father and your mother, that you may live long in the land which the Lord your God is giving you.

The commandment to honor one's parents offers a reward: long life. We should note that Hebrews generally thought of rewards and punishments as being given on earth and in one's lifetime. The notion of rewards given in a future life or an afterlife was a later development.

You shall not commit murder.

This commandment does not prohibit all killing but prohibits murder—that is, unlawful and undeserved killing of human beings. Killing human beings in wartime and in self-defense was allowable, and execution was expected as the punishment for many types of crime.

You shall not commit adultery.

The commandment against adultery is only incidentally concerned with sex. Primarily it is a property law, because a man's wife was legally considered his property. This commandment is linked with the commandments immediately before and after it, because all three refer to property rights. To murder is to take unlawful possession of another person's body; to commit adultery is to disregard a man's right to sole possession of his wife; and to steal is to take unlawful possession of another person's goods.

You shall not steal.

You shall not give false evidence against your neighbor.

You shall not covet your neighbor's house; you shall not covet your neighbor's wife, his slave-girl, his ox, his ass, or anything that belongs to him.

In this last commandment, property rights are linked together and spelled out clearly.

The Judges and Kings

After Moses' death, the Israelites were led by men and women who had both military and legal power, called judges. To think of them as military generals is more accurate than to envision them as modern-day courtroom judges. The Books of Joshua and Judges describe this period.

Joshua is the general who leads the Hebrews across the Jordan River after Moses' death. Under his leadership, the Hebrew tribes take the town of Jericho, with the help of spies and the assistance of Rahab, a prostitute of the town, who hides them. After this victory, the Israelites take additional territory, and the land of Canaan is divided up among eleven of the tribes. Only the tribe of Levi is not given land, because members of this tribe are to serve as priests and assistants in worship; instead of land, members receive a portion of religious offerings and other forms of regular support. Realizing that they need to be unified for their protection, the people of Israel soon establish a king, select a capital city, impose a system of laws, and build a temple for centralized worship. The biblical Books of 1–2 Samuel and 1–2 Kings describe the process.

The first king, Saul (whose reign began c. 1025 B.C.E.), became a tragic figure, suffering repeatedly from depression and then dying after a battle—one tradition says from suicide (1 Sam. 31:4). The next king was David (c. 1013–973 B.C.E.), a young man from Bethlehem, a town in the tribal area of Judah. As an accomplished military leader, David oversaw the buildup of the kingdom. Recognizing the need for a central city, he took over the hilltop town of Jebus, renaming it Jerusalem and establishing it as the national capital. Because David was described as a musician, many psalms are attributed to him, and because he had a strong interest in religious ritual, he is also said to have planned to build a temple in Jerusalem where national religious ceremonies could be carried out. He died, however, before he could accomplish that goal.

David's son Solomon built and dedicated the First Temple in Jerusalem, thus creating a home for Yahweh, whose presence it was hoped would protect the kingdom. The exact design of Solomon's temple is not certain, but it was probably a long, tall rectangular building—designed according to similar temples in the region—that featured an interior sanctuary and outdoor courtyards for sacrifices and gatherings. Services included prayers by priests, with hymns sung by choirs and accompanied by musical instruments, such as trumpets, lyres (harplike stringed instruments), and cymbals. Incense and grain were common offerings, and animals were ritually killed and offered as burnt sacrifices to Yahweh. Some sacrifices, called holocaust offerings, demanded that all the animal be burnt and thus transported upward to God. Other sacrifices involved the offering of the animal's blood and fat to God, thus allowing the priests and the offerer to share in a meal of cooked meat from the animal parts that remained.[11]

Having a royal palace and the national temple in Jerusalem unified the separate Hebrew tribes for a time, but the taxes required to fund these and other extensive building projects made the people rebellious. After the death of Solomon, the northern tribes broke away from the control of the king in Jerusalem and set up their own kingdom.

Division weakened the two kingdoms, and in 721 B.C.E. Assyria, an expanding power in the northeast, took over the northern kingdom. A theological explanation for the destruction of the northern kingdom came from prophets of the time. Although **prophets**—human beings who spoke in God's name—were significant figures—both as groups and individuals—from the earliest days of the kingdom, individual prophets became important in the three hundred years after 800 B.C.E. Typically the prophet experienced a life-changing revelation from God and then felt commissioned by God to speak his message to the people. The prophet Isaiah, who was active in the eighth century B.C.E., is possibly the best known. He had a vision of God in the temple of Jerusalem, which he described as being filled with smoke (symbolic of the divine presence) and the voices of the angels crying out "Holy, holy, holy" in the presence of God (Isa. 6). His feeling of unworthiness dissolved when an angel touched a lighted coal to his lips, thus purifying and empowering Isaiah. From then on, he could speak his message. Isaiah and other prophets explained that political losses were punishment from Yahweh for worshiping other gods and for not having kept his laws. The losses were not a sign of God's weakness but rather of his justice and strength.

The southern kingdom, the kingdom of Judah, carried on alone, although with constant anxiety, for more than a century. Unfortunately, another power had emerged—Babylonia—and at first the remaining southern kingdom paid tribute; but when tribute was refused, Babylonia took control. In 586 B.C.E. Nebuchadnezzar II destroyed Solomon's temple, tore down the city walls of Jerusalem, and took the aristocracy and a great part of the Jewish population off to Babylonia (modern-day Iraq) into an exile that would last almost fifty years. Because the kingdom had ended and temple worship was no longer possible, the religion of Israel seemed to lose its heart.

Exile and Captivity

The period of exile in Babylonia (586–539 B.C.E.) was a monumental turning point and one of the greatest emotional strains in the history of Judaism. Psalm 137 is a manifestation of the sorrow felt by the Jews during their captivity. It tells of their inability to sing happy songs as long as they were in exile: "By the rivers of Babylon—there we sat down and there we wept when we remembered Zion."[12]

Without a temple, public ritual had come to an end, but in its place the written word took on new importance. During their exile in Babylonia, the Jews began to meet weekly to discuss the scriptures and to pray. What developed was the **Sabbath** service of worship, study, sermon, and psalms, performed in a meetinghouse, or *synagogue* (Greek: "lead together"). The period of exile also made it clear that the oral Hebrew religious traditions had to be written down if they were to survive.

During their exile, the Jewish people began to assimilate influences from the surrounding Babylonian culture. Knowledge of the Hebrew language declined, while Aramaic, a sister language, emerged as the common tongue. (Aramaic eventually even crept into the sacred literature: while Hebrew is the canonical language of scripture, a few passages, and in some cases whole chapters, are in Aramaic, although the reason for this is not clear.[13]) Also emerging at this time was a growing sense of an active spirit of evil, often called Satan, and of a cosmic antagonism between good and evil. The sense of moral opposition, while present in the Israelite religion from an early time, may have been sharpened from this time on, both by the pain of exile and by subsequent contact with the Persian religion of Zoroastrianism.

Return to Jerusalem and the Second Temple

In 540 B.C.E., Cyrus came to the throne of the Persian Empire and, after taking over Babylonia, allowed the Jews to return to their homeland. The returning exiles rebuilt their temple, dedicating it in 515 B.C.E., and the sacrificial cult was reestablished. The Book of Psalms, containing the lyrics of 150 hymns, is often called the hymnbook of the Second Temple, and when we read in the closing psalms of all the instruments used in temple worship, we get a sense of the splendor of the ceremonies performed there.

The new temple inaugurated an era, called the period of the Second Temple, in which the work of priests took on great importance. Priests worked out in detail the ceremonies of the Second Temple, because it played an expanded role as the religious center not only for the land of Israel but also for all Jews who lived abroad. Some Jews, we might note, had remained in their adopted country of Babylonia; as a result, a significant Jewish presence was established there that would last more than a thousand years. There was also a large population of Jews living in northern Egypt.

At the same time, the work of recording oral traditions and editing written material also grew in importance. Scribes did not want the history of their people to be lost, and the result of their work was to become the Hebrew Bible. A final edition of the Torah (Pentateuch) was made, the prophetic books were compiled, and new books were written as well. Several of the last books written were literary—such as Ecclesiastes, a dark meditation on life, and the Song of Songs, a collection of love poetry. One work, the Book of Daniel, was apocalyptic, envisioning a final judgment at the end of the world—a vision possibly influenced by Zoroastrianism. Among these late, literary works, the Book of Job is one of the world's first written attempts to understand the suffering of an innocent person. The

Zoroastrianism

Although Zoroastrianism today is a small religion (found mostly in India), it was once a religion of millions, and its influence spread far beyond its home in Persia. It was begun by the prophet Zarathustra (or Zoroaster), who was born (c. 650 B.C.E.) in what is now Iran. Zarathustra was surrounded by the worship of the gods of nature, common to the Aryan religion, which was also practiced in India. As in Indian Vedic religion, the religion of Zarathustra's culture involved the worship of gods at fire altars, the use of a ritual drink (*haoma,* like the Vedic *soma*), and a hereditary priesthood. Like the Buddha after him, Zarathustra was distressed by the sacrifice of animals at the fire altars and by the power of the priests.

At about the age of 30, Zarathustra experienced a vision that changed his life. He felt himself transported heavenward by a spirit he called *Vohu Manah* ("good mind"), into the presence of the High God, *Ahura Mazda* ("wise lord"), a god associated in Zarathustra's mind with cosmic justice. Like the calls of Isaiah and Muhammad, this revelation led Zarathustra to preach his new message. At first Zarathustra was met with strong rejection, which he blamed on demons (*daevas*) and the satanic head of evil forces, *Angra Mainyu* ("wicked spirit"), and Zarathustra's bitter experiences deepened his sense that evil forces constantly oppose the forces of goodness. Zarathustra was undaunted, however, and his preaching eventually converted an Iranian king, Vishtaspa, who used his power to spread Zarathustra's new religion. Zarathustra condemned animal sacrifices, but he maintained the ceremonial use of the Aryan fire altar: although fire was not to be worshiped, Zarathustra considered it to be symbolic of divine goodness. Tradition relates that Zarathustra died in his 70s, killed by invaders while praying at his fire altar.

What we know of Zarathustra comes from the most ancient part of the Avesta, the Zoroastrian scriptures. They teach of a high God, Ahura Mazda, who expresses himself through good spirits, whose names are virtues. Whether these spirits are simply aspects of Ahura Mazda or independent beings is unclear. The most important is called *Spenta Mainyu* ("holy spirit"). Others, for example, have the names *Power, Devotion, Immortality,* and *Obedience.* (We find some tantalizing similarities in the Jewish mystical literature of the Kabbalah, in Gnosticism, and in some New Testament letters.)

Although Zoroastrianism is ultimately monotheistic, it sees the universe in morally dualistic terms. Forces of good are in perpetual conflict with forces of evil—a conflict that mysteriously began at the start of time. Each person is involved in this cosmic struggle and thus must make moral choices between good and evil. Good actions include telling the truth and dealing honestly with others—in the Avesta, good actions include cultivating farmland and treating animals kindly. There is a belief in divine judgment and in an afterlife of reward or punishment, which begins at death when each individual's soul must cross a bridge that can lead to paradise. If the individual has been good, the bridge is wide and the journey to paradise is easy; but if the individual has been evil, the bridge becomes so narrow that the soul falls into the depths of hell.

Zoroastrianism also presents an apocalyptic vision of the end of time: when the world comes to an end, there will be a resurrection of all bodies and a great general judgment; at this time the world will be purified by fire, which will punish the evil but leave the good untouched. Because Zoroastrianism was widespread in the Near East and Middle East for centuries, some see its influence in the worldviews of the Essenes, in some later books of Jewish scripture (such as Job and Daniel), in early Christianity, and in Islam. Today, the religion is small, with no more than 200,000 followers, the majority of whom live in western India.

role of Satan (or "the Satan," because his name is really a title meaning "adversary") in this book is important, possibly reflecting a Zoroastrian sense of a cosmic struggle between good and evil. The books that would eventually be accepted into the Hebrew canon were finished by about 200 B.C.E.[14]

CULTURAL CONFLICT DURING THE SECOND-TEMPLE ERA

The historical record in the canonical Hebrew scriptures ends with the building of the Second Temple. But the history of the region did not end here. Because of the geographic location of Israel, it seemed that the Jews in Israel would continually have to contend with invasions—and in some cases conquests—by foreign powers.

The Seleucid Period

When the army of Alexander the Great was on its way to conquer Egypt, it made Israel part of the Greek Empire, and after Alexander's death in 323 B.C.E, his generals divided up his empire. Israel at first was controlled by Egypt, which was ruled by the descendants of Alexander's general Ptolemy. Later, Israel was controlled by Syria, ruled by the descendants of Alexander's general Seleucus.

In 167 B.C.E. a Seleucid ruler, Antiochus IV (Antiochus Epiphanes) took over the temple, apparently with the intention of introducing the worship of the Greek god Zeus to the site. His deliberately placing pork (a forbidden meat) on the altar and his prohibition of circumcision caused such hatred among the Jews that they rebelled. Led by a Jewish family of five brothers, the Maccabees (or Hasmoneans), the Jews took back the rule of their country and the temple was rededicated to the worship of Israel's one God. (The winter festival of **Hanukkah,** widely kept today, is a joyous memorial that recalls that rededication of the Second Temple.) The country retained its autonomy for almost a century, until the Roman general Pompey took control in 63 B.C.E.

Antagonism between Jewish culture and the dominant Greek-speaking culture in the region was inevitable, because Jewish culture had values and practices that made absorption into Greek culture difficult, if not impossible. For example, all Jewish males were circumcised, which meant they were easily identified in the public baths or while exercising in gymnasiums. There were also Jewish dietary restrictions, which forbade the eating of pork and shellfish, and strict prohibitions against work on the Sabbath. These practices conflicted with the sophisticated Greek-speaking culture called Hellenism (from *Hellas,* "Greece"), a culture that was becoming the dominant culture in the entire Mediterranean area, even after the Romans took control of the region. Greek plays and literature were read everywhere around the Mediterranean; Greek history, science, medicine, and mathematics were considered the most advanced of their day; and Greek architecture and city planning were becoming the norm. Because of its sophistication, Hellenistic culture was hugely attractive to educated people.

Responses to Outside Influences

Contact with Hellenistic culture led to a variety of responses. Some welcomed and adopted it, either in whole or in part; some rejected it, clinging passionately to their own ethnic and religious roots; and the rest took a position in between. Tensions led to the rise of several religious factions among the Jews in Israel during this period, after 165 B.C.E.

The **Sadducees** were the first of the factions to emerge.[15] They were members of the priestly families, living primarily in Jerusalem, and were in charge of the temple and its activities. The fact that they derived their living from temple worship would have made them traditional—or at least in their public behavior. They accepted the Torah as sacred, but generally did not accept other books as being equally inspired—a position that brought them into conflict with other groups.

The **Pharisees** were the second faction that arose.[16] Their focus was on preserving Hebrew piety through careful observation of religious laws and traditions. Because of their emphasis on daily religious practice, the Pharisees relied heavily on the scriptures for devotional guidance. They accepted as canonical a wider number of books than did the Sadducees—a source of conflict with the priests—and they valued the oral tradition that accompanied the written Torah, a tradition they traced back to Moses.

A third faction, eventually called the **Zealots,** was opposed to foreign influences and after 6 C.E. was bitterly opposed to Roman rule of Israel. The patriots sometimes used violent means to achieve their ends.

The **Essenes** were the fourth group. Not a great deal is known with certainty about them, although current interest in them is intense. They were written about by three authors of the classical world: Philo (c. 10 B.C.E.–50 C.E.), a Jewish theologian of Alexandria; Josephus (c. 37–100 C.E.), a Jewish general and historian; and Pliny the Elder (23–79 C.E.), a Roman writer. These classical writers indicate that the Essenes numbered several thousand; lived a communal, celibate life, primarily in the desert area near the Dead Sea; rejected animal sacrifice; and avoided meat and wine. We also are told that the Essenes were skilled in medicine; dressed in white; followed a solar calendar, different from the lunar calendar used in the temple; studied the scriptures assiduously; and kept separate from the rest of society.

A common theory holds that the Essenes began as a breakaway group of priests opposed to the Maccabee family's takeover of the high priesthood. They saw themselves as an advance guard, preparing for the time when God would end the old world of injustice and bring about a new world of mercy and peace. They described themselves as "sons of light" who were fighting against the forces of "darkness."[17] Because their center was no more than fifteen miles east of Jerusalem, they would have had some contact with the political currents of their day, and they may have shared some of the ideals of the Zealots and Pharisees.

Scrolls and scroll fragments, called the Dead Sea Scrolls, were uncovered between 1947 and 1955 in caves near Qumran, above the northwestern

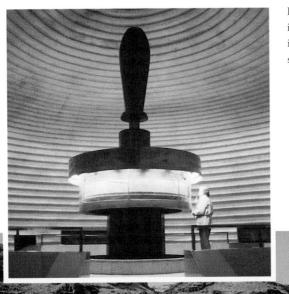

Inside the Shrine of the Book in Jerusalem, a visitor inspects examples of the Dead Sea Scrolls. The building is in the shape of one of the jars in which the scrolls were stored.

The Dead Sea Scrolls were preserved for 2000 years in these caves at Qumran.

shore of the Dead Sea. It is possible that the scrolls constituted the library of the Essenes or that they were a more general library of Jewish sacred books brought from Jerusalem for safekeeping during the rebellion against the Romans that began in 66 C.E. Besides containing all or part of nearly every book of the Hebrew scriptures, the cache of scrolls contained works that commented on scriptural books, gave details about the organization and practices of the Essenes, and spoke of a coming judgment and end of the world. Not all the work of editing and translating these scrolls has been completed, but once it has we hope to know more about their origin and about the beliefs of the Essenes.

It seems that during the later part of the Second-Temple period, there was no universally accepted norm of correct religion, and the canon of scripture was still in the process of formation. Instead, there were many books and interpretations of correct practice, each competing for acceptance.

Although the Second Temple was flourishing, the older, ceremonial, temple-based religion was in fact giving way to a more decentralized religion, based on the Hebrew scriptures and on religious practice in the synagogues.

THE DEVELOPMENT OF RABBINICAL JUDAISM

The Roman Empire assumed direct political control of much of Israel in 6 C.E, and it ruled with severity. Consequently, there was much anti-Roman fervor and a widespread hope that, as in the time of the Maccabees, the foreigners could be expelled and a Jewish kingdom reestablished. A major revolt broke out in 66 C.E., but Roman legions crushed it brutally in 70 C.E., when they destroyed the temple and much of Jerusalem.

The end of the Second Temple was a turning point for the Jewish faith, producing two major effects. It ended the power of the priesthood, whose sacrificial rituals were no longer possible. It also forced the religion to develop in a new direction away from temple ritual, moving Judaism toward a central focus on scripture and scriptural interpretation.

The Canon of Scripture and the Talmud

Once the temple-based religion had been destroyed, it was necessary to clearly define which religious books, of the several hundred being revered and read by various groups, constituted the sacred canon. Tradition holds that in about 90 C.E., twenty years after the destruction of the Second Temple, Jewish rabbis gathered together in Israel at the town of Jabneh (Jamnia). There, it is said, they examined each book individually to decide which books would be included in the canon. (Some books, like the Song of Songs and Ecclesiastes, were hotly debated and were almost excluded.) The canon of the land of Israel resulted from this process of selection. (A slightly larger number of books had already been accepted by Jews in Egypt and came to be known as the Alexandrian canon.)

Another revolt began in Israel in 132 C.E. Some declared its leader, Bar Kokhba, to be the **Messiah,** the long-awaited savior sent by God to the Jews. In 135 C.E., the Romans put down this second revolt even more cruelly than the first, with many public executions. Jerusalem was demolished and rebuilt as a Roman city, with a new name, Aelia Capitolina, and Jews were forbidden to live there. Jewish families who had remained in Israel even after the destruction of the Second Temple now fled. They went not only to Egypt but settled around the Mediterranean, expanding the number of Jews living in the **diaspora** (dispersion) outside Israel. The existence of a canon of scripture, which could be copied and carried anywhere, brought victory out of apparent defeat. Rabbinical Judaism, based on interpreting sacred scripture and oral tradition, could spread and flourish.

Once the Hebrew scriptures were declared complete, the next logical development was their protection and explanation. Interpretive work, called midrash ("seeking out"), became a central focus of evolving Judaism. Some Jewish teachers held that the teachings of God had been passed on not only in the written Torah but also in an oral form to Moses, who came to be called "our Rabbi." Rabbis held that the "oral Torah" was passed on by Moses to Joshua and from him to others in an unbroken line. This concept of an oral Torah given by God as a counterpart of the written Torah is sometimes called "the dual Torah," and it helped give great authority to later rabbinical commentary.

The work of interpreting the Hebrew scriptures and applying their principles to everyday problems went on in stages. By about 200 C.E. there existed a philosophical discussion in six parts of specific biblical laws and their application, called Mishnah ("repetition"). By about 400 C.E., the Mishnah had received further commentary (Gemara, "supplement"), and the result was the Palestinian **Talmud** ("study"), or Talmud of the Land of Israel.

When people use the word *Talmud,* however, they usually are referring to a second, larger collection of material—called the Babylonian Talmud to distinguish it from the earlier, shorter commentary—completed by about 600 C.E. and compiled by religious specialists in Babylonia. After the Hebrew Bible itself, the Babylonian Talmud became the second most important body of Jewish literature, and it continued to be commented on over the centuries by rabbinical specialists. (A modern edition by Rabbi Adin Steinsaltz is the most recent example.)

The Babylonian Talmud is vast, sometimes being compared to an ocean in which a person can sail or swim. In the Babylonian Talmud, rabbis of different generations add their insights and solutions to problems. The growth of opinion is visible, because the earliest material is printed in the center of each page, and later commentary is arranged around it. The Babylonian Talmud contains legal material (*halakhah,* "direction") and nonlegal anecdotes

Two rabbis speak:
[Rabbis] Hillel and Shammai received the tradition from [earlier rabbis]. . . . [Hillel] used to say: If I am not for myself, who will be for me? Yet if I am for myself only, what am I? And if not now, when?

Shammai said: Set a fixed time for thy study of the Torah; say little and do much; and receive all men with a cheerful countenance.

—from The Sayings of the Fathers[18]

and tales (*haggadah*, "tradition"). It is really a large encyclopedia, organized into sections, or tractates, according to subject matter. Its size and complexity, along with the difficulty of mastering it, contributed to a strong scholarly orientation in later Judaism.

Islam and Medieval Judaism

The diaspora introduced Jewish vitality to places far from Israel, such as Spain and Iraq. After the ninth century, this Jewish presence was possible because of the tolerance with which Islam (now dominant in Spain, North Africa, and the Middle East) usually treated the Jews. Islam has held that Jews and Christians have a special status: called "peoples of the Book," they are members with Muslims in the same extended religious family. The result was that cities such as Alexandria, Cairo, Baghdad, and Córdoba became havens for Jewish thought.

Jewish academies in Babylonia continued the tradition of learning that had produced the Babylonian Talmud. The great scholar Saadia ben Joseph (Said al-Fayyumi, 882–942 C.E.) translated the Hebrew scriptures into Arabic and wrote commentaries that synthesized Jewish and Greek thought. He also composed a prayer book, which has been used throughout the Jewish world. The other great center of learning was in Islamic Spain. Saadia's thought was carried there, providing a matrix for the philosophy and poetry of the Jewish Academy of Córdoba, which flourished in the tenth and eleventh centuries.

Foremost among the Jewish medieval thinkers was Moses Maimonides (called Rambam, 1135–1204), who was born in Córdoba but who fled that city with his family when it was occupied by Muslim forces hostile to both Jews and Christians. He eventually settled in Cairo, where he practiced medicine at the court of Salah-al-Din (Saladin). The work that made him famous was his book *The Guide of the Perplexed,* in which he argued that Judaism was a rational religion and that faith and reason were complementary. He wrote this work in Arabic in order to make it accessible to a wide readership. Maimonides is also known for his *Mishneh Torah,* a scholarly work written in Hebrew, which is a religious code of fourteen books that summarizes the legal formulations of the Talmud and other rabbinical writings. Maimonides is renowned for his list of the basic principles of Jewish belief, which we will discuss later in this chapter.

Jewish thought has consistently shown several approaches in its interpretation of the Hebrew Bible. The more conservative tendency, which produced the Talmud, has interpreted the Hebrew scriptures fairly strictly, using them as a guide for ethical living. This tendency has generated much written commentary about the application of principles that had developed in an earlier agrarian society for later, often urban lifestyles.

Another trend has been speculative, using the scriptures imaginatively as a way to understand more about the nature of God and the universe. Out of this second tendency came works of Jewish mysticism, which we look at next.

This statue of Maimonides sits in the old Jewish Quarter of Córdoba in Spain.

The Kabbalah

The Middle Ages saw renewed interest in Jewish mysticism. The whole body of Jewish mystical literature, called **Kabbalah** ("received," "handed down"), began to emerge even before the common era in works that speculated on mysterious passages of the Hebrew Bible. For example, kabbalistic literature speculated about Enoch and Elijah, who had not died but had simply been transported upward to God's realm (Gen. 5:24 and 2 Kings 2:11). It also speculated about Yahweh's throne (*merkebah*) and the sound of the surrounding angels (see Isa. 6:2), using the scriptures as a tool for understanding more about the reality of God and the hidden structure of the universe. A frequent mystical assumption was that the Hebrew Bible was written in coded language, which could be interpreted only by those who had solved it. Much biblical language, this view held, was to be read not literally but symbolically.

A special key for mystical interpretation was *gematria*—the practice of transposing words into numbers. (The term *gematria* is related to the word *geometry*.) For example, *aleph,* the first letter of the Hebrew alphabet, would be given a value of 1; the second letter, *beth,* a 2; and so on. In this way, the letters of every word could be added up and correspondences between similar sums could be found.

New mystical speculation arose in the medieval period, sometimes as a response to the growing persecution of Jews. Common themes were the divine origin of the world, God's care for the Jews, and the eventual coming of the Messiah (spoken of in Dan. 7 and elsewhere). The human world was frequently seen as the microcosm of a greater heavenly world beyond the earth and the human being as a microcosm of the universe: "the superior and inferior worlds are bound together under the form of the Holy Body, and the worlds are associated together."[19] What was learned about the microcosm would then give insight into the larger realm, and vice versa.

The most famous book of the Kabbalah is the *Zohar* ("splendor"). It was long believed to have been written in the first centuries of the common era, but in actuality it was probably written about 1280 in Spain by Rabbi Moses de León. The *Zohar* sees the universe as having emerged from a pure, boundless, spiritual reality. From the divine Unity come the ten *sefiroth*—ten active, divine powers, such as wisdom, intelligence, love, and beauty. The *Zohar* compares these sefiroth to individual colors: "from the innermost center of the flame sprang forth a well out of which colors issued and spread upon everything beneath, hidden in the mysterious hiddenness of the Infinite."[20] The sefiroth of God manifest themselves in the structure of the physical world and are a bridge between the world of God and the human world. Human beings are particularly significant in creation, blending the divine and the earthly, for within their bodies is a spark of divine light that seeks liberation and return to God. Other texts included the *Sefer Yetzira* and the *Sefer HaHasidim.* Some Jewish circles valued the mystical texts of the Kabbalah as much as, or even more than, the Talmud.[21]

Christianity and Medieval Judaism

The mystical movements gave comfort to European Jews as their persecution increased. Christianity had become the dominant religion in all Europe by the late thirteenth century, and Christianity unfortunately carried with it an anti-Jewish prejudice that had been present since the first century C.E., when Christianity was separating—sometimes angrily—from its Jewish origins (see, for example, Matt. 27:25 and Acts 7:31–60 in the Christian New Testament).

The dominant position of Christianity in medieval Europe also had political implications, because Christians were thought of as loyal citizens

whereas Jews were treated as suspicious and even traitorous persons. Because so much of Jewish religious practice was carried out in the home, superstitious stories circulated among Christians that Jews needed the blood
of Christian children for their Passover meal or that they stole and misused
the consecrated Christian communion bread. Because Jews were often forbidden to own farmland, they were excluded from agriculture; and because
they were kept out of the guilds (the medieval craft unions), they were excluded from many types of urban work. Furthermore, because Christians in
the Middle Ages were generally prohibited from lending money at interest,
this role became a Jewish occupation, but it generated much ill will among
those to whom money was lent. In many places, Jews were forced to wear
a special cap or display some other identifying detail. They were sometimes
also forced to live in a separate section of town, called a ghetto, which might
be walled so that Jews could be locked in at night. During the period of the
bubonic plague, also known as the Black Death (1347–1351 and sporadi-
cally afterwards), Jews sometimes were blamed for the deaths. Many Jews
were killed, even by being burned alive in their synagogues.

Beginning in the late Middle Ages, European Jews were forced into exile. Often the motive was economic as much as religious, because exiling the
Jews would allow the Christian rulers to confiscate their property and to be
freed of debt to them. Over a period of two centuries, Jews were expelled
from England, France, Spain, and Portugal. In Spain, they were forced in
1492 to become Christians or to leave. Some Spanish Jews converted to
Christianity but continued Jewish practice in their homes. As a result of the
Spanish Inquisition, which sought out Jews who had converted only in order to remain in Spain, Jews fled elsewhere—to Morocco, Egypt, Greece,
Turkey, Holland, central Europe, and the New World. It is at this time that
two great cultural divisions of Judaism emerged—Sephardic Judaism in the
Mediterranean region, North Africa, and the Middle East, and Ashkenazic
Judaism in Germany, central Europe, and France. We will look at their cul-
tural differences later, when we examine the branches of Judaism.

QUESTIONING AND REFORM

The Renaissance of the fifteenth and sixteenth centuries began a new era
for Europe. As people began to travel more, they were exposed to a multitude of previously unknown religions, cultures, and regions of the world.
The invention of printing with moveable type quickened this process by
making written material widely available. Discoveries in science and instruments like the telescope revolutionized people's perception of the
earth and its relationship to the larger universe. These changes, which presented challenges to the Christian worldview, also affected Judaism.

After the Renaissance, Judaism began to move in two directions, both
of which continue today. One direction cherished traditional ways; the
other saw a need for modernization.

The traditionalist way, strong in eastern Europe, offered refuge from an uncertain world. In central Europe, traditionalism expressed itself both in Talmudic scholarship and in the devotional movement *Hasidism* ("devotion," "piety"). The Hasidic movement was founded by Israel ben Eliezer (c. 1700–1760), a mystic and faith healer known affectionately as the Baal Shem Tov (the "good master of the Holy Name"), who felt that living according to the rules of the Torah and Talmud was important but also that devout practice should be accompanied by an ecstatic sense of God who is present everywhere.[22] Hasidism emphasized the beauty of everyday life and the physical world, teaching that "only in tangible things can you see or hear God."[23]

> The Creator and the objects of His creation are a Unity inseparable.
> —Hasidic saying[24]

The other direction in which Judaism moved was toward modernization. The liberal direction, which was strongest in Germany and France, urged Jews to move out of the ghettos, to gain a secular education, and to enter the mainstream in their countries. In Germany, the modernizing movement, called the Reform, began in the late eighteenth century. With the goal of making worship more accessible, the Reform movement translated many of the Hebrew prayers into German and introduced musical elements (such as organ and choir music) that derived from current Protestant Christianity. (Choir music and instrumental accompaniment had existed much earlier, however, in the religious practice of the temple, as we see in Psalm 150.) In France and Italy, legal liberation began at the time of Napoleon. In many places, Jews were no longer barred from entering universities, which helped to enlarge the pool of highly educated, generally liberal thinkers in Judaism. The Reform movement generated many counterresponses—among them, an attempt to preserve traditional Judaism (Orthodox Judaism) and an attempt to maintain the best of tradition with some modern elements (the Positive-Historical School and Conservative Judaism.) We will look at all these movements later in more detail.

JUDAISM AND THE MODERN WORLD

The growth of freedom for European Jews over the nineteenth century did not end anti-Jewish activity. The Russian Empire, where Eastern Orthodox Christianity was the established religion, continued its restrictions on Jews, with occasional outbreaks of persecution. In response, Jews from Russia, Poland, and the Baltic area emigrated, and from 1880 to 1920 more than a million Jews came to the United States, most coming to or through New York City. Their children and grandchildren sometimes moved further, settling in Los Angeles, Chicago, Miami, and elsewhere. Jews also emigrated to other large cities in North America and Latin America, such as Montreal, Toronto, Mexico City, and Buenos Aires—bringing a new freedom to Judaism, but at a price. Jewish identity was compromised because many Jews wished to assimilate with the surrounding culture, and intermarriage grew in frequency.

Traditional Jewish life continued in Europe until the end of the 1930s, particularly in Poland and the Baltic region, where there were still more than three million Jews. Beautiful evocations of this warm, traditional lifestyle are evident in paintings by Marc Chagall and in the book that he and his wife Bella created together, *Burning Lights*.[25] This centuries-old culture, however, would be destroyed within ten years by Adolf Hitler.

Hitler and the Holocaust

The rise of Adolf Hitler in 1933 as German chancellor and head of the Nazi Party began a prolonged wave of anti-Jewish activity that ended in the most dreadful sufferings. Hitler was fueled by several irrational notions. One was a theory of racial classes, which imagined Jews and Gypsies to be subhuman polluters of a pure but mythical "Aryan race." Another was Hitler's belief that Jewish financiers and industrialists had conspired against Germany and helped make possible the Allied victory over the Germans during World War I. Hitler sought both an imaginary "racial purity" and political revenge.

At first, the Nazis put pressure on Jews to emigrate by forcing them out of government and university positions, by boycotting their stores, and eventually by physically persecuting them. Many Jews did emigrate, particularly to North America—Albert Einstein is a well-known example. After the annexation of Austria and the invasion of Poland (1939), Nazi control eventually spread to Holland, Norway, northern France, and Czechoslovakia; and as Nazi domination spread to these countries, so too did the persecution of Jews. Jews who wanted to flee found it hard to find refuge, because many countries, including the United States, refused to take in large numbers of Jews. Moreover, France and England did not forcefully protest Hitler's policies against the Jews, and the Catholic leader Pope Pius XII signed a concordat of understanding with Hitler in 1939. The Jews were without defenders, and when World War II was declared, they were caught in a trap.

Hitler began plans to exterminate all European Jews. Jews in countries under Nazi control were officially identified, made to wear a yellow star in public, and eventually deported via train to concentration camps. Because there was a large number of Jews in Poland, most major concentration camps were constructed there. Some camps are well known—Auschwitz, Bergen-Belsen, Maidanek, Mauthausen—but there were also hundreds of smaller camps, such as at Melk (in Austria, on the Danube River) and Dachau (in Germany, near Munich).

The path to death at Auschwitz.

Upon arrival at the extermination camps, Jews were often divided into two groups: (1) those who were strong enough to work and (2) the rest—mostly women, children, the sick, and the elderly—who were to be killed immediately. (The psychologist Viktor Frankl has described the process in his book *Man's Search for Meaning.*) At first the killings were done by guns, but as the numbers of internees increased, gas chambers and crematoria (to incinerate the victims) were constructed. Those who were kept as workers lived in horrible conditions and were routinely starved, insufficiently clothed, and attacked by all kinds of vermin and disease. Few ultimately survived.

By the end of World War II in 1945, about twelve million people—Jews, Gypsies, homosexuals, Jehovah's Witnesses, prisoners of war, and political enemies—had died in the concentration camps. Of these, it is estimated that as many as six million were Jews, and of that number about a million and a half were Jewish children. This immense loss is called the **Holocaust** (Greek: "completely burned") or *Shoah* (Hebrew: "extermination"). It is one of the greatest crimes ever committed against humanity.

The extermination has left a shadow on civilization and a great scar on Judaism. About a third of the Jews of the entire world were killed, and of those who died, a large number had been devout, traditional Jews. Their death, in such painful circumstances, raised haunting questions about the faith and future of Judaism.

Creation of the State of Israel

A major result of the Holocaust was the creation of the state of Israel after more than a century of hope, thought, and work. Centuries of virulent anti-Jewish restriction and persecution had created in many Jews a desire for a Jewish nation, where they could live without fear and in the traditional historic home of their faith. The movement came to be called **Zionism,** after Mount Zion, the mountain on which Jerusalem is built.

The state of Israel emerged through several steps. The first was the notion of a separate Jewish nation, popularized by the influential book *The Jewish State,* written by the Hungarian-born Austrian writer Theodor Herzl (1860–1904) following an outbreak of antisemitism in France. The second step was the Balfour Declaration, a political statement issued in 1917 by the British government, which endorsed the notion of a Jewish homeland. When World War I ended, the British received control of the area then called Palestine and authorized a limited immigration of Jews to their territory, the British Mandate of Palestine. The third step came after World War II. Prodded by the Nazi slaughter of Jews, the newly created United Nations voted to divide the old British Mandate of Palestine, and from this territory, a new Jewish state of Israel was created. Palestinians who left or who lived in surrounding areas, however, sometimes became a very hostile part of the neighboring population.

The difficult relationship between Jews and Palestinians has continued to the present day. There have been repeated wars and terrorist activities against Israel, and surrounding Arab populations have in some cases refused to accept Jewish control of the region. On the other hand, Jews everywhere have gained pride through the resurrection of their homeland and of the Hebrew language. Once again there is a homeland of which any Jew may become a citizen.

Because European Judaism was almost completely destroyed, Jewish life today has three centers: Israel, Russia, and the United States. The estimated Jewish populations of Israel and Russia total about six million each and that of the United States is another six million. Judaism in the United States is largely liberal and enjoys general freedom of practice. In Israel, Judaism presents a wide spectrum of opinions and practices, ranging from liberal and even atheistic to highly conservative and traditionally religious. Some important control of government policy and daily life is in the hands of traditionalists, but for perhaps a majority of the population Judaism is more a culture than a religion.

PERSONAL EXPERIENCE: A VISIT TO ANNE FRANK'S HOUSE

In high school I read the diary of Anne Frank, a teenage Jewish girl of Amsterdam who had hidden with her family and others throughout most of World War II. Her sensitive diary covers her years from ages 13 to 15. In August of 1944, Nazi soldiers found the family and took them away to the concentration camp of Bergen-Belsen, where Anne died in March of 1945—just months before the war ended. Her father was the only family member who survived, and when he returned to Amsterdam he found her diary on the floor of the house where they had hidden.

In her diary she wrote of her discovery of the beauty of nature—something she'd never appreciated before. Hiding in the attic rooms, she began to look out an upstairs window for long periods of time. One night she wrote: "the dark, rainy evening, the gale, the scudding clouds held me entirely in their power; it was the first time in a year and a half that I'd seen the night face to face."[26] Anne described having fallen in love there and her first kiss—with her friend Peter, who was also in hiding. As she described it, "suddenly the ordinary Anne slipped away and a second Anne took her place, a second Anne who is not reckless and jocular, but one who just wants to love and be gentle."[27] She wrote as well of God, religion, and belief.

During my first trip to Europe, at the end of college, I sought out the narrow house beside the canal in Amsterdam where Anne and her family and others had all lived in hiding. After climbing the steep, narrow stairs, I looked out through the same window that Anne had looked out many

Anne Frank and her family hid in a secret annex beyond this door in a house in Amsterdam.

times and realized that the life and young intelligence that had once lived here had been so meaninglessly destroyed. As I stood there in thought, gazing through the open window, the bells of a nearby church rang out. What feelings, I wondered, had the sound of those bells evoked in her? As for me, I could feel only loss and emptiness.

Afterwards, when reading her diary again, I marveled at the sweet hopefulness she expressed there, near the end of the book, and near the end of her short life: "in spite of everything I still believe that people are really good at heart."[28]

JEWISH BELIEF

There is no official Jewish creed, but there is a set of central beliefs, first formulated by the medieval scholar Maimonides. Among them are:

- Belief in God. God is one, formless, all-knowing, and eternal. God is master of the universe as its creator and judge. God is both loving and just.
- Belief in the words of the prophets.
- Belief that God gave the law to Moses.
- Belief that the Messiah, the savior to be sent by God, will come someday.
- Belief that there will be a resurrection of the good "in the world to come."

Regarding these beliefs, there is no universal agreement about the precise meaning of the Messiah, the resurrection of the good, or "the world to come." In the past, these were understood literally. The Messiah would be a heaven-sent leader who would inaugurate a new age, and at that time the deceased who had followed God's laws would come back to life. Some Jews no longer interpret these beliefs literally but see them as symbols of the ultimate triumph of goodness in the world.

Belief in personal immortality or in the resurrection of the dead has been frequently debated. One can find several references in the Hebrew scriptures to an afterlife and to a resurrection of the good (see 1 Sam. 28:13–14 and Dan. 12:2), but other passages express doubt about any afterlife at all (Eccles. 3:20). In the postbiblical period, however, the Pharisees defended the notion of a future resurrection of the good, and rabbinical Judaism accepted this position. Although the notions of resurrection and even of an immortal soul have been defended by many, Judaism strongly emphasizes the kind of immortality that comes from acting virtuously in this world, living on in one's children, and leaving behind some charitable contribution to the world.

In Judaism, human beings have a special role. Because they are created in God's image, they have the ability to reason, to will, to speak, to create, and to care; and they have the responsibility to manifest these divine characteristics in the world. Jews believe that among human beings, the Jewish people have a special role—a role that some believe is to witness to the one God and to do his will in the world. Others believe that their role is to suffer for a purpose known only to God. And others have said that their role is to bring a sense of justice to a world that often has none. Although there is no agreement about *the* Jewish role, there is general consensus among Jews that they hold a unique place in this world.

RELIGIOUS PRACTICE

To be a Jew, however, does not come only from holding a set of beliefs; it is even more a way of living. Scholars explain this by saying that Judaism is less interested in *orthodoxy* (correct belief) and far more interested in *orthopraxy* (correct practice). The Ten Commandments, of course, are at the heart of Jewish morality, and they direct behavior, but there are many additional laws and specific customs that dictate how time is to be used, what foods are to be eaten, and how prayer is to be conducted. And although Judaism promotes congregational worship, many Jewish celebrations are carried on in the home. Moving like wheels within wheels, the week, month, and year all have their devotional rhythms, established by religious laws and customs. The goal of all laws, however, is the recognition of God's presence and the sanctification of human life.

The Jewish Sabbath

Central to all forms of Judaism is keeping the Sabbath, the seventh day of the week, as a special day. The Sabbath, when kept properly, is felt to sanctify the entire week. Recalling the royal rest of God after the six laborious days of creation, the Sabbath is a day of special prayer and human relaxation (see Exod. 20:11 and 31:12–17).[29] In earlier times, before watches and clocks were invented, a "day" began in the evening at sundown; thus the Jewish Sabbath begins on Friday at sunset and lasts until Saturday at sunset.

The traditional purpose of the Sabbath was a compassionate one: it was to allow everyone, even slaves and animals, regular rest. The prohibition against work has been interpreted variously over the centuries. Shops, of course, would be closed. Traditionally, fires could not be built on the Sabbath because of the work involved; and related to this, some traditionalist Jews today will not even turn light switches or kitchen stoves on or off during the Sabbath. The prohibition against making fires meant that food consumed during the Sabbath period would have to be cooked beforehand or eaten uncooked (see Exod. 35:1–3). Interpreting the requirement of rest in the modern world, some Jews do not drive a car or use a telephone during the Sabbath. Although some restrictions might seem excessive, their purpose is to separate the everyday world of labor from the one day of the week in which everyone can enjoy leisure.

The Sabbath is meant to be joyous and is often remembered that way by adults who have grown up in traditional households. The Talmud recommends that the mother of the household welcome the Sabbath on Friday night by lighting candles, and it recommends that the family drink wine at the Sabbath meal as a sign of happiness. During the Jewish exile in Babylonia, synagogue study and worship became a regular way to mark the Sabbath, and today it is common for religious Jews to attend a synagogue service on Friday night or Saturday morning. Friends are often invited over to share the main Sabbath meal, and on Saturday evening the Sabbath is at last bid farewell. "More than the Jews have kept the Sabbath, has the Sabbath kept the Jews" is an old adage.

Jews speak with pride of their observance of the Sabbath, pointing out that the great gift of Judaism to the world has not been the creation of a beautiful temple in physical space but rather the creation of a beautiful "temple" in time. Jews were once called lazy by the Romans for stopping their work one day out of every seven. But the Jewish practice has triumphed and one day of the week is generally set aside as a day of rest throughout the world.

Holy Days

Just as the week is sanctified by the Sabbath, so the months and the entire year are sanctified by regular holy days and periods, each marked by a distinctive emotional tone—happiness, sadness, repentance, gratitude.

Before speaking of specific festivals, we must point out that the Jewish religious calendar is lunar, meaning that each month begins with the new moon. However, adjustments must be made in order to keep the lunar years in general harmony with the regular, solar calendar. Because a year of twelve lunar months lasts 354 days, one lunar year is eleven days shorter than one solar year. Therefore, in the Jewish religious calendar an extra month is added approximately every three years. The lunar months of the Jewish year thus vary somewhat, as do the holy days.

Like the lunar calendar, many Jewish holy days derive from an earlier time when most Jews lived an agricultural life. The earliest holy days arose at seasonal turning points; but later, additional holy days were instituted to recall important events in Jewish history.

The Jewish New Year, **Rosh Hashanah,** recalls the creation of the world and occurs during the autumn, in the seventh lunar month (see Lev. 23:23–24). Coming at the end of the agricultural season, this celebration allows people to consider their obligations and to pay off their debts. It is preceded by a month of daily blowing of the *shofar* (a ram's horn), which produces a solemn tone of warning to remind people that they stand before God.

Ten days later comes the most sacred day of the year, **Yom Kippur,** the Day of Atonement (see Lev. 16). To atone means to make up for one's faults, and this day has traditionally been kept by prayer and strict fasting, with no food or drink during the entire day. Devout Jews spend most of the day in the synagogue or in quiet private prayer at home, seeking God's forgiveness and making resolutions to better their lives. Rosh Hashanah and Yom Kippur are called the High Holy Days, and even quite secular Jews frequently keep them in some way, refraining from work or school and often attending synagogue. The entire period is called the Days of Awe, because of the mood of solemn judgment.

Not long afterwards, and complementing the Days of Awe, comes a joyful harvest celebration, called **Sukkot** ("shelters," "booths"; see Deut. 16:12–15). In early days it was common for families to sleep outdoors in the fields during the autumn harvest season—which allowed them to begin work in the fields early, to stay late, and to protect what they had harvested. The small sleeping shed that was used began to be built and slept in as part of the celebration, and sleeping in the shelters came to symbolize the period of wandering in the desert, before the Israelites entered the land of Canaan. Today, a shelter made of light wood (referred to in Hebrew as a *sukkah*) is set up in or near the home and is commonly decorated with branches and fruits to suggest the bounty of the earth. (The biblical description of this harvest festival helped to shape the first American holiday of Thanksgiving.) The eighth day of Sukkot, called the day of Rejoicing in the Torah (*Simhat Torah*), ends the festival with readings from the end of the Torah—the final chapters of Deuteronomy—and the cycle of readings from the Torah can begin again. Men carry the Torah in procession, kiss the Torah scrolls, and sometimes even dance with the scrolls to show gratitude for the guidance of the Torah.

Hanukkah, the Feast of Dedication, is an early winter festival full of joy. Often called the Feast of Lights, it is a welcome celebration during the growing gloom of winter. Each day, over an eight-day period, one more candle is lit on a special nine-branched candelabrum—a **menorah**—until at the end of the festival, all are alight. The festival commemorates the time in 165 B.C.E. when after a period of desecration by the Syrian forces of Antiochus IV, the Second Temple was rededicated. Tradition says that oil that was enough for only one day miraculously kept burning for eight days. Consequently, over an eight-day period, families gather in the evening, light the Hanukkah candles, play traditional games with their children, and give them small gifts each night. Over time, Hanukkah developed into an important holiday, particularly as the efforts to renew Jewish independence intensified with the creation of modern Zionism.

A late-winter feast just before spring commemorates another important event. **Purim** recalls a time when the Hebrews were in danger of annihilation in Mesopotamia, as told in the book of Esther. When Haman, a government minister, wished to destroy the Hebrews, they were saved by Esther, the queen, and her uncle, Mordecai.[30] This happy festival is marked by the reading of the book of Esther, by costume plays that reenact the story, and by parties.

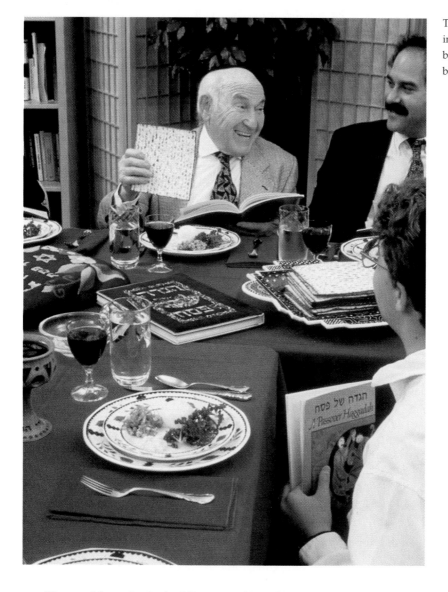

The Passover Seder includes unleavened bread, wine, haroseth, and bitter herbs.

The weeklong festival of Passover (Pesach) occurs in the first lunar month and may have originally begun as a springtime nature festival of renewal.[31] Its primary role now, however, is to recall the Hebrews' exodus from Egypt and to symbolize their liberation (see Deut. 16:1–8). The blood of the lamb killed for the Passover meal, as the book of Exodus relates, was placed over the doors of the Hebrews (Exod. 12), thus keeping the angel of death from entering their homes while the power of God "passed over" Egypt. The most significant event of Passover is a memorial meal, the **Seder** ("order"), at which Jews eat several symbolic foods. The bread is a thin, flat bread (*matzah*), made without yeast, which helps recall how there was no time for bread to rise in the Hebrews' rush to leave Egypt. The meal also includes a shank bone of lamb or other animal, representing the sacrificial lamb. A salad of nuts and fruits (*haroseth*) recalls the mortar used by the Hebrews in their forced labor. Diners dip parsley in salt water and eat bitter herbs to remind themselves of the suffering of the Hebrews during their oppression. During this memorial meal, the story of the exodus is retold. An additional place is set at the table for the prophet Elijah, and a cup of wine is reserved for him—actions representing the hope that he will return to earth to announce the coming of the Messiah. A delicious meal follows the ritual part of the supper. Today, many Jews invite non-Jews to share in their Seder and celebration of Jewish customs.

The Holocaust, or Shoah, is memorialized on the day of Yom Hashoah in April or May. It is a new memorial, kept in late spring, and rituals for it are still being worked out, including services in honor of those who died. Television programs show films documenting the Holocaust, and memorial concerts feature music by Jewish composers (such as Leonard Bernstein). The theme of the memorials is "Never again!"

The period after Passover is kept with general austerity until the summer festival of Shavuot, called the Feast of Weeks because it occurs at the end of a week of weeks—fifty days after Passover (see Deut. 16:9–12). It began as a summer grain-harvest festival. Later, Shavuot gained a special religious meaning as an invitation to renew the covenant, because it was believed that God gave Moses the Ten Commandments at this time of year.

Nine weeks after Shavuot occurs a day of fasting that recalls the destruction of the two temples. Called Tisha Be-Av, this fast, and the week preceding it, have traditionally been marked by lamentations and a very serious mood; but since the creation of the state of Israel, this period of solemnity is not as widely observed.

The month before Rosh Hashanah is marked by the daily blowing of the shofar, and with Rosh Hashanah the religious year begins anew.

Jewish Dietary Practices

From its earliest biblical origins, Judaism has valued cleanliness and care about food. What were once basic rules of hygiene developed into rules about ritual purity—rules about what is, from a religious point of view, considered to be clean and unclean. Traditionally, these rules were intended particularly for those who conducted the temple services, but in many ways they were meant for all Israelites, who thought of themselves as a "nation of priests." In recent centuries, some Jews have relaxed their observance of certain dietary rules, keeping them to a greater or lesser degree as they think suitable and according to the branch of Judaism to which they belong.

One of the basic tenets of traditional Jewish dietary practice is that food consumption and food handling be done according to religious laws. The term *kosher* (Hebrew: *kasher*) means "ritually correct" and particularly applies to food consumption and preparation. In regard to meat, all blood must be drained before the meat is cooked and eaten, because blood, which gives life, is sacred to God. In temple services, blood was offered on the altar separately from the rest of the sacrificed animal, and only meat without blood could be eaten by the priests and sharers in the sacred meal (see Lev. 17). This rule also ensured that animals that had died in the field or were killed by larger animals—carcasses that might be unsafe to eat—could not be consumed (see Exod. 22:31). In practice, there are very specific methods of kosher slaughter, inspection, and preservation.

Pork and shellfish are forbidden (see Lev. 11), probably because these animals were considered scavengers and thus easily contaminated by what they ate. (Pork sometimes contains a parasite, *Trichinella spiralis,* which can be killed only by cooking at high temperatures.)[32] For traditional Jews, meat and dairy products may not be mixed or eaten together at the same meal. This also means that a household that "keeps kosher" must maintain separate sets of cooking implements, pans, dishes, and utensils—one for meat and one for dairy products. Some households even have separate sinks. These practices derive from a rule of uncertain origin that forbids the cooking of a baby goat or lamb in its mother's milk (Exod. 34:26). It is possible the practice was forbidden for being cruel: some fetal animals, cut from the womb before birth, were considered tender delicacies. The practice of cooking a kid in its mother's milk may also have been associated with non-Hebrew religious practice and therefore forbidden.

Other Religious Practices

Regular daily prayer is practiced by devout Jews at dawn, noon, and dusk, and private prayer is often done at bedtime as well. When they pray in the morning during the week, traditionalist males use the **tefillin,** or phylacteries, which are two small boxes containing scriptural passages; one is attached to the forehead by leather straps tied around the head, and the other is attached to the upper left arm by straps wound down around the arm and hand. They signify quite literally that God's law is in the mind and heart of the person at prayer (see Deut 6:8). The **talit** (a prayer shawl)—usually white, with dark stripes and fringes—covers the man's head and body during prayer and signifies humility in the sight of God. In less traditional forms of Judaism, the prayer shawl is sometimes not used, but men wear the skullcap (*kippah* in Hebrew and **yarmulke** in Yiddish, the old language of eastern European Jews). Devout males sometimes express their reverence before God during their waking hours by keeping their heads continually covered by the skullcap.

Remembrance of God is also assisted by the presence of a *mezuzah,* which is placed on the doorpost of the entrance to a home and sometimes on the doorposts of interior rooms (see Deut. 6:9). Like the tefillin, the

mezuzah is a small container that holds scriptural words; it can be touched upon entering the house or room. Unlike the tefillin, it is used even by secular Jews.

Perhaps because sexuality and the origin of life are considered especially sacred, Judaism has a number of practices relating to them. Eight days after birth, when a male receives his name, he is circumcised—the foreskin of the penis is cut off (see Gen. 17 and Lev. 12:3) by a specialist—in a ceremony that recalls God's covenant with the Hebrew people. The origin of the practice of circumcision in Judaism is uncertain. It began possibly as a health measure, because in hot climates germs easily grow in loose tissue; but it is also possible that circumcision began as a way of recognizing divine control over sex and generation.

Males mark puberty with a coming-of-age ceremony at age 13, when a young man legally becomes an adult, or "son of the commandment" (**bar mitzvah**). In some branches of Judaism, girls ages 12 to 18 are honored in a similar ceremony, called a bat mitzvah. For women, menstruation and childbirth have also been considered special times, and have come to involve rituals of bathing and purification. Although in ancient days priests on duty in the temple and soldiers in the field were expected to be temporarily celibate, sex has been viewed positively in Judaism. With the exception of the Essenes, marriage has been honored and children are a major goal of life (see Gen. 1:28 and 12:2).

DIVISIONS WITHIN CONTEMPORARY JUDAISM

We find in Judaism both cultural differences and differences in the observance of traditional rules. Some commentators, as a result, talk not of "Judaism" but of "Judaisms."

Culturally Based Divisions

The great ethnic diversity among Jews has resulted in a number of cultural divisions within Judaism. It is important to understand these divisions in order to appreciate the richness of Judaism, as well as the challenges that face Israel, where members of these groups have come to live together.

Sephardic Jews The name Sephardic comes from a mythic land of Sephar (or Sepharad), once thought to exist in the distant west of Israel and often identified with Spain. After the Roman victories over the Jews in Israel (70 and 135 C.E.), Jews emigrated from Israel and settled in lands far away. Southern Spain particularly became a center of flourishing Jewish life, especially under Muslim rule, but this ended with the expulsion of the Muslims and Jews by the Christian rulers in 1492 C.E. After their expulsion from Spain, Sephardic Jews (**Sephardim**) from Spain

A traditional Jewish man, dressed in tefillin and a prayer shawl, reciting morning prayer. ◄

Devout Jews place a mezuzah, containing words from the Torah, beside their doors and touch it reverently when they enter.

carried their language and culture to Morocco, Greece, Egypt, and elsewhere in the Mediterranean region, as well as to Holland and England. The common language of the Sephardic Jews, termed Ladino in recognition of its ultimate derivation from Latin, was a type of Spanish mixed with Hebrew words and often written in Hebrew characters. Sephardic Jews lived in significant numbers in Morocco until recent times, when most emigrated to Israel. More than half of the Jews of Israel are of Sephardic background.

Ashkenazic Jews   The name Ashkenazic comes from Ashkenaz, a descendant of Noah who settled in a distant northern land (see Gen. 10:3). The term **Ashkenazim** refers to those Jews who at one time lived in or came from central Europe. A very large population of Jews flourished for centuries in Poland, the Ukraine, Lithuania, Latvia, Germany, and Hungary, and before the Holocaust it is estimated that three million Jews lived in Poland alone, where sometimes entire towns (called shtetls) were Jewish.

The origin of Ashkenazic Judaism is unclear, but the most common opinion is that it arose when Jews after 1000 C.E. migrated from France and other countries of western Europe to central Europe. Another theory, advanced by Arthur Koestler in his book *The Thirteenth Tribe,* holds that a whole kingdom in southern Russia, called Khazaria, converted to Judaism after the seventh century C.E. This theory argues that the conversion to Judaism was a highly political decision: conversion to Christianity would have brought absorption into the Byzantine Empire, and conversion to Islam would have brought control by Muslim forces. Invasions from the north that occurred several centuries later forced the Jewish Khazars into Hungary, Poland, and the rest of central Europe.

The common language of central European Judaism was *Yiddish* ("Jewish"), a medieval form of German mixed with Hebrew words and written in Hebrew characters. While it flourished, Ashkenazic Judaism produced a rich culture of books, stories, songs, and theater in Yiddish. Ashkenazic culture virtually ended in Europe with the Holocaust, but Yiddish language and culture lived on in the United States, Canada, and Israel, and although it once seemed to be rapidly declining, there are recent signs of revival. Yiddish-speaking culture has contributed Yiddish words and ideas to American life, and Yiddish literature is being translated into many languages.

Other Jewish Cultures   A mysterious form of Judaism exists in Africa in Ethiopia among the Falashas. These Ethiopian Jews practice a religion that accepts as canonical only the five books of the Torah—a sign that Ethiopian Judaism could be quite ancient. Possibly an archaic form of Judaism, once practiced in southern Egypt, penetrated into Ethiopia and continued there, cut off from contact with later Jewish development. However, there may be other explanations for the existence of the

Falashas. In the 1980s, when they were subject to Marxist persecution in Ethiopia, many Falashas were airlifted by the Israeli government to Israel.

Elsewhere, Judaism established itself in a small community on the western coast of India, though today it is very small. Even into this century, a form of Chinese Judaism could also be found in western China, but it has now evidently disappeared. Distinctive Jewish cultures exist as well in Yemen, Iraq, and elsewhere.

Observance-Based Divisions

Within Judaism today, divisions also exist based on variations in religious observance. As described earlier, a movement for reform began in eighteenth-century Germany with a questioning of traditional Jewish practices, creating a distinction between traditionalist Jews and those who wished to modernize Jewish practice. Although some Jews have held to traditional practices, other branches have developed out of the conviction that Judaism will stay vital only if it reinterprets its traditions, just as it did after the destruction of the First and Second Temples. Those who reinterpret Judaism have naturally come to varied conclusions about what should be kept, discarded, or viewed symbolically rather than literally. Disagreements abound about observance of the laws of the Torah and Talmud, the use of Hebrew in services, the role of women in traditionally male roles, support for the nation of Israel, and the relationship of Judaism with the non-Jewish world. Four branches have emerged. We begin with the most traditional and move to the least traditional, although the branches did not emerge in this order.

Orthodox Judaism   Traditional Judaism is often called **Orthodox,** but we might recall that until the Reform movement began, there was no need to give a special name to traditional Judaism, because all Jews were traditional in belief and practice. In a sense, Orthodox Judaism came into being only after the Reform began, and as a response to it. When we use the term *Orthodox* to refer to traditional Jews, we should also recognize the great variety among Orthodox Jews—particularly regarding social and political positions. Some, termed integrationists, seek to play a role in civil society, while others, called separatists, want to live their traditional lifestyle apart from society, sometimes without political activity. Most Orthodox Jews support the state of Israel, and many accept the need for secular education in addition to traditional learning, but some are opposed to both.

With this said, we can describe Orthodoxy as a branch of Judaism committed to retaining traditional practice and belief. Orthodox Jews are hesitant to discard any traditional practices, even those not demanded by the Torah but simply revered as reasonable later developments that are said to "guard" the Torah from being lost or misinterpreted. Some specific practices follow.

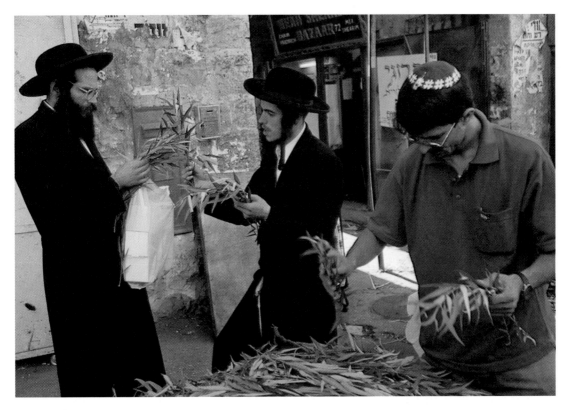

Traditional Jews in Jerusalem buy branches for Sukkot.

- Orthodox synagogues separate males and females, with females often sitting in an upstairs gallery.
- For a service to take place, there must be a quorum (*minyan*) of ten Jewish males.
- Services are conducted completely in Hebrew and led by male rabbis.
- Only males may celebrate the coming-of-age ceremony (bar mitzvah).
- Men at prayer use the talit and at weekday morning prayer use the tefillin.
- Males must keep their heads covered (with the skullcap, prayer shawl, or hat) as a reminder that God is above all.
- Social roles (especially among "ultraorthodox" Jews) are strictly separate. Men are the breadwinners of the family, and women are responsible for running the household.
- The hair of the beard and in front of the ears is sometimes left uncut by males, in response to a command in the Torah (Lev. 19:27).
- Some Orthodox Jewish males (and particularly those affiliated with a specific Hasidic community) also wear a style of dress that developed in central Europe during the nineteenth century—a black hat and black coat (originally a beaver-skin hat and a black smock).

- Orthodox women who are married sometimes cover their heads with a kerchief when outside the home. (Some cut their hair short and wear a wig, although this practice is condemned by certain rabbis.) The hair is covered as an expression of modesty, because a woman's hair is considered to be seductive to men.
- The Orthodox household keeps strictly the traditional laws about diet.
- Orthodox Jews closely follow rules that prohibit any manual labor on the Sabbath. Cooking is not allowed, nor is driving a car, walking long distances, dialing a telephone, or even turning on an electric light.

Outsiders might consider the strictness of this lifestyle burdensome. But the Orthodox themselves say that it is not difficult (particularly those who have been raised as Orthodox) and that it is even fulfilling, because every waking moment is consciously devoted to the worship of God.

In continental Europe, Orthodox Judaism was nearly destroyed by the Nazis. In Israel, although only a tenth of the population can be considered traditionalist or Orthodox, that segment has considerable political power. In the United States, Orthodoxy is a small but visible minority among those who practice Judaism.

Conservative Judaism   For some Jews, the European movement for reform seemed too radical. **Conservative Judaism** traces itself back to the Positive-Historical School of Judaism in Germany, but it took strong root in the United States among Jews who desired moderate change that was coupled with a protection of beloved traditions, such as use of Hebrew in the services. Conservative Judaism recognizes that change has always been a part of the religion, that the centuries have seen many additions and deletions—for example, the temple sacrifices ceased but the Talmud was written. Thus this branch of Judaism accepts change but uses study and discussion to guide change carefully, valuing all traditions and weighing them thoughtfully. Conservativism itself has also changed over time by altering its positions on several important issues. For example, it once opposed Zionism and forbade the ordination of women as rabbis, but it has reversed itself in both instances. In the United States, almost half of all practicing Jews belong to this branch.

Reform Judaism   Reform Judaism began in Germany out of a desire of some Jews to leave ghetto life completely and enter the mainstream of European culture. An early influence on this movement was Moses Mendelssohn (1729–1786), a major thinker and writer. Mendelssohn, although he was not a Reform Jew, had influence on Reform and Orthodox Judaism. He argued for religious tolerance, held that Judaism could be combined with civil culture, and embraced many of the ideals of the European Enlightenment of the eighteenth century—human dignity, equality, individual liberty, democracy, secular education, and the development of science. These ideals brought radical changes in the Jewish circles that espoused them, because in the name of reform, every traditional Jewish belief and practice could be questioned.

The result has been that in Reform synagogue worship, women and men do not sit separately, services are conducted in both the native language and Hebrew, choirs and organ music are common, and use of the talit and tefillin has been dropped or made optional. Traditional ways of dressing, common among the Orthodox, have disappeared. Perhaps more important, equality is espoused for men and women. As a result, women may become rabbis, and girls have coming-of-age ceremonies in which they are declared "daughters of the commandment" (*bat mitzvah*).

The goal of the Reform movement has been to thoroughly modernize Judaism, in the hope that it will survive in the contemporary world. However, because several of the Reform ideals are considered to be injurious to traditional Judaism, Orthodox Jews view it with suspicion and see it as a dangerous dilution of Judaism.

Reconstructionist Judaism   This newest and smallest branch of Judaism grew out of the thought of its founder, Mordecai Kaplan (1881–1983), a Lithuanian who came to the United States as a child. Kaplan was influenced by the American ideals of democracy and practicality. As a leader in the Society for the Advancement of Judaism, Kaplan promoted a secular vision that encourages Jews to become familiar with as many elements of traditional Judaism as possible but that allows them the freedom of individual interpretation. Elements of belief that traditional Jews interpret literally (such as angels, prophecy, revealed law, and the Messiah) are taken as useful symbols in **Reconstructionism;** even the notion of God is seen from a pragmatic viewpoint as "the Power which makes me follow ever higher ideals."[33] Instead of searching for a minimum number of beliefs and practices that are the unchanging essence of Judaism, Reconstructionism sees Judaism as a changing cultural force, with many elements and manifestations. Judaism, in this view, is a whole civilization "which expresses itself . . . in literature, art, music, even cuisine. It never stands still but evolves."[34]

THE CONTRIBUTIONS OF JUDAISM

Judaism's unique contributions to civilization are products of the Jewish view of life. Although postbiblical Judaism embraced a belief in a resurrection of the dead who had lived holy lives and in their life "in the world to come," the focus of Judaism has been primarily on the importance of loving—and contributing to—*this* world. As described in the Book of Genesis, the world has not only been created by God but is also the object of his admiration, and human beings, an important part of God's plan, are of unique value. Just as when God speaks, acts, and gives form to the universe, human beings imitate him when they shape the world and better it.

The emphasis on living fully in this world has shaped the ways in which members of the Jewish faith achieve fulfillment. Jewish culture values the following:

Individuality and independence

Self-improvement

The body, medicine, and medical care

Marriage, family life, and children

Psychology, psychotherapy, and counseling

Education, books, journalism, and debate

Economics, business, and finance

Law and social justice

Philanthropy and social contribution

Comedy and humor

As a consequence, prestige in the Jewish community has attached itself historically to vocations that express the preceding values—physician, professor, scientist, writer, merchant, manufacturer, producer, comedian, lawyer, and counselor.

Several vocations are represented less frequently by Jews, either for religious reasons or because of past social restrictions. For example, until recent times the label *Jewish artist* was almost a contradiction in terms. We might recall that one of the Ten Commandments forbade the making of human and animal images. Although this commandment has not always been interpreted strictly (and some examples of religious Jewish image making do exist), the visual fine arts in general were not thought of as appropriate forms of religious expression for devout Jews. The area of nonfigurative decorative arts, however, was acceptable. Judaism has produced beautiful religious objects, such as candelabra, wine cups, Sabbath bread plates, and scroll covers. (Many fine examples can be seen in the Jewish Museum in New York City.)

Until the last century, however, artistic instincts generally have been channeled into other paths, such as music and architecture. We should, though, be aware of the artistry that exists in the images, records of visions, and patterns of sound to be found in Jewish religious literature and poetry.

Although Jews are a small minority in every country except Israel, their achievements on the world stage, especially over the last two centuries, have been exceptional. Jews often feel a justifiable pride in their contributions to the world.

Philosophy was enriched by the thought of Martin Buber (1878–1965), whose book *I and Thou* has become one of the seminal works of the twentieth

> All real living is meeting.
> —Martin Buber[35]

century. In it, Buber described the "I-Thou" relationship with someone or something in the world as a relationship of openness and dialogue. Buber held that in every I-Thou relationship in the world the divine is encountered. Buber also pointed scholarly attention to mysticism and Hasidic wisdom through his anthologies of Hasidic stories.

Many great Jewish authors have contributed to literature: Saul Bellow (b. 1915), Elie Wiesel (b. 1928), Chaim Potok (b. 1929), and Isaac Bashevis Singer (1904–1991), to name just a few. Their themes have often been religious—spiritual self-discovery, individuality in interplay with religious tradition, and the Jewish response to the Holocaust.

The fairly new discipline of psychology owes its advancement to the great work of people of Jewish background, such as Sigmund Freud (1856–1939), Abraham Maslow (1908–1970), and Viktor Frankl (1905–1997). (The striking examples of dream analysis in the Books of Genesis and Daniel are ancient precursors to psychoanalysis.) All three thinkers concerned themselves with the role of religion—Freud being nonreligious and quite skeptical but Maslow and Frankl seeing the significance of religion in bringing essential meaning to human life.

In recent times, classical music has been particularly enriched by notable Jewish composers who have brought an explicitly religious dimension to their music. Gustav Mahler (1860–1911) introduced religious themes into several of his works (for example, his Second and Eighth Symphonies). Another composer, Ernest Bloch (1880–1959), is known for his works inspired by Judaism, especially his *Kol Nidre* and *Schelomo*. Leonard Bernstein (1918–1990), although best known for his secular musical *West Side Story*, also created serious works on explicitly Jewish themes—such as his *Jeremiah Symphony*, his *Chichester Psalms*, and his *Kaddish Symphony*, which is a disturbing memorial to an ancient, dying God.

Albert Einstein *(left)* is considered by many to be the preeminent scientist of the twentieth century. Elie Wiesel *(right)* was imprisoned in a concentration camp as a teenager. His writings about the Holocaust helped earn him the Nobel Peace Prize.

The image-making restrictions that discouraged the development of Jewish painting began to weaken for some artists in the late nineteenth century. Marc Chagall (1887–1985) had to leave his small hometown in Russia in order to learn to paint, but in his imagination he recreated the Jewish world he had left behind. His paintings are full of the Jewish figures he learned about in childhood—angels, rabbis, Jewish violinists, Jewish brides and grooms. This use of figurative painting was in line with Chagall's training in Paris, which at the beginning of Chagall's career was still the world center of painting. There the academic study of painting had at its core the Renaissance love of the human figure.

Possibly the most important influence of Jewish values on world culture in the last one hundred years has come through film. (The traditional Jewish prohibition on the making of human images apparently did not apply to filmmaking.) In California, the film industry was built up largely by men of Ashkenazic background, whose Orthodox parents and grandparents had emigrated from Europe. It is significant that *The Jazz Singer* (1927), the first successful talking film, is a Jewish story that tells of a young Jewish man eager to make a career singing popular songs. To do this, he must oppose his own father, a cantor in a synagogue, who wants his son to have the same career as he. The story epitomizes the struggle in the life of every young Jewish man of the time: to live a traditional life in a Jewish world or to find a new style of life within the secular world. (The story is so powerful that it has been remade several times.) The advent of the talking film opened up a whole new area for development—the written, sung, and spoken word of film—and unleashed the potential of scriptwriters, songwriters, lyricists, and comedians, many of whom were (and are) of Jewish background. They brought into their work the traditional Jewish values—particularly the love of home and family, of words and books, of humor and song.

Modern feminist values, sometimes in conflict with Jewish tradition, can be seen in the film work of Barbra Streisand (b. 1942). The film *Yentl*, for example, is a demand for gender equality in Judaism. Set in eastern Europe in 1904, it tells the story of the daughter of a rabbi who cuts off her hair and pretends to be a male—all so she can enter a rabbinical school. The film *Hello, Dolly* also presents Streisand (in the character of Dolly Levy) as a strong Jewish woman and role model.

Similar talent at writing and entertaining was called for with the arrival of television. Today, television writers of Jewish backgrounds often introduce elements of Jewish culture, such as Jewish rituals, Yiddish words and phrases, scriptural references, and insider jokes (in such television shows as *Seinfeld, The Simpsons, Laverne and Shirley,* and *Dinosaurs*). Television series sometimes address quite sensitive issues that face modern Jews. One program, for example, showed an interreligious married couple—in which the husband was Jewish but the wife was not—trying to decide whether to have the ritual of circumcision performed after their boy is born. (They did.) Another show explored the religious significance of a student's absence from school on Yom Kippur. Shows like this make welcome use of the powerful medium of television to explain Judaism to a wide audience.

JEWISH IDENTITY AND THE FUTURE OF JUDAISM

Judaism today is particularly concerned with two great questions, which are inescapably linked. What is essential to being a Jew? Will Judaism survive?

Appreciating the cultural and religious divisions among Jews demonstrates how difficult it is today to define what makes a Jew. Two hundred years ago, the question of identity was nonexistent, because Jews were those people who practiced traditional Judaism. Now, however, Jewish identity is no longer so easy to ascertain. Although Orthodox Judaism holds that a person is born a Jew if his or her mother is Jewish, this does not address the matter of practice, and today there are many nonobservant Jews. A person may also convert to Judaism, although some Orthodox rabbis have refused to accept conversions to non-Orthodox branches of Judaism. Judaism is certainly a religion, but there is great disagreement about the essentials of belief and practice, and many people consider themselves Jews even though they do not practice the religion.

Furthermore, any attempt to define a Jew as a person belonging to a single culture or ethnic group is virtually impossible. Jews are as ethnically diverse as they are ideologically diverse, a fact that becomes quite clear when one visits Israel. Although there is as yet no clear answer to the question of Jewish identity, the topic becomes more important as Jews increasingly intermarry with non-Jews.

The history of Judaism has been marked by displacement and disasters. In the twentieth century alone, nearly a third of the world's Jewish population was destroyed. Nevertheless, Jewish history has also been marked by the will to endure. The resilience of Judaism has in large part resided in its ability to adapt to changing circumstances and environments. This ability suggests that in the decades ahead, Judaism will again take new forms and gain new life.

RELIGION BEYOND THE CLASSROOM

Because Judaism is a religion that emphasizes practice, to experience Judaism one should see how it is and has been lived. This can be done by attending services and visiting with Jewish families. If travel abroad is possible, touring Israel is an unforgettable way to experience Jewish life.

North America Jewish life is vibrant in the United States and Canada. People with specifically religious interest may visit most synagogues to experience their Sabbath prayer. (It is thoughtful to phone beforehand to make arrangements.) There are architecturally significant synagogues in some major cities, especially New York and Los Angeles.

Some Jewish families are happy to include non-Jews in Passover Seders; this can sometimes be arranged through synagogues in one's area. Non-

Jews are frequently invited, too, to bar mitzvah and bat mitzvah celebrations and to weddings; such celebrations are wonderful opportunities for non-Jews to experience the visual and oral richness of Jewish practice. Jewish contributions to the arts can be seen in several places, such as the Jewish Museum in New York City. The Holocaust Museum in Washington, D.C., provides powerful insight into the buildup of antisemitism in Germany and the virtual destruction of European Judaism during World War II.

Europe The continent is dotted with significant sites and museums, particularly where there was once a strong Jewish presence. Jewish museums (some housed in former synagogues) are located, for example, in Vienna, Prague, Copenhagen, Berlin, Budapest, Toledo, and Amsterdam. Amsterdam is also the city of the Anne Frank house— which should have particular meaning for anyone who has read her diary. Former ghetto areas in some cities still retain a flavor of Jewish life, for example, in Venice (near the train station), Paris (the Rue des Rosiers area in the Marais district), Amsterdam (Jodenbuurt, around Jodenbreestraat), and Córdoba (the Judería, Synagogue, and Plaza Juda Levi). A few former concentration camps have been kept intact as museums and memorials to the Holocaust, such as Dachau (near Munich) and Auschwitz (Oświęcim, near Krakow).

Israel This country is, of course, full of significant Jewish sites, of which Jerusalem is the most important. The Western Wall of the Second Temple is a place for prayer; the Shrine of the Book displays examples of the Dead Sea Scrolls; and Yad Vashem is a memorial to the Holocaust. Other places in Israel are also worth visiting, time permitting. One such site is the fortress ruins of Masada, where Jewish Zealots resisted Roman soldiers, even to the point of suicide. The tomb of Abraham is venerated at Hebron, and Mount Carmel (near Haifa) is associated with the life of the prophet Elijah. Finally, visitors might be interested in arranging to visit, stay, and even work at one of Israel's many communes (*kibbutzim*).

FOR FULLER UNDERSTANDING

1. If your area has a synagogue or a museum that chronicles Jewish history, visit it and make an oral report to your class on what you learned.
2. With a few classmates, undertake a comparative study of women's roles in several religions, including Judaism. Pay particular attention to changes that have taken place over the twentieth century, and speculate on changes that might occur during the twenty-first century.
3. Using library and computer-lab resources, examine architectural models and diagrams of the Second Temple. Prepare an illustrated report in which you explain the various temple courts and the services held there.
4. Choose an artist, composer, or writer whose work suggests the influence of Jewish thought and practice. Study several of that person's works, making note of any elements on which Judaism has left its mark.

RELATED READINGS

Buber, Martin. *I and Thou.* New York: Simon and Schuster, 1984. An influential book that speaks of the holiness of all close personal relationship, which Buber calls I-Thou relationship.

Chagall, Bella, with drawings by Marc Chagall. *Burning Lights.* New York: Schocken, 1962. A book that evokes through words and drawings the warm Orthodox Jewish world of central Europe before the Holocaust.

Flanders, Henry Jackson, Robert Wilson Crapps, and David Anthony Smith. *People of the Covenant.* 4th ed. New York: Oxford University Press, 1996. A good introduction to Hebrew scriptures and history, from Abraham to the Second-Temple period.

Frank, Anne. *The Diary of a Young Girl.* New York: Bantam, 1993. The diary of a Jewish girl who hid with her family in Holland during World War II.

Frankl, Viktor. *Man's Search for Meaning.* New York: Pocketbooks, 1988. A two-part book that describes the author's horrifying experiences in several concentration camps and then gives his reflections on the human need for meaning.

Friedman, Maurice. *Martin Buber: The Life of Dialogue.* New York: Harper & Bros., 1960. A lucid explanation of the thought of Buber, by a foremost disciple.

Friedman, Richard. *The Disappearance of God: A Divine Mystery.* Boston: Little, Brown, 1995. A look at the books of the Hebrew scriptures in chronological order, with the conclusion that the role of God is greatest in the earlier books but declines severely in the final books.

Kushner, Harold. *When Bad Things Happen to Good People.* New York: Schocken Books, 1989. A compelling book in which a rabbi tackles the question of evil in a world created by a good God.

Scholem, Gershom. *Major Trends in Jewish Mysticism.* New York: Schocken Books, 1995. A classic by a major specialist in Jewish mystical literature.

Seltzer, Robert M. *Jewish People, Jewish Thought.* New York: Macmillan, 1980. A good general introduction to Judaism.

Singer, Isaac Bashevis. *Collected Stories.* New York: Farrar, Straus & Giroux, 1982. A collection of stories by a highly acclaimed Jewish author, including the story of Yentl, the girl who wished to be a rabbi—the story on which the movie *Yentl* was based.

KEY TERMS

Ashkenazim (*ash-ken-ah'-zeem*): Jews who lived in or came from central Europe.

Bar (bat) mitzvah: "Son (daughter) of the commandment"; the coming-of-age ceremony that marks the time when a young person is considered a legal adult within the Jewish community.

Biblical Judaism: Judaism before the destruction of the Second Temple (70 C.E.).

Canaan (*kay'-nun*): An ancient name for the land of Israel.

Conservative Judaism: A branch of Judaism that attempts to blend the best of old and new Judaism.

Covenant: A contract; the contract between the Hebrews and their God, Yahweh.

Diaspora (*dai-as'-po-rah*): The dispersion of Jews beyond Israel, particularly to Persia, Egypt, and the Mediterranean region.

Essenes: A semimonastic Jewish community that flourished from c. 150 B.C.E. to 68 C.E.

Hanukkah (*ha'-nuk-kah*): An early-winter festival recalling the rededication of the Second Temple, celebrated with the lighting of candles for eight days.

Holocaust: The destruction of European Judaism by the Nazis; also known as Shoah (Hebrew: "extermination").

Kabbalah (*kab-bah'-luh* or *kab'-bah-luh*): "Received," "handed down"; the whole body of Jewish mystical literature.

Kethuvim (*ke-tu-veem'*): "Writings"; the third section of the Hebrew scriptures, consisting primarily of poetry, proverbs, and literary works.

Kosher (*koh'-shur*): "Ritually correct"; said particularly about food consumption and food preparation.

Menorah (*me-noh'-ruh*): A candelabrum usually containing seven—and occasionally nine—branches, used for religious celebrations.

Messiah (*mes-sai'-uh*): A savior figure to be sent by God, awaited by the Jews (see Dan. 7:13–14).

Midrash (*mid'-rash*): "Search"; rabbinical commentary on the scriptures and oral law.

Nevi'im (*ne-vee-eem'*): "Prophets"; the second section of the Hebrew scriptures, made up of historical and prophetic books.

Orthodox: The most traditional branch of Judaism.

Passover (Pesach): A joyful spring festival that recalls the Hebrews' exodus from Egypt and freedom from oppression.

Pharisees: A faction during the Second-Temple period that emphasized the observation of biblical rules.

Prophet: A person inspired by God to speak for him.

Purim (*poo'-reem*): A joyous festival in early spring that recalls the Jews' being saved from destruction, as told in the Book of Esther.

Rabbi (*rab'-bai*): A religious teacher, Jewish minister.

Rabbinical Judaism: The Judaism that developed after the destruction of the Second Temple (70 C.E.).

Reconstructionism: A modern, liberal branch of Judaism that emphasizes the cultural aspects of Judaism.

Reform: A modernizing movement and a liberal branch of Judaism.

Rosh Hashana (*rosh-ha-sha'-nah*): "Beginning of the year"; the celebration of the Jewish New Year, occurring in the seventh lunar month.

Sabbath: "Rest"; the seventh day of the week (Saturday), a day of prayer and rest from work.

Sadducees (*sad'-dyu-sees*): A priestly faction, influential during the Second-Temple period.

Seder (*say'-dur*): "Order"; a special ritual meal at Passover, recalling the Hebrews' exodus from Egypt.

Sephardim (*se-far'-deem*): Jews of Spain, Morocco, and the Mediterranean region.

Sukkot (*soo-koht'*): "Booths"; a festival in the late autumn that recalls the Jews' period of wandering in the desert after their exodus from Egypt.

Talit (*tah'-lit*): A prayer shawl worn by devout males.

Talmud (*tahl'-mood*): An encyclopedic commentary on the Hebrew scriptures.

Tanakh (*ta-nak'*): The complete Hebrew scriptures, made up of the Torah, Prophets (Nevi'im), and Writings (Kethuvim).

Tefillin (*te-fil'-in*): Phylacteries; two small boxes containing biblical passages that are worn by Orthodox males on their head and left arm at morning prayer during the week.

Theophany: A revelation or appearance of God.

Torah (*toh'-rah*): "Teaching," "instruction"; the first five books of the Hebrew scriptures; also, the additional instructions of God, believed by many to have been transmitted orally from Moses through a succession of teachers and rabbis.

Western Wall: The foundation stones of the western wall of the last temple of Jerusalem, today a place of prayer.

Yarmulke (*yar'-mool-kah*): The skullcap worn by devout males.

Yom Kippur (*yohm kip-puhr'*): Day of Atonement.

Zealots: An anti-Roman, nationalistic Jewish faction, active during the Roman period of control over Israel.

Zionism: The movement that has encouraged the creation and support of the nation of Israel.

CHAPTER **9**

Christianity

 FIRST ENCOUNTER

On a Sunday morning in Rome you make your way by taxi to Saint Peter's Basilica, perhaps the best-known church in the world, to attend the Pope's Sunday Mass. You enter the piazza on foot, passing the tall columns that form two encircling arms around a great open space. The first thing that you see is the dome over the church, which was designed by Michelangelo and refined by others. The dome is a work of special beauty: it is not a half-circle as you might expect but is shaped more like an egg stretching upward. The rise of the dome is accentuated by the "lantern," or viewing room, on top, which ties the dome to the sky.

Walking toward the entrance, you pass one of two huge tiered fountains. The breeze throws some of the falling water onto the stones of the pavement, and you feel mist on your face. As you get closer to the church and ascend the stairs, the dome overhead, now hidden by the porch, disappears. You pass two eagle-eyed guards who inspect you and the hundreds of others entering the church to make sure that every person's arms and legs are clothed modestly.

The vastness and magnificence of this sacred space (Saint Peter's Basilica) can only be understood firsthand.

Once inside the church you see two famous sights: the thirteenth-century bronze statue of Saint Peter (attributed to Arnolfo di Cambio) whose right big toe shines from being touched by so many visitors, and Michelangelo's marble statue, called the *Pietà*, of Mary holding the body of her crucified son Jesus across her lap. Wonderful as these statues are, once your eyes adjust to the light inside the body of the church itself, you are taken by the true magnificence of this vast room. The interior space is so enormous that the view to the far end of the church is softened by a kind of mist. Sunlight streams down diagonally through windows in the dome, caught in beams by the atmospheric haze of the air. Above the high altar is a huge copper roof (called a baldachin and designed by Giovanni Bernini), supported by four pillars that twist upward into space. At the very back of the church, a magnificent oval window of yellow and white glass portrays the Holy Spirit of God as a dove in flight.

The church fills with people. After candles are lit on the high altar, the pope enters and begins the ceremony called Mass. The choir sings in Latin as the pope slowly carries a silver pot of incense around the altar. You watch the smoke rise in clouds through the air. There are readings from a large book, and finally wafers of bread are blessed and offered to the people. As the ceremony moves solemnly through its stages, you wonder about the origins of it all. You know that the Mass originated as a simple meal—the Last Supper of Jesus with his twelve followers. The high altar, up a multitude of stairs, you know is essentially a table. But the incense, the robes, the chant sung in Latin—where did these originate, and why are they still used?

The Christian System of Chronology: B.C and A.D

The influence of Christianity is apparent in the European dating system, which has now generally been adopted worldwide. The Roman Empire had dated events from the foundation of Rome (753 B.C.E.), but a new system was devised by a Christian monk, Dionysius Exiguus (Dennis the Little) at the request of Pope Gregory I (c. 540–604 C.E.). The new system made the birth of Jesus the central event of history. Thus we have "B.C.," meaning "Before Christ," and "A.D.," Latin for "in the year of the Lord" (*anno Domini*). The date selected as the year of Jesus' birth may have been incorrect, and scholars now think that Jesus was born about 4 B.C.E. (The historical facts given in Matt. 2:1 and Luke 2:2 about the year of Jesus' birth are not compatible.) Also, the new dating system began not with the year zero but with the year one because there is no zero in Roman numerals. Because of the Christian orientation of this dating system, many books (including this one) now use a slightly altered abbreviation: "B.C.E.," meaning "before the common era," and "C.E.," meaning "common era."

After Mass, you walk around the church, absorbing it from different angles and perspectives. You stand under the dome. Why, you wonder, are high ceilings so common in churches? You go outside and wait in the piazza with tens of thousands of other visitors of every nationality and origin. Precisely at noon the pope appears to the right of the church in a high window of his apartments; he speaks, then blesses the crowd. What thoughts, you wonder, would Jesus have if he were with you now? How have these ceremonies come to be? What will be the future of this church and of Christianity?

THE LIFE AND TEACHINGS OF JESUS

Christianity, which grew out of Judaism, has had a major influence on the history of the world. Before we discuss its growth and influence, we must look at the life of Jesus, who is considered its originator, and at the early scriptural books that speak of his life.

At the time of Jesus' birth and long before that, the land of Israel had been taken over repeatedly by stronger neighbors. During Jesus' time, Israel was called Palestine by the Romans and was part of the Roman Empire—but not willingly. The region was full of unrest, a boiling pot of religious and political factions and movements. Patriots wanted to expel the Romans. The Sadducees, a group of priests in Jerusalem, kept up the Jewish temple rituals while accepting the Roman occupation as inevitable. Members of a semimonastic movement, the Essenes, lived an austere life in the desert and provinces; for the most part, they deliberately lived away from Jerusalem, which they thought was corrupt. The Pharisees, a lay movement of devout Jews, preoccupied themselves with meticulously keeping the Jewish law.

Many Jews in Jesus' day thought that they were living in the "end times." They expected a period of turbulence and suffering and a final great

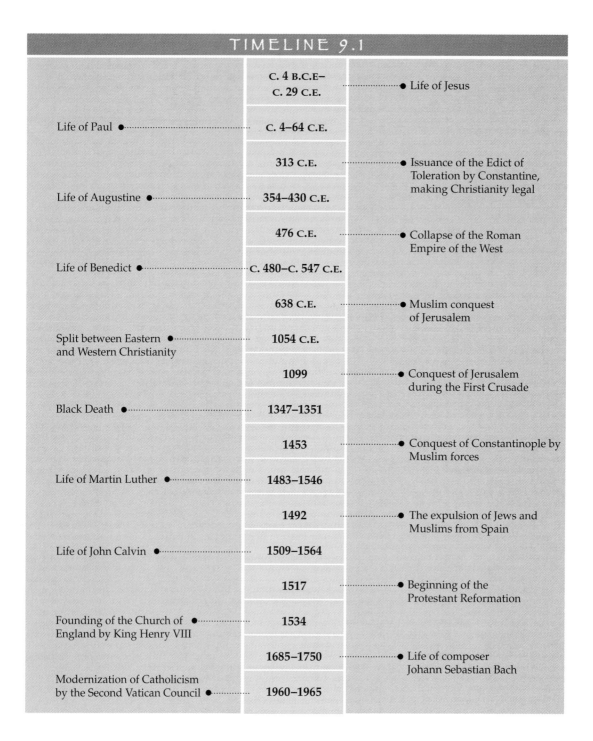

TIMELINE 9.1

	C. 4 B.C.E.– C. 29 C.E.	● Life of Jesus
Life of Paul ●	**C. 4–64 C.E.**	
	313 C.E.	● Issuance of the Edict of Toleration by Constantine, making Christianity legal
Life of Augustine ●	**354–430 C.E.**	
	476 C.E.	● Collapse of the Roman Empire of the West
Life of Benedict ●	**C. 480–C. 547 C.E.**	
	638 C.E.	● Muslim conquest of Jerusalem
Split between Eastern and Western Christianity ●	**1054 C.E.**	
	1099	● Conquest of Jerusalem during the First Crusade
Black Death ●	**1347–1351**	
	1453	● Conquest of Constantinople by Muslim forces
Life of Martin Luther ●	**1483–1546**	
	1492	● The expulsion of Jews and Muslims from Spain
Life of John Calvin ●	**1509–1564**	
	1517	● Beginning of the Protestant Reformation
Founding of the Church of England by King Henry VIII ●	**1534**	
	1685–1750	● Life of composer Johann Sebastian Bach
Modernization of Catholicism by the Second Vatican Council ●	**1960–1965**	

Timeline of significant events in the history of Christianity.

battle, when God would destroy all the enemies of pious Jews. God, they believed, would then inaugurate a new age of justice and love. Some expected a new Garden of Eden, where the good people who remained after the Judgment would eat year-round from fruit trees and women would no longer suffer in childbirth. Most Jews shared the hope that the Romans would be expelled, that evildoers would be punished, and that God's envoy, the **Messiah,** would appear. (The name *Messiah* means "anointed" and refers to the ceremony of anointing a new king with olive oil.) Many held that the Messiah had been foretold in some of their sacred books—such as Isaiah, Micah, and Daniel—and they expected him to rule the new world.

Into this complicated land Jesus was born about two thousand years ago (Timeline 9.1). Traditional teaching tells of a miraculous conception in Nazareth, a town of northern Israel, and of a birth by the virginal mother Mary in Bethlehem, a town in the south not far from Jerusalem. It tells of wise men who followed a guiding star to the baby soon after his birth. The traditional portrait of Jesus, common in art, shows him in his early years assisting his foster father Joseph as a carpenter in the northern province of Galilee. It is possible that the truth of some of these traditional details—as it is regarding the lives of many other religious founders—may be more symbolic than literal.

There have been many attempts to find the "historical Jesus." Although artists have portrayed Jesus in countless ways, no portrait that we know of was ever painted of Jesus while he was alive. Of course, we can guess at his general features, but we cannot know anything definitive about the individual face or eyes or manner of Jesus.

Almost everything we know of Jesus comes from the four Gospels of the New Testament. (**Testament** means "contract" or "covenant," and **gospel** means "good news.") The Gospels, however, tell very little of Jesus until he began a "public life" of teaching and healing. He probably began his public life in his late twenties, when he gathered twelve disciples and moved from place to place, teaching about the coming of what he called the Kingdom of God. After a fairly short period of preaching—no more than three years—Jesus was arrested in Jerusalem at Passover time by the authorities, who considered him a threat to public order. From the point of view of the Sadducees, Jesus was dangerous because he might begin an anti-Roman riot. In contrast, Jewish patriots may have found him not anti-Roman enough. From the Roman point of view, however, he was at least a potential source of political unrest and enough of a threat to be arrested, whipped, nailed to a cross, and crucified—a degrading and public form of execution. Death came from shock, suffocation, and loss of blood.

Dying on a Friday, Jesus was buried near the site of his crucifixion shortly before sunset, just as the Jewish Sabbath was to begin. On the following Sunday, the Gospels report, the followers who went to care for his body found his tomb empty. Some followers reported apparitions of him, and his disciples became convinced that he had returned to life. Forty days later, the New Testament says, he ascended into the sky, promising to return again.

This bare outline does not answer many important questions: Who was Jesus? What kind of personality did he have? What were his teachings? For the answers to these questions we must turn to the four Gospels. They are the core of the Christian New Testament.

Although never portrayed during his life or even physically described, Jesus has been the subject of innumerable paintings. This fresco of Jesus appears in a dome of the monastery dedicated to Saint John of Rila in Bulgaria.

Jesus in the New Testament Gospels

The four Gospels describe the life and words of Jesus, but the New Testament is not the equivalent of a well-documented research report. The Gospels are instead written remembrances of Jesus' words and deeds, recorded some time after his death by people who believed in him. All the books of the New Testament are strongly colored by the viewpoints of their writers and by the culture of the period, and scholars consequently debate how much they reflect the views of later Christian believers as opposed to the actual teachings of Jesus. In fact, it is difficult to establish the historical accuracy of New Testament statements about Jesus or the words attributed to him. (Perhaps an analogy can clarify the problem: the Gospels are like paintings of Jesus, not photographs.) In compiling our picture of Jesus, we must also recognize that the Gospels are not a complete record of all essential information. There is a great deal we cannot know about Jesus. Nevertheless, although we accept a possibly irresolvable uncertainty about the historical Jesus, a definite person does emerge from the Gospels.

However obvious it may seem to point this out, Jesus believed and trusted in God, just as all contemporary Jews did. But while Jesus thought of God as creator and sustainer of the universe, he also thought of God in a very personal way, as his father. It is Jesus' extremely special relationship to God that is central to Christianity.

Raised as a Jew, Jesus accepted the sacred authority of the Law and the Prophets (the Torah and the books of history and prophecy). As a boy, he learned the scriptures in Hebrew. He kept the major Jewish holy days common to the period, and he often traveled to Jerusalem and its temple for some of these events. He apparently kept the basic food laws and laws about Sabbath observance, and he attended synagogue meetings on Saturdays as part of the observance of the Jewish Sabbath (Luke 4:16). It seems he was a devout and thoughtful Jew.

Nonetheless, one striking personal characteristic of Jesus, alluded to frequently in the Gospels, was his independence of thought. He considered things carefully and then arrived at his own opinions, which he was not hesitant to share. Jesus, the Gospels say, taught differently: "unlike the scribes, he taught them with authority" (Mark 1:22).[1]

Perhaps Jesus' most impressive characteristic was his emphasis on universal love—not just love for the members of one's own family, ethnic group, or religion. He preached love in many forms: compassion, tolerance, forgiveness, acceptance, helpfulness, generosity. When asked if a person should forgive up to seven times, he answered that people should forgive seventy times seven times (Matt. 18:22)—in other words, endlessly. He rejected all vengeance and even asked forgiveness for those who killed him (Luke 23:34). He recommended that we respond to violence with nonviolence. "But I tell you who hear me: Love your enemies, do good to those who hate you, bless those who curse you, and pray for those who mistreat you. If anyone hits you on one cheek, let him hit the other one too; if someone takes your coat, let him have your shirt as well. Give to everyone who asks you for something, and when someone takes what is yours, do not ask for it back. Do for others just what you want them to do for you" (Luke 6:27–31).[2]

Although Jesus' nonviolent, loving message has often been neglected over the centuries, it is spelled out clearly in the Sermon on the Mount sections of the New Testament (Matt. 5–7, Luke 6). In the world of Jesus' day, which esteemed force and exacted vengeance, his message must have been shocking.

Jesus was wary of an overly strict observance of laws that seemed detrimental to human welfare. About keeping detailed laws regarding the

Do not judge others, and God will not judge you; do not condemn others, and God will not condemn you; forgive others, and God will forgive you. Give to others, and God will give to you. Indeed, you will receive a full measure, a generous helping, poured into your hands—all that you can hold. The measure you use for others is the one that God will use for you.

—Luke 6:37–38[3]

Sabbath, he wisely commented, "The sabbath was made for man, not man for the sabbath" (Mark 2:27).[4] He did not confuse pious practices, common among the Jews of his day, with the larger ideal of virtue. He disliked hypocrisy and "show" (Matt. 23:5–8).

From what we can see in the Gospels, Jesus showed many human feelings. He had close friends and spent time with them (John 11:5) and was disappointed when they were less than he had hoped for (Matt. 26:40). He wept when he heard of the death of one of his dearest friends (John 11:33–36).

Jesus urged simplicity. He recommended that people "become like little children" (Matt. 18:3). He liked directness and strived to go beyond details to the heart of things.

Much of Jesus' advice is good psychology, showing that he was a keen observer of human beings. For example, we are told that as you give, so shall you receive (Matt. 7:2) and that if you are not afraid to ask for what you want, you shall receive it (Matt. 7:7).

Jesus also showed an appreciation for nature (Matt. 6:26–30), but not with the detachment of a scientist. He knew scripture well but was not a scholar. As far as we know, he was not a writer and he left behind no written works. He showed almost no interest in money or in business. In adulthood he probably did not travel far from his home territory, between the Sea of Galilee and Jerusalem. While he may have spoken some Greek in addition to his native Aramaic, he did not apparently have much interest in the Greco-Roman culture of his day.

Whether Jesus had a sense of humor is hard to know. The four Gospels never record him as having laughed, thus giving him an image of solemnity. But some of his statements come alive when we see them as being spoken with ironic humor and even laughter (see, for example, Matt. 15:24–28). We do know that although he sometimes sought seclusion, Jesus seems to have enjoyed others' company.

Some people would like to see Jesus as a social activist. He cared about the poor and the hungry, but he apparently was not a social activist of any specialized type. For example, the Gospels do not record words of Jesus that condemn slavery or the oppression of women. Perhaps, like many others of his time, Jesus believed that the world would soon be judged by God, and this may have kept him from working for a specific reform. Instead, he preached basic principles of humane treatment, particularly of the needy and the oppressed (Matt. 25).

For those who would turn Jesus into a protector of the family and family values, the Gospels present mixed evidence. When asked about the divorce practice of his day, Jesus opposed it strongly. He opposed easy divorce because it meant that a husband could divorce his wife for little reason, often leaving her unable to support herself or to remarry. He stated that the marriage bond was given by God (Mark 10:1–12). And at his death, Jesus asked a disciple to care for his mother after he was gone (John 19:26). But Jesus himself remained unmarried. If Jesus had had a wife, that fact almost certainly would have been mentioned somewhere in a gospel or other New Testament book or would have survived in tradition. Moreover, there is no mention anywhere that Jesus ever had children.

Indeed, Jesus spoke highly of those who remained unmarried "for the sake of the kingdom of heaven" (Matt. 19:12).[5] As an intriguing confirmation of Jesus' unmarried state, we now recognize that celibacy was valued by the Essenes, the semimonastic Jewish community of that era, which may have had some influence on him.[6] In any case, Paul—one of the most influential of the early Christians and missionaries—and generations of priests, monks, and nuns followed a celibate ideal that was based on the way Jesus was thought to have lived. In fact, the ideal of remaining unmarried for religious reasons has survived over the centuries and remains influential in several branches of Christianity today.

The Gospels mention Jesus' brothers and sisters (Mark 6:3). Some Christian traditions have held that these relatives were cousins or stepbrothers and stepsisters, hoping thereby to preserve the notion of his mother Mary's permanent virginity. But it is now widely accepted that Jesus had actual brothers and sisters who were children of his mother Mary and of Joseph. When we inspect his relationship to his family members, it seems that Jesus at times was alienated from them. They quite naturally worried about him and apparently wished he were not so unusual and difficult. But Jesus, irritated by their claims on him, said publicly that his real family consisted not of his blood relatives but of all those who hear the word of God and keep it (Mark 3:31–33).

The Two Great Commandments

What then was Jesus' main concern? His teachings, called the Two Great Commandments, combine two strong elements: a love for God and an ethical call for kindness toward others. These commandments already existed in Hebrew scripture (Deut. 6:5 and Lev. 19:18), but Jesus gave them new emphasis by reducing all laws to the law of love: Love God and love your neighbor (Matt. 22:37–40). Being fully aware of God means living with love for all God's children. Like prophets before him, Jesus had a clear vision of what human society can be at its best—a Kingdom of God in which people care about each other, the poor are looked after, violence and exploitation are abandoned, and religious rules do not overlook human needs.

It may be that Jesus' emphasis on morality was tied to the common belief in an imminent divine judgment. This belief seems to have been a particularly important part of the worldview of the Essenes, who thought of themselves as preparing for this new world. It was also essential to the thinking of John the Baptizer (also called John the Baptist), the cousin of Jesus. John preached that the end of the world was near, when God would punish evildoers. As a sign of purification, John immersed his followers in the water of the Jordan River. Jesus allowed himself to be baptized, and when John died, Jesus had his own followers carry on John's practice by baptizing others. Whether Jesus shared John's view of the coming end of the world is much debated. Some passages would seem to indicate that he did (see Mark 9:1, Mark 13:30, Matt. 16:28). This vision of impending judgment is called **apocalypticism.** In the apocalyptic view, the Kingdom of God would soon be a social and political reality.

Whatever Jesus' views about the "end times," his focus was on bringing about the Kingdom of God in each human heart. This would occur when people followed the Two Great Commandments and lived by the laws of love. Some of Jesus' closest followers, as well as others, seem to have expected him to be a political leader, wanting him to lead the fight against the Roman overlords to establish a political kingdom of God. But Jesus refused. The Gospel of John records him as saying, "My kingdom is not of this world" (John 18:36).[7] Instead of political violence, Jesus chose a path of nonviolence.

EARLY CHRISTIAN BELIEFS AND HISTORY

The Book of Acts records that after Jesus' ascension to heaven forty days following his resurrection, his disciples were gathered, full of fear, wondering what to do next. The Book of Acts then tells how the Spirit of God came upon them in the form of fire, giving them courage to spread their belief in Jesus as the Messiah. As they began to preach, they found that people of different countries and languages understood them, even though they did not necessarily speak the same language (Acts 2). This symbolic scene conveys the Christian belief that the spread of the Christian message was guided by God. The Book of Acts sees it as a reversal of the disunity that had afflicted human beings since the emergence of separate human languages (Gen. 11). (The Book of Genesis tells of an ancient time when people had begun to build a tower to reach God. Because God was not too eager for their intrusion, he created separate languages so that people could no longer communicate with each other and thus could not continue building their tower.) This first preaching of the Christian message has been called the Birthday of the Church.

The early Christian message was not complex. It is summarized in the **apostle** Peter's speech in Acts 2, which says that God is now working in a special way; Jesus was the expected Messiah, God's ambassador; and these are the "final days" before God's judgment and the coming of a new world. Early Christian practice required those who believed to be baptized as a sign of rebirth, to share their possessions, and to care for widows and orphans.

The early Christian group that remained in Jerusalem seems to have been almost entirely Jewish and was led by James, called the Just because of his careful observance of Jewish practice. James may have been one of Jesus' real brothers, and, if so, he carried great authority. This Jewish-Christian Church, however, was obliterated by the Roman destruction of the temple and other parts of Jerusalem in 70 C.E. Meanwhile, the non-Jewish, Greek-speaking branch of early Christianity, led by Paul and others like him, began to spread throughout the Roman Empire.

Paul and Pauline Christianity

As the Jewish Christianity of Jerusalem and Israel weakened, Christianity among non-Jews grew because of the missionary Paul. Paul is occasionally called with much seriousness the cofounder of Christianity because of the way that Jesus' teachings and Paul's interpretation of them blended to form a viable religion with widespread appeal. Paul's preaching in Greek, his energetic traveling, and his powerful letters spread his form of belief in Jesus far beyond the limits of Israel.

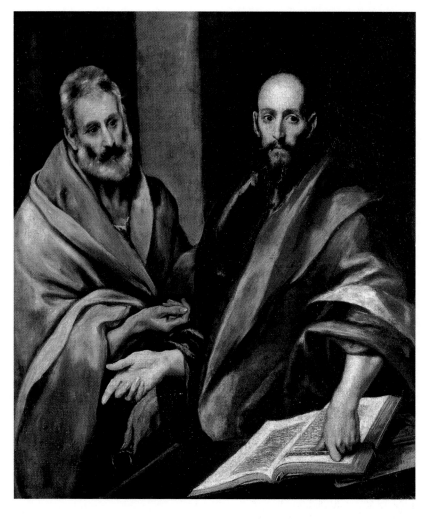

The Apostles Saint Peter and Saint Paul, by El Greco. This famous portrait gives human faces to the mythic figures who did much to spread Christianity and emphasizes Paul's contribution to New Testament writings.

Originally named Saul, Paul was born of Jewish parentage in Tarsus, a town in what is today southern Turkey. He was earnest about traditional Judaism and went to Jerusalem for study. At that time he was a Pharisee. There, he was adamantly opposed to the new "Jesus movement," which he saw as a dangerous messianic Jewish cult that could divide Judaism.

Although he never met Jesus during Jesus' human life on earth, the Book of Acts relates that while Paul was on the road from Jerusalem to root out a cell of early Christian believers, he experienced a vision of Jesus. In it Jesus asked, "Saul, Saul, why do you persecute me?"[8] (See Acts 9, 22, 26.) Temporarily blinded by the vision, Saul went on to Damascus, where he learned more about Jesus and was baptized. He spent several years of study in seclusion, and by the end of this period he became convinced that Jesus' life and death were the major events of a divine plan to renew the world.

Paul discovered his life's mission: to spread belief in Jesus around the Mediterranean, particularly among non-Jews, whom he found more receptive to his message. Many of the Pauline Epistles (or letters) that are part of the New Testament are addressed to regions and towns in Asia Minor (now Turkey) and Greece, which were then part of the Roman Empire. Paul also preached in Rome, where, tradition says, he was executed. (He had hoped to travel as far as Spain, but he probably did not realize that ambition.) His use of the Greco-Roman name Paul, instead of his Jewish name Saul, shows his orientation to the non-Jewish world.

Paul's missionary technique was the same in most towns. If the Book of Acts is correct in its portrayal of Paul's missionary work, he would begin by visiting the local synagogue or other Jewish place of worship (in Philippi, for example, the Jews worshiped beside a river). There, Paul would use Jewish scriptures, such as the Book of Isaiah, to explain his own belief that Jesus was the Messiah whom Jews had long been awaiting. He was unsuccessful with most Jews, who sometimes treated him like a traitor, especially when he said that it was unnecessary to impose Jewish laws about diet and circumcision on non-Jewish converts to Christianity.

Whether all Christians had to keep Jewish religious laws was a subject of intense debate in early Christianity. Christianity had begun as a movement of Jews who believed that Jesus was the expected Messiah, but it soon attracted followers who did not come from a Jewish background. Questions about practice led early Christianity to differentiate itself from Judaism, to define itself on its own terms. Did adult males who wished to be baptized also have to be circumcised? (Needless to say, adult male converts were not always enthusiastic about the practice of circumcision.) Did new converts have to keep the Jewish laws about diet? Did they have to keep the Jewish Sabbath? Should they read the Jewish scriptures?

Some early Christian preachers decided not to impose Jewish rules on non-Jewish converts, while others insisted that all Jewish laws had to be kept. The faction that insisted on upholding all Jewish laws, however, did not prevail. Ultimately, some elements of Judaism were retained and others were abandoned. For example, circumcision was replaced by **baptism** as a sign of initiation, but Jewish scriptures were retained.

These efforts to define what it meant to be a Christian signaled a major turning point in Christianity. Paul's conclusions, in particular, played a prominent role in shaping the movement. His views on the meaning of Jesus, on morality, and on Christian practice became the norm for most of the Christian world. This happened because of his extensive missionary activities in major cities of the Roman Empire and because he left eloquent letters stating his beliefs. Copied repeatedly, circulated, and read publicly, these letters (and letters imitating his thought and style) have formed the basis for all later Christian belief.

Paul's training as a scholar of Jewish law made him acutely aware of human imperfection. He wrote that "all have sinned and fall short of the glory of God" (Rom. 3:23).[9] He came to feel, in fact, that external written laws, such as those of Judaism, hurt more than they helped; the imposition of laws that could not be fulfilled could only make human beings aware of their inadequacies. For him, Jesus came from God to bring people a radical new freedom. Believers would no longer have to rely on written laws or to feel guilty for past misdeeds. Jesus' death was a voluntary sacrifice to take on the punishment and guilt of everyone. Human beings have been **redeemed** from punishment. Believers need only follow the lead of the Spirit of God, which dwells in them and directs them.

Thus Paul preached that it is no longer by the keeping of Jewish laws that a person comes into right relationship (**righteousness**) with God; rather, it is by the acceptance of Jesus, who shows us God's love and who was punished for our wrongdoing. What brings a person into good relationship with God "is not obedience to the Law, but faith in Jesus Christ" (Gal. 2:16).[10]

Despite his newfound freedom, Paul did not abandon moral rules. But his notion of morality was no longer based on laws that are imposed externally—and are kept grudgingly—but rather on an interior force that inspires people to do good deeds spontaneously.

> God's love has been poured into our hearts.
> —Rom. 5:5 [11]

The life of Jesus was for Paul a proof of the love of God, because God the Father had sent Jesus into the world to tell about his love. According to Paul, our awareness of God's love will inspire us to imitate him in a new and loving way of life.

Paul saw Jesus not only as teacher, prophet, and Messiah but also as a manifestation of divinity. For Paul, Jesus was a cosmic figure—the preexistent image of God, the Wisdom of God (see Prov. 8), and the Lord of the universe. Jesus was sent into the world to begin a process of cosmic reunion between God and his human creation. Sin had brought to human beings the punishment of death. But Jesus' death was an atonement for human **sin** (wrongdoing), and the result is that the punishment of death is no longer valid. Jesus' return to life was just the beginning of a process of eternal life for all people who have the Spirit of God within them.

Coptic Christians from Ethiopia carry the gospel book in this Palm Sunday procession at the Church of the Holy Sepulchre in Jerusalem.

The New Testament: Its Structure and Artistry

What we know of Jesus and early Christianity comes largely from the New Testament. The New Testament, which is also at the core of Christianity, is used in religious services, read regularly, and carried throughout the world.

The New Testament is divided into four parts: (1) the Gospels, (2) the Acts of the Apostles, (3) the Epistles, and (4) Revelation. The Gospels describe the life and teachings of Jesus and are traditionally attributed to early followers of Jesus and their disciples—the **evangelists** (Greek: "good news person") Matthew, Mark, Luke, and John. The Acts of the Apostles tells of the initial spread of Christianity, although its historical accuracy cannot be confirmed. The Epistles are letters to early Christians, primarily by Paul. The New Testament ends with a visionary book, Revelation, which foretells in symbolic language the triumph of Christianity. Altogether, there are twenty-seven books in the New Testament.

The New Testament is history, literature, and artistic creation all together. We should recall that because Judaism generally forbade image making, Christians did not produce much art in the first century of the new era, which meant that the aesthetic impulse had to express itself in writing, rather than in painting or sculpture. And because Christianity was not a legal religion until the early fourth century, Christian architecture, which would later flourish in public church buildings, could not easily develop at

The Books of the New Testament

GOSPELS

The Synoptic Gospels

Matthew (75–80 C.E.)

Mark (65–70 C.E.)

Luke (85 C.E.)

John (90–100 C.E.)

HISTORY

Acts of the Apostles (85 C.E.)

EPISTLES

The Pauline Epistles (c. 50–125 C.E.)

Romans

1–2 Corinthians

Galatians

Ephesians

Philippians

Colossians

1–2 Thessalonians

1–2 Timothy

Titus

Philemon

Hebrews

The Catholic (Universal) Epistles (c. 90–125 C.E.)

James

1–2 Peter

1–3 John

Jude

PROPHECY

Revelation (c. 95 C.E.)

first. A great deal of the writing in the New Testament, however, is genuinely artistic.

The New Testament is a mirror image of the books of the Hebrew Bible. For early Christians, the Gospels were considered the new Torah, equivalent to the teachings of Moses. The record of the buildup of the Hebrew kingdom in the historical books (Former Prophets) of the Hebrew Bible is paralleled by the record of the growth of early Christianity in the Book of Acts. The Epistles are the Wisdom Literature of the New Testament. And the Latter Prophets of the Hebrew Bible are paralleled by the Book of Revelation.

All the books of the New Testament were written in Greek, the language of culture and commerce in the classical Mediterranean world in the first century of the common era. The quality of the Greek varies; in the Book of Revelation it is considered rough, while in the Books of Luke and Acts it is considered particularly graceful.

The Gospels   We know of the life of Jesus primarily from the Gospels, which are written in an extremely pictorial way. They are filled with powerful stories and images and have been the source of great inspiration for much later Christian art. Each of the Gospels is as unique in its artistry and style as would be four portraits of the same person painted by four different artists: the resulting portraits would certainly be recognizably similar but also different in such details as choice of background, clothing, angle of perspective, and so on. The same is true of the "portrait" of Jesus that is painted in the Gospels: each gospel writer shows Jesus in a different way.

Because the first three gospels, despite their differences, show a family resemblance in stories, language, and order, they are called the Synoptic Gospels (*synoptic* literally means "together-see" in Greek, implying a similar perspective). The synoptic writers show Jesus as a messianic teacher and healer sent by God. It is generally thought that the Gospel of Mark was written first and seems to be the primary source for the later Gospels of Matthew and Luke. The Gospel of John, however, is recognizably different and relies on its own separate sources.

The Gospel of Matthew is thought to have been written (about 75–80 C.E.) for an audience with a Jewish background. For example, it portrays Jesus as the "new Moses," a teacher who offers a "new Torah." Furthermore, its organization into five thematic sections recalls the five books of the Torah. These five sections are framed by an introductory section (the "infancy account"), which tells of the birth of Jesus, and a conclusion (the "passion account," from the Latin term *passio,* "suffering"), which tells of his death and resurrection. The five middle sections are based on themes, such as God's Kingdom and discipleship. Including the introduction and conclusion, the Gospel of Matthew contains seven parts—and the number seven in Judaism suggests completeness and perfection.

The Gospel of Mark is the shortest and simplest of the four Gospels, which suggests that it is the oldest (around 65–70 C.E.) because it has the least elaboration. This gospel contains no infancy stories and begins instead with the adult public life of Jesus. In the original version, it ends with an account of Jesus' empty tomb. The resurrection account in Mark was added later. Some have argued that pages were lost from the end of the gospel (a view that has virtually no scholarly support), while others hold that the original gospel ended without the resurrection account.

The Gospel of Luke (about 85 C.E.) is filled with a sense of wonder, perhaps because it speaks repeatedly of the miraculous action of the Spirit of God at work in the world. It has been called the women's gospel because of its delicate portraits of Mary (Jesus' mother), her cousin Elizabeth, and other women. This is a gospel of mercy and compassion, with a strong focus on the underdog, which the story of the Good Samaritan illustrates very well (see Luke 10:29–37): A man who has been robbed and beaten is left beside the road to die. People pass by, including officials from the temple in Jerusalem, but they do nothing. At last the beaten man is helped by a Samaritan, a member of a race of people who were looked down upon by many Jews. The audience of the story, probably Greco-Roman, would have appreciated the assurance that in God's sight all people are equal and everyone is a neighbor.

The Gospel of John stands by itself. The time of its writing is difficult to pinpoint. Traditionally, it has been dated quite late—about 90 or 100 C.E.—because of its apparent elaboration of Christian doctrines. But details that might have come from an eyewitness suggest that parts may be earlier. Because it views human life as a struggle between the principles of light and darkness, students of the Gospel of John have wondered whether it was influenced by one or more religious movements of the period, such as the Persian religion of Zoroastrianism, Greek mystery religions, or Gnosticism (see Chapter 8)—a movement that saw human life as a stage of purification to prepare the soul to return to God.[12] The discovery of the Dead Sea Scrolls in 1947 near Qumran has shown many similarities of language between the Gospel of John and certain phrases found in the Qumran literature (for example, "sons of light and sons of darkness"). The Jewish origins of the gospel are now clear.

In the Gospel of John, the portrayal of Jesus is full of mystery. He is the **incarnation** of God, the divine made visible in human form. He speaks in cosmic tones: "I am the light of the world" (John 9:5). "I am the bread of life" (John 6:35). "You are from below; I am from above" (John 8:23).[13] Scholars frequently question the historicity of these exact words, seeing them more as representing the author's vision of the heavenly origin and nature of Jesus.

The central aesthetic image of the gospel is of a ray of divine light that descends like a lightning bolt into our world, passing through and lighting up the darkness, but ultimately returning to its heavenly source and enabling human beings to follow. Most people, the gospel states, do not really understand the truth; but the true nature of Jesus as divine light can be seen by those who have an open heart. Water, bread, the vine, the shepherd, and the door are additional symbols used in the Gospel of John to indicate aspects of Jesus and his meaning for the believer. These symbols later became regular features of Christian art.

Symbols for the four Gospels themselves eventually appeared in manuscript illustrations and other art forms. They derived from a vision of the prophet Ezekiel (Ezek. 1:10). The winged lion represents the Gospel of Mark, since that gospel opens in the desert, the lion's home. The winged ox represents Luke, because that gospel begins in the temple of Jerusalem, where oxen were sacrificed. The winged angel represents Matthew, since that gospel tells of angelic help at the time of Jesus' infancy. The eagle represents the Gospel of John, which begins soaringly with an account of the heavenly origin of God's Word.

The Acts of the Apostles   This book (dating from about 85 C.E.) is really the second part of the Gospel of Luke, and scholars sometimes refer to the two books together as Luke-Acts. It is possible that the single work of Luke-Acts was divided in two in order to place the Gospel of John after the Gospel of Luke. Just as the Gospel of Luke portrays Jesus as moving inevitably toward his sacrifice in Jerusalem, so Acts portrays Paul in a parallel journey to his final sacrifice in Rome. At the heart of both books is a single beautiful image of a stone, dropped in a pond, that makes ever widening ripples. Similarly, the life of Jesus makes ever widening ripples as it spreads in a growing circle from its origin in Jerusalem to the ends of the earth.

The Epistles   The word *epistle* means "letter" and is an appropriate label for most of these works, which were written to instruct, to encourage, and to solve problems. Some epistles are long and formal; a few are brief and hurried. Some epistles seem to have been written to individuals; some to individual churches; and others for circulation among several churches. And it appears that a few of the epistles were originally sermons (for example, 1 Peter) or treatises (Hebrews).

The wide category of works called the Epistles can be divided into two groups. The first includes those books that traditionally have been attributed to the early missionary Paul—the Pauline Epistles. The second group includes all the other epistles—called the catholic ("universal") Epistles because they seem to be addressed to all believers. The genuine Pauline letters are the earliest works in the New Testament, dating from about 50 to 60 C.E. The dating of the other epistles is debated, but some may have been written as late as about 150 C.E.

Of the so-called Pauline Epistles, it is now recognized that several were not written by Paul. Hebrews is most clearly not by Paul, because the Greek is quite different from that of Paul's genuine letters. And because the "pastoral" Epistles (1–2 Timothy and Titus) show strong interest in church organization, they were probably written after Paul's time. The authorship of several others (such as Ephesians, Colossians, and 2 Thessalonians) is less clear and much debated. However, writing in the name of a famous teacher after that person's death was a common practice in the ancient world; it was meant not to deceive, but to honor the teacher.

One factor that has made the Epistles so much loved is their creation of memorable images, many of which come from the Pauline letters. For example, life is compared to a race with a prize given at the end (1 Cor. 9:24); good deeds are like incense rising to God (2 Cor. 2:15); and the community of believers is like a solid building set on secure foundations (1 Cor. 3:9–17). Effective images also appear in the non-Pauline Epistles: new Christians are compared to babies who long for milk (1 Pet. 2:2); and the devil is like a roaring lion, seeking someone to devour (1 Pet. 5:8).

The themes of the Epistles vary widely, but they focus generally on proper belief, morality, and church order. The topics include the nature and work of Jesus, God's plan for humanity, faith, good deeds, love, the ideal marriage, community harmony, Christian living, the conduct of the Lord's Supper, and the expected return of Jesus.

Revelation   This final book of the New Testament was originally written (around 100 C.E.) as a book of encouragement for Christians who were under threat of persecution. Through a series of visions, the book shows that suffering will be followed by the final triumph of goodness over evil.

The last chapters show the descent of the New Jerusalem from heaven and the adoration of Jesus, who appears as a lamb.

The language of Revelation is highly symbolic, deliberately using numbers and images in a way that would make the meaning clear to early Christians but obscure to others. Although long attributed to the author of the Gospel of John, Revelation is plainly—because of stylistic differences—by another hand. Some of its images were seminal to the development of later Christian art—particularly the adoration of the Lamb, the Four Horsemen of the Apocalypse, the Book of Life, and the vision of heaven.

We should recognize that some of the books in the New Testament were not accepted universally for several centuries and that their status involved much debate—Hebrews, James, and Revelation are the most prominent examples. Agreement on which books belonged to the sacred **canon** of the New Testament took several hundred years.[14]

Early Christians continued for the most part to accept and read the Hebrew scriptures, particularly those books—such as Genesis, Exodus, Isaiah, the Psalms, and the Song of Songs—that they saw as foreshadowing the events of Christianity. The New Testament books, therefore, were added to the Hebrew scriptures already in existence. Christians thought of the Hebrew scriptures, which they called the Old Testament, as being fulfilled by the Christian scriptures, which they called the New Testament. The Christian Bible thus includes the Hebrew scriptures and the New Testament.

There is a whole spectrum of ways in which the Christian Bible is read and interpreted by Christians. One approach emphasizes the subjective aspect of the scriptures, interpreting them primarily as a record of *beliefs*. A contrasting approach sees the Christian Bible as a work of objective history and authoritative morality, dictated word for word by God. To illustrate, let's consider how the two approaches interpret the stories of creation in the Book of Genesis. The conservative position interprets the six days of creation and the story of Adam and Eve quite literally, as historical records, while the liberal approach interprets these stories primarily as moral tales that express God's power, love, and sense of justice. There are similar contrasts between the conservative and liberal interpretations of miracles (for example, the virgin birth) in the New Testament.

Interpretation of the Bible causes much controversy among Christians and poses a serious problem for them because it has major implications for their understanding of God's will and their understanding of the life of Jesus. It also affects the question of how strictly to apply rules of conduct, codified (for example) in the Torah and in the Epistles for quite different cultures several thousand years ago. Most contemporary Christians hold a position that is somewhere in between the conservative and liberal poles of the spectrum. They believe that the Bible was inspired by God in its essentials, but they see it as requiring human understanding and thoughtful human interpretation. Interpretation of the Bible has been and still is a major cause of conflict and division in Christianity; however, the debate has also been a great source of intellectual vitality.

Stories from the life of Jesus are often portrayed in art. Above this Spanish church door is a depiction of his birth.

THE ESSENTIAL CHRISTIAN WORLDVIEW

Although the New Testament reveals the essentials of the Christian way of looking at the world, it took four more centuries for the Christian worldview to fully develop. The Christian worldview has remained basically the same since then, with some differences among denominations, although scientific discoveries and biblical studies have begun to stimulate debate and reinterpretation.

God the Father Behind the activity of the universe is an invisible intelligence that created the cosmos as an expression of power and love. Human beings are an important part of the divine cosmic plan. They may not understand the reasons behind specific events in their lives, but there are underlying reasons that only God knows. This creative aspect of God is called Father because of its love and strength, and also because Jesus used this term for God. In art, God the Father is represented by a robed and bearded man, elderly but powerful. Michelangelo's imagery in the Sistine Chapel in Rome is an excellent example.

Jesus Christ Jesus was an ideal human being, but even more he was the visible manifestation of God's gentleness and love. He showed God's power in his healing and his performing of other miracles. Jesus is thus often called the Word and Image of God to emphasize his divine origin and nature. Throughout most of its history, Christianity has emphasized Jesus' divinity. In art, however, especially since the Renaissance, the humanity of Jesus has emerged. Moreover, scholarly interest in Jesus as a human being has grown in recent centuries as a result of insights from psychology and new directions in biblical studies.

Jesus' life as a human being and his death were part of God's plan, and during his earthly life Jesus taught about the mind and will of God. Jesus died voluntarily in order to take upon himself the punishment that justice demands should fall on other human beings who have done wrong. Some forms of Christianity also teach that Jesus' death redeemed a basic sinfulness in humanity, called **original sin,** inherited from Adam by his descendants. After his resurrection and ascension, Jesus continued to live physically beyond the earth. Although he is not physically visible now, he is alive and is therefore worthy of human adoration and prayer. He will return in the future to judge human beings and to inaugurate a golden age.

Jesus has been given many devotional titles. The best-known, *Christ*, means "anointed." (Anointment is a ceremony in which a leader is consecrated with olive oil, a symbol of health and strength.) To refer to Jesus as *Christ*, therefore, means that he is a special leader, sent by God. This title is the Greek equivalent of the Hebrew title Messiah.

The Holy Spirit In Jewish and Christian thought, God makes use of his Spirit to create and vivify. The Gospel of John records Jesus as saying that although he himself must leave the earth, the Spirit of God will come to strengthen his followers (John 16). Traditional Christian belief speaks of the Holy Spirit (or Holy Ghost) as a separate power of God that guides all believers. In art, the Holy Spirit is usually represented as a white dove, appearing over the head of Jesus or coming to Mary at the time of her conception of Jesus.

The Holy Trinity The word **Trinity** does not appear in the New Testament. The term, in common use by the fourth century, expresses the belief that God, although one, has three "persons": Father, Son, and Holy Spirit. (The names of Father, Son, and Holy Spirit do appear together at the end of the Gospel of Matthew.) The doctrine of the Trinity is called a mystery, meaning that it is beyond complete human explanation or understanding, but it hints that the nature of God is essentially a relationship of love.

Angelic forces Invisible personal forces have powerful influence on individuals and on events. They were created by God as intelligent but bodiless beings. Those that are benevolent are called angels ("messengers"), while those that are malevolent are called devils. Devils are said to be rebellious angels led by a former angel, once called Lucifer ("lightbearer") and now called Satan ("adversary"). In art, angels and devils are shown with wings to represent their spiritual nature and ability to appear anywhere.

The Bible God's will and his plan for human beings are expressed in the **Bible,** a collection of books written down by many human beings, all of whom were inspired by God. The first three-quarters of the Christian Bible is made up of the Hebrew Bible (in a somewhat different arrangement than that used by Jews), which Christians adopted and called the Old Testament. The last quarter of the Christian Bible is called the New Testament. It is called "new" because it is thought of by Christians as a new contract or covenant with God and as a fulfillment of the Hebrew scriptures.

Human life Human beings are a major part of God's plan. They are on earth to perfect themselves, to help other human beings, and to prepare for the afterlife. Suffering, when accepted and put to use, allows human beings to grow in virtue, and good people are eventually rewarded in the afterlife. God's Word became embodied in Jesus in order to show human beings God's solidarity with them and to provide a model for how to live in harmony with God's will. Human beings can pray to God the Father and to Jesus to receive help from them.

Life after death Almost universally, Christianity accepts the view of the human being as consisting of two realities: body and soul. After the death of the body, the soul of a person is believed to be rewarded or punished permanently for the way the individual has lived on earth. Heaven, the reward of the good, is the presence of God. In art, heaven is often shown as a place of angels, light, joy, dance, and song. Hell, the punishment of the wicked, is shown as fire, smoke, suffering, and despair. Many Christians believe in a temporary intermediate state of the afterlife, called purgatory, which prepares less worthy but not wicked souls for heaven. At the end of the world, there will be a great public judgment, and at this time the bodies of all who have died will

Inspired by the biblical story of three supernatural visitors who ate with Abraham, this icon by Andrei Rublev portrays the Trinity. ◄

come to life again and be reunited with their souls. The theme of the last judgment is frequently presented in Christian painting, sculpture, and music. Michelangelo, for example, painted it above the altar in the Sistine Chapel, and Mozart portrayed it in his *Requiem.* With a few early exceptions, reincarnation has not been a Christian belief.

These basic beliefs, which allow a great deal of room for individual interpretation, were added to and further refined over many centuries by powerful personalities. Just as Christianity was initially influenced by Paul, it was later influenced by major historical figures, such as Constantine, Benedict, Luther, and others. It has also been much shaped by historical events, whose influence we will now examine.

THE EARLY SPREAD OF CHRISTIANITY

As we have already seen, Christianity is a missionary religion. The Gospel of Mark tells how Jesus sent out his disciples in pairs to preach throughout the land of Israel (Mark 6:7). Then the Gospel of Matthew ends with Jesus' command, "Make disciples of all nations" (Matt. 28:19).[15] In the following discussion, we will see how Christianity spread in stages: from being a Jewish messianic movement in Israel, Christianity spread around the Mediterranean; then it became the official religion of the Roman Empire; and after the end of the empire in the West, Christianity spread to the rest of Europe. (Figure 9.1; later, we will see how it spread to the New World and beyond.) Paul's eagerness to spread his belief in Jesus took him to Asia Minor (Turkey), Greece, and Italy. Tradition holds that Peter, one of the original twelve apostles of Jesus, was already in Rome when Paul arrived and that both Peter and Paul died there under the Emperor Nero about 64 C.E. At that point, early Christianity was only loosely organized, but it was clear even then that some kind of order was necessary. Influenced by the Roman Empire's hierarchical political organization, the Christians developed the monarchical (Greek: "one ruler") model of church organization. Population centers would have a single **bishop** (*episkopos,* "overseer"), who would be in charge of lower-ranking clergy.

In those days, before easy communication, a truly centralized Christianity was impossible. The bishops of the major cities thus played a significant role for the churches of the neighboring regions. Besides Rome, several other great cities of the Roman Empire also became centers of Christian belief—particularly Antioch in Syria and Alexandria in Egypt. Because the bishops of these important cities had more power than bishops of other, smaller cities, four early patriarchates arose: Rome, Alexandria, Antioch, and Jerusalem. The word **patriarch** (Greek: "father-chief") came to apply to the important bishops who were leaders of an entire region.

However, when serious questions arose about doctrine and practice, the early church leaders needed some way to answer them. On the one hand, they could seek a consensus from all other bishops by calling a church

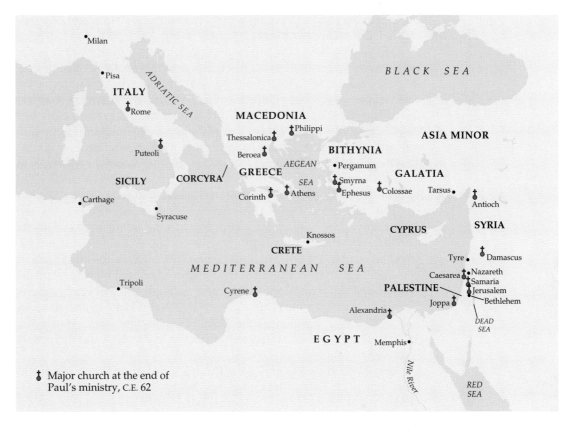

FIGURE 9.1
Historical centers of early Christianity.

council—an approach that the churches in the eastern part of the Roman Empire held to be the only correct practice. On the other hand, they could designate one bishop as the final authority. The bishop of Rome seemed to be a natural authority and judge for two reasons. First, until 330 C.E. Rome was the capital of the empire, so it was natural to think of the Roman bishop as a kind of spiritual ruler, like his political counterpart, the emperor. Second, according to tradition, Peter, the head of the twelve apostles, had lived his last days in Rome and had died there. He could thus be considered the first bishop of Rome. The special title **pope** comes from the Latin word *papa* ("father"), a title now applied exclusively to the bishop of Rome.

The nature of papal authority and the biblical basis for it (Matt. 16:18–19) have been much debated. Nonetheless, this hierarchical model of Christianity became common in western Europe. Although the Protestant Reformation of the sixteenth century, which we will discuss later, weakened the acceptance of papal authority, the Catholic bishops of Rome have continued to claim supremacy over all Christianity, and the Catholic Church maintains this claim. (Critics of this claim see it as exaggerated and call it a form of triumphalism.) Christianity in eastern Europe, however, as we will see later in the chapter, developed and has maintained a different, less centralized form of organization.

The Roman Empire made many contributions to Christianity. In the first two centuries of the common era, Christianity was often persecuted because it was associated with political disloyalty. But when Constantine became emperor, he saw in Christianity a glue that would cement the fragments of the entire empire. In his Edict of Toleration, Constantine decreed that Christianity could function publicly without persecution, and he supported the religion by asking its bishops to meet and define their beliefs. This they did at the first major church council, the Council of Nicaea, held in Asia Minor in 325 C.E. By the end of the fourth century, Christianity had been declared the official religion of the Roman Empire.

Thus the partnership of Christianity with the Roman Empire marked an entirely new phase and a significant turning point for the religion. Christianity formalized its institutional structure of bishops and priests, who had responsibilities within the set geographical units—based on imperial political units—of dioceses and parishes. And because it now had the prestige and financial support that came with government endorsement, Christianity could enthusiastically adopt imperial Roman architecture, art, music, clothing, ceremony, administration, and law. Most important, through church councils and creeds, Christianity clarified and defined its worldview.

Because Christianity in western Europe spread from Rome, much of it was distinctively Roman in origin—especially its language (Latin) and subsequently its alphabet (Roman). Latin was the language of church ritual and scholarship in the West. The Bible had also been translated into Latin. Because of all this, scholars often say that though the Roman Empire disintegrated in the late fifth century, it actually lived on in another form in the Western Church. The emperor of Rome was replaced by the pope, but the language, laws, architecture, and thought patterns of Rome would continue fairly undisturbed in the West for more than a thousand years.

There are some fascinating examples of Roman influence on the Western Church. The typical design for church architecture, for instance, was the basilica—a long, rectangular, pillared building, originally used in Roman times for meetings and judicial proceedings. To the original design, Christian churches added one or two bell towers at the front of the building and a baptismal pool inside or outside. The clothing that Western Church clergy wore during worship ceremonies continued the fashions of the late Roman aristocracy. The undergarment was a long, white linen robe, called the *alb* ("white"), tied by a cloth belt, the *cincture*. Over the alb the priest wore the late-Roman *chasuble* ("little house"), which was originally worn as a poncho.

Roman influence was also incorporated in church ritual. Incense, once used by government dignitaries to purify the air, was used to symbolize prayer and the ascent of the spirit to God. Candles in tall candlesticks, originally carried to light the way for government authorities, were used in services to illuminate readings from scripture. Their light also came to symbolize spiritual understanding and new life. These are just a few of the many elements of the liturgy that were adapted from imperial court ceremony.

INFLUENCES ON CHRISTIANITY AT THE END OF THE ROMAN EMPIRE

As the Roman Empire was collapsing in the West (it would end in 476 C.E.), new sources of energy and direction influenced the next stage in the development of Christianity. Two individuals who had a great impact on Christianity were a bishop, Augustine, and a monk, Benedict.

Augustine

Augustine (354–430 C.E.) was born in North Africa in the later days of the western part of the Roman Empire. Although we think of North Africa today as being quite different and separate from Europe, in Augustine's day it was still a vital part of the Roman Empire.

Augustine's mother, Monica, was a devout Christian, but his father was not. As a result, Augustine was pulled in two directions: he loved the classical non-Christian culture of Greece and Rome, but he was searchingly religious. As a young man, he became involved in a movement called Manicheism (influenced by Zoroastrianism), which saw the world as being strictly divided between the forces of good and the forces of evil. In this view, goodness expressed itself in the mind and spirit, and evil manifested itself in the body and the physical world. Although Augustine eventually rejected this movement, traces of its pessimistic view of the body and the physical world remain in Augustinian Christianity.

As an adult, Augustine left his home in North Africa for Italy to make his name as a teacher of rhetoric. After a short time in Rome, he acquired a teaching position in Milan. He became seriously interested in Christianity as a result of his acquaintance with Ambrose, the bishop of the city, and a priest named Simplicianus. While in his garden one day, Augustine thought he heard a child's singsong voice repeating the phrase, *Tolle et lege, tolle et lege* ("pick up and read").[16] Augustine, who had been studying the letters of Paul, picked up a copy of the epistles that lay on a nearby table. When he opened the book, what he read about the need for inner change pierced him to the heart, and he felt that he must totally reform his life. Augustine sought out Ambrose and asked to be baptized.

Augustine returned to North Africa to devote himself to church work. Ordained first as a priest and then as a bishop, he decided to live a semimonastic life in the company of other priests. Although he had had a child with a mistress before his conversion, Augustine now preached a negative attitude toward sex and marriage that encouraged a growing Christian suspicion of the body. A reversal of those attitudes began only a thousand years later with the thought and work of the reformer Martin Luther, who had been a celibate member of the Augustinian order but who later married and rejected its idealization of celibacy.

In the years after his conversion, Augustine wrote books that were influential in the West for centuries. His *Confessions* was the first real autobiography in world literature, and it details Augustine's growth and conversion. *The City of God* was a defense of Christianity, which some people in his day blamed for the decline of the Roman Empire. *The Trinity* was Augustine's explanation of the relationship between God the Father, Jesus, and the Holy Spirit.

Augustine had incalculable influence on Western Christianity. He was *the* authority in Christian theology until the Protestant Reformation of the sixteenth century and was an influence on Reformation thinkers (such as John Calvin) as well. In short, Western Christianity was basically Augustinian Christianity for over a thousand years.

Benedict and the Monastic Ideal

As mentioned earlier, Augustine, after his conversion, chose to become a priest and live with other priests and monks in a life devoted to prayer and study. This monastic way of life became an important part of Christianity. Although it may be hard to imagine the appeal this kind of life had in the past, it is important to remember that it was not just a religious choice. In the days when life was less secure, when work options were severely limited, and when marriage inevitably brought many children (of whom up to half might die young), the life of a monk offered extraordinary freedom. The monastic life provided liberation from daily cares, leisure to read and write, a wealth of friendships with interesting people, and a strong sense of spiritual purpose and devotion. In fact, monks and nuns are found in many religious traditions today, and monasticism, far from being odd or rare, is a fairly universal expression of piety. Monasticism appears not only in Christianity, but also in Hinduism, Buddhism, and Taoism; and in Judaism, the celibate monastic life was carried on by the Essenes for approximately two hundred years.

A monk is not necessarily a priest, nor need a priest be a monk. A monk is simply any male who chooses to leave society to live a celibate life of religious devotion; a priest is a person authorized to lead public worship. In the early days of Christianity, priests were often married and thus were not monks. However, under the influence of monasticism, Western priests began to be expected to resemble monks and to be unmarried.

Christian monasticism probably sprang from a number of influences. One was the Essene movement and another was the fact that Jesus had never married. We might recall that he praised those who do not marry "for the sake of the kingdom of heaven" (Matt. 19:12).[17] Paul also was without a wife and recommended that state heartily for others (1 Cor. 7:32–35). Another influence came from Egypt, where hermits had been living in caves

Benedict of Nursia's *Rule for Monks* prescribed a simple way of life. Nonetheless, the followers of his *Rule* sometimes became more famous for their libraries than for their simplicity. We see here the library of Saint Gall's monastery in Switzerland. ▶

even before Jesus' time. Contact through trade between India and Egypt had also brought Buddhist monks to Alexandria at the time of Jesus, and their lifestyle might have influenced the Christian monastic movement as well. Lastly, once Christians were no longer being persecuted by the government, becoming a monk or nun was an important way for a Christian to show special religious fervor.

The first Christian monks that we know of are called the Desert Fathers: Paul the Hermit, Antony of Egypt, Paphnutius, Pachomius, Simon Stylite. There were also women (of apparently shady origins) among them: Saint Pelagia the Harlot and Saint Mary the Harlot. These individuals all turned away from the world to live what they thought of as a more perfect type of life. We can criticize the movement for its lack of interest in the needs of the world, but the movement also expressed a longing for the life of paradise—for joy, lack of conformity, individuality, and love of God. In fact, the monastic style of life was often called the life of the angels.

The monastic movement in the West was greatly influenced and spread by a Latin translation of the *Life of Antony*, the Egyptian hermit. The movement took root in southern France and Italy. The real founder of Western monasticism was Benedict of Nursia (c. 480–c. 547 C.E.). Benedict was born into a wealthy family in Rome but fled to live in a cave, where he began to attract attention and followers who joined him in the monastic life. Eventually, Benedict and his followers built a permanent monastery on the top of Monte Cassino, south of Rome. From there the movement spread and became known as the Benedictine order.

> What can be sweeter to us, dear brethren, than this voice of the Lord inviting us? Behold, in His loving kindness the Lord shows us the way of life.
>
> —Saint Benedict's
> *Rule for Monks*[19]

Benedict's influence came from his *Rule for Monks.* Based on the earlier *Regula Magistri* ("rule of the master") and the New Testament, the *Rule* gives advice about how the monks should live together throughout the year. It stipulated that monks should pray each week the entire group of 150 psalms (biblical poems), spend time in manual labor, and remain at one monastery. It opposed excess in any way, yet it was sensible; for example, it allowed wine, because, as it lamented, the monks could not be persuaded otherwise. The *Rule* became the organizing principle for all Western monasticism and is still followed today by Benedictines.[18]

Benedictine monks became the missionary force that spread Christianity—and Roman architecture and culture—throughout western Europe.[20] Among the great Benedictine missionaries were Augustine (d. 604), who was sent as a missionary to England by Pope Gregory I, and Boniface (c. 680–755 C.E.), who spread Christianity in Germany.

From monastic ideals and practices have come several key elements of Christianity. For example, because monastic life segmented time into periods of work and prayer, it hastened the development of the clock. Even more significant was the ideal of celibacy. Living without family ties gave priests, nuns, and monks much mobility and freedom from care, yet it also promoted the ideal of a studious life somewhat detached from the outer world. It fostered the belief that the unmarried, celibate way of life was more perfect than noncelibacy—a belief that would not be seriously challenged in Christianity until the Protestant Reformation of the sixteenth century.

THE EASTERN ORTHODOX CHURCH

Up to this point, we have focused on Christianity in western Europe. But another form of Christianity, known as the Eastern Orthodox Church, developed and spread in Russia, Bulgaria, the Ukraine, Romania, Greece, and elsewhere. These were regions that learned their Christianity from missionaries sent out from Constantinople, which Constantine had established as his imperial capital in 330 C.E.

The word **orthodox** means "correct belief" (from the Greek *orthos,* "straight," and *doxa,* "opinion," "thought"). It is used to designate Christianity in the East because of attempts by that church to define its beliefs and keep them unchanged.

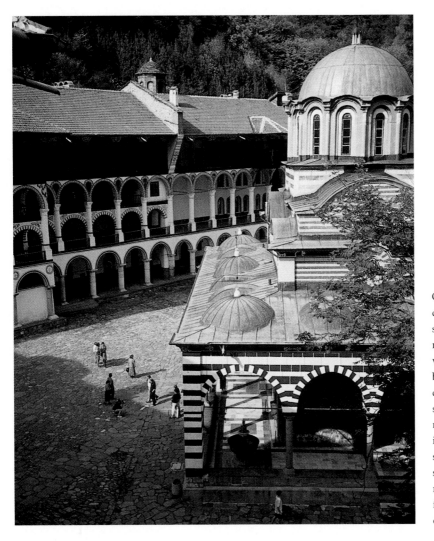

Orthodox churches developed architectural styles that typically were more intimate than the vast spaces of Roman basilicas and Gothic churches. Here we see the spherical domes of the monastery church at Rila in Bulgaria. A common sound within is the scraping of the floor to remove the wax dropped from hundreds of devotional candles.

Early Development

In the earliest centuries of Christianity, when communication was slow and authority was rather decentralized, the bishops of Jerusalem, Antioch, Rome, and Alexandria, though often at odds in their theology, were looked to for guidance and authority. They were eclipsed, however, when a small fishing village named Byzantion (or Byzantium, now the site of Istanbul in Turkey) was renamed Constantinople ("Constantine's city") and was made the new capital of the Roman Empire. The large population of Constantinople, its importance as a governmental center, and its imperial support of Christianity all united to elevate the status of the bishop of Constantinople. Now called a patriarch, he became the most influential of all the bishops in the East.

By moving the capital of the Roman Empire to his new capital at Constantinople, Constantine had hoped to strengthen the empire by placing its capital closer to the northern frontier. From there, soldiers could be sent quickly to protect the frontier against the many barbarian tribes that lived in the north. But Constantine had in fact planted the seeds for an inevitable division of the empire into East and West. Following his death, for a time there were two emperors—of East and West—although this did not work well. The Latin-speaking Western empire, as we have seen, ended in the fifth century, and Western Christianity developed independently. The Greek-speaking Eastern empire, centered in Constantinople, continued until its fall in the Muslim conquest of 1453.

The Orthodox Church is generally divided along ethnic and linguistic lines—Russian, Greek, Serbian, Bulgarian, and Romanian. But all these churches accept the statements of faith of the first seven Church councils, and particularly those of Nicaea (325 C.E.) and Chalcedon (451 C.E.). The Orthodox Church has always held to a decentralized, consensus-based model. Although it does accept in theory that the bishop of Rome has a "primacy among equals," it holds that decisions concerning all of Christianity should be made collectively, in consultation with all patriarchs and bishops. Thus it holds that only church councils are of ultimate authority.

Monasticism in the Eastern Church

As in the West, the monastic movement was an important aspect of the Eastern Church. It spread northward from Egypt and Syria into Asia Minor, where its greatest practitioners were the fourth-century church leaders, Gregory of Nyssa, Gregory Nazianzen, and Basil, who set the pattern for the monastic movement in **Orthodoxy.** Basil (c. 330–379) wrote recommendations for monastic living that are still followed today in Orthodox Christianity. Greek-speaking monks of the eastern part of the Roman Empire carried Christianity from Constantinople into Russia and eastern Europe. The ninth-century brothers Cyril and Methodius are the most famous of these missionary monks, because they are said to be the authors of the Cyrillic alphabet, based on the Greek alphabet, which is in common use in eastern Europe and Russia today.

Eastern Orthodoxy has created great monastic centers. The most famous is on Mount Athos in Greece, the current center of monasticism in this region. All Orthodox branches have sent representatives there for monastic training, and to visit or study there is considered a great honor.[21] Other monastic centers grew up in Romania, Bulgaria, the Ukraine, and Russia. Because Kiev was the city where the first Russians were converted, it took on a role as a traditional religious center, and its monasteries were famous. The northeast section of Romania contains extraordinary monasteries, many of their walls covered with frescoes. Other great centers of monasticism grew up in the regions around Moscow and Saint Petersburg.

Eastern Orthodox Beliefs

Several questions in its early development helped define and differentiate the Orthodox Church. One issue was the nature of Jesus Christ: How is Jesus related to God? Is God the Father greater than Jesus? If Jesus is divine as well as human, is he two persons or one person? And how did Jesus exist before his human life began? Some believers stressed the human nature of Jesus, while others stressed his divinity. The controversies eventually led to the creation and adoption in the fourth century of the Nicene Creed, which is accepted not only by the Orthodox but also by all traditional Western Christians. Because the creed was created to overcome several heresies, it speaks of the nature of Jesus in some detail:

> We believe in one God, the Father Almighty, maker of all things visible and invisible. And in one Lord Jesus Christ, the Son of God, begotten of the Father, the only-begotten; that is, of the essence of the Father, God of God, Light of Light, very God of very God, begotten, not made, being of one essence with the Father; by whom all things were made, both in heaven and on earth; who for us men, and for our salvation, came down and was incarnate and was made man.[22]

Even after the Nicene Creed, one school held that the divine and human natures of Christ were two separate persons, not one. Others argued that Jesus had only one nature, not two. The Council of Chalcedon (in 451 C.E.) declared that Jesus had two natures—divine and human—that were united in only one person.

After the major church councils of the fourth and fifth centuries, certain groups of Christians, with differing views about the nature of Jesus, were labeled heretical. They continued to exist, however, though not in communion with the mainstream. The Nestorian Christian Church, existing primarily in Syria today, continues to teach that Jesus had two separate natures that were not united in a single person. The Coptic Christian Church, existing today primarily in Egypt and Ethiopia, maintains its belief that Jesus had only one nature, which was divine—a belief called *monophysitism*

(Greek: "one nature"). (The views of these two churches exemplify the diversity of thought that existed among Christian groups in the first four centuries.)

It is hard for us today to realize the vehemence with which these doctrinal battles were fought. The questions seem more like arguments over words. But at stake was the important question of the union of God and humanity. The insistence on the union of the divine and the human in Jesus left a strong mystical tendency in the theology of Orthodoxy, which equally emphasizes the potential for union between each human being and God. This mystical tendency expressed itself in every aspect of Orthodoxy—particularly in theology and art—and it still exists today.

Another defining controversy, which has had lasting influence, occurred over the use of images for religious practice. We might recall that one of the Ten Commandments prohibits the making of images (Exod. 20:4), and Jews, as a result, have generally refrained from doing so. Islam has a similar prohibition, as do some forms of Protestant Christianity today. The argument over making and using images reached a crisis when the Byzantine Emperor Leo III (717–740 C.E.) commanded the destruction of all images of Jesus, Mary, and the angels. It is possible that he did this for political as well as religious reasons, hoping to build bridges to Islam. But John, bishop of Damascus, came strongly to the defense of religious images—or **icons,** as they are often called (the Greek term *eikon* means "image"). John argued that images served the same purpose for the illiterate as the Bible did for those who could read. He also argued that God, by becoming incarnate in Jesus, did not disdain the material world. Icons, he said, were simply a continuation of that manifestation of divine love shown through the physical world. Church councils in 787 and 843 affirmed the use of images, thus putting an indelible stamp on the practices of the Orthodox Church, which glories in the veneration of religious images.

Cracks in the unity of Christianity appeared early, but the first great division occurred in 1054, when disagreements brought the bishops of Rome and Constantinople to excommunicate each other. The separation remains today. Although cultural and linguistic differences lay behind the separation, there were small doctrinal differences, as well. The most famous concerned the doctrine of the Trinity. Did the Holy Spirit come from the Father or the Son or from both? The oldest and traditional position held that the Father generated the Spirit, but it became common in the West to attribute the generation of the Spirit to both Father and Son together. The Latin word **filioque** ("and from the Son") was added to creeds in the West from an early period. The Eastern Church rejected the notion as an improper addition to the Nicene Creed and cited it as a main reason for splitting off from the Western Church.

Orthodox belief is, in summary, quite similar to that which emerged in the West and eventually became mainstream Christianity. The doctrinal differences are quite small, but the Orthodox Church differs in emphasis. Western Christianity (Catholicism and Protestantism) has focused on the

Inside a Greek Orthodox Church

In his book *Eleni*, Nicholas Gage documents his childhood in Greece during World War II and the civil war that followed it. His memories include this description of the Greek Orthodox church in his native village of Lia. The church was destroyed by the Nazis.

> For seven centuries the Church of the Virgin had nourished the souls of the [villagers of Lia]. Its interior was their pride and their Bible. No one needed to be literate to know the Holy Scriptures, for they were all illustrated here in the frescoes painted by the hand of monks long vanished into anonymity. In the soaring vault of the cupola, Christ the All-Powerful, thirty times the size of a mortal man, scrutinized the congregation below, his Gospel clasped in his hand. In the spaces between the windows, the prophets and apostles, painted full-length with bristling beards and mournful eyes, made their eternal parade toward the altar.

The villagers of Lia never tired of staring at the wonders of the Church of the Virgin: the walls glowed with every saint and martyr, the twelve feast days, the Last Supper, the life of the Virgin, and as a final warning, on the wall near the door, the Last Judgment, where bizarre dragons and devils punished every sort of evil, with the priests in the front rank of the sinners.

The jewel of the church was the magnificent golden carved iconostasis, the shimmering screen which hid the mysteries of the sanctuary until the priest emerged from the Royal Doors carrying the blood and body of Christ. The iconostasis held four tiers of icons, splendid with gold leaf and jewels, and between the sacred pictures the native wood-carvers had allowed their imagination to create a fantasy of twining vines and mythical birds and beasts perched in the lacy fretwork.[23]

death of Jesus as an atonement for sin. Some scholars have said that focus indicates a more "legal" emphasis: God is viewed as a judge, and punishment and repentance are paramount. Eastern Christianity has put more emphasis on a mystical self-transformation that human beings can experience through contact with Christ. As a consequence, Orthodox Christian art and literature focus less on the crucifixion of Jesus and more on the resurrection.

With the collapse of Communism in Russia and eastern Europe, the Orthodox Church may be expected to regain some of its earlier strength. Although it is unlikely the church will become a state-supported institution as it once was, church buildings that were banned from religious use will increasingly be transferred back to church ownership and restored. It is notable that after the fall of Communism, Russian authorities decided to rebuild the Cathedral of the Holy Savior in Moscow, which Stalin had destroyed and replaced with a swimming pool. The Russian Orthodox Church was also successful in having laws passed in 1997 that affirmed its special status, thereby giving it assistance against the missionary efforts of some other religious groups.

PERSONAL EXPERIENCE: INSIDE THE MONASTERIES ON MOUNT ATHOS

Mount Athos is a finger of rocky land, jutting into the Aegean Sea in the far north of Greece. The peninsula is a monastic state, where monks and hermits have lived for at least a thousand years. Although politically it is part of Greece, it is semi-independent and conducts its own affairs through a monastic council. At the center of the peninsula is a high mountain, and

The Simonopetra
Monastery at Mount
Athos, Greece, sits on a
precipice overlooking
the sea.

scattered around it, close to the shore, are twenty large monasteries. One spring, after getting the proper approvals from the government, I spent the week of Orthodox Easter at Athos.

From Athens I went to Thessaloníki, and from there I took a bus filled with people going back home to celebrate the festival. After staying the night in the village of Ierissos, I got on a ferry boat to Athos before dawn the next morning. In the small capital of Kariaí, where monks run the shops, I received my passport. Over its Greek words was a picture of the peninsula and of Mary, appearing protectively over its mountain. This passport allowed me to stay overnight in any monastery I visited. Each day I walked from one monastery to the next, a trip of about four hours, and was received graciously everywhere. One day I even hitched a ride on the back of one of three donkeys that were being used to carry supplies to several monasteries for the Easter celebration. The two drivers of the animals gave me brandy and Easter candy as the donkeys ambled along. Spring flowers blossomed everywhere next to innumerable streams, which were fed by water from snow melting on the mountain.

The monasteries have high walls designed to protect the monks from the pirates who once roamed the coast. The lower half of each monastery is generally without windows, rising about 70 feet in height, and above that are six or seven stories of wooden balconies. In the center of each monastery is a separate church building in the shape of a Greek cross, usually painted a reddish-brick color. Each arm of the church building is equal in size and is topped by a dome. At the intersection of all the arms is the large, central dome.

I can never forget the services of Easter, celebrated in those mysterious spaces. Being inside the churches felt like being in a group of caves. The floors were covered with sweet-smelling laurel leaves, an ancient symbol of victory. Chandeliers full of candles hung from the domes, illuminating the darkness like stars. For the predawn Easter service, monks used long sticks to make the chandeliers swing back and forth. As the chandeliers swayed, they lit up the murals and mosaics on the walls. I could see images of the prophet Elijah in his cave and the prophet Isaiah speaking with a six-winged angel. Jesus stood on a mountaintop, surrounded by an almond-shaped, rainbow-colored halo. Mary held her child and looked at me serenely. Above them all, an austere cosmic Christ held his hand up in blessing. Below him, each holding a lighted, orange beeswax candle that smelled like honey, the monks sang in Greek, "Christ is risen." In response, the other monks sang, "Truly, he is risen."

CHRISTIANITY IN THE MIDDLE AGES

From its earliest days, when it was just another exotic "Eastern" religion in the Roman Empire, Christianity had made astonishing leaps—at first facing persecution, then becoming the official religion of the empire, and finally rising as *the* religion of all Europe. By 1200 C.E., the only non-Christians in Europe were small communities of Jews, primarily in cities; Muslims in Spain and Sicily; and followers of the old native religions in Scandinavia.

There were many reasons for the growth of Christianity. It preached a gospel of mercy and hope, offered divine help, promised an afterlife, treated the sick, and aided the poor. It taught skills in agriculture and architecture, introduced books, and spread use of the technology of the time. Imagine how a candlelit church at Easter—with its music, incense, candles, jeweled books, glass windows, and gorgeously robed priests—must have appeared to people who were not yet Christians. The effect must have been intoxicating. A legendary story is told of how Russian ministers attended a service at Saint Sophia's Cathedral in Constantinople about 988 C.E. When they returned home to Kiev, they said that during the cathedral service they had not known whether they were on earth or in heaven.

Although many of the religious practices in both Rome and Constantinople were Roman in origin, the two centers, as we have seen, eventually split over differences. The existence of several patriarchates in the East kept any one from becoming a single ruling power. But the Roman Church in the West had no competitors for power in its region and thus grew in authority and strength. The pope, as the bishop of Rome, asserted his dominion over all Christians, an assertion that was not widely opposed in the West until the Protestant Reformation of the sixteenth century. The long-term effect was that the practices of the Roman Church would set the standard for language, practice, doctrine, church calendar, music, and worship throughout western Europe and then beyond.

The growing size of the Christian population and the increasing cultural dominance of Christianity created a climate for a wide variety of religious expression: devotional and mystical movements, the founding of new religious communities, the Crusades and the Inquisition, reform movements, and new interpretations of the Christian ideal. Over time, traditional church authority was questioned, giving rise to a search for new sources of authority.

Christian Mysticism

The word *mysticism* in theistic religions indicates a direct experience of the divine and a sense of oneness with God. Although not always approved of by church authorities, this sort of transcendent experience is nevertheless an important part of Christianity. Christian mystics have spoken of their direct contact with God, sometimes describing a dissolution of all boundaries between themselves and God. Accounts of their experiences speak of intriguing states of consciousness.

The fact that Jesus felt an intimate relationship with God, whom he called Father, provided a basis for seeing Jesus as a role model for all Christian mystics. The Gospel of John, which has a strong mystical tendency, sees Jesus in this light. We also see mysticism in some letters of Paul. For example, Paul describes himself as having been taken up to "the third heaven" and having heard there things that could not be put into words (2 Cor. 12:1–13). Many monks and nuns from the earliest days of Christianity yearned to experience God, and mystical passages are common in the writings of Origen, Augustine, and Gregory of Nyssa.[24] Origen (c. 185–254) was the first of many Christians who would interpret the biblical Song of Songs mystically. He saw the young lover as Jesus and his beloved as a symbol of the mystic, "who burned with a heavenly love for her bridegroom, the Word of God."[25]

Mystical experience was especially prized in the West during the Middle Ages and early Renaissance. Saint Francis of Assisi (1182–1226 C.E.) is possibly the best-known medieval mystic. Originally a playboy and son of a wealthy trader, Francis embraced a life of poverty in order to imitate the life of Jesus. He also showed a joyful love of nature, calling the sun and moon his brother and sister. One of the greatest Christian mystics was Meister Eckhart (c. 1260–1328), a German priest whose description of God as being beyond time and space, as "void," and as "neither this nor that" [26] has captured the interest of Hindus and Buddhists as well as Christians.

Many mystics were women. In recent years, the mystical songs of the medieval Benedictine nun Hildegard of Bingen (c. 1098–1179) have become popular through the availability of numerous recordings. An English-woman, Julian (or Juliana) of Norwich (c. 1342–1416) had a series of mystical experiences, which she later described in her book *Revelations of Divine Love.* She wrote of experiencing the feminine side of God. "God is as really our Mother as he is our Father. He showed this throughout, and particularly when he said that sweet word, 'It is I.' In other words, 'It is I who am the strength and goodness of Fatherhood; I who am the wisdom of Motherhood.' " [27] One of the most famous female mystics was Teresa of Avila (1515–1582), a Spanish nun who wrote in her autobiography about her intimacy with God. A dramatic statue by Bernini at the Roman church of Santa Maria della Vittoria shows Teresa lost in ecstasy.

The mystical approach to Christianity was counterbalanced by Christian attempts to offer reasoned, philosophical discussion of primary beliefs. The religious communities of Franciscans and Dominicans (who will be discussed later in this chapter) were especially active in this work. Thomas Aquinas (1225–1274), a Dominican priest, is the best known. In two major works, the *Summa Theologica* and *Summa Contra Gentiles,* he blended the philosophical thought of Aristotle with Christian scripture and other Christian writings to present a fairly complete Christian worldview. Even he, however, was swayed by the appeal of mystical experience. At the end of his life, after a particularly profound experience of new understanding brought on by prayer, he is said to have remarked that all he had written was "like straw" in comparison to the reality that could be understood directly through mystical experience.

> Lord, make me an instrument of your peace. Where there is hatred, let me sow love; where there is injury, pardon; where there is doubt, faith; where there is despair, hope; where there is darkness, light; and where there is sadness, joy.
>
> —Prayer attributed to Francis of Assisi [28]

The Crusades, the Inquisition, and the Founding of Religious Orders

During the fourth and fifth centuries and thereafter, Christians all over Europe made pilgrimages to visit the lands where Jesus had lived and died, and the Emperors Constantine and Justinian had built churches there to encourage this practice. But Muslims took control of Jerusalem in the eighth century, and by the eleventh century, Christian pilgrimage had become severely restricted. To guarantee their own safety in pilgrimage and their access to the Holy Land, some Europeans felt they had a right to seize control over the land of Israel and adjacent territory. Attempts to take back the Holy Land were called the Crusades—military expeditions that today might be described as religious enthusiasm gone badly astray. At the time, however, the militant, crusading spirit was considered a high religious ideal.

The First Crusade began in 1095, and Jerusalem was taken after a bloody battle in 1099. Europeans took control of Israel and kept it for almost two hundred years, until they lost their last bit of Israel, at Acre near the port of Haifa, in 1291. Looking back on the events, we see the Crusades as a form of early colonialism, stemming from a questionable notion that European Christians had a right to control Israel. The suffering inflicted on Muslims and Christians alike was appalling; and most crusaders died not of wounds but of illness. Many Eastern Christians, too, died at the hands of crusaders because they were mistaken for Muslims. The Crusades also did ideological damage, for they injured Christianity in their promotion of the ideal of a soldier who kills for religious reasons—something quite foreign to the commandments of Jesus. The romantic notion of the Christian soldier, "marching as to war," has remained in some forms of Christianity ever since.

There were, however, unexpected benefits that resulted from Europe's contact with the Islamic Near East. When crusaders returned home from Israel and Syria, they brought back foods and recipes, medicines, Persian carpets, architectural ideas, songs and musical instruments, poetry, and new ways of appreciating life. Because crusaders and pilgrims needed funds while far away from home, methods for transferring money had to be refined. Moreover, hospitals and religious workers to staff them were established along Crusade routes. Thus even though the Crusades did not succeed in their primary purpose, they were valuable for European culture in general and for European religion in particular.

One significant development in Christianity was the founding of non-monastic religious communities, called religious orders. An *order* is a religious organization of men or women who live communal celibate lives, fol-

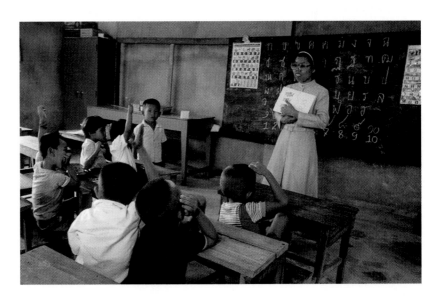

This nun, a contemporary member of a religious order founded in the Middle Ages, engages in the traditional practice of teaching, here with Cambodian refugees in Thailand.

low a set of written rules (Latin: *Ordo*), and have a special purpose, such as teaching or nursing. (It is possible that contact with Sufism may have influenced the emergence of Christian religious orders. Sufism is a general term for mysticism in Islam—see Chapter 10—and it encompasses many orders. Although the Sufi orders have not demanded celibacy, some were semimonastic in lifestyle, with followers living in religious compounds as disciples of a Sufi master.) The most famous medieval order was the Franciscan order, begun by Saint Francis of Assisi, who idealized poverty and worked to help the poor. (Francis may have made contact with Sufism during a visit to Egypt.) Other orders were the Dominicans, who became teachers and scholars, and the Knights Templar, who protected the pilgrimage sites and routes. Most orders also accepted women, who formed a separate division of the order.

In another development of the times, as western Europe became almost fully Christianized, Jews, Muslims, and heretics were considered to be religiously and politically dangerous. The Inquisition received its name from its purpose—to "inquire" into a person's religious beliefs. Church authorities set up an organization to guarantee the purity of Christian belief, and its aim was to root out variant forms of Christianity that were considered "heretical"—divisive and dangerous to public order. Heretics were ferreted out, questioned, tortured, and, if found guilty, burned to death.

The Inquisition was first active in southern France in the twelfth century, and the same inquisitorial procedures were later employed in Spain. We might recall that in the fifteenth century there was a large-scale attempt by Christian rulers to "reconquer" all of Spain. When all Spanish territory had been taken over by Christian rulers, Jews and Muslims were forced to convert to Christianity or to leave Spain, and many did leave, particularly for Morocco and Egypt. Those who stayed had to accept baptism and to publicly practice Christianity. Some of these new converts continued, however, to practice their old religions in private.

The Inquisition attempted to discover who these "false Christians" were, and the religious order of Dominicans was especially active in this pursuit. Tomás de Torquemada (c. 1420–1498), a Spanish Dominican, was appointed first inquisitor general by King Ferdinand and Queen Isabella in 1483 and grand inquisitor by Pope Innocent VIII in 1487. As he oversaw the Inquisition in Spain, he became notorious for his cruelty. The Reconquista, as the Christian movement was called, took over all Spanish territory in 1492. After this date, the Inquisition acted as a religious arm of the Spanish government both in Spain and in Spanish colonies in the New World.

The Late Middle Ages

The complete ousting of the crusaders from Israel (1291) marked the end of the Christian optimism that had been typical of the earlier Middle Ages. The loss was widely viewed as some kind of divine punishment for religious laxity. The feeling of pessimism deepened a half century later, when an epidemic of bubonic plague—called the Black Death for the black swellings that appeared on people's bodies—began to spread throughout Europe. The first major outbreak of disease occurred largely between 1347 and 1351. Beginning in France and Italy, as the plague swept throughout western Europe, whole towns were emptied, with no one left to bury the corpses. Priests often fled, refusing to attend the dying—a neglect which brought the church into great disrepute. Between a quarter and a third of the population died, and the plague continued to break out in many places for years afterward.

We now know that the disease was bacterial, caused by a bacillus found in fleas, which carried the disease to human beings. Rats that carried the fleas had arrived on ships that came from the Black Sea to ports in southern France and Italy. But the medical origin of the plague was not understood at the time, and people saw it instead as punishment from God. Some blamed the Jews, who were accused of poisoning wells or of angering God by their failure to accept Christianity. Others saw the plague as punishment for the lax behavior of church authorities.

It is natural that a successful institution will take its authority for granted. By the late Middle Ages it was common for bishops and abbots to be appointed to their positions purely for financial or family reasons. Some even lived away from their monasteries or dioceses. Indeed, for most of the fourteenth century, the popes lived not in Rome but in southern France. This papal dislocation led to a weakening of church authority, until finally two and then three factions claimed the papacy.

The Middle Ages saw many changes in European society, as travelers to the Middle East and Asia returned home with new goods and ideas. New forms of trade and economy developed. Imagination and independence grew.

By far the greatest development of the late Middle Ages was the invention of printing with moveable type. Before that time, all writing had to be done laboriously by hand, making the Bible and other works available only to scholars and clergy. Although the first book to be printed (c. 1450) was a Latin Bible, translations were soon necessary. Printing also made possible the spread in modern languages of new and revolutionary ideas.

THE PROTESTANT REFORMATION

As institutions age, they naturally lose some of their earnestness and purity, prompting attempts at reform. The Eastern Church, weakened by the Muslim invasions and its own decentralization, had less need for reform. In contrast, the Roman Church in the West had been enormously successful, spreading throughout western Europe and building a centralized power structure that had not been seriously challenged in the first thousand years of its growth.

Printing made biblical texts readily accessible. Two pages of a Gutenberg Bible are shown above.

The Western Church establishment had become wealthy from bequests of the rich. To endow monasteries with land and money was a natural form of piety, which aristocrats hoped would benefit them in the afterlife. Collections in local parish churches also generated funds, some of which were sent to Rome, just as they are today.

By the late medieval period, people resented the lands and wealth of the church and its monasteries. Thoughtful people also were troubled by what seemed to be the multitude of superstitious practices—particularly the veneration of relics of saints. Significant relics included the bones of saints and any object supposedly touched by Jesus or Mary or the saints, such as Mary's veil and the nails used at Jesus' crucifixion. Many of these items were not genuine.

Other events also were leading the world in the direction of religious exploration and change. The fall of Constantinople to Muslim forces in 1453 drove Greek scholars to live in Italy. Their scholarly presence and their books sparked great interest in Greek language, which contributed to an examination of the Gospels in their original language. The dissemination of printed Bibles encouraged anyone who could read to turn to the Bible—rather than to a priest, bishop, or pope—as the ultimate religious authority.

Earlier attempts at reform had not been successful. John Wycliffe (c. 1320–1384), an English priest, preached against papal taxation and against the special authority of the clergy. He labeled as superstition the doctrine of transubstantiation (the notion that the sacrament of bread and wine, when blessed at the Mass, literally turned into Jesus' flesh and blood). He also oversaw the first translation of the Latin Bible into English. Accused of heresy by Pope Gregory XI in 1377, he was forbidden to teach. He died a natural death by stroke, but after the Council of Constance (1414–1418) condemned his teachings, his body was dug up and burned and the ashes were thrown into a river.

Jan Hus (c. 1369–1415), rector of the University of Prague, continued many of Wycliffe's criticisms. Excommunicated in 1410 and condemned by the same council that condemned Wycliffe, Hus was burned to death at the stake in 1415.

Reform was inevitable. Soon another great turning point would occur in Christianity. The north and south of Europe would painfully split along religious lines, and Western Christianity would divide into Protestantism and Catholicism.

Martin Luther

Martin Luther (1483–1546), a German priest, was the first reformer to gain a large following and to survive, and his success encouraged others who also sought reforms. Their joint influence ultimately created the Protestant branch of Christianity, so called because the reformers protested some of the doctrines and practices of the Roman Church.

The psychologist Erik Erikson paints a riveting portrait of Martin Luther in his book *Young Man Luther*.[29] Luther, convinced of his own personal sinfulness, entered religious life (the Augustinian order) as the result of a vow made to Saint Anne (the supposed mother of Mary) during a lightning storm. To enter religious life, he had to disobey his father, who wanted him to be a lawyer. His difficult relationship with his father, Erikson argues, colored Luther's understanding of God. After ordination as a priest, Luther still did not experience the inner peace he had expected.

Luther became a college professor in the university town of Wittenberg, teaching courses in the Bible, with a specialty in the New Testament—particularly the Pauline Epistles. At a time when he felt overwhelmed by his own sinfulness, he was struck by Paul's words at the beginning of the Epistle to the Romans: "The just shall live by faith" (Rom. 1:17).[30] Luther admitted that upon reading this epistle he felt as if he had been "born anew," and sensed that now "the gates of heaven" were open to him.

What Luther came to understand was that no matter how great the sinfulness of a human being, the sacrifice of Jesus was enough to make up for all wrongdoing. An individual's good deeds could never be enough, but to become sinless in God's eyes, a person could rely on the work of Jesus.[31]

Emphases of Protestant Christianity

Protestantism seeks to find—and live by—what is essential to the Christian experience. It places great emphasis on the individual's own ability to establish a personal relationship with God.

Return to simple Christianity The New Testament outlines the essentials of Christianity, both in belief and in practice. Christians should imitate the early tradition and avoid unnecessary, later alterations.

Centrality of Jesus Jesus is the one way to God the Father. Devotion to Mary and the saints has distracted believers from their faith in Jesus and should be deemphasized or even abandoned. Trust in relics of Mary and the saints borders on superstition.

Guidance of the Bible The Bible is a divinely inspired guide for human lives. Believers should read it regularly, and ministers should explain it in sermons.

Importance of faith One's deeds alone cannot bring salvation. Faith in Jesus brings righteousness in God's eyes.

Direct relation to God Although ministers assist in religious services, they are not necessary as intermediaries between God and the individual. Every individual has a direct relationship with God.

Individual judgment The Holy Spirit helps each believer make decisions about the meaning of biblical passages and about how to apply Christian principles to everyday life. (The ability of each individual to question and rethink accepted interpretation is sometimes called the **Protestant Principle.**)

Luther also recognized the importance of his reading of the Bible as an important factor in receiving his new spiritual insight. Luther's main focuses have sometimes been summarized by the Latin phrases *sola scriptura* ("scripture alone") and *sola fides* ("faith alone").

Luther's teaching came at a time when the papacy was asking for contributions for the building of the new Saint Peter's Basilica in Rome. In return, donors were promised an **indulgence,** which would shorten the time after death that an individual would spend in purgatory, a preparatory state before the soul could attain heaven.

To show his opposition and to stir debate, Luther posted his demands for change and reformation in the form of *Ninety-Five Theses* on the door of the main church of Wittenberg in 1517. Despite reprimands, Luther was unrepentant, and in 1521 Pope Leo X excommunicated him. Luther's efforts at reform might have failed—and he also might have been burned at the stake—if he had not received the support of and been hidden by the prince of his region, Frederick III of Saxony. During this period of refuge, Luther translated the New Testament into German, and he soon translated the Old Testament, as well. Luther's translation of the Christian Bible was to become for the Germans what the King James Bible became for the English-speaking world—it had an incalculable influence on language and culture.

After his insight into the sufficiency of faith, Luther firmly rejected celibacy and the monastic style of life. He married a former nun, Katharina von Bora, had children, and opened his home to a wide range of visitors interested in his work on church reform.

Forms of Protestantism

The ability of individuals to interpret the Bible for themselves is an essential aspect of Protestant Christianity. This so-called Protestant Principle has been responsible for the generation of several branches of Protestantism.

Lutheranism   Martin Luther's version of the reform emphasized faith and the authority of the Bible. To encourage greater participation, Luther called for services to be conducted in German as well as in Latin. He also wrote hymns that were to be sung in German by the entire congregation, thus beginning the strong musical tradition in Lutheranism, which has particularly valued choral and organ music. (Johann Sebastian Bach [1685–1750] is the greatest composer of this tradition.)

Luther's version of the Protestant reform spread throughout central and northern Germany and then into Scandinavia and the Baltic states. It came to the United States with German and Scandinavian immigrants, who settled primarily in the upper Midwest. Over the years, Lutheranism has retained Luther's original enthusiasm for the Bible, a trust in God, and excellent church music.

Calvinism   Once the notion of reform was accepted, it was adopted and reinterpreted by others who also sought change. Among them was the French theologian John Calvin (1509–1564). Calvin's thought was less optimistic than Luther's because he saw human nature as being basically sinful and almost irresistibly drawn to evil. He also took the notion of God's power to its logical end: if God is all-powerful and all-knowing, then God has already decreed who will be saved and who will be damned (a doctrine known as **predestination**). One's deeds do not cause one's salvation or damnation; rather, they are a sign of what God has already decreed.

Calvin's view of God as judge may have been influenced by his study of law at the University of Paris, where he first began to push for reform. When only 26, Calvin published a summary of his ideas in *The Institutes of the Christian Religion.* Persecuted in France, he was forced to flee and eventually settled in Geneva, Switzerland. Because of the work of the reformer priest Huldrych Zwingli (1484–1531), the Swiss were already considering reforms. Calvin's great success in Geneva made the city a center for the expansion of the reform movement.

Where Luther had allowed much latitude in preserving elements of the Mass and other traditional Catholic practices, Calvin had a more austere view. Looking exclusively to the Bible for what might be approved, he encouraged the removal of all statues and pictures from the churches and the adoption of a style of congregational singing that had no organ accompaniment. The focus of the Calvinist service was on the sermon.

Ministers were not appointed by bishops—there were to be none in Calvinism—but were "called" by a council from each congregation. This practice, being highly democratic, threatened the political and religious leaders of the time, and believers were often forced into exile. Among such believers were the Puritans, who immigrated to New England, and the Huguenots (French Protestants), who were forced out of France in 1685 and settled in several areas of North America. Calvinism spread to Scotland through the efforts of John Knox (1514–1572), who had studied with Calvin in Geneva. It was in Scotland that a church structure without bishops was refined, providing a pattern for Calvinism in other countries. Calvinism ultimately became important in Holland, Scotland, Switzerland, and the United States. The Presbyterian Church is the best-known descendant of Calvinism. It gets its name from the Greek word *presbyter,* meaning "elder" or "leader."

The Church of England (Anglican Church)   A third form of Protestantism, which originated in England under King Henry VIII (1491–1547), unites elements of the Reformation with older traditional practices. Some see the Anglican Church as a compromise between Catholicism and Protestantism. Perhaps it is a compromise, because it was born not so much out of Henry's interest in reform as it was out of his interest in marriage. His story is complicated. Henry's older brother Arthur had been married for political reasons to Catherine of Aragon, a Spanish princess. When Arthur died, Henry was forced to marry Catherine in order to continue the political relationship with Spain. This marriage produced a daughter but no living male heir—to Henry's terrible disappointment. When Henry fell in love with Anne Boleyn, a lady-in-waiting at the court, he sought to annul his first marriage. The pope and papal bureaucracy refused.

As a result, Henry began to dismantle papal power in England. He dissolved the monasteries and cleverly gave their lands to nobles and friends—an action that strengthened their loyalty to him. Henry had parliament declare that the "bishop of Rome" had no jurisdiction in England and that he, as the monarch, was the head of the Church in England. He maintained the traditional church structure of bishops and priests. (It is called an episcopal structure, from the Greek word *episkopos,* meaning "bishop" or "overseer.") He also kept the basic structure of religious services much as before, although they were conducted in English. He even maintained priestly celibacy, although this was repealed soon after he died. As a concession to reformers, Henry had an English translation of the Bible placed in each church for all to read. The Church of England had a shaky beginning, but Henry's daughter Elizabeth, when she finally became queen, established it firmly.

The Church of England produced several works of great significance in its first century of existence. *The Book of Common Prayer,* containing all the major prayers for church use, was issued in 1559. Its rhythmic sentences set a standard by which other works in English have been measured. Throughout the sixteenth century, composers were commissioned to write choral music in English for religious services. The result was a wonderful body of music, still in use today (a description appears later in the chapter). In 1604 the King James Bible was published, named for its sponsor, James I, who had succeeded Queen Elizabeth I. It became the single greatest influence on the English language.

The Church of England has been deliberately tolerant of a wide spectrum of interpretation and practice. Some churches have buildings and services of great simplicity (their style is called Low Church), while in others the worshiper will find incense, statues of Mary, and stately ritual (called High Church). Furthermore, in spite of great opposition, the Church of England has recently accepted the ordination of women to the priesthood and episcopate.

Sectarianism   The powerful notion that every individual can interpret the Bible has encouraged—and still encourages—the development of an abundance of independent churches or sects. Most have been formed by a single, charismatic individual, and many have been small. Some have interpreted the Bible with literal seriousness, thus producing special emphases—among them, the rejection of the outside world and its technology; the adoption of extremely simple lifestyles, total pacifism (rejection of war and violence), or complete celibacy; and the expectation of the imminent end of the world. As a loosely defined group, this branch of Protestantism is called Sectarianism. Here, only the most prominent sects are mentioned.

The Anabaptists (meaning "baptize again"), a Swiss movement that developed during the sixteenth century, stressed the need for believers to be baptized as a sign of their inner conversion—even if they had been baptized as children. Their worship was simple. From this general movement arose several Mennonite and Amish sects, some communities of which maintain a simple, agricultural lifestyle without the use of cars or electricity. The Baptists, a denomination that began in England, have grown up as a major force in the United States. Baptists espouse some of the Anabaptist principles, including the need for inner conversion, baptism of adults only, simplicity in ritual, independence of personal judgment, and freedom from government control.

The Quakers were founded by George Fox (1624–1691) in England. Those who came to the United States settled primarily in Pennsylvania. Quakers are ardent pacifists; they have no clergy; and they originated a type of church service conducted largely in silence. Their official name is Society of Friends, but the name Quaker came about from George Fox's belief that people should "quake" at the Word of the Lord.

The Shakers grew out of the Quaker movement. They were begun by an Englishwoman, "Mother" Ann Lee (1736–1784), who came from England to New York State. The Shakers accepted both women and men but preached complete celibacy. Their religious services were unusual because they included devotional dance, from which their name derives. Settling in New York State and New England, the Shakers founded communities primarily dependent on farming. Although there are only a handful of Shakers today, their vision of Christian simplicity lives on in their architecture and furniture, which is unadorned but elegant.

The Pentecostal movement, although it has ancient roots, has been especially active since the beginning of the twentieth century. It emphasizes the legitimate place of emotion in Christian worship. At such services one might encounter "speaking in tongues" (*glossolalia*), crying, fainting, and other forms of emotional response, which are thought of as gifts brought by the presence of the Holy Spirit.

The Methodist Church at first was simply a devotional movement within the Church of England. It was named for the "methodical" nature of prayer and study followed by Charles Wesley (1707–1788) and his followers at Oxford. But under the strong guidance of John Wesley (1703–1791), Charles's brother, Methodism took on an independent identity. Charles Wesley wrote more than six thousand hymns, which helped spread the movement.

THE DEVELOPMENT OF CHRISTIANITY FOLLOWING THE PROTESTANT REFORMATION

The Catholic Reformation (Counter Reformation)

Although the Protestant Reformation was a powerful movement, Catholicism not only withstood its challenges but also grew and changed in response to it. That response, in the sixteenth and seventeenth centuries—called the Catholic Reformation, or the Counter Reformation—strongly rejected most of the demands of the Protestant reformers. Protestants rejected the authority of the pope; Catholics stressed it. Protestants demanded the use of native languages; Catholics retained the use of Latin. Protestants emphasized simplicity in architecture and music; Catholics created churches of flamboyant drama.

Nevertheless, the Catholic Church recognized that some institutional reform was necessary. The church's first response was a long council, held in the northern Italian town of Trent between 1545 and 1563. The council set up a uniform seminary system for the training of priests, who had sometimes in the past learned their skills simply by being apprenticed to older priests; it made the Roman liturgy a standard for Catholic services; and it defended traditional teachings and practices (see the box "Emphases of Catholic Christianity"). This council took a defensive posture that erected symbolic walls around Catholic belief and practice.

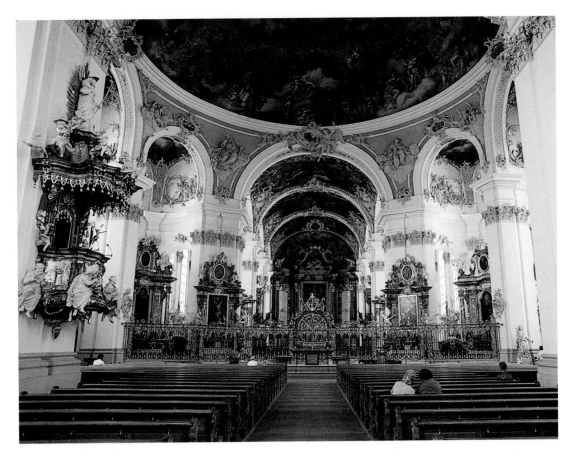

Baroque church interiors, here represented by Saint Gall in Switzerland, are seen by some to celebrate the triumphalism of Roman Catholicism after the Protestant Reformation.

Several new religious orders came into existence to defend and spread Catholic teaching, of which the most influential was the Society of Jesus, or the Jesuits. The Spanish founder of the Jesuits, Ignatius of Loyola (1491–1556), was a former soldier, and with this background, he brought a military discipline to the training and life of his followers. Ultimately, Jesuits made a lasting contribution through their establishment of high schools and colleges for the training of young Catholics, and many continue this work today.

Because of the varied interpretations of the Bible and of Christian doctrine that began to emerge as a result of the Protestant Reformation, a major part of the Catholic Church's response was to stress discipline and centralized authority. The First Vatican Council (1870) continued this emphasis when it declared that the pope is infallible when he speaks officially (that is, *ex cathedra*, "from the chair" of authority) on doctrine and morals.

The International Spread of Christianity

The New Testament contains the injunction to "baptize all nations" (Matt. 28:19). As a result of this order, powerful missionary and devotional movements arose within all branches and denominations of Christianity (Figure

Emphases of Catholic Christianity

Catholicism accepts all traditional Christian beliefs, such as belief in the Trinity, the divine nature of Jesus, and the authority of the Bible. In addition, particularly as a result of the Protestant Reformation, it defends the following beliefs and practices.

Importance of good works The Christian must accompany faith with good works to achieve salvation.

Value of tradition Along with the Bible, church tradition is an important guide for belief and practice.

Guided Interpretation of the Bible Individual interpretation of the Bible must be guided by church authority and tradition.

Hierarchical authority The pope, the bishop of Rome, is the ultimate authority of the church, and bishops are the primary authorities in their dioceses (regions of authority).

Veneration of Mary and the saints Believers are encouraged to venerate not only Jesus but also Mary and the saints, who reside in heaven. As an aid to faith, believers may also honor relics (the bodies of saints and the objects they used while alive).

Sacraments There are seven **sacraments** (essential rituals), not just two—as most Protestant reformers held. They are baptism, confirmation, the **Eucharist** (the Lord's Supper, Mass), matrimony, holy orders (the ordination of priests), reconciliation (the confession of sins to a priest), and the anointing of the sick (unction).

9.2). Over the last five hundred years, these movements have spread Christianity to every continent and turned it into a truly international religion.

An early wave of missionary work was conducted by the Catholic Church. Wherever Spanish, Portuguese, and French colonists took power, their missionaries took Catholic Christianity. The Jesuit Père Jacques Marquette (1637–1675) propagated Catholicism in Canada and the Mississippi River valley, and the Franciscan Padre Junípero Serra (1713–1784) spread it

FIGURE 9.2
Branches and denominations of Christianity.

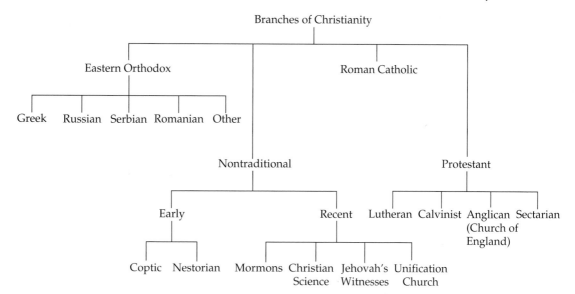

Branches of Christianity

Eastern Orthodox — Greek, Russian, Serbian, Romanian, Other

Roman Catholic

Nontraditional — Early (Coptic, Nestorian), Recent (Mormons, Christian Science, Jehovah's Witnesses, Unification Church)

Protestant — Lutheran, Calvinist, Anglican (Church of England), Sectarian by establishing missions in California. In Latin America, the Christianity that Jesuit and Franciscan missionaries introduced frequently mixed with native religious customs to produce unique hybrids. In Asia, early Catholic missionaries at first had little success. Jesuit missionaries were sent out from such missionary centers as Goa in India and from Macau in China to convert the Chinese and Japanese. The Spanish Jesuit Francis Xavier (1506–1552) and Italian Jesuit Matteo Ricci (1552–1610) were industrious, but their attempts in China and Japan were repressed by the government authorities, who wisely feared that conversion would bring European political control. Catholicism was, however, successful in the Philippines and Guam, where Spanish colonization contributed to the widespread acceptance of the religion. In the nineteenth century, French Catholic missionaries worked in Southeast Asia and the Pacific region. Tahiti, after being taken over by the French, became heavily Catholic; and Vietnam, too, now has a sizable Catholic population. In sub-Sahara Africa, wherever France, Portugal, and Belgium established colonies, Catholicism also became common.

Protestant Christian missionaries and British conquests also spread their faith throughout the world. Protestant settlers who came to North America represented the earliest wave. The Church of England (Anglican Church) traveled everywhere the English settled—although in the United States at the time of the American Revolution the name of the church was changed to the Episcopal Church, to avoid the appearance of disloyalty to the new United States. The Anglican Church is widespread in Canada, Australia, New Zealand, and other former British colonies. It is also a major force in South Africa—as the work against apartheid (the former government policy of racial segregation) by Anglican Bishop Desmond Tutu has shown.

Methodism in the United States was highly successful in reaching people who lived far from the large cities. Methodist and Presbyterian missionaries were active in spreading their vision of Christianity even further afield, particularly to Asia and the South Pacific. About a quarter of South Koreans are now Christian, and Protestant Chinese have been prominent in the political life of Taiwan.

Missionaries spread Orthodox Christianity across Russia to Siberia and even into Alaska (a Russian Orthodox church is located in Sitka). The Orthodox Church also spread to North America through emigration from Russia, Greece, and eastern Europe.

Christianity has been less successful in China, Japan, Southeast Asia (except Vietnam and the Philippines), the Middle East, and North Africa. But elsewhere it is either the dominant religion or a powerful religious presence.

Nontraditional Christianity

Because Christianity is a fairly old religion and has flourished in cultures far from where it originally developed, it has produced some significant offshoots. These denominations differ significantly from traditional Christianity, and although they are not usually considered a part of the three traditional branches of Christianity—Roman Catholic, Protestant, and Eastern Orthodox—they all sprang from Protestant origins. Although mainstream Christian churches often do not accept them fully, these offshoots manifest many Christian elements. Those that are growing rapidly present a special challenge to traditional Christianity.

Church of Jesus Christ of Latter-day Saints   The Mormon Church is the largest branch of this religion, with its headquarters in Salt Lake City, Utah. (A much smaller branch, which does not refer to its followers as Mormons, is the Reorganized Church of Jesus Christ of Latter-day Saints.) The Latter-day Saint movement was begun by Joseph Smith (1805–1844), an American who is believed to have had special revelations that began in 1820. According to tradition, the *Book of Mormon* was divinely inspired and is a translation of golden plates to which Smith was led by an angel in New York State. The *Book of Mormon* tells of the history of descendants of Israelites who came to North America. It also describes the ministry of Jesus in North America after his resurrection. Joseph Smith organized a group of believers, but he and his followers were continually persecuted. In 1844, Smith was shot and killed in Illinois by a non-Mormon mob.

Led by Brigham Young (1801–1877), early church members settled in what is now the state of Utah in order to practice their religion freely. A split occurred in the midnineteenth century, which produced the Reorganized Church, centered in Independence, Missouri.

The Latter-day Saints Church accepts the Christian Bible, along with its own scriptures, as being sacred. It combines elements of Judaism and traditional Christianity with its own beliefs. The church initially accepted polygamy, such as is found in the biblical stories of Abraham and others, although that custom is no longer allowed. The church has a priesthood: males may join the priesthood of Aaron and then that of Melchizedek. It also teaches that God the Father has a physical body, just as Jesus does. Although Sunday services are conducted in local churches ("stakes"), regional temples have been constructed for the performance of some special rites—among which are proxy baptisms for the dead and a marriage ceremony that "seals" the couple and their children together for all eternity. Church members are forbidden to use tobacco, caffeine, or alcohol. And young males go on "mission" for two years, seeking converts. In Utah and some other western states, Mormons are a major religious force.

Mormon temples are architecturally interesting in that they are deliberately unlike older styles, such as Romanesque or Gothic or Byzantine. Instead, the building designs reflect an imaginative style that has been called Temple Revival. Elements of the style include large, flat building surfaces that are ornamented with elaborate grillework and decorated with tall, narrow spires. The temples in Salt Lake City and Los Angeles are good examples. Mormon art inside the temples and other public buildings tends to be realistic and representational, showing Jesus and scriptural scenes. Mormonism also has a strong choral tradition. Hymns and solo works are sung at services, and the Mormon Tabernacle Choir uses a traditional Christian repertory of hymns, oratorios, and organ music.

Christian Science and the Unity Church   The Christian Science, Unity, and other similar churches emerged in England and the United States in about 1880, coming from a larger movement called New Thought. The movement emphasizes positive thinking and the ability of the individual to grow through a belief in inner power. The use of positive affirmations is a technique that these groups share.

Christian Science, founded in 1879, has its mother church in Boston. The founder, Mary Baker Eddy (1821–1910), began the church following her recovery from a serious illness, a recovery she attributed to divine power. The book *Science and Health with a Key to the Scriptures* gives her interpretation of biblical passages and is read along with the Bible in Christian Science services. Eddy emphasized the healing role of Jesus, and her church maintains that not only negative emotions but also physical sicknesses are the result of an inadequate understanding of the divine nature within each individual. Healing comes when the individual discovers that physical and mental evils are actually illusions. Christian Scientists generally avoid hospitals and doctors and instead seek healing through "practitioners" who visit and pray with the ill. The Christian Science Church supports "reading rooms" in urban locations, where passersby can acquaint themselves with the literature and religious views of the church.

Unity Church (or the Unity School of Christianity) is another religious denomination that emerged, like Christian Science, from the New Thought movement. It puts little stress on traditional Christianity, although it makes use of some of its language and practice. The Unity Church seeks wisdom in every religious tradition, and its groups often invite members of other religions to speak at their meetings. Services avoid mention of sin or punishment and instead rely on inspirational talks, peaceful music, and guided meditations to help individuals discover the hidden possibilities within themselves.

Jehovah's Witnesses   The Jehovah's Witnesses, founded by Charles T. Russell (1852–1916), are an apocalyptic group that puts the Bible, literally interpreted, at the center of belief and practice. The Witnesses hold that God (Jehovah), after punishing evildoers and nonbelievers with annihilation, will create in the near future a paradise-like world for virtuous believers. At one time the Witnesses thought this event would occur on earth in 1914, but they argue now that the process only began in 1914. Strongly influenced by the Book of Revelation, the members believe that 144,000 people of the past and present will be taken to heaven as a special reward, while all other good people of the past will rise from death and join the rest of the faithful on a restored earth. The Jehovah's Witnesses do not believe in the divinity of Jesus, the Trinity, or a permanent hell, which they say are not biblically based. Neither do they allow blood transfusions, because of the biblical prohibition against the ingestion of blood. They do not celebrate Christmas (or birthdays), which they consider to be non-Christian. And because they believe that the Bible demands freedom from the world, they are strongly nonpolitical, refusing to salute a flag or to give allegiance to any country. They spread their faith door-to-door as a part of their religious practice.

Unification Church   This church blends elements of Christianity and Confucian social principles. The founder, Reverend Sun Myung Moon, escaped from North Korea after great personal suffering and founded his church in South Korea in 1954. His church has associated Communism with demonic powers. Reverend Moon believes that evil forces will overtake the world unless they are opposed, and against these forces he hopes his church will help create "the kingdom of heaven on earth." He calls himself "the Jesus of the second coming." (This view might also be influenced by the Korean devotion to Miruk, the Buddha of the future.) Reverend Moon offers his vision of the new society as a great, well-ordered family. He and his wife claim to be the father and mother of the just new society, and in order to create this society, he arranges marriages between his followers, which he and his wife solemnize in large ceremonies. Outsiders see Confucian and Buddhist elements, conjoined with messianic Christianity, in the Unification Church.

CHRISTIAN PRACTICE

We have seen how Christian beliefs have developed and been interpreted in varied ways over two millennia. While Christianity is very much a religion of doctrines, it is also a religion of ritual, and after more than two thousand years, these rituals have become rich and complex. Although Christian ritual practice varies among branches and denominations, many elements are shared.

Sacraments and Other Rituals

The most important rituals are called sacraments. These are the rituals that are considered the most essential to the practice of Christianity.

> *Baptism* A ritual cleansing with water, or baptism, is universally used in Christianity as an initiation rite. The ritual originally involved complete immersion of the body, but some forms of Christianity require that only the head be sprinkled with water. Baptism came to Christianity from Judaism, where ritual bathing was an ancient form of purification (see, for example, Lev. 14:8). It was also commonly used to accept converts to Judaism, and the Essenes practiced daily ritual bathing. John the Baptizer, the cousin of Jesus, used baptism as

Contemporary Protestants often use baptism by immersion for adults. The white robes and the water work together as symbols of inner purification and new life.

a sign of repentance, and Jesus himself was baptized and had his followers baptize others. Early Christians continued the practice as a sign of moral purification, new life, and readiness for God's kingdom. In early Christianity, because baptism was done by immersion in water, the act helped recall vividly the death, burial, and resurrection of Jesus. Although early Christians were normally baptized as adults, the practice of infant baptism became common within the first few hundred years. Catholicism, Orthodoxy, and the more ceremonial forms of Protestantism practice infant baptism. Other forms of Protestantism insist that the ritual should be done only as a voluntary sign of initiation, and, as such, baptism should be reserved for adults only.

Eucharist Another sacrament is the Eucharist, or Lord's Supper. Early Christians, particularly Paul's converts, met weekly to imitate the Last Supper, which was probably a Passover meal. At this meal of bread and wine, they prayerfully recalled Jesus' death and resurrection. Sharing the Lord's Supper is a symbolic sharing of Jesus' life and death, but beliefs about it are quite varied. Some churches see the bread and wine as quite literally the body and blood of Jesus, which the believer consumes; other groups interpret the bread and wine symbolically. All Christian denominations have some form of this meal, but they vary greatly in style and frequency. Catholic, Orthodox, and traditional Protestant churches have a Lord's Supper service every Sunday. Less ceremonial churches prefer to focus their Sunday service on preaching and Bible study; but they usually have the Lord's Supper once a month. All churches use bread, but some use grape juice or water in place of wine.

In addition to these two main sacraments, accepted by all Christians, some churches count the following rituals as full sacraments:

Confirmation The sacrament of confirmation ("strengthening") is a blessing of believers after baptism. In the Orthodox Church, confirmation is often administered with baptism, but in Catholicism and in some Protestant churches, it is commonly administered by a bishop in the believer's early teen years.

Reconciliation The sacrament of reconciliation (or penance) takes place when a repentant person admits his or her sins before a priest and is absolved.

Marriage This is the sacrament in which two people publicly commit themselves to each other for life. The two individuals administer the sacrament to each other while the priest acts as a public witness of the commitment.

Ordination This sacrament involves the official empowerment of a bishop, priest, or deacon for ministry. (Some denominations ordain ministers but do not consider the action to be sacramental.)

Anointing of the sick In this sacrament (formerly called extreme unction), a priest anoints a sick person with oil—an ancient symbol of health—and offers prayers.

In addition to the sacraments, a multitude of smaller devotional rituals has arisen over the two thousand years of Christianity. Making the sign of the cross—in which the fingers of the right hand touch the forehead, the chest, and the two shoulders—is used to begin and end prayer and to call for divine protection. Genuflection—the bending of the right knee—which originated as a sign of submission to a ruler, is a ritual performed by Catholics and some Anglicans on entering and leaving a church. Christians in general often pray on both knees as a sign of devotion to and humility before God.

Devotional objects are also widely used in Christianity. Blessed water (holy water) reminds one of baptism; it is used in the blessing of objects and in conjunction with making the sign of the cross on entering a Catholic church. Oil and salt are used in blessings, as symbols of health. Lighted candles symbolize new understanding. Ashes placed on the forehead at the beginning of **Lent** (a time of preparation before Easter) recall the inevitability of death. Palms are carried in a procession on the Sunday before Easter to recall Jesus' triumphal procession into Jerusalem. Incense is burned to symbolize

Common Christian
symbols.

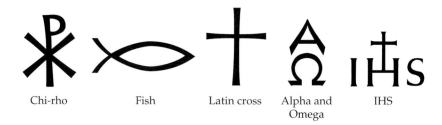

Chi-rho   Fish   Latin cross   Alpha and   IHS
                                               Omega

prayer and reverence. Statues and pictures of Jesus, Mary, angels, and saints
are common in traditionalist forms of Christianity. Often the statues of saints
have special insignia for identification, such as the X-shaped cross on which
the apostle Andrew is believed to have been executed.

In addition to devotional rituals and objects, Christianity is a source of
much religious symbolism. The fish is an ancient symbol of the Christian
believer. It probably began as a reference to Jesus' desire that his followers
go out "as fishers of men" (Luke 5:10), seeking converts. It was also used to
represent the Greek word *ichthus* ("fish"), which could be read as an
acronym for the Greek words that mean "Jesus Christ," "God's son," and
"savior." The cross is used to recall Jesus' death; when Jesus is pictured
hanging on this cross, it is called a crucifix.

Letters of the Greek alphabet are frequently found in Christian art. Alpha
(A) and Omega (Ω), the first and last letters of the Greek alphabet, symbolize
God as the beginning and end of all things. The logo IHS (from the Greek let-
ters iota, eta, and sigma) represents the first three letters of the name *Jesus*.
The logo XP (usually written as a single unit and called "chi-rho"—
pronounced *kai-ro*) represents the first two letters of the name *Christ* in Greek.
(It is also the basis for the abbreviation of *Christmas* as *Xmas*.)

The Christian Year

By the sixth century a fairly complete church calendar had evolved, which
is still followed by most denominations of Christianity in varying degrees.
The most important celebrations are Christmas and Easter. Additional festivals developed around these two focal points. The complete traditional
calendar is kept by Catholic, Orthodox, and traditionalist Protestant
churches (Anglicans and Lutherans). Because of the Reformation and later
developments, many Protestants rejected parts of the traditional church calendar. (Because the Orthodox generally follow the old Julian calendar of the
Roman Empire, Orthodox celebrations can occur several weeks after
Catholic and Protestant celebrations.)

Easter The celebration of the resurrection of Jesus was the first
Christian festival to develop. Its origins are in the Jewish Passover, a
lunar festival of springtime during which Jews recall their exodus
(from Egypt). Christians have added another layer of meaning by

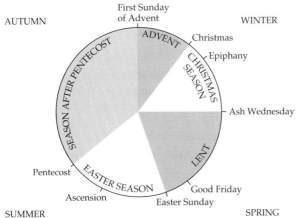

The Christian Church Year

using the festival to recall Jesus' return to life, which they believe occurred on the Sunday after the Jewish Passover. (The Western Church came to celebrate Jesus' resurrection on the first Sunday after the full moon that follows the spring equinox, while the Eastern Orthodox Church celebrates Easter later.) Although there have been attempts—all unsuccessful—to give Easter a permanent date such as Christmas has, Easter is still an ancient moveable feast, connected with the full moon.

Christmas The celebration of Jesus' birth was a later development than the celebration of the resurrection. Although no one knows the exact date of his birth, it was once celebrated on January 6 and also on other dates in the spring. In Rome, however, Christians began to use the Roman midwinter solstice festival called Saturnalia to celebrate the birth of Jesus. Thus the festival of Christmas ("Christ-Mass") was born and began its spread across the globe.

From these two major festivals of birth and resurrection have grown two cycles of celebrations and memorial days. Two somber, reflective periods were introduced to help prepare for Christmas and Easter—Advent and Lent, respectively.

Advent The four-week preparation for Christmas that recalls the period before the coming of Jesus is called Advent ("approach"). It was once thought that the period from the Creation to the birth of Jesus was four thousand years, and each week of Advent thus represents one thousand years.

Lent The period of forty days of repentance and preparation for Easter is called Lent. The forty days recall the period of fasting and prayer that Jesus spent in the desert before his public life began. For many centuries, people were expected during Lent to do without meat, dairy products, and wine—all foods that were once associated with luxury.

The days just before its start are given over to the last pleasures possible, before the abstinence of Lent begins. On the Tuesday before Lent, meat eating must stop at the end of the carnival (from the Latin *caro* "meat" and *levare* "to remove"). Because meat and butter are used up on that day, it came to be called in French *Mardi Gras* ("fat Tuesday") and is the day of a special pre-Lenten celebration in some countries.

Lent begins with Ash Wednesday, when the devout wear ashes on their foreheads to recall the inevitability of death and to show sorrow for wrongdoing. It has been customary during Lent for devout Christians to attend daily church services, to restrict their intake of food, and to give up pleasures. Secular entertainment, music, and marriage are sometimes forbidden until the end of Lent.

Holy Week The week before Easter, called Holy Week, has particular meaning for Christians. Palm Sunday, celebrated on the Sunday before Easter, recalls Jesus' entry into Jerusalem and the acclaim he received in the form of people waving palm and olive branches. The Thursday before Easter recalls the Last Supper. It is sometimes marked by a washing of the feet of twelve people, reenacting Jesus' act of service to his followers. The Friday before Easter (called Good Friday) recalls his death, and services are often held between 12:00 P.M. and 3:00 P.M. in remembrance of the time that Jesus suffered on the cross. Saturday is a day of quiet but signals a strong change of mood, from sad to hopeful: on Saturday evening, a long vigil service is held, which ends with the first celebration of Easter at dawn.

Ascension and Pentecost Forty days after Easter, Jesus' ascension into heaven is celebrated. And ten days later the feast of Pentecost recalls the first preachings of the early Christians. The Sundays after Pentecost are devoted to meditations aimed at furthering the Christian life of the believer. Thus a whole church year centers around the drama of the life of Jesus and belief in him.

Saints' days and other practices This primary yearly cycle, mainly celebrated on Sundays, has been supplemented by a secondary yearly cycle that memorializes the saints—the heroes of Christianity. It is kept (with some variations) by Catholics, Orthodox, and Anglican Protestants. Saints include Mary, Joseph, the twelve apostles, the four gospel writers, early bishops, leaders who were renowned for their holiness, and martyrs ("witnesses") who died in persecutions. In the West, Valentine's Day (February 14) and Saint Patrick's Day (March 17) are the best-known of these saints' days and are celebrated in popular culture. Halloween derives from pre-Christian practice, but the name refers to the evening before All Saints' (All Hallows') Day, November 1. Almost every day of the year is dedicated to a special saint or saints, and in some countries children are still often named after the saint on whose feast day they are born.

Western Christianity has developed a symbolic system of colors to be used for church decoration and ministers' robes. This system is used by Catholics, Anglicans, some Lutherans, and others. White and gold, representing joy, are used for the greatest festivals, such as Christmas and Easter. Violet (or sometimes blue) is associated with Advent and Lent because of its more somber nature. Red represents the shedding of blood and consequently has been used for the feasts of martyrs—those who died for their faith. Because red is associated with the flamelike love of the Holy Spirit (see Acts 2), it is also used at Pentecost. Black, representing death, may be used on Good Friday to represent the death of Jesus. (Black was also formerly used for adult funerals but has been replaced nowadays by white.) Green, signifying growth in the Christian life, is used between Pentecost and Advent— appropriate during the agricultural summer months.

The cycle of festivals and use of symbolic colors weakened after the Protestant Reformation, when reformers eliminated what they felt was inessential in Christian practice.

Devotion to Mary

Devotion to Mary, the mother of Jesus, appeared in Christianity quite early. In the Eastern Church, its strength was evidenced in the fifth century by arguments concerning the titles that could be given to Mary. For example, although some objected, Mary was called *theotokos* ("God bearer"). In churches she was pictured in frescoes and mosaics as a large figure holding a small infant Jesus. Sometimes she was paired with the adult Jesus. Icons and carvings began to show scenes from her life, and devotees prayed to Mary for their needs.

In the West, Roman Catholic devotion to Mary began to flourish in the Middle Ages. Many of the new churches built after 1100 C.E. in the Gothic style in France were named for *notre dame* ("our lady"), and statues of Mary, often tenderly holding her child on her hip, appeared in almost every church. Praying the rosary became common in the West after 1000 C.E. A rosary is a circular chain of beads used to count prayers, with the prayer *Ave Maria* ("Hail, Mary") said on most of the beads. (The use of rosaries for counting prayers is also found in other religions, such as in Hinduism, Islam, and Buddhism.)

Protestant reformers in the sixteenth century in the West criticized the devotion to Mary as a replacement for a devotion to Jesus. For this reason, devotion to Mary is less common in Protestant Christianity, although Lutheran and Anglican (including Episcopal) churches sometimes feature statues and pictures of her.

Today, devotion to Mary remains strong in Orthodox and Catholic branches of Christianity. In the nineteenth century, the Catholic Church

Pilgrims hold lighted candles and hope to be healed at Lourdes in southern France.

declared that Mary's conception was an "immaculate conception," meaning that because she would be the mother of Jesus, she did not inherit the original sin that came from Adam (Rom. 5:17). The Catholic Church believes that Mary has appeared in several countries (for example, Lourdes in southern France and Fatima in Portugal) to deliver messages to the faithful.

CHRISTIANITY AND THE ARTS

Particularly because of its ritual needs, Christianity has contributed much to architecture, the visual arts, and music. The stories and lessons of the Christian Bible and the rich symbols that are part of the tradition have inspired centuries of artists, artisans, composers, and architects. This artistic legacy is one of the greatest gifts of Christianity to world culture—a gift that can be experienced easily through travel, through visits to the great churches and museums of major cities, and through the experiencing of concerts and recordings of Christian music.

Architecture

When Christianity began, its services first were held in private homes. As it grew in popularity, larger buildings were needed to accommodate the larger groups, particularly for rituals such as the Lord's Supper. For their public services, early Christians adapted the basilica, a rectangular building used in the Roman Empire as a court of law. In larger Roman basilicas, interior pillars and thick walls helped support the roof. Windows could be numerous but not too large, because large windows would have weakened the walls. Rounded arches were placed at the tops of windows and doors and between the lines of pillars.

This style—known as Romanesque because of its Roman origins—spread throughout Europe as a practical church design and predominated across western Europe until about 1140. Sometimes two arms were added at each side of one end in order to allow more people to view the ceremonies. Adding two arms also gave the building the symbolic shape of the Latin cross (a cross with the lower part longer than the upper three parts).

Eastern Orthodox Christianity used the basilica shape but also developed another shape. The model was a perfect square covered by a large dome; it was based on the design of the Roman Pantheon. Soon four domed extensions were added on the sides of the main building, which allowed more people inside and offered better structural support to the roof. Like the two arms of the basilica, the four arms gave this building another symbolic shape—that of the Greek cross (a cross with all parts the same length). Because the windows around the domes had to be small, so as not to weaken the roof support, they shed little light, making the interior dark and mysterious. Mosaics with gold backgrounds help to magnify the sometimes dim light.

In the West, probably as a result of contact with Islamic architecture, a new style arose after 1140, known as Gothic style. (The designation *Gothic* was applied to this new style of architecture by a later age, which considered this style primitive and thus named it after barbarian Gothic tribes. The Gothic style, however, is neither primitive nor a product of Goths. It seems to have developed first in Persia, between 600 and 800 C.E., and elements of it may have been carried to Europe by Europeans returning from Syria and Israel.) The first example of Gothic architecture appeared in France; the cathedral of Saint Denis near Paris is still open to visitors today.

Gothic architecture is light and airy; it leaps upward toward the sky. Typical of Gothic style are pointed arches, high ceilings, elongated towers, and delicate stone carving. The walls and roofs are held up externally by stone supports (called flying buttresses) that extend outward from the walls and down to the ground. Because these supports do much of the work of holding up the roof, they allow the walls to be filled with large windows, frequently of colored glass. Smaller Gothic churches retain the rectangular shape of the basilica, but large Gothic churches add extensions on each side. Notre Dame Cathedral in Paris and Westminster Abbey in London are beautiful examples of this style. Gothic style was especially popular in France and England but also spread to Germany, Italy, and Spain. Most of the great European Gothic churches were begun in a single century, from about 1200 to 1300.

During the time that the Gothic churches were being built, every town of any importance wanted to have a church built in the new style. This was

especially true in towns that featured a cathedral. (A cathedral is a bishop's church and takes its name from the bishop's special chair, the *cathedra*, which symbolizes his teaching authority.) The great Gothic cathedrals were so impressive that Gothic style remains *the* style associated with Western Christianity. As a result, later grand churches outside Europe were built in Gothic style: for example, St. Patrick's Cathedral and the Cathedral of St. John the Divine in New York City; Grace Cathedral in San Francisco; the National Cathedral in Washington, D.C.; and the Notre Dame Basilica in Montreal.

The soaring spaces of the Gothic cathedral (here, at Amiens, in northern France) were seen to represent Christian faith—and perhaps human aspiration. ◄

In addition to the influence of the Gothic style in the West, other styles have also been important. The Catholic (Counter) Reformation popularized the theatrical baroque style. The word *baroque* is thought to come from the Portuguese name for an irregular pearl, *barroco*. Baroque style uses contrasts of light and dark, rich colors, elegant materials (such as marble), twisting pillars, multiple domes, and other dramatic elements to create a sense of excitement and wonder. Beginning in Italy, baroque style also became popular in Austria and southern Germany, and because it was used by the Jesuits in their missions around the world, it is often called the Jesuit style. Fine examples are found in Rome, such as the church of Il Gesù and Santa Maria della Vittoria, and in Austria, such as Melk Abbey and Salzburg Cathedral. (For an example of baroque style, see the photograph on page 368.)

While Catholicism was adopting the baroque style with enthusiasm, Protestantism generally moved in a more sober direction. Older Gothic churches were simplified and brightened by having much of their stained glass, statues, and paintings destroyed. Although the artistic loss was terrible, the result was a striking focus on basic architectural structure. Good examples of this can be found in the Netherlands and in the Protestant parts of Germany (the cathedral of Ulm is a fine example). With the focus of worship placed on hearing the Bible read aloud and listening to a sermon, new churches were built with pews, clear-glass windows, high pulpits, and second-floor galleries to bring people closer to the preacher. In larger churches, classical Greco-Roman architecture was drawn upon to produce the neoclassical style. Saint Paul's Cathedral in London, the masterwork of Christopher Wren (1632–1723), is the finest example of the style. Neoclassical style became common in the United States, particularly in New England and the South, where it has been commonly used for both churches and other public buildings.

In the twentieth century, partly because new materials were developed (such as steel and concrete) or because old materials were used in a new way (such as large sheets of plate glass), experimentation led to innovations in church design, particularly in the United States. The Crystal Cathedral, designed by the noted architect Philip Johnson for a congregation in southern California, is made entirely of glass. Looking up, the participant sees only the sky. The Wayfarer's Chapel at Palos Verdes, California, is made of plate glass and large beams of wood. Designed by Lloyd Wright, the son of Frank Lloyd Wright, it is set in a grove of tall trees on a bluff near the ocean

The Crystal Cathedral, an all-glass church near Los Angeles, was designed by Philip Johnson. Particularly well known for its Christmas and Easter presentations, it is a spectacular example of contemporary American Protestant architecture.

and allows the worshiper an experience of closeness with surrounding nature. Concrete has been used as well to create unusual, modern soaring shapes, such as in the Catholic Cathedral of Saint Mary in San Francisco.

Art

Christianity has made immense contributions to art, despite the fact that it emerged from Judaism, which generally forbade the making of images. Mindful of the biblical prohibition against images (Exod. 20:4), a few Christian groups still oppose religious images as a type of idolatry. But because Christianity first began to flourish in the Greco-Roman world, it abandoned the prohibition of images and quickly embraced the use of statues, frescoes, and mosaics, which were already common there. By the second century, statues and pictures of Jesus had begun to appear, based on Greco-Roman models. The Christian Bible provided innumerable stories and images that could be illustrated, and these illustrations, used in churches, served as both decoration and instruction.

Orthodox Christianity has tended to avoid statues but has concentrated instead on frescoes, mosaics, and icons (paintings on wood). A solemn style (sometimes called hieratic) was developed by Byzantine monks and painters in Constantinople and continues to be reproduced today. The unmoving, stylized figures often gaze full-face at the onlooker. They do not appear as ordinary human beings but more frequently as majestic universal types—prophets, monks, kings. The backgrounds are

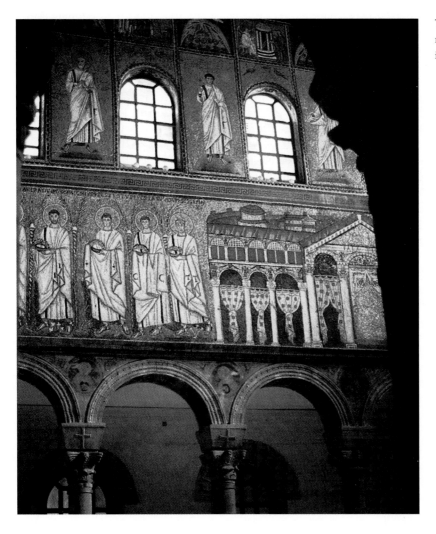

These Byzantine style mosaics appear in a church in Ravenna, Italy.

usually gold, sometimes with stylized rocks and trees. The Orthodox de-pictions of Jesus emphasize his radiant divine nature and pay less attention to his human suffering than does Western art. Perhaps because of its em-phasis on human beings' becoming divine through their contact with God, there is a strong otherworldly character to Orthodox art. Although the figures are rigid and sometimes not warmly human, they have an austere fascination that hints at a supernatural realm beyond, and the gold back-grounds of the artworks suggest timelessness and the light of eternity.

Icons play a special part in Orthodoxy. Churches usually have a high screen that separates the altar area from the body of the church. This screen is called an *iconostasis* ("image stand") because it is covered with icons. Doors through the iconostasis are closed during much of the service, cut-ting off the congregation's visibility of the priest and altar; the priest's chanting, however, can be heard as it comes over the screen. Thus the iconostasis becomes an important focus of attention for worshipers. Indi-vidual icons also stand around the church, and during services worshipers may kiss them and place candles nearby. Many homes also display icons.

In western Europe, Christianity favored artworks of sculpture, fresco, and painting (first on wood, later on canvas). Some of the earliest examples derived from older models; for example, statues of Jesus were based on ear-lier Roman sculptures. The Byzantine style of Constantinople was influen-tial in frescoes and painting for many centuries, particularly in Italy, until the end of the Middle Ages.

New directions appeared in Western Christian art in the later Middle Ages, as wealth and population increased, and after 1300, an interest in the individual person and the human body is evident. This change in direction can be seen on the exterior statues of Chartres Cathedral in France: the ear-lier sculptures are elongated and unearthly, suggesting spirituality, while the later sculptures look more like real human beings. As the Middle Ages waned, statues and paintings of Mary began to show her less like a goddess and more like a human mother, and representations of Jesus began to em-phasize his bodily suffering. The plain gold backgrounds of earlier paint-ings began to disappear, and the backgrounds became crowded with scenes of cities and of human activity, like farming, boating, and trading. Real people—such as donors with bowl-shaped haircuts—were painted kneel-ing in front of Jesus and Mary. This humanistic tendency eventually flow-ered in the Renaissance, when biblical persons often served as simply a pre-text for quite secular painting and sculpture. Michelangelo's statue of David is a prime example.

During the baroque era, painting and sculpture tended toward the dra-matic and showy. Paintings of saints often showed the saints' eyes lifted to the skies, the robes blown by wind, and sunlit clouds parted in the back-ground. Sculptures were made of rich marbles, and the figures employed dramatic gestures and poses. Paintings and statues were mixed together on the walls and in the domes of the churches, creating effects that often fool the eye. For example, an angel might be painted on the wall of a dome, with one of the angel's legs sculpted and dangling below. Sometimes the effect of baroque style is garish, but it can also be astonishingly beautiful.

Many Protestant groups rejected religious painting and sculpture as being unnecessarily sensual, wasteful, or idolatrous, and because artists in Protestant countries were not greatly patronized by churches, their subjects tended to be secular, often depicting home life, civic leaders, and landscapes. Sadly, Christian art has been in some decline for the last two hundred years, partly because the greatest artists of the time have not been commissioned by visionary Christian leaders.

Music

From the beginning, Christianity has been a religion of music. Jesus himself is recorded as having sung a psalm hymn (Matt. 26:30, Mark 14:26). Because of its early musical involvement, Christianity has contributed much to the development of both theory and technique in music. A Benedictine monk, Guido d'Arezzo (c. 995–1050), worked to help monks sing the notes of religious chants correctly; he is thought to have systematized the basic Gregorian musical notation system (of lines, notes, and musical staffs) from which modern musical notation derives.

For the first thousand years, both Eastern and Western church music was chant—a single line of melody usually sung in unison without instruments. The origins of chant are uncertain but probably emerged from both Jewish devotional songs and folk music. Various modes developed, using scales of differing intervals. Each mode conveys its own feeling—some light, some sad, some exalted.

Music in the Orthodox Church is sung without accompaniment, thus remaining closer to ancient church music and to its origins in the synagogue and the Near East. The only instruments commonly found are bells and wooden clappers. The choral music of the Russian Orthodox Church tends to be done in harmony and is typified by extremely deep bass notes, so deep as to recall the pedal notes on an organ.

The ancient Greeks were familiar with the principles of harmony as they related to mathematics. But the use of harmony in terms of musical composition (called *organum*) seems to have first developed in Paris, in the cathedral of Notre Dame, about 1100. In the West, initial experiments with harmonized singing eventually led to the introduction of instruments, such as the flute, violin, or organ, which could easily be used to substitute for a human voice or to accompany the chant. Even though it is now considered a primarily religious instrument, the organ was opposed for use in some churches because it was considered a secular instrument.

Harmonic experimentation in church music continued in four directions: (1) voices alone (called *a capella or* "chapel"—style because it was thought appropriate for churches); (2) voices and instruments together;

(3) organ alone; and (4) instruments in harmony (this was more common outside churches and eventually gave birth to the symphonic orchestra).

The most important early pattern for Western religious music was the Catholic Mass[32] (Lord's Supper), with its five sections of *Kyrie, Gloria, Credo, Sanctus,* and *Agnus Dei.* (The first section is in Greek, and the others in Latin.) The five sections vary greatly in mood. The *Kyrie,* which prays "Lord, have mercy" (in Greek *Kyrie eleison*), is a plea for forgiveness. The *Gloria,* which begins "Glory to God in the highest places," is a joyous hymn of praise. The *Credo* ("I believe") affirms belief in God and recalls major events in the life of Jesus. The *Sanctus* ("holy") is the song of angels who are in the presence of God. The *Agnus Dei* ("Lamb of God") is a quiet prayer to Jesus for mercy and peace. On Sundays and at special celebrations, these five sections were traditionally sung, rather than spoken, and innumerable composers have put the five-part Mass to music.

A variant of the regular Mass is the Requiem ("rest") Mass, the Mass for the dead. It excludes the relatively cheerful *Gloria* and *Credo* and adds some more somber texts. Psalms and other short biblical passages were also put to music for the services. These relatively short works, usually in Latin, are called motets. All church music sounds best in the appropriate surroundings, such as in large stone churches, where sounds can resonate and echo.

After the Protestant Reformation, the tradition of composing Masses and motets was continued by Catholic composers. Renaissance composers, such as Giovanni da Palestrina (c. 1526–1594) and William Byrd (c. 1540–1623), composed Masses for voice alone. Later composers (such as Joseph Haydn, Wolfgang Amadeus Mozart, Franz Schubert, and Ludwig van Beethoven) all made use of organ or orchestra in their Masses. Although the Catholic Church officially endorsed the purer musical style of unaccompanied singing, many dramatic Masses and motets were created; sometimes the line between sacred and secular music was hard to define. The dramatic style of church music reached an artistic peak in the Masses of Mozart.

Continuing the Catholic tradition in the late-nineteenth and twentieth centuries, the French have made notable contributions to both choral and organ music. Two Requiem Masses of extraordinary beauty are those by Gabriel Fauré (1845–1924) and Maurice Duruflé (1902–1986). Rather than grimly emphasizing divine judgment, they radiate joy and peace.

The Protestant Reformation greatly expanded the variety of religious music, as each branch created its own musical traditions. Luther, we might recall, wrote hymns in German, and although he encouraged some church use of Latin for its educational value, he recommended that services be conducted primarily in the language of the people. The Lutheran tradition also supported the use of the organ, both on its own and to accompany hymns. The supreme genius of the Lutheran tradition was Johann Sebastian Bach (1685–1750). A church organist and choirmaster for most of his career, Bach composed many beautiful musical pieces for church use, both solo organ music and choir music. His *Saint Matthew Passion,* a musical reflection on the last days of Jesus, is one of the world's most complex and moving religious compositions. He also wrote in forms that derived from the Roman Catholic tradition, producing a *Magnificat* in Latin and his *Mass in B-minor.*[33]

After the Church of England decreed that services be in English, a body of church music began to develop in England. Much of this music was written for choirs, which traditionally have been supported by Anglican cathedrals. One of England's great twentieth-century composers, Ralph Vaughan Williams (1872–1958), wrote much religiously inspired music, some of which was intended for church performance. His *Fantasia on a Theme of Thomas Tallis* is a meditation on an Elizabethan hymn, and his soaring *Mass in G minor* was used at the coronation of Queen Elizabeth II.

Other forms of Protestant Christianity have been cautious about the types of music used in church services. Wanting to keep the music popular and simple, Protestant churches have supported the writing and singing of hymns but often have avoided more complex compositions. They have allowed use of the organ and piano but until recently have generally discouraged the use of other instruments. The churches that have been the most influential creators of hymns have been the Methodist and Baptist Churches, and as a result of the creativity of these and other sects there is now a whole genre called gospel music. Spirituals, based on biblical themes, are a distinctive African American contribution to Protestant Christianity.

In recent decades, a liberalization of practice has brought about great experimentation in both Protestant and Catholic church music. Guitars, synthesizers, and full rock bands are now common in church services. Christian songs are being created in a wide variety of styles, especially rock and reggae. The influence of church music on the secular musical world is also evident; Elvis Presley, Aretha Franklin, Whitney Houston, and a multitude of others have risen to celebrity from a gospel-music background.

CHRISTIANITY FACES THE TWENTY-FIRST CENTURY

Christianity—in spite of the strength of its varied interpretations and its international influence—faces obstacles that arise from new nonreligious worldviews.

The Challenge of Science

The greatest challenge to Christianity as a whole has been the growth of science, and it will remain so. With science have come the demand for scientific proof and a nonsupernatural way of looking at the world. (For example, Carl

The Neo-Gothic towers of
Saint Patrick's Cathedral
in Manhattan contrast
with surrounding
skyscrapers, expressing
the notion of Christianity
as an island amid
the swirling river
of modern life.

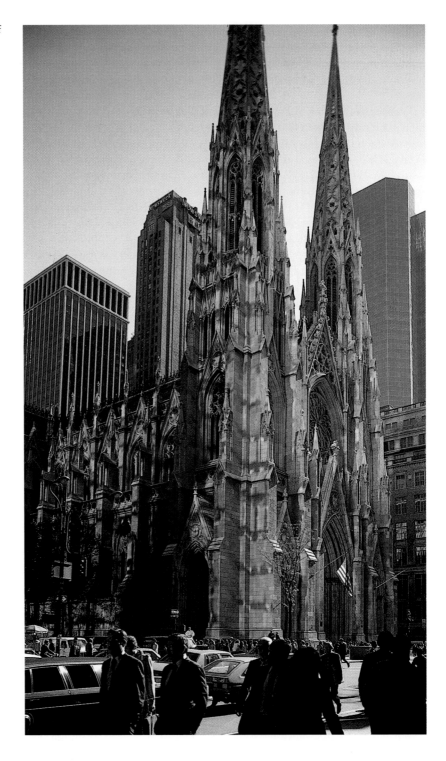

Sagan, the well-known astronomer, often said, "I am a devout agnostic.") Biblical miracles, such as those written about in the Gospels, have been questioned, and proof sought. Critical approaches to the study of scripture have also raised many questions, as have comparative religious studies. These tendencies appeared regularly in the eighteenth century, but the theory of evolution in the next century became a focus for angry public debate. At that time, the theory of evolution seemed to conflict with the biblical account of creation. Today, however, many churches have accepted evolutionary theory and see no conflict between it and the basic religious intent of the biblical story of creation. Perhaps this pattern of accommodation with science will repeat itself in other problem areas.

The three great traditional branches of Christianity have been affected to varying degrees by the challenges of the scientific worldview. Catholicism initially fought emerging biblical scholarship, which it condemned as dangerous "Modernism." Up until the early twentieth century, Orthodox Christianity was less touched by conflict with science, because Orthodoxy existed in mostly preindustrial countries; with the introduction of Communism and new technology, however, many Orthodox countries began experiencing conflict between science and religion. In the nineteenth century, Protestant scholars, particularly in Germany, enriched biblical understanding, as they examined the cultures that produced the biblical texts, the meaning of the texts to their writers, and the historical facts of the stories. Biblical scholars have been particularly eager to find the "historical Jesus." That search continues in the Jesus Seminar, a group of biblical scholars who meet regularly to ascertain the historical accuracy of New Testament passages about Jesus' actions and the sayings that have been traditionally attributed to him.

Contemporary Influences and Developments

Mainstream Christian denominations now look for common ground and work together in a movement called **ecumenism,** from the Greek word for "household." Ecumenism sees all mainstream Christian groups as part of a single "household" of Christianity and tries to encourage dialogue between all its major branches. Marriages between partners of different Christian denominations are no longer discouraged and are sometimes witnessed by ministers of both churches. Several denominations often participate together in community welfare projects.

Cooperation and dialogue have occurred, too, at official and institutional levels. The best known of the ecumenical organizations is the World Council of Churches, which emerged in 1937 from the Church of England. It now includes mainstream Protestant churches, all Eastern Orthodox churches, and observers from the Roman Catholic Church. Churches with similar beliefs have united or are discussing possible

While retaining some flavor from the past, the old cathedral of Cuernavaca in Mexico has been refurbished to accommodate the changes brought about by the Second Vatican Council.

▶

unions. At the international level, there have been formal meetings of many world religions. The first, held in 1893, was followed by a second parliament in 1993, which was represented by an even wider range of religions, including Native American religions. We can assume that an even more inclusive parliament will meet in 2093.

The Catholic Church, after four centuries of a defensive approach, took a new course in the mid–twentieth century. Pope John XXIII (Angelo Roncalli, 1881–1963), who had been elected as an elderly interim pope, convened a council of bishops in 1960. This council, named the Second Vatican Council (or Vatican II), proceeded to make the first major changes since the Council of Trent in the sixteenth century. The most obvious was to use the living languages of the people instead of Latin in ordinary church services. Another result is that Catholic documents now endorse the value of other major religions and dialogue with Christian groups. More authority rests with laypeople, and consultation with them is officially encouraged. Modern approaches to understanding the Bible, pioneered by Protestant scholars, are now permitted. In addition, many church buildings have been stripped of inessentials, and their decoration has been simplified.

These changes have initiated intense debate over other elements of traditional Catholic life, such as the celibacy of priests, the ordination of women, the role of Catholic schools, and traditional positions on divorce, sex, and birth control. In other words, just about everything is being questioned. These topics just mentioned will gain in importance in the twenty-first century.

What is happening in Catholicism can be seen as a new wave of the Protestant Principle of individual judgment that emerged in the sixteenth century. Some of the same events that occurred in Protestantism several centuries ago are happening again—but this time within Catholicism. Certain effects are predictable. There is already a spectrum of opinions, from ultraconservative to extremely liberal, on every question, and there is more emphasis on the authority of the Bible and individual judgment. To prevent a breakup of the Catholic Church into factions, Church authorities have responded to these various questions with conservative policies in recent years. Although authorities have tried to lessen the debate, it is quite possible that Catholicism will eventually move in the same direction as many Protestant churches already have, with more liberal positions on most of these issues.

Christianity has a long tradition of helping the poor. A Catholic movement (which can be traced back to European ideas in the 1930s but only began in the 1950s) called Liberation Theology began in South America as a way of extricating the church from the power structure of politicians and land owners. Critics have accused the movement of identifying religion with social work, but it has done much to realign the Catholic Church with the poor. Evangelical and Pentecostal Protestant churches in South America have also been socially active against poverty.

At a Pentecostal service in Los Angeles, participants are exuberant in their fervor.

Another development in Protestant Christianity has been the emergence (beginning in the 1920s) of **evangelical** denominations. With an emphasis on the Bible, a conservative morality, and religious services that often encourage the expression of individual emotion, this approach has helped Protestant Christianity develop in several often interrelated ways. One has been the rise of nondenominational churches, often begun by charismatic ministers who have little or no affiliation with established churches. Another has been the development of televangelism (television evangelism), which grew out of the work of radio evangelists (such as Billy Sunday, 1862–1935). Evangelism, which often places an emphasis on healing, is significant because of the millions of people who can be reached by one minister. Lastly, because a great deal of Protestant religious television and radio programming is given to singing, Christian rock music and gospel music have entered the mainstream. All these trends will be significant in the next century.

Women have assumed more leadership in Christian denominations over the last fifty years. The earliest examples of women in the ministry were in the charismatic and nondenominational churches. People like Aimee Semple McPherson (1890–1944), the founder of the Foursquare Gospel Church, advanced the cause of women in the churches. A vital radio preacher in Los Angeles in the early days of radio, McPherson accustomed people to the notion of a woman preacher.

Feminist theory is adding its insights to Christianity, which according to many is overly patriarchal and male-dominated. Some churches have responded by including more women in the ministry, and in some branches of the Church of England and the Lutheran Church women have recently become not only priests but also bishops. The male-oriented religious language that describes God in the Bible and in hymns ("king," "lord") is giving way to more inclusive language ("ruler," "creator").

The environment and the natural world have not been strong concerns of Christianity in the past, but this is changing. Based on the notion that the world is the creation of God and reflects God's love, Christians are beginning to work out a theology of environmentalism. The design of some modern churches reflects a new interest in nature. For example, modern churches often feature large glass windows to reveal the surrounding sky and trees. The new cathedral of Evry, in France, designed by Mario Botta, even has trees growing on its roof!

Another current development is a renewed interest in Christian mysticism. The rereading of great medieval classics has also led to further interest in Hindu spirituality, Buddhist meditation, and other forms of mysticism. One form of mystically oriented Christian thought, called Creation Spirituality, is gaining renown. Begun by a priest, Matthew Fox, it unites contemporary concerns—mystical experience, feminism, ecology, and individual judgment—with traditional Christianity.

In summary, traditionalists see much to worry about, such as the scientific questioning of belief in the supernatural and the growth of secular values. But optimists see great vitality in Christianity because of its respect for the individual, its ethic of practical helpfulness, its love of the arts, and even its openness to debate.

RELIGION BEYOND THE CLASSROOM

Christianity has been a major patron and protector of the arts. The following list is long enough to highlight some of the significant examples of Christian art, but it represents a mere sampling of the multitude of artistic expressions that has been produced by Christianity.

The best time to visit Christian churches is when they come alive, that is, during services or concerts. Almost every Christian church has at least one service on Sundays. In cathedrals and major churches the choral service is the most important and usually begins at about 10:00 or 10:30 in the morning. The great festivals, like Christmas and Easter, are a particularly good time to attend a religious service. Concerts are often held in churches, too—usually in the evening. Consult local sources of information, such as newspapers, hotels, and travel bureaus.

North America Fine church buildings are located in many places, particularly in major cities. In New York: Saint Patrick's Cathedral, Cathedral of Saint John the Divine, Saint Thomas Church (its choir school sings at services during the school year). In Boston: Trinity Church. In Washington, D.C.: the National Cathedral and the Shrine of the Immaculate Conception. In San Francisco: Grace Cathedral. In Los Angeles: the Wayfarer's Chapel (Palos Verdes) and the Crystal Cathedral (Orange County), which has special programs at Christmas and Easter.

There are many smaller churches of interest as well. Some historical churches include the Old North Church in Boston and the Franciscan missions of California (fine ones are located in Carmel and San Juan Capistrano). Other churches are modern, designed by well-known architects, such as Frank Lloyd Wright's Unity Church in Madison, Wisconsin, and Marcel Breuer's Abbey Church at Saint John's Abbey, Collegeville, Minnesota.

In Canada, of special beauty is the neo-Gothic Notre Dame Basilica in Montreal. In Mexico, the cathedral of Mexico City is exceptional and is on the site of an Aztec temple.

Europe The most important countries in Europe for visitors interested in the art and architecture of Christianity are England, France, Italy, Germany, Spain, and Greece. Below are some of their major religious sights.

In England, visitors should include in their itineraries Saint Paul's Cathedral and Westminster Abbey. The cathedrals of York, Durham, Lincoln, Wells, Salisbury, and Winchester are also fine buildings. Sunday services are usually held at about 10:00 A.M. (mattins) and 4:00 P.M. (evensong).

In France, organ concerts are held on Sunday afternoons at Notre Dame Cathedral in Paris. Other churches of interest in Paris are Sainte Chapelle (featuring exquisite stained glass), Saint Severin, Sacre Coeur (in neo-Byzantine style), and the Madeleine (in the style of a Greek temple). The cathedral of Chartres is a masterpiece of Gothic style, with much original stained glass and sculpture. Other significant Gothic cathedrals are located in Amiens, Rouen, Rheims, Laon, and Strasbourg. Major museums located in Paris are the Louvre and the Musée de Cluny.

Italy is the home to so much fine religious art and architecture that limiting examples to a small sampling is difficult. First-time travelers might want to visit the following in Rome, Florence, and Venice. In Rome: Saint Peter's Basilica (there is a papal blessing at noon on most Sundays), Saint Mary Major, Saint John Lateran, Il Gesù (a baroque church with a spectacular ceiling), Santa Maria della Vittoria (featuring Bernini's statue of Saint Teresa in ecstasy), and Santa Sabina (in very pure basilica style). In Florence: the cathedral (Duomo; with baptistery doors by Ghiberti and a bell tower by Giotto), Santa Maria Novella, Santa Croce, Orsanmichele, and the Convent of San Marco. In Venice: Saint Mark's Cathedral (featuring mosaics), Zanipolo, Salute, and Frari. Other cathedrals of worth are located in Milan, Siena, and Orvieto. Assisi and its basilica are wonderful to visit because of their association with Saint Francis and the frescoes attributed to Giotto. Major museums are located in Rome (the Vatican Museum), Florence (Uffizi Gallery, Pitti Palace, Bargello, San Marco, and Accademia), and Venice (Accademia).

In Germany, an especially fine Gothic cathedral (Dom) is located in Cologne. Other cathedrals of note can be found in Munich, Freiburg, Mainz, Dresden, and Ulm. Major museums are in Berlin (Pergamon and Dahlem).

In Spain, the center of the Catholic Church is Toledo, one of the most beautiful hill towns in the world. Two sights not to miss there are the cathedral and the church of Santo Tomé. In Barcelona, of particular interest are the cathedral and the incomplete Sagrada Familia church (by Antonio Gaudí), which looks like melting ice cream. Other cathedrals of note are located in Seville (the location of one of the largest cathedrals in the world), Salamanca, and Madrid. The cathedral of Córdoba is a beautiful former mosque, still almost entirely intact. The major museum is the Prado in Madrid.

In Greece, two buildings of interest in Athens are the Little (Old) Cathedral and the New Cathedral. In Thessaloníki, visitors should see Agios Georgios, Agios Dimitrios, and Agia Sophia. Monastic life can also be experienced at the monasteries of Meteora, built on mountains. The Byzantine Museum in Athens contains many fine pieces of Christian artwork.

FOR FULLER UNDERSTANDING

1. Compile an inventory of questions (perhaps by rereading this chapter), and conduct interviews with the pastors of different denominational churches. Write up a report that compares and contrasts the beliefs and practices of these churches.
2. Locate important examples of Christian art and architecture in your area. Prepare a self-guided tour tailored to a visitor who is interested in religious art and architecture.
3. Imagine that you have been offered an all-expenses-paid one-month trip to Europe in exchange for guiding a tour group to cities and sites that played major roles in the early spread of Christianity. Do research to help you put together an itinerary. Then write a "script" of the history and details you will share with your tour group at each site.
4. If you belong to a Christian congregation, arrange an interview with both longtime church members and relative newcomers. What does being a member of the congregation mean to members of each group? What particular satisfaction do they gain from their church membership? What do the elders miss from the "old days," and what sorts of things do younger members hope to change? Prepare a display that celebrates the members you interview.
5. See if there are any Christian nuns in your area. Arrange an interview with several nuns and, if possible, a visit to their convent. Ask the nuns to relate their personal stories of their choice to join the convent. Ask them also about their joys and their hopes. Write up your report as a collection of life stories or as part of a study on the status of women in various religions.
6. Experience the choral Sunday service at an Episcopal cathedral (or major Episcopal church) in your area. Make a report on the composers of the music performed.

RELATED READINGS AND MUSICAL RECORDINGS

Books

Erikson, Erik. *Young Man Luther.* New York: Norton, 1993. A fascinating study of the early development and psychology of Luther.

Henry, Francoise, ed. *The Book of Kells.* New York: Knopf, 1977. A reproduction of important pages from the *Book of Kells,* the most beautiful of all European illuminated manuscripts.

James, Janet, ed. *Women in American Religion.* Philadelphia: University of Pennsylvania Press, 1980. Studies of the roles of women in American religious life.

Norris, Kathleen. *Cloister Walk.* New York: Putnam, 1996. A personal account by a Protestant writer who describes her discovery of monastic life and its rituals.

Pelikan, Jaroslav. *Jesus Through the Centuries.* New Haven: Yale University Press, 1985. A famous study by a Protestant scholar on the changing image of Jesus.

Progoff, Ira, ed. and trans. *The Cloud of Unknowing.* Garden City, NY: Image/Doubleday, 1996. A modern translation of a medieval English classic of mystical experience.

Robinson, John. *Honest to God.* Philadelphia: Westminster Press, 1963. A seminal book by an Episcopal bishop who questions traditional Christian understanding of key beliefs.

Ware, Timothy. *The Orthodox Church.* Baltimore: Penguin, 1993. A new edition of a classic on the history, beliefs, and practices of Orthodox Christianity.

Music

Christianity cannot be appreciated fully without experiencing some of its music. Following is a short list of selections, all available on CD by various recording houses. Especially approachable compositions are starred.

Bach: *Magnificat, Mass in B-minor,* *motets
Britten: *A Ceremony of Carols
Byrd: Masses
Duruflé: *Requiem, Mass "Cum Jubilo,"* *motets
Fauré: *Requiem
Gregorian chant: *Masses of Christmas and Easter
Handel: *Messiah
Hildegard of Bingen: Hymns and antiphons
Mozart: *Coronation Mass, Requiem,* *motets
Palestrina: Masses
Rachmaninoff: *Evening Vigil* (other Orthodox music is available in collections)
Vaughan Williams: *Mass in G minor,* *Fantasia on a Theme of Thomas Tallis
Vivaldi: *Gloria

KEY TERMS

Apocalypticism: The belief that the world will soon come to an end; this belief usually includes the notion of a great battle, final judgment, and reward of the good.

Apostle (*a-paw'-sul*): One of Jesus' twelve disciples; also, any early preacher of Christianity.

Baptism: The Christian rite of initiation, involving immersion in water or sprinkling with water.

Bible (Christian): The scriptures sacred to Christians, consisting of the books of the Hebrew Bible and the New Testament.

Bishop: "Overseer" (Greek); a priest and church leader who is in charge of a large geographical area called a diocese.

Canon (*kaa'-nun*): "Measure," "rule" (Greek); a list of authoritative books or documents.

Ecumenism (*e-kyoo'-men-ism*): Dialogue between Christian denominations.

Eucharist (*yoo'-ka-rist*): "Good gift" (Greek); the Lord's Supper.

Evangelical: Emphasizing the authority of scripture; an adjective used to identify certain Protestant groups.

Evangelist (*ee-van'-je-list*): "Good news person" (Greek); one of the four "authors" of the Gospels—Matthew, Mark, Luke, and John.

Filioque (*fee-lee-oh'-kway*): "And from the Son"; a Latin word added to the creeds in the Western Church to state that the Holy Spirit arises from both Father and Son. The notion, which was not accepted by Orthodox Christianity, helped cause a separation between the Western and Eastern Churches.

Gospel: "Good news" (Middle English); an account of the life of Jesus.

Icon (*ai'-kahn*): "Image" (Greek); religious painting on wood, as used in the Orthodox Church; also spelled "ikon."

Incarnation: "In flesh" (Latin); a belief that God became visible in Jesus.

Indulgence (*in-dul'-jens*): "Kindness-toward" (Latin); remission of time spent in purgatory (a state of temporary punishment in the afterlife); an aspect of Catholic belief and practice.

Lent: "Lengthening day," "spring" (Anglo-Saxon); the preparatory period before Easter, lasting forty days.

Messiah: "Anointed" (Hebrew); a special messenger sent by god, foretold in the Hebrew scriptures, and believed by Christians to be Jesus.

Original sin: An inclination toward evil, inherited by human beings as a result of Adam's disobedience.

Orthodox: "Straight opinion" (Greek); correct belief.

Orthodoxy: The Eastern branch of Christianity.

Patriarch: The bishop of one of the major ancient sites of Christianity (Jerusalem, Rome, Alexandria, Antioch, Constantinople, and Moscow).

Pope: "Father" (Latin); the bishop of Rome and head of the Roman Catholic Church.

Predestination: The belief that because God is all-powerful and all-knowing, a human being's ultimate reward or punishment is already decreed by God; a notion emphasized in Calvinism.

Protestant Principle: The ability of each believer to rethink and interpret the ideas and values of Christianity.

Redemption: "Buy again," "buy back" (Latin); the belief that the death of Jesus has paid the price of justice for all human wrongdoing.

Righteousness: Being sinless in the sight of God; also called *justification*.

Sacrament: "Sacred action" (Latin); one of the essential rituals of Christianity.

Sin: Wrongdoing, seen as disobedience to God.

Testament: A contract; the Old and New Testament constitute the Christian scriptures.

Trinity: The three "persons" in God: Father, Son, and Holy Spirit.

CHAPTER **10**

Islam

 FIRST ENCOUNTER

With much anticipation you have taken a train from New Delhi to the town of Agra, not far away. You stop by your hotel room—with its slowly turning ceiling fan and its four-poster bed—long enough to drop off your bags. After bargaining with a driver in front of the hotel, you hop in a pedicab and merge with the currents of the Indian street. Alongside, in the human tide, you see what seem like a thousand bicycles and hundreds of other pedicabs—many filled with women with packages and schoolgirls with ribbons in their braided black hair. You see countless pedestrians, some of whom seem eager to collide with your pedicab. You pass tea shops and candy shops and photo shops and a movie theater, where a recording of a woman's song pierces the air and huge red and yellow posters advertise her latest film.

The pedicab turns suddenly and then stops next to a white wall. This must be it. You hop down and pay the driver, enter a gate into a dark enclosure, and let your eyes adjust to the dim light. Beyond the darkness is a bright light at the end of a long channel of water. You see it—perhaps the most delicate domed building in the world: the Taj Mahal.

You have seen so many photos of this fragile-looking building, yet experiencing it firsthand evokes many feelings. The first is relief. You think to yourself: Here I am, at last. You also feel as if you are standing in a postcard. The building seems like a mirage.

After seeing the Taj Mahal for the first time, some people say, "It was huge!" And yet others say, "It was so much smaller than I expected." Part of its hallucinatory quality is that there is nothing to give it scale—no mountains or buildings behind it, which would give a clue to its size. (It is built on a riverbank, with the river invisible behind it.) Beyond the Taj Mahal is only open sky. The effect is dreamlike, a quality that is enhanced by the ambiguous color of the building. Covered in glistening white marble, the Taj Mahal takes on different light and hue, depending on the time of day. In the morning it is golden. At noon it is bright white. At sunset it grows pink. In moonlight it is a mysterious blue-violet.

To reach the building, you must walk through a long, formal garden, with grass and dark green bushes. The entire garden is enclosed by a wall with a fountain in the center, where channels of cooling water move in the four directions of a compass. The grass is being cut by a lawn mower pulled by two oxen.

Before you enter the Taj Mahal building itself, you must leave your shoes at the entry stairs. (In Islam, shoes are not allowed in holy places for reasons of cleanliness.) As you enter, you see a filigree of Arabic writing and stylized flowers around the arches. Inside, there are no statues or pictures— only empty space under the great, tall dome. Two little boys come in with their parents just behind you and make loud birdlike calls, which echo wonderfully. They repeat their calls, listening for the echo. You want to experiment along with them but realize with a sigh the price of being an adult.

Although the Taj Mahal is not a place of worship, it is a sacred place, for it is a monument to Mumtaz Mahal, the best-loved wife of the Muslim ruler Shah Jahan (1592–1666), who built the monument in her honor. Their tombs are below, side by side. As you enjoy the sights, you ask yourself, How did such architecture come from a religion that emerged in desertlike Arabia? How did the Muslim religion get to India from Arabia? And, why are there no pictures, paintings, or statues?

THE LIFE AND TEACHINGS OF MUHAMMAD

Muhammad[1] (570–632 C.E.) was born in Mecca, in what is today Saudi Arabia (Timeline 10.1). Much of what we know about him comes from his sermons and revelations in the Muslim sacred book, the **Qur'an** ("recitation"), and from the **hadiths** ("recollections," "narratives"), the remembrances of him by his early followers.

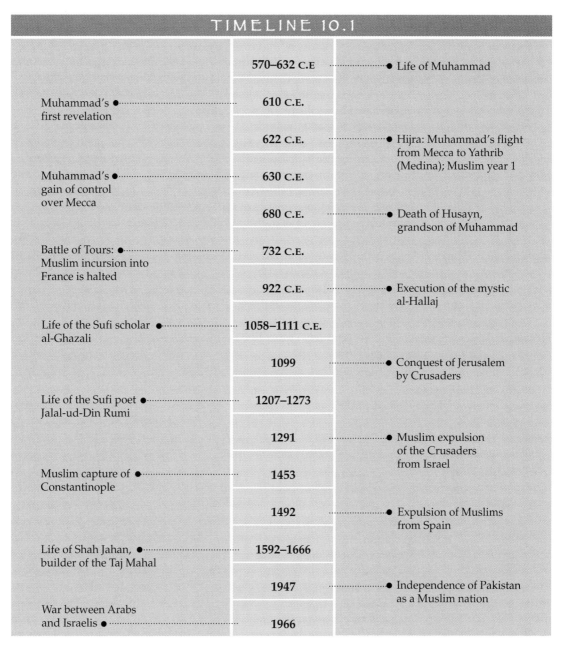

	570–632 C.E	● Life of Muhammad
Muhammad's ● first revelation	**610 C.E.**	
	622 C.E.	● Hijra: Muhammad's flight from Mecca to Yathrib (Medina); Muslim year 1
Muhammad's ● gain of control over Mecca	**630 C.E.**	
	680 C.E.	● Death of Husayn, grandson of Muhammad
Battle of Tours: ● Muslim incursion into France is halted	**732 C.E.**	
	922 C.E.	● Execution of the mystic al-Hallaj
Life of the Sufi scholar ● al-Ghazali	**1058–1111** C.E.	
	1099	● Conquest of Jerusalem by Crusaders
Life of the Sufi poet ● Jalal-ud-Din Rumi	**1207–1273**	
	1291	● Muslim expulsion of the Crusaders from Israel
Muslim capture of ● Constantinople	**1453**	
	1492	● Expulsion of Muslims from Spain
Life of Shah Jahan, ● builder of the Taj Mahal	**1592–1666**	
	1947	● Independence of Pakistan as a Muslim nation
War between Arabs and Israelis ●	**1966**	

Timeline of significant events in the history of Islam.

In the days before Islam arose, the religions of the Arabian Peninsula were Judaism, Christianity, Zoroastrianism, and traditional local religious practices. These local practices worshiped tree spirits, mountain spirits, tribal gods, and *jinni* (the origin of the English word *genie*)—capricious spirits that were thought to inhabit the desert and even to enter people. The supreme god Allah was an object of faith but not of worship. Allah "was the creator and sustainer of life but remote from everyday concerns and thus not the object of cult or ritual. Associated with Allah were three goddesses who were the daughters of Allah: al-Lat, Manat, and al-Uzza,"[2] goddesses related to nature, the moon, and fertility.

At the time of Muhammad's birth, Mecca was already a center of religious pilgrimage. Located in Mecca was a black meteorite that had fallen to earth long before Muhammad's time. It was venerated because it was believed to have been sent from heaven. A squarish shrine had been constructed to contain it, called the Kabah[3] ("cube"). By Muhammad's day, as many as 360 religious images of tribal gods and goddesses had been placed within the Kabah, and tradition tells that 24 statues, perhaps associated with the zodiac, stood around the central square of Mecca. By Muhammad's time, yearly pilgrimages to Mecca were already common, and a four-month period of regular truce among the many Arabian tribes was kept in order to allow this.

Muhammad's grandfather, Abd al-Muttalib, played an important role among the Quraysh (Quraish), the dominant tribe of Mecca, and is even thought to have been custodian of the Kabah. Muhammad's father died not long before Muhammad's birth, and his mother seems to have died when he was just a child. Muhammad then lived with his grandfather, and after his grandfather's death two years later, he went to live with his uncle, Abu Talib.[4]

As an adult, Muhammad worked as a caravan driver for a widow named Khadijah,[5] who had inherited a caravan company from her deceased husband. The friendship between Khadijah and Muhammad grew over time. They married in about 595 C.E., when Muhammad was 25 and she (tradition says) was about 40.[6] This marriage brought financial, spiritual, and emotional support to Muhammad; Khadijah proved to be his mainstay until her death. Together they had at least six children, but no boy—who could be Muhammad's hereditary successor—survived into adulthood. After Khadijah's death, Muhammad remarried a number of times. It is possible he married several of his wives out of compassion, because in his society widows of soldiers often needed a husband for financial support and legal protection.

From his travels as a caravan worker, Muhammad undoubtedly learned a great deal about several religions, including the differences within and among them. Although the monotheistic religions of his region believed in one "High God" and emphasized the need for morality, there was much disagreement as well. Jews and Christians disagreed about the role of Jesus and the nature of God. Christians disagreed with each other about the nature of Jesus. Jews and some Christians forbade image making, while other Christians allowed it. Many people also worshiped nature spirits. And the Persian religion Zoroastrianism, a major influence in the Near East of the time, so emphasized the moral struggle in human life that many people saw the world as being subject to two cosmic forces—good and evil.

As a religious person, Muhammad spent time pondering and meditating. To do this, he frequently went to caves in the hills that surrounded Mecca, which had long been used for prayer. When he was 40, during a religious retreat in a cave at Mount Hira, he received his first revelation, as recorded in the Qur'an. A bright presence came to him and held before his eyes a cloth covered with writing. It commanded three times that he recite what was written there:

> Recite in the name of the Lord who created—created man from clots of blood.
> Recite! Your Lord is the Most Bountiful One, who by the pen taught man what he did not know.
> Indeed, man transgresses in thinking himself his own master; for to your Lord all things return. . . .
> Prostrate yourself and come nearer.[7]

At first, Muhammad doubted the nature of this revelation. Could it be madness or hallucination or some kind of demonic apparition? He confided in his wife Khadijah, who knew him well and encouraged him to accept his experience as a true communication from God. He became convinced that the bright presence was the angel Gabriel, and when further revelations came to him, Muhammad began to share them with his closest friends and family members—particularly his wife, his cousin Ali, and his friend, Abu Bakr. These were the first **Muslims,** meaning "people who submit" to God (Allah).

When Muhammad began to proclaim his revelations more openly, he was not well received. Although much of his message was unthreatening (promoting the need for honesty, kindness, support of the poor, and protection of the weak), the revelations insisted that only the One God, Allah, should be worshiped. The revelations forbade the worship of other gods and demanded the destruction of statues and images. Muhammad also denounced usury (lending money at exorbitant rates) and the failure to make and keep fair contracts. These messages threatened business people, particularly those involved in the pilgrimage trade, because the revelations denounced both common business practices and the multiple tribal gods whose images were kept in the Kabah. In 615 C.E., some of Muhammad's followers fled for safety to what is today Ethiopia. In 619 C.E. Khadijah died. When Abu Talib, Muhammad's protective uncle, died soon after, Muhammad became concerned for his safety; he and the rest of his followers considered eventually leaving Mecca.

During this stressful time, Muhammad, in 620 C.E., experienced himself being carried to Jerusalem and ascending from there into paradise. In this experience, called his Night Journey or Night of Ascent, the angel Gabriel guided him upward. As Muhammad ascended toward the highest heaven,

Muhammad, accompanied by angels, is portrayed during the Night of Ascent on the back of the steed Buraq.

he encountered angels and the great prophets of the past, including Abraham and Jesus, and at last entered into the presence of God. Muslims disagree about whether this event constituted a personal vision or an actual physical ascension from Jerusalem. Regardless, artistic tradition treats Muhammad's experience as a physical and bodily ascent from the city of Jerusalem.[8] He is pictured as being carried on the back of the celestial steed Buraq, surrounded by flames and flying through the sky. This experience confirmed for Muhammad his vocation as a prophet and messenger of God.

Persecution of Muhammad and his followers in Mecca intensified. At the invitation of leaders of Yathrib, a city about three hundred miles to the north, Muhammad and his followers finally left Mecca in 622 C.E. Muhammad's migration, called in Arabic the **Hijra** (or Hegira, often translated as "flight" or "migration"), is a central event in Islam. It marks (1) the point at which Muhammad's message began to be favorably received and (2) the start of the Islamic community (*umma*). For these reasons, the Muslim calendar dates the year of the Hijra as year 1. (In the West, dates according to the Muslim calendar are given as A.H.—*anno Hegirae,* Latin for "in the year of the Hijra.")

Muhammad's initial success in Yathrib was not complete. Jews there allied with his political enemies and rejected his beliefs because he recognized Jesus a prophet and disputed the completeness and correctness of the Hebrew scriptures. Muhammad eventually banished or executed these enemies, and over time he gained control of the city. He set up the first Islamic **mosque** (*masjid*) in Yathrib, where many early rules about worship and social regulation were worked out. Yathrib is now called Medina (*madinat an-nabi,* "city of the prophet"). Along with Mecca and Jerusalem, Medina has become one of the three most sacred cities of Islam.

In spite of his success in Yathrib, Muhammad's goal was always to return to Mecca, the religious center of Arabia. In a battle in 624 C.E. at Badr between citizens of Mecca and Medina, Muslim soldiers triumphed against great odds. There were skirmishes and threats and a tentative treaty over the following few years until, finally, Muhammad returned as the victor to Mecca in 630 C.E. where he then took control of the city, destroyed all images in the Kabah and marketplace, and began to institutionalize his religious ideals.

Muhammad extended his control over further territory in Arabia; at the time of his death, he was planning to spread his religion into Syria. In his final sermon, he opposed merely tribal loyalties and preached the brotherhood of all believers. Muhammad died in Medina in 632 C.E.

Muhammad viewed himself, as did his followers, as the last of the long line of prophets who transmitted God's word to humanity. He did not consider himself to be divine but simply an instrument in the hands of God, a messenger transmitting God's will to the human world. Muslims view Muhammad as a man who showed perfection in his life, and they revere him as an ideal human being, a model for all believers.

ESSENTIALS OF ISLAM

Islam literally means "surrender" or "submission," indicating whole-hearted surrender to God, and a Muslim is one who submits to God (Allah). The words *Islam* and *Muslim* are related to several words for peace, such as the Arabic word *salam* and the Hebrew *shalom*. They suggest the inner peace that is gained by surrendering to the divine. The word *Islam* also connotes the community of all believers, suggesting inclusion in a large family. As the Qur'an states, "the believers are a band of brothers."[9]

At the heart of Islam is a belief in an all-powerful, transcendent God who has created the universe and who controls it down to the smallest detail. Islam is thus a cousin to the other monotheistic religions of Judaism and Christianity, and all three religions worship the same God. It is possible, however, that the notion of God's power and transcendence receives the greatest emphasis in Islam. Some observers have commented that in Islam, prostration of the entire body during prayer fittingly indicates a belief in divine power and the believer's submission to it—as compared to other characteristic prayer postures, such as kneeling (common in Christianity) and standing (common in Judaism). The physical posture of prostration illustrates well the Muslim attitude of total surrender to God.

Muslims refer to God as Allah. The word is a contraction of *al* ("the") and *ilah* ("God") and simply means "the God" or "God." (The Arabic word *Allah* is related to *El*, the general Hebrew word for "God.") Muslims explain that the word *Allah* is not the name of God—it simply means "God." It is said that Allah has ninety-nine names, among which are "the Merciful," "the Just," and "the Compassionate." These names demonstrate that Allah is not abstract—not just an impersonal force—but has characteristics of a personal being. In the Qur'an, Allah describes himself as personal and caring, as well as all-knowing, all-seeing, and all-powerful. Allah, because of this personal nature and the attribute of power, is referred to in Islam as being "male," although, strictly speaking, God has no gender.

It is sometimes hard for non-Muslims to understand the Muslim notion that God is omnipresent and controls every detail of life. The name of God is invoked in daily conversation, particularly in the frequently used phrase, "if God wills." People are called to prayer several times a day by a **muezzin,** a chanter who announces that Allah is great, greater than anything else. The chanted voice suggests that God is as active in the world as sound is active in the air, unseen but present. Some visitors to Muslim countries have remarked that people there live in a shared belief in God as easily as fish live in water or birds fly in air. God's active, present reality is taken for granted.

In Islamic belief, God has spoken repeatedly through human beings—prophets—revealing his mind and will. Muslims believe that divine revelation began just after the creation of the human race, when God spoke to Adam and Eve. It continued to occur, as when God spoke to patriarchs and prophets such as Abraham (Ibrahim) and Moses (Musa). Islamic belief also thinks of Jesus (Isa) as a prophet of God, although Muslims reject both the

Muslims pray at Kuala Lumpur's Sultan Abdul Aziz Mosque, a modern adaptation of traditional architectural style. ▶

notion of Jesus' divinity and the Christian doctrine of the Trinity. Muslims believe that both Judaism and Christianity express true revelation from God but that in various ways those religions have contaminated God's word with human misunderstanding. It was Muhammad, Muslims believe, who freed the divine message from human error and offered it, purified, to all people. Because he is considered the last and greatest figure in the long line of prophets, Muhammad is called the "seal of the prophets."

Muslims trace their ancestry back to Abraham, the same patriarchal ancestor of the Jews, and to his son Ishmael (Ismail). Ishmael (as discussed in Chapter 8) was conceived by Abraham and Hagar, who was a maid to Sarah, Abraham's wife. When Sarah, at an advanced age, became pregnant and gave birth to her son Isaac, Hagar and Ishmael were forced to leave Abraham's care, purportedly because of Sarah's jealousy. They survived in the desert only because an angel revealed to them a source of water, which Muslims believe was found near Mecca. Thus Islam and Judaism trace themselves back to a common ancestor, Abraham.

Muhammad learned about Judaism from the Jews who lived in Arabia. He also absorbed and considered religious elements from Christianity and Zoroastrianism—religions that share with Islam a belief in souls, bodily resurrection, a final judgment (the Day of Doom), and an afterlife of hell [10] for the wicked and paradise for the good. All three religions also share with Islam a belief in angels and devils, who can have influence on human beings. Indeed, there are numerous similarities between Islam and other religions, and non-Muslims might speculate that Muhammad was influenced by these religions. However, Muslims hold that Muhammad's religious ideas came directly from God.

The overall worldview of Islam (as with the other three religions) is highly dramatic. Muslims believe that good and evil forces are in constant battle and that life on earth is filled with choices that lead to the most serious consequences. This conception goes hand in hand with the overall emphasis of all Western prophetic religions on morality. Religion is viewed as a strongly ethical enterprise: one of its most important purposes is to regulate human life. This moral emphasis appears clearly in the essential Five Pillars of Islam, which we will now consider.

The Five Pillars of Islam

All Muslims must accept and practice the following Five Pillars, so called because they hold up one's faith. The Five Pillars are mentioned in the Qur'an.

Creed (Shahadah)   "There is no God but Allah, and Muhammad is his messenger." This single sentence, when recited with belief, makes a person a Muslim. It is the first sentence whispered into the ears of a newborn infant, it is recited daily in prayer, and it is written in Arabic everywhere inside mosque domes and over their doors.

The most noticeable quality of the Muslim creed is its simplicity, for it emphasizes that there is only one God and that God is a unity. As the Qur'an says, "Your God is one God. There is no God but him."[11] The simplicity of the creed is in deliberate contrast to the rather long and complicated creeds of Christianity, and within it is a rejection of several Christian notions. It rejects the Christian doctrine of the Trinity, which Muslims see as a belief in three gods. It also rejects the idea that Jesus was divine or that any human being can be divine. It emphatically does not see Muhammad as a divine or supernatural figure but specifies his role as God's prophet and messenger.[12]

Prayer (Salat)   Much like the traditional Jewish practice of prayer at dawn, noon, and dusk, devout Muslims are called on to pray five times a day: before dawn and at midday, midafternoon, sunset, and nighttime.[13] Times for prayer are announced by a muezzin, who calls out from the top of a tower called a **minaret.** (Nowadays, recordings of the call to prayer are often played over loudspeakers.) The muezzin's call to prayer begins with *Allahu akbar* ("God is great"),[14] and it continues, "I witness that there is no God but Allah; I witness that Muhammad is the messenger of Allah; hasten to prayer." In towns and cities with many mosques, the call to prayer comes from the most prestigious mosque first and is then followed up by other mosques.

Before prayer, the individual is normally expected to perform a ritual purification with water, in which the hands, arms, face, neck, and feet are washed. If water is unavailable, purification may be done with sand.

Those who pray face toward Mecca—inside a mosque the direction (**qiblah**) is indicated by a special arched niche (**mihrab**). In the earliest days of Islam, Muslims faced Jerusalem for prayer, but later revelations received by Muhammad in Medina changed this direction to Mecca. The Qur'an directs: "Turn your face toward the holy mosque; wherever you be, turn your faces toward it."[15] When several people are praying together, one person acts as the leader, standing at the head of the group in front of the mihrab. Passages from the Qur'an and other prayer formulas are recited from memory in Arabic, accompanied by several basic bodily postures: standing, bowing, prostrating, and sitting. Each time of prayer demands a certain number of sets (*rakas*) of prayers: two at morning prayer, three at dusk, and four at the other times of prayer.

Friday is the day of public prayer. On other days, people may pray privately, at home or at work, as well as in a mosque. Originally, the day of prayer was Saturday, following the Jewish practice; but Muhammad received a revelation that public prayer on Friday was God's will. In most Muslim countries, public prayer is performed at midday on Friday. Usually only men perform public prayer at a mosque, while women ordinarily pray at home; but where women are allowed to pray with men at a mosque, they are assigned their own area, separated by a curtain or screen or located in an upstairs gallery. The Friday service usually includes a sermon by a

Whether from a simple tower in a desert town or from this prominent minaret near the Atlantic Ocean, Muslims are called to prayer five times each day.

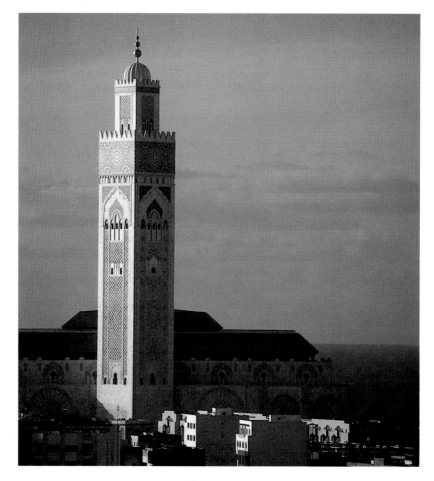

religious leader. Although Friday is a day of public prayer, it is not necessarily a public day of rest. In many Muslim countries, offices are open on Fridays, and because of European colonial influence, the public day of rest is Sunday. Some Muslim countries, however, recognize Friday as the weekly day of public rest.

Charity to the Poor (Zakat) Muhammad was troubled by injustice, inequality, and poverty, and the demand that people give to the poor was a part of his overall vision of a more just society. Islamic practice demands that believers donate certain percentages of their total income, herds, and produce from fields and orchards each year to the poor. This is not a tax on yearly income, but rather a tax on all that one owns. The percentages vary depending on what is taxed but are commonly about 2.5 percent. Nowadays, government involvement in this taxation varies among Muslim countries. (In industrialized countries, we are used to government taxes paying for systems of welfare, disability compensation, social security, and other forms of assistance. This is a fairly recent phenomenon, however, that is practical only in money-based economies. Nonindustrial societies, which often use barter instead of money, depend much more on voluntary care for the poor.) In addition to established yearly donations, a good Muslim is expected to perform isolated acts of generosity and charity for the poor when such acts are called for in everyday life.

Fasting during Ramadan (Sawm)   To fast means to abstain from food for a specified period of time. The purpose of fasting is to discipline oneself, to develop sympathy for the poor and hungry, and to give to others what one would have eaten. Fasting is thought to be good for individual spiritual growth, and it is also an important bond that unites Muslims during the period of shared discomfort—**Ramadan.**

Ramadan, the ninth month of the Muslim calendar, is the time during which Muhammad first received his revelations. Fasting during this month, followed by a celebration at the month's end, is considered a fitting way to remember this special event. During the month of Ramadan, Muslims avoid all food, liquid, tobacco, and sex from dawn until dusk. Exceptions are made with regard to food and drink for travelers, pregnant women, and the sick, but these people are expected to make up the days of fasting at a later time.

Because Islam follows a strictly lunar calendar, Ramadan occurs at a slightly different time each year. Twelve lunar months equal only 354 days; thus, Ramadan falls 11 days earlier each year than the previous year. As a result, Ramadan can fall in any season. When Ramadan falls in winter, when the days are cool and short, it involves the least discomfort. But when the month of Ramadan falls in the summer, fasting can be a great hardship; when evening finally comes and the day's fast is ended, water and food seem miraculous. The entire month of fasting is followed by a feast of celebration.

We should note that periods of abstinence are common in many religions. The Christian observance of Lent, for about a month before Easter, is a well-known example, as is the Jewish practice of fasting on Yom Kippur, the Day of Atonement, in autumn.

Pilgrimage to Mecca (Hajj)   Pilgrimage—a religious journey by a believer to a sacred city or site—is a common practice in many religions. Besides fulfilling religious demands, pilgrimage offers other, less obvious rewards. It allows people to travel and experience new sights, brings people of different backgrounds together, and engenders a sense of unity. Best of all, it becomes a powerful symbol of an interior journey to the spiritual goals of new understanding and personal transformation. All Muslims, both men and women, unless prevented by poverty or sickness, are expected to visit Mecca at least once in their lifetime. Because Islam is central to the nature of Mecca, only Muslims may visit the city.

Pilgrimage to Mecca, or **Hajj,** was already a practice before Muhammad was born, possibly because worshipers wanted to visit the mysterious black meteorite that had fallen in the area. Muhammad, following divine revelation, continued the practice of pilgrimage to Mecca and many earlier aspects of that pilgrimage—including veneration of the black meteorite. Although this veneration might seem to contradict Muhammad's call for pure, nonidolatrous worship of the One God, the meteorite was thought of as a special gift from God. It was also connected with Abraham and even with Adam, who are said to have venerated it, and with the angel Gabriel, who was thought to have carried it to earth.

Because the present-day form of pilgrimage offers many deeply emotional experiences for believers, it deserves special description.[16] Contemporary pilgrims generally arrive by plane at Jiddah, the port city on the west coast of Saudi Arabia. In earlier times, people came by more romantic (and dangerous) methods—by boat or camel caravan. Air travel, however, has allowed people to come in great numbers. In the past, about 30,000 people visited Mecca each year; now two million make the journey. In earlier days, the pilgrimage took months or even years. Some pilgrims died along the way, particularly when the special month of pilgrimage (as we already noted) fell in the summer. Often it was the only long trip a person might ever take from a home village. Despite the numbers of pilgrims, to return home as a *hajji* (male pilgrim) or *hajjiyah* (female pilgrim) still confers much prestige.

Muslims distinguish between the "greater pilgrimage," which is made only during the special month of pilgrimage (*dhu'l-Hijjah*) and the "lesser pilgrimage," made at other times of year. The lesser pilgrimage consists simply of a visit to Mecca and nearby holy sites. The greater pilgrimage, which is described in the following paragraphs, adds several days of arduous travel and ritual in the plains beyond Mecca; a trip to the city of Medina is often included.

Pilgrims first come to Mecca and are expected to arrive by the seventh of the month for the Hajj. For men there is special clothing, called the robe of Abraham, consisting of two pieces of white, seamless cloth. One piece is worn around the waist and lower body; the other covers the upper body and the left arm. (Women have no special clothing, but many dress in white. They do not veil their faces when they are participating in the pilgrimage.) The uniformity of clothing for males emphasizes their basic equality before God. In addition to the robe of Abraham and special prayers, all pilgrims are expected to refrain from sex, violence, and hunting. (It is easy to see how these pilgrimages and the associated practices drastically reduced intertribal warfare on the Arabian Peninsula.)

After settling into their hotels or hostels, pilgrims proceed to the great mosque. Inside the huge rectangle of the mosque area is a large courtyard, open to the sky. The four sides of the courtyard consist of pillared colonnades, which open out onto the central area and offer shade. At the center of the courtyard is the Kabah shrine. It is a building approximately 50 feet high and 40 feet wide and deep. It is covered with a black cloth, remade every year, whose edges are embroidered in gold with words from the Qur'an. The interior of the Kabah is empty and is entered only by caretak-

Worshipers pray facing the Kabah in the Great Mosque of Mecca.

ers and dignitaries, who ritually cleanse the interior with rosewater. The black meteorite, known as the Black Stone, is embedded in one external wall of the building and is visible on the outside from the courtyard.

After ceremonially purifying themselves with water, pilgrims immediately walk counterclockwise around the Kabah seven times. As they pass the east corner, they kiss or salute the Black Stone, which extends from the shrine about 5 feet above the ground. Today the Black Stone is surrounded by silver and has become concave from being touched and kissed over the years by so many millions of people.

Pilgrims reenact important events in the life of Abraham, their forefather. Islam holds that Hagar and Abraham's son, Ishmael, lived in the region of Mecca and that Abraham visited them here. Muslims believe that Abraham was asked by God to sacrifice his son Ishmael—not Isaac, as Judaism and Christianity teach—and that the near sacrifice took place in Mecca. In their actions, they relive Abraham's spiritual submission as a means of emulating his close relationship to God.

After walking around the Kabah, pilgrims ritually recall Hagar. A long covered corridor nearby connects the two sacred hills of Safa and Marwah, which the Qur'an calls "signs appointed by Allah."[17] Between these two hills Hagar is believed to have searched desperately for water for her son Ishmael. Pilgrims walk speedily seven times along the corridor (the *Masa*), reenacting

Hagar's thirsty search. They drink from the well of Zamzam in the mosque area, which is believed to be the well shown to Hagar by an angel.

On the eighth day of the month, after another visit to the Kabah, pilgrims go to Mina, a few miles outside Mecca, where they pray through the night. The next morning, the ninth day, they travel to the plain of Arafat, about 12 miles from Mecca, where Muhammad preached his final sermon. At noon they hear a sermon and stand all afternoon in prayer, exposed to the sun; the day of prayer at Arafat is often crucial to the experience of exaltation that the pilgrimage experience can bestow. That night is spent outdoors at Muzdalifa, halfway between Arafat and Mina.

The following day, the tenth of the month, is called the Day of Sacrifice (**Id al-Adha**). Pilgrims return to Mina, where they throw small stones at three square pillars, a ritual that recalls how Abraham responded to a temptation: when a demon tempted him to disobey God's command to sacrifice his son, Abraham threw stones at the demon and drove it away.

Pilgrims then select for themselves and their families one animal (sheep, goat, cow, or camel) to be sacrificed to reenact another important incident in Abraham's life: after showing his willingness to sacrifice his son Ishmael to God, Abraham was divinely directed to substitute a ram for his son. The slaughtered animal is then cooked and eaten. (This act of animal sacrifice is carried out throughout the Muslim world at the same time during the month of pilgrimage.) After the sacrifice, the men's heads are shaven, the women's hair is cut, and all fingernails and toenails are trimmed to signify a new, purified life and a return to ordinary activities. Pilgrims then return to Mecca to again walk around the Kabah. Although this concludes the essential ritual of the Hajj, many pilgrims go on to visit Medina to honor the memory of Muhammad, who is buried there.

Additional Islamic Religious Practices

Islam aims at providing patterns for ideal living. Controls and prohibitions are imposed not to signify a love of suffering but to increase social order and happiness. Where outsiders might see only limitations, Muslims see instead the benefits that sensible regulations bring to individuals and societies. People who visit Muslim cultures often comment on the rarity of crime and the sense of security that people regularly feel on city streets.

Although it is strict, Islamic practice also values pleasure and happiness in this world. Believers must fast during the daylight hours of Ramadan, but each night families gather to enjoy a good meal together. The same general attitude applies toward sexuality. Although sex is regulated, Muslims do not value celibacy. Muhammad was no celibate and opposed celibacy as being unnatural. In this regard, Muslims are puzzled by Jesus' never having married and by the religious ideal of monasticism. It is within this framework of an ideal society that we should view some of the prohibitions of Islam.

The Islamic Religious Calendar: Festivals and Holy Days

Like other religions, Islam has developed a sequence of religious festivals and holy days. The main observances follow.

- The Day of Sacrifice, or Id al-Adha, is celebrated during the month of the Hajj. The head of every Muslim household is expected to sacrifice (or to pay someone to sacrifice) a sheep, goat, cow, or camel to recall Abraham's sacrifice of a ram in place of his son. The meat is cooked, eaten by the family, and shared with the poor.
- The Day of Breaking the Fast, or **Id al-Fitr,** is observed just after the month of Ramadan (the ninth lunar month) has ended. People have parties and often visit the graves of ancestors. Sometimes the festival goes on for up to three days.
- During Muharram (the first month of the Muslim year), believers remember the migration of Muhammad and his followers to Medina. For the Shiite branch of Islam, found primarily in Iran, Iraq, and Pakistan, the month has additional significance because it is associated with the death of Husayn, the son of Muhammad's son-in-law Ali. The first nine days of the month are solemn, and on the tenth day the devout reenact publicly the assassination of Husayn. Plays and processions vividly recall his death, sometimes with devotees cutting themselves and crying aloud during processions in the street.
- Muhammad's birthday occurs on the twelfth day of the third month of the year. In some countries it is a public holiday, and in some regions the whole month is given to celebrating and reading religious texts.
- Birthdays of other holy men and women are variously marked by devotees in different regions and groups. Shiites observe the birthday of Ali; religious communities honor the birthdays of their founders; and the birthdays of regional saints are celebrated locally.

Dietary Restrictions   The Qur'an forbids pork and wine. Both Judaism and Islam view the pig as a scavenger animal, whose meat can transmit disease. Wine is forbidden because of its association with violence and frequent addiction. Although only wine is forbidden in the Qur'an, Islam has interpreted that prohibition to include all alcohol.[18]

Usury and Gambling   Charging interest on loans is not allowed. We might recall that in Muhammad's day money was lent at very high rates of interest, which impoverished and exploited the borrower. (Some Muslims today get around this prohibition by charging a "commission" for making a loan, although the loan itself is officially without interest.) Gambling is forbidden because it is considered a dangerous waste of time and money for the individual and is a practice that can ruin the gambler's family.

Circumcision   Male circumcision is a religious requirement in Islam, although it is not actually demanded by the Qur'an. Circumcision at about age 7 or 8 is common. In circumcision, a small amount of loose skin (called the foreskin) is cut off from the end of a boy's penis. (We might recall that Jews circumcise boys on the eighth day after birth. Circumcision is also common among many Christians, although for them it is not a religious commandment; and it occurs frequently in native religions.) Explanations for the practice of circumcision vary. One is that the practice shows submission to the role of God in human procreation. Another relates to reasons of hygiene; in a hot climate, where daily bathing is not always possible, circumcision might have served as a preventive measure against infection. Perhaps both are true. In Islam, however, it is also done in emulation of Muhammad, who was circumcised.

In some primarily Muslim countries, particularly those in East Africa, Muslim girls are also circumcised at puberty. The act involves the removal of part or all of a girl's external sexual organs. A common explanation is that it decreases sexual desire in the circumcised young woman, helping her to remain a virgin before her marriage and to be faithful to her husband afterward. Non-Muslims in the West commonly criticize the practice as being repressive and dangerous; but some traditionalists see it as a valuable initiation rite and a preparation for marriage. In any case, we should recognize that it is not a Qur'anic command, nor does it have the same religious authority as does male circumcision.[19]

Marriage   In Islam, marriage is basically a civil contract, although a certain amount of ritual has grown up around it. In traditional Muslim societies, marriage is arranged by the parents and formalized by a written contract. Usually the bridegroom's family makes an offer of money or property to the family of the bride as a part of the contract. The marriage ceremony, which is held at home, is essentially the witnessing and signing of the contract. A passage from the Qur'an might be read, and there is usually a feast following the signing of the contract. Marriages can be annulled for serious reason, and divorce is possible and can be initiated by a wife as well as by a husband. Neither annulment nor divorce, however, is frequent. After marriage, a woman takes on a new, more responsible role. As a wife she has left the protection of her father and is now the legal responsibility of her husband.

Female Roles   Islamic practice sees male and female social roles as different but complementary. Girls are prepared for traditional female roles, such as wife and mother, although in many Muslim societies today women also work as nurses, doctors, and teachers. Nevertheless, a woman is expected to be circumspect in public, particularly after marriage. In some societies, a woman must be veiled when she goes out of the house, and she allows only her husband and relatives to see her face. Quite conservative societies keep women from jobs outside the home, and women are expected to socialize only with female friends and relatives.

Death Rituals   The same general simplicity of marriage ceremonies is also characteristic of death and funerals. Prayers from the Qur'an are

The simple gravestones of this Islamic cemetery surround a small shrine dedicated to a local saint. The desert location is a vivid reminder of the landscape from which Islam arose.

recited for the dying person, and after death the body is buried in a plain white shroud. Ideally, for a male who has made the pilgrimage, the shroud is the white robe of Abraham that he wore in Mecca. The face of the deceased is turned toward Mecca at the burial, and the headstone is usually an undecorated stone marker, which signifies equality of all people in death.[20]

Scripture: The Qur'an

The name *Qur'an* (*Koran*) means "recitation" and recalls the origins of these sacred writings in the sermons of Muhammad. The name also suggests the way in which the Qur'an is best communicated—by being recited. Although the Qur'an has been translated into many languages, only the Arabic version is considered to be fully authoritative. The beautiful sounds of the original are considered a part of its nature and are essential to its spiritual power.

The Qur'an is believed to be of divine origin, for it is God's Word, which was revealed to Muhammad during the approximately twenty years from his first revelation in 610 C.E. until the end of his life. Disciples wrote down the words of Muhammad's revelations, but after his death, when people became concerned that variations would arise and spread, it was thought necessary to establish a single authorized version. This work was begun by Abu Bakr, Muhammad's first political and religious successor, or **caliph** (*khalifa,* "successor"), and it was finished in the caliphate of Uthman, which ended in 656 C.E. The authorized edition that was created became the basis for all later copies.[21]

There is a repetitive quality about the Qur'an, common to memorized material, due largely to the fact that the Qur'an is not a carefully constructed argument divided into segments, nor is it a series of stories. Rather, it is a body of sermons and utterances that repeat images and themes in a natural way.

The Qur'an covers a wide variety of topics, as well as discusses figures who are also found in the Jewish and Christian Bibles: Adam, Eve, Noah, Abraham, Isaac, Jacob, Joseph, Moses, David, Solomon, Jesus, Mary, and others. It also gives practical admonitions about everyday life—about property rights, money, inheritance, marriage, and divorce. It refers to events in the life of Muhammad and to specifically religious beliefs and regulations—angels, divine judgment, fasting, and the pilgrimage. The topics and types of material are often blended together.

The Qur'an has 114 chapters, or **suras.** Each sura has a traditional name, derived from an image or topic mentioned in it, and many of these names are evocative: "The Elephant," "Light," "Dawn," "Thunder," "The Cave," "Smoke," "The Mountain," "The Moon," "The High One." The order of the suras does not reflect the exact order in which they were revealed. Except for the first sura, which is a brief invocation, the suras are arranged so that the longest is given first. This means that the last chapters are extremely short (and the easiest for beginners). The placement is generally, in fact, in reverse chronological order, with some intermixture of periods. The short suras are probably the earliest teachings of Muhammad, while the long ones are the products of his final years, when the details of Islamic life were being revealed to him. The suras of the Qur'an have been compared to leaves that have fallen from a tree: the first-fallen leaves are on the bottom.

Islamic art has been profoundly affected by the Qur'an. Indeed, some handwritten copies of the Qur'an are great artworks in themselves, often filled with gold letters and colorful geometrical designs. Because Islam generally prohibits the making of images, artists have developed the most wonderful calligraphy to record the sacred words of the Qur'an.

Frequently the words of a phrase from the Qur'an are also cunningly interlaced to make integrated designs, which are used to beautify mosques

In the name of God
The Compassionate
The Merciful.
Praise be to God, Lord
of the Universe,
The Compassionate,
    the Merciful,
Sovereign of the Day of
    Judgment!
You alone we worship,
    and to You alone
we turn for help.

—Opening (Al-Fatihah)
of the Qur'an[22]

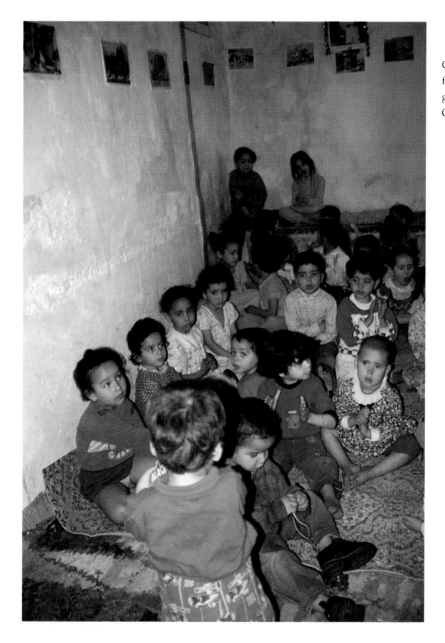

Children memorize verses from the Qur'an through group recitation in a Qur'anic school.

and religious schools (*madrasas, medersas*). On buildings, passages from the Qur'an are carved in stone or wood or set in mosaic. Of the many writing systems in the world, cursive Arabic, with its wondrous curves, is possibly the most visually beautiful of all. The fluid form of this writing is suggested nicely by the word *arabesque,* a French word that has entered the English language to describe a pattern of interlacing lines that are curving and graceful.

The repetition of phrases and images from the Qur'an is comforting to Muslims who have heard them recited aloud in daily prayers and in sermons since childhood. Passages are recited regularly on the radio, particularly during Ramadan, and in some countries are part of the signoff of television broadcasts. Present everywhere, every day, such phrases have a hypnotic resonance. Because Arabic is an especially beautiful language, chanting the Qur'an in Arabic is an art form, and some chanters have even become famous for the beauty of their voices and their interpretation of Qur'anic material.

THE HISTORICAL DEVELOPMENT OF ISLAM

Because his sons had died in infancy, Muhammad died without a clear hereditary male successor.[23] He apparently had not appointed anyone to succeed him,[24] and the result was confusion and an unclear line of succession—a fact that ultimately created significant divisions in Islam, whose effects remain today.

Muhammad had asked Abu Bakr, his friend and the father of his youngest wife, to be the principal leader of prayer. Because of this position, Abu Bakr was recognized as the first caliph. When Abu Bakr died two years later, he was succeeded by Umar, the second caliph, and followed by Uthman, both of whom were assassinated. The fourth caliph was Muhammad's cousin and son-in-law, Ali, the husband of his daughter Fatima. Ali was also assassinated, and control of Islam was taken over in 661 C.E. by his opponents, who ruled from Damascus. This period marks the first and most significant division of Islam, which broke into two factions, Shiite and Sunni (which we will discuss in the following section).

The earliest stage of growth of Islam came during the time of the first four rulers, called the orthodox caliphs. These men had been close to Muhammad, and their home was Arabia. A major change occurred, however, as Islam spread outside Arabia. From an early, deliberate simplicity, Islam would now become more urbane and complex.

Expansion and Consolidation

Islam arose at a time (seventh century C.E.) that was congenial to the growth of a new political and religious power. The Byzantine Empire, ruling from Constantinople, had fought repeatedly with the Persian Empire, and both were weakened by the effort. Areas theoretically controlled by the Byzantine emperor, such as regions of North Africa, were far away from the capital.

The weakness of the Byzantine and Persian Empires—and what Muslims believe was divine purpose—helped Islam quickly expand into their territory. Islamic armies took Syria in 635 C.E. and Persia in 636 C.E. They began to move westward, taking control of Egypt in about 640 C.E. The success was intoxicating. Islam spread across most of North Africa within the

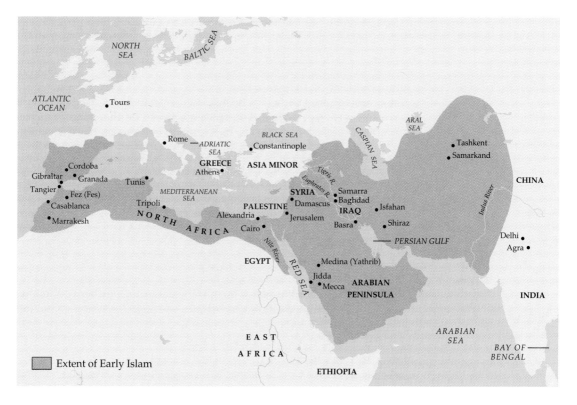

Figure 10.1
Map of the early Islamic world.

next seventy years and spread across the Red Sea and Indian Ocean from Arabia to much of East Africa (Figure 10.1).

Islamic forces entered Spain in 711 C.E., when a Muslim general named Tariq landed in the south—the name of Gibraltar ("mountain of Tariq") recalls this event. In fact, Muslim forces might have spread Islam through much of western Europe if they had not been stopped in southern France by the Christian forces of Charles Martel, the grandfather of Charlemagne, in 732 C.E. at the Battle of Tours.[25] This battle—just a hundred years after the death of Muhammad—was one of the defining battles of world history, because it prevented the further expansion of Islam into western Europe.

Although Islam was stopped from expanding northward, Islamic rulers remained in Spain for nearly eight hundred years, with capitals in Córdoba and Granada. The Islamic period in Spain is remembered with nostalgia and longing by many, for it is universally thought to have been a paradise-like time, when the arts flourished and Muslims, Jews, and Christians lived together in general harmony. The only other significant incursion into the West in these early centuries was into Sicily, where Islam was a force for about two hundred years.

From 661 C.E. to 750 C.E., Islam was controlled by the Umayyad dynasty—a period called the Damascus caliphate (the caliphate was now hereditary). During this period Islam adopted elements—from architecture to cuisine—that were introduced to Syria by the Roman Empire. It also adopted and refined the administrative and military apparatus of a political state. This fruitful contact with Roman-influenced Syria is just one example of the genius that Islam has shown in absorbing elements from other cultures and giving them new life.

Control of Islam shifted to Baghdad in 750 C.E. under the Abbasid dynasty—a hereditary line that claimed connection to Muhammad. It is often thought that this period, also known as the Baghdad caliphate, which did not end until 1258, was the golden age of Islam—its cultural peak. Just as the Umayyads had adopted Roman-inspired elements from Syria, so the Abbasids adopted much that was Persian—music, poetry, architecture, and garden design. Classical Greek texts on philosophy, science, and the arts were translated into Arabic. Under the influence of Indian artists, the prohibition on images was relaxed in court art, and miniature paintings and drawings of dazzling images were created. Baghdad became a world center of civilization and taste.

Islam continued to spread eastward. From Persia it moved into present-day Azerbaijan, Kazakhstan, Afghanistan, Pakistan, northern India, and Bangladesh. It then spread northward into western China, where millions of Muslims still live today.

After Baghdad was invaded and sacked by the Mongols in 1258, the center of Islam shifted to Egypt. Then in 1453, Muslims captured the ancient Christian capital of Constantinople, making it the center of the Ottoman Empire as well as of the Muslim world until 1921, when the Ottoman Empire ended. During this long period Islam spread, primarily through trade, to southeast Asia—to what is today Malaysia, southern Thailand, Indonesia, and the southern Philippines.

Because of the great size of Islamic territory—a span from Spain and Morocco to Indonesia and the Philippines—completely centralized control was impossible. Thus, secondary centers, which were sometimes totally independent caliphates, were established. In Spain, the cities of Córdoba and, later, Granada became local political capitals, until Muslims were expelled from Spain in 1492. In India, Delhi became the center of the Muslim Mogul (Mughal) Empire, until the British took control of the subcontinent. The fiction of a single caliph ruling all of Islam, however, was kept alive until the Ottoman caliphate in Turkey was dissolved in 1924.

The Shiite and Sunni Division within Islam

Over the centuries of its growth, Islam has experienced several divisions. The most important division is between the **Shiites** (from *shia*, "faction") and **Sunnis** (*sunna*, "tradition"). Today about ten to fifteen percent of Islam is Shiite, and the remaining majority is Sunni (Figure 10.2). The division began as a political argument over who should succeed Muhammad, but it has widened over the centuries into a division over belief, practice, and general religious approach.

The real argument over succession centered on different conceptions of the caliphate. Some thought that it should be held by a man of Muhammad's tribe (the Quraysh), someone chosen by his peers as being the person who was strongest and most capable of governing. This was a fairly practical notion of leadership. Others, however, saw the caliph as a spiritual leader, and they believed that God gave the spiritual power of the caliph to only those males who were descended directly from Muhammad's immediate family.

Shiite Islam   Shiites derive their name from the word *shia*, which means "faction"—namely, the faction, or party, of Ali, the son-in-law and cousin of Muhammad. We might recall that the legitimacy of the first four successors of Muhammad (Abu Bakr, Umar, Uthman, and Ali) was accepted by most early Muslims. Some early Muslims, however, held that Muhammad had assigned Ali to be his first successor but that a series of political and religious intrigues had initially kept Ali from the caliphate. These disagreements led to further arguments during the period of Uthman and continued even into Ali's eventual caliphate. Muawiya, leader of the Umayyad clan, rejected Ali's leadership, but when arbitration declared Ali the legitimate leader, Ali was assassinated. Following Ali's death, some believers held that succession rightfully belonged to his two sons, Hasan and Husayn. Ali's first son, Hasan, renounced his rights to succession; he was poisoned nonetheless by enemies. Ali's second son, Husayn, fought against Umayyad control but was killed and beheaded after being defeated in 680 C.E. at the battle of Karbala (or Kerbela), in Iraq. This death allowed the Umayyad dynasty to maintain control for a hundred years, but it also created strong opposition, which became the Shiite movement. Shiites, who trace Muhammad's line of succession as going from Ali to Husayn, see Husayn as a martyr whose heroic death is a redeeming sacrifice that invites imitation.

Shiite Islam believes that the legitimate succession was hereditary, descending from the immediate family of Muhammad. A God-given, hereditary spiritual power, called the Light of Muhammad, is thought by most Shiites to have passed to a total of twelve successors, or **imams.** For them, the first legitimate imam was Ali. The line ended with the disappearance of the last imam, Muhammad al-Mahdi, about 900 C.E. According to tradition,

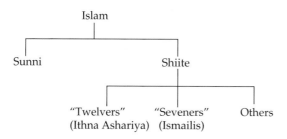

FIGURE 10.2
Branches of Islam.

he did not die but entered a hidden realm from which he works by guiding Shiite scholars and leaders. Some Shiites believe that he will emerge from this state in the future to help restore Shiite Islam and that his reappearance in the world will usher in a messianic age, heralding the end of the world. There is much speculation about this figure, and he is thought to be sinless. (The Ayatollah Khomeini [1900–1989] was considered by some in Iran to be the reappearance of this figure.)

There are several divisions within Shiite Islam that differ on how many imams there were and on the exact line of succession. Most Shiites believe in twelve imams, as previously mentioned, and thus are sometimes called Twelvers—Ithna Ashariya. And members of one group, the Ismailis, are often called the Seveners because they disagree with the Twelvers about the identity of the seventh imam; they trace descent from Ismail, whom they consider to be the seventh imam. Ismailis have split further into two main groups, the Nizari and Mustali Ismailis, and several smaller groups, a few of whom (like the Druzes of Lebanon) are not considered orthodox Muslims.

Shiite Islam has been attractive to non-Arab Muslims, who have sometimes felt that they were relegated to an inferior role in a religion whose origins were in Arabia. Iran is the center or home of the majority of Shiites, although smaller populations exist in Iraq, Pakistan, India, Lebanon, Syria, Yemen, and elsewhere.

Sunni Islam   Sunni (or Sunnite) Islam, the other great division of Islam, takes its name from a word (*sunna*, "tradition," "example") that refers to the entire body of traditional teachings that are based on the life and teachings of Muhammad, as given in the Qur'an and the authoritative hadiths. Such a great majority of Muslims belong to this branch of Islam that the history of Islam is predominantly Sunni.

Sunni Islam developed to some degree in response to the claims of Shiite Islam. Because they accepted the legitimacy of the orthodox caliphates, the Sunnis were compelled to develop a religious, political, legal, and cultural system that was consistent with their beliefs. The system included the caliphs, who were thought to rule in God's name; the Qur'an and hadiths, seen as expressing God's will; the schools and scholarly debate that interpreted the Qur'an and hadiths to apply to everyday life; and the scholars who carried on this debate. Traditional Islam does not separate political life from religious life; it aims to create a public life that is shaped by the Qur'an. Although scholarly debate has been a tradition of Shiite Islam, it is central to the ideology of Sunni Islam, which is distinctive in its openness to reasoning and practicality.

Because Mecca is located in Saudi Arabia, it is one center of power in modern Sunni Islam. This (and the influence of a reformist movement) has meant that the government of Saudi Arabia expects its country to be a model of proper Muslim belief and behavior—as tourists and foreign workers who have been forbidden from importing alcohol have sometimes been shocked to discover. It has also led to occasional friction, particularly with

Iran, which reflects the long-standing differences between Shiite and Sunni points of view.

Another center of power in the Sunni world is Egypt. Its universities, particularly Al-Azhar in Cairo, give it prestige as an interpreter of Islam; and its large Muslim population makes it politically important in the Muslim world.

SUFISM: ISLAMIC MYSTICISM

Islam began as a rather austere religion. But as it moved beyond Arabia, Islam came into contact with the luxurious lifestyle of the settled old cities in the Near East and North Africa. The Umayyad dynasty, we recall, ruled Islam for one hundred years from Damascus, which even then was an ancient city. Damascus had become one of the most important cities in the eastern part of the Roman Empire, and it had retained its prominent role under the Byzantine Empire. The caliphate of Damascus simply carried on the aristocratic style of life already present.

Islam had contact not only with sophisticated city dwellers but also with the Christian monks and hermits who lived in Israel, Syria, and Egypt. Their simple lives made a great impression on Muslims, who seemed to desire something similar for Islam. Because Islam rejected celibacy as a religious ideal, the Christian model of monasticism could not be imitated exactly. What emerged, however, were lay individuals who cultivated the spiritual life on their own and groups of devotees, loosely organized around charismatic spiritual leaders.

Sufism is the name of an old and widespread devotional movement—or group of movements—in Islam. The name *Sufism* is thought to be derived from the Arabic word *suf* ("wool"), because early Sufis wore a simple robe made of common wool. It is possible that this type of ordinary cloth was not only practical but also a statement opposing needless luxury. Sufism has been a religious movement that values deliberate simplicity.

But Sufism was not only a reaction against superficial luxury. The movement also grew out of a natural desire to do more than the merely formalistic. As Islam defined itself further, establishing religious practice in even the smallest areas of life, it was possible for some people to think that "keeping the rules" was all there was to being a good Muslim. Sufism, however, recognized that it is possible to "go through the motions" but to leave the heart uninvolved. As a result, Sufism has sought the involvement of emotions. Because of this it has been called the heart of Islam.

Sufi Beliefs

The core of the Sufi movement is its mysticism, its belief that the highest experience a person can have is a direct experience of God. It has held that an individual can, on earth, experience God "face to face." It has even held that this is the whole purpose of life, not something that has to wait until after death.

Sufi mysticism was encouraged by several religious movements that had been active in Egypt and Syria long before Sufism began to arise in the seventh and eighth centuries C.E. One was Neoplatonism, a mystical philosophical school that began in Alexandria in Egypt with Plotinus (c. 205–270 C.E.). Plotinus's work *The Enneads* spoke of the emergence of the entire cosmos from the One and the journey of the soul as it returns to its divine origin. Another movement that influenced Sufism was Gnosticism, which saw life as a spiritual journey. Gnosticism produced its own literature and interpreted other religious literature symbolically. Christian forms of Neoplatonism and Gnosticism flourished in Syria not long before the Umayyad period and produced such books as *The Divine Names* and *The Mystical Theology* by Pseudo-Dionysius, who is thought to have been a Syrian Christian monk of the sixth century. It is also possible that influences from Hindu mysticism, coming from India into Persia, were behind a great flowering of mystical poetry.

> To God belongs the east and the west. Whichever way you turn, there is the face of God.
>
> —Qur'an[28]

Sufis saw in the Qur'an a number of passages that invited mystical interpretation. These became their favorites. A beloved passage says that Allah is so near to every human being that he is even "closer than the jugular vein."[26] Another favorite passage says, "Whether you hide what is in your hearts or manifest it, Allah knows it."[27]

The image of Muhammad also took on new meaning. To the Sufis, Muhammad was himself a mystic. He lived a life of deliberate simplicity, sought God, and had profound revelations. Because he submitted himself so fully to God's will, in his Night Journey, he was carried up to the highest heaven, where he spoke with God as a friend speaks to another friend. This event, the scholar A. J. Arberry remarks, "for the Sufis constitutes the Prophet's supreme mystical experience and an example which they may aspire to follow."[29]

One of the great early Sufi saints was a woman mystic, Rabia (c. 717–801 C.E.), who left behind ecstatic writings that speak of God as her divine lover. She is famous for her statement that she sought God not because of fear of hell or desire for heaven but simply for himself alone. In other words, she sought God not for her sake but for his.

Sufis have commonly spoken about the sense of loss of self (*fana*, "extinction") that occurs in mystical experience: when the self is gone, all that remains is God. Some Sufis have spoken about this experience in language that has been shocking to the orthodox—their mystical descriptions seeming to weaken the distinction between God and his created world, which is strong in orthodox Islam, and even seeming to embrace pantheism, the belief that everything is God. Abu Yazid (d. 875 C.E.), when he was in ecstasy, is reputed to have said, "Glory be to me—how great is my majesty."[30] Al-Hallaj (d. 922 C.E.) was one of the most alarming Sufi figures; he publicly and repeatedly applied a name for God to himself, calling himself *al-Haqq*—

"the Truth," "the Real," or "Reality Itself." His comments were so shocking to his contemporaries that they executed him.

Sufis continued to come into conflict with religious authorities who feared that Sufi meeting places would supplant the mosques and that a vague command simply to love would replace the clearer, specific commands of traditional Islam. The veneration of both living and dead Sufi masters also seemed to the orthodox to be opposed to the traditional demand to worship God alone.

Al-Ghazali and Sufi Brotherhoods

The conflict was softened when al-Ghazali (or al-Ghazzali, 1058–1111), a respected scholar and teacher of philosophy and theology in Baghdad, adopted Sufism. Al-Ghazali relates in his autobiography that despite the respect his job gave him, he was deeply unhappy. What he was doing did not seem important to his own spiritual life. He was torn between leaving his post or staying on in comfort and at last followed an inner voice that demanded he go "on the road." He did this for more than ten years, traveling in Syria and Arabia and living simply. He eventually returned to Baghdad and formed a brotherhood of Sufis, but he insisted on keeping orthodox law and practice as well. His blend of Sufism with traditional practice, his later books on Sufism, and his scholarly reputation made an indelible mark on Islam. He explained that the Sufi language of "extinction" (fana) is metaphorical, which he compared to "the words of lovers passionate in their intoxication,"[31] or to a diver lost in the sea.[32] His explanations of Sufism and his prestige gave a legitimacy to Sufism that it had not had before. Sufism and orthodoxy no longer needed to run like parallel lines, never meeting. Now they could enrich each other.

After al-Ghazali, more Sufi brotherhoods were founded and a certain institutionalization developed. Disciples gathered around a master. The disciple—in Arabic called *faqir* and in Persian *darwish,* meaning "poor"—would learn a distinctive spiritual discipline (*tariqa*) from the *shaykh,* a Sufi expert. Often a master and his disciples lived in a compound of many buildings, and the life was semimonastic. Laypersons could also be associated with the religious order, even while living an entirely secular life.[33]

Many Sufi orders emerged and spread widely. One of the most famous was the Maulawiya (in Turkish, Mevlevi), founded by Jalal-ud-Din Rumi (1207–1273). Born in Persia, Rumi eventually settled in what is today Turkey. Rumi's exquisite poetry is now becoming well known beyond the Muslim world through translations. His great work is called *Mesnevi* (or *Mathnawi*). The Maulawiya order became famous for its type of circular dance, which Rumi asserted could assist mystical experience. (The English phrase *whirling dervish* refers to a member of this order, and the Mevlevi dance is still performed in Konya on Rumi's birthday in early December.)

Sufis of the Mevlevi order dance in Turkey.

Among other orders to emerge, with different emphases, were the Qadiri, Suhrawardi, and Naqshbandi.[34]

Sufi Practice and Poetry

Sufism has incorporated many techniques to encourage spiritual insight, some possibly derived from Hindu yoga or from Christian monastic practice in the Near East. One technique involved jerking the head to encourage an upward flow of blood during prayer. Two other techniques were deep, regular breathing during meditation and the repetition of the ninety-nine names of Allah, sometimes counted on a rosary, to enable a constant remembrance of God (**dhikr**). Some groups used music and others used spinning or dancing in circles or occasionally ingesting wine and psychedelic plants to alter consciousness. Some groups reportedly howled and walked on fire, among other unusual techniques. And all groups made use of allegorical interpretations of Qur'anic passages and of Islamic practices (such as the pilgrimage to Mecca), which they saw as living metaphors for their mystical search.

Sufism has also used poetry in the same allegorical and symbolic ways. When read one way, a poem might resemble the lyrics of a romantic song. Read another way, the same poem might suggest a longing of the spirit for God, a search for God, or the ecstasy of final union with God. Sufism has inspired some of the world's greatest poets, as famous in the Muslim world as are Shakespeare and Goethe in Western countries.

Until recently, only one Muslim poet was well known in English-speaking countries. Omar Khayyám (c. 1048–1122), who was also an astronomer and mathematician, gained fame in the West from a late-Victorian translation (by Edward FitzGerald) of the long poem *The Rubaiyat*. Many people are familiar with "a loaf of bread, a jug of wine, and thou," which is paraphrased from the poem and brings to mind a romantic picnic. But a Sufi could interpret a loaf of bread symbolically as the depth of ordinary reality, the jug of wine (intoxicating but suspect) as ecstasy, and "thou" as the divine *Thou*—God. Through translations, many great Sufi poets, such as Hafiz (c. 1325–1390) and Jami (1414–1492), are nowadays becoming better known and appreciated.

There is a warmth about Sufism that appeals to the ordinary layperson, and some Sufi groups have served as fraternal societies in people's lives—providing comfort, helping the poor, and even burying the dead. Its characteristic warmth and practicality helped Islam spread to countries far from its place of origin, such as Malaysia and Indonesia.

The Sufi connection with common people, however, has sometimes made the orthodox think of Sufism as a superstitious folk religion. For example, Sufi practice has encouraged devotion to deceased shaykhs and has promoted visits to their tombs, hoping for miracles. To the orthodox, this recalls the Christian veneration of saints, who may be prayed to for favors—a practice that, according to the orthodox, takes attention away from the sole worship of God. Sufis also have sometimes substituted their spiritual practice for the regular daily prayer expected of all Muslims, and some Sufis have held themselves exempt from certain religious laws. Therefore, despite the esteem generated by al-Ghazali and the Sufi poets, Sufism is still held by some in disregard and is not always practiced openly by its devotees. Although mosques are plentiful and visible in the Islamic world, Sufi meeting places are hard to find, as are individuals who will actually admit to being Sufis. Luckily, however, Sufism has been buoyed in recent years by a growing appreciation of Sufi poetry and practice.

❧ PERSONAL EXPERIENCE:
RAMADAN IN MOROCCO

During my first trip to Europe as a college student, I found myself spending a very cold February in "sunny" Spain. No one had told me that snow falls in Madrid. But there it was, pure, white, everywhere. The air was so cold in our unheated youth hostel that everyone slept under mounds of blankets. Trudging back to the hostel one evening, ice in my veins, I realized that if I were to survive, I had to go south—quickly.

I took a train from Madrid, then a ferryboat across to Morocco, and finally a bus inland. At first the land was sandy, dry, and flat, but soon the countryside grew greener, with small hills and low trees. I saw children watching over flocks of sheep, and donkeys pulling carts and carrying food on their backs. Animals seemed to be as much a part of everyday life as cars are in Los Angeles. As I traveled south, Morocco appeared to be much like Spain, except that many of the men were dressed in long, hooded robes, and I could hear the call to prayer regularly during the day and early evening.

I reached Fès at the beginning of Ramadan. Old Fès is a traditional, Islamic-style city on a hill, brimming with mosques, shrines, and medersas (religious schools). Its streets, just wide enough for two people to pass, twisted and curved. Mules laden with saddlebags rushed past, their drivers yelling *Balek!*— "Watch out!" On each side of the narrow streets, tiny shops sold fruit, vegetables, sweets, spices, perfumes, robes, brass, and leather. All kinds of fruit were piled high; spices were arranged in neat pyramids of red, yellow, and orange; and sweet desserts made of honey and almonds were heaped in thick stacks. People were buying for the evening meal that would end the day's fasting, but I never saw anyone eat or drink during the daytime. In the evening, the recitation of the Qur'an could be heard loudly, coming from radios placed in shops and on windowsills.

Many shops sold spiral candles with paper decorations on them, meant as offerings at shrines. At a shop where I stopped to buy a candle, the old owner was reading a copy of the Qur'an. I was hesitant to disturb him, but then two young customers came and helped. They each bought a candle, too, then introduced themselves. Moulay and Noureddine were students in Casablanca and were in Fès on vacation. Moulay was Berber, a member of the native tribal people of Morocco, and his parents lived in the north, near Oujda. Noureddine was Arab, from Ourzazate in the south. He told me proudly that his name (which he pronounced *nur-deen'*) means "light of faith." The two friends were making a religious pilgrimage together to the main religious sights of Fès, Meknes, and places in central Morocco. Soon their pilgrimage would end with a visit to the shrine of the saint after whom Moulay was named, in the hilltop town of Moulay-Idriss. They invited me to join them, and I accepted without hesitation.

All along the way we talked about religion—about my beliefs and theirs. They explained that their way of practicing Islam was not strict. They did not pray at all the times of daily prayer, and they did not keep all

The green roofs of the main shrine stand out as one looks down upon the pilgrimage town of Moulay-Idriss.

the customs. But, they told me, they prayed at the public prayer on Fridays, and they kept Ramadan. I could see that: they rose before dawn to eat and would not eat or drink again till after sunset. They kindly encouraged me to eat whenever I was hungry, thinking I must be weaker than they were. "You have no practice in fasting," Noureddine explained. They recommended, however, that during the day I not let others see me eat the bread and oranges or drink the water that I carried in my shoulder bag.

From our conversations, I discovered that Moulay and Noureddine were both interested in Sufism. Commenting on its teachings, Moulay said, "Allah is not something always clear and certain, like a tree or a mountain, that you only have to look at to see. Allah is a reality that you have to look for and discover for yourself. The word *Allah* is an invitation, like an invitation to a meeting or a party. You don't quite know what will happen until you go there yourself. Europeans and Americans seem to think of themselves as believers or unbelievers, just based on their ideas. But I am somewhere in between. I practice my religion to see what will happen. I think you have to do it in order to know it."

Noureddine pointed to some boys on the road who were riding bicycles. "Maybe it's like that," he said. "You don't know how to ride a bicycle until you do it. In fact, it looks a little crazy. It even looks impossible. But when you do it, it works, and you get where you need to go."

Our first vision of Moulay-Idriss was from a distance: a white town at the top of two steep hills. "They say it's shaped like a camel's back," said Noureddine. When we arrived, the town was mobbed with people. Luckily, we found a small place to stay and left our things there. We then walked down to the entrance to the shrine, the burial site of Moulay Idriss I (d. 791 C.E.), a descendant of Muhammad and an early Muslim ruler of Morocco. My friends bought colorful spiral candles, decorated with cut paper, and asked me to wait for them. They went up a long corridor and disappeared; a small sign high up on the wall said, "No entry for non-Mussulmans." I passed the time observing people's faces and their clothing. One thing that struck me were the contrasting elements of some women's appearance: their faces were modestly veiled, almost to the point of being entirely covered, yet their gowns attracted one's attention because of their bright colors—purple, red, yellow, chartreuse.

When my friends returned, they took me up a seemingly endless flight of stairs to the top of the town. We looked down on square towers with roofs of green tile and across to the beautiful green mountains beyond. "That is the shrine down there," Moulay said, "but I'm sorry you cannot go inside." Noureddine smiled but looked serious. Then he had an idea. He asked me, "Wouldn't you like to become a Muslim, too?"

ISLAMIC LAW AND PHILOSOPHY

Islamic thought focuses on both practice and belief. It asks, How should I live my life according to God's will, and how am I to understand and relate to God? Over the first five hundred years of Islam, these questions were debated intensely and some basic principles were acknowledged. Islam also recognized that there could be reasonable disagreement. Thus, various schools of opinion emerged.

Because the Qur'an does not give specific laws for every possible human situation, Muslims have found it necessary to discuss how to interpret the Qur'an. Muslims believe that the Qur'an offers principles for correct guidance in all of human life; as such, regulations for specific instances have to be worked out by considering parallels and utilizing those basic principles.

In addition to the primary authority of the Qur'an, the hadiths—other people's recollections of Muhammad's words and actions—have been consulted. The most authoritative collection of recollections has been that of al-Bukari (died c. 870), which contains almost three thousand hadiths. The use of hadiths enlarged the body of material that could be drawn on, but it also created problems of its own. Disagreement about which hadiths were genuine prevented their universal acceptance. Also, even apparently worthy hadiths were not always consistent with each other.

Islam has a long history of scholarly debate. Over the centuries (from the eighth century on), four major schools of Islamic law have emerged in Sunni Islam and three schools in Shiite Islam, each school differing on what it has looked to as an authoritative guide for making judgments on particular cases: On what grounds may a wife request a divorce? Can a village without a mosque be taxed and forced to build one? How many witnesses are necessary to legitimize a marriage? In arriving at decisions, scholars have relied (to varying degrees) on the Qur'an (which has been interpreted both literally and symbolically), the hadiths, logic, precedents, analogy (*qiyas*), the consensus of early jurists, and the decisions of religious scholars.

Islamic Law and Legal Institutions

Islamic law, called **Sharia,** is the entire body of laws that guide the believer in this life. The legal ideal of Islam is different from what is now considered the norm in many countries. Most modern industrialized countries expect laws to reflect a kind of civilized minimum, something that all citizens, of any background or belief, can be expected to accept and obey in their public life. Often these laws have a distant religious background or origin, but they are framed for very diverse populations and are deliberately secular in nature. We see this division in the United States, for example, in debates about the propriety of having prayer at a public high school graduation or at the beginning of a legislative session. In industrialized countries, the two realms—secular and religious—generally exist somewhat apart.

The traditional Islamic ideal, however, does not separate religious and secular spheres, and this ideal is the subject of intense argument in Muslim countries today—especially in Afghanistan, Pakistan, Egypt, Algeria, and Iran. In the traditional Islamic ideal, laws bring everyday life into ever closer harmony with the regulations of the Qur'an and traditional teaching.

Traditional Islam is theocratic, seeking the "rule of God" in all aspects of everyday life, for in its view there is one God and one correct religion. Nature is orderly because it follows the laws of God spontaneously—for example, gravitation governs the movement of the planets and the change of tides. Similarly, in Islamic thought God presents human beings with laws of human order. There cannot be different sets of laws for different human beings; otherwise, chaos would ensue. The laws of God must be obeyed not only because they are his commands but also because they lead to human fulfillment.

This ideal of a single religion guiding an entire society has, of course, not often been attained. Muhammad himself recognized that there must be exceptions. Although he demanded that people who followed tribal folk religion convert to Islam, he was more lenient about Jews and Christians. In fact, he allowed Jews and Christians to continue their own laws and practices in the hope that they would eventually convert to Islam voluntarily. In Muhammad's eyes, Jews and Christians were "people of the book" and were thus considered to be within the same general "religion of Abraham" as Muslims—although living at a less perfect level.

Nonetheless, Islam has always held that the "rule of God," as presented in the Qur'an and Muslim tradition, is universally binding. Islamic practice teaches the ideal that a devout Muslim will spread knowledge and practice of the will of God. This ideal lies behind the notion of **jihad,** which has been interpreted in various ways, sometimes endorsing a militant fight for what is considered to be true and right. Some governments, such as that of Iran since 1979, have even imposed a theocratic rule. There and in a few other strongly Muslim countries, the rules of the Qur'an and the rulings of religious scholars have had great political power. Although Islam does not have an official clergy, it does have religious specialists and scholars (*ulama, mullahs*) who have various levels of influence, both religious and political.

Islamic Philosophy

Many profound questions about the religion emerged quite naturally as early thinkers began to consider the basic beliefs of Muhammad and of Islam. One of the first questions regarded intellectual investigation itself. Is a good Muslim allowed to question religious topics? Does the philosophical study of religion (*kalam*, "theology") hurt a person's spiritual life, or can it deepen it? Do faith and reason contradict each other, or can they coexist happily?

These early thinkers posed important questions that had to be addressed. Some questions were simply intriguing, while others presented serious philosophical problems. For example, the Qur'an calls God both just and merciful. But how is it possible to be strictly just and also to be really merciful? Doesn't one virtue exclude the other? Or a second question: If God is truly all-powerful, how can a human being really be free to make a choice? Doesn't God make everything happen? And even when human beings think they are acting by their own choice, isn't God really doing the choosing? Or another question: If God is all-loving, why does he allow bad things to happen? Wouldn't an all-loving God prevent evil things from happening in the world? The list of many other similar questions goes on.

Some philosophical questions arose early as a result of studying the Qur'an. Others, however, emerged as Islam encountered the philosophies and religions of its neighbors, such as when Greek philosophical works began to be translated into Arabic and were then taught in the great schools of Baghdad, Córdoba, and Cairo: Aristotle, for example, taught that the universe was eternal. But didn't this conflict with the Qur'an's vision of God as Creator of the universe? Further questions arose when Islam moved into India and had contact with a monistic Hindu spirituality: certain schools of Hindu thought taught that everything, ultimately, was God. But didn't this conflict with the Muslim notion that Allah, as Creator, is different from his creation?

In general, there have been two philosophical poles within Islam. The more liberal view values reason and maintains that everything can be examined intellectually. It argues that human beings are basically free and that reason is a God-given gift that illuminates and complements faith. The other, more conservative view is suspicious of reason, which it sometimes sees as an expression of false human pride. It therefore values intellectual submission, believing that ultimately neither God nor anything else can be explained fully by reason. It tends to see the entire universe, including human lives, as being strongly determined by God. Like a pendulum, the history of Islamic thought has swung back and forth between these two poles.

One of the first intellectual movements, the eighth-century Mutazilite school, was an early form of rationalism. In attempts to defend the young religion of Islam, this movement tried to answer several perplexing questions. When the Qur'an speaks of God in human terms (for example, the "face of God"), does this mean that God has a body, or is the language simply symbolic of God's characteristics? And regarding the Qur'an itself, what is its ultimate origin and nature? Is the Qur'an an earthly creation of God? Or is the Qur'an—because it is God's thought and words—uncreated and eternal? The Mutazilites argued that the anthropomorphic speech of the Qur'an is symbolic and that the Qur'an is not eternal but was created by God. But the Mutazilites were opposed by other thinkers.[35]

The voice of conservatism responded firmly about a century later in the work of al-Ashari (died c. 935 C.E.). He spoke of God as being entirely sovereign and transcendent and stressed the power of God to determine human lives. It is said that al-Ashari was one of the most important influences on the common Muslim emphasis on the absolute power of God.

The emphasis on the value of philosophical reasoning appears in the works of two Muslim thinkers who are considered prominent figures of world philosophy. They are Ibn–Sina (980–1037) and Ibn-Rushd (1126–1198), known in medieval European philosophy by their Latin names Avicenna and Averroës, respectively. Because of their interest in medicine and the natural sciences, as well as philosophy, they thought that using reason to explore nature would give insight into nature's Creator.

Perhaps the most influential philosophical formulations, however, were more conservative. They came from al-Ghazali (mentioned earlier) and his intellectual disciple al-Arabi (d. 1240), who rejected rationalism in favor of the conservative approach of al-Ashari. In his books, *The Incoherence of the Philosophers* and *The Revival of the Religious Sciences,* al-Ghazali showed the inconsistency of several philosophers who based their thought on Aristotle's. He criticized philosophy for generating arguments and false pride, and he distanced himself from both rational theology and legalism. The elements that he thought to be the core of religion, instead, were the submission of the heart to God and direct religious experience—ideals attainable by anyone, not just philosophers.

Al-Arabi continued this line of thought, but, influenced also by Sufism, he moved even further in a mystical, monistic direction. For him, all apparently separate realities were images of God and all activity was ultimately the activity of God.[36] Submission to God meant a lived awareness of God's active presence in all things.

ISLAM AND THE ARTS

Islam has had a unique influence on the arts. Its prohibition of much figural art, its love of the chanted word, its weekly public worship, and its focus on the Qur'an have channeled the work of its artists in intriguing directions and helped create works of great imagination.

Architecture

The delicate minarets of the Sultan Ahmet mosque, the celebrated Blue Mosque of Istanbul, stand as timeless sentinels overlooking a timely game of soccer.

Perhaps the greatest art form of Islam is its architecture. When we think of Islam, we envision tall towers and immense domes. It takes only a few visits—to the Umayyad Mosque in Damascus, to the Sultan Ahmet "Blue Mosque" in Istanbul, to the former grand mosque of Córdoba, or to the brand-new Hassan II mosque of Casablanca—to sense the architectural genius of Islam, whose uniquely shaped spaces express beauty in what is vast and empty.

Islamic architecture expresses itself most importantly in the place of public prayer, the mosque (*masjid*, meaning a space for prostration). Because a mosque can be any building or room where Islamic prayer is offered, its design can be quite simple, especially in villages or in any city where the Muslim population is small. Grand mosques, however, provide greater opportunity for artistic attention to the design of basic elements. A mosque has at least one formal entry to the compound, where shoes (which may not be worn inside) are to be taken off and left outside. Inside the compound, because purification is necessary before prayer, there is at least one fountain for washing one's hands, face, neck, and feet. There is a high pulpit indoors or outdoors for sermons—although as an act of humility the speaker does not stand at the very top. Worshipers stand and prostrate themselves in rows, facing the mihrab (the special marker that indicates the direction of Mecca). The floor is usually covered with rugs or mats. Frequently, there are covered porches for protection from the sun and rain. Other wings or buildings—used for schoolrooms and libraries—are often a part of the complex. Outdoors there is also usually a minaret—a tall tower, either round or square, from which people can be called to prayer. Although only one minaret is needed, there are frequently two; in grand mosques there might be four or even six. Inside the minaret is a staircase, which leads up to a balcony near the top, from which the muezzin can chant his call.

Most styles of religious architecture in the world emphasize ornamentation, but the aesthetic principles of Islamic religious architecture are more austere. This simplicity enhances one's appreciation of space and balance, particularly in the mosque and its attendant structures.

The value of empty space is one of an art student's first lessons. Some paintings, for example, are partially devoid of paint or drawing, and although those parts seem to have no function, the student learns that the empty space actually acts in harmony with whatever is depicted. The space gives rest to the eye and directs the viewer's focus. In art this necessary emptiness is called negative space. In architecture, negative space is the space above or beside or around a building. The building shapes the space within and without, and both the space and the building work together to balance each other. Large mosques especially demonstrate a skillful use of negative space, such as in the shaped space between a dome and a minaret.

Because many mosques, particularly in dry climates, have extensive open courtyards, the negative space of most importance is the sky. It is beautifully balanced and complemented by the columns, arches, and walkways below. Other types of mosques, particularly in wetter climates, are almost entirely enclosed, frequently covered with one or more domes. But even inside, a person can experience the beauty of negative space—especially in the large mosques (such as those in Turkey) that are primarily domed buildings. A vast dome (although it shelters one from the sky) is itself like the sky in its feeling of expansiveness. The internal and external shaping of space also helps one experience the divine, for in Islam space is an important symbol of God, invisible but present everywhere.

Dwarfed by the magnificent arches of the modern Great Mosque of Casablanca, visitors experience the tranquility evoked by the balance of architectural elements.

In Islamic architecture, balance is an important feature especially as it relates to the use of color. Perhaps because Islam spread throughout hot, sunny regions, the most typical color of its architecture is white, to reflect the sunlight. White is balanced by black, particularly in the dark shadows that are created by windows and doors, covered porches, and colonnades. Sometimes, too, alternating lines of black and white are painted on walls for decorative effect.[37] This white-black contrast is a fundamental theme of much Islamic architecture. A second color scheme contrasts blue with gold, often in the form of ceramic tiles on domes, where the dome is covered in one color and its base is covered in another. (Good examples are the golden Dome of the Rock in Jerusalem and the blue domes of Isfahan in Iran.) The blue can vary in shade from sea-blue to blue-green. It is interesting to note that the Islamic tendency toward the color blue-green is hinted at by the original meaning of the word *turquoise*, which in French means "Turkish."

Fine Art

To talk of "Islamic art" might seem a contradiction in terms because of the prohibition, noted earlier, against making images of human beings or animals. Yet Islam has created a rich tradition of pictorial art.

Paradise as a Theme in Art   One theme that seems to have inspired much Islamic art—as well as architecture and garden design—is the theme of paradise. In the Qur'an and the Muslim imagination, paradise is quite concrete and sensuous. It is not just a heaven of diaphanous angels, singing hymns and resting on wispy clouds. Paradise is more like a fertile oasis, a large park, or an enclosed garden. The Qur'an repeatedly says that paradise is "watered by running streams."[38] Wildflowers are at our feet, we sit comfortably under date palms and other fruit trees, whose fruit is ready to be eaten.[39] In the afternoon, we feel cooling breezes. Paradise is safe, too. (Literally, the word *paradise,* from Middle Iranian, means "wall around.") We can stay outdoors in this garden, enjoying nature without fear.

This image of paradise in Islamic art often appears in symbolic, stylized form in the prayer carpet. Although the carpet is not usually recognized as religious art, it is to Islam what stained-glass windows are to Christianity. Both are objects of contemplation for people at prayer. Interestingly, both manifest the same fundamental color scheme—every shade of red and blue. A major difference between the stained-glass window and the prayer carpet is that the latter does not depict human images. Instead of portraying figures of saintly persons, prayer carpets often contain a symbolic image of the garden of paradise. At the center of the carpet might be a stylized fountain that sends water in straight lines to each of the four directions and then around the entire border, the four sides of the border representing the walls of the garden. The rest of the carpet might be filled with stylized flowers. To walk into a large mosque where immense carpets are laid out side by side, such as the Umayyad Mosque in Damascus, gives the feeling of entering a magical garden.

The paradise theme is carried over in Muslim architecture as well: slender pillars resemble the trunks of trees, and arches that come to a point, suggest adjoining tree branches. Ceilings often suggest a night sky full of stars: blue ceramic tiles may form a backdrop for golden six-pointed stars, clustered in complex patterns. Or delicate wood and plaster stalactites hang from the ceiling, suggesting light coming from heaven. The paradise theme is sometimes evident in and around mosque buildings, shrines, palaces, and even homes. It may express itself in fountains and narrow canals, in a grove of orange trees, in a garden full of fragrant plants (such as rose and jasmine), or in a decorated porch from which one can enjoy the sights and sounds of the garden.

The Islamic love of the Qur'an often continues the theme of paradise. The words of the Qur'an are symbolically the sounds of heaven: they are the voice of God, heard not only by human beings but also by angels. In spoken and chanted form, they fill the air and remind us of God and paradise. In written form, they decorate the domes, doors, walls, and windows to remind us of the divine presence. The care and beauty that are lavished on handwritten copies of the Qur'an extend the sense of paradise: because the Qur'an is the book of God's speech, to open the Qur'an is to psychologically enter God's presence. Thus, beautiful writing has become an integral part of the Islamic art of creating paradise on earth.

In both this complex dome and in the elaborately grilled door and window we see some of the elements that create a paradise in the imagination and characterize Islamic fine arts.

The Generalife gardens, constructed when Granada was the center of Islamic power in Spain, illustrate the Muslim ideal of Paradise.

Despite what has been said about the Islamic love of simplicity, Islamic art, particularly in manuscript writing and illustration, demonstrates an appreciation for ornamentation. Extremely fine, handwritten copies of the Qur'an feature pages surrounded by filigree. Similarly, geometrical designs on doors and walls create an effect of hallucinatory complication. Although Islamic ornamentation is complex, it is usually also subtle, allowing the eye to wander and inviting the mind to lose itself in the experience. Because many geometrical designs have no visual center, experiencing them can be like looking at stars or waves, inducing a gentle ecstasy.

Exceptions to the Prohibition against Image Making The prohibition against the making of images has been quite strong in Islam, but there have been three important exceptions. One is the imagery surrounding Muhammad's Night Journey—his ascent to the highest heaven (see the illustration on page 406). As shown by many Muslim artists, Muhammad rises through the air on his human-headed horse Buraq. Both are surrounded by golden flames and by hovering angels. As a bow to the Muslim prohibition against image making, however, Muhammad's face often appears as a rather ghostly blank space.

The second exception to image making is a whole category of art called Persian miniatures. (The tradition was continued in Turkish Mogul art, as well.) Influenced by artistic traditions from nearby India, the Persian court commissioned innumerable small paintings of its personages and its activities— rulers on horseback, picnicking courtiers, and lovers enjoying the afternoon in a garden pavilion. The topics are almost invariably secular, but the treatment has that same hallucinatory quality—evoked by complex designs—that we see in Islamic mosaic, stucco, and woodwork. Thousands of tiny flowers seem to carpet the meadow, and tens of thousands of leaves cover the trees. The eye becomes lost in infinity.

The third exception to image making belongs to the realm of folk art. Pilgrims who return successfully from Mecca have a natural pride in their accomplishment, as have their families. Often they will make or commission a picture of the pilgrim on the way to or from Mecca—nowadays looking happily out of an airplane. Sometimes this picture is even placed outside the house, near the front door, where it cannot be missed.

Over the last century, the prohibition against making images has begun to break down. Statues are still not made, but photographs are common, and Western-style figure art is being taken up by Muslim artists. It is possible nowadays to see carpets and wall hangings woven with recognizable human figures.

ISLAM AND THE MODERN WORLD

Modern life presents great challenges to traditional Islam. Industrial work schedules make daily prayer and other religious practices difficult; women are demanding total equality with men and complete independence; and individualism is weakening family ties and social responsibility. Islam is being pulled in many directions.

Islam and Contemporary Life

Soon after its beginnings, Islam became and remained a world power for about eight hundred years. During that period, Islamic universities— in Baghdad, Córdoba, and Cairo—were among the great centers of learning and scientific investigation in the world. Islamic cities were centers of civilized living. During this period, Islamic strength contrasted with the general weakness of western Europe: the Roman Empire had ceased to exist in the West in the late fifth century, not long before Muhammad was born. Ruling from Constantinople, the Byzantine

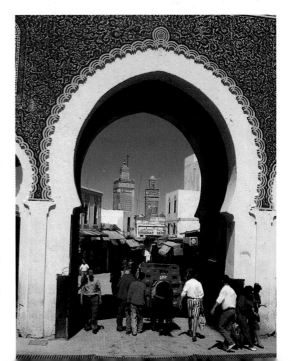

Here, passing through one of the gates of the ancient city of Fès, we see, juxtaposed before minarets, a cartload of modern bottled cola pulled by a donkey.

emperors continued the Eastern Roman Empire in weakened form. Islam's last great military victory was the conquest of Constantinople, and thus of the Eastern Roman Empire, in 1453. It continued to spread and consolidate eastward, as far as Indonesia and the Philippines, but after that its expansion slowed.

Toward the end of the fifteenth century, the pendulum of power swung in the opposite direction. While Islam became fairly settled in its territory, western Europe gained strength and began to expand its control. Significant turning points were Columbus's journeys to the New World, beginning in 1492, and Vasco da Gama's journey around Africa and his arrival in India in 1498. These explorations changed the patterns of trade. Before then, trade was conducted primarily by land routes, which were frequently controlled by Muslim rulers. Now journeys could be made by ship, a form of travel that greatly enlarged the opportunity for travelers to influence others. These journeys were just the beginning of powerful waves of expansion by European traders, soldiers, political figures, and Christian missionaries. Coupled with circumnavigation were the growth of scientific understanding during the European Renaissance of the fifteenth and sixteenth centuries, the Enlightenment of the seventeenth and eighteenth centuries, and the development of technology during the Industrial Revolution of the eighteenth and nineteenth centuries. As Islamic and European cultures came into more frequent contact with each other, their differing values and social ideals led to conflict. That conflict continues today, although now the sources are less military and more cultural. The spread of European American culture (called Coca-Colonization by some critics) is manifested in many forms: clothing (blue jeans, T-shirts, and shorts), food (hamburgers, pizza, french fries), music (rock), technology (radio, film, television, cars, airplanes, computers), modern Western medicine, and sociopolitical philosophy (industrial capitalism, democracy, nationalism, and individualism.) Although Muslim countries have adopted Western technology and medicine, individualistic Western social behavior has caused alarm. Modern Islam is an often unwilling partner in a tug-of-war that has been going on with European culture for hundreds of years.

The Challenge of Secularism   The most difficult of the Western models for Islam to accept has been secularism. The word *secularism* comes from a Latin word for "world" (*saeculum*) and implies a focus on this world, without reference to values or entities beyond this world. Secularism seeks to create political institutions that are independent of any established religion.

Secularism is not necessarily antireligious. In its political form, it actually developed in part for religious reasons—to avoid religious fights and to allow all religions to flourish. The point of the secular model was not to destroy religion but to allow all religions to exist without hindrance from any one religion or from government. But secularism is based on a governmental system of laws, courts, and legislatures that operate independently from any religion. That ideal of independence from religion has caused dismay in many Islamic countries.

Science has also promoted secularism. While investigators like Isaac Newton (1642–1727) once looked into the properties of light in order to better understand the nature of God, scientists nowadays rarely carry on their work in this spirit. Science pursued for its own sake has led to a view of the universe that does not include God, as either its creator or its moral guide. In this worldview, God is not necessarily excluded but is simply not mentioned. (To appreciate this fact, look for the word *God* in a textbook on biology, chemistry, or physics.) But Islamic tradition holds that to view the universe apart from God is to live without God.

A Range of Solutions   One of the great challenges for Islam, therefore, has been to adopt from the West what is obviously useful, to avoid what is dangerous, and to continue holding on to what it thinks valuable. There are a variety of intriguing solutions to this challenge—a few are extreme responses, yet the majority are attempts at compromise.

Turkey has arrived at the most clearly secular solution. For centuries, Islam had had a caliph, God's representative on earth, who united in himself religious and political power. As we discussed earlier in the chapter, the last caliphate existed for centuries in Istanbul. But in 1924, trying to build a modern country, Kemal Atatürk (1881–1938) dissolved the caliphate and created a new secular nation, modeled after the European pattern. He replaced the Arabic alphabet with the Roman alphabet for writing Turkish; he created a legal system independent of Muslim religious authorities; and he set up a democratic form of government that allowed women to vote. In his desire to Europeanize, he even outlawed men's wearing the fez (a traditional round hat) and women's wearing the veil, and he encouraged European styles of clothing. Turkey has generally kept to this secular vision, although religious conservatives have made regular attempts to establish an Islamic government. Furthermore, Atatürk's hope of transforming Turkey into a European-style nation has not yet been fully realized.

In contrast, Iran represents a country that has responded in an extreme fashion to Western influence. For decades, Iran seemed to be moving inexorably toward westernization. After World War II, the ruling families of Iran traveled regularly to Europe (particularly to France) and adopted European ways of thinking and living. For example, the royal family spoke French and English fluently, and for the 1971 celebration of the twenty-fifth centennial of the Persian Empire, the food for the reception was flown in from Maxim's restaurant in Paris. Iran also had close political ties to the United States, and Tehran was an international city, a hub for most major airlines. All this ended in 1979, when an exiled mullah, the Ayatollah Khomeini, returned to Iran and Shah Mohammad Reza Pahlavi went into exile himself. Iran rapidly became a Muslim theocracy. A new constitution was written by the religious authorities, who also held a majority of the seats in the legislature. Khomeini had a new post created for himself as

Women in Islam: Contrasting Notions of Liberation

Islam grew up within a culture that restricted many rights of women. The exact details of pre-Islamic Arabian culture are sketchy, but we know that female children, if unwanted, were routinely killed by being smothered or buried alive soon after birth. Wives were often treated as property, to be bought and sold, and a husband took as many wives as he pleased. Divorce meant that an ex-wife could be sent away with nothing for her financial support.

This background is important in understanding the new climate that Muhammad established for the rights of women:

- He forbade infanticide, thus saving many baby girls from death.
- He limited to four the number of wives a man could have and demanded that all wives be treated equally. Although this number of wives may seem excessive to non-Muslims, we should recall that in the past, marriage offered a woman economic and legal protection and was often entered into for these reasons. Today, most Muslim men have only one wife.
- He considered women and men equal in basic rights. Muhammad legislated that wives as well as husbands could institute divorce, and he demanded that a wife receive financial support in the event of a divorce. He also allowed remarriage for divorcées and widows. He affirmed property rights for women as well as men.

- Finally, he prescribed the basic religious duties, such as prayer, fasting, and the pilgrimage to Mecca, for both women and men.

Despite Muhammad's efforts on women's behalf, however, traditional Islam reinforces major social distinctions between women and men. While men may still have up to four wives, women may have only one husband. The Qur'an demands that both men and women dress modestly in public, but social custom dictates that women alone must cover their hair, because it is considered to be especially seductive; and although the Qur'an does not demand the veiling of a woman's face, it has become customary in some areas as an extension of the demand for public modesty. While men must wear the robe of Abraham during the pilgrimage, women have no special clothing for the pilgrimage. Women usually do not pray in the mosque with men at the Friday prayer, and if they do, it is in a separate section. In the past, women did not receive formal education; some countries even today have separate schooling for men and women. Women in general are still expected—even pressured—to play a role that is primarily domestic, centering around marriage and children. Public life is reserved for men, and men have greater freedom to enjoy themselves outside the home.

Some proponents of women's rights find certain passages in the Qur'an distressing. For

"legal guide," from which he could oversee and validate all legal and political developments. Mosques became centers of civil as well as religious activity, women were forced to veil themselves in public, and alcohol was strictly forbidden. Iran thus became a fully Muslim state.

Egypt, on the other hand, is typical of those countries that have tried to work out a compromise, partly out of necessity. At least ten percent of its population is Christian, and Jews and Greeks living primarily in Alexandria have also played an important role in Egyptian shipping and business. Moreover, because Egypt is dependent on foreign tourism for its economic survival, it must have at least a limited acceptance of alcohol in tourist hotels. Laws that were solely Islamic would not work for everyone.

Other countries that are working out a modern vision of Islam are India, Pakistan, and Bangladesh. Modernizing thinkers there have used two strong arguments. One is that reason does not contradict revelation, be-

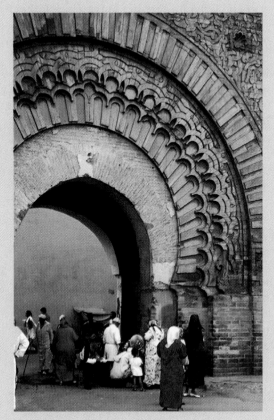

Muslim women are typically fully covered and sometimes even veiled in public.

example, in Sura 4 ("Women") we find the statement, "Men have authority over women because God has made the one superior to the other"; and the Qur'an states that although "good women are obedient," those women who could become disobedient are to be beaten.[40] Critics also point out that before Islam, women derived some security from their clan or tribe, and they already had independent property rights and the right to initiate divorce. Islamic reform replaced that with the patriarchal nuclear family and female legal dependence on a male. As an example of this change in the status of women, critics point to the difference between Muhammad's first wife, Khadijah, who was a property owner and strong figure in her own right, and Muhammad's later wife A'isha, who was married at a young age and was expected to be secluded and submissive.

Contemporary thinking in even staunchly Muslim countries has led to a questioning of some traditional limitations placed on women. Women now usually receive public education, sometimes in coed settings, and growing numbers of women are taking roles in public life. On the other hand, traditionalist movements in some countries (the Taliban movement in Afghanistan being the most extreme) strongly oppose some of these changes, characterizing them as dangerous secularization and insisting on the most conservative interpretations of women's roles and behavior.

cause God is the source of both—an argument that undergirds the study of the sciences. The other argument holds that Muhammad was a humane, moral reformer who would have supported all attempts to change inhumane laws. A strong belief in the possibility of a modern Islamic state was the reason behind the separation of Pakistan from India (1947) and the eventual emergence of Bangladesh (1971). However, exactly how to create the ideal Muslim state has been the cause of interminable debate and practical compromise.

Islam in the West and Beyond

Islam has begun to spread to the West through immigration and conversion. It has spread to England, Canada, and Australia through emigration from some former British colonies, particularly Pakistan and India; and many French cities have large populations of immigrants from Algeria (about three million Muslims now live in France). Large cities in North America have also attracted Muslim immigrants, particularly from Iran, Lebanon, and Africa; for example, there are now more than 300,000 Muslim émigrés from Iran living in Los Angeles.

Because of its simplicity and strong moral guidance, Islam has also been successful in attracting converts in places far away from traditionally Muslim regions. For example, Koreans who worked in the oil fields of Saudi Arabia have taken Islam back to South Korea. It is spreading in some large Western cities, such as Chicago and Detroit, where it has had special appeal to minorities. It is growing strongly in sub-Sahara Africa. Islam is attractive to some converts because it is a way of expressing a deliberate rejection of Christianity, which many people associate with European exploitation. Islam is also attractive in sub-Sahara Africa because of its acceptance of the traditional practice of polygamy.

Some relatively new forms of Islam have emerged that are not as inclusive as orthodox Islam, and their relation to mainstream Islam has occasionally been questioned. The movement known at first as the Nation of Islam, for example, was begun as an Islamic religious movement meant exclusively for African Americans. Its founders were Wali Farrad Muhammad (W. D. Fard, born c. 1877; he mysteriously disappeared in 1934) and his successor Elijah Muhammad (Elijah Poole, 1897–1975), who set up the first centers of worship in Detroit and Chicago. The Nation of Islam, whose members are known as Black Muslims, attempted to bring pride to African Americans by instilling the virtues of thrift, hard work, education, and self-defense. It created an organization for young men, called the Fruit of Islam, and one for young women, called Muslim Girl Training.

The Nation of Islam's original vision was anti-white, but this emphasis has softened due to the preaching of one of its most important members. Malcolm X (Malcolm Little, Malik Shabazz, 1925–1965) split from the organization over the matter of race in 1963. Malcolm X, initially violently anti-white, experienced a profound change of thought as a result of his pilgrimage to Mecca, where he met Muslims of many races and ethnicities. His journey gave him new understanding of the spiritual implications within Islam for universal brotherhood, and as a result, he founded his own group, the Organization of Afro-American Unity. Under the son of Elijah Muhammad, the Nation of Islam has renounced its purely racial basis, changed its name to the American Muslim Mission, and worked to integrate itself into mainstream Sunni Islam.

A follower of the early views of Malcolm X, Louis Farrakhan (b. 1933), has attempted a revival of the Nation of Islam, particularly through preaching the values of hard work and social responsibility. His Million-Man March on Washington in 1995 was a successful attempt to generate self-pride and political activism among African American men.

It is hard to predict the development of Islam over the next few centuries. The model of the democratic, secular state with a written constitu-

The Million-Man March, organized by Louis Farrakhan in 1995, emphasized renewed dedication to social responsibility.

tion guaranteeing individual rights seems to be taking hold worldwide; and monarchy, theocracy, and imperial dominion appear to be generally in decline. Thus it seems unlikely that Islam will ever again have a single caliph or be a single empire. Where Islam is the predominant religion, there might sometimes be a theocratic government—as in Iran. This may occur elsewhere, where extremely traditionalist Muslim movements gain political control—as they hope to do in Afghanistan, Algeria, and Pakistan. But the long-term future for theocracies seems doubtful. There are simply too many areas of possible disagreement. It is more likely that Islam will remain divided into nation-states, each with its own interpretation of the Muslim religion and its own path.

Also, secular practices are spreading now not only from the West but also from some countries of the Far East. These practices and values will be reinforced by television, film, and travel. Even in Saudi Arabia—where there are no movie theaters—VCRs abound in private homes. Television satellites and satellite receiving dishes are beginning to spread world culture beyond all national boundaries. The cultural clash is evident in Muslim countries of North Africa, where it is possible to see via satellite television not only international news but also quiz programs, rock videos, and soap operas from Europe and the United States. It's not hard to understand why the government of Iran has legally banned the use of satellite dishes. Those responsible for making the films and generating the programs seen by the world on television may ultimately have the greatest influence on Islam's future.

There are elements of Western culture that orthodox Islamic societies will quite rightly wish to avoid: alcohol use and abuse, gambling, divorce, urban violence, and other social problems. There will be regular debate about the behavior of women—their proper dress, their education, their social roles. And nations will continue to grapple over how much traditional Islamic law can be imposed in a modern society. Particularly under pressure from traditionalist movements, Islamic countries will do what they can to oppose what they see as dangerous elements. In the long run, however, we should expect them to hold on to what seems best—especially the mosque, regular prayer, charity, the Ramadan fast, pilgrimage to Mecca, and the ideals of honesty, generosity, and justice.

RELIGION BEYOND THE CLASSROOM

Great Islamic art and architecture can be experienced most easily today in Egypt, Morocco, and Turkey—countries with well-developed infrastructures for travelers. Southern Spain also contains much Islamic architecture, although the mosques have been converted to other uses. Note that some mosques are open only to Muslims (especially in Morocco); but a few of these have tours for non-Muslim visitors, and all of course can be viewed from the outside. Only Muslims may visit Mecca.

Egypt   In spite of being a modern city, Cairo has much that is old and traditionally Islamic. Among its Islamic treasures are the al-Azhar Mosque and University and the Mosque of Ibn Tulun.

Turkey   Istanbul is one of the most fascinating cities in the world. Its skyline, although constantly changing, is dominated by domes and minarets. Aya Sofia, first a cathedral and then the central mosque of the city, is now a museum; but its architecture set a pattern for much subsequent mosque design. The Mosque of Sultan Ahmet is famous for its six minarets; it is called the Blue Mosque for its interior tile work. The Süleymaniye Mosque is also famous for its size and domes.

Morocco   One of the greatest sights in Morocco is the new Hassan II Mosque at the edge of the ocean in Casablanca. The mosque—whose interior is as impressive as its exterior—is open for morning tours. Although most mosques in Morocco are closed to non-Muslims, visitors are welcome at the many medersas (religious schools). The cities of Fès and Marrakesh should not be missed and have good museums of Islamic art.

Spain   Southern Spain is rich in Islamic art. One of the world's architectural masterpieces is the Alhambra palace in the hilltop city of Granada; worth visiting nearby are the gardens of Generalife, a thirteenth-century country estate. In Córdoba, the cathedral is a former mosque (called Mezquita); its interior is a forest of columns and Islamic arches. In Seville, the minaret of the former central mosque remains in use as the cathedral bell tower, called La Giralda.

United States   Many of the more than 1,000 mosques in the United States are small and are often converted houses or stores. But large mosques and Islamic centers exist in some places, such as in Perrysburg, Ohio (near Toledo), in Washington, D.C., and in New York. Mosques in the United States often provide guided tours to Muslim and non-Muslim visitors alike.

FOR FULLER UNDERSTANDING

1. List some differences in attitudes toward women in Islam, Protestant Christianity, and Hinduism. Organize a panel to discuss this topic.
2. Research the differences in the attitudes toward and treatment of death in Islam and Hinduism.
3. Islam is becoming an important presence in Europe and North America. Discuss what contributions Islam might make there. Also discuss how non-Islamic cultures might influence or change the practice of Islam. (For example, could Islamic worship begin to adopt regular congregational music of some kind?)

RELATED READING

Akbar Ahmed. *Living Islam*. New York: Facts on File, 1994. A popular, nicely illustrated appreciation of Islam by a knowledgeable believer.

Dawood, N. J., trans. *The Koran*. London: Penguin, 1993. A clear, understandable translation of the Qur'an.

Denny, Frederick. *Islam and the Muslim Community*. San Francisco: Harper and Row, 1987. An overview of the history, practice, and spread of Islam.

Esposito, John. *Islam: The Straight Path*. 3d ed. New York: Oxford University Press, 1998. A book that is especially helpful in its treatment of contemporary developments in Islam.

Malcolm X. *The Autobiography of Malcolm X*. New York: Grove, 1964. The story of the development of a young African American—a convert first to the Nation of Islam and then to traditional Islam—who has been a major influence on American political thinking.

Schimmel, Annemarie. *Islam: An Introduction*. Albany: State University of New York Press, 1992. A study that focuses on Islamic mysticism, theology, and piety.

Shah, Idries. *The Sufis*. Garden City, NY: Doubleday, 1971. A readable introduction to Sufism by a writer who, through many books on the topic, has been instrumental in spreading the knowledge of Sufism.

KEY TERMS

Caliph (*kay'-lif*): "Successor" (Arabic: khalifa); a religious and political leader.

Dhikr: A devotional remembrance of Allah through the recitation of his ninety-nine names and other devotional practices.

Fana (*fah-nah'*): "Extinction"; the sense of loss of self in mystical experience.

Hadith (*huh-deeth'*): A "recollection" of an act or saying of Muhammad.

Hajj: Pilgrimage to Mecca.

Hijra (*hij'-ra*): "Flight"; Muhammad's escape from Mecca to Yathrib (Medina).

Id al-Adha: The Day of Sacrifice during the month of the Hajj, when an animal is sacrificed to recall the submission of Abraham.

Id al-Fitr: The festival at the end of the month of Ramadan, during which people feast and visit friends and often the graves of ancestors.

Imam (*ee-mahm'*): A religious leader; specifically, one of the hereditary successors of Muhammad, venerated in Shiite Islam.

Islam: "Submission"; the Muslim religion and the community of believers who have submitted themselves to Allah.

Jihad (*jee-hahd'*): "Struggle"; the ideal of spreading Islamic belief and practice.

Kabah (*kah'-bah*): "Cube"; the square shrine at the center of the great mosque of Mecca.

Mihrab (*meeh-rahb'*): The decorated niche inside a mosque that indicates the direction of Mecca.

Minaret (*min-a-ret'*): A tower used by a chanter to call people to prayer.

Mosque: (Arabic: masjid); a Muslim place of worship.

Muezzin (*mu-edz'-in*): A chanter who calls people to prayer.

Muslim: A person who submits to Allah.

Qiblah: The direction toward Mecca; the direction toward which Muslims pray.

Qur'an: "Recitation"; God's words as revealed to and recited by Muhammad; an authorized edition of the written words that appeared after Muhammad's death.

Ramadan: The month of fasting; the ninth month of the Muslim calendar.

Sharia (*shah-ree'-uh*): "Path"; the whole body of Islamic law, which guides a Muslim's life.

Shiite (*shee'-ait*): A minority branch of Islam, which holds that Muhammad's genuine successors descended from his son-in-law Ali.

Sufism (*soof'-ism*): A group of devotional movements in Islam.

Sunni (*soon'-ee*): The majority branch of Islam, which holds that genuine succession from Muhammad did not depend on hereditary descent from his son-in-law Ali.

Sura (*soo'-rah*): A chapter of the Qur'an.

The Religious Search in the Modern World

 FIRST ENCOUNTER

It's the middle of April. You're scanning the newspaper's long list of upcoming events that will celebrate Earth Day—April 22. The local university will be showing a series of films on the great mountain ranges of the world; a nearby high school plans to hold something called "Energy Workshops"; and the city has scheduled an Earth Day fair and an exhibition at City Hall of art objects made from recycled materials. At one church, you read, there will be an "interreligious Earth Day service with dance processional." You also see a notice for a sunset service at a park, the newspaper says, "in honor of the Goddess." Articles in the newspaper talk about recycling programs at area hotels and offices, the improving water quality of a local river, and the celebration of Earth Day in Europe. Even the comic strips take up the theme. One shows a smiling globe topped by a lighted birthday candle.

Also listed are many volunteer events in the upcoming week. Various civic organizations have adopted environmental projects such as clearing a stream and cleaning litter from several roads. If you want to join the stream-clearing group, the newspaper advises, bring gloves and waterproof boots.

You have already agreed to join some neighbors on Saturday to plant flowering trees at a park near your house. When you arrive with your shovel just before ten in the morning, you see a much larger group than you had anticipated. The mayor is there, although you don't recognize her readily in her baseball cap, blue jeans, and work shirt. About ten ribboned shovels have been laid out for dignitaries. The Channel 4 van is parked on the street, and a man with a heavy video camera is getting ready to do some taping for the evening news. The young trees, wrapped in burlap, have been carefully laid out in the spots where they are to be planted.

Before the planting begins, you listen to a speech from the head of the department of parks. "Parks are the lungs of a city, and trees in cities help us all breathe," he says, before thanking everyone for volunteering to help. The president of the Nature Circle, a longtime civic organization, speaks of some great parks of the world, and, of course, the mayor says a few words. The program director then divides the volunteers into small teams.

As you begin working, you think about Earth Day, which began only in 1970. What does all this interest in nature mean? Will Earth Day survive? Will it someday be seen as the holy day of a new religion? Is this part of an emerging religion of nature? Will ocean explorer Jacques Cousteau and Jane Goodall, the protector of chimpanzees, someday be thought of as saintly role models?

MODERN INFLUENCES ON THE FUTURE OF RELIGION

It is obvious that religions in the modern world face both challenge and inevitable change. Women are demanding roles in arenas traditionally dominated by males—including institutional religions. Science asks for proof of everything once believed to be miraculous. Many Western cities are homes to religions, such as Hinduism and Islam, that just a few years ago were considered to be exotic and foreign. Finally, television and travel expose the world to new cultures and their religions.

Change is happening so quickly that we must wonder about the future. What if we could return to earth a thousand years from now? Would the religions that we know now have changed a great deal? What religions would even still exist? Would there be new great religions?

We cannot know exactly how the religious landscape will look in another millennium, but we can make a guess based on the influences at work today—influences that are pulling religions in different directions. As we've seen throughout this book, religions in general tend to be conservative and often change more slowly than their surrounding societies. But, indeed, they do change. They change as a result of forces both from within themselves and from their surrounding cultures.

In this chapter we will first look at a few of the modern developments—including globalism, multiculturalism, women's rights movements, and science—that are shaping our future and the future of religions. Then we will look at two alternatives to organized religion. The first is the environmental movement and its almost religious view of nature. The second is what has come to be called eclectic spirituality, a tapping into various sources of inspiration, often through art and music frequently associated with spirituality.

The New World Order

A century ago, the majority of earth's population lived an agricultural life on farms and in villages, and many countries were ruled by kings and queens. In a relatively short amount of time, however, most kings and queens have either disappeared or become largely symbolic; democracy has become a common (though not fully realized) ideal; and large numbers of people live in cities.

The political and economic landscape has changed dramatically over the last ten or so years. After decades of dividing the world symbolically into Communist and capitalist halves, the Berlin Wall came down in 1989. After many of its republics declared their independence, the Soviet Union dissolved in 1991 and abandoned Communism. And mainland China, although it remains a Communist nation, now includes highly capitalistic Hong Kong (returned in 1997) and tolerates, even encourages, free enterprise.

At one time, people would travel to experience different cultures and cuisines. Now, a person can buy a donut and coffee at a Dunkin' Donuts in Japan or a McDonald's hamburger in Israel. International companies are becoming significant entities—sometimes with more real power than many nations. Once, foreign countries were genuinely foreign and far away. Now, through the use of satellites, news events in distant countries can be broadcast instantaneously across the world. And reruns of *Dallas*, which can be seen as far away as Russia, will be shown somewhere on the globe, one feels sure, until the world ends.

We cannot help but wonder how this cultural unification will affect religion. So far, most of the world's religions have remained fairly separate traditions—even those that have spread to different countries and cultures. But globalism may make it impossible for separate religions to remain separate.

Modern capitalism will also challenge religion, primarily by exposing relatively broad segments of populations to its promotion of a fairly positive attitude toward money. In the past, many religions preached the value of poverty, simplicity, and detachment—values that at one time were consistent with life as experienced by the vast majority. Now, many religions are influenced by capitalist ideals, which esteem individual and group betterment; but it is a betterment that can be measured in material terms and can be paid for with money. As Robert Ellwood has commented, the "idea that poverty could be a state of blessedness in itself, a favorite of preachers

Old world boundaries are disappearing through the spread of technology. Here a woman in rural Bangladesh uses a cellular telephone.

as recently as a century ago, is now hopelessly discredited. . . . Even the most conservative pulpiteers nowadays exhort their poor to get ahead, but to do it by non-violent means."[1] We know that money can be used just as selfishly in the modern world as it was in the past. But money is not always used for selfish and useless reasons—take, for example, medicine, books, scholarships, nursing care for the aged. The modern culture of money-based betterment will increasingly challenge religions to adjust to and produce what material cultures value. It will challenge the religious idealization of poverty and will question religions carefully about how much they contribute to measurable human betterment.[2]

Globalism will also challenge parochialism and thus will contest any incomplete visions of reality offered by traditional religions. Finally, urbanism will challenge traditional religions to (1) confront the tribulations of large-scale city life and (2) take advantage of its opportunities.

Multiculturalism and Interfaith Dialogue

The new world order makes crosscultural contact practically unavoidable as television, radio, film, travel, books, and the Internet all work to narrow the gulfs that once separated people, nations, and even religions. Aside from crosscultural contact, there is a good amount of religious interchange, some of it unintentional. Consider, for example, how language—always quick to reflect new influences—picks up trendy words and concepts, including those of a religious nature. Today's international English includes the words *nirvana* (the name of a former rock band), *karma* (in the title of the Boy George song "Karma Chameleon"), *samsara* and *zen* (the names of perfumes), and *Dharma* (the name of a principal character in a television sitcom). We find a similar appropriation of some religious symbols: the Christian cross is now an international fashion item, often worn with little regard for its historical associations; and the symbol for yin and yang is a logo for at least one company (and is a feature of the South Korean flag).

It will be very difficult for any religion in the future to belong to a single culture or to be unaware of the teachings and practices of other religions. With awareness often comes adaptation, a phenomenon we have already seen with current religions. Certain forms of Pure Land Buddhism outside Japan, for example, make use of hymns and offer Sunday school. In Western forms of Zen and Tibetan Buddhism, married laypersons sometimes take leadership roles that have traditionally been performed by monks. African and Native American forms of Christianity now deliberately make use of native art and music. Roman Catholicism, which only a generation ago celebrated its rituals in Latin with uniform prayers and music, is today often as much a reflection of its specific community or church group as it is of Rome. Some Christian monasteries and other religious groups have adopted Zen meditation. People who convert to a religion—as a result of marriage, perhaps, or immigration—will bring their cultural and religious background with them and will influence the religion they have chosen. Entirely new religions may frequently blend elements from several religions. We see this, for example, in religions like the Unification Church, which began in Korea and blends Christianity and Confucianism, and in new Shinto religious offshoots, some of which blend elements of Shinto, Buddhism, and Christianity.

Another response to the growing awareness of cultural multiplicity can be seen in the increasingly frequent meetings held by representatives of

Religion and Rock Music

Popular rock music illustrates how religion is a frequent vehicle for multicultural expression. Rock videos of popular songs—the main fare of MTV, now seen around the world—often use religious images in interesting, new ways. It is not uncommon for videos to include images of Buddhist and Christian monks, churches, temples, crosses, candles, angels, statues. The singer Madonna (note her name) has been especially adept at using such images: the video for "Like a Prayer" uses crosses and stigmata, and "Bedtime Story" features Sufi dancing.

Religious and spiritual themes permeate the world of popular music, whatever the country of origin. Any number of internationally popular musical groups of the present or recent past reflect religious influence (Genesis, Nirvana, and Judas Priest are just a few examples). Popular lyrics are a particularly rewarding focus for study. They often delve into serious questions about the purpose of the universe and how people should live, about overcoming social problems and finding meaning. Sometimes lyrics even borrow directly from religions, for example, "*Kyrie Eleison*" by the group Mister Mister and the earlier "My Sweet Lord"—about Krishna—by George Harrison. Singers and groups that have emphasized such themes include Bob Marley, the Beatles, Genesis, Phil Collins, Billy Joel, U2, and the previously mentioned Madonna. Rock concerts—which are becoming more and more internationally uniform, whether held in Tokyo or Chicago—offer multiple parallels with a religious service: the stage is like a lighted sanctuary; the rock stars are like priests or shamans; and the audience, often holding lighters that are aflame, constitute a congregation of enthusiastic believers.

different religions. Although religions have too often battled each other or promoted war, they all preach human harmony and offer visions of peace. They have much to gain from and share with each other as they investigate their religious similarities and differences. One natural focus of discussion concerns basic rules of living—all religions seem to value honesty and display a concern for the disadvantaged. Another possible discussion focus concerns mystical experience, which is described similarly in quite different religions. A third focus for discussion is the changing role of women in religion. And a fourth focus will increasingly be the practical problems of the world—poverty, overpopulation, destruction of resources—and what religions can do jointly to help.

One of the first examples of modern religious dialogue was the first World Parliament of Religions, held in Chicago in 1893. Swami Vivekananda, a disciple of Ramakrishna, brought the inclusivist Hindu approach to the attention of the world through his insistence at that conference that all religions value holiness and love. In 1986, Pope John Paul II held a conference in Assisi, Italy, for more than a hundred leaders of many religions. In 1990, a world conference was held in Moscow that brought together government leaders, scientists, and religious figures to work to save the environment. And in 1993, Chicago hosted a second World Parliament of Religions, with simultaneous meetings of religious leaders at many places around the world. At the tenth annual Convocation for Peace, held in Rome in 1996, Yasumi Hirose, a Japanese representative of Omoto, used the language of several religions to speak of his hope. "Unless we awake to the

Shinto offering trays and tables set up in the Cathedral of St. John the Divine in New York City demonstrate the cathedral's openness to other religions. ▶

love and compassion of the God who created the heavens and earth, and realize that all creatures are filled with Divine Spirit and live by the grace of Amida Buddha, it will be impossible to change history to bring about a new century of co-existence. By rethinking the significance of human life and returning to the sources of religion, it is my deep hope that all the world's religions can work and pray together to realize a . . . future where peaceful co-existence between the races and nations of this earth is possible."[3] Dialogue is a constant in less spotlighted circles, such as the Ecumenical Institute at St. John's Abbey in Minnesota, where scholars of different faiths spend months in conversation, study, and reflection. These dialogues may well chart a new path for religion in the future.

Women's Rights Movements

Some of the most significant movements of the last hundred years have involved efforts to liberate women from oppression and inequality. Just as the nineteenth century is seen as the century in which slavery was abolished worldwide, the twentieth century may well be seen by future generations as the century in which women, at least in some quarters, achieved fundamental equality and political freedom.

In many societies, women have been restricted by tradition in multiple ways—they have been kept from acquiring an education, owning land, having professional careers, traveling, marrying or divorcing as they wished, voting, and holding office. But education and women's political movements—along with advances in science that produced contraceptives and minimized the complications of pregnancy and childbirth—have slowly changed attitudes toward women's roles and rights. As a result, women are now indispensable in the workplaces of many cultures, earning their own incomes and making use of their new economic power. This new independence of spirit and action has led women closer to equality in government, business, and the arts.

Despite the controversy (even turmoil) engendered by women's movements, a few religious groups have permitted women to hold leadership roles for more than a century. This has been especially true of smaller, more charismatic groups, such as some of the New Religions derived from Shinto and those Christian churches (such as the Christian Science Church and the Foursquare Gospel Church) whose founders were female. Christian churches in the Lutheran and in the Episcopal and Anglican traditions now ordain women priests and bishops (although this has caused great opposition, and some congregations have broken away in order to maintain their traditions).

Resistance to allowing women in key roles is, however, strong in other religions. In Christianity, the Catholic and Orthodox Churches so far have staved off pressures to ordain women or otherwise allow them full participation in decision making. In Judaism, females have been ordained in the Reform and Conservative branches, but the Orthodox still will not accept

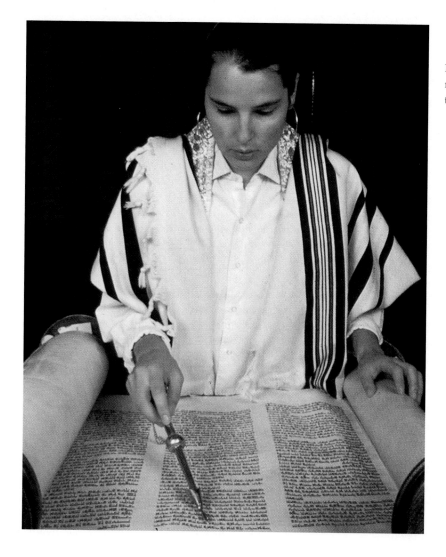

Rabbi Leeza Taylor uses a ritual pointer to read from the Torah.

the notion of a female rabbi. (Even in more liberal branches of Judaism, female rabbis complain that they are relegated to posts of lesser responsibility—to small congregations and to assistantships at the larger synagogues. The movie *Yentl* was a strong protest against the unequal treatment of women in Judaism.) Buddhism is seeing stirrings in its communities of nuns, who traditionally have played only a small role in the religion. Today, Buddhist nuns are still only one-tenth the number of all Buddhist monks, and they clearly cannot have the same influence; but some—Western women among them—want to have an equal voice.

Women's gains have been broader in areas that can be addressed without changing a religion's basic power structure. Thus we find new translations of sacred literature and prayer forms that attempt to be more gender neutral. For example, words like *Ruler, Creator,* and *Parent* are used in place of the exclusively male terms *Lord* and *Father* in some translations of the

Bible. (A controversial feminist exhibit at the Jewish Museum in New York included an artwork that showed all "patriarchal" passages of the Bible marked for deletion.) Unity Church congregations address God as *Father-Mother*—a term used as early as 1875 by Mary Baker Eddy (see Chapter 9), the founder of Christian Science, in her explanation of the Lord's Prayer.

There is also a heightened interest in religions that have envisioned the divine as being female or that have valued its feminine aspect. This explains the renewed attention paid to early nature religions that worshiped a major female deity (such as Astarte) or in which women have had an important role. A religious movement called Wicca worships "the Goddess" in nature and in all women. In Judaism and Christianity, research into the contributions of women—contributions often readily evident when scholars move beyond the patriarchal stances assumed to be "natural" in the past—are common and even encouraged. Bible studies now talk of the great matriarchs, as well as the patriarchs, of Hebrew history. In Christianity, there is growing interest in medieval female mystics such as Hildegard of Bingen, Margery Kempe, and Mechtilde of Magdeburg. Likewise, Hinduism is being appreciated not only for its female divinities but also for the many female gurus it has produced; Shinto and shamanistic religions are being studied for the important roles women have played; and Taoism is receiving attention for its female imagery and its expressions of yin.

Much of this new insight, however, remains academic and theoretical. As welcome as practical changes might be, they are in most cases only modest steps toward a religion's perception and treatment of all persons as equal in value, regardless of gender. Often, of course, the underlying inequality is not acknowledged by a religion's leaders; for example, women might be told that their silent witness is equal in importance to men's vocal deliberations. Such arguments have been received with at least outward meekness in countries and cultures where challenges to patriarchal institutions run counter to long-standing tradition, but they have been downplayed or even ignored in cultures where women's gains have been marked. How long religions will be able to stand firm against the arguments and momentum of women's movements is anyone's guess, but many observers assume that women's liberation efforts in the religious mainstream, at least in industrialized countries, will eventually succeed.

Reassessment of Human Sexuality

The developments—scientific, economic, ideological—we have been discussing thus far in this chapter have all contributed to a reexamination of human sexuality. Through the introduction of contraception, science has helped divert the focus of human sexuality away from the sole purpose of procreation; yet, at the same time, through its development of artificial insemination, in vitro fertilization, and so on, science has expanded the possibilities for reproduction that were once left to chance (or predetermination, some might say). Medicine, clean water, and public sanitation have led to an explosion of the world population—a fact which in turn has forced the rethinking of the purpose of marriage. Psychology has contributed an understanding of sexuality as being essential to the makeup of human beings. Biology has shown the human connection with the animal world and the great variety of animal sexual expression. Anthropology has made people aware of the variety in attitudes toward sex among different peoples and across historical periods.

As a result of these advances, many people now grant that sex has key functions in human existence beyond the creation of children. Primary among these functions are the fulfillment of intimacy, pleasure, self-expression, and even self-understanding. The acknowledgment of these (and other) functions has led many to question traditional sexual ethics and to rethink the appropriateness of sexual prohibitions in religious traditions.

Religions and sects that stress morality have tended to react to sexual liberation movements by defending, often staunchly, the primacy of procreation as the purpose for sex, and marriage as its proper context. Typically, more conservative sects argue that procreation is the only justification for sex, while more liberal sects recognize other purposes as being equally valid and even go so far as to condemn only sexual acts that cause harm.

The ongoing discussion of human sexuality has brought to the fore numerous questions about the relationship between sex and religion and about the history of religious teachings on sex. Looking across the spectrum of the world's religions, we find great variety in the attitudes toward sex. Some religions see sex as having a sacred aspect. Other religions seem almost preoccupied with controlling sexual expression. At certain times and in some religions, any sexual expression has been held inferior in virtue to virginity and celibacy. In some quarters, male and female sexual expression are viewed quite differently; often, female sexuality is repressed. Unfortunately, it is far easier to document the variety in attitudes than it is to explain where the attitudes came from and why they have been maintained.

The ongoing clash between traditional views of sexuality—views often codified in religions—and modern insights probably will not be resolved any time soon. What we are likely to see, however, is greater tolerance for beliefs and practices that are somewhat contradictory—as is evident in teachings about the indissolubility of marriage as compared to the toleration of divorce (or annulment) in practice. The arena of birth control is particularly fertile ground for debate; although forbidding the practice of birth control acknowledges the primacy of the procreative purpose of sex, it also risks pushing people and even world populations beyond the point where they can satisfy physical and educational needs.

Another area of controversy exists regarding same-gender sexual expressions and relationships. Some religions hold that all homosexuality runs counter to divine or natural laws. Some sects approach homosexuality as an orientation that occurs naturally in some people but say that acting out that orientation in sexual behavior is wrong. Still other sects value love,

This chapel in Grace Cathedral in San Francisco is dedicated to persons with AIDS. At the right hangs a portion of the AIDS Quilt with panels celebrating the lives of those who have died of the disease. A memorial triptych, the last work of Keith Haring, adorns the altar.

compassion, individuality, and privacy more than universal judgment of sexual acts and thus accept gay men and lesbians as full members. Of course, "full membership" for heterosexual men and women allows religious marriage and ordination to leadership roles, but few religions have yet to move that far for gays and lesbians as well. However, as the contradictions in a partial acceptance of gay members become more obvious and even painful, sects and religions will begin to reconsider past practice. Same-gender marriage is now legal in Denmark, and church marriage by the Lutheran Church may soon be possible in Scandinavian countries. Same-gender "commitment ceremonies" are celebrated in increasing numbers of liberal Christian religious congregations—examples are to be found among Unitarians, Quakers, the Metropolitan Community Church, and the Unity Church.

While debate over what constitutes legitimate sexual expression will continue, there is no denying the impact the sexual revolution has had on religion. Until the twentieth century, religions were able to avoid complex debates on sexual matters because their teachings on sexual morality were regarded as obvious and "natural." Now, however, it is difficult for religious leaders to gather officially without discussing the matter of sex and having it reported on later as front-page news. Even the Dalai Lama faces press-conference questions about Buddhist views on sex. Traditions that emphasize conservative positions will be most challenged by the changing views on sexuality.

Science and Technology

One of the engines that powers to some degree all of the movements we are analyzing has been science. Modern science made great early progress in the sixteenth and seventeenth centuries, with the work of Copernicus (1473–1543), Galileo (1564–1642), Kepler (1571–1630), Newton (1642–1727), and others. At first, the developments were theoretical, without much practical application. While theoretical science continued to advance, applied science in the eighteenth and nineteenth centuries led to many practical benefits, including the invention of machinery that could do the work that human beings had formerly done by hand. Scientists investigated the mysteries of lightning and electricity; inventors made engines powered by steam and coal; researchers made advances in understanding and preventing diseases; engineers designed train tracks that linked large cities to each other; and the telephone and electric light became commonplace. In the next century came the airplane, radio, television, and computers. Simultaneously, scientific theory advanced: the theory of evolution, molecular theory, the theory of relativity, and theories regarding astronomy and quantum physics. These accomplishments have transformed both our physical world and our view of the universe.

Some religions have tried to reject or even ignore the contributions of science, arguing that science displaces God, questions religious belief, and undermines morality. Scientists, however, argue that science gives us a valuable view of the universe that should be appreciated. It represents, they say, the collective work of thousands of people over many centuries. If we think about how long it took for human beings to draw a map of the whole earth (accomplished by Gerardus Mercator in 1538), we can admire the efforts of science to give us an even grander "map"—a general view of reality.

The current scientific view of reality can be summarized quickly. Scientific theory and research states that the universe emerged in a great explosion approximately ten to fifteen billion years ago. (What came before the explosion is not known and possibly cannot be known by science.) In fact, the universe is still expanding from that explosion—although scientists debate whether the universe will contract or continue to expand indefinitely. As the universe cooled, galaxies formed; there are at least a hundred billion galaxies, each containing about a hundred billion stars. Our planet, earth, is about six billion years old, belongs to a galaxy we call the Milky Way, and travels around a sun whose energy will be exhausted in another six billion years. All physical things are made of smaller units, called molecules, which in turn consist of even smaller units, called atoms, electrons, neutrons, and other particles; and, ultimately, the physical world can

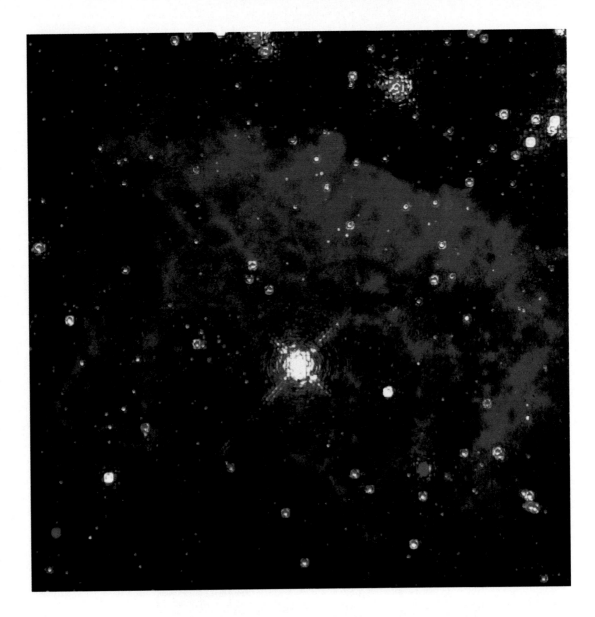

The Hubble Space Telescope photographed the stars near the center of the Milky Way Galaxy. The telescope's findings challenge not only some traditional religious formulations, but also some commonly accepted scientific hypotheses. Science, like religions, evolves.

be seen as various forms of energy. Events in the world, such as lightning and earthquakes, have natural causes. Carbon-based life forms—possibly assisted by lightning, volcanic eruptions, and matter from comets—began to emerge on earth in one-celled form several billion years ago and, growing more complex, evolved in many directions on land and sea, finally producing the plants and animals we know today. The human being, which first appeared on earth about one or two million years ago, is part of the same evolutionary process but is the most complex life form known so far.

Although some scientific positions, such as those concerning evolution and molecular structure, are still called theories, they have enough proof underpinning them that they will almost certainly not be supplanted. The current general scientific vision of reality thus seems fairly firm; and although intriguing new discoveries will certainly be made over the next centuries, the basic vision will probably not be totally overturned.

Just as science has advanced our understanding of reality, so it has replaced earlier worldviews: for example, we now see the earth not as a flat surface but as a sphere, in orbit around the sun; we understand most sickness to be caused by germs; and we know that earthquakes are generally caused by the movement of tectonic plates. Just as surely as electricity, television, and basic literacy are penetrating to the far corners of the world, so also will the scientific model of reality. Prescientific religions may continue to exist in the remotest cultures and wherever there is prescientific mentality, but major religions will have to accommodate the scientific view of reality. It is the anvil on which all religions will be hammered and tested.

The scientific approach to reality generally has helped—at least potentially—to make the earth a more interesting and pleasant place for human beings to inhabit than it was in past centuries. Granted, applied science has done a great deal to alter the landscape for the worse, to damage nonindustrial cultures, to destroy animal habitats, and to pollute the physical environment. But science has also done much to help—by reducing infant mortality, extending human life spans, and making many human lives more physically secure, primarily through medicine, water purification, and modern sanitation practices. Today, life spans are double what they were two hundred years ago in industrialized countries, and scientists are working to extend lifespans even further. When this happens, death and the afterlife will seem increasingly distant, and the earth will seem more like our permanent home. The resultant feeling of security that has grown up in industrialized countries may have helped human beings within them to place a new value on the earth and on earthly life. It has helped to foster an approach to living that is not traditionally religious but rather secular.

Secularism

The word *secular* is often used as the opposite of *sacred*. As mentioned in earlier chapters, *secularism* refers to the modern tendency to separate religion (which deals with the sacred) from everyday life (the secular). In earlier centuries, as we have seen in much of this book, religion and everyday life were quite commonly intertwined. Today, they remain intertwined primarily in societies in which a single religion is the state religion or the predominant religion.

The impetus to separate religion from public life found its greatest support in Europe. Primarily because of the horrific religious wars of the sixteenth and seventeenth centuries, influential thinkers there began to envision a type of nation in which there would be no state religion and where individuals would be free to practice their religions as they chose. This model was drawn on in the creation of the new United States and was detailed in the Bill of Rights, which was appended to the Constitution.

Because the model is based on a general separation of church and state, it has led to a secular type of government.[4]

Furthermore, the model of no established religion has encouraged a secular style of life. After all, if people are free to practice any religion, they are equally free to practice no religion at all. *Secularism* thus has come to refer to a way of looking at life in which human values and rules for living are taken from experience in *this world*, not from divine revelation, from a world beyond this one, or from religious authorities or religious traditions.

Secularism seems to be gaining ground as science finds ways to extend human life and make it more secure. Consequently, traditional religious worldviews have, for many people, lessened in influence. Religions of the future will continue to be challenged by the secular vision, particularly when they have to work within secular political entities. To survive on a large scale, they will have to add to and give greater meaning to the modern secular world. This may not be impossible, however. After all, science seeks to describe reality, but religions seek to describe and create meaning. As the philosopher K. N. Upadyaya explains, "Religion is not antagonistic to science. . . . The antagonism comes only through a misunderstanding. It has to be understood that science deals with the physical. Religion, on the other hand, deals with something that is beyond the physical. But the methodology of the two is—or should be—exactly the same: observation, experimentation, and verification."[5] We might note, too, the many contemporary scientists, such as physicists Paul Davies (b. 1946) and Fritjof Capra (b. 1939), who have shown considerable interest in religion.

Agnosticism is a concept often associated with a secular worldview. The English biologist T. H. Huxley (1825–1895), who coined the term, was of the opinion that the existence of God could be neither proven nor disproven from a scientific point of view. He argued that agnosticism—a middle ground between theism and atheism—was the most reasonable theoretical position to hold. It is a view that is commonly held by scientifically minded people, because it accommodates the study and teaching of science without reference to God or gods. Some people have found that everyday life can be carried on, too, without reference to God or gods. Both this kind of practical agnosticism and scientific-theoretical agnosticism may begin to replace traditional theistic religious belief and practice. This tendency may also generate attempts to redefine the conceptions of God; it may inspire a turn toward the nontheistic religions (such as Jainism or Theravada Buddhism); and it may promote the development of nontheistic expressions of values and beliefs.

Some would say that Marxist Communism, which began in nineteenth-century Europe but took root elsewhere, is an example of a nontheistic religion. Although it is explicitly atheistic, Communism in some forms took on many of religion's attributes. The tomb of Lenin in Moscow was for a long time a site of pilgrimage, with long lines of people. The writings of Marx and Lenin have been treated with an almost scripturelike reverence, and Mao's "little red book" of sayings took on a near-magical quality in China during his lifetime—hospital patients could even be seen clutching it on their way to the operating room. Although Communism has weakened considerably (it has been called the God that failed), the factors that first produced it have not disappeared. It failed not because of its atheism but because of its lack of economic realism.

Communism, even where it has now been abandoned as an official ideology, succeeded in creating a fairly secular milieu. In Russia and many parts of eastern Europe, new generations of people have been raised without religion. Schools there often spoke of religion as an outdated method for providing solutions to life's problems—as outdated as horse-drawn carriages and whale-oil lamps. (There are exceptions, of course, such as Poland, but in Poland religion has been inextricably linked with nationalist aspirations.) The same antireligious stance has also been true of China, particularly since the Communist Revolution of 1949. The resultant secularism among the Chinese may have a significant influence on the world, as China, with its population of more than a billion, gains power in the international arena.

Some people welcome secularism—possibly with the same relief felt by some in the early confederation of the United States—because they want life to be carried on without religiously inspired rancor. Machines, such as

Prior to the breakup of the Soviet Union, citizens waited in a long line to view the body of Lenin displayed in the Lenin Mausoleum outside the Kremlin walls in Moscow. This photo recalls the visits of pilgrims to the relics of saints.

computers, cars, and telephones, are secular in that they do not ask the religion of the person who operates them. In secular cultures, some wish human beings could be similarly accommodating.

Science offers explanations of reality that once came only from religion. Secular governments often promote values that were once primarily espoused by religion. What then does this leave for religion? Will current religions move in the direction of secularism? Will religions survive as pockets of belief and practice in a basically secular environment?[6] Could completely secular "religions" emerge? Or will religious instincts be expressed in increasingly nontraditional forms?

Environmentalism

Four centuries ago, the total human population was about 500 million. Now, the world's population is more than 6 billion. This growing population has migrated to cities to find jobs, and cities with a million people— once extremely rare—are now sprouting like mushrooms. Megacities— such as Mexico City, São Paulo, Shanghai, Tokyo, New York, and Cairo—are becoming more common, even though most of them find it difficult to cope with their unchecked growth. Some cities are becoming bleak, inhospitable urban environments.

At the same time, the natural environment is being ravaged to provide resources for the increasing world population. The rainforests of Malaysia, Indonesia, and Brazil are disappearing to provide wood and farmland, and the habitat of many animals, including all great apes in the wild, is threatened. Nuclear energy is used to make electricity, but no one knows where to safely store the spent fuel. Pesticides are used for growing and storing many foods, despite the health dangers.

The great religions of the past grew up in a quite different world and did not have to deal with the moral issues raised by population growth, urban life, corporate business policies, nuclear waste, and environmental pollution. Faced with these entirely new problems, old religions must try to discover within themselves the wisdom to handle these challenges. They will have to fundamentally rethink morality. Doing so is not easy or straightforward, as we will see in a moment.

THE RECURRING CHALLENGE OF CHANGE

If our textbook pilgrimage of world religions has revealed a common denominator among religions, it is this: All religions that survive must ultimately adapt to changing circumstances, whether they acknowledge the adaptations or not. If there is a second common denominator, it is probably the fact that adaptation is seldom achieved without confusion, struggle, and pain. Indeed, we might argue that struggle, debate, "swings of the pendulum," the breaking off of splinter groups, and even the founding of new

The view from the moon . . . gave new meaning to the word "religion." The English word for religion came from the Latin word *religare*. It means to connect. Religion is about how we are all connected to each other and to every creature and to the earth. Religion is about including, about every part belonging to the whole. "Religion" is the old word and "ecology" is the new word. The view from the moon shows that religion and ecology share the same meaning of connectedness."

—James Parks Morton, Dean Emeritus of the Cathedral of St. John the Divine in New York, speaking of the 1969 photo of the earth taken from the moon[7]

This NASA photo of Earth has sometimes been called a religious icon that makes viewers realize the beauty of the earth and the interrelatedness of all its parts.

sects are all part of the process by which religions seek to remain relevant in a changing world.

A good case study of a religion's processes of adaptation is found in the twentieth-century history of Roman Catholicism. Catholicism, because it has adherents in so many parts of the world, is always being challenged somewhere by changing circumstances. At the beginning of the twentieth century, Catholicism was challenged by new "scientific" understanding, particularly Darwinism and modern biblical criticism. Its response was initially a set of proclamations against the evils of Modernism and secularism, movements that might bring the gradual elimination of the need for religious explanations.

To some extent, Catholicism's warnings against these new movements seemed vindicated by the instabilities of World War I and, shortly thereafter, of worldwide economic depression. Nonetheless, in some ways Catholicism was already adapting to the changing world order, particularly in the evolution of new Catholic social doctrine that was spelled out in several papal encyclicals. The horrors of World War II provided new opportunities for the expression of religious faith, but the same war ultimately fostered crosscultural contacts, female emancipation, secularization, and—through the use of atomic fission—the power of science. The war also exposed a chronic contradiction in a Catholicism that preached love but also appeared silent in the face of the Holocaust.

The aftermath of the war only increased the pace of change, and the movement of "tectonic plates" eventually produced a Catholic earthquake in the person of Pope John XXIII. This elderly, mild-mannered pope stated his desire to open the church to the modern world, and he initiated meetings of the world's Catholic bishops that were intended to help Catholicism remain relevant in ways other than through single-minded opposition to change. By the end of the Second Vatican Council in 1965, Roman Catholicism had a different face, a face marked by an emphasis on human rights, a new tolerance for the secular world, an acceptance of separation between church and state, and an openness to diversity—perhaps most immediately evident in Catholicism's abandonment of the Latin language in everyday liturgical forms that had been unchanged since the sixteenth century. This was the face of an old religion taking major steps to adapt itself to the modern world.

But the case study does not end with the liberalization initiated by John XXIII. As history would have predicted, the pendulum swung back, particularly at the urging of Pope John Paul II, the first pope from a Communist country. Perhaps the most telling mark of the swing away from change was the new pope's open embrace of the cult of the Virgin Mary, a cult that had been deemphasized by the Catholicism that emerged from Vatican II. Pope John Paul II insisted that only males could be priests and bishops. He also appointed bishops who reflected his own conservative beliefs, reasserted the primacy of Rome, and condemned the thought of certain Catholic theologians. Nonetheless, he also furthered his church's defense of human social rights, condemned the excesses of capitalism, and fought capital punishment. And, while reasserting the traditional Catholic opposition to divorce, the tribunals of his bishops oversaw overwhelming growth in the number of Church-granted marriage annulments.

The phenomena in this small case study are by no means unique to Roman Catholicism (although we must grant that it is a more monolithic religion than most). We review them here simply to illustrate the tensions and vacillations that surface when the traditions of a powerful religion are confronted by new developments that are incompatible with some of the old ways. Ultimately, as we saw in preceding chapters, religions adapt and change. Often they initially fight the forces of change and in the process possibly become even more conservative, but such conservatism can be a stage of adaptive development that eventually grows into new forms of religious belief and practice.

The inevitability of conservative reaction to the onslaught of change is one way to understand a phenomenon that is sometimes called fundamentalism. Fundamentalist movements—occurring in many parts of the world—are often fueled by calls for a "return to the values of our founders" and to an earlier, more traditional vision. Interestingly, fundamentalist religious movements are quite compatible with nationalistic movements, which are often nostalgic for earlier times.

The term *fundamentalism* was first used in the early twentieth century to describe certain conservative Christian movements. These movements sought to counter doubts about traditional beliefs by asserting what they held to be the "fundamentals" of Christian faith. Among the traditional beliefs being reasserted were several that had been called into question by science: belief in the physical resurrection of Jesus, in the virgin birth, and in the inerrancy of the Bible. From that limited usage of the word *fundamentalism,* the term has come to be used more broadly (perhaps too broadly) to refer in general to conservative movements in virtually all religions, most notably Hinduism, Islam, Judaism, and Christianity.

Fundamentalist movements reflect an effort to simplify a religion. They emphasize what followers see as the basics, the essential elements, of a religion. Many fundamentalists claim to be returning to the beliefs and practices of the early days of a religion, times when accommodation to political structures, to secular powers, and to the latest "fashions" of society had not yet contaminated the originating spirit. The personal rewards of fundamentalism are multiple: a sense of bettering society, of uniting with like-minded people, and of repairing a religion to make it useful once again as a clear guide to what is right and wrong. Although fundamentalist movements are motivated by many reasons, they represent primarily a response to the threat of change. The embrace of fundamentalist beliefs is also quite often a declaration of superiority over those who hold different (and often newer) values.

The best-known example of late-twentieth-century fundamentalism is possibly the Islamic Revolution in Iran, initiated by the late Ayatollah Khomeini (see Chapter 10); but Islamic fundamentalist movements are also occurring in many other countries, such as Egypt, Turkey, Pakistan, Afghanistan, and Algeria. We see fundamentalism active in other religions, as well—in Christianity, especially in the United States; in Hinduism in India; and in Judaism, particularly in Israel. In some of these countries, fundamentalist movements also serve to help assert ethnic or national identity. However, it may be increasingly difficult for fundamentalist religious movements to avoid being influenced by the pervasive secular environment that is spreading throughout the modern world.

The image of a swinging pendulum is a recurrent metaphor in this chapter. We return to it one last time, as we imagine the pendulum swinging away from fundamentalism toward another phenomenon, which may well be at the other end of the arc: a kind of neopantheism expressed through a semideification of nature. Just as the Ayatollah Khomeini and Pope John Paul II articulated the aspirations of monotheistic fundamentalist movements, so twentieth-century thinkers such as Julian Huxley (1887–1975), Aldous Huxley (1894–1963), René Dubos (1901–1982), Rachel Carson (1907–1964), and E. F. Schumacher (1911–1977) have articulated the "doctrines" of the "nature movement." Major religions, perhaps less anxious over the "nature" movement than over other forces of change, are now taking note of these doctrines. Older religions that grew from nature (such as oral religions, Shinto, and early Taoism) are being looked at with new respect. The potential of this movement for growth and for assimilation by existing religions suggests that it is a possible emerging scaffolding for the cathedral of humankind's future religious expressions.

NATURISM: A NEW RELIGIOUS PHENOMENON?

For a long time, human beings have been asking questions about how to relate to the natural world. On the one hand, nature is obviously beautiful and awe inspiring, and human beings are clearly dependent on "Mother Nature" for food, water, and air. On the other hand, anyone who has been lost on a hike or adrift in a boat understands that the natural world can be very unmotherly, dangerous, and uncaring. Nature can be too cold or too hot, too wet or too dry; it endangers us with disease, insects, and wild animals; it can hurt as well as help. Survival in nature can be precarious.

Out of necessity, human beings have tried to control the power of nature in two ways. One way has been to modify nature. We have discovered how to use fire, make clothing, grow food, and "influence" nature through religious rituals. In more recent times, we have invented many more ways to make life safer and more comfortable: water purification, electric lighting, central heating, air-conditioning, indoor plumbing, vaccination, and antibiotics. The second way to control nature has been internal and psychological—by modifying our thoughts and perceptions. Human beings have used philosophy, religious belief, psychology, meditation, and yogic practices to overcome suffering and to increase happiness.

In the drive to overcome the injurious power of nature, however, some religions have virtually denied that human beings are a part of nature. They have viewed the earth as merely a way station on the road to a more permanent life after death and human beings as primarily spirits, temporarily imprisoned in their bodies. Some religions have architecturally separated their believers from nature in buildings that resemble bank vaults. Those religions that see nature as dangerous have too often paid little attention to its beauty.

Technology and commerce have also exhibited a limited vision of nature, treating it merely as a resource to be exploited. Nature has been valued not for its forests but for its lumber; not for its sand and soil but for its concrete; not for its rivers and waterfalls but for its energy potential in the form of dams and hydroelectric power.

Now, however, human beings are at a new place in the history of their relationship with nature. Because human life for a good number of people is less subject to the earlier discomforts and diseases, nature seems less fearsome than was the nature that once needed to be placated through ritual. The more recent exploitive approach to nature is coming to be seen as inappropriate. People are beginning to recognize that the exploitation of nature must give way to the protection of nature. This new attitude respects nature for itself and refuses to view it simply as something that helps or hurts human beings. It sees nature not only as a pool of natural resources but also as a source of wonder. This approach has led thinkers to reexamine religious views of nature and has generated new interest in all those religions that esteem nature. Native religions are appreciated for their reverence for the rights of trees, birds, and animals to continue in their own particular modes of existence. Taoism is looked to for its sensitivity to the mystery of the universe and for its influence on the Chinese artistic rendering of nature. This approach also looks to those forms of Mahayana Buddhism that have seen nature as "the body of the Buddha."

In Europe, a contemplative interest in nature is not entirely new. Its origins can be traced back many centuries to the nature mysticism of some medieval Cistercian monks and Franciscan friars. It gained strength in those thinkers and artistic creations that are now recognized as part of the European Renaissance: an interest in nature is evident in the writings of Petrarch (1304–1374), in the poetry of Chaucer (c. 1340–1400), in Italian and English madrigals, and in many Renaissance paintings. Nature played a major role in the Romantic movement of the eighteenth and nineteenth centuries, which held that nature is the major manifestation of the sublime. It was thus of great importance in many manifestations of the Romantic sensibility during that period—in English and French painting, in German music, and in English garden design.

The spread of Chinese ceramics in the eighteenth century and Japanese art in the late nineteenth century may have added to the growing appreciation of nature. Chinese painting on ceramics (which we significantly call chinaware) frequently portrayed trees, birds, and nature scenes; and Japanese scrolls and woodblock prints, which revolutionized European painting, often showed the power and color of mountains and ocean.

In the late nineteenth and early twentieth centuries, the movement toward nature was strikingly evident in the painting of the Impressionists, among whom Claude Monet (1840–1926) was a significant example. Monet not only painted occasional scenes of nature in the countryside, but he left Paris to create a country home with a garden featuring a large waterlily pond, which he painted regularly for the last forty-three years of his life. The garden he created at Giverny is virtually a place of pilgrimage today; his paintings of nature hang in many major museums; and reproductions of his paintings of waterlilies have made his work well known and loved throughout the world.

The great open spaces of North America have inspired a feeling for the spirituality of nature—as depicted in the works of European and American painters of the nineteenth century, such as the German-born Albert Bierstadt (1830–1902) and American Asher Durand (1796–1886). Travelers who visited the western part of North America wrote of its extravagant beauty. One of these was Scottish-born naturalist John Muir (1838–1914), author of

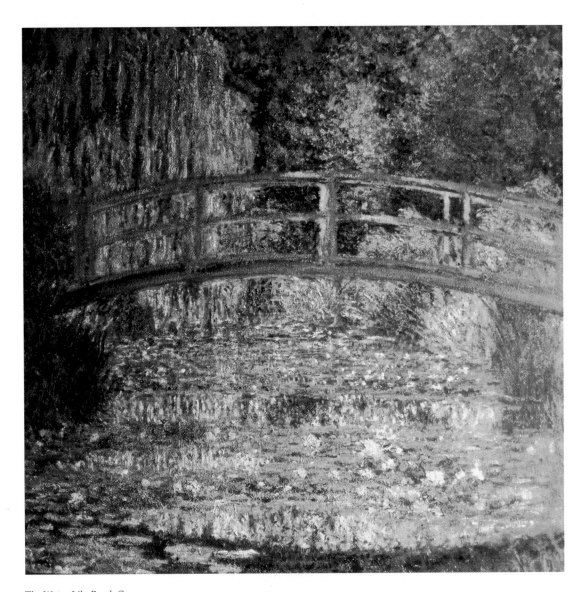

The Water Lily Pond: Green Harmony (1899), Claude Monet. Monet's paintings provide many people with a new way to contemplate nature. His garden near Paris, shown here in one of his paintings, has become a contemporary pilgrimage site.

The Mountains of California (1894) and *Our National Parks* (1901). Largely because of his efforts, Yosemite was made a national park, and his work helped to protect and develop the growing national park system, because he demanded that beautiful regions important to the whole nation be protected.

Today, signs of this new approach to the natural world—an approach that is both practical and spiritual—are evident everywhere. Earth Day was established only a few decades ago, but it grows yearly in importance as a festival of nature. Television is crowded with wonderfully photographed programs on animals and insects, forests and lakes, coral reefs, fish, and oceans—films that have become an art form in their own right. Specialty stores now sell items that express the theme of nature—from semiprecious stones and interesting mineral formations to posters of dolphins and whales, to recorded music that incorporates the sounds of waves and rain. A whole new type of environmentally sensitive travel is becoming popular: *ecotourism* takes people to places like the Amazon and the Galápagos Islands. Zoos, which used to be little more than prisons for animals, are undergoing a revolution in design; they now try to provide a familiar, comfortable, and spacious environment for their animals. Legal protections are being created for endangered species. Art and music (discussed in more detail later in this chapter) have actually pointed the way, through over a century of works that have been strongly inspired by the world of nature.

This entire movement, which we might call Naturism, is influencing our lives in important ways in the industrialized world. It is actually a network of related interests, including groups that work for the protection of forests and jungles and endangered species. It has worked to set up sanctuaries for whales and dolphins. It has produced ardent animal rights groups, which oppose the use of fur, the killing of animals for sport, unnecessary animal testing, and the inhumane breeding and slaughter of animals for food. It has generated efforts to recycle and to minimize pesticide use. It inspires those groups that are seeking to reduce energy consumption and to use forms of energy that do not endanger human and animal life. It encourages energy efficiency in architecture and car design. It expresses itself, as well, in efforts that encourage a healthy diet, regular exercise, vitamin supplements, and non-Western forms of medical treatment. As examples of its organizational expression, there are a whole host of organizations dedicated to bettering the earth: Greenpeace, the Sierra Club, the Audubon Society, the Nature Conservancy, and People for the Ethical Treatment of Animals.

What I have called Naturism has interesting parallels with traditional religions. For example, it has a strongly prophetic aspect because of its moral rules. Like many religions, it dictates what a person should or should not eat, wear, and do. (Some bumper stickers illustrate this: "Love animals, don't eat them," "Fur looks good on animals," and "Think globally, act locally.") Naturism also has a mystical aspect in its emphasis on the fundamental unity of human beings and the universe. In fact, it offers as its supreme experience the sense of oneness with animals and the rest of nature.

So far, this movement is deficient in the sacramental, ritualistic element that usually characterizes religions—although this aspect has great potential for development and may grow in the next centuries. Events like Earth Day and summer solstice festivals may be a beginning of such rituals, and the religion of Wicca attempts to re-create pre-Christian nature rituals. We might see the evolution of nature-based ritual for the major seasons: Earth Day already marks spring, summer solstice rites mark summer, and autumn is marked by Thanksgiving or similar end-of-harvest ceremonial meals and rituals.

Like religion, Naturism also has its "sacred places." Destinations of eco-pilgrimage include Yosemite, the Rocky Mountains, wildlife preserves in East Africa and Costa Rica, Mount Everest, the whale sanctuary at Maui, Glacier Bay and Denali National Park in Alaska, and many others. (The word *sanctuary,* used in reference to animal preserves, is religiously significant.) Naturism is also developing its role models, many of whom—interestingly—are women: Dian Fossey (1932–1985), Jane Goodall (b. 1934), Rachel Carson (1907–1964), and Brigitte Bardot (b. 1934). There is a growing body of environmentalist "scripture," for example, *Walden* by Henry David Thoreau (1817–1862) and *Animal Liberation* by Peter Singer (b. 1946). And sacred iconography extends, for example, from the nature photographs of Yosemite by Ansel Adams (1902–1984) to popular paintings of whales and porpoises by Christian Lassen (b. 1956), Robert Wyland (b. 1956), and others.

ECLECTIC SPIRITUALITY

It is quite common now to hear people say that they are not particularly interested in any one religion but that they are interested in spirituality. It is not always clear what they mean by *spirituality,* but the fact that people use this word to describe their religious stance does reveal an important contemporary phenomenon: increased knowledge of the world's religions, coupled with the popularization of certain schools of psychology (discussed later in this section), has led a number of people to assemble elements of different belief systems in an attempt to satisfy needs that once were assumed to be addressed only through participation in a single intact religious tradition.

As has occurred with Naturism, "eclectic spirituality" has become associated with a particular set of attitudes and practices. Highly valued are practices that promote inner peace and a feeling of harmony between oneself and the outer world. The key belief of those who embrace eclectic spirituality involves some understanding of the interrelatedness of all elements in the universe. That belief is often expressed through a moral earnestness about the need to express respect and reverence for other persons and other creatures. The respect and reverence are often cultivated through contemplative acts that dissolve separateness and promote ways of seeing beyond the superficial to the essential relatedness, even oneness, of all beings.

Traditional religions often engender spirituality, and eclectic spirituality is marked by borrowings from traditional religions, ranging from meditative practices inspired by Buddhism to dancing inspired by Sufism. But there are other means to attain spirituality, and many find it outside traditional religion. We have all had the experience, for example, of going to a movie theater, sitting down in the darkness, and being progressively drawn into a film that does far more than merely entertain. At a certain point, we recognize that the film is evoking in us a response that is somehow funda-

Religion and Movies

From their earliest days, movies have explored religious themes and the questions of spirituality—from the silent film *Intolerance* and films based on the Bible to the more recent movies *Yentl* and *Little Buddha*. Less overtly religious films also have explored moral and spiritual topics. Frank Capra (1897–1991), in his film *Lost Horizon* (based on a novel by the same title by James Hilton [1900–1954]), contrasted the utopian world of Shangri-la, hidden in the Himalayas, with the superficiality of the modern industrial world. The message of the movie is given by the "high lama," the founder of Shangri-la, whose very last words are, "Be kind." Another film by the same director, *It's a Wonderful Life* (which regularly appears on television at Christmas time), shows a man discovering the value of his life only when he is on the brink of suicide. At that moment he sees all the good he has done, and he receives the affectionate care of his neighbors.

Some films bring a kind of enlightenment through their revelation of the value of everyday life. The film version of the play *Our Town*, by Thornton Wilder (1897–1975), shows a girl going back in time to her sixteenth birthday and seeing her family in a new light. *Peggy Sue Got Married* does the same thing, when a woman is transported back to her high school days. *Late Summer* and other films by the Japanese director Yasujiro Ozu (1903–1963) reveal the beauty of the everyday through careful attention to the details of human life. They typically show a family at a turning point in its life, such as when a daughter gets married and must move away. Akira Kurosawa (b. 1910), in his *Ikiru (To Live)*, depicts a man's reflections upon discovering he is dying of cancer. The man, up to now an undistinguished city bureaucrat, fights to create a city park for children as the one major gift of his life, and in that struggle he becomes a spiritual hero.

Science fiction films about space travel also show interesting parallels with mythic religious stories of visitations by angels and deities or human ascensions to heavenly realms. Sometimes—as in the *Star Trek* series on television and in film or in the *Star Wars* series—these films touch on the semireligious struggle between the forces of good and evil. Many times (as in the film *E.T.*) they suggest that human beings need to learn lessons that can only be taught by representatives from other worlds.

mental to the human experience and at the same time transcendent—an experience of the "spiritual." Often we sense that others in the audience are sharing in the experience. At the end of many films, there is silence rather than applause, a silence that may prevail even in the lobby as people leave the theater. Musical concerts can also induce a similar experience.

Psychologists such as Jung (1875–1961; see Chapter 1) and Abraham Maslow (1908–1970) have written extensively of the necessary spiritual development of the human being. Maslow became preoccupied with it, first describing what he called "peak experiences," which are rare and transient, and then describing what he called "plateau experiences," which are contemplative experiences in everyday life that may be frequent and long-lasting. Maslow's most famous books were *Toward a Psychology of Being* and *Religions, Values, and Peak Experiences.* These works focus on contemplative experiences of many types, which Maslow identified through numerous interviews. He belonged to the school that has been called Humanistic Psychology. Another related school was Logotherapy, begun by Viktor Frankl (1905–1997).

The notion of spirituality, within but also increasingly apart from religion, permeates modern culture. Almost any big-city record store has a

Who would have thought that Gregorian chant, used only by a small number of cloistered monks, would in the late twentieth century reach the top ten charts? Many people understand this popularity as an indication of the public's hunger for spiritual nourishment.

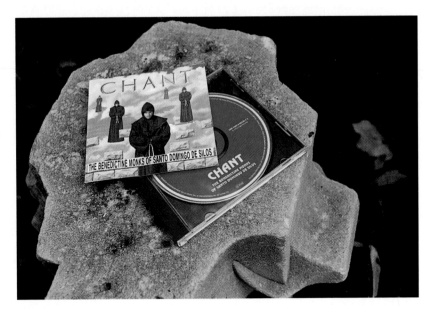

"spiritual music" section. There you may find the compositions of Arvo Pärt (b. 1935) alongside New Age synthesizer music, recordings of birdsong and ocean waves, and recordings of monastic chant from the Catholic and Tibetan religious traditions.

Because eclectic spirituality is difficult to define, we will try now to understand it through examples. We will look particularly at three aspects frequently thought of as characterizing modern spirituality: the sense of interrelatedness; an attitude of respect and reverence; and a contemplative approach to experiencing reality.

Interrelatedness   As we saw in earlier chapters, many religions have pointed to a relatedness among all beings, expressed perhaps most strongly in Buddhist and Hindu thought but also in the mystical teachings of many other religions. Interest in interrelatedness resurfaced as a cultural phenomenon in the 1980s, when a book on contemporary physics—which ordinarily would have had a readership of at most a few thousand—became a best-seller. Its title, *The Tao of Physics*, was a clear signal of the willingness of its author, Fritjof Capra (mentioned earlier), to leap across the traditional boundaries between religion and science. Its exploration of the subatomic world helped many readers understand that the relationality we can observe in the visible world mirrors what occurs in the very building blocks of the universe. This same interest in interrelatedness helps account for the popularity of such abstruse topics as chaos theory, cosmology, and the meteorological relations between ocean temperature and distant weather patterns and of such books as *The Whole Shebang* by Timothy Ferris (b. 1914) and *A Brief History of Time* by Stephen Hawking (b. 1942).

Religion and Pop Culture

Popular culture often presents religious themes. Comic strips and animated cartoon films, for example, look uncomplicated but sometimes have a depth that belies their appearance. (Pablo Picasso ([1881–1973] and other artists have highly valued comics for their economy of line—a great deal can be said with minimal drawing.) Some comic strips indict society in a prophetic way (such as *Doonesbury* or *Mallard*); other comic strips are explicitly religious (such as *Peanuts, Family Circus,* and *B.C.*). In many of Disney's animated films (*Snow White, Fantasia, Dumbo, Bambi, Cinderella, Little Mermaid, Lion King*), a host of loving animals have been created with such personality and charm that their portrayal as conscious, feeling beings on a par with human beings may have contributed to the growing animal liberation movement.

The creation of Superman and other heroic comic-book figures may be a popular form of biblical messianism. Like the messianic agent given authority by the Ancient of Days in the seventh chapter of the Book of Daniel, Superman comes to earth from another world to bring justice and compassion. Biblical influence may have inspired semi-biblical "Krypton names" of Superman and of his father: Kal-El and Jor-El. (We might recall that *El* means "God" in Hebrew and occurs in names such as *Israel, Samuel,* and *Michael.*) Superman and other similar heroes help reinforce the human desire for justice and compassion.

The cult of Elvis Presley ("Presleyanity"), while perhaps not what one would call "spiritual," has multiple religious parallels: the death of Elvis at an early age, his later "apparitions" to the faithful, the supposed healing power of his photos, the common image of him dressed in white, the commemoration of his birth and death, the pilgrimage to Graceland and other sites where Elvis lived and worked, and the marketing of some of his songs as gospel music. The cult of Elvis suggests that the religious urge remains, though its forms of expression change.

Popular interest in interrelatedness is also evident in the reinterpretation of some artworks. The paintings of Georgia O'Keeffe (1887–1986) provide a particularly good example. Her paintings (which have become so popular that one has been reproduced on a United States postage stamp) of flowers and animal bones and close-to-the-earth architectural forms have always been regarded as technically excellent. Their recent popularity, however, may hinge more on their expression of interrelatedness and interchangeableness: because many of her paintings depict objects at close range, the viewer is often unable at first glance to tell if the painting represents a flower, a part of human or animal anatomy, an adobe church, a hillside, or even a seashell. This ambiguousness is surprising because, in fact, O'Keeffe's work is often closer to realism than abstraction. However, even that distinction is broken down by O'Keeffe's highlighting of the abstract within the specific. Overall, her paintings express interrelatedness on several levels; they invite the viewer to contemplate patterns and underlying similarities. Some reproductions of O'Keeffe's paintings have become almost icons of spirituality.

Abstraction has been used repeatedly to suggest both the state of interrelatedness and the human experience of oneness. Georgia O'Keeffe's nonrepresentational works frequently use curves of color with this intent, as in *Music: Pink and Blue, Blue,* and the *Series 1* paintings.[8] Mark Rothko (1903–1970), in his mature style, achieves a similar effect by superimposing squares of subtle color, which seem to float luminously above their

White Flower on Red Earth by Georgia O'Keeffe. Contemplation of works of art based on nature is as meaningful today as was contemplation of stained-glass windows and mandalas in earlier ages.

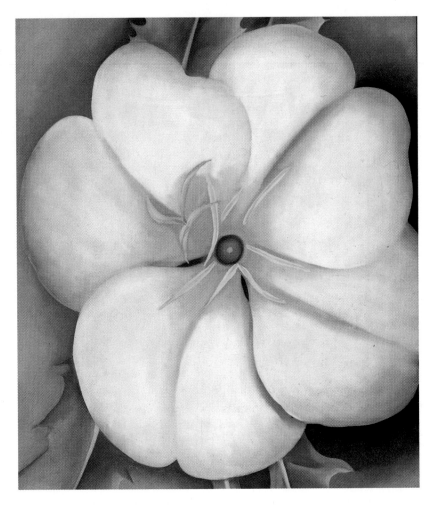

backgrounds. Jackson Pollock (1912–1956) created spontaneous but very complicated worlds of relationship in color by spattering paint on canvases that he had placed on the ground. Viewing these artists' works can give the viewer a feeling of being either out in space, surrounded by stars and blackness, or within an atom, amid the active particles and surrounding emptiness.

Reverence and Respect   As we've already discussed, nature came to be seen during the late twentieth century not as something to use, exploit, and abuse, but rather as a part of ourselves that must be nurtured for the well-being of all. Beyond this reconceptualization of nature, best expressed in environmental movements, is a turn to nature as revelation—nature as an expression of the spirit that permeates all reality, nature as a phenomenon to be revered. This attitude is perhaps best expressed in the art of photography.

In an article that compares the qualities of some creative photographers with the virtues of the Taoist sage as espoused in the Zhuangzi, writers Philippe Gross and S. I. Shapiro describe Taoistic ideals, often using both the words of the Zhuangzi and of modern photographers themselves, placed side by side. The authors conclude that the vision of the Taoist sage and of many great photographers is the same: "Both the Sage and the taoistic photographer have the capacity for seeing with unconstricted awareness and are therefore capable of seeing the miraculous in the ordinary."[9] According to Gross and Shapiro, the virtues shared by the Taoist sage and the contemplative photographer include freedom from the sense of self, receptivity, wu wei, spontaneity, acceptance, and nonattachment—attributes that promote a general attitude of respect and reverence.

Contemplative photography reached a peak of sorts in the nature photography of Ansel Adams (mentioned earlier). His black-and-white photographs of Yosemite National Park, whose mountains and waterfalls recall the subject matter of traditional Chinese landscape painting, evoke a feeling of respect for the power and the beauty of nature. Another devotee of nature, Eliot Porter (1901–1990), photographed in brilliant color to let nature speak fully of its beauty. He became well known for his photographs of trees turning yellow in autumn, of reflections in ponds, and of river canyons. These photographs often elicit the same reverence in the viewer as a Taoist sage might have experienced in contemplating a waterfall or a distant mountain.

Photography has been particularly effective in recording the most minute details of the human face and of human life, once again inviting insight, respect, and reverence. Photography of the American Civil War by Matthew Brady (c. 1823–1896) includes portraits of people in terrible circumstances. Not long after, Edward Curtis (1868–1952) sensitively documented the vanishing indigenous life of Native Americans. Dorothea Lange (1895–1965) and Walker Evans (1903–1975) produced moving studies of people during the Great Depression. More recent masters have been Edward Steichen (1879–1973) and Diane Arbus (1923–1971). Steichen's published anthology of photographs, called *The Family of Man,* includes studies of the spiritual expressed in human faces and actions from around the world. Arbus drew our respectful attention to marginalized people in our urban societies.

The ability to evoke an attitude of respect and reverence is by no means limited to the art of photography. The details of ordinary human life can be treated with reverence in painting as well. Vincent van Gogh (1853–1890) did this repeatedly in his works—from his earlier portrayal of peasants, in *The Potato Eaters,* to the later paintings of his neighborhood postman, of sunflowers arranged in a vase, and of a neighborhood cafe at night. The same attitude of respectful attention is given to cartoons (consider the role of Lisa in the popular *Simpsons*) and to music (for example, John Corigliano's *First Symphony,* inspired by the human sense of loss and grief

I'm not responsible for my photographs. Photography is not documentary, but intuition, a poetic experience. It's drowning yourself, dissolving yourself. . . . First you must lose your self. Then it happens.

—Henri Cartier-Bresson, photographer[10]

caused by AIDS). In fact, this attitude can be expressed by any art form or technique that promotes contemplation—the method for revealing spirituality to which we now turn.

Contemplative Practices   Although eclectic spirituality emphasizes the interrelatedness of all creation, it does not maintain that each person is able to see interrelatedness. However, one can promote the seeing of relatedness, as well as attitudes of respect and reverence, by preparing the eyes to see, the ears to hear, and the mind to understand. This is done through a variety of practices that might best be described as contemplative approaches to experiencing reality.

As we saw in the earliest chapters of this book, native forms of religious practice often have made use of practices that result in trance states, in which ordinary reality is viewed in a transformed way. In later chapters we reviewed the forms of mysticism that exist in many of the world's religions and touched upon the different contemplative activities—such as meditation, Sufi dancing, tea ceremony, and hatha yoga—that have to some extent supplanted the cultivation of trance states. The fact is that anyone—even the person who does not practice a traditional religion—is free to try any of the following contemplative practices that have been developed.

Traditional religions can provide a number of the practices that attract people who are eclectically charting their own spiritual path. Most religions make use of songs, chants, and other forms of music—some of them elaborate. Mahayana and Vajrayana Buddhism use complex chant, often accompanied by bells, drums, gongs, trumpets, conch shells, and cymbals. Christianity has produced a great amount of chant and other choral music. Shinto uses chants and gagaku (the solemn instrumental music derived from ancient Chinese court music). Much religious music is intended to help listeners experience a connectedness with the sacred. Until recently, however, there were few opportunities to experience religious music without attending a religious service. Today, however, through recordings, people can listen to this music and use it as part of contemplative practice.

Along with traditional religious music, some secular forms of music are also used for contemplative purposes. Today, a common form of contemplative practice is to listen to these types of music in a meditative way. During the late nineteenth century and early twentieth century, the Impressionist schools (particularly in France) developed not only a style of painting but also of music. What is notable about Impressionist music is that it aims not so much to satisfy classical requirements of form but to convey a sensual impression, through music, of a primarily nonmusical experience, such as the coming of dawn or the feeling of standing in a verdant forest.

Much Western contemplative music today is a direct descendant of that earlier evocative music. One example of Impressionist music is *Prelude to the Afternoon of a Faun* by Claude Debussy (1862–1918). In his tone poem *La Mer* ("the sea"), Debussy uses music to describe a sunrise and a storm on the

New Age devotees regard crystals in much the same way as traditional religions treat certain objects as sacred—the vajra in Buddhism, for example, and the mirror in Shinto.

ocean. His *Nocturnes* for orchestra include a meditation on clouds (*Nuages*), and his *Clair de Lune* creates the feeling of a quiet, moonlit night. Another French composer, Maurice Ravel (1875–1937), even used a wind machine to evoke nature in the full version of his *Daphnis and Chloe*. And both Ravel and Debussy created serene music for quartets as well as music for piano that suggests the relaxing play of fountains. A third composer in this contemplative line was the Englishman Frederick Delius (1862–1934), whose works are generally short impressions of seasonal moods. Among the finest are *On Hearing the First Cuckoo in Spring* and *The Walk to the Paradise Garden.* The English composer Ralph Vaughan Williams (1872–1958), who studied with Ravel, suggests with a solo violin the flight of a bird in *The Lark Ascending*—a delicate work that, when experienced in a quiet environment, has helped many a listener experience a connectedness with the sacred (the composition is also often used as a subject for modern ballet). His *Fantasia on Greensleeves* and *Fantasia on a Theme of Thomas Tallis* are equally contemplative. The moods created by these composers are today frequently echoed in what has come to be called New Age music, some of which is performed on synthesizers.

In addition, the spread of modern orchestral instruments in Asia and the use of the synthesizer have made it possible for Asian composers to create complicated crosscultural works that offer new windows through which listeners can experience that which is within and beyond. The contemporary Japanese composers Toshiro Mayazumi (b. 1928) and Toru Takemitsu (b. 1930), for example, are often cited for their efforts to transport listeners through transcultural and transpersonal music.

Whether eclectic spirituality will develop into a fully developed religion is impossible to say. It is easier to predict that world growth will result in more crowded spaces, more noise, greater competition, and increased stress. Under such circumstances, the need for contemplation can only grow.

PERSONAL EXPERIENCE: *2001* AND BEYOND

Recently in the local newspaper I read some prophecies by Arthur C. Clarke, author of many science fiction books and of the book on which the film *2001* was based. Clarke says that in the future human beings will stop eating meat. To me, that seems a realistic prophecy. He also says that in the future religions will be banned. At first I found myself disagreeing: How could anything so powerful be banned? Clearly, from what we have just seen of religion in contemporary culture, the religious instinct is alive, and it is being expressed even as it undergoes transformation. It may not always be found in temples and churches, but it certainly seems to be alive and strong.

On second thought, perhaps religion *should* be banned. After all, Clarke is a respected writer whose thoughts should be taken seriously. Indeed, various religions have wielded dangerous power throughout history. Some have been divisive by being maddeningly conservative, and still others have been frustratingly prophetic and idealistic, pointing to "another way" that differs from the status quo.

Nonetheless, depending on how one sees it, religions have stymied progress, helped maintain the patriarchy, and prompted wars; yet at the same time they've fueled the arts, been a source of personal and communal comfort, and kept humankind from destroying itself. Whatever one's point of view, it is easy to come up with reasons why at least certain religions should be banned. From there it is not much of a leap to argue that all religions should be banned—as vestiges of a superstitious past and obstacles to a scientifically charted better future.

Yet I don't know, Mr. Clarke. I am not quite ready for an updated version of your computer HAL to replace the religious authorities and scriptures. But I am sure of two things, Mr. Clarke. First, if you want to stamp out religion, you will have to achieve a worldwide ban, because history has shown that religious ideas and emotions are tenacious, obliterated over here only to reemerge, sometimes in a different guise, over there. And second, although the banning of religions is possible, what is impossible is the elimination of the religious urge, which has been with us since the first person looked up and asked, Why? And it is likely to be around at least until either a great comet wipes us out or until we—unable to get our hearts and minds to work together—muddle our way to self-destruction.

But even then, who knows? Life just could reevolve, and down the road one of our successors might one day gaze upon the setting of an older sun and ask, Why? If you wonder what that successor might answer, you are coming close to religious wondering.

RELIGION BEYOND THE CLASSROOM

The national park movement is an expression of the growing sensitivity to nature. It shows an awareness of the spiritual experiences that contact with nature can make possible. In the continental United States, there are parks of special importance: Yosemite, Yellowstone, the Grand Tetons, the Grand Canyon, and Bryce Canyon. In Alaska, there are Denali National Park and Glacier Bay. In Hawai'i, there are Volcano National Park on the island of Hawai'i and the Na Pali Coast on Kauai. In Canada, Banff and Lake Louise are two sites worth visiting in the Canadian Rockies. In Central America and South America, the system of national parks is less developed but is under way, particularly in Costa Rica, Belize, Venezuela, and Brazil. In Africa, there are major wildlife refuges in Kenya, Tanzania, and South Africa.

FOR FULLER UNDERSTANDING

1. Visit a museum that has a good sampling of art covering many centuries. Name some artists who paint explicitly religious paintings. At what point in history do explicitly religious paintings seem to drop off? What are the themes of modern painting? List any that convey spiritual themes.
2. Islam and Buddhism are spreading in North America. How do you think each religion will be changed by contact with the widespread behavior and values of the surrounding culture?
3. How do you see feminism changing traditional religions over the next hundred years?
4. Design a ritual that expresses human relationships with nature. What music might accompany it? Where would it occur? How frequently would it be celebrated?
5. With a partner, write both sides of a debate on the assertion "Religions have in human history done more harm than good and therefore should be banned."

RELATED READINGS

Ellwood, Robert. *The History and Future of Faith.* New York: Crossroad, 1988. A work by a noted scholar of religion that describes stages in the development of major religions, debates secularism, and projects the future of religion.

Fox, Matthew. *Creation Spirituality.* San Francisco: Harper San Francisco, 1993. A reinterpretation of Christianity by a Christian priest that emphasizes basic human goodness and mystical awareness.

Huxley, Aldous. *The Human Situation.* New York: Harper and Row, 1973. A seminal early book that points to the spirituality of nature and calls for environmental responsibility.

Mitchell, Stephen, ed. *The Enlightened Mind.* New York: HarperCollins, 1991. An anthology of spirituality from many religions.

Tuchman, Maurice, ed. *The Spiritual in Art: Abstract Painting 1890–1985.* New York: Abbeville Press, 1986. A large and well-illustrated collection of essays by many writers on the fascinating topic of spirituality in modern art.

Van Gogh, Vincent. *Letters from Provence.* Edited by Martin Bailey. London: Collins and Brown, 1990. A book that offers insight into van Gogh's unique spiritual vision.

Notes

Chapter 1

1. The original painting is part of the permanent collection of the Boston Museum of Fine Arts.

2. William James, *The Varieties of Religious Experience* (New York: Collier, 1961), p. 377.

3. Rudolf Otto, *The Idea of the Holy* (New York: Oxford University Press, 1963), p. 62.

4. Some have criticized Otto's notion of the *mysterium tremendum,* arguing that his theorizing was overinfluenced by Protestant Christianity, in which he was raised.

5. Carl Jung, *Memories, Dreams, Reflections* (London: Collins, 1972), p. 222.

6. *Webster's New World Dictionary,* 2d ed. (New York: William Collins, 1972). Other Latin roots are also possible.

7. *Cassell's New Latin Dictionary* (New York: Funk & Wagnalls, 1960).

8. Similar lists can be found, for example, in William Alston, "Religion," in *The Encyclopedia of Philosophy,* vol. 7 (New York: Macmillan, 1972), 141–42; and Ninan Smart, *The Religious Experience,* 4th ed. (New York: Macmillan, 1991), 6–10.

9. Julian Huxley, *Religion Without Revelation* (New York: Mentor, c. 1957), p. 33.

10. "Between Mountain and Plain," *Time,* 20 October 1952, p. 33.

11. Alston, "Religion," 143–44.

12. Catholics touch the left shoulder first; Orthodox Christians touch the right shoulder first.

13. Kusan Sunim, *The Way of Korean Zen* (New York: Weatherhill, 1985), 168.

14. New Oxford Annotated Bible (New York: Oxford University Press, 1991).

15. Good News Bible (New York: American Bible Society, 1976). This version is a paraphrase.

16. For example, the Srimaladevisimhananda Sutra speaks of the enlightenment of a female lay ruler.

17. Martin Luther King, Jr., *Strength to Love* (New York: Harper & Row, 1963), p. 3.

Chapter 2

1. Nancy Parezo, "The Southwest," in *The Native Americans,* ed. Colin Taylor (New York: Salamander, 1991), p. 58.

2. Geoffrey Parrinder, *Religion in Africa* (New York: Praeger, 1969), pp. 21, 18.

3. Foreword to Peter Knudtson and David Suzuki, *Wisdom of the Elders* (Toronto: Stoddart, 1993), p. xxiv.

4. Gladys Reichard, *Navaho Religion* (Princeton: Bollingen, 1963), p. 286.

5. Florence Drake, *Civilization* (Norman: University of Oklahoma Press, 1936), quoted in John Collier,

Indians of the Americas (New York: New American Library, 1947), p. 107.

6. Frank Willet, *African Art* (London: Thames and Hudson, 1993), p. 35.

7. One entire room at the Gauguin Museum in Tahiti illustrates Gauguin's interest in discovering a "primary religion." It also shows the religious origin of much imagery in his paintings. A significant collection of Gauguin's paintings and carvings can be seen at the Musée d'Orsay in Paris.

8. See Parrinder, *Religion in Africa*, pp. 47–59 for more detail.

9. Quoted in T. C. McLuhan, ed., *Touch the Earth* (New York: Promontory Press, 1971), p. 42.

10. McLuhan, *Touch the Earth*, p. 56.

11. Knudtson and Suzuki, *Wisdom of the Elders*, p. xxv.

12. Ibid., p. 29.

13. Ibid., p. 27.

14. Parrinder, *Religion in Africa*, p. 43.

15. Ibid., p. 32.

16. Joseph Campbell, *The Power of Myth* (New York: Doubleday, 1988), p. 6.

17. Parrinder, *Religion in Africa*, pp. 80–81.

18. Collier, *Indians of the Americas*, p. 105.

19. Parrinder, *Religion in Africa*, p. 81.

20. For details, see William Sturtevant, "The Southeast," in *The Native Americans*, pp. 17–21.

21. From Florence Drake, *Civilization*, quoted in Collier, *Indians of the Americas*, p. 107.

22. See John Mbiti, *Introduction to African Religion* (London: Heinemann, 1986), pp. 143–44.

23. Joan Halifax, *Shaman: The Wounded Healer* (London: Thames and Hudson, 1994), p. 5.

24. Quoted in Knudtson and Suzuki, *Wisdom of the Elders*, p. 70.

25. For a detailed study of the religious use of peyote by Native Americans, see Omer C. Stewart, *Peyote Religion: A History* (Norman: University of Oklahoma Press, 1987).

26. John Fire/Lame Deer and Richard Erdoes, *Lame Deer: Seeker of Visions* (New York: Simon and Schuster, 1972), p. 220.

27. Mbiti, *Introduction to African Religion*, p. 165.

28. Ibid., p. 166.

29. These are the commonly used names; nomenclature is in a process of change for some Northwest tribes.

30. Pat Kramer, *Totem Poles* (Vancouver: Altitude, 1995), pp. 48–49.

31. Richard W. Hill, Sr., "The Symbolism of Feathers," in *Creation's Journey* (Washington, DC: Smithsonian Institution Press, 1994), p. 88.

Chapter 3

1. Arthur Basham, *The Wonder That Was India* (New York: Grove, 1959), p. 16. Chapter 2 of Basham's book contains a detailed description of the Harappa culture.

2. Ibid., p. 23.

3. Also spelled *Rg Veda*. For representative prayers, see William T. deBary, ed., *Sources of Indian Tradition*, vol. 1 (New York: Columbia University Press, 1958), pp. 7–16.

4. Rig Veda 10:129, quoted in Basham, *The Wonder That Was India*, p. 16.

5. The same tendency toward philosophy existed in Greece at the time and a few centuries later in the Roman Empire.

6. The philosopher Shankara offered another interpretation—"to wear away completely."

7. These five concepts are not fixed concepts in the Upanishads. They are more like centers around which speculation revolves, and there may be differences in how they are described, even within the same Upanishad. The notion of Brahman, for example, sometimes varies from that of a divine reality quite beyond the world to a spiritual reality that exists within the world.

8. Chandogya Upanishad 6:13, in *The Upanishads*, trans. Juan Mascaró (New York: Penguin, 1979), p. 118.

9. Shvetasvatara Upanishad, end of part 3, *The Upanishads*, pp. 90–91; emphasis added.

10. Ibid., part 4, p. 91.

11. Ibid.

12. See, for example, ibid., p. 92.

13. Ibid.

14. Brihadaranyaka Upanishad 2:4, *The Upanishads*, p. 132.

15. *The Song of God: Bhagavad-Gita*, trans. Swami Prabhavananda and Christopher Isherwood (New York: Mentor, 1972), chap. 5, p. 57.

16. Ibid., chap. 1, p. 34.

17. Ibid., chap. 18, p. 127.

18. Ibid., chap. 2, p. 38.

19. Rig Veda 10:90, as quoted in deBary, *Sources of Indian Tradition*, vol. 1, p. 14.

20. See Chapter 2 of the Bhagavad Gita.

21. Sometimes the term *caste* is reserved for what I call here subcastes—the hundreds of occupation-based social divisions (*jati*).

22. I follow the common practice of using the word *brahmin* (priest)—rather than the Sanskrit term *brahman*—to avoid confusion with the term *Brahman* (spiritual essence of the world) with a capital *B*.

23. See, for example, the description of Gandhi's "fast unto death" for untouchables in Louis Fischer, *Gandhi* (New York: New American Library, 1954), pp. 116–19.

24. The six orthodox schools of Hindu philosophy all developed as systems of personal liberation but disagreed about the views and methods that would bring liberation. The six schools are Nyaya, Vaisheshika, Sankhya, Yoga, Mimamsa, and Vedanta. Nyaya ("analysis") valued the insight that comes from clarity, reason, and logic. Vaisheshika ("individual characteristics") taught what it considered to be the correct way of understanding reality—seeing reality as essentially being made up of atoms. Sankhya ("count") was originally an atheistic philosophy that considered the universe to be made of two essential principles—soul and matter. Yoga ("union," "spiritual discipline") emphasized meditation and physical disciplines. Mimamsa ("investigation") defended the authority of the Vedas as a guide to salvation. Vedanta developed several sub-schools but tended to see a unifying principle—Brahman—at work behind the changing phenomena of everyday life; the individual can find salvation by attaining union with this principle.

25. Shankara's conception of Brahman is debated. For him, Brahman may have been a positive spiritual reality, or it may have been closer to the notion of emptiness found in Buddhism.

26. Shankara (attrib.), *Shankara's Crest-Jewel of Discrimination* (New York: Mentor, 1970), p. 72.

27. *The Song of God: Bhagavad-Gita,* chap. 2, p. 40.

28. Ibid., chap. 18, p. 128.

29. Although these sutras are attributed to an ancient grammarian named Patanjali, who lived before the common era, they may have been written later, from about 200 C.E.

30. Basham, *The Wonder That Was India,* p. 326.

31. Heinrich Zimmer, *Myths and Symbols in Indian Art and Civilization* (Princeton: Princeton University Press, 1972), p. 153.

32. Basavaraja, quoted in *Sources of Indian Tradition,* vol. 1, p. 352. Basavaraja was a twelfth-century Indian government official who founded a religious order devoted to Shiva.

33. *The Gospel of Ramakrishna,* quoted in deBary, *Sources of Indian Tradition,* vol. 2, p. 86.

34. *The Upanishads,* trans. Swami Prabhavananda and Frederick Manchester (New York: Mentor, 1970), pp. 70–71.

35. The term *darshan* also extends to viewing images of deities in order to experience the divine presence that they mediate.

36. When the Mother died, her role was taken over by an Indian girl, now called Mother Meera. See Andrew Harvey, *Hidden Journey: A Spiritual Awakening* (New York: Penguin/Arkana, 1992) for his description of Mother Meera.

37. See Ainslie T. Embree, ed., *The Hindu Tradition* (New York: Vintage, 1972), p. 279.

38. Fischer, *Gandhi,* p. 11.

39. Quoted in Fischer, *Gandhi,* p. 18.

40. Gandhi compromised his position on nonviolence somewhat during World War I, when he urged Indians to join the war effort on the side of the British. Later, he said that this position had been a mistake.

Chapter 4

1. Arthur Basham put it nicely: "Much doubt now exists as to the real doctrines of the historical Buddha, as distinct from those of Buddhism." *The Wonder That Was India* (New York: Grove, 1959), p. 256.

2. The tree may have been a form of banyan, which today is called the *Ficus religiosa* (religious fig) because of its supposed connection with the Buddha.

3. As quoted in William T. deBary, ed., *Sources of Indian Tradition* (New York: Columbia University Press, 1958), vol. 1, p. 110.

4. Some scholars think that the Reclining Buddha images may also depict the Buddha sleeping, sometimes with his cousin Ananda looking on protectively.

5. Sometimes the term "Sangha" is used more widely to include devout laypersons.

6. See David Kalupahana, *Buddhist Philosophy: A Historical Analysis* (Honolulu: University Press of Hawaii, 1976), pp. 38–41.

7. *Buddhist Suttas,* trans. T. W. Rhys Davids (New York: Dover, 1969), p. 148.

8. *The Dhammapada: The Sayings of the Buddha,* trans. Thomas Byrom (New York: Vintage, 1976), chap. 15, p. 76.

9. From the *Sammanaphala Suttanta,* in E. A. Burtt, *The Teachings of the Compassionate Buddha* (New York: New American Library, 1955), p. 104.

10. Sometimes the order is reversed, and the vinaya is designated as the first basket, with the sutra listed second.

11. The commonly accepted view about the introduction of form into Buddhist imagery has been questioned. See Stanley Abe, "Inside the Wonder House: Buddhist Art and the West," in *Curators of the Buddha: The Study of Buddhism under Colonialism,* ed. Donald S. Lopez, Jr. (Chicago: University of Chicago Press, 1995), pp. 63–106.

12. Hirakawa Akira, *A History of Indian Buddhism* (Honolulu: University of Hawaii Press, 1990), p. 258.

13. For details about the origins of Mahayana, see John Koller, *The Indian Way* (New York: Macmillan, 1983), p. 163.

14. For information about Buddhist schools of philosophy, see John Koller, "The Nature of Reality," in *Oriental Philosophies* (New York: Scribner's, 1970), pp. 146–79.

15. Kenneth Ch'en, *Buddhism in China* (Princeton, NJ: Princeton University Press, 1972), p. 385.

16. For more information see Richard Robinson and Willard Johnson, *The Buddhist Religion,* 4th ed. (Belmont, CA: Wadsworth, 1997), pp. 181ff.

17. Robert Buswell, *Tracing Back the Radiance: Chinul's Korean Way of Zen* (Honolulu: University of Hawaii Press, 1991), p. 5. See the introduction for a description of Korea's early Buddhist contacts with China and central Asia.

18. For a traveler's description of the monastery complex in the seventeenth century, see Li Chi, *The Travel Diaries of Hsü umlau Hsia-k'o* (Hong Kong: The Chinese University of Hong Kong, 1974), pp. 29–42.

19. The meditation guidebook *Shikantaza: An Introduction to Zazen* (Kyoto: Kyoto Zen Center, 1990) contains instructions for zazen and a good selection of passages by Zen masters on the practice and effects of zazen.

20. See the story of Rinzai, who received a beating from his master Obaku as a koan-like response to his simple-minded questioning, in D. T. Suzuki, *Studies in Zen* (New York: Delta, 1955), pp. 68–70. Suzuki gives many examples of koan, with commentary. The actual use of the koan in Japanese monasteries over the last three centuries has become more formalized. Instead of working through a koan, a person in training (who hopes to take over his father's temple) now often refers to books for the appropriate answers.

21. For connections between Christianity and the tea ceremony see Heinrich Dumoulin, *A History of Zen Buddhism* (Boston: Beacon, 1963), pp. 214–24.

Chapter 5

1. Mahapurana 4:16; cited in William T. deBary, ed., *Sources of Indian Tradition,* vol 1. (New York: Columbia University Press, 1958), p. 76.

2. Acaranga Sutra 1.6,5, cited in deBary *Sources of Indian Tradition,* vol. 1, p. 65.

3. See John Koller, *The Indian Way* (New York: Macmillan, 1982), pp. 114–15.

4. Selection from the Mul Mantra, cited in M. A. Macauliffe, *The Sikh Religion* (Oxford: Oxford University Press, 1901) vol. 1, p. 195.

5. From Asa Ki Var, Mahala I. Cited in Macauliffe, *The Sikh Religion* vol. 1, p. 221.

Chapter 6

1. *Tao Te Ching,* trans. Gia-fu Feng and Jane English (New York: Random House, 1972), chap. 1. This translation is used unless stated otherwise.

2. *Lao Tzu: Tao Te Ching,* trans. Robert Henricks (New York: Ballantine, 1989), p. 72.

3. *Tao Te Ching.*

4. *The Wisdom of Laotse,* trans. Lin Yutang (New York: Modern Library, 1948), p. 76.

5. *Chuang Tzu: Basic Writings,* trans. Burton Watson (New York: Columbia University Press, 1964), p. 36 (sec. 2).

6. Ibid., p. 113 (sec. 18).

7. Ibid.

8. Cited in *The Way and Its Power,* trans. Arthur Waley (New York: Grove, 1958), p. 181.

9. Wing-Tsit Chan, "Man and Nature in the Chinese Garden" in Henry Inn and Shao Chang Lee, eds., *Chinese Houses and Gardens* (Honolulu: Fong Inn's Limited, 1940), p. 33.

10. Ibid., pp. 35–36.

11. *The Doctrine of the Mean* 20:18; in *Confucius: Confucian Analects, The Great Learning, and The Doctrine*

of the Mean, trans. James Legge (New York: Dover, 1971), p. 413. (Legge's translation of the Four Books—the major Confucian books, which include the sayings of Confucius and Mencius—is used unless otherwise noted.) In the original translation, the word *right* is italicized and the word *way* is not. I have changed this to make my point clearer.

12. Ibid., 12:4.

13. *Analects* 5:25, 4.

14. Ibid., 2:4, 1–6.

15. See *The Doctrine of the Mean* 22:8 for a different order.

16. *Analects* 12:1, 1.

17. See *Analects* 12:1, 2 and *The Doctrine of the Mean* 13:3.

18. R. D. Baird and Alfred Bloom, *Indian and Far Eastern Religious Traditions* (New York: Harper & Row, 1972), p. 169.

19. George Kates, *The Years that Were Fat* (Cambridge, MA: MIT Press, 1976), pp. 28–29.

20. *The Doctrine of the Mean* 20:18; adapted.

21. *Analects* 4:16; trans. Arthur Waley (New York: Vintage, c. 1938), p. 105.

22. Ibid. 4:24; trans. Waley.

23. *The Great Learning*, "Text of Confucius" verse 6.

24. *The Doctrine of the Mean* 1:1–2; adapted.

25. Ibid. 1:5.

26. *Mencius* 4:2, 12, trans. James Legge (New York: Dover, 1970); adapted.

27. See Chapters 18–20 of the *Tao Te Ching*.

28. See Chapter 80 of the *Tao Te Ching*.

29. *Mencius* 4:1, 9.2.

30. Ibid., 6:1.6.7.

31. Given in an introductory chapter of Ibid., p. 81.

32. Cited in William T. deBary, ed., *Sources of Chinese Tradition* (New York: Columbia University Press, 1960), vol. 1, pp. 45–46.

33. Ibid., vol. 1, p. 436.

34. Since this visit, the Confucian Temple has been renovated.

Chapter 7

1. This myth begins the Kojiki ("chronicle of ancient events"); see *Translation of Ko-ji-ki*, trans. Basil Hall Chamberlain, 2d ed. (Kobe: J. L. Thompson, 1932), pp. 17–23.

2. Ibid., pp. 21–22. The same story, with many variants, appears at the beginning of another ancient work, the Nihongi.

3. Ibid., pp. 50–51.

4. Also called Shrine Shinto. For details, see H. Byron Earhart, *Religions of Japan* (New York: Harper & Row, 1984), pp. 43–45 and 93–100.

5. Sometimes a distinction is made between the spirits of nature and the spirits of the deceased. It is debated whether a belief in one type of spirit was the origin of a belief in the other. See, for example, Carmen Blacker, *The Catalpa Bow* (London: Allen & Unwin, 1975), pp. 45–46.

6. For a translation, see *Nihongi*, trans. W. G. Aston (London: Allen & Unwin, 1956).

7. Such imagery was apparently much more common before Western influence—and its sense of decorum—entered Japan in the nineteenth century.

8. The sense that death is polluting and dangerous explains the regular rebuilding of some Shinto shrines and the destruction of the clothing and personal effects of a deceased person.

9. The torii is used as a gateway, but it can be placed anywhere to indicate the presence of kami.

10. See H. Byron Earhart, *Japanese Religion: Unity and Diversity*, 2d ed. (Encino, CA: Dickenson, 1974), p. 21.

11. Keiichi Nakayama, *Tenrikyo Kyoten Kowa* (Tenri: Tenrikyo, 1951), p. 3; cited in Harry Thomsen, *The New Religions of Japan* (Rutland, VT: Tuttle, 1963), p. 34.

12. A translation of Miki's poetic work, *Mikagura Uta*, can be found in Thomsen, *The New Religions of Japan*, pp. 41–48.

Chapter 8

1. Scholars commonly hold that the Torah is composed of four strands of material, each coming from a different author or school. This theory is called the Documentary Hypothesis. For details, see Stephen Harris, *Understanding the Bible*, 3d ed. (London: Mayfield, 1992), pp. 53–59.

2. The Greek translation of the Hebrew Bible is commonly called the Septuagint. For details about the Septuagint translation, see Henry Jackson Flanders, Robert Wilson Crapps, and David Anthony Smith, *People of the Covenant*, 4th ed. (New York: Oxford University Press, 1996), p. 21.

3. Translation from *Tanakh—The Holy Scriptures* (Philadelphia: The Jewish Publication Society, 1985).

4. Emphasis added.

5. The New Oxford Annotated Bible (New York: Oxford University Press, 1991).

6. The translation by the Jewish Publication Society (1985) simply gives the Hebrew phrase "Ehyeh-Asher-Ehyeh"; it adds a footnote, saying that the exact meaning of the Hebrew is uncertain but that a common translation is "I am who I am" (p. 88).

7. The words "Yahweh" and "Adonai" were ultimately blended to create the name "Jehovah," used in English Bibles.

8. It is possible that the Book of Deuteronomy constitutes the first volume of a history about the Hebrews' entry into Canaan, which is continued in the Books of Joshua and Judges.

9. Exodus 20:2–17, from *Tanakh—the Holy Scriptures.*

10. The most famous is at Dura-Europos, in southern Syria.

11. Although today we might recoil at the thought of animal sacrifice, we must realize that it was common throughout the world of the time, even in India and China. It fulfilled several functions. Worshipers often thought the ritual of sharing a sacred meal would unite them with their deity. Punishment that might have fallen on human beings was thought to be transferred to the sacrificial animal. It was also a sign that the deity was in charge of all life.

12. The New Oxford Annotated Bible.

13. There are two long passages in Aramaic: Daniel 2:4–7:28 and Ezra 4:8–6:18. Short Aramaic passages also appear in Genesis (31:47) and Jeremiah (10:11).

14. Many other religious books were popular but were not finally accepted as canonical by Jews in Israel. A few additional books, however, were accepted as canonical by Jews living in Egypt, such as Sirach, the Wisdom of Solomon, and Maccabees. (Later, they were also accepted as canonical by Catholic and Eastern Orthodox Christians.)

15. The name *Sadducee* may derive from the name *Zadok* (or *Sadoc*), a priest of the time of King David.

16. The name *Pharisee* may derive from a Hebrew word meaning "separate"—referring to a ritual purity associated with the careful practice of religious laws.

17. It is possible that the dualistic worldview of the Essenes was influenced by the Persian religion of Zoroastrianism and that their semimonastic lifestyle was influenced by monastic ideals that had come from India to Egypt.

18. Union Prayerbook (New York, 1959), part 1, pp. 166–67.

19. A passage from the *Zohar,* quoted in *The Wisdom of the Kabbalah,* ed. Dagobert Runes (New York: Citadel, 1967), p. 172.

20. Quoted in Gershom Scholem, *On the Kabbalah and Its Symbolism* (New York: Schocken, 1969), p. 103.

21. The beginning of the movie *Yentl* illustrates the value put on the mystical interpretation of the Book of Genesis.

22. Martin Buber, the great Jewish writer, collected and published two volumes of Hasidic sayings. Many tales of the Baal Shem Tov appear in the first volume, *Tales of the Hasidim: Early Masters* (New York: Schocken, 1973).

23. Louis Newman, *Hasidic Anthology* (New York: Schocken, 1975), p. 148.

24. Ibid., p. 149.

25. Bella Chagall, *Burning Lights* (New York: Schocken, 1972). This book contains thirty-six drawings by Marc Chagall.

26. Anne Frank, *Diary of a Young Girl* (New York: Pocket Books, 1959), p. 222.

27. Ibid., pp. 192–93.

28. Ibid., p. 233.

29. The origin of the Sabbath is uncertain. It may have been inspired by Babylonian culture, or perhaps it was unique to the Hebrews. It is natural, however, to divide a lunar month into four seven-day periods.

30. The literal truth of this story is doubtful. We might note that the names of Esther and Mordecai are suspiciously close to the names of the Babylonian divinities Ishtar and Marduk. As such, the festival may derive from a Babylonian fertility festival.

31. The fact that Passover occurs in the first month of the Jewish lunar calendar may be an indication that it was once the Jewish New Year.

32. It is also possible that pigs and shellfish were considered "imperfect" animals. Perfect land animals (such as sheep and goats) chewed a cud and had divided hooves; perfect sea animals had scales. All others were considered less "perfect."

33. Leo Trepp, *Judaism: Development and Life* (Belmont, CA: Dickenson Publishing, 1966), p. 75.

34. Ibid.

35. From *I and Thou,* quoted in *The Writings of Martin Buber,* ed. Will Herberg (Cleveland: Meridian/World, 1961), p. 46.

Chapter 9

1. Jerusalem Bible (Garden City, NY: Doubleday, 1966).

2. American Bible Society translation, in *Good News Bible* (Nashville: Nelson, 1986). This version is not a strict translation, but is a paraphrase.

3. Ibid.

4. Jerusalem Bible translation.

5. Ibid.

6. See James Charlesworth, *Jesus and the Dead Sea Scrolls* (New York: Doubleday, 1992).

7. King James Version (Cambridge: Cambridge University Press, n.d.).

8. Acts 9:4, Revised Standard Version (New York: New American Library, 1974).

9. RSV translation.

10. Jerusalem Bible translation.

11. RSV translation.

12. For more information on Christian Gnosticism, see Elaine Pagels, *The Gnostic Gospels* (New York: Random House, 1979) and *Adam, Eve, and the Serpent* (New York: Vintage, 1989).

13. Jerusalem Bible translation.

14. Earlier lists, such as the Muratorian Canon, differ from the present-day canonical list of New Testament books. The list, as we now have it, is mentioned in the *Festal Letter* of Athanasius of Alexandria, circulated in 367 C.E., and is the same list of books translated by Jerome into Latin. For further details, see Dennis Duling and Norman Perrin, *The New Testament* 3d ed. (New York: Harcourt Brace, 1994), p. 134.

15. Jerusalem Bible translation.

16. *The Confessions of St. Augustine,* trans. Rex Warner (New York: New American Library, 1963), 182–83.

17. Jerusalem Bible translation.

18. See David Knowles, *Christian Monasticism* (New York: McGraw-Hill, 1972), which emphasizes the development of Benedictine monasticism.

19. *St. Benedict's Rule for Monasteries* (Collegeville, MN: Liturgical Press, 1948), chap. 1, pp. 2–3.

20. See Christopher Brooke, *Monasteries of the World* (New York: Crescent, 1982), for excellent maps, diagrams, and photographs.

21. The author Nikos Kazantzakis lived for a time on Mount Athos and considered becoming a monk.

22. *The Disciplinary Decrees of the General Councils,* trans. H. J. Schroeder (St. Louis: B. Herder, 1937), p. 19; quoted in Colman Barry, ed., *Readings in*

Church History, vol. 1 (Westminster, MD: Newman Press, 1960), p. 85.

23. Nicholas Gage, *Eleni* (New York: Ballantine Books, 1983), pp. 122–23.

24. For the mysticism of Gregory of Nyssa, see *From Glory to Glory: Texts from Gregory of Nyssa's Mystical Writings* (New York: Scribners, 1961), particularly the introduction by Jean Daniélou. For Augustine's mysticism, see *The Essential Augustine* (New York: Mentor, 1964), pp. 127 and 148.

25. Origen, prologue to the "Commentary on the Song of Songs," in *Origen,* trans. Rowan Greer (New York: Paulist Press, 1979), p. 217.

26. From Sermon 6, in *Meister Eckhart,* trans. Raymond Blakney (New York: Harper, 1941), p. 131.

27. Julian of Norwich, *Revelations of Divine Love,* trans. Clifton Wolters (New York: Penguin, 1982), Chap. 59, p. 167.

28. Pamphlet, *Prayer of Saint Francis,* (Columbus, OH: Christopher House, 1996), p. 4, adapted.

29. Erik Erikson, *Young Man Luther: A Study in Psychoanalysis and History* (New York: Norton, 1962).

30. King James Version.

31. A similar development occurred in the Buddhist Pure Land movement. In Japan, Shinran concluded that only trust in Amida Buddha's grace was enough for the devotee.

32. The term *Mass* comes from the dismissal at the conclusion of this ceremony, when the priest said in Latin, *Ite missa est* ("Go, it is the dismissal").

33. Albert Schweitzer's classic study *J. S. Bach* (Neptune, NJ: Paganiniana, 1980) emphasizes the religious character of all of Bach's work.

Chapter 10

1. Also spelled *Mohammed,* although this spelling is now considered less accurate than *Muhammad.* We might also note that there is some disagreement about the details of Muhammad's life, particularly those regarding his early years.

2. John Esposito, *Islam: The Straight Path,* 3d ed. (New York: Oxford University Press, 1998), p. 3.

3. Also spelled *Kaaba, Ka'bah,* and *Kaba.*

4. For further details see Thomas Lippman, *Understanding Islam* (New York: New American Library, 1982), pp. 34–38.

5. Also commonly spelled *Khadija.*

6. It is possible that Khadijah was younger than this, given the fact that she gave birth to at least six children.

7. 96:1–19 passim; from *The Koran*, trans. N. J. Dawood (London: Penguin, 1993), p. 429. This translation is used unless otherwise noted.

8. Lippman, *Understanding Islam*, p. 44. Guides in Jerusalem sometimes point to marks in stone, which they say are footprints left by Muhammad. The account of Muhammad's journey may have influenced Dante's vision of paradise in the *Divine Comedy*.

9. 49:10.

10. In Islamic belief, punishment in hell is not necessarily eternal for all.

11. 2:163; from *Holy Qur'an*, trans. M. H. Shakir (Milton Keynes, England: Mihrab Publishers, 1986).

12. In Islam, a "messenger" is a prophet with a special call from God.

13. Some Shiite Muslims combine these into three periods of prayer.

14. Another translation is, "Allah is greater (than anything else)."

15. 2:144.

16. Although only Muslims may make the pilgrimage to Mecca, many films document the practice. See, for example, the classic film *Mecca: The Forbidden City* by Iranfilms.

17. 2:158 (Shakir translation).

18. Muslims were originally permitted to drink wine, but later revelations to Muhammad prohibited it. There is, however, some variation in the keeping of this regulation. Although some governments have tried to eliminate all alcohol, absolute prohibition is nearly impossible, because even countries with large Muslim majorities have minorities of Christians and Jews, who use wine in religious rites. Countries that have experienced strong European influence (such as several in North Africa—Morocco, Algeria, Tunisia) often produce wine, and countries that depend heavily on tourism usually allow the serving of alcohol in tourist hotels.

19. Female circumcision is sometimes said to be based on a hadith (a remembrance of Muhammad's early followers); see Annemarie Schimmel, *Islam: An Introduction* (Albany: State University of New York Press, 1992), p. 55.

20. An exception is made in some cases, such as the tombs of rulers and publicly recognized holy persons.

21. Although the first version did not contain vowels or diacritical marks, later versions do; consequently, some differences exist between versions.

22. 1:1–5.

23. Esposito, *Islam: The Straight Path*, p. 6.

24. There is some disagreement over this matter among Sunni and Shiite Muslims.

25. Also called the Battle of Poitiers.

26. 50:16. See also John Williams, ed., *Islam* (New York: Washington Square, 1963), pp. 122–58.

27. 3:29 (Shakir translation). See A. J. Arberry, *Sufism* (New York: Harper, 1970), pp. 17–22.

28. 2:115.

29. Arberry, *Sufism*, p. 28.

30. Ibid., p. 228.

31. Afkham Darbandi and Dick Davis, introduction to *The Conference of the Birds*, by Farid Ud-Din Attar (Hammondsworth, England: Penguin, 1984), p. 10.

32. Quoted in F. C. Happold, *Mysticism* (Baltimore: Penguin, 1963), p. 229.

33. Esposito, *Islam: The Straight Path*, pp. 105–106.

34. Idries Shah, *The Way of the Sufi* (New York: Dutton, 1970), p. 113 ff.

35. For representative samples of the writings of theologians, see the chapter "Kalam" in Williams, *Islam*, pp. 159–96.

36. Williams, *Islam*, pp. 138–41. Williams claims that al-Arabi influenced the Spanish mystics and poets John of the Cross and Ramón Lull and possibly Benedict de Spinoza, a Dutch philosopher.

37. Islamic influence on Christian architecture is demonstrated by the use of these alternating lines of color, such as in the cathedrals of Siena, Pisa, and Florence.

38. See 2:25, 3:136, and 10:9.

39. See 2:25.

40. 4:34.

Chapter 11

1. Robert Ellwood, *The History and Future of Faith* (New York: Crossroad, 1988), p. 137.

2. Ibid., p. 141.

3. "Which Humanism for the Third Millennium?" *Aizen* 16 (July–August 1997): 3.

4. Government in the United States, however, is not fully secular. We might note, for example, the use of prayer and chaplains in legislative houses, the mention of God in the Declaration of Independence,

the use of the word *God* in court and on currency, and tax benefits given to churches and church property. See Ronald Thiemann, *Religion in Public Life* (Washington: Georgetown University Press, 1996), in which the author argues against the complete separation of church and state.

5. *Honolulu Advertiser,* 26 July 1997, sec. B, p. 3, adapted.

6. For a good discussion of secularism in the modern world and its relation to religion, see Ellwood, *The History and Future of Faith,* chap. 5, pp. 96–117. Ellwood sees religions surviving in the future within a secular milieu but existing rather separately from it.

7. "Speech of the Very Rev. James Parks Morton at the Esperanto Conference, 1996, July 22, Prague," *Aizen* 16 (July–August 1997): 6.

8. See Maurice Tuchman, ed., *The Spiritual in Art: Abstract Painting 1890–1985.* (New York: Abbeville Press, 1986) for many examples.

9. Philippe Gross and S. I. Shapiro, "Characteristics of the Taoist Sage in the *Chuang-tzu* and the Creative Photographer," *Journal of Transpersonal Psychology* 28:2 (1996), p. 181.

10. *Modern Photography,* October, 1988, p. 94; quoted in ibid., p. 177.

Credits

Index

Aaron, priesthood of, 371
Abbasid dynasty, 424
Abel, 271
abhidhamma, 120
abhidharma, 120
aboriginal religions. *See* oral religions
aborigines, 27
Abraham, 266, 272, 410, 414, 415, 416, 419
Abu, Mount, 174
acceptance, Buddhism and, 111
accommodation
    Shinto with Buddhism and Confucian-
      ism, 239–241
    See also exclusiveness and inclusiveness
Acoma Pueblo, 35
Acre, 358
action, effortlessness in, 197–198
Acts, Book of, 328, 330, 332, 335–336
A.D., 321
Adam and Eve, 270–271, 337, 414
Adi Granth "original collection"; the pri-
    mary scripture of the Sikhs, 178,
    180–181
Adonai, 276
adultery, 40, 278
Advaita, 74
Advent, 377, 379
Afghanistan, 424, 435, 449, 451, 475
Africa
    ancestor spirits, 35, 37
    art, 29–30, 44
    child naming, 37
    Christianity in, 351–352, 370

circumcision in, 37, 418
death rituals, 39
deities, 32
divination, 43
female circumcision, 418
initiation rites, 37–38
Islam and, 418, 422–423, 450
Judaism in, 306–307
magic, 42–43
marriage, 38
North, 345, 422–423
origin stories, 35
religions of population, 50
sacrifice, 40
taboos, 40
African Americans, 389, 450
afterlife
    Chinese traditional beliefs and, 189, 220
    Christianity and, 341, 363
    Islam and, 410, 441
    Japanese view of, 239, 258
    Judaism and, 297, 310
    Zoroastrianism and, 282
    See also reincarnation
aging
    Confucianism and, 209–210, 213
    Hindu life stages, 72–73
    religion and, 5
Agni, 60, 78
agnosticism literally meaning "not
    know"; the position that holds that
    the existence of God cannot be
    proven, 8, 470

Agnus Dei, 388
A.H., 407
ahimsa "nonharm," "nonviolence," 75,
    113–114, 115, 117, 148, 154, 156
Ahura Mazda, 282
AIDS, 485–486
Ainu, 27
A'isha, 449
ajiva matter without soul or life, 167
Ala, 32
Alaska, 50
alb, 344
alchemy, Taoist, 198–199, 200
alcohol, prohibition on, 417, 426, 448
    See also wine
Alexander the Great, 283
Alexandria, 342
Algeria, 435, 450, 451, 475
Ali, 422, 425
Allah, 405, 408, 410–411, 436–438, 439, 441
    ninety-nine names of, 408, 430–431
    of pre-Islamic religion, 403–404
    rule of, 435–436
    Sufism and, 427–429, 430–431, 433
    as term, 408
Alpert, Richard. *See* Ram Dass
Alpha and Omega, 376
altars
    of the Aryans, 61
    Eastern Orthodox, 386
    flower arrangement and, 144
    Hindu, 77
    Jainist, 172

altars (*continued*)
    in Native American Church, 42
    Shinto, 251
    to High God, 35
altered consciousness
    Hindu methods, 60, 63, 89
    psychedelic substances, 42, 60, 431
    Sufis and, 429, 431
    trance, 42–43
    See also contemplative practices; self,
        lessening sense of
Amanita muscaria, 42
Amar Das, 178
Amaterasu "shining in heaven"; goddess
    of the sun, 15, 238, 242, 256
Ambrose, 345
American Muslim Mission, 450
Amish, 366
Amitabha Buddha the Buddha of the
    Western Paradise, a bliss-body Bud-
    dha in Mahayana, 127, 137
Anabaptists, 366
Analects the book of the sayings of Con-
    fucius, 212, 217
ananda, 66
anatta "no self"; the doctrine that there is
    no soul or permanent essence in peo-
    ple and things, 109
ancestor worship
    Chinese traditional beliefs, 189
    oral religions and, 35, 37, 39
    origins of religion and, 4
    Shinto and, 236, 245
Andrew, Saint, 376
androgyny
    Guanyin and, 128
    High Gods and, 35
    Hinduism and, 84
Angad, 178
Angas, 173–174
angels and devils, 341
anger, Buddhism and, 112
Angkor Wat, 94
Anglican Church (Church of England), 50,
    365–366, 367, 370, 375, 378, 379, 389,
    395, 462
Anguttara Nikaya, 120
anichcha impermanence, constant change,
    108
Animal Liberation, 480
animals
    Buddhism and, 114, 120
    contemporary worldview of, 33
    habit destruction, 472
    Hinduism and, 79, 83, 85–86
    Jainism and, 166, 168–169
    Judaism and, 271
    Naturism and, 477, 479, 480
    oral religions and, 32–33, 477
    pop culture and, 483
    rights groups, 479, 480

sacrifice of, 40, 61, 113, 146, 277, 279,
        416, 417
    sanctuaries for, 480
    sexuality research and, 465
    Shinto and, 245
    as totems. *See* totems
    zoos, 479
    Zoroastrianism and, 282
    See also nature
animated films, 483, 485
animism from the Latin *anima*, meaning
    "spirit," "soul," "life force"; a world-
    view common among oral religions
    that sees all elements of nature as be-
    ing filled with spirit or spirits, 5,
    31–32, 189
Aniruddha (king of Myanmar), 120
Anne, Saint, 362
annulment of marriage, 365, 418, 474
anointing of the sick, 375
anointment, 339
anthropology
    oral religions as recovered by, 29, 31
    sexuality attitudes and, 465
    studies of religion and, 17
Antioch, 342
Antiochus IV, 283, 300
Antony of Egypt, 347
Apache, 38, 39
apartheid, 93
Aphrodite, 15
apocalypticism the belief that the world
    will soon come to an end; this belief
    usually includes the notion of a great
    battle, final judgment, and reward of
    the good, 328
    Christianity and, 326, 327–328, 341–342,
        372
    Judaism and, 281, 286, 321–323
    Zoroastrianism and, 282
apostle one of Jesus' twelve disciples;
    also, any early preacher of Christian-
    ity, 328
arabesque, 421
al-Arabi, 437, 438
Arabian Peninsula
    religions of, 403, 404, 413–414
    warfare on, 404, 414
Arafat, plain of, 416
Aramaic, 281
Aranyakas, 62
Arberry, A. J., 428
archeology
    biblical figures and, 269
    studies of religion and, 17–18
architecture
    Buddhist, 121, 123
    Chinese, 203
    Christian, 332–333, 344, 353, 371, 379,
        380–384, 395
    Confucian, 226–228

    Islamic, 401–402, 438–440
    Jainist, 172, 174
    Japanese, 247
    Orthodox Christian, 353, 355
    as pattern element, 17
    Shinto, 254–255, 260
    tropical Gothic, 49
arhat in Theravada, a person who has
    practiced monastic disciplines and
    reached nirvana, the ideal, 118
Aristotle, 436, 437
Arjan, 178–179
Arjuna, 70, 75
art
    Buddhist, 121–123, 125, 128–129, 132,
        137, 142–146, 151–152, 154–156,
        158–159
    Buddhist influence on, 142–146, 155–156
    of China, 144, 146, 201–203, 223–225
    Christianity and. *See under* Christianity
    Confucianism and, 208, 213–214, 223–228
    eclectic spirituality and, 480–488
    film, 313, 451, 478–479, 480–481, 483
    Hindu, 79, 80, 88–90
    Islam and, 352, 401–402, 407, 420–421,
        424, 438–445, 452
    Jainist, 174
    of Japan, 142–146, 155, 254–256
    Judaism and, 278, 293, 311–314, 315
    Naturism and, 477–479, 480
    Omoto and, 258
    of oral religions, 28–30, 43–47
    origins of religion and, 2–3, 5
    permanence vs. impermanence of,
        28–29
    Shinto and, 254–256, 258
    studies of religion and, 17, 20
    Taoism and, 201–203
    See also music
artha, 73
Aryans, 15, 60–61
    Nazi ideas of, 293
Ascension, 378
asceticism
    Buddhism and, 104–105, 137, 148, 171
    Hinduism and, 62, 64
    Jainism and, 165, 166, 170, 171
    Judaism and, 284
    Shinto and, 250–251
Ashanti, 32
al-Ashari, 437
Asherah, 15
ashes, 10, 375, 378
Ashkenazim Jews who lived in or came
    from central Europe, 291, 306, 313
Ashoka, 115, 117
ashram a spiritual community, 73, 84
Ash Wednesday, 378
Asia
    eclectic music of, 487–488
    See also specific countries and religions

Assyria, 280

Astarte, 15

Atatürk, Kemal, 447

Atharva Veda, 62

atheism literally meaning "not God"; the position that holds that there is no God or gods, 8

    Buddhism and, 115

    Communism and, 470–471

    of Jainism, 164, 167

Athos, Mount, 351, 353–355

Atman the spiritual essence of all individual human beings, 66

    Buddhist rejection of, 109

atonement

    in Christianity, 331, 352–353

    in Judaism, 299–300

    for taboo, breaking, 40

Audubon Society, 479

Augustine, 345–346, 356

Augustine (Benedictine monk), 347

Aurangzeb, 180

Aurobindo, Sri, 87–88

austerity. *See* asceticism

Australia, 370

authority, 360

    Eastern Orthodox Church and, 350, 360

    Islam and, 424, 434–436

    Protestantism and, 363, 364–365

    Roman Catholic Church and, 343–344, 350, 356, 360–362, 363, 365, 368, 369, 392, 474

    See also government and politics; persecution

Avalokiteshvara, 128, 149

avatar an earthly embodiment of a deity, 79

Ave Maria, 379

Averroës, 437

Avesta, 282

Avicenna, 437

Awakened One. *See* Buddha (Siddhartha Gautama)

Axis Age, 62

Ayers Rock, 34

Azerbaijan, 424

Aztecs, 40

Baba, Sai, 96

Babel, tower of, 271, 328

Babylonia, 266, 270, 271, 277, 280–281, 288, 299, 300

Babylonian Talmud, 287–288

Bach, Johann Sebastian, 364, 388–389

Badr, 407

Baghdad, 424

Bahadur, Tegh, 180

Bakr, Abu, 405, 420, 422

Bakuta, 35

Balfour Declaration, 294

Bali, 94, 113

Baltic region

    Christianity and, 364

    Judaism and, 292, 293

Bangkok, Thailand, 101–102

Bangladesh, 424, 448, 449

baptism the Christian rite of initiation, involving immersion in water or sprinkling with water, 327–328, 330, 331, 345, 366, 371, 373–374, 375

Baptist Church, 366, 389

BaPunu, 44

bar (bat) mitzvah "son (daughter) of the commandment"; the coming-of-age ceremony that marks the time when a young person is considered a legal adult within the Jewish community, 305, 308, 310, 315

Bardot, Brigitte, 480

Bar Kokhba, 287

baroque style, 383, 386–387

Bartók, Béla, 29

Basham, Arthur, 59

Basho, 142

basic religions. *See* oral religions

Basil, 350

basilicas, 380–381

basketry, 45

Basu, Sobharani, 87

B.C., 321

B.C.E., 2, 321

beading, 45

Beatles, 96, 460

"Bedtime Story," 460

Beethoven, Ludwig von, 388

Beijing, China, 158–159

belief system. *See* worldview

bell, 150

Bellow, Saul, 312

Benedictine order, 347, 387

Benedict of Nursia, 347

Berbers, 432

Bernini, Giovanni, 320

Bernstein, Leonard, 312

Bhagavad Gita a religious literary work about Krishna, 68–76, 95, 96

bhakti devotion to a deity or guru

bhakti yoga the spiritual discipline of devotion to a deity or guru, 74–75, 77, 89

Bible

    Christian. *See* Bible, Christian

    Hebrew. *See* Hebrew Bible

    Qur'an as discussing, 420

    as term, 267

    on women, 15

Bible, Christian the scriptures sacred to Christians, consisting of the books of the Hebrew Bible and the New Testament, 337, 341

    interpretation of, 337, 363, 364, 366, 368, 369, 372, 392

    Mormons and, 371

    New Testament. *See* New Testament

    Old Testament, 269, 337, 341

    printing and translations of, 360, 361, 362, 363

    scholarship on, 391

biblical Judaism Judaism before the destruction of the Second Temple (70 C.E.), 266

Bierstadt, Albert, 477

Billy Sunday, 395

biology, 465

biophilia, 29

birth. *See* childbirth; reincarnation

bishop "overseer" (Greek); a priest and church leader who is in charge of a large geographical area called a diocese, 342–343, 350, 352

Black Death, 291, 360

Black Elk, 32, 34

Black Heads, 201

Black Muslims, 450

Black Stone, 404, 413–414

    See also Kabah

bliss-body Buddhas, 127

Bloch, Ernest, 312

blood

    taboos and, 39

    See also meat eating

blood transfusions, 373

Blue (O'Keeffe), 483

Boas, Franz, 29

bodhi enlightenment, 105

Bodhidharma, 138–139

bodhisattva "enlightened being"; in Mahayana, a person of deep compassion, especially one who does not enter nirvana but is constantly reborn to help others; a heavenly being of compassion, 125, 128–129, 151

Bodhi Tree, 105

body

    Buddhism and, 123, 147–148

    Christianity and, 341–342, 345–346

    Jainism and, 167–168

    Shinto and, 246

    Sikhism and, 177

    See also asceticism; nature; sexuality; soul

Boleyn, Anne, 365

Boniface, 347

Book of Changes, 215–216

Book of Common Prayer, The, 365

Book of History, The, 215

Book of Mormon, 371

Book of Poetry, 215, 218

Book of Rites, The, 217

Bora, Katharina von, 363

Boy George, 459

boys

    circumcision of. *See* circumcision

    initiation rituals for, 37–38

Brahma god of creation, 79
Brahman the spiritual essence of the universe, 64, 65–66, 74
    Buddhism and, 115
Brahmanas, 62
brahmin member of the priestly caste, 71
Brahmo Samaj, 90
Brazil, 50, 472
breath
    Buddhist meditation and, 140
    control of, Hinduism and, 75, 76
    Taoist internal alchemy technique, 199
Brief History of Time, A (Hawking), 482
Brihadaranyaka Upanishad, 68
Britain. *See* Great Britain
Britrail Pass, 19
Buber, Martin, 311–312
bubonic plague, 291, 360
Buddha (Siddhartha Gautama)
    as ideal, 107, 125–128, 130, 221
    life of, 79, 102–107, 115, 126, 138
Buddhism
    atheism and, 115
    in Bali, 94
    basic teachings of, 107–113
    Buddha. *See* Buddha (Siddhartha Gautama)
    Christianity and, 347, 357
    compassion and, 123, 124–125, 128, 134, 150, 156
    Confucianism and, 131, 132, 139, 221
    festivals of, 147
    Hindu influence on, 94, 113–115, 118, 123, 125, 126, 135, 148
    Jainism compared to, 164, 165, 171, 174
    Mahayana. *See* Mahayana Buddhism
    multiculturalism and, 459
    nonattachment, 111, 118, 125, 147–148
    nonviolence (ahimsa) and, 70, 113–114, 115, 117, 148, 154, 156
    persecution of, 132, 155, 156, 243, 255
    and Shinto, 147, 236, 239–240, 242, 243, 245, 253–254, 255
    spread of, 115–118, 459
    Taoism and, 132, 139, 140, 199–200, 201
    Theravada, 118–123, 126, 147, 154–155
    Vajrayana, 136, 146–154
    as Western influence, 154–156
    women and, 16, 105, 113, 156, 463
Bukari, 434
Bulgaria, 349, 350, 351
Burma. *See* Myanmar
Burning Lights (Chagall and Chagall), 293
bushido "warrior knight way"; military devotion to a ruler, demanding loyalty, duty, and self-sacrifice; an ideal promoted by State Shinto, 243
business, Confucianism and, 210, 211, 230
Butchart Gardens, 158
Byrd, William, 388

Byzantine Empire, 350, 422, 424, 427, 446
    See also Eastern Orthodox Church
Byzantine style, 385–386
Byzantium, 350

Cain, 271
Cairo, 452
calendars
    Christian, 376
    Jewish, 284, 299
    Muslim, 407, 413
caliph "successor" (Arabic: khalifa); a religious and political leader, 422, 425–426
calligraphy, 146, 223–225
calumet a long-stemmed sacred pipe used primarily by many native peoples of North America; it is smoked as a token of peace, 42
Calvin, John, 364
Calvinism, 364–365
Cambodia, 94, 120
Campbell, Joseph, 9
Canaan an ancient name for the land of Israel, 272–273
    See also Israel
Canada, 50, 314–315, 449
    See also North America
candles, Christianity and, 344–345, 375
cannabis, 42
cannibalism, 40
canon "measure," "rule" (Greek); a list of authoritative books or documents, 227
capitalism and modern religion, 457–459
Capra, Frank, 481
Capra, Fritjof, 470, 482
Caribbean
    intermixed religions, 51
    magic and, 42
carpets, prayer, 441, 445
Carson, Rachel, 475, 480
cartoons, 313, 483, 485
Cassino, Monte, 347
caste one of the five major social classes sanctioned by Hinduism, 70–71, 91
    Sikhs as abolishing, 180
Cathedral of the Holy Savior, 353
cathedrals, 382–384
Cathedral of St. John the Divine, 383
Catherine of Aragon, 365
Catholic Cathedral of Saint Mary, 384
Catholic Church. *See* Roman Catholic Church
Catholic (Counter) Reformation, 367–368, 383
C.E., 2, 321
celibacy
    Buddhism and, 131, 132, 133, 148
    Christianity and, 326–327, 345–347, 362, 365, 366

    Hare Krishna movement and, 96
    Hinduism and, 72, 73
    Islam and, 416
    Jainism and, 170
    See also marriage; sexuality
Central America, 51
ceramics, Japanese, 144, 254
ceremony. *See* ritual
chado, 142–144
Chagall, Bella, 293
Chagall, Marc, 293, 313
chakras, 76
Chan, Wing-Tsit, 205
Chan Buddhism, 138–139, 140
Chandogya Upanishad, 64, 65
change
    Buddhist acceptance of constant, 108–109, 129–130
    Jainist view of, 167
    Judaism and, 309–310
    Taoist view of, 195, 196
    See also exclusiveness and inclusiveness
Chango. *See* Shango
chant
    Aryan, 61
    Buddhist, 135, 137, 138, 151, 482
    Christian, 387, 482
    Muslim, 422
    of oral religions, 29, 44
    See also music
charity. *See* good deeds; poverty; social responsibility
chastity
    Jainism and, 170
    See also celibacy
chasuble, 344
Chaucer, 477
Ch'en, Kenneth, 130
Chicago, 450
Chichester Psalms (Bernstein), 312
childbirth
    baptism of, 366, 374
    desire for, 80, 83, 305
    rituals of, 37, 305
    safety in, women's rights and, 462
    taboos and, 37, 39
    virginal, 192, 323, 327
    See also death
children
    Confucianism and, 209, 210, 213
    Shinto and, 249
    Taoism and, 195
China
    art of, 144, 146, 201–203, 223–225
    beliefs of, traditional, 189–191
    Buddhism, 123, 126, 130–132, 135–137, 138–139, 147, 158–159, 199–200, 201, 221
    calligraphy, 146
    Christianity and, 370

Communism of. *See* Communism
Confucianism. *See* Confucianism
gardens of, 144, 203, 205–231
Islam in, 424
Japan and, 133, 135, 238–241, 249, 255
Judaism in, 307
language of, transcription systems for, 188
secularism and, 471
Taoism. *See* Taoism
Tibet and, 156
travel to, 158–159
See also Taiwan
Chinul, 133
chi-rho, 376
ch'i. *See* qi
chit, 66
Chogye Buddhist order, 133
Christianity
the arts and, 332–334, 342, 344, 376, 380–389, 395, 441
architecture, 332–333, 344, 353, 371, 379, 380–384, 395
Eastern Orthodox Church, 352, 353, 385–386
God, representation of, 339
Jesus, images of, 323
Mormon, 371–372
painting, 385–387
Protestant, 364–366, 367, 383, 387, 388–389
sculpture, 320, 357, 376, 379, 386–387
Augustinian, 345–346
baptism and, 327–328, 330, 331, 345, 366, 371, 373–374, 375
beliefs and history
Catholic Reformation (Counter Reformation), 367–368, 369
early, 328–337
influences on, 345–347
in Middle Ages, 290–291, 355–360
modern developments and influences, 391–395
nontraditional, 370–373
Protestant Reformation, 360–367
science and, 389–391, 473, 475
spread of, 342–345, 347, 355, 368–370
bubonic plague and, 291, 360
Buddhism and, 347, 357
Crusades, 357–358, 359
dating system of, 321
deeds, 362, 363, 364, 369, 392
dominance of, 290–291, 356
Eastern Orthodox. *See* Eastern Orthodox Church
ecumenism, 391–392, 459–460, 462
environmentalism and, 395
founder of. *See* Jesus Christ

fundamentalism, 474–475
Gandhi as influenced by, 92–93
Goddess worship and, 15
heretics and, 351–352, 359, 362, 363
Hinduism and, 357
Islam and, 288, 357–359
Judaism and, 290–291, 305, 306, 330–331, 332, 333, 334, 335, 337, 373, 376–377, 387
in Korea, 156
as missionary religion, 50, 90, 330, 331, 342, 347, 368–370
multiculturalism and, 459
mysticism of, 352, 353, 356–357, 395, 428
persecution by, 291, 351–352, 359, 360, 362, 363, 364, 365
persecution of, 332, 344, 347, 371
philosophy and, 357
practice of, 373–380
pre-Christian influence on, 46
Protestant. *See* Protestantism
religious orders, 358–359
Roman Catholic. *See* Roman Catholic Church
study of, 396–397
Sufism and, 336, 341
Two Great Commandments of, 327–328
women and, 347, 357, 359, 366, 366–367, 392, 395, 462, 464
worldview, 338–342
Zoroastrianism and, 282
See also specific people and churches
Christian Science, 372, 462, 464
Christmas, 46, 376, 377, 379
Christ, as term, 339
See also Jesus Christ
Chuang Tzu. *See* Zhuangzi
Chunda, 107
Church of England (Anglican Church), 50, 365–366, 367, 370, 375, 378, 379, 395, 462
Church of Jesus Christ of Latter-day Saints, 371–372
cincture, 344
circle, 5, 8, 32, 146
circumcision
Christianity and, 330, 331, 417–418
Islam and, 417–418
Judaism and, 272, 283, 305
rites of passage and, 37, 418
cities, 472
City of God, The (Augustine), 346
civil service, 215, 221
Clair de Lune (Debussy), 487
Clarke, Arthur C., 488
class
caste system as system of, 70–71
See also economics

clergy
Christian, 343–345, 360, 462
Jewish, 266, 268, 281, 286, 308, 310, 462–463
Shinto, 248, 249–250
Taoist, 201
See also authority; monastic life; priests; religious orders
clock, development of, 347
clothing
Buddhism and, 118, 148
Christianity and, 344, 379
Islam and, 414, 434, 439, 448
Jainism and, 166, 171
Judaism and, 308–309, 310
Shinto and, 249–250, 254, 256
Sikhism and, 177, 178, 179
Turkish modernization and, 447
See also hair
coca, 42
Coca-Colonization, 446
Collins, Phil, 460
colonialism, 358, 370, 446, 450
colors, use of, 47, 379, 440
Columbus, 446
comic strips, 483
Coming of Age in Samoa (Mead), 20
coming-of-age rituals, 37–38, 305, 308, 310
Communism
Christianity and, 353
Confucianism and, 226, 228, 229, 230
fall of Soviet, 353, 457
free enterprise within, 457
as religion, 470–471
secularism of, 471
Taoism and, 200–201, 204
community, as key characteristic of religion, 7
comparative religion, 18
compassion
Buddhism and, 123, 124–125, 128, 134, 150, 156
Christianity and, 325
Confucianism and, 212
Hinduism and, 68, 79
Jainism and, 168
Judaism and, 298, 299, 303
popular culture and, 483
concentration camps, 293–294, 315
Confessions (Augustine), 346
confirmation, 375
Confucian Imperial Academy, 226, 227
modern world and, 228–230
Confucianism, 206–231
Buddhism and, 131, 132, 139, 221
Christianity and, 373
development of, 218–223
Five Great Relationships, 209–212
government and, 211, 215, 220–221, 228–230

Confucianism (*continued*)
ideals and beliefs of, 208–215
Neo-Confucianism, 221–223
as philosophy, 208, 218–223
philosophy and, 211, 215, 220–221,
228–230
as religion, 208, 221–223
Shinto and, 254–256, 258
Tao in, 206
Taoism and, 191, 201, 206, 219, 221
texts of, 206, 212, 215–218
virtues of, 206, 212–215, 218–221, 223,
229–230, 240–241
women and, 16, 229, 230
Confucian Temple, 226–227
Confucius, 206–209, 215, 219, 221
Conservativeism a branch of Judaism that
attempts to blend the best of the old
and new Judaism, 292, 309
Constantine, 349, 350, 357
Constantinople, 349, 350, 361, 422, 424
Constitution, U.S., 469–470
contemplative practices, 486–488
contraception, 462, 464, 465
conversion
Judaism and, 314
multiculturalism and, 459
Convocation for Peace, 460, 462
Cook, James, 33
Copernicus, 467
Coptic Christian Church, 351–352
Córdoba, 288, 423, 524
Corigliano, John, 485–486
corporations, multinational, 457
Council of Chalcedon, 350, 351
Council of Constance, 362
Council of Nicaea, 344, 350
Council of Trent, 367
Counter Reformation, 367–368, 383
covenant a contract; the contract between
the Hebrews and their God, Yahweh,
272, 277, 302, 305
cows, 85–86
Creation Spirituality, 395
creation stories. *See* origin stories
Creator God
Buddhism and, 115
Islam and, 408
Jainism and, 167
Judaism and, 270–271
See also God; High God
Credo, 388
cross
in architecture, 381
Jungian interpretation of, 5
sign of, 11, 375
as symbol, 376
crucifix, 376
crucifixion, 323
Crusades, 357–358, 359
Crystal Cathedral, 383

Cultural Revolution, 156, 226, 228, 229
culture
Europe American, spread of, 446,
451–452
multiculturalism, 459
pop, religion and, 459, 460, 483
pre-Islamic, 448
religious influence on, 18–20, 29, 46, 51,
154–156, 459
spirituality and, 480–482
taboo determined by, 40
See also art; government and politics
cummings, e. e., 155
Cyril, 350–351
Cyrillic alphabet, 350–351
Cyrus, 281

Dallas, 457
Damascus, 422, 423, 427
dance
Buddhism and, 151
Hindu, 90
oral religions and, 43, 44
Shakers and, 367
Shinto, 256
Sufi, 429, 431
See also movement and exercise
Daniel, Book of, 281
Daphnis and Cloe (Ravel), 487
darkness, Taoism and, 195
darshan, 85
darwish, 429
datura, 42
David (king of Canaan), 279
Davies, Paul, 470
Day of Doom, 410
day of rest, 278, 299, 411–412
Day of Sacrifice, 416, 417
Days of Awe, 300
d'Arezzo, Guido, 387
Dead Sea Scrolls, 284–286, 335
death
acceptance of, 3
bubonic plague and, 291, 360
Buddhism and, 104, 107, 114–115, 131,
137, 150–151
Christianity and, 388
Crusades and, 358
Hinduism and, 56–57, 67, 80, 90–91
Islam and, 418–419
Judaism and, 297
oral societies and, 38–39
origin of religion and, 3
preparation for and origin of religion, 5
psychological, shamans and, 41
Shinto and, 239, 246, 250, 252
suicide. *See* suicide
symbolic, as rite of passage, 37
taboo and, 39

Taoism and, 196
See also childbirth; immortality;
longevity
Debussy, Claude, 486–487
Delhi, 424
Delius, Frederick, 487
Dengyo Daishi, 137
Denmark, 466
Derain, André, 30
Desert Fathers, 347
desire
Buddhism and, 110–111
Taoism and, 194
destruction, 80
detachment. *See* nonattachment
Detroit, 450
Deuteronomy, 277
Devi "goddess"; the Divine Feminine,
also called the Great Mother, 83–84
Dewey, John, 229
Dhammapada, 120
Dharamsala, India, 152–153
Dharma the totality of Buddhist teaching,
107, 459
dharma, 73
Dharmakaya, 125–126
Dhikr a devotional remembrance of Allah
through the recitation of his ninety-
nine names and other devotional
practices, 431
dhoti, 177
dhyana "meditation"; focusing of the
mind; sometimes, stages of trance,
75, 113
diaspora the dispersion of Jews beyond Israel, particularly to Persia, Egypt,
and the Mediterranean region, 287
Digambara "Clothed in sky"; a member
of the Jain sect in which monks do
not wear clothing, 171, 172, 174
Digha Nikaya, 120
Dinosaurs, 313
Disney productions, 483
Divali, 86
divination a foretelling of the future or a
discovery of the unknown by magi-
cal means, 43
Confucian, 215, 217
traditional Chinese, 191
Divine Feminine. *See* Goddess worship
Divine Names, The (Pseudo-Dionysius), 428
divorce, 38, 326, 418, 448, 449, 465, 474
Doctrine of the Mean, 206
Doctrine of the Mean, The, 218
Dominicans, 357, 359
dream quest, 38
dreams
ancient analysis of, 312
religion as source of, 9
subconscious as source of, 8
Druzes, 426

dualism the belief that reality is made of two different principles (spirit and matter); the belief in two gods (good and evil) in conflict, 2–3
  Jainism and, 167–168
  Zoroastrianism and, 282
Dubos, René, 475
dukkha sorrow, misery, 109–110
Durand, Asher, 477
Durga "awe-inspiring," "distant,"; a goddess, a form of Devi, 15, 83, 86
Durga Puja, 86
Duruflé, Maurice, 388
Dyaüs Pitr, 60, 78

Earth Day, 455–456, 478, 479
earth. *See* nature; world
Easter, 46, 355, 376–378, 379
Easter Island, 33
Eastern Orthodox Church, 349–355
  art and, 352, 353, 385–386
  Crusades and, 358
  as decentralized, 350, 360
  ecumenism and, 391–392
  festivals of, 376–379
  Mary, devotion to, 15, 379
  missionaries of, 370
  music in, 387
  papal authority and, 343–344, 350
  sacraments and rituals of, 374–379, 386
  science and, 391
  See also Christianity
Ecclesiastes, 281
Eckhart, Meister, 357
eclecticism. *See* exclusiveness and inclusiveness
eclectic spirituality, 480–488
ecology. *See* environment
economics
  Buddhist persecution and, 132
  Confucianism and, 230
  future of religion and, 457–459, 459
  Hinduism and, 73
  Jewish persecution and, 291, 293
  Protestant Reformation and, 361, 363
  women's equality and, 462
  See also poverty; social responsibility
ecotourism, 479, 480
Ecumenical Institute at St. John's Abbey, 462
ecumenism dialogue between Christian denominations, 391–392, 459–460, 462
Eddy, Mary Baker, 372, 464
education
  Confucianism and, 206, 208–209, 211, 213–214, 215, 218–221, 228–229, 230
  in India, 92
  Judaism and, 307

Muslim, 427, 445, 448, 449
  Roman Catholicism and, 368–369
  Taoism and, 198, 206, 219
  of women, 92
effortlessness, 197–198
egotism, liberation from, 67–68, 168
  See also self, lessening of
Egypt
  Christianity and, 351–352, 448
  government of, 448
  Islam and, 422–423, 424, 427, 428, 435, 452, 475
  Judaism and, 273–276, 281, 283, 287
Ehrlich, Paul, 29
Einstein, Albert, 293
Elderhostel, 19
Eleni (Gage), 353
Elijah, 302
Elizabeth I, 365
Ellwood, Robert, 457–458
ema, 250
Emerson, Ralph Waldo, 95
emotions
  Buddhism and, 111, 112, 113
  Christianity and, 326, 367, 394
  Islam and, 414
  Judaism and, 299
  key, as characteristic of religions, 7
endangered species, 472, 479
"end times." *See* apocalypticism
energy consumption, 472, 479
England. *See* Great Britain
enlightenment, Buddhism and, 105, 123, 125, 130, 134–135, 137, 139–140, 147–148, 151,
Enlightenment, European, 266, 309–310
Enneads, The (Plotinus), 428
enso, 146
environment
  Buddhism and, 156
  challenge of, for religion, 472
  Christianity and, 395
  oral religions and, 29, 32–33, 50
  world conference on, in Moscow, 460
  See also body; nature; world
Episcopal Church, 370, 379, 462
  See also Anglican Church
episcopal structure, 365
Epistles, 330, 331, 332, 333, 336, 345, 356, 362
eremitical way of life, 199
Erikson, Erik, 362
esoteric, 146
Esperanto, 258
Essenes a semimonastic Jewish community that flourished from c. 150 B.C.E. to 68 C.E., 282, 284, 286, 305, 327, 346, 373
Esther, 300
E.T., 481
ethics. *See* moral codes and ethics

Ethiopa, 306–307, 351–352, 405
ethnomusicology, 29
Eucharist "good gift" (Greek); the Lord's Supper, 369, 374–375
Eurailpass, 19
Europe
  Aryan ancestors of, 60
  Christianity and. *See* specific countries
  Crusades and, 358
  Goddess worship and, 15
  Hinduism as influenced by, 90–91
  Judaism and, 288, 290–294, 295, 306, 309, 315
  Middle Ages and. *See* Middle Ages
  nature and, 477
  Zen Buddhism centers in, 156
evangelical emphasizing the authority of scripture; an adjective used to identify certain Protestant groups, 392, 394–395
evangelist "good news person" (Greek); one of the four authors of the Gospels—Matthew, Mark, Luke, and John, 332
Eve, Adam and, 270–271, 337, 414
evil. *See* good vs. evil
evolution
  of religion, movement away from idea of, 5
  theory of, Christianity and, 391, 473
exclusiveness and inclusiveness
  Buddhism and, 125, 134–135, 239
  Chinese thought and, 201
  Hinduism and, 86–87, 460
  Islam and, 435–436
  multiculturalism and, 459
  patterns of, 14
  Shinto and, 259
  See also interfaith dialogue
exercise. *See* movement and exercise
Exiguus, Dionysius, 321
exile, of Jews, 280–281, 291, 299
Exodus, 274, 276–277, 337
exorcism, 201, 249
extreme unction, 375

faith, 363, 369
Falashas, 306–307
falsehoods. *See* honesty
family
  Buddhism and, 131, 132
  Chinese architecture and, 203
  Christianity and, 326–327, 347
  Confucianism and, 209–212, 213
  Islam and, 448–449
  study of religions and, 20
  See also marriage
fana "extinction"; the sense of loss of self in mystical experience
Fantasia on Greensleeves (Vaughan Williams), 487

Fantasia on a Theme of Thomas Tallis
(Vaughan Williams), 389, 487
faqir, 429
Farrakhan, Louis, 450
fasting
Christianity and, 377–378
death rituals and, 39
Islam and, 413
Jainists and, 170, 172–173
Judaism and, 299–300, 302
as religious practice, common, 413
suicide by, 170
vision quest and, 38
Father, God as, 339
father-son relationship, 209–210
Fauré, Gabriel, 388
Feast of Lights, 300
Feast of Weeks, 302
feathers and featherwork, 45–46
female circumcision, 418
females
as divine. *See* Goddess worship
patterns of religions regarding. *See* gender; women
feminism. *See* women's rights movements
Ferdinand (king of Spain), 359
Ferlinghetti, Lawrence, 155
fertility, Hinduism and, 80, 83, 86
See also childbirth
fertility treatments, 464–465
Fès, 432–434
festivals and holy days
Buddhist, 147
Christian, 46, 355, 376–379
Confucian, 231
Hindu, 86
Jainist, 172
Jewish, 45, 276, 283, 299–302
Muslim, 413, 416, 417
of nature, 455–456, 478, 479
Shinto, 250–251, 256
Taoist, 201
See also pilgrimage; ritual
fez, 447
filial piety, 213
filioque "and from the Son"; a Latin word
added to the creeds in the Western
Church to state that the Holy Spirit
arises from both Father and Son. The
notion, which was not accepted by
Orthodox Christianity, caused a sep-
aration between the Western and
Eastern Churches, 352
film, 313, 451, 478–479, 480–481, 483
fire
Buddhism and, 123, 135
Christianity and, 328, 379
Hinduism and, 61
Jewish Sabbath and, 298
Shinto and, 238
Zoroastrianism and, 282

First Symphony (Corigliano), 485–486
First Temple (Judaism), 279–280
fish, 376
Five Classics the classical literature of the
time preceding Confucius, including
poetry, history, and divination, 215, 217
Five K's of the Sikhs, 178
Five Pillars of Islam, 410–416
flower arrangement, 144
food
Islamic restrictions, 417
Judaism and purity of, 277, 283,
302–303, 309, 417
longevity and, 199
Naturism and, 479
sacrifice of, 40
symbolic, 301–302
taboos, 40
vegetarianism. *See* vegetarianism
forgiveness, Christianity and, 325
Fossey, Dian, 480
Four Books the major Confucian books,
which include the sayings of Confu-
cius and Mencius, 215, 217–218, 222
Four Noble Truths, 110–112
Four Passing Sights, 103
Foursquare Gospel Church, 395, 462
Fox, George, 366
Fox, Matthew, 395
France
Christianity and, 364, 365, 369–370, 379,
388
Islam and, 450
Judaism and, 291, 292, 293, 306
Francis of Assisi, Saint, 356–357, 359
Franciscans, 357, 359, 369
Frank, Anne, 295–297, 315
Franklin, Aretha, 389
Frankl, Viktor, 294, 312, 481
Frazer, James, 4
Frederick III of Saxony, 363
freedom
Christianity and, 331
Hinduism and, 67–68
Jainism and, 166–168
See also enlightenment
Freia, 15
Freud, Sigmund, 4, 312
dream interpretation, 8
friendships, Confucian relationship hier-
archy and, 211
Fruit of Islam, 450
Fuji, Mount, 245, 251, 260
fundamentalism, 474–475

Gabriel (angel), 405, 414
gagaku the stately ceremonial music of
Shinto, 255–256
Gage, Nicholas, 353
Galileo, 467
Gama, Vasco da, 446

gambling, 417
Gandhi, Indira, 182
Gandhi, Mohandas, 70, 71, 92–94, 165
Ganesha, 83, 85, 86
Ganga, 84
Ganges River, 56–57, 58, 84
Garden of Eden, 270–271, 322
gardens
Chinese, 144, 203, 205, 231
Islamic, 441
Japanese, 144–145, 251
of Monet, 477
garlic, 199
Gauguin, Paul, 2–3, 30
Gautama, Siddhartha. *See* Buddha (Sid-
dhartha Gautama)
gay men, 465–466
Gelug-pa, 148
gematria, 290, 337
gender
Allah and, 408
Christianity and, 395, 464–467, 474
Confucianism and, 16, 229, 230
Hinduism and, 77, 83–84, 90–92
Islam and, 418, 448–449
Jainism and, 171
Judaism and, 264–265, 270–271, 278,
307, 308, 309, 310, 313, 462–464
patterns of views on, 14–16, 462–464
sexual expression and, 465
See also women
Genesis, Book of, 270–273, 337
Genesis (rock band), 460
genie, 403
gentleness, Taoism and, 198
genuflection, 375
Germany
Christianity and, 347, 357, 362–364,
388–389, 391
Judaism and, 291, 292, 293–294,
295–297, 306, 309
al-Ghazali, 429, 437–438
ghee, 61
ghettos, 291, 292, 309, 315
Ghost Dance, 46
Gibraltar, 423
Gilgamesh, 271
ginger, 199
Ginsberg, Allen, 155
ginseng, 199
girls
circumcision of, 418
initiation rituals for, 38
Gloria, 388
glossolalia, 367
glottal stop, 25
Gnosticism, 335, 428
Gobind, Har, 179
God
Buddhism and, 115, 148
Chinese traditional beliefs, 189

of Christianity, 327–328, 331, 339, 341, 352–353, 356–357, 362, 363, 364, 371
Creator. *See* Creator God
High God. *See* High God
as immanent, 8
of Islam. *See* Allah
of Judaism (Yahweh), 270–273, 274–276, 277, 289–290, 297, 309, 310–311
questioning existence of. *See* agnosticism; atheism; nontheism
Sikhism and, 176, 177, 180
as transcendent, 8, 276
Goddess worship, 15–16, 32, 464
Hinduism and, 15, 78, 83–84, 86–87
pre-Aryan, 78, 83
pre-Islam, 404
Shinto and, 237–239
Wicca, 15, 464, 479
See also individual goddesses
gods
Aryan, 60, 78
Hindu, 77–83, 86–87
Pre-Islam, 403–404
Shinto, 237, 242, 245–249, 254, 255, 256, 257
Taoist, 200, 201
See also specific gods
Gogh, Vincent van, 155, 485
Golden Bough, The (Frazer), 4
Golden Gate Park, 158
Golden Rule, 213
Golden Temple, 178, 180, 182, 184
Goma, 135
Goodall, Jane, 480
good deeds
Christianity and, 334, 362, 363, 364, 369, 392
Islam and, 412–413
Judaism and, 297, 311
good vs. evil
Christianity and, 335, 345, 364
human nature and, 218–220, 246–247, 364
Islam and, 410
Judaism and, 281, 284, 297
Zarathustra and, 282
Good Friday, 378, 379
Good Samaritan, 334
gopis, 80
gospel music, 389
gospels "good news" (Middle English); accounts of the life of Jesus, 323, 324–327, 333–335
Gothic style, 379, 381–383
government and politics
Buddhism and, 138, 156
capitalism and modern religion, 457–459
Christianity and, 344–345, 347, 350, 352, 353, 359, 365, 370, 392

Communism. *See* Communism
Confucianism and, 211, 215, 220–221, 228–230
democratic, secular model, 450–451, 457
Islam and, 426–427, 435–436, 447–449, 450–452
of Japan, Shinto and, 238, 241–245, 252
Jehovah's Witnesses and, 373
Jesus and, 323, 328
Judaism and, 279–280, 309
Mormons and, 372
nationalism, 241–245, 474–475
Naturism and, 479
secularism, 435, 446–447, 469–472, 475
theocracy, 435
world changes in, 457
See also authority; culture; persecution
Grace Cathedral, 383
Graham, Billy, 11
Gram, 370
Granada, 423, 424
Great Britain
Christianity and, 50, 365–366, 367, 370, 375, 378, 379, 389, 395, 462
India and, 90–91, 92, 93–94, 181
Islam and, 449
Judaism and, 291, 293, 294
Great Flood, 271
Great Going Forth, 103–104
Great Learning, The, 218
Great Mother, 15, 83–84
Great Ultimate, 222–223
Greece
Buddhist sculpture, as influence on, 121
Christianity and influence of, 329, 330, 333, 349
Islam and influence of, 424, 436
Judaism and influence of, 283–284
Greek, 329, 330, 333, 376
Greek cross, 381
Greek Orthodox Church, 353–355
See also Eastern Orthodox Church
Greenpeace, 479
Gregorian chant, 482
Gregorian musical notation, 387
Gregory I, 321
Gregory of Nyssa, 350, 356
Gregory XI, 362
group, vs. individualism, 111
Growing Up in New Guinea (Mead), 29
Guanyin a popular bodhisattva of compassion in Mahayana, 15, 128–129, 137
Guide for the Perplexed, The (Maimonides), 288
guilt
Jesus as sacrifice for, 331
Shinto as lacking, 246
gurdwara a Sikh temple, 180, 182
guru a spiritual teacher, such as Guru Nanak (the founder of Sikhism) and his nine successors, who are the

mouthpiece of God, the fundamental Guru, 177, 180
guru spiritual teacher, 75, 84–85, 148
Gypsies, 293, 294

hadith a "recollection" of an act or saying of Muhammad, 402, 434–435
Hafiz, 431
Hagar, 410, 415–416
haggadah, 287–288
Haida, 33, 44
haiden, 247
haiku, 142, 155
hair
Islam and, 416, 448
Judaism and, 308–309
Sikhism and, 178
See also clothing
hajj pilgrimage to Mecca, 413–416, 417
halakhah, 287
al-Hallaj, 428–429
Halloween, 46, 378
Haman, 300
Hammurabi, 277
Han dynasty, 219, 220–221
Hanukkah an early-winter festival recalling the rededication of the Second Temple, celebrated with the lighting of candles for eight days, 283, 300
Hanuman, 79, 85
happiness, vs. peace, 111
Harappa culture, 59–60, 77–78, 80
Hare Krishna movement, 96
Harkishan, 179
harm, avoiding. *See* nonviolence
harmonized singing, 387–388
Harney Peak, 34
Harrison, George, 96, 460
Hasan, 425
Hasidic Jews, 292, 308, 312
Hasmoneans, 283
hatha yoga the spiritual discipline of postures and bodily exercises, 76
Hawai`i, 25–27
ancestor worship, 37
childbirth, 39
dance, 44
music, 30
refuge, 47–50
revival of oral religion, 51
sacrifice, 40
Shinto in, 259, 260
taboos, 33, 39–40, 47
time, 33
Haydn, Joseph, 388
H. D., 155
healers
Christian Science and, 372
evangelism and, 395
oral religions and, 43
healing, Tenrikyo, 257–258

Heard, Gerald, 95
heaven. *See* afterlife
Hebrew Bible, 266–269
  history in, 269–282
  interpretation of, 287–290
  as term, 269
  Torah, 268–277, 281, 284, 300, 307
  See also Judaism
Hebrew language, 281, 295, 306
Hebrews, 266, 268
  See also Judaism
Hebrews, Book of, 336
Hegira. *See* Hijra
heiau, 47
hell, 341
Hellenism, 283–284
Hello, Dolly, 313
Henry VIII, 365
heretics, 351–352, 359, 362, 363
hermits
  Christian, 347
  Egyptian, 346–347
  Taoist, 199, 204
  See also asceticism
Herod the Great, 264
Herzl, Theodor, 294
hexagram, 191
hieratic style, 385–386
High Church, 366
High God
  disagreement about, 404
  as female, 35
  oral religions and, 35
  of Zoroastrianism, 282
  See also Creator God; God
High Holy Days, 300
Hijra "Flight"; Muhammad's escape from
  Mecca to Yathrib (Medina), 407
Hildegard of Bingen, 357, 464
Hill, Richard W., 45–46
Hilton, James, 481
Hinduism
  animals and, 79, 83, 85–86
  arts and, 79, 80, 88–90
  the Bhagavad Gita, 68–76, 95, 96
  Buddhism, as influence on, 94, 113–115,
    118, 123, 125, 126, 135, 148
  caste system, 70–71, 91, 180
  Christianity and, 357
  concepts of, 64–68
  devotional, 77–87
  festivals, 86
  fundamentalism, 475
  Gandhi and, 70, 71, 92–94, 165
  goddesses of, 15, 78, 83–84, 86–87
  gods of, 79–83, 84, 86–87
  gurus, 84–85, 87–88
  Islam and, 174, 176, 430
  Jainism and, 164, 165, 172
  life goals, 73
  life stages, 72–73

modern challenges to, 90–92
multiplicity and, 86–87, 88
nonviolence (ahimsa) and, 75, 92, 93–94,
  156
origins of, 57–64
practice of, 68–87
prayer in, 379
Sikhism and, 176, 177, 178, 180
Sufism and, 430
the Upanishads, 62–68, 95
Vedas, 61–62
as Western influence, 94–97
women and, 77, 84, 90–92
the yogas, 73–76
Hitler, Adolf, 293
Holi, 86
holidays. *See* festivals and holy days
holistic organic, integrated; indicating a
  complete system, greater than the
  sum of its parts; here, refers to a culture whose various elements (art,
  music, social behavior) may all have
  religious meaning, 30
Holland, 365
Holocaust the destruction of European Judaism by the Nazis; also known as
  Shoah (Hebrew: "extermination"),
  293–294, 295–297, 302, 306, 309, 312,
  315
Holst, Gustav, 95
holy days. *See* festivals and holy days
Holy Spirit, 339, 341, 363, 379
Holy Trinity. *See* Trinity
Holy Week, 378
home exchanges, 19
homosexuality, 465–466
homosexuals, 294
Honen, 137
honesty
  Buddhism, 113
  Jainism and, 169–170
  See also stealing
Hong Kong, 457
Honmichi, 258
Hopi, 35
horses
  Aryans and, 60, 61
  Shinto and, 249
Houston, Whitney, 389
hsiao. *See* xiao
Huguenots, 365
Huizi, 196
hula Kahiko, 44
human excellence, Confucianism and,
  208–209, 214, 217–218
humanism, 386
Humanistic Psychology, 481
human nature, as good vs. bad, 218–220,
  246–247, 364
human purpose
  Christianity and, 341

Judaism and, 297–298
  patterns of views of, 13
humor
  Jesus and, 326
  Judaism and, 311
  Taoism and, 195
Hungary, Judaism and, 306
Husayn, 417, 425
Hu Shih, 228–229
Hus, Jan, 362
Huxley, Aldous, 95, 475
Huxley, T. H., 470, 475
hylozoism the belief that all physical mat-
  ter has life and feeling, 167

Ibn Rushd, 437
Ibn Sina, 437
Ibo, 32
I Ching. *See* Yi Jing
icon "image" (Greek); religious painting
  on wood, as used in the Orthodox
  Church; also spelled "ikon," 352, 385,
  386
iconostasis, 386
Id al-Adha the Day of Sacrifice during the
  month of the Hajj, when an animal is
  sacrificed to recall the submission of
  Abraham, 416, 417
Id al-Fitr the festival at the end of the
  month of Ramadan, during which
  people feast and visit friends and often the graves of ancestors, 417
Idea of the Holy, The (Otto), 4–5
identity
  Buddhist impermanence of, 109, 114,
    129
  Jewish, 292, 314
Ignatius of Loyola, 368
ikebana, 144
Ikiru (To Live) (Kurosawa), 481
Il Gesù, 383
imam a religious leader; specifically, one
  of the hereditary successors of
  Muhammad, venerated in Shiite Is-
  lam, 425–426
immaculate conception, 379–380
immanent existing and operating within
  nature, 8
immigration
  Buddhism and, 155–156
  Hinduism and, 97
  Islam and, 449–452
  Judaism and, 280–281, 287, 291, 292,
    293, 295
  Shinto and, 259–260
  Sikhism and, 183
immortality
  Christianity and, 331, 341–342
  Judaism and, 11, 297, 310
immortality. *See* death; longevity
Imperial Rescript on Education, 242

Impressionism, 155, 477, 486

Inari, 260

incarnation "in flesh" (Latin); a belief that God became visible in Jesus, 335

incense, 279, 344, 375–376

incest taboo, 40

inclusiveness. *See* exclusiveness and inclusiveness

Incoherence of the Philosophers, The (al-Ghazali), 437

India, 55–60
    colonization of, 90
    Islam and, 424, 426, 437, 448, 449
    Judaism in, 307
    religions begun in. *See* Buddhism; Hinduism; Jainism; Sikhism
    Sikh independence and, 182
    women in, 77, 84, 90–92

indigenous religions. *See* oral religions

individuality
    Christianity and, 325, 363, 364, 366, 369, 392
    Confucianism and, 212, 230
    desire and suffering and, 111
    as ideal, 67
    Islam and, 436, 446
    liberation from, 67–68
    See also authority; self; social responsibility; soul

individuation, origin of religion and need for, 5

Indonesia, 50, 94, 424, 472

Indra, 60, 78, 94

indulgence "Kindness-toward" (Latin); remission of time spent in purgatory (a state of temporary punishment in the afterlife); an aspect of Catholic belief and practice, 363

infanticide, 448

Inquisition, 291, 359
    heretics, 351–352, 359, 362, 363

Institutes of the Christian Religion (Calvin), 364

interfaith dialogue, 391–392, 459–460, 462
    See also exclusiveness and inclusiveness

internal alchemy, 198–199, 200

International Society for Krishna Consciousness (ISKCON), 96

Intolerance, 481

Inuit, 27, 35

Iran, 60, 426, 435, 436, 447–448, 451, 475

Iraq, 307, 426

Isaac, 272, 415

Isabella (queen of Spain), 359

Isaiah, 280, 330, 337

Ise location in eastern Honshu of a major shrine to Amaterasu, 242, 255, 260

Isherwood, Christopher, 95–96

Ishmael, 272, 410, 415

Islam "Submission"; the Muslim religion and the community of believers who have submitted themselves to Allah, 408
    art and, 352, 401–402, 407, 420–421, 424, 438–445, 452
    calendar of, 407, 413
    Christianity and, 288, 352, 357–359, 404, 408, 410, 411, 423, 427, 430, 436
    Crusades, 357–358
    fundamentalism, 475
    Hinduism and, 86, 94, 174, 176
    historical development of, 422–427, 445–446
    Judaism and, 288, 305, 306, 404, 407, 408, 410, 423, 436
    law and philosophy, 434–438
    modern world and, 445–452
    Muhammad. *See* Muhammad
    pantheism and, 428–429, 438
    persecution by, 288, 428–429
    persecution of, 305, 359
    practices of, 410–419
    as proselytizing religion, 50
    Qur'an. *See* Qur'an
    rosaries in, 379
    Shiite/Sunni division, 424–427, 435
    Sikhism and, 176, 177, 178, 180
    Sufism, 176, 359, 427–431, 433–434, 438
    as term, 408
    women and, 411, 413, 414, 418, 434, 447, 448–449
    Zoroastrianism and, 282, 404, 410

Ismailis, 426

Israel
    Crusades, 357–358, 359
    Goddess worship and, 15
    Jewish history and, 266, 272–273, 276–277, 279–281, 283, 286–287, 294–295
    Jewish support for, 307
    naming of, 272–273
    as nation, 294–295
    Orthodoxy in, 309
    sites in, 315
    Tisha Be-Av and, 302

Israelites. *See* Judaism

Istanbul, 452

Istanbul, ancient. *See* Constantinople

Italy, Judaism and, 292

Ithna Ashariya, 426

I and Thou (Buber), 311–312

I-Thou relationship, 311–312

It's a Wonderful Life (Capra), 481

Izanagi "male who invites"; primordial male parent god, 237–238

Izanami "female who invites"; primordial female parent god, 237–238

Jacob, 272–273

Jahangir, 178

Jahan, Shah, 402

Jainism, 165–174, 184

Buddhism compared to, 164, 165, 171, 175
    Hinduism and, 164, 165, 172
    nonviolence and, 70, 164, 165, 167, 168–169
    Sikhism and, 164

James the Just, 328

James, William, 4, 229

Jami, 431

Japan
    art of, 142–146, 155, 254–256
    Buddhism, 123, 126, 129, 133–146, 147, 155, 158, 252–254
        and Shinto, 236, 239–240, 242, 243, 245, 253–254
    China and, 133, 135, 238–241, 249, 255
    Christianity and, 370
    Confucianism and, 210, 211, 215, 230, 240–241
    eclectic music of, 487–488
    gardens of, 144–145, 251
    Goddess worship and, 15
    Korean occupation by, 133
    national identity of, 241–245
    origins of, 236–239
    shamanism of, 257–258
    Shinto. *See* Shinto
    travel to, 158
    Western influence on, 241, 243

Japji a poem by Guru Nanak that begins the Adi Granth; the poem is recited daily by pious Sikhs, 180–181

Jazz Singer, The, 313

Jehovah's Witnesses, 294, 372

jen. *See* ren

Jeremiah Symphony (Bernstein), 312

Jerusalem, 263–265, 279, 287, 328–329, 342, 358, 406–407

Jesuits, 368, 369, 370, 383

Jesus Christ, 339, 341
    doctrinal battles concerning, 351–353
    Gospels, portrayed in, 333–335
    life and teachings of, 321–328, 374
    Muslim view of, 409–410, 411
    Protestant emphasis on, 363
    as redeemer, 331, 339, 362–363
    relics of, 361
    as role model, 352, 356

Jethro, 274

Jewish Academy of Córdoba, 288

Jewish-Christian Church, 328–329

Jewish State, The (Herzl), 294

Jiao rite, 201

jihad "struggle"; the ideal of spreading Islamic belief and practice, 436

Jimmu, 238

jina "conqueror"; the Jain term for a perfected person who will not be reborn, 167

jinja a Shinto shrine, 247–251, 254–255

jinni, 403

jiva spirit, soul, which enlivens matter, 167

Jizo, 147

jnana yoga the spiritual discipline of knowledge and insight, 73–74

Job, Book of, 281–282

Jodo. *See* Pure Land Buddhist school

Joel, Billy, 460

John the Baptizer, 327–328, 373–374

John (bishop of Damascus), 352

John, Gospel of, 328, 334–335, 339, 356

John Paul II, 460, 474, 475

Johnson, Philip, 383

John XXIII, 392, 474

Joseph, 273

Joseph, Saint, 323, 327, 378

Josephus, 284

Joshua, 287

Joshua, Book of, 279

Judah, kingdom of, 266, 280

Judaism, 263–315
  arts and, 278, 293, 311–314, 315
  Ashkenazi, 291, 306, 313
  beliefs of, 297–298
  biblical, 266
  Christianity and, 290–291, 305, 306, 330–331, 332, 333, 334, 335, 337, 373, 376–377, 387
  cultural contributions of, 310–314
  divisions within, 305–310
    Conservative, 292, 309
    cultural, 305–307
    Orthodox, 292, 307–309, 310, 314
    Reconstructionist, 310
    Reform, 266, 292, 309–310
  Falashas, 306–307
  fundamentalism, 475
  history of, 264–267, 283–295
    in Hebrew Bible, 269–282
  Holocaust and, 293–294, 295–297, 302, 306, 309, 312, 315
  identity and, 292, 314
  Islam and, 288, 305, 306, 404, 407, 408, 410, 423, 436
  and Israel. *See* Israel
  of Jesus, 325–326
  language and, 281, 295, 303, 306, 313
    of services, 308, 309, 310
    written, 266, 281–282, 287
  Latter-day Saints Church and, 371
  moral codes and, 277–278, 281, 288
  mysticism of, 289–290
  name of God and, 275, 276, 278
  persecution of, 288, 290–291, 292–294, 295, 305–307, 359, 360
  practice of, 298–305
    holy days, 45, 276, 283, 299–302
    Sabbath. *See* Sabbath
  rabbinical, 266–267, 286–295, 297
  Reform of, 266, 292, 309–310

scripture
  canon of, 286–287
  Dead Sea scrolls and, 284–286
  Hebrew Bible. *See* Hebrew Bible
    interpretation of, 287–288
  Sephardic, 291, 305–306
  study of, 314–315
  traditionalism, 291–292
  women and, 15, 264–265, 270–271, 272, 278, 279, 305–310 *passim*, 313, 462–464

Judas Priest, 460

Julian of Norwich, 357

Jung, Carl Gustav, 5, 9, 481

junzi "noble person," the refined human ideal of Confucianism, 214, 223

Jupiter, 60

justice
  Christianity and, 331, 339
  Judaism and, 297–298
  See also government and politics

Justinian, 356

Kabah "Cube"; the square shrine at the center of the great mosque of Mecca, 404, 405, 407, 414–416

Kabbalah "received," "handed down"; the whole body of Jewish mystical literature, 289–290

Kaddish Symphony (Bernstein), 312

kadomatsu, 250

Kali a form of Devi; a goddess associated with destruction and rebirth, 15, 83–84

kama, 73

Kamehameha II (king of Hawai`i), 47

kami a spirit, god, or goddess of Shinto, 237, 242, 245–249, 254, 255, 256, 257

kamidan a shelf or home altar for the veneration of kami, 251

kamikaze "spirit wind"; suicide fighter pilots of World War II, 243

Kampuchea. *See* Cambodia

Kanjur, 149

Kannon. *See* Guanyin

Kaplan, Mordecai, 310

kapu. *See* taboos

Karbala, 425

karma the moral law of cause and effect that determines the direction of rebirth, 67, 114, 459
  Buddhism and, 114, 120
  Jainism and, 168
  Sikhism and, 177

karma yoga the spiritual discipline of selfless action, 74

karuna compassion, empathy, 124–125
  See also compassion

Kates, George, 214

Kauravas, 68, 70

Kazakhstan, 424

Kempe, Margery, 464

Kepler, Johannes, 467

Kerouac, Jack, 155

Kethuvim "writings"; the third section of the Hebrew scriptures, consisting primarily of poetry, proverbs, and literary works, 268

Khadijah, 404, 405, 449

Khajuraho, 89

Khalsa, 178, 180

Khayyám, Omar, 431

Khazaria, 306

Khmer, 120

Khomeini, Ayatollah, 426, 447–448, 475

Khuddaka Nikaya, 120

kibbutzim, 315

Kiev, 351

ki`i, 47

Kilimanjaro, Mount, 34

kindness. *See* compassion

Kingdom of God Is Within You (Tolstoy), 93

King James Bible, 366

King, Martin Luther, Jr., 94, 165

kings, taboos and, 39–40

Kings, Books of, 279

Kinkaku-ji, 158

kippah, 303

Kiyomizu-dera, 158, 252–254

Knights Templar, 359

Knox, John, 365

koan in Chan and Zen Buddhism, a question that cannot be answered logically; a technique used to test consciousness and bring awakening, 140

Kobo Daishi, 135

Koestler, Arthur, 306

Kojiki the earliest chronicle of Japanese history, 245

Kol Nidre (Bloch), 312

Kong Fuzi. *See* Confucius

Kongo-kai, 135

Kong Qiu. *See* Confucius

Koran. *See* Qur'an

Korea
  Buddhism, 123, 126, 133, 135, 147, 158
  Christianity in, 370, 373
  Confucianism in, 210, 211, 215, 229, 231
  Goddess worship and, 15
  religious blending in, 133
  shamanism of, 50–51, 257
  travel to, 158

Koryo dynasty, 133

kosher "ritually correct"; said particularly about food consumption and food preparation, 277, 283, 302–303, 309

Koyukon, 33

Krishna a god associated with divine playfulness; a form of Vishnu, 70, 80, 88

kshatriya caste, 71, 103

Kuan-yin. *See* Guanyin

Kukai, 135
Kundalini Yoga, 76
Kurosawa, Akira, 481
Kusan, 12
Kwakwaka`wakw (Kwakiutl), 44
Kyoto, Japan, 133, 158, 252–254, 260
Kyrie, 388
"Kyrie Eleison" (Mister Mister), 460

labor, Zen Buddhism and, 140, 142
Ladino, 306
Lakshmi, 84, 86
lama a Tibetan Buddhist teacher, 148–149
lamb, sacrificial, 276, 301, 302
La Mer (Debussy), 486–487
language
    appropriation of religious, 459
    Aramaic, 281
    archeology and, 17–18
    and Babel, tower of, 271, 328
    Chinese transcription systems, 188
    Christianity and, 328, 329, 330, 333, 344,
        351, 360, 361, 362, 365–366, 392,
        395, 474
    as concealing reality, 109, 140, 141
    Confucian influence on, 210
    Esperanto, 258
    gender-neutral, 463–464
    Hebrew, 281, 295, 306
    inadequacy of, 194
    Indo-European, 60
    Islam and, 420–422
    Ladino, 306
    revival of, 51
    Tibetan, 148
    written
        calligraphy and value of, 223–224
        Christianity and, 344, 350–351
        of Harappa culture, 59
        of Islam, 419–421, 441, 444
        Japanese use of, 245
        Judaism and, 266, 281–282, 287
        vs. oral, and study of religion,
            28–29
        printing press and, 360
        Turkish, 447
    Yiddish, 303, 306, 313
    See also texts
Laos, 120
Lao Tzu. *See* Laozi
Laozi the legendary founder of Taoism,
    192–195, 221
Lark Ascending (Vaughan Williams), 487
last judgment, 341–342
Last Supper, 374
al-Lat, 404
Late Summer, 481
Latin, 344, 392, 474
Latin cross, 376, 381
laughing Buddha, 126
Laverne and Shirley, 313

law, 435
    Islam and, 435–436
Leah, 272
Leaves of Grass (Whitman), 95
Lebanon, 426
Lee, "Mother" Ann, 366
Legalists the strictest of the Chinese philo-
    sophical schools, which advocated
    strong laws and punishments,
    220–221
lei, 44
Lenin, Vladimir Ilich, 470
Lent "lengthening day," "spring" (Anglo-
    Saxon); the preparatory period be-
    fore Easter, lasting forty days, 375,
    377–378, 379
Leo III, 352
León, Moses de, 290
Leo X, 363
lesbians, 465–466
Let's Go (Harvard Student Agencies), 19
Leviticus, 277
Levi, tribe of, 279
Lhasa, Tibet, 159
li appropriate action, ritual, propriety, eti-
    quette, 212, 222
libation the act of pouring a liquid as an
    offering to a god, 40
Liberation Theology, 392
Li Bo, 203
Life of Antony, 347
Life Divine, The (Aurobindo), 87
Light of Muhammad, 425
"Like a Prayer" (Madonna), 460
lingam, 77–78, 83
literature
    Judaism and, 312
    See also texts
Little Buddha, 481
logging, 50
Logotherapy, 481
Lonely Planet (Harvard Student Agencies),
    19
longevity, Taoism and, 198–199, 200
Lono, 33
Lord's Supper. *See* Eucharist
Lost Horizon (Capra/Hilton), 481
lotus, 151
Lotus Sutra, 130, 137, 138
love, universal. *See* universal love
Low Church, 366
Lucifer, 341
    See also Satan
Luke-Acts, 335–336
Luke, Gospel of, 334, 335
Lutheranism, 364, 379, 388, 395, 462, 466
Luther, Martin, 346, 362–363, 364, 388
lying. *See* honesty

Mabuchi, Kamo, 243
Maccabees, 283, 284

McPherson, Aimee Semple, 395
Madhva, 74
Madonna, 460
magic
    Buddhism and, 131, 135, 148
    divination. *See* divination
    malevolent vs. beneficial, 43
    in oral religions, 42–43
    origins of religion and, 2
Magnificat (Bach), 389
Mahabharata, 68, 80
Mahapurana, 167
Maharishi Mahesh Yogi, 96
Mahavira, 166–167, 168, 170, 171, 172,
    173
Mahayana Buddhism, 123–138
    in China, 130–133
    festivals of, 147
    Goddess worship and, 15
    in Japan, 133–134, 239–240
    in Korea, 133
    literature of, 130
    major schools of, 134–138
    Naturism and, 477
    Vajrayana and, 146
al-Mahdi, Muhammad, 425–426
Mahendra, 117
Mahinda, 117
Mahler, Gustav, 312
Maimonides, Moses, 288, 297
Maitreya a Buddha (or bodhisattva) ex-
    pected to appear on earth in the fu-
    ture, 126
Majjhima Nikaya, 120
Makahiki, 33
Malaysia, 50, 424, 472
Malcolm X, 450
males, High Gods as complementary
    male/female, 35
Manat, 404
Manchus, 132
mandala a circular design containing
    deities, geometrical forms, symbols,
    and so on that represent totality, the
    self, or the universe, 5, 135, 151
Manicheism, 345
Man's Search for Meaning (Frankl), 294
mantra a short sacred phrase, often
    chanted or used in meditation, 75,
    135, 137, 138, 151
    See also chant
Manu, 92
Maori, 27, 51
Mao Zedong, 229, 470–471
Mara, 105
Mardana, 176, 177
Mardi Gras, 378
margas, 73
marijuana, 42
Mark, Gospel of, 334, 335, 342
Marley, Bob, 460

marriage, 38
  annulment of, 365, 418, 474
  caste system and, 71, 91
  Christianity and, 326–327, 345–346, 371, 373, 375
  Confucian relationship hierarchy and, 210–211, 213
  divorce, 38, 326, 418, 448, 449, 465, 474
  intermarriage, 292, 313, 314, 391
  Islam and, 404, 418, 448, 449, 450
  Judaism and, 305, 309, 313, 314
  monogamy, 38
  oral societies and, 38
  pre-Islamic culture and, 448
  same-gender, 465–466
  Unification Church and, 373
  See also family
Marx, Karl, 470
Mary the Harlot, Saint, 347
Mary (mother of Jesus), 15, 323, 327, 334, 361, 363, 369, 378, 379–380, 386
  devotion to, 363, 369, 379–380, 474
masks, 29–30, 44
Maslow, Abraham, 312, 481
Mass, 388
Mass in B minor (Bach), 389
Matisse, Henri, 30
matriarchal cultures, 15–16
matriarchs, 272, 464
matter
  Jainism and, 167–168
  See also body
Matthew, Gospel of, 334, 335, 341, 342
matzah, 302
Maulawiya, 429
maya "illusion"; what keeps us from seeing reality correctly, 66–67
Mayazumi, Toshiro, 488
Ma Yuan, 203
Mbiti, John, 442
Mead, Margaret, 29
meat eating
  Islam and, 174
  Judaism and, 303
  Sikhism and, 177
Mecca, 402, 404, 405, 407, 410, 411, 413–416, 417, 426, 450
Mechtilde of Magdeburg, 464
medicine men
  as term, 41–42
  See also shamans
Medina (Yathrib), 407, 416
meditation
  Buddhist, 105, 113, 138–142, 148
  Chinese gardens and, 205
  Christian, 372
  Hindu, 75–76
  Transcendental Meditation, 96
  See also chant; contemplative practices; prayer; ritual
Meiji (emperor of Japan), 235, 236, 243
Meiji Restoration, 243, 255

Meiji Shrine, 235–236, 249
Melchizedek, priesthood of, 371
Melinda, 117
Melk Abbey, 383
Memories, Dreams, Reflections (Jung), 5
Menander, 117
Mencius, 215, 218, 219, 222
Mencius, The, 218
Mendelssohn, Moses, 309–310
Mengzi. See Mencius
Mennonites, 366
menorah a candelabrum usually containing seven—and occasionally nine—branches, used for religious celebrations, 300
men. See gender; women
menstruation
  coming-of-age rituals for, 38, 39
  rituals for, 305
  taboos and, 39
mental health, physical health dependent on, 258
mentor relationships, 211
Mesnevi (Mathnawi) (Rumi), 429
Messiah "anointed" (Hebrew); a special messenger sent by God, foretold in the Hebrew scriptures, and believed by Christians to be Jesus, 323, 328, 330, 331, 339
Messiah a savior figure to be sent by God, awaited by the Jews (see Dan. 7:13–14), 287, 297, 302
messianism
  Buddhism and, 126
  Superman comic and, 483
Methodist Church, 367, 370, 389
Methodius, 350–351
Metropolitan Community Church, 466
Metteya. See Maitreya
Mevlevi, 429
mezuzah, 303–304
Michelangelo, 319, 320, 339, 386
Middle Ages
  bubonic plague, 291, 360
  Christianity and, 290–291, 355–360, 379, 386
  European religion during, 355, 359
  European society during, 358, 360
  Islam and, 288, 359
  Judaism and, 288–291, 359
middle way, 105–106
midrash "search"; rabbinical commentary on the scriptures and oral law, 266–267, 287
mihrab the decorated niche inside a mosque that indicates the direction of Mecca, 411, 439
Miki, Nakayama, 257–258
militancy
  Shinto and, 243, 245
  Sikhism and, 178–180, 181–182
Million-Man March, 450

Mi-lo-fo, 126
Mina, 416
minaret a tower used by a chanter to call people to prayer, 411, 439
Ming dynasty, 223
mining, 50
miracles, 391
Miroku, 126
Miruk, 126, 373
Mishnah, 287
Mishneh Torah (Maimonides), 288
misogi a ritual of purification that involves standing under a waterfall, 250–251, 253–254
missionaries
  Buddhist, 117, 130–135
  Christian, 50, 90, 330, 331, 342, 347, 368–370
  exclusiveness/inclusiveness and, 14
  Hinduism affected by, 90
  oral religions as weakened by, 50
  Russian Orthodox Church and, 353
  Shinto and, 259–260
Mister Mister, 460
mlechcha caste, 71, 91
mochi, 250
Modern Man in Search of a Soul (Jung), 5
Mohists a Chinese school of philosophy that taught universal love, 220
moksha "liberation" from personal limitation, egotism, and rebirth, 67–68
monastic life, 346
  Buddhist, 105–106, 118–120, 123, 135–137, 140, 148, 156, 346, 347, 463
  Christian, 345–347, 350–351, 353–355, 356–357, 427, 477
  Hindu, 346
  Islamic (Sufi), 408
  Jainist, 166–167, 170, 171, 172
  Jewish, 284, 346
  Orthodox Christian, 350–351, 353–355
  Taoist, 199, 346
  See also authority; clergy; religious orders
Monet, Claude, 155, 477
money lending
  Islam and, 405, 417
  Judaism and, 291, 293
  See also economics
Mongols, 132, 133, 424
monism, 74
  See also unity
monks. See monastic life
monophysitism, 351–352
monotheism the belief in one God, 5
  of Christianity, 339, 341
  in Hinduism, 78–79
  of Islam, 408
  of Judaism, 275–276
  of Sikhism, 164
  of Zoroastrianism, 282

moon
    male god as, 15, 238
    as symbol, 105
Moon, Sun Myung, 373
moral codes and ethics
    the arts and, 225
    Christianity and, 325, 327, 331, 336, 337,
        394
    environmental issues and, 472
    human significance and existence of, 13,
        218–220
    Islam and, 410
    of Jainism, 168–170
    Judaism and, 277–278, 281, 288
    karma. *See* karma
    as key characteristic of religions, 7
    Naturism and, 479
    sexuality and changing, 465–467
    Shinto and, 246, 259
    Western religions and, 410
    Zoroastrianism and, 282
    See also values; virtues
Mordecai, 300
Moriah, Mount, 272
Mormons, 371–372
Mormon Tabernacle Choir, 372
Morocco, 306, 432–434, 452
mortality. *See* death
Moscow, 351, 353
Moses, 274–277, 297, 410
Moses and Monotheism (Freud), 4
mosque a Muslim place of worship, 407,
        439–440, 452
motets, 388
Mother-Goddess, 15
Moulay Idriss I, 434
mountain, as symbol, 10
Mountains of California, The (Muir), 478
movement and exercise
    hatha yoga, 76
    Shinto purification, 250
    Taoist, 198–199
    See also dance
movies, 313, 451, 478–479, 480–481, 483
Mozart, Wolfgang Amadeus, 388
Muawiya, 425
mudra a symbolic hand gesture, 151
muezzin a chanter who calls people to
        prayer, 408, 411
Muhammad
    heirs of, 404, 422, 425–426
    life of, 402–407, 420
    Night Journey of, 405, 407, 428, 444
    as prophet, 409–410, 411, 428
    as role model, 407, 418
    See also Islam
Muhammad, Wali Farrad, 450
Muhammad, Elijah, 450
Muir, John, 477–478
mullas, 436
multiculturalism, 459–462
Mulungu, 35

Mumtaz Mahal, 402
murder, 278
museums, Buddhist art and, 156, 159
mushrooms, psychoactive, 42, 60
Music: Pink and Blue (O'Keeffe), 483
music
    Buddhism and, 151
    Christianity and, 364, 365–366, 367,
        371–372, 387–389, 395
    contemplative practices and, 486–488
    development of Western, 387–389
    eclectic spirituality and, 485–488
    ethnomusicology, 29
    Hindu and Hindu influence, 89–90, 95,
        96
    Impressionist, 486–487
    Judaism and, 279, 281, 292, 312
    New Age, 482, 487
    as patterned element, 17
    rock music, 389, 459
    Shinto, 244–256
    spiritual music, 481–482
    See also art; chant
music theory, 387
Muslim a person who submits to Allah,
        405
    See also Islam
Muslim Girl Training, 450
Muslim Mogul Empire, 424
Mustali Ismailis, 426
Mutazilites, 437
al-Muttalib, Abd, 404
Myanmar, 120, 121, 156
mystery, origin of religion and, 4–5
mystical orientation, 11–12
    multiplicity and, 88
Mystical Theology (Pseudo-Dionysius),
        428
mysticism, 395, 433–434
    Christian, 352, 353, 356–357, 395, 428
    defined, 356
    of Islam (Sufism), 359, 427–431,
        433–434, 438
    Jewish, 289–290
    of Naturism, 477, 479
    Neoplatonism, 428
"My Sweet Lord" (Harrison), 96, 460
mythology, 16–17
    origin stories. *See* origin stories
myth, as term, 17

Nanak, 176–178
Nandi, 83, 84
Nao, Deguchi, 258
Naqshbandi, 430
Nara, 158
Natchez, 39
National Cathedral, 383
nationalism, 241–245, 474–475
National Palace Museum (Taipei), 187–188
national park system, 478, 489
Nation of Islam, 450

Native American Church, 42, 51
Native Americans (North America), 28
    art, 28, 43, 44
    death rituals, 39
    ecumenism and, 392
    Gods, respect for, 35
    marriage, 38
    nature, reverence toward, 32, 33
    origin stories of, 34–35
    peyote use, 42
    pipe ceremony, 42
    revival of oral religions, 51
    sacrifice, 40
    sandpaintings, 28, 43
    social behavior enforcement, 40
    taboos, 40
    time and, 33, 34
    vision quest, 38
native religions. *See* oral religions
nature
    animals. *See* animals (nonhuman)
    animism. *See* animism
    Buddhism and, 125–126, 129, 477
    Chinese traditional beliefs and,
        189–190
    Christianity and, 326, 356–357
    Confucianism and, 206
    conservation of. *See* environment
    eclectic spirituality and reverence of,
        484–485
    Islam and, 436–437, 441
    Judaism and, 271
    mysticism of, 477, 479
    oral religions and, 31–33, 34, 477
    origin of religion and, 2, 3–5
    patterns of views of, 12–13, 476–478
    religion of (Naturism), 475–480
    Shinto and, 236, 245–247, 259, 260
    Taoism and, 194–198, 201–203, 205, 477
    transcendence vs. immanence and,
        7–8
    See also body; environment; world
Nature Conservancy, 479
Naturism, 475–480
Navajo, 28, 29, 43
Nazianzen, Gregory, 350
Nazis, 293–294, 295, 309, 353
Nebuchadnezzar, 280
negative space, 439
Nemi, 172
neoclassical style, 383
Neo-Confucianism, 221–223
Nepal, 94, 113, 159
Nero, 342
Nestorian Christian Church, 351
Nevi'im "prophets"; the second section of
        the Hebrew scriptures, made up of
        historical and prophetic books, 268
New Age music, 482, 487
New Culture Movement, 228–229
New Guinea, 40, 50
New Religions, 256–259

New Testament, 269, 337, 341
  Acts, Book of, 328, 330, 332, 335–336
  Epistles, 330, 331, 332, 333, 336, 345, 356, 362
  Gospels, 323, 324–327, 333–335
  interpretation of, 337
  Jesus, life of, in, 323, 324–327
  on Judaism, 290
  literary qualities of, 332–333
  Protestantism and, 363
  Revelation, 332, 333, 336–337, 372
  structure of, 332–337
  on women, 15
  See also Bible, Christian
New Thought, 372
Newton, Isaac, 447, 467
New Year
  Jewish, 299, 300, 302
  Shinto, 250
New Zealand, 51, 370
Nez Perce, 32
Nicene Creed, 351
Nichiren Buddhist school, 137–138, 156
Nichiren Sho-shu, 138, 156
Night Journey (Night of Ascent), 405, 407, 428, 444
Nihongi the second chronicle of Japanese history, 245
Ninety-Five Theses (Luther), 363
Nineveh, 17
Nirmanakaya, 126
nirvana the release from suffering and re-birth that brings inner peace, 111–112, 114–115, 123, 459
Nirvana (rock band), 459, 460
Nizari, 426
Noble Eightfold Path, 112–113
Nocturnes (Debussy), 487
Noh dramas performed in mask and cos-tume, associated with Shinto, 256
nonattachment
  Buddhist, 111, 118, 125, 147–148
  Jainist, 166–167, 170
nondenominational churches, 394
nonharm. *See* nonviolence
nonliterate religions. *See* oral religions
nontheistic not asserting or denying the existence of any deity; unconcerned with the supernatural, 8
nonviolence
  Buddhism and, 75, 113–114, 115, 117, 148, 154, 156
  Christianity and, 325, 366
  Hinduism and, 75, 92, 93–94, 156
  Jainism and, 70, 164, 165, 167, 168–169
  See also vegetarianism; warfare
"no pain, no gain," 198
Norinaga, Motoori, 243
North Africa, 345, 422–423, 451
North America
  Christianity and, 364, 365, 366, 367, 370
  Judaism and, 292, 293, 314–315

natives of. *See* Native Americans (North America)
  Naturism and, 477–478
notre dame, 379
Notre Dame Basilica, 383
Notre Dame Cathedral, 381
nuclear energy, 472
nudity, Jainists and, 166–167, 171, 174
Numbers, 276, 277
numerology. *See* gematria
numinous awe, 5
nuns. *See* monastic life; women
Nzambi, 35

O-Bon, 147
occupations and religion
  Buddhists and, 113, 114
  Hindus and, 71
  Islam, 418, 448, 449
  Jainists and, 168–169
  Judaism and, 291, 311–314
  monastic life and choices of, 346
Oglala Sioux, 32
`ohi`a lehua, 25
oil, 375
oil interests, 50
O'Keeffe, Georgia, 482
Old Testament, 269, 337, 341
Om, 75
omnipotence, 7
Omoto a New Religion, which stresses art and beauty, 258, 460, 462
"On Civil Disobedience" (Thoreau), 93
On Hearing the First Cuckoo in Spring (Delius), 487
Onisaburo, Deguchi, 258
"onward and upward," 198
opium, 42
oral religions, 27–31
  of Arab Peninsula, 403–404, 405, 413–414, 435–436
  biases against, 28–29, 31, 43
  defined, 27
  of India, 59–61, 77–78, 80
  modern societies, influence on, 46, 476
  nature and, 31–33, 34, 477
  patterns of, 31–37
  practices of, 37–47
  pre-Buddhist, 134, 146, 147, 148
  recovery of, 29–31
  survival of, 50–51
orders, religious, 358–359, 429–430
  See also monastic life
ordination, 375
Organization of Afro-American Unity, 450
organ music, 387–389
Origen, 356
original sin an inclination toward evil, in-herited by human beings as a result of Adam's disobedience, 339, 380

origin stories
  in Hebrew Bible, 269–271
  oral religions and, 34–35
  of Rig Veda, 62
  Shinto, 237–239
  time and, 13
Orthodox "straight opinion" (Greek); cor-rect belief, 349
Orthodox the most traditional branch of Judaism, 292, 307–309, 310, 314
Orthodoxy the Eastern branch of Chris-tianity, 350
  See also Eastern Orthodox Church
Ottoman Empire, 424
Otto, Rudolf, 4–5
Our National Parks (Muir), 478
Our Town (Wilder), 481
ozoni, 250
Ozu, Yasujiro, 481

Pachomius, 347
Padmasambhava, 148
Pagan, Myanmar, 120
Pahlavi, Mohammad Reza, 447
painting
  Buddhist, 128, 137, 146, 151–152
  Chinese, 201–203, 224–225, 231
  Christian, 385–387
  Confucian influence on, 225
  eclectic spirituality and, 483–484, 485
  Hindu, 88–89
  Islamic, 424, 439
  Judaism and, 278, 313
  Naturism and, 477
  negative space, 439
  Taoist influence on, 201–203
  Zen, 146
Pakistan, 94, 424, 426, 435, 448, 449, 451, 475
Palestinians, 294–295
Palestrina, Giovanni da, 388
Pali, 107
Pali Canon, 120
Palm Sunday, 378
Pandu, 68
pantheism the belief that everything in the universe is divine, 8, 428–429
  See also Naturism
Paphnutius, 347
paradise, of Islam, 441
  See also afterlife
parent-child relationship, 209–210
Paris, France, 313
Parrinder, Geoffrey, 29
Parshva, 165, 172
Pärt, Arvo, 482
Parvati, 84
Passover (Pesach) a joyful spring festival that recalls the Hebrews' exodus from Egypt and freedom from op-pression, 45, 276, 301, 302, 315
Patanjali, 75

patriarch the bishop of one of the major ancient sites of Christianity (Jerusalem, Rome, Alexandria, Antioch, Constantinople, and Moscow), 342, 350

patriarchal religion, 15–16

   India and, 60–61, 91–92

patterns among religions, 10–16

   beliefs and practices, focus of, 11–12

   male and female, views of, 14–16

   in oral religions, 31–37

   world and life, views of, 12–14, 31–34

Paul, 327, 329–331, 342

Paul the Hermit, 347

Pauline Epistles, 330, 331, 332, 336, 345, 356, 362

peace

   Buddhism and, 108, 111–113

   interfaith dialogue and desire for, 460, 462

   Omoto and, 258, 460, 462

Peggy Sue Got Married, 481

Pelagia the Harlot, Saint, 347

Pele, 26–27

Pentateuch. *See* Torah

Pentecost, 378, 379

Pentecostal movement, 367, 392

People for the Ethical Treatment of Animals, 479

Père Jacques Marquette, 369–370

persecution

   of Buddhism, 132, 155, 156, 243, 255

   Christianity and. *See under* Christianity

   Islam and. *See under* Islam

   of Jews, 288, 290–291, 292–294, 295, 305–307, 359, 360

   of Protestantism, 364–365

   of religion, in China, 200–201

   of Sikhism, 178–180

   See also authority; government

Persia, 281, 358

Persian Empire, 422, 424, 447

   See also Iran

Persian miniatures, 424, 445

pesticides, 472, 479

Peter, 328, 342, 343

Petrarch, 477

peyote, 42

Pharisees a faction during the Second-Temple period that emphasized the observation of biblical rules, 284, 297, 330

Philippines, 370, 424

Philo, 284

philosophy

   Christianity and, 357

   Confucianism as, 208, 218–221

   Islam and, 436–438

   Jewish contributions to, 311–312

   religion compared to, 17

   Taoist, 191–198

photography, 29, 445, 480, 484–485

phylacteries. *See* tefillin

Picasso, Pablo, 29, 30, 483

Pietà (Michelangelo), 320

pilgrimage

   Christian, 357–358, 359

   Communist, 470

   Hindu, 87

   Jainist, 173, 184

   Muslim, 413–416, 417, 445, 448, 450

   Naturism and, 477, 480

   pre-Islamic, 404

   Shinto, 251, 260

   to Giverny, 477

   trade and, 358, 405

pinyin system, 188

pleasure, Hinduism and, 73

Pliny the Elder, 284

P. L. Kyodan, 258

Plotinus, 428

poetry, 142, 155, 180–181, 201, 203, 281, 429, 431, 477

Poland

   Communist secularism and, 471

   Judaism and, 292, 293, 306

politeness, Confucianism and, 212–213

politics. *See* government and politics

Pollock, Jackson, 484

pollution. *See* purity and purification

polygamy, 371, 450

polytheism the belief in many gods, 5, 8, 189

   Christianity and, 411

   Judaism and, 275–276

pope "father" (Latin); the bishop of Rome and head of the Roman Catholic Church, 343–344, 350, 356, 360, 361–362, 363, 365

   as infallible, 368

Pope Gregory I, 347

popular culture, religion and, 459, 460, 483

population explosion, 464, 472

pork, 283, 303, 417

Porter, Bill, 204

Portugal, 369

Positive-Historical School of Judaism, 292, 309

Postimpressionism, 155

Potato Eaters, The (van Gogh), 485

Potok, Chaim, 312

Pound, Ezra, 155

poverty

   Christianity and, 356, 359, 392

   idealization of, capitalism and, 457–459

   Islam and, 412–413

   See also economics; government and politics; social responsibility

power

   Buddhism and, 149–150

   Hinduism and, 73

   Judaism and, 290

   Taoism and, 196

Prabhavananda, 96

Prabhupada, Bhaktivedanta, 96

Prajnaparamita Sutras, 130

prayer

   Buddhist, 150, 379

   Christian, 375, 379, 408, 441

   Hindu, 379

   Islamic, 408, 411–412, 441, 448

   Jewish, 303, 308, 408

   rosaries for, 379

   See also meditation; ritual

prayer flags, 150

prayer shawl, 303

prayer wheel, 150

predestination the belief that because God is all-powerful and all-knowing, a human being's ultimate reward or punishment is already decreed by God; a notion emphasized in Calvinism, 364

prejudice. *See* persecution

Prelude to the Afternoon of a Faun (Debussy), 486

Presbyterian Church, 365, 370

Presley, Elvis, 389

Presley, Elvis, cult of, 483

priests

   Hindu caste of, 71, 115

   monks distinguished from, 346

   Mormon, 371

   training of, 367

   See also clergy; monastic life; religious orders; shamans

primal religions. *See* oral religions

printing press, invention of, 360

property

   Hebrew Bible and, 277, 278

   Islam and, 448, 449

prophet a person inspired by God to speak for him, 280, 408–409

   See also Christianity; Islam; Judaism

prophetic orientation, 11

Prophets (of Hebrew Scripture). *See* Nevi'im

proselytizing. *See* missionaries

Protestantism

   architecture and, 383

   arts and, 364–366, 367, 383, 387, 388–389

   beliefs of, 352–353, 363

   Evangelical, 392, 394–395

   festivals of, 376–379

   forms of, 364–367

   Mary in, 363, 379

   missionaries of, 370

   modern world and, 391–392, 394–395

   music and, 364, 365–366, 367, 388–389, 395

   nontraditional denominations, 371–373, 394–395

   Pentecostal, 367, 392

   persecution of, 364, 365

Protestantism *(continued)*
  Reformation of, 360–363, 367, 368, 376,
    379, 388–389
  sacraments and rituals of, 374–375,
    376–379
  science and, 391
  See also Christianity
Protestant Principle the ability
    of each believer to rethink and inter-
    pret the ideas and values of Chris-
    tianity, 363, 364, 366, 392
Protestant Reformation, 360–363, 367, 368,
    376, 379, 388–389
Psalms, 280, 281, 337
psychedelic substances, 42, 60, 431
psychology
  Jesus and, 326
  Judaism and contributions to, 312
  nirvana and, 115
  on origin of religion, 4–5
  on sexuality, 465
  spirituality and, 481
  studies in religion, 16
Psychology and Alchemy (Jung), 5
puja offerings and ritual in honor of a de-
    ity; ritual in honor of tirthankara, 172
Pulguk-sa, 158
Punjab, 174
Puranas, 80
Pure Land Buddhist school, 133–134, 137,
    459
purgatory, 341, 363
Purim a joyous festival in early spring
    that recalls the Jews' being saved
    from destruction, as told in the Book
    of Esther, 300
Puritans, 365
purity and purification
  Christianity and, 327, 335
  Hindu, 71
  Islam and, 411, 415, 439
  Judaism and, 277, 283, 302–303, 373
  Shinto and, 238, 239, 246–247, 248,
    250–251
Purusha, 62, 70–71
Purvas, 173
Pu`uhonua `o Honaunau, 47

Qadiri, 430
qi the life force, 198, 222
qiblah the direction toward Mecca; the di-
    rection toward which Muslims pray
Quakers, 366, 466
Quan Yin. *See* Guanyin
Qumran, 284, 335
Qur'an "recitation"; God's words as re-
    vealed to and recited by Muham-
    mad; an authorized edition of the
    written words that appeared after
    Muhammad's death, 419–422
  Allah, 408, 411

  art and, 420–421, 441, 444
  circumcision and, 417, 418
  death, 418–419
  dietary restrictions, 417
  law and, 434–436
  marriage, 418
  Muhammad and, 402, 404, 420
  philosophy and, 436–437
  Sufis and, 428, 431
  Sunnis and, 426
  on women, 418, 448–449
Quraysh, 404

rabbi a religious teacher, Jewish minister,
    266
rabbinical Judaism the Judaism that de-
    veloped after the destruction of the
    Second Temple (70 C.E.) 266–267,
    286–295, 297
Rabia, 428
race
  Holocaust and, 293
  Malcolm X and, 450
Rachel, 272
racial segregation, 93, 94
Radha, 80
radio
  Christian evangelism, 395
  Muslim, 422
ragas, 89–90
Rahab, 279
Rai, Gobind, 180
Rai, Har, 179
rainbows, 271
rainmakers, 43
raja yoga the "royal" discipline of medita-
    tion, 75–76
Ramadan the month of fasting; the ninth
    month of the Muslim calendar, 413,
    416
Ramakrishna, 83, 95, 460
Ramanuja, 74
Rama a god and mythical king; a form of
    Vishnu, 79, 86
Ramayana, 79
Ram Das, 178
Ram Dass, 96
rationalism, 437
Ravan, 79
Ravel, Maurice, 487
reality. *See* sacredness; worldview
Rebecca, 272
rebirth. *See* reincarnation
reciprocity, Confucianism and, 213
Reclining Buddha, 107, 123, 158
reconciliation, 375
Reconquista, 359
Reconstructionism a modern, liberal
    branch of Judaism that emphasizes
    the cultural aspects of Judaism, 310
recording technologies, 29

rectification of names, 211
redemption "buy again," "buy back"
    (Latin); the belief that the death of Je-
    sus has paid the price of justice for
    all human wrongdoing, 331, 339,
    362–363
Red Heads, 201
Reform a modernizing movement and a
    liberal branch of Judaism, 266, 292,
    309–310
refuge, Hawaiian, 47–50
reggae music, 389
Regula Magistri, 347
Reichard, Gladys, 29
reincarnation
  Buddhism and, 112, 114–115, 126,
    148–149, 154
  Hinduism and, 67–68, 79, 86
  Jainism and, 168
  oral religions and, 37
  Sikhism and, 177
relationships
  Confucian hierarchy of, 209–212
  I-Thou, 311–312
relativity
  Jainism and, 169–170
  Taoism and, 198
relics, 361, 363
religions
  animals and. *See* animals
  authority in. *See* authority
  capitalism and, 457–459
  change as integral to, 11, 78
  eclectic spirituality, 480–481
  economics and. *See* economics
  ethics and morals. *See* moral codes and
    ethics
  evolutionary hierarchy of, as discred-
    ited, 5, 31
  exclusivity. *See* exclusiveness vs. inclu-
    siveness
  fundamentalism in, 474–475
  globalism and, 457–459
  interfaith dialogue, 391–392, 459–460,
    462
  interrelatedness and, 482–484
  key characteristics of, 6–7
  multidisciplinary approaches to, 16–18
  nature and. *See* nature
  oral. *See* oral religions
  origins of, theories regarding, 2–5
  patterns among. *See* patterns among re-
    ligions
  politics and. *See* government and politics
  repression of. *See* persecution
  ritual of. *See* ritual
  sacredness. *See* sacredness; worldview
  secularism and, 435, 446–447, 469–472,
    475
  specialists in. *See* clergy; monastic life;
    priests; religious orders; shamans

study of, 18–21, 31, 51
　See also travel (study)
symbolism in. *See* symbols and symbolism
as term, 6–7
time and. *See* time
urge for, as tenacious, 488
worldviews of. *See* worldview
　See also specific religions
Religions, Values, and Peak Experiences
　(Maslow), 481
religious orders, 358–359, 429–430
　See also clergy; monastic life
ren empathy, consideration for others, humaneness; a Confucian virtue, 212
Renaissance
　Christianity and, 362–368, 386, 388
　Judaism and, 291
　nature mysticism and, 477
Reorganized Church of Jesus Christ of
　Latter-day Saints, 371
replacement, cycle of, 49–50
Requiem Mass, 388
resurrection
　Christianity and, 323, 339,
　　376–378
　Judaism and, 297
　See also afterlife; death; immortality
retirement, Hindu, 72
Revelation, 332, 333, 336–337, 372
Revelations of Divine Love (Julian of Norwich), 357
Revival of the Religious Sciences, The (al-Ghazali), 437
Ricci, Matteo, 370
righteousness being sinless in the sight of
　God; also called *justification*, 331
right livelihood, 113, 114
Rig Veda, 62, 70–71, 95
Rinzai Buddhist school, 139–140
Rishaba, 172
rishis, 61
rites of passage
　in oral societies, 37–39
　See also circumcision
ritual
　Buddhism and, 123, 135–137, 138, 146,
　　149–151
　of Christianity, 344–345, 369, 373–376
　circumcision. *See* circumcision
　of Confucianism, 221, 223, 229
　of Hinduism, 77–78
　of Islam, 417–419
　of Jainism, 172–173
　of Judaism, 279, 280–281, 286
　as key characteristic of religion, 7
　Naturism and, 479
　oral religions and, 35, 37–47
　patterns of views on, 11
　rites of passage. *See* rites of passage
　of Roman Empire, 344–345

shamanic, 146
of Shinto, 239, 247–252, 254, 255–256, 259
of Sikhism, 180–181
of Taoism, 200, 201
　See also meditation; pilgrimage; prayer
*Road to Heaven: Encounters with Chinese
　Hermits* (Porter), 204
rock music, 389, 459
Roman Catholic Church
　architecture and, 380–384
　authority of and in, 343–344, 350, 356,
　　360–362, 363, 365, 368, 369, 392,
　　474
　changes in, 392, 459, 473–474
　Counter Reformation, 367–368, 383
　cross, sign of, 11
　Eastern split from, 350, 351–353, 356
　ecumenism and interfaith dialogue and,
　　391, 460
　festivals of, 376–379
　in Hawai`i, 47, 49–50
　Hitler, agreement with, 293, 474
　Mary, devotion to, 15, 379–380
　multiculturalism and, 459
　papal authority and, 343
　Protestant Reformation and, 360–363,
　　367
　sacraments and rituals of, 369, 374, 375,
　　376–380, 379
　See also Christianity
Roman Empire
　Christianity and, 323, 328–329, 330,
　　342–347, 350
　collapse of, 344, 345, 350
　dating system of, 321
　Islam and, 424
　Israel ruled by, 283, 284, 286, 287, 305,
　　322–323
Romanesque style, 380–381
Romania, 349, 350, 351
Romantic movement, 477
Rome, as seat of Christianity, 342, 343
rosaries, 279, 431
Rosetta Stone, 18
Rosh Hashana "beginning of the year";
　the celebration of the Jewish New
　Year, occurring in the seventh lunar
　month, 299, 300, 302
Rothko, Mark, 483–484
Roy, Ram Mohan, 90
Rubaiyat, The (Khayyám), 431
Rudra, 60, 80
Rule for Monks (Benedict), 347
Rumi, Jalal-ud-Din, 429
Russell, Bertrand, 229
Russell, Charles T., 372
Russia
　Christianity and, 349, 350, 351, 370
　Communism of. *See* Communism
　Judaism and, 292, 295, 306
　secularism and, 471

Russian Orthodox Church, 353, 370, 387
　See also Eastern Orthodox Church
Russo-Japanese war, 243
Ryoan-ji, 158

Saadia ben Joseph, 288
Sabbath "Rest"; the seventh day of the
　week (Saturday), a day of prayer and
　rest from work, 278, 280–281, 283,
　298–299
　Jesus and, 325–326
　See also day of rest
sacrament "sacred action" (Latin); one of
　the essential rituals of Christianity,
　369, 373–375
sacramental orientation, 11
sacredness
　concepts of, as varying, 7–8, 12
　as key characteristic of religion, 7
　patterns of. *See* patterns among religions
sacred space, oral religions and, 33–34, 38
sacrifice
　ancestor worship and, 37
　of animals, 40, 61, 113, 146, 277, 279,
　　416, 417
　death rituals and, 39
　of food, 40, 61
　of humans, 40
　Islam and, 416, 417
　Judaism and, 272, 279, 284
　taboo, atonement for, 40
　Zoroastrianism and, 282
Saddharma Pundarika Sutra, 130
Sadducees a priestly faction, influential
　during the Second-Temple period,
　284
sadhanas, 76
Sagan, Carl, 391
Saicho, 136–137
Saint Matthew Passion (Bach), 389
St. Patrick's Cathedral, 383
Saint Patrick's Day, 378
Saint Peter's Basilica, 319–321
Saint Petersburg, 351
saints
　Catholics and, 369
　days of celebration, 378–379
　Jainist, 165–167, 168, 172, 174
　Muslims and, 417, 431, 432
　Protestants and, 363
　relics of, 361, 363
Saint Sophia's Cathedral, 355
sake, 250–251
Salat, 411–412
sallekhana "holy death"; death by self-
　starvation, valued in Jainism as a no-
　ble end of a long life of virtue and
　detachment, 170
salt, 375
　purification with, 250

Salt March, 93–94

Salzburg Cathedral, 383

samadhi a state of deep awareness, the result of intensive meditation, 75

Sama Veda, 62

Sambhogakaya Buddhas, 126–127

same-gender relationships, 465–466

Samhain, 46

samsara constant rebirth and the attendant suffering; the everyday world of change, 114–115, 123, 459

See also moksha

Samuel, Books of, 279

samurai feudal soldier, 243

Samyutta Nikaya, 120

sanctuary, 480

Sanctus, 388

sangats, 178

Sangha the community of monks and nuns; lowercased, *sangha* refers to an individual monastic community, 105–106, 107, 111, 118, 120, 156

of China, 132, 221

of Japan, 133–134

of Korea, 133

of Tibet, 148–149, 156

Zen, 140, 142

Sankhya school, 177

sannyasin a wandering holy man, 72–73, 118

Sanskrit, 107

Santa Maria della Vittoria, 383

Santeria, 51

Sarah, 272, 410

sat, 66

Satan, 282–283, 341

See also good vs. evil

satellite television, 451, 457

sati, 90–91

satori in Zen, the enlightened awareness, 140

Saturnalia, 377

satyagraha, 93, 94

Saudi Arabia, 426–427, 451

Saul (king of Canaan), 279

Scandinavia, 364, 466

Schelomo (Bloch), 312

Schmidt, Wilhelm, 5

Scholar and His Servant on a Terrace, A (Ma Yüan), 203

Schubert, Franz, 388

Schumacher, E. F., 475

science

agnosticism and, 470

Christianity and, 389–391, 473, 475

Confucianism and, 229, 230

cultural conflicts and, 446

future of religion and, 467–469

Islam and, 437, 448–449

Judaism and, 291

origins of religion and, 3–4

secularism and, 447, 470

sexuality and, 464–465

spirituality and, 482

women's rights and, 462

science fiction, 481, 488

Science and Health with a Key to the Scriptures (Eddy), 372

Scotland, 365

scriptures. *See* texts

scullcap, 303, 308

sculpture

Buddhist, 107, 121–123, 128–129, 132, 137, 158

Christian, 320, 357, 376, 379, 386–387

Hindu, 89

Jainist, 174

wood carving, 45, 47

seasons, 196, 250, 377, 479

Second Temple of Jerusalem, 265–267, 281, 283–286, 300

Second Vatican Council, 392, 474

Sectarianism, 366–367

Sect Shinto, 243

secularism, 435, 446–447, 469–472, 475

security, origin of religion and, 4

Seder "order"; a special ritual meal at Passover, recalling the Hebrews' exodus from Egypt, 301–302

Sefer HaHasidim, 290

Sefer Yetzira, 290

sefiroth, 290

Se-icho-no-le, 258

Seinfeld, 313

Seleucid period, 283

self, lessening sense of, 11–12, 67–68, 168

in Buddhism, 135, 140

meditation, 75

Sufis and, 428, 429

See also altered consciousness; soul

Sephardim Jews of Spain, Morocco, and the Mediterranean region, 291, 305–306

Serbia, 350

Series 1 (O'Keeffe), 483

Sermon on the Mount, 325

Serra, Junípero, 369–370

sewage systems, 59

sexuality

adultery, 40, 278

Buddhism and, 113, 147–148, 151

Christianity and, 345–346

Hinduism and, 75, 80, 89

Islam and, 416

Jainism and, 170

Judaism and, 278, 305

modern reassessment of, 464–467

same-gender, 465–466

Shinto and, 246

taboos and, 39, 40

Tantric Buddhism and, 147–148, 151

Taoism and, 200

See also celibacy; chastity; marriage

Shahadah, 410–411

Shakers, 366–367

shaktis, 84

shalom, 264

shaman a human being who contacts and attempts to manipulate the power of spirits for the tribe or group, 41–43, 257

shamans

as female, 41–42, 50–51, 250, 257–258, 464

Japan and, 257–258

Korea and, 50–51, 257

Tibetan, 146, 151

See also clergy; oral religions

Shang Di, 189

Shang dynasty, 189

Shango, 32

Shankara, 74

Shankara's Crest-Jewel of Discrimination, 74

Sharia the whole body of Islamic law, which guides a Muslim's life, 435–436

Shavuot, 302

shaykhs, 429, 431

shellfish, 283, 303

Shetrunja, Mount, 184

Shiite a minority branch of Islam, which holds that Muhammad's genuine successors descended from his son-in-law Ali, 417, 422, 424–426, 435

shimenawa twisted rope, marking a sacred spot, 255

Shingon Buddhist school, 133, 135–136

Shinran, 137

Shinto, 235–260

arts and, 254–256, 258

beliefs of, 245–247

Buddhism and, 147, 236, 239–240, 242, 243, 245, 253–254, 255

Confucianism and, 240–241, 243, 245

development of, 239–245

Goddess worship and, 15

Japanese national identity and, 241–245

modern world and, 259–260, 476

O-Bon festival and, 147

offshoots of, 256–259, 459, 462

origins of, 236–239

practice of, 247–254

study of, 260

women and, 250, 257–259, 462, 464

Shiva a god associated with destruction and rebirth, 59–60, 80–83, 84, 85–86, 89

Shoah. *See* Holocaust

shofar, 299

shrines, Shinto, 247–251, 254–255

shtetls, 306

shu reciprocity; a Confucian virtue, 213

shudra caste, 71

shunyata the Mahayana notion of emptiness, meaning that the universe is empty of permanent reality, 129

Shvetambara "clothed in white"; a member of the Jain sect in which monks and nuns wear white clothing, 171–172, 173

Shvetasvatara Upanishad, 65, 66

siblings, 210
 of Jesus, 327

Sicily, 423

Siddhartha Gautama. *See* Buddha (Siddhartha Gautama)

Sierra Club, 479

Sikh "Disciple"; a follower of the Sikh religion, 176

Sikhism, 174–184
 Hinduism and, 164
 Islam and, 176, 177, 178, 180
 Jainism compared to, 164

Silla kingdom, 133

Silver Rule, 213

Simon, Paul, 29

Simon Stylite, 347

Simplicianus, 345

simplicity, Taoism and, 198

Simpsons, The, 313, 485

sin wrongdoing seen as disobedience to God, 331, 339, 380

Sinai, Mount, 277

Sinai Peninsula, 276–277

sincerity, 214–215, 246–247

Singapore, 230

Singer, Isaac Bashevis, 312

Singer, Peter, 480

Singh, Gobind, 180

singing, 387–389
 See also chant; music

Sioux, 32

Sistine Chapel, 339

Sita, 79, 86

sitar, 90

skillful means, 125, 130, 134–135

slaves, Buddhism and, 113

Smith, Joseph, 371

Smoholla, 32

snake, as symbol, 15

Snyder, Gary, 155

social behavior, taboos and, 39–40

social nature of human beings, origins of religion and, 3

social responsibility
 Buddhism and, 138, 156
 Christianity and, 326, 327, 328, 356, 359, 392, 474
 Confucianism and. *See* Confucianism
 Hinduism and, 74
 interfaith dialogue and, 460
 Islam and, 412–413, 431
 Judaism and, 297–298

Sikhism and, 177–178
 Sufism and, 431
 taxes and, 412–413
 See also good deeds; individuality; poverty

Society for the Advancement of Judaism, 310

Society of Friends, 366

Soka Gakkai, 138

Solomon (king of Canaan), 279–280

solstice festival, 377, 479

Soma, 60

Song dynasty, 201

Song of Songs, 281, 337, 356

Song-tsen-gam-po, 148

Soto Buddhist school, 139

soul
 Atman as unity of, 66
 Buddhist impermanence of, 109, 114, 129
 Christianity and, 341–342
 permanence of, 111, 297
 See also self

sound recording, 29

South Africa, 93, 370

South America, 370, 392

South Korea, 158, 370, 373, 450, 459
 See also Korea

Spain
 Christianity and, 291, 359, 369, 370
 Inquisition and, 291, 359
 Islam and, 359, 423, 424, 452
 Judaism and, 288, 291, 305, 359

"speaking in tongues," 367

spirit, Jainism and, 167–168

spirituality, eclectic, 480–488

spiritual path
 study of religions and, 20
 as term, 6

spirituals, 389

spirit world
 ancestor worship. *See* ancestor worship
 animism and, 32
 Chinese traditional beliefs of, 189
 death rituals and, 38–39
 Halloween/Samhain and, 46
 magic and, 42
 Zoroastrianism and, 282

Spring and Autumn Annals, 217

Sri Lanka, 117, 118, 120, 121, 156, 158

stained-glass windows, 441

Stalin, Joseph, 353

stars, 2

Star Trek, 481

State Shinto, 243, 245

stealing
 Buddhism and, 113
 Jainism and, 170
 Judaism and, 278
 oral religions and, 40

Steinsaltz, Adin, 287

Sthanakavasi "building person"; a member of the youngest Jain sect, which rejects the use of statues and temples, 172, 174

Stonehenge, 34

Streisand, Barbra, 313

stupa a shrine, usually in the shape of a dome, used to mark Buddhist relics or sacred sites, 121, 158

submission. *See* Islam

suffering
 Buddhism and, 103–105, 108, 109–113
 Christianity and, 336, 341
 Islam and, 416
 Jainism and, 167
 Judaism and, 297
 nature and, 476

Sufism a group of devotional movements in Islam, 176, 359, 427–431, 433–434, 438

Suhrawardi, 430

suicide
 Buddhism and, 171
 Hinduism and, 170
 Jainism and, 170
 kamikaze pilots and Shinto, 243
 of Saul, 279

Sukkot "booths"; a festival in the late autumn that recalls the Jews' period of wandering in the desert after their exodus from Egypt, 300

Summa Contra Gentiles (Thomas Aquinas), 357

Summa Theologica (Thomas Aquinas), 357

summer solstice, 377, 479

sun, female god as, 15, 238

Sunni the majority branch of Islam, which holds that genuine succession from Muhammad did not depend on hereditary descent from his son-in-law Ali, 422, 424–425, 435, 450

Superman (comic), 483

superstition, Roman Catholic Church and, 361, 362

Supreme Court, U.S., 42

Sura a chapter of the Qur'an, 420

Surya, 60

Susanowo, 238

sutra a sacred text, especially one said to record the words of the Buddha, 120, 130

sutta. *See* sutra

suttee. *See* sati

Suzuki, David, 29

Switzerland, Christianity and, 364, 366

symbols and symbolism
 appropriation of, 459
 Buddhist, 121, 150–151, 154
 Christian, 323, 328, 335, 337, 339, 344–346, 375–376, 379

symbols and symbolism (*continued*)
defined, 8
of the female divine, 15
of founders' lives, 323
in haiku, 142
of Hindu art, 88
of Islam, 415–416, 419, 431
Judaism and, 289–290, 301–302
Jungian interpretation of, 5, 9
of Native American Church, 42
of oral religion art, 45–47
pre-Christian sources of, 46
universality of, 8–10, 46
synagogues, 281
Synoptic Gospels, 334
Syria, 283, 351, 358, 422, 424, 426, 428

taboo a strong social prohibition (Tongan: tabu; Hawaiian: kapu), 39–40
in modern societies, 40
in oral societies, 39–40, 47
taboos, ecology and, 33
tabu. *See* taboos
T'aego Buddhist order, 133
Tagore, Rabindranath, 94
Tahiti, 37, 370
Tai, Mount, 204
Taiwan, 50, 187–188, 199, 200–201, 204, 229, 231, 370
Tai-zo, 135
Taj Mahal, 401–402
Takemitsu, Toru, 488
Talib, Abu, 404, 405
Taliban movement, 449
talit a prayer shawl worn by devout males, 303, 310
Talmud an encyclopedic commentary on the Hebrew scriptures, 287–288, 290, 298–299
Tanakh the complete Hebrew scriptures, made up of the Torah, Prophets (Nevi'im), and Writings (Kethuvim), 268
tanha, 110
Tan Luan, 137
Tantric Buddhism, 147–148, 151
Tantrism, 76, 89
Tao the mysterious origin of the universe which is present and visible in everything, 194, 197, 206
Taoism, 191–205
arts and, 201–203
Buddhism and, 132, 139, 140, 199–200, 201
Confucianism and, 191, 201, 206, 219, 221
education and, 198, 206, 219
future of, 204
longevity and, 198–199, 200
nature and, 194–198, 201–203, 205, 477
philosophical, 191–198

religious, 191, 199–201
study of, 230–231
Western culture and, 204–205, 476, 477
women and, 195, 464
Tao of Physics, The (Capra), 482
Tao Te Ching the classic scripture of Taoism, 193–195, 203, 219
Tara, 152
Tariq, 423
tathata "thatness," "thusness," "suchness"; the uniqueness of each changing reality, 129–130
Tattooed Serpent, 39
taxes, 412–413
Ta Yao, 32
tea ceremony, 142–144
tefillin phylacteries; two small boxes containing biblical passages that are worn by Orthodox males on their head and left arm at morning prayer during the week, 303, 310
Tehran, 447
televangelism, 394–395
television
appropriation of religion and, 459
Confucianism taught on, 230
cultural unification and, 457
culture clashes and, 451
evangelism on, 394–395
Islam and, 422, 451
Judaism and, 313–314
nature shows on, 478–479
spirituality and, 481
Ten Commandments, 277–278, 302, 311
Tendai Buddhist school, 133, 136–137
Tenjur, 149
Tenri City, 258
Tenrikyo a New Religion devoted to human betterment, 257–258
Teotihuacán, 34
Teresa of Avila, 357
testament a contract; the New Testament constitutes the Christian scriptures, 323
texts
Buddhist, 120, 130–131, 133, 137–138, 148, 149
Christian. *See* Bible, Christian
Confucian, 206, 212, 215–218
Hindu, 61–62, 62–76, 95, 96
Islamic. *See* Qur'an
Jainist, 173–174
Jewish. *See* Judaism: scripture
Shinto, 245, 258
Sikh, 178, 180–181
Taoist, 192–196, 200, 203
Tenrikyo, 258
Zoroastrian, 282
Thailand, 94, 101–102, 120, 121, 424
travel to, 158
thangkas, 151–152

theocracy, 435, 436, 447–448, 450–451
theology, 17
theophany a revelation or appearance of God, 272
theotokos, 379
Theravada Buddhism, 118–123, 126, 147, 154–155
Thirteenth Tribe, The (Koestler), 306
Thomas Aquinas, 357
Thoreau, Henry David, 93, 95, 480
Three Doctrines of China, 132, 201, 221
Three Jewels, 107
thusness. *See* tathata
Tian, 189, 220
Tibet
pre-Buddhist religion of, 146, 148
travel to, 159
Tibetan Buddhism, 136, 146–154, 155–156
tikis. *See* ki`i
time
Hinduism and, 66
oral religions and, 33–34
patterns of views of, 13
tipis, 32
Tipitaka. *See* Tripitaka
ti plants, 26, 27, 47
tirthankara "crossing maker"; in Jainism, one of the twenty-four ideal human beings of the past, Mahavira being the most recent, 165–167, 168, 172, 174
Tisha Be-Av, 302
Tolstoy, Leo, 93
Torah "teaching," "instruction"; the first five books of the Hebrew scriptures; also, the additional instructions of God, believed by many to have been transmitted orally from Moses through a succession of teachers and rabbis, 268–277, 281, 284, 300, 307
torii a gatelike structure that marks a Shinto sacred place, 235, 247, 255
Torquemada, Tomás de, 359
totem poles, 45
totem an animal (or image of an animal) that is considered to be related by blood to a family or clan and is its guardian or symbol, 45
Totem and Taboo (Freud), 4
Toulouse-Lautrec, Henri de, 155
tourism
alcohol availability and, 426, 448
ecotourism, 479, 480
See also travel (study)
Tours, Battle of, 423
Toward a Psychology of Being (Maslow), 481
trade, 358, 405, 424, 446
See also economics
traditional religions. *See* oral religions
training. *See* education

trance
  shamanic, 42–43
  See also altered consciousness; contemplative practices
transcendent not limited by the physical world, 8, 276
Transcendentalism, 95
Transcendental Meditation, 96
transformation, as symbol, 10
transubstantiation, 362, 374
travel (study), 19, 20, 158–159, 184, 230–231, 260, 452
  See also pilgrimage
trees, 46, 47, 84, 105
tribal religions. *See* oral religions
Trichinella spiralis, 303
trikaya the three "bodies" of the Buddha, the Dharmakaya (cosmic Buddha nature), the Sambhogakaya (celestial Buddhas), and the Nirmanakaya (historical Buddhas), 125–127
Trimurti "three forms" of the divine—the three gods Brahma, Vishnu, and Shiva, 79–83
Trinity the three "persons" in God: Father, Son, and Holy Spirit, 341, 352, 411
Trinity, The (Augustine), 346
Tripitaka the three "baskets," or collections, or Buddhist texts, 120, 130, 133, 149
trishna, 110
"True Name," 176
truth, Jainism and, 169–170
Tsimshian, 44
Tsong Kha-pa, 148, 149
Tsukiyomi, 238
Turkey, 447, 452
  See also Constantinople
Tutu, Desmond, 370
Two Great Commandments, 327–328
Tylor, E. B., 4

U2, 460
Ukraine, 349, 351
ulama, 436
Uma, 84
Umar, 422
Umayyad dynasty, 423–424, 425, 427
umma, 407
Unification Church, 373, 459
Unitarians, 466
United Nations, 294
United States
  architecture and, 383–384
  Christianity and, 364, 365, 366–367
  Islam and, 450, 452
  Judaism and, 292, 293, 295, 309, 310, 314–315
  Naturism and, 477–478
  secularism and, 469–470

unity
  Buddhism and, 124–125, 140
  Hinduism and, 67–68, 74, 84
Unity Church, 372, 464, 466
universal love
  Confucianism and, 219, 220
  Jesus and, 325
  Mohists and, 220
universe
  origins of religion and nature of, 2, 3–5
  patterns of views of, 12
  See also nature; world; worldview
untouchables, 71, 91
Upangas, 174
Upanishads written meditations on the spiritual essence of the universe and the self, 62–68, 95
Ushas, 60
usury, 417
Utah, 371
Uthman, 422, 425
al-Uzza, 404

vaishya caste, 71
vajra the "diamond" scepter used in Tibetan and other types of Buddhist ritual, symbolizing wisdom; when used with the bell, the vajra symbolizes the union of knowledge and compassion, 150
Vajrayana Buddhism, 136, 146–154
Valentine's Day, 378
valley, Taoism and, 195
values
  of Jewish culture, 311
  See also moral codes and ethics; virtues
Vardhamana, Nataputta. *See* Mahavira
Varuna, 60
Vatican II, 392, 474
Vaughan Williams, Ralph, 29, 95, 389, 487
VCRs, 451
Vedanta, 73–74, 95
Vedas four collections of ancient Aryan prayers and rituals, 61–62
vegetarianism
  Buddhism and, 114
  Hinduism and, 85, 86, 92, 96
  Jainism and, 168
  Naturism and, 479
  See also meat eating
Vietnam, 210, 215, 370
Vimalakirti Sutra, 130
violence
  nonharm. *See* nonviolence
  Taoist position against, 198
  Zealots and, 284
virgin birth, 192, 323, 327
Virgin Mary. *See* Mary (mother of Jesus)
virtues
  Christianity and, 341

Confucianism and, 206, 212–215, 218–221, 223, 229–230, 240–241
  Zoroastrianism and, 282
Vishnu a god associated with preservation and love, 60, 79, 84, 85
vision quest, 38
Vivekananda, 95
Vivekananda, Swami, 460
Vlaminck, Maurice, 30
Vohu Manah, 282
Voodoo, 51

Wade-Giles system, 188
Walden (Thoreau), 480
Walking on a Mountain Path in Spring (Ma Yuan), 203
Walk to the Paradise Garden, The (Delius), 487
Wang Yangming, 223
warfare
  of Arabian tribes, 404, 414
  Aryans and, 60
  Buddhism and, 115, 117
  Christianity and, 357–358, 423
  Hinduism and, 70
  Judaism and, 278
  Muslims and, 357–358, 407, 422–424
  Native Americans and, 40
  Taoism and, 198
  See also nonviolence
Wat Benchamabophit, 101–102
water
  floods, 271
  holy water, 375
  as symbol, 9, 9–10, 15, 374
  Taoism and, 195
Wayfarer's Chapel, 383–384
Way. *See* Tao
weaving, 45
weddings, Shinto, 249
wen cultural refinement; a Confucian virtue, 213–214
Wesley, Charles, 367
Wesley, John, 367
Western culture, Buddhism and, 154–156
Western Paradise, 127, 137
Western Wall the foundation stones of the western wall of the last temple of Jerusalem, today a place of prayer, 264–265
Westminster Abbey, 381
West Side Story (Bernstein), 312
Where Do We Come From? What Are We? Where Are We Going? (Gauguin), 2–3
whirling dervish, 429
Whitman, Walt, 95
Whole Shebang, The (Ferris), 481
Wicca, 15, 464, 479
widows, 90–91
Wiesel, Elie, 312

Wilder, Thornton, 481
Williams, William Carlos, 155
Wilson, E. O., 29
wine, 347, 362, 374–375, 417, 431
winter solstice, 46
wisdom, Buddhism and, 124, 150
Wisdom of the Elders (Suzuki), 29
Wittenberg, Germany, 362, 363
women
    Buddhism and, 16, 105, 113, 156, 463
    Christianity and, 347
    Confucianism and, 16, 229, 230
    Hinduism and, 84, 90–92, 464
    in India, 77, 84, 90–92
    Islam and, 411, 413, 414, 418, 434, 447,
        448–449
    Jainism and, 171
    Judaism and, 264–265, 270–271, 272,
        278, 307, 308, 309, 310, 313,
        462–464
    Naturism and, 480
    New Religions and, 257–259
    patterns of views about, 14–16, 462–464
    rights of. *See* women's rights move-
        ments
    Shinto and, 250, 257–259, 462, 464
    Taoism and, 195, 464
    See also gender
women's rights movements
    Christianity and, 395
    future of religion and, 462–464
    Islam and, 448–449
    Judaism and, 313
    See also authority; government and poli-
        tics
wood carvings, 45, 47
    See also masks
words
    patterns of emphasis on, 13
    Zen and, 140, 142
world
    Buddhism and, 123–124, 138
    Christianity and, 328, 346–347, 352, 395
    Hinduism and, 66–67, 73, 89
    Islam and, 416
    Judaism and, 310–311
    Shinto and, 258
    See also environment; nature
World Council of Churches, 391–391

World Parliament of Religions, 392, 460
worldview
    Buddhism, 108–110, 125–130
    Christianity, 338–342
    Confucianism, 222–223
    eclectic spirituality, 480
    globalism contesting incomplete, 459
    Hinduism, 66–67
    Islam, 408, 410
    Jainism, 167–168
    Judaism, 290
    as key characteristic of religion, 7
    of Naturism, 476–477
    of science, 467–469
    secularism, 435, 446–447
    Sikhism, 177–178
    Taoism, 194–196
    traditional China, 190–192
World War I, 474
World War II, 243, 245, 293–297, 353,
    473–474
Wright, Lloyd, 383
Writings. *See* Kethuvim
Wu, 229
wu wei "no action," "no strain"; doing
    only what comes spontaneously and
    naturally; effortlessness, 197–198
Wycliffe, John, 362

Xavier, Francis, 370
xiao family devotion, filial piety; a Confu-
    cian virtue, 213
Xunzi, 220, 222

Yahweh, 15, 270–273, 274–276, 277, 279,
    280, 289–290, 297, 309, 310–311
    as term, 275
Yajur Veda, 62
Yama, 60
yang the active aspect of reality that ex-
    presses itself in speech, light, and
    heat, 190, 196, 205
yantra, 76, 88
yarmulke the skullcap worn by devout
    Jewish males, 303, 308
Yathrib (Medina), 407, 416
Yazid, Abu, 428
Yellow Hat sect, 148
Yellow Turban sect, 199

Yemen, 307, 426
Yentl, 313, 463, 481
Yiddish, 303, 306, 313
Yi dynasty, 133
Yi Jing an ancient Confucian book of div-
    ination, one of the Five Classics, still
    in use today, 191
yin the receptive aspect of the universe
    that expresses itself in silence, dark-
    ness, coolness, and rest, 190, 196, 205
yoga a spiritual discipline; a method for
    perfecting one's union with the di-
    vine, 73–76
    Taoist, 198–199
Yoga Sutras, 75
Yom Hashoah, 302
Yom Kippur Day of Atonement, 299–300
yoni, 15, 83
Yoruba, 27, 32
Yosemite, 478
Young, Brigham, 371
Young Man Luther (Erikson), 362
Youth Hostel Association, 19

Zarathustra, 282
zazen, 140–142
Zealots an anti-Roman, nationalistic Jew-
    ish faction, active during the Roman
    period of control over Israel, 284, 315
Zen Buddhism, 134, 138–146, 155, 243, 459
Zeus Pater, 60, 283
Zhang Daoling, 199
Zhang Jue, 199
Zhuangzi author of the Zhuangzi, a book
    of whimsical stories that express
    themes of early Taoist thought,
    195–196
Zhu Xi, 222–223
Zimmer, Heinrich, 80
Zionism the movement that has encour-
    aged the creation and support of the
    nation of Israel, 294, 309
zodiac, 404
Zohar (de León), 290
zoos, 479
Zoroastrianism, 281, 282, 335, 345, 403,
    404, 410
Zwingli, Holdrych, 364